The political economy of colonialism in Ghana

The political economy of colonialism in Ghana

a collection of documents and statistics 1900-1960

Edited with an introduction by

G. B. KAY
Lecturer in Economics
The City University, London

with a statistical abstract prepared in collaboration with

STEPHEN HYMER

CAMBRIDGE
At the University Press, 1972

Published by the Syndics of the Cambridge University Press
Bentley House, 200 Euston Road, London NW1 2DB
American Branch: 32 East 57th Street, New York, N.Y.10022

Library of Congress Catalogue Card Number: 70–158551

ISBN: 0 521 07952 7

Printed in Great Britain by
The Eastern Press, Limited
London and Reading

To my mother and
the memory of my father

Contents

Documents

Tables

Chapter 10. External trade—*continued*

Chapter 11. Public finance

Maps

Acknowledgements

The author and publisher would like to thank the following for permission to include copyright material:

The Controller of Her Majesty's Stationery Office for Document 2 (from *Private Enterprise in British Tropical Africa*, Cmd 2016), Documents 11 and 13 (from *Report of a Committee on Trade and Taxation for British West Africa*, Cmd 1600), Documents 17, 25 and 36 (from *The Report by the Hon. W. G. A. Ormsby-Gore on his visit to West Africa 1926*, Cmd 2744), Documents 3, 4, 28 (b), 35 and 38 (from *Report of the Commission of Enquiry into Disturbances in the Gold Coast*, Colonial Office, London 1948), Document 33 (from *Report of the Commission on the marketing of West Africa cocoa*, Cmd 5845) and Document 34 (from *Report on Cocoa Control in West Africa*, Cmd 6554).

The Leverhulme Trust Fund for Document 28 (a) (from *The West African Commission, 1938–39*).

The Ghana Government for all the remaining documents.

Preface

When the British finally pulled out of Ghana in 1957 they left behind them a country which bore all the most important features of under-development. In particular it suffered the acute form of structural dislocation characteristic of an open dependent economy: production and consumption were not integrated within the country but through external trade. Thus the colony exchanged commodities which it produced but did not consume or even fully process, such as cocoa, gold and manganese, for other, mainly manufactured goods, that it did consume but did not, and in many cases could not, produce itself. In addition its rate of growth depended upon the performance of its export sector: when export earnings were buoyant, as in the twenties and fifties, the colony enjoyed mild prosperity; when they slumped in the thirties it was engulfed by depression. The ' model colony ' was also the ' fragile economy ': foreign political domination on the one hand and external economic dependence on the other constitute the main aspects of the political economy of colonialism.

Colonialism, it is now clear, represents a particular moment in the history of imperialism when trade and the flag moved together. To satisfy the imperial requirements of British capital, the British state took upon itself the task of creating a global economy: political dominion was established over huge areas and whole populations were precipitated into the vortex of the world market. While the drive behind this venture ultimately found its origin and logic in the interests of a small segment of the British population, in the minds of the colonial administrators it not surprisingly assumed a much wider significance that transcended sectional interests altogether. As an ideology colonialism saw the convergence of several important streams of nineteenth century British thought: evangelical Christianity and social Darwinism on the one hand; free trade and *laisser-faire* on the other. As a practice it reverted more closely to the sectional interests that engendered it; and *laisser-faire* and free trade were as much ideological distortions and justification of practice as Christianity and Darwinism, though less obviously so. Certainly this was the case in Ghana.

At first sight the reverse seems to be the case and free trade and *laisser-faire* present themselves as the key to understanding colonial policy in Ghana. Not only was Ghana part of an empire that has been characterised by historians as a free trade empire, but colonial policy met all the formal requirements of free trade. There were almost no physical or fiscal restrictions imposed on the free flow of commodities into and out of the colony whose currency was held at parity with the pound sterling. Inside the colony government intervention in the economy appeared to be kept to a minimum, and government revenue and expenditure as a percentage of trade was among the lowest for all British colonies in Africa. In addition the colonial government constantly emphasised the importance of trade for progress, and the colonial ' growth model ' is identical in all important respects to recent analyses of the ' open economy '. Yet, as I argue in the introductory essay, the colonial authorities in Ghana did not pursue free trade and *laisser-faire* to their logical conclusion: in fact quite the reverse. Economic policy in Ghana reveals a continual reluctance on the part of the colonial government to maximise the trade of the colony.

The explanation put forward for this apparent anomaly can be quickly summarised: free trade and trade maximisation were only of interest to the colonial government: (1) insofar as they were consistent with the profitability and accumulation of British capital; and (2) only to the extent that they did not threaten to undermine the social basis of British power in the colony. In Ghana both these constraints operated with particular force with the result that the colonial government in the words of one of its officials ' had occasion to act as brake rather than as an accelerating force '.

In this work I have limited myself to the presentation of documentary and statistical material on Ghana and comments upon this material. Despite continuous temptation no attempt has been made to generalise the most important conclusions substantively or theoretically beyond the immediate scope of this enquiry: such generalisation requires a book very different from this. However, it is hoped that this study will be of interest to economists and other social scientists concerned with the problems of development and under-development, despite the limited nature of its object of study and the fact that in the introductory essay which sets forth the framework of analysis and the most important conclusions, little use is made of the concept of economic growth while those of development and under-development are deliberately not deployed at all.

The book is divided into three Parts. The Introduction forms Part 1. Part 2 consists of selected documents on key areas of colonial policy extracted with one exception from official publications and reports of the colonial government in Ghana, and the British government and Colonial Office in London. These documents are organised into six chapters: General Economic Policy, Finance, Transport, Agriculture, Cocoa and Education. In the main they are drawn from the period 1920–50, though one or two fall just outside these years: within each chapter they are organised on a chronological basis. Each chapter is prefaced with a brief introductory note which explains the background of the documents included, what I believe to be their most important points and how they relate to each other. Direct editing has been kept to a minimum and the original paragraph enumeration has been retained wherever possible so that the reader who wishes can easily check back to the original sources.

While this part of the book was in preparation the 'fifty year rule' was lifted and replaced by a 'thirty year rule' which meant that a great volume of previously classified information on the inter-war period became available for public inspection. However, I have deliberately made no use of this, since any attempt to work through it systematically would have delayed publication indefinitely. A further consideration that determined my decision concerns the value of classified material. Generally speaking my belief is that this type of information, particularly in the field of economic policy, can only add further detail to what can be discovered from published sources. It can perhaps reveal something of the motives of those in office and the immediate pressures that acted upon them, but my analysis does not rest upon such things. Insofar as various interests put pressure upon the colonial government evidence will be found in what it did, which in turn is quite independent of motives: as Adam Smith pointed out, the ends men achieve are often quite different from their intentions. Readers concerned with the analysis of colonial motivation or some form of interest group theory of colonial practice will find little of direct interest to them here.

In any collection of documents the principles of selection and editing are equally important, often more important, than the nature of the sources. All collections of documents reflect the interests and biases of those putting them together and it is necessary for the criteria of selection to be made explicit. This is particularly true in this case as the two most important criteria exercised might well appear contradictory. On the one hand I have aimed to reproduce representative material in considerable detail in the hope that it will be of interest and use to those who do not necessarily accept the conclusions I draw from it. But on the other hand the selection of areas and the choice of particular documents has been *consciously* guided by my interpretation of colonialism; and to a considerable extent the introductory essay and all of Part 2 should be understood as a single whole. In other words this part of the book should be understood as a thesis about the political economy of colonialism in Ghana in which the vast bulk of the evidence is presented in more or less its original form so that it might simultaneously act as a source of reference for others whose positions differ from my own.

Similar problems arise with the abstract of colonial statistics presented in

Part 3, though not in so acute a form as the volume of material from which selection could take place was much more limited. These data, again gleaned almost entirely from official sources, are organised into eight chapters: Population, Wages, Development plans, External trade and balance of payments, Public finance, Transport and communications, Education and Miscellaneous. Covering the period 1900–60 the attempt has been to present all relevant series on an annual basis in a way that makes it possible to link them on to the statistical abstracts published by the government of Ghana from the early sixties. Important data on such matters as prices and agricultural production are omitted because they were not available. A note at the beginning of Part 3 provides details of sources and methods of compilation.

This book was originally planned as a joint venture with Stephen Hymer and Reginald Green. The statistical abstract was finally completed in collaboration with Stephen Hymer, but his influence on the whole work goes much further. Without the advantages of long discussions with him, his comments on my numerous drafts and his many brilliant insights this book could hardly have been written. My debt to Reginald Green is less recent but hardly less great for that. In 1964–5 we taught a joint course in the University of Ghana on colonial history and it was there under his influence that many of my basic ideas began to crystallise. I would like to think that had pressing reasons not ended our collaboration by isolating us in three continents the book we would have produced together would have been little different in all essential features from this one; nevertheless beyond expressing my very considerable indebtedness to them both I do not wish to implicate them in the many defects for which I alone am responsible. Numerous people have helped me directly and indirectly with the introductory essay and the theoretical skeleton of this book. In particular I would like to extend my thanks to Roger Genoud, Roger Murray, Tom Wengraf, Paul Semonin, Andrea Hopkinson, Brian van Arkadie, and John Merrington. Before his sad death Robert Seresweski was a constant source of inspiration and encouragement and his pioneering work, particularly on the statistical front, paved the way for much that is included here. I would like especially to record my gratitude to Polly Hill. Not only did her own work on cocoa farmers, acknowledged in the text, provide the vital insight into the nature of the colonial formation, but her many helpful suggestions on the arrangement and presentation of the documents and statistics were extremely valuable. Her critical reading of the Introduction was particularly useful.

Numerous people in Ghana and Britain helped with the preparation of tables and the documents. J. Sarblah, H. Dougan, J. Atta, K. Wiredu and J. Amarti did enormous amounts of work in helping put the first draft together. The completion of Part 2 would have proved impossible without the assistance of Helene Lackner whose enthusiasm and attention to detail generally exceeded my own. Together with Wendy Smith she helped turn numerous scraps of paper into an organised manuscript. Edward Stanton provided assistance in the final arrangement of Part 3 and Susan Bennett gave generously of her time in the preparation of the final draft of the Introduction.

Gratitude is due to the University of Ghana, The Economic Growth Center, Yale University and The City University for the facilities they made available. I must also thank the Nuffield Foundation which made funds available to me at a crucial moment for the final preparation. Without this institutional and foundation assistance it would have been quite impossible to prepare this work, particularly the statistical abstract.

GEOFFREY KAY

The City University
March 1971

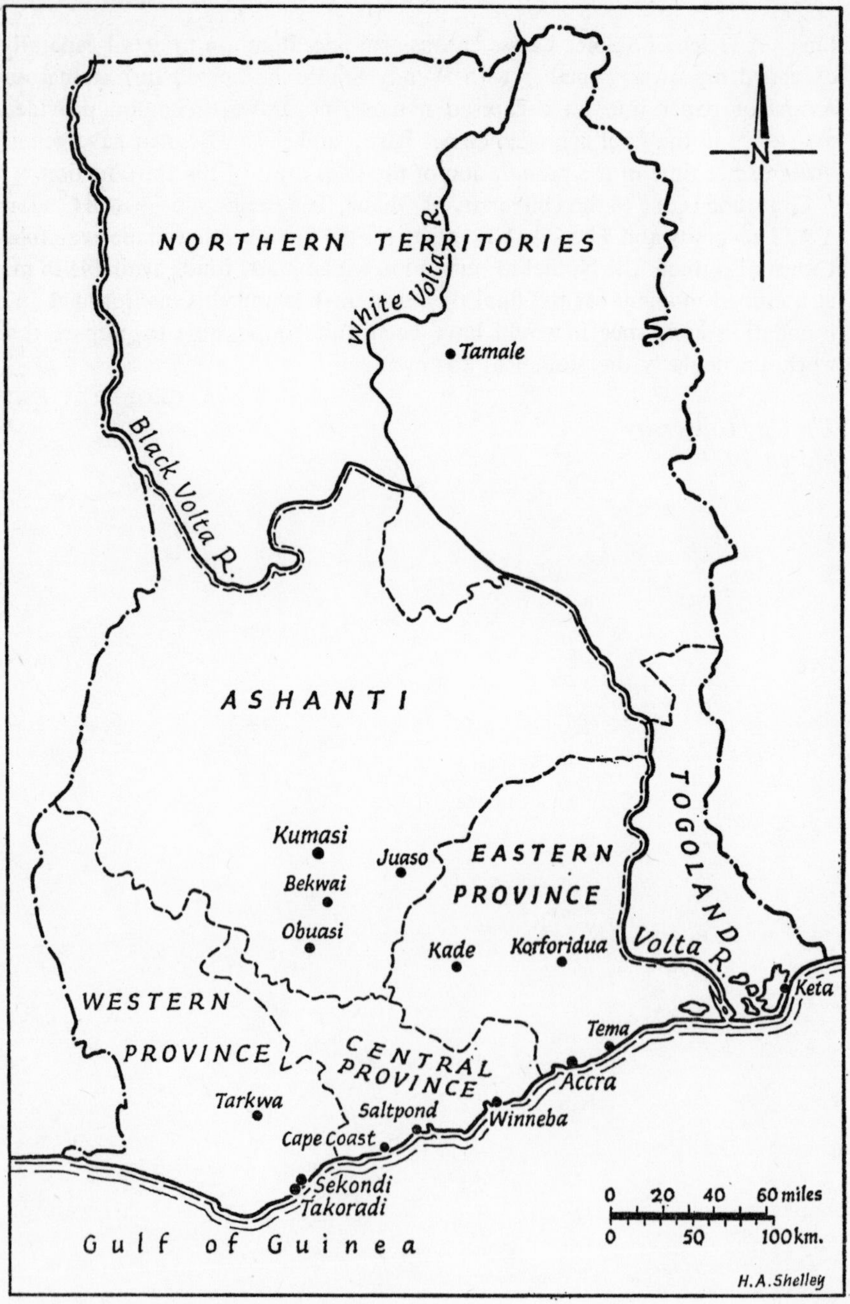

Map 1. The Gold Coast with Togoland under British mandate, 1945 (from Gold Coast Survey Department, Accra 1945).

Part 1

Introduction. The political economy of colonialism in Ghana

The producers of cocoa in this colony . . . are natives in a most elementary state of civilisation whose sole aim as yet appears to be the attainment of a maximum amount of money with a minimum expenditure of energy.

ACTING DIRECTOR OF AGRICULTURE, 1917 [1]

The part of West Africa that became the Gold Coast and subsequently Ghana [2] had ties with the outside world that started long before its formal colonisation by the British at the end of the nineteenth century. The heartland of the Ashanti Empire, centred upon Kumasi, in the hinterland of what is now contemporary Ghana, carried on a substantial trade with the Arab world across the Sahara to the north, and with European powers through the trading forts the latter had established on the coast to the south. The main exports of Ashanti were gold and slaves, both going north and south, but with the bulk of the gold going to the north and the majority of the slaves going to the south. The build-up of the trade in slaves to the south reached its climax during the heyday of the slave trade in the second half of the eighteenth century. The consequences of this trade were so important that its abolition by the British at the beginning of the nineteenth century precipitated a crisis in the area that lasted until its formal colonisation almost one hundred years later. For Ghana the abolition of the slave trade was crucial; for Britain the implications for West Africa were among the last factors to enter into consideration. A step which the British in their self-righteousness like to view as a triumph of their civilisation was taken chiefly for economic reasons and furthermore the economic calculations behind it did not refer primarily to West Africa.[3] British colonialism in the twentieth century faithfully retained these elements and the balance between them.

Following abolition, the British attempted to establish what they called ' legitimate ' trade in the area and were particularly keen on trading gold. This attempt foundered on the reluctance of the Ashanti, who controlled the production of the commodity, to trade it with the British on any substantial scale. The British sent two missions to Kumasi, the capital of Ashanti, in an

[1] Papers relating to the cocoa industry, *Sessional Paper no. II, 1916–17.*

[2] Throughout this essay we refer to the country as Ghana, although it was known as the Gold Coast when it was a colony.

[3] See Eric Williams, *Capitalism and Slavery*, Russell and Russell, New York 1961.

attempt to establish much wider trade relations, in which Kumasi would become an entrepot for British imports as well as a gold exporting centre.[4] Their failure ultimately brought the Ashanti and the British, fast becoming the most important European power on the coast, into conflict and led to a series of wars, whose eventual outcome was the conquest and colonisation of the Ashanti at the end of the century. Such a development seemed highly unlikely in the 1860s, when British failure to establish any substantial trade, coupled with the strong current of anti-colonial feeling that was running so high at home, pointed towards British evacuation. Events turned dramatically in the next two decades. The partition of Africa in the 1870s and 80s had less to do with developments specific to the continent than with the changed terms of competition among the imperial powers following the Franco-Prussian War.[5] Here again the interests of West Africa influenced only marginally an event that had a profound effect upon the future of the region.

In 1874 Britain formally colonised the southern part of the country, but this left unresolved the major political and economic issues that gave rise to their conflict with the Ashanti. In fact it served to heighten the political struggle, as the area that was colonised was considered by the Ashanti as part of their empire. At the economic level no sound basis for British colonialism yet existed, as the gold trade remained small and no alternative export crop had emerged – cocoa did not become important until after the turn of the century. As the name of the colony suggests, it was gold that provided its economic significance for the British in the early years. The limitations of this vision were demonstrated by subsequent events.

The reluctance of the Ashanti to trade gold in substantial quantities left British capital with the choice between ignoring the commodity or seeking control over its production. It opted for the latter. Despite the flotation of a large number of companies, however, no significant breakthrough was achieved until a railway was built at the end of the nineteenth century, since heavy equipment had to be imported for mining, which could not be carried economically except by rail. But the establishment of an industry involving substantial amounts of capital required a measure of political stability that could only be achieved by the subjugation and colonisation of the Ashanti. The construction of the railway proved an inspired solution to both problems. Running inland to the gold areas it carried the vital mining equipment, and

[4] 'Were the Ashantees a commercial people they might be brokers between the interior and the Europeans', T. Edward Bowdich, *Mission from Cape Coast to Ashantee*, John Murray, London 1819, pp. 335–6.

[5] See K. O. Dike, *Trade and politics in the Niger Delta*, Oxford University Press, London 1956, Ch. IX. See also John Gallagher and Ronald Robinson, 'The imperialism of free trade', *Economic History Review*, 2nd Series, VI, no. 1, August 1953.

its continuation through to Kumasi, which had suffered a military defeat, secured the establishment of administrative control over the Ashanti.[6] The close ties between British rule and the railways that were established right at the beginning of the colonial period barely slackened during it.

The coastal terminus of the railway was the town of Sekondi in the west, despite the fact that equally good harbour facilities were available or could easily have been made available in the more important towns to the east, particularly Accra. Sekondi was the nearest town on the coast to the gold producing areas and the colonial government had every reason at the time to believe that the west would remain the economic centre of gravity of the newly formed colony. Events beyond its control were to confound this belief. While British capital was establishing itself in gold production to the west, important developments were taking place in the east; for this was the time when the cocoa industry sprang into existence. While British colonialism was successfully meeting the Ashanti challenge in the west, in the east a new problem was emerging with which it was never adequately able to cope. This was cocoa: not simply the industry as such, but the social relations of production which it engendered.

In many parts of pre-colonial Ghana the social division of labour was quite advanced and petty commodity production, exchange and monetisation were all firmly established. The simple uninformed view of many development economists that so-called traditional societies were more or less completely dominated by subsistence production is less applicable to southern Ghana than perhaps any other region of sub-Saharan Africa. Colonial officials, coping with the concrete tasks of political administration, rarely subscribe to what Polly Hill has called the 'myth of the amorphous peasant' and were more aware of Ghanaian realities than are many contemporary economists. This does not mean that they were free of mythology; their own was a reflection of both their situation in Ghana and their British backgrounds.[7] Their commitment to indirect rule on the one hand, requiring, as it did, concrete knowledge of the actual social situation, combined with their public school education in Britain on the other, made them particularly sensitive to the class divisions of Ghanaian society.

[6] A similarity exists with the Post Office in Great Britain, of which Thorold Rogers wrote: 'It was instituted under Cromwell's government, and the Act of the Commonwealth which created it states that it was to be "for the benefit of commerce, for the conveyance of government despatches, and for the discovery of wicked and dangerous designs against the commonwealth."' James E. Thorold Rogers, *The economic interpretation of history*, T. Fisher Unwin, London 1891.

[7] The background of colonial administrators is discussed by R. Heussler, *Yesterday's rulers*, Syracuse University Press, New York 1963; the selection of personnel by Sir R. Furse, *Aucuparius: recollections of a recruiting officer*, Oxford University Press, London 1962. See also R. Symonds, *The British and their successors*, Faber and Faber, London 1966.

The nature of these divisions was transformed during the colonial period. Not only did the appearance of foreign companies in mining and commerce, plus the economic activities of the colonial government itself, foster the beginnings of wage labour, but also, and more importantly, commodity production spread rapidly throughout the countryside, giving rise to wholly new social relations and institutions. Cocoa lay at the centre of these changes. Introduced in the last quarter of the nineteenth century, the crop was cultivated on a rapidly increasing scale in the south eastern part of the country by Ghanaians, whose enterprise alone was responsible for its success. By 1910 it had become the colony's most important export. The complexity of social arrangements in the countryside can be gauged by the ' classification of agricultural labour ' worked out by A. W. Cardinal, the Census Officer, in 1931, who identified the following groups: (*a*) peasant proprietors cultivating solely for themselves and their families; (*b*) peasant proprietors cultivating crops for sale and export; (*c*) hired labourers; (*d*) employers of labour and non-working land-holders; (*e*) distribution agents, buyers, middlemen, transport owners, transport employees, porters, etc.[8] Although Cardinal himself made little of this framework – his main concern was with the types of house in which the different groups lived – its importance is obvious.

What this list of categories suggests is that alongside subsistence production (group *a*) there was developing not only a sector of petty commodity production (group *b*) but also, and growing out of it, a sector of capitalist production (groups *c* and *d*) which was pushing out beyond agricultural production, as narrowly defined, into distribution and transport. Polly Hill's work on the development of the cocoa industry confirms the conclusion to which Cardinal's observations point and significantly she sub-titles her book on this subject *A study of rural capitalism.*[9] The emergence of a capitalist mode of production in the Ghanaian countryside, and in particular the emergence of a Ghanaian capitalist class that rivalled British capital in the colony, is the key to understanding the evolution of colonial policy.

Alongside agricultural production other forms of economic activity were pursued in the colonial period. Although agriculture remained the largest sector, as we shall see later, these others exercised an influence on the course of the economy's development out of proportion to their size, measured in terms of employment. The two most important non-agricultural employers of labour were the colonial administration and expatriate business, mainly

[8] A. W. Cardinal, *The Gold Coast, 1931*, Government Printer, Accra 1931, p. 201.

[9] Polly Hill, *The migrant cocoa-farmers of southern Ghana, a study in rural capitalism*, Cambridge University Press, Cambridge 1963. This exemplary study establishes the crucial fact of Ghanaian history; namely that the cocoa industry was organised upon a capitalist basis. For a discussion of some of the wider aspects of her work see foreword by Stephen Hymer to her book, *Studies in rural capitalism in West Africa*, Cambridge University Press, Cambridge 1970.

British. The administration offered not only the much sought after clerical and teaching jobs, and a small number of higher administrative posts, but was also, through its transport and public works departments, the largest employer of manual and technical workers. A similar range of jobs was offered by the two important sections of British capital present in the colony: the commercial firms that engaged in cocoa-exporting and general importing employed substantial numbers of clerical workers, while the mining companies, as one would expect, offered more manual and technical jobs. Migrant workers played an important part in the labour force and it was not only the administration and the mines that relied upon them to perform unskilled manual work, but also the cocoa industry. The competition for labour was often acute, particularly during periods of cocoa boom, in the years immediately following the First World War and generally throughout the twenties. As a consequence, except for the depression and the difficult years following the end of the Second World War, there was little of the widespread urban unemployment which has recently become a characteristic feature of so many underdeveloped countries in Africa and elsewhere.[10]

Census data provide some idea of the occupational structure of the population,[11] but the information they offer on class structure is hardly more than impressionistic.[12] The most significant point that emerges from these data is that, aside from agriculture, commercial activities engaged more people than anything else. The majority of the people aggregated under this head were independent petty traders. The relative size of this group is another indication of the extent to which the economy fails to fit the profile of a traditional society engaged in subsistence production and affected only at its margins by a modern monetised sector introduced and controlled from outside. To investigate the importance of this it is necessary to rely upon qualitative rather than quantitative material. It is significant that Cardinal's observations tell us more of importance than the statistical material of the 1931 census, which he conducted.[13]

[10] See C. R. Frank Jr, 'Urban unemployment and economic growth in Africa', *Oxford Economic Papers*, 1968, pp. 250–75; and W. Baer and M. E. Herve, 'Employment and industrialisation in developing countries', *Quarterly Journal of Economics*, 1966, pp. 88–107.

[11] See Tables 9 and 10 below.

[12] An interesting attempt to use the 1960 census data as a guide to social structure is made by Roger Genoud, *Nationalism and economic development in Ghana*, Praeger, New York 1969, pp. 24–50.

[13] The following is a particularly illuminating and relevant passage. 'The inevitable result of the rapid increase of the people's wealth (due to cocoa) has been to bring about what almost amounts to a revolution. The communal ownership of land is being largely repudiated for individual ownership; the sale of land, an almost unheard of practice, has become a matter of every-day life; the tendency for the maker of a cocoa plantation to leave his property to his son rather than his sister's

The picture that emerges from this brief survey of pre-colonial Ghana and the social and economic structure of the colony is one of considerable complexity, whose salient feature is the emergence of an authentic Ghanaian capitalist class. The policies of the colonial government have to be understood not only against this background, but also in the context of the fact that the country was only a small part of a world wide empire.

The colonial state and the determinants of policy [14]

In a country such as Britain it is easy enough to draw an institutional and constitutional distinction between the government and the state. The government is only one part of the state. It performs particular executive functions but is usually, and in principle, quite distinct from the legislature, the judiciary, the permanent civil service which staffs the administrative departments, the police, the army and the public bodies which control large parts of the social and economic infrastructure, such as education and transport. The crown colony system of rule, such as existed in Ghana until after the Second World War, makes such a distinction difficult, as the various branches of government and state were fused tightly together. This fusion, which is clearly expressed in the colonial concept of political administration, was realised through the constitution of the legislative council.

As its title suggests, this council was the supreme legislative organ in the colony, but unlike the Commons in Britain it was not an elected body. Presided over by the Governor, it was dominated by the directors of the main

---

son has almost brought a change from matrilineal to patrilineal descent; the industrious planter has been forced to hire labour in order to cope with the fruits of his industry and is generally ceasing to be a working farmer with the inevitable result that in the course of time he will be a non-working landlord; an influx of strangers drawn as it were to El Dorado has opened up the country to an extent that no man could have foreseen as possible within so short a period; fresh problems of the gravest nature, such as preservation of forests, slum conditions, unemployment, spread of disease, transport and shipment, and a people which has learnt to gallop before it could crawl have been set for government to solve.' Cardinal, *The Gold Coast, 1931*, p. 84.

Sir Gordon Guggisberg, Governor of the colony 1919–27, who launched a Ten Year Development Programme, felt the need shortly after his arrival to issue the caveat that 'history shows that too quick an advance at any period in the development of a race means delay in the end'. *Legislative Council Debates, 1920–1*, p. 2.

14 A case could be made out for denying the existence of any such entity as the *colonial state*, which, it could be argued, is a contradiction in terms. The point would be that a state must have sovereignty, which a colony, by definition, lacks. However, sovereignty is a relative and not an absolute concept, and it can be reasonably doubted that the attainment of formal independence always creates a situation fundamentally different from that which preceded it. Andre Gunder Frank steers round this problem by talking of satellites, which can be formally sovereign or not as the case may be. See A. G. Frank, *Capitalism and underdevelopment in Latin America*, Monthly Review Press, New York 1967.

administrative departments – the official members – who worked alongside unofficial members, representing British business interests on the one hand and local interests on the other. In some cases Ghanaian unofficial members were elected, but most Ghanaians were not enfranchised; and although the ethos of the British colonial administrator was in keeping with the sense of neutral service and scrupulous honesty which became a characteristic feature of government and administration in Britain after 1870, the constitution of the legislative council was reminiscent of the Old Corruption of the eighteenth century. This had important consequences for politics and economics in the colony. The separation of government from state in Britain, which allows governments to be changed in response to changes in the political situation, serves to stabilise the permanent apparatus of state. The colonial state in Ghana, by the very fact of its being colonial (i.e. imposed from outside), enjoyed none of the stabilising advantages that accrue from parliamentary democracy and its ramifications. It confronted civil society directly. But although force was implicit in this confrontation – as indeed force is implicit in all present and hitherto existing states – it was used sparingly after the subjugation of Ashanti and cannot be adduced as the main explanation of the stable polity that was achieved in the colony for almost half a century. The magnitude of this achievement becomes clearer when it is realised that British colonial officials were numbered only in their hundreds and that for many Ghanaians a glimpse of a white man was no more than an occasional experience. The question at once arises, how was the colony managed?

It was managed by extreme caution. The political administrators of the colonial state were instinctively aware, if not fully conscious, of the frailty of their position and knew they could never maintain their power in the face of organised opposition among the mass of the Ghanaian people. When such opposition did emerge in the late forties the colonial government, after initial hesitation and an attempt to quell it by force, retired from the stage. The attempt, wherever possible, to avoid such opposition by exercising deliberate restraint, runs like a thread through the official actions and statements: colonial administrators were practised exponents of the maxim that those who wish to rule must first learn to govern themselves. The result of this caution was what Stephen Hymer has called 'sluggishness',[15] and, as we shall see, one of its most important consequences, aside from the perpetuation of British rule, was to reduce the rate of growth of the economy.[16]

[15] Stephen Hymer, 'The political economy of the Gold Coast and Ghana', *Center Discussion Paper no. 73*, Economic Growth Center, Yale University 1969.

[16] 'One of the most prominent features in the history of this country has been its persistent advances in cultural progress by leaps rather than by the process of gradual and continuous evolution. Since the beginning of the twentieth century these leaps have been even more exaggerated and the past decade has witnessed a

While the constitutional and institutional fusion of government and state determined the form of politics and defined the limits of policy in the colony, it did not obliterate their separate identities, which expressed themselves in different aspects of policy. Corresponding to their conceptually distinct identities, as opposed to their actual inter-penetration, we can elaborate a framework with two poles for analysing the substance of policy. At one pole there are the economic determinants of policy,[17] at the other the political.[18] For the British, these were on the one hand the promotion of trade, and on the other the use of the resources generated by this trade to ' raise the level of civilisation '. What the British hoped would prove a harmonious combination turned out altogether different in practice.

The integration of these two aspects of colonial policy in Ghana, in other words, the political economy of colonialism as seen through British eyes, can be readily summarised. The people of Ghana were ' natives in a most elementary state of civilisation ', far below the British on the evolutionary ladder both materially and in other no less important ways. The task of the British was clear, their trust sacred: progress had to be made on both fronts. Fortunately simultaneous advance on both fronts was not only possible but a necessary precondition of advance on either: Adam Smith and William

---

rate of progress which might even be considered dangerous. The sudden acquisition of very great wealth may upset the equilibrium of an individual but in the Gold Coast it seems to have acted over the nation as a most potent stimulant for greater effort, even the set-back of over-production and the disappearance of markets having had but little effect. It is probable that the nation is advancing faster than may seem good to Government who actually has had occasion to act as a brake rather than as an accelerating force.' Cardinal, *The Gold Coast, 1931*, p. 75.

17 We must also mention here the technical and administrative determinants of policy, but as the main theme of this essay is the contradiction between the political and economic determinants of policy, we shall be concerned with them only in passing.

18 At this pole there must also be included the structural determinants of policy: structural in the sense that they correspond to the structure of the economy. During the colonial period the structure of the Ghanaian economy was becoming increasingly capitalist; it is those policies or aspects of policy that correspond to this development that we call structural. Insofar as this development required positive actions, such as pacification and the establishment of a legal framework to confirm the emerging relations of production, the structural aspects of policy were highly defined. But such positive actions were not frequently required after the establishment of the colonial state, and instead of actively shaping policy, they increasingly assumed the form of constraints. (They constituted a second set of limits on colonial policy, together with those that arose from the constitutional and institutional structure of the colonial state which we have just discussed.) Thus colonial policy, while never jeopardising the institution of property or wage labour – though it modified their conditions, particularly those of the latter, on occasions – did not refer to them continuously and explicitly. Although they remained an implicit aspect of policy after 1920, i.e. in the period that concerns us here, they were taken more or less for granted and we will have little occasion to refer to them directly.

Table I. *Value of major exports, 1900–60 (five year average) (£000s)*

	Total	Cocoa	Gold	Manganese
1900–4	803	90	152	—
1905–9	2,019	467	931	—
1910–14	3,788	1,761	1,314	—
1915–19	6,221	4,145	1,489	46
1920–4	8,720	6,896	872	208
1925–9	12,324	10,012	758	681
1930–4	8,183	5,397	1,616	435
1935–9	12,314	6,499	4,123	790
1940–4	12,059	3,654	6,088	1,195
1945–9	32,433	21,890	5,343	2,636
1950–4	88,088	61,638	9,161	6,878
1955–9	95,835	59,718	9,624	7,330

Source: See Table 21a below.

Wilberforce marched forward hand in hand.[19] On the one hand the colonial government was to build the economy with a policy of free trade and by concrete efforts through railway construction and assistance to farmers; on the other, by a low and judicious taxation of the expanding trade that resulted from this, it could raise the revenue necessary for building such things as schools, which would bring to the colony the less tangible advantages of British progress.[20] If in the process British capital was to profit, then this was further evidence, if any were needed, of the marvellous order of things: philanthropy at 5 per cent was the vision of the epoch.

Table I, which presents a summary of the trade returns for the colony for the period 1900–60, shows how substantial was the growth of external trade during this period, even allowing for the valuation of imports and exports at current prices. As these returns were considered the most important economic indicator – apart from the accounts of public revenue and expenditure, they were the most reliable economic statistics that the colonial government gathered and presented – the message they relate might reasonably have been expected to meet with official approval. In part it did, but it was also a source of profound disquiet. For, aside from the growth in the total value of export

[19] 'British colonial policy can be symbolised as an alliance between Wilberforce and Adam Smith . . . One man took it for granted that any individual of any race could find a fuller life within the expanding Christian Church: the other took it for granted that he would live more abundantly within the expanding economy of Europe.' W. K. Hancock, *The wealth of colonies,* Marshall Lectures, Cambridge University Press, Cambridge 1950, pp. 18–20.

[20] 'For Progress we must have education. For Education of the right kind we must have a bigger Revenue. To get a bigger Revenue we must have a bigger trade, and to get a bigger trade we must have more agriculture and far better systems of transport than at present exist.' The Governor, *Legislative Council Debates, 1920–1,* p. 6.

trade, the fact that emerges from these data is the massive importance of cocoa. This presented major economic and political problems for the colonial government. Firstly, to the extent that cocoa was important and profits from its production accrued to Ghanaians, British capital captured a diminished share of the total profits that arose from the trade of the colony. Thus the coincidence of colonial progress and the prosperity of British enterprise was far from complete. Secondly, Ghanaian capital competed with British capital for resources, such as labour and the provision of transport facilities by the state, and prevented its expansion in sectors of the economy where it might otherwise have settled. The challenge of Ghanaian business grew with the prosperity of cocoa and it is not surprising that the colonial government cast desperately around for an alternative crop whose production it could control more easily. Thirdly, the capitalist organisation of cocoa production acted as a dissolvent on the 'traditional' structures of Ghanaian society, through which the British would have liked to exercise their power: indirect rule. The progress of the cocoa industry therefore threatened to erode the very roots of the colonial state. For all these reasons the colonial government was never anything but ambiguous about the trading success of the colony.

The dilemma of the colonial government is now apparent. At one moment it was dependent upon the cocoa trade to generate the revenue it needed, not only to fulfil its civilising mission but more importantly to finance the apparatus of state and the social and economic infrastructure which British capital needed to do business in the colony. At the same time the very success of the cocoa industry undermined the opportunities it created, and the frailty of the colonial state, arising from its particular institutional and constitutional structure, made it impossible for the colonial government to impose any effective form of control over cocoa producers. This dilemma came to a head at the end of the First World War and affected all the details of colonial policy after this date.

COLONIAL POLICY

In this section four areas of colonial policy are discussed: agriculture, transport, finance and education. The period mainly under consideration is that between the two world wars, though the discussion is not narrowly restricted in a temporal sense. Nor does it attempt to provide a comprehensive survey of policy; rather its aim is to illustrate the way in which the colonial government coped with the basic dilemmas that faced it.

Agriculture

Agriculture was the largest sector of the colonial economy, employing more labour and producing more output than any other, and cocoa was the colony's most important export. Had the colonial government's only concern been to maximise the trade of the colony it would almost certainly have done more to promote the production of this crop. Yet the steps it took to encourage technical progress and increased productivity in the cocoa industry, and also in agriculture generally, were few, hesitant and mainly misdirected.[21] At times actual attacks were launched against the industry.

In the period after 1910 the Department of Agriculture started a sustained campaign against the cocoa industry, which reached its peak towards the end of the First World War. This attack was concentrated on two issues: the department contended, first, that the methods of cultivation employed by Ghanaian cocoa farmers paid inadequate attention to disease control; and second, that the cocoa brought to market was of poor quality. On both issues the department was wrong.[22]

The substance of the first complaint was that cocoa farmers who owned more than one farm could not give proper attention to disease control. Certainly Ghanaian cocoa farmers had no scientific measures for dealing with disease, but then neither had the Department of Agriculture. Its solution of weeding and keeping farms tidy, doubtless based on the vision of the well-ordered English countryside, would have proved useless even if it could have prevailed upon the farmers to perform these chores; and when farms in the eastern region were severely struck by disease (swollen-shoot) in the late forties it had nothing to suggest but cutting out infected trees.[23] In fact the Ghanaian cocoa farmer's own intuitive reactions to the disease were the best in the circumstances: their farms were generally scattered through the bush

[21] 'It is extraordinary . . . that until 1937 there was no single agricultural station in the cocoa belt proper at which research could be carried out on the requirements of the crop. It is difficult to see how any officer of the department (of agriculture) could be expected to offer correct advice on cultural or other treatments as he had no opportunity to acquire knowledge under local conditions. Thus when diseases and pests became serious, the technical officers of the department had no means of knowing how any remedial measures they might suggest would affect the general health of the trees. At one stage they suggested cutting out diseased parts of the trees, but this opened the canopy with disastrous results.' *The West Africa Commission 1938–9*, Leverhulme Trust, London 1943. Extracts from this report are included as Document 28a below. According to the Commission very few agricultural research stations in the colony were well located: except for those in the Northern Territories 'none of them appears to be typical of the country it is intended to serve'. Agricultural policy was also criticised just after the Second World War by the Watson Commission, which commented upon 'the lack of interest in technical problems shown by many members of the Administration'. *Report of the Commission of enquiry into disturbances in the Gold Coast, 1948*, Colonial Office, London 1948. See p. 202 below and Document 28b below.

[22] See R. H. Green and S. H. Hymer, 'Cocoa in the Gold Coast: a study in the relations between African farmers and agricultural experts', *Journal of Economic History*, XXVI, September 1966, no. 3. The argument of the next few pages is largely based upon this article.

[23] See below p. 241 and Document 35.

and their practice of leaving infected farms to recuperate by themselves worked more often than not. Not only was the department's advice technically inadequate, it was also economically inappropriate, as it would have involved reducing acreages and increasing the use of scarce labour. The Ghanaians' response was the rational one to the factor endowments of the area. The proposals of the Department of Agriculture would have restricted the growth of the industry as existing techniques, both those used by farmers and even more those suggested by the department, did not allow for any substantial increase in yields per acre, so that expanding output could only be achieved by increasing the area under cultivation.

On the issue of quality the department was similarly incorrect both technically and economically. On technical grounds it was wrong because it mistook Ghanaian cocoa for a crop equivalent to West Indian cocoa, whereas the two are in fact quite distinct and have separate uses in the confectionery industry.[24] Its economic error followed logically from its technical ignorance, for, had it understood more about the uses to which Ghanaian cocoa was put, it might not have persisted with the groundless belief that improvements in quality would have to lead to substantial increases in price. 'Much of the work of the department' commented the West Africa Commission in the forties, 'had been devoted to setting up standards for marketed cocoa and a Special Produce Inspection Branch was established. Their work has not been backed up by appreciable price bonuses for better quality.'[25] Both farmers and the European buying firms knew that the return on improved quality was often less than the cost of grading and that efforts to better the quality of cocoa were not therefore an economic proposition. In addition grading, like the recommendations on disease control, would have slowed down the growth of the industry by absorbing considerable amounts of labour. Nevertheless the department continued its efforts in this field for over 30 years.[26]

24 West Indian *criollo* is a fine quality cocoa used in limited quantities for flavouring: the *amerlonado* is used in much greater quantities and makes up a high proportion of the net bulk of the finished product. The two types of cocoa are not direct substitutes for each other, but are qualitatively quite distinct and complement each other.

25 See p. 231 below.

26 As early as 1904 the Governor, Sir John P. Ridger, sought to 'impress on both the growers and purchasers of this product the necessity of shipping, as far as possible, Cocoa of the best quality that can be grown here, and not mixed consignments containing a large proportion of immature, unclean and improperly prepared beans. I am informed [he continued] that there is no reason whatever why Gold Coast Cocoa should not equal a price to that grown in St Thome...' Governor's statement on the 'State of Trade in 1904', *Legislative Council Debates, 1905*; cited in G. E. Metcalfe, *Great Britain and Ghana: documents of Ghana history, 1807–1957*, University of Ghana (Thomas Nelson) Legon, Accra and London 1964, p. 531. Shortly before this the recently constituted Department of Agriculture complained that 'the quality of cocoa appears to deteriorate yearly.

While Ghanaian opinion rejected the charges made against cocoa farmers that they were lazy, careless of the future of their industry and indifferent to the quality of the crop,[27] organised opposition never got under way. In fact the colonial government itself stepped in and refused to give the department the sweeping powers of control it sought, precisely in order to prevent just such an occurrence.[28] This is one of the few occasions in which the political and economic polarities of policy stand in sharp and palpable opposition to each other. As this political action resulted from the weakness of the colonial state it worked in the Ghanaian interest.

Despite the activities of the Department of Agriculture, cocoa production continued to grow rapidly and accounted for 83 per cent of the total exports of the colony in 1920.[29] The colonial government's response to this phenomenal success of Ghanaian enterprise was to try and do by stealth what its over-zealous Department of Agriculture had failed to do by confrontation. It launched a policy of export diversification.

The economics of diversification in the context of colonial Ghana are not as unambiguous as they appear at first sight. First, diversification, as

---

This is largely due to plants being raised from immature beans and to the ignorance of natives in the proper method of preparing their crop.' To prove that better prepared cocoa fetched a higher price the department shipped off two special consignments: one to Hamburg the other to London. In Hamburg, the graded cocoa received a premium of 'nearly 3 percent' and on this basis, without any estimates of the costs of preparation the department 'assumed it would pay the grower to wash cocoa intended for the Hamburg market'. In London the department's consignment received no premium at all, making the results of the tests 'somewhat contradictory': 'judging from the London brokers' opinion it would appear that it would be more profitable for the grower to send his cocoa to market unwashed, as its weight is decreased by this operation and a certain amount of extra labour is entailed'. *Report of the Department of Agriculture, 1904.* Three years later the department made a second attempt to prove its point with further trial shipments to London: the average premium these received was £2 a ton on a prevailing market price of about £65 a ton. Again no attempt was made to estimate the costs of special preparation. *Report of the Department of Agriculture, 1907.* Despite this the department and the colonial government persisted with the attempt to improve the quality of cocoa until the 1930s. See 'Memorandum on the creation of a fund for improving the quality and marketing of Cocoa', *Sessional Paper no. XVIII, 1930–1*; 'The report of the cocoa exportation committee', *Sessional Paper no. II of 1934*; and the *Cocoa industry regulation ordinance 1934.*

27 See Document 32 below.

28 The Department of Agriculture made a strong call for legislation to control the activities of cocoa farmers after a fact-finding tour by its director in 1916–17. The Governor, Sir Hugh Clifford, resisted it on the grounds of 'political consideration' which the colonial government could not 'afford to ignore or neglect', p. 239 below. His successor, Sir Gordon Guggisberg, somewhat hesitantly affirmed this stand in 1923: 'The policy of this Government is to increase cocoa production up to the full working capacity of the population. In view of the right of every man to grow as much as his land can produce I do not see what other policy this Government could adopt.' p. 240 below.

29 See Table 21a below.

attempted by the colonial government, amounted to a practical rejection of the theory of comparative advantages, which provided the classical economic justification for the trading policy of the British Empire, and the international division of labour that it engendered. If one thing was clear by 1920 it was that Ghana had a comparative advantage in the production of cocoa: and since the colonial government was formally committed to the promotion of trade, the decision to diversify must ultimately have been politically determined. Second, the argument of the colonial government which prompted the attempt at diversification, that the colonial economy was unstable due to its heavy dependence upon the export of a single primary commodity, was essentially correct; but the policy conclusion, that the economy could be stabilised by widening the range of agriculture exports, was essentially incorrect.[30] For the instability of the colonial economy arose not from its dependence upon cocoa as such, but from its role in the world economy as an exporter of primary goods, and this would not have been changed by the type of diversification the colonial government had in mind.[31] It is possible that a greater degree of stability might have resulted if, first, the diversification policy had substantially increased the output of alternative crops and, second, their world market prices had not had the same pattern of fluctuation as that of cocoa. Neither condition held; and when the depression of the thirties led to sharp price falls in *all* primary exports, the limited schemes the colonial government had launched in the twenties did not fulfil the aims of stabilisation.[32] In fact all the schemes failed in the thirties and only cocoa survived the collapse of world trade.

[30] See p. 51 below.

[31] Some measure of stability might have been achieved had the diversification programme turned in the direction of industry and if Ghana had entered the world market as an exporter of manufactured goods. But a diversification policy of this type was unthinkable for the colonial government and when it was suggested over twenty years later to the Watson Commission it was turned down on the grounds that the climate was too enervating to make industry feasible. See p. 78 below.

[32] For details of expenditure on agriculture under the Ten Year Development Programme of the twenties, see p. 200 below. Details of the various schemes are contained in a number of sessional papers: 'Report of the shea-butter areas of the Northern Territories', *Sessional Paper no. VIII, 1922–3*; 'Shea butter industry of the Northern Territories by G. C. Coull', *Sessional Paper no. VII, 1925–6*; 'Despatches relating to the shea nut industry in the Northern Territories', *Sessional paper no. XI, 1929–30* (see Document 27 below); 'Report on the Accra seisal hemp plantation', *Sessional Paper no. IX, 1922–3*; 'Report on the Accra seisal plantation', *Sessional Paper no. XIX, 1927–8*; 'Report on communal coconut plantations', *Sessional Paper no. X, 1922–3*; and 'Report on the palm-oil industry', *Sessional Paper no. IV, 1924–5*; 'Despatch relating to the oil palm industry with particular reference to a subsidiary scheme for palm oil mills', *Sessional Paper no. III, 1930–31* (see Document 26 below). An interesting attempt to promote palm oil

The success of cocoa on the world market was reflected inside Ghana by the higher wages that cocoa farmers were able to pay their rapidly expanding labour force. The initial difficulty faced by the colonial government in its bid to diversify agricultural exports was in attracting labour. The comparative advantage of the cocoa industry meant that productivity in cocoa was higher than in any other export crop, so that the task that faced the colonial government was to achieve even higher levels of productivity in the new agricultural projects. This could not have been done without considerable investment in techniques and organisation, for the high productivity of labour in cocoa was not due simply to the natural advantages the crop enjoyed in Ghana but also to the high degree of organisation and enterprise that Ghanaian farmers had brought to the venture of growing it – cocoa did not simply 'grow on trees' as the colonial government fondly imagined. The problem of the colonial government boiled down to finding the financial resources to undertake an ambitious programme of agricultural investment: but all sources of investment were politically unsatisfactory.

First, it could have attempted to raise funds by borrowing in London, but as we shall see when we look at financial policy, the colonial government would only borrow money against projects that yielded a return sufficient to cover both current and capital costs by an early date, and this could not be guaranteed here. Second, it could have invited expatriate business to enter directly into foreign production. Although it did subsidise a venture by the United Africa Company in the oil palm industry in the late twenties, it was generally reluctant to pursue this line too far, because of the risk to the political stability of the countryside. From this perspective expatriate capital was barely preferable to Ghanaian capital. Thirdly, it could have attempted to raise revenue itself, but this course of action was subject to many difficulties that arose directly from the colonial dilemma.

The colonial government raised the vast bulk of its revenue by taxing external trade, which was so heavily dominated by cocoa that any attempt to increase revenue would have involved increasing the taxation on cocoa farmers, either directly through export duties or indirectly through import duties. They could hardly have been expected to help finance rival activities without strong opposition. So the colonial government in its attempt to find a rival to the cocoa industry was more or less dependent upon the self-same

---

cultivation was made before the First World War; see the Debate on the Second Reading of the Palm Oil Bill, 1913, *Legislative Council Debates, 1913*; cited by Metcalfe, *Great Britain and Ghana*, pp. 540–2. Details of the progress of the various schemes can be found in the annual *Reports of the Department of Agriculture*; and the annual addresses by the Governor in the *Legislative Council Debates* (see Document 24 below).

industry, and since it could not risk a full-scale confrontation with cocoa farmers on the issue of 'no taxation without representation', its diversification programme remained small and insignificant for the development of the colony.

The various schemes it did manage to get off the ground bring all the elements of its dilemma into sharp focus and make clear the real significance of diversification, irrespective of the immediate motives that inspired it. No scheme relied upon Ghanaian capital, and expatriate capital was admitted only hesitantly, belatedly and in a limited fashion. The first choice of the colonial government was to work within the 'traditional' framework of Ghanaian society; it favoured communal ventures or projects under the control of chiefs and overseen by expatriate managers. But as it recognised itself on at least one occasion, this type of economic activity had limited possibilities for success in the Ghanaian countryside, where capitalism in Cardinal's words 'almost amounted to a revolution'.[33] Through its diversification policy the colonial government was vainly trying to shore up pre-capitalist forms of activity while depending upon capital for the resources to make this possible.[34] The aim of the diversification policy, and indeed of all colonial agricultural policy, was also the principal cause of its failure.

[33] 'Economic conditions have changed in the Gold Coast largely as a result of the successful development of the cocoa industry. The average farmer instead of being as formerly a labourer himself has now become an employer of labour. Likewise cocoa has been responsible for the development of an individualistic spirit in production as against the communal co-operative system under which palm-oil was produced in former days.' p. 215 below.

[34] In addition diversification, had it succeeded in weakening the cocoa industry, might also have worked to the advantage of the mines. 'During 1919 and the early part of 1920 the cocoa industry was booming with the result that unnecessarily high wages were paid to labourers engaged in carrying cocoa to the depots. These high wages attracted a large percentage of the available labour and caused a shortage for other purposes. The mines were naturally affected by the shortage. To attract labour the Mining Companies have constructed good houses for the labourers, installed water supplies, provided food at cost price and raised wages as high as they could afford. These measures should be effective in securing a better labour supply, and with a return to normal conditions in the cocoa industry an improvement in the labour situation might be expected.' *Annual Report of the Department of Mines, 1920*, p. 3. The same year the Department of Agriculture commented, 'The abnormal demand produced a curious situation which in other words meant to the farmers a maximum return for a minimum expenditure of energy expended. Today the position is the antithesis of that described; greater effort must be put forth not only in the cultivation of cocoa but also in the cultivation of other crops, and the sooner this is realised the better for all concerned.' *Annual Report of the Department of Agriculture, 1920*, p. 12. Ten years later Cardinal provided the following interesting justification for diversification: 'the Gold Coast peasant-farmer if he is to survive must remember and be always taught to remember that the crops which produce small but certain profits are those upon which his existence depends, since they do not draw upon him the envious eye of the usurer or the greedy one of the capitalist.' Cardinal, *The Gold Coast, 1931*, p. 99.

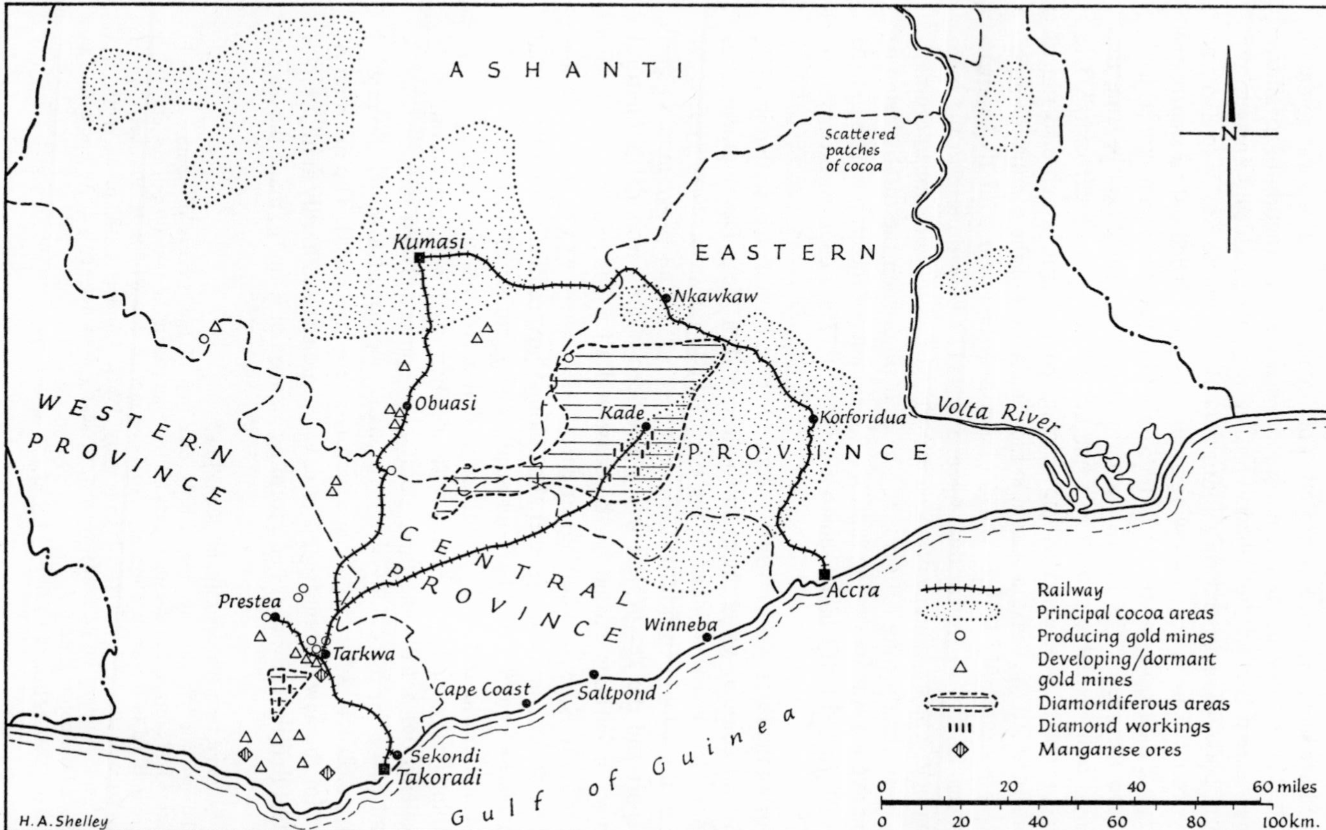

Map 2. The Gold Coast Railway, 1945 (from Gold Coast Survey Department, Accra 1945).

Transport

As we have seen, the original attraction of Ghana for the British was gold and almost the very first act of colonialisation was the construction of a railway in the western part of the country, linking the gold-producing areas to the nearest port, Sekondi, and running on inland to Kumasi (see Map 2). Far away from the main cocoa growing areas, this line carried only a small percentage of the crop to the coast: in 1905 only 12 per cent of cocoa exports were taken to the sea by the railway, and in 1910, the year cocoa became the colony's most valuable export, this had actually fallen to 8 per cent.[35] The second railway constructed by the colonial government, which also ran to Kumasi but left the coast at Accra, in the eastern part of the country, changed matters considerably in the course of the next few years, for its southern stretches – Accra to Korforidua, opened in 1912 – passed close to the main cocoa belt. The percentage of cocoa exports carried by rail jumped dramatically with the opening of this new line at a time when the total volume of cocoa exports was increasing rapidly: 23,000 tons of the crop were exported in 1910; in 1914 this had risen to 52,900 and 77 per cent were carried by rail.[36]

During the First World War the second line was completed, so that in 1920, when the colonial government introduced a Ten Year Development Programme, Kumasi was linked to the coast by two railways. Seventy-five per cent of the actual expenditure undertaken as part of this programme was on transport and the key project was a new deep-water harbour.[37] No natural deep-water harbour existed on the coast and all goods had to be taken by surf-boats to ships standing out in deep water. There was considerable dispute in the colony as to whether the colonial government should undertake the construction of a new harbour at all. The argument of those in favour of construction was technical, pointing out that surf-boats were inadequate for handling heavy loads; cocoa deteriorated when it got wet; and so on. Their opponents did not dispute these points, but contended that greater benefits would ensue for the colony if the colonial government lowered the rate of taxation, instead of undertaking expensive new investment. The question of a site for the new harbour seems to have been discussed hardly at all, despite the fact that the railway system, forming an apex at Kumasi, made the choice

[35] Calculated from Tables 21b and 32c below.

[36] 'To provide the railway line is only one step in the process of change . . . Only limited advantage can accrue unless all the changes in the structure of society which are implied in the application of capital are carried through.' S. H. Frankel, *Capital investment in Africa*, Oxford University Press, London 1938, p. 6. While this judgement might be generally correct, it clearly does not apply to southern Ghana during the colonial period.

[37] See pp. 54–5 below and Table 15 below.

of either Accra or Sekondi feasible.[38] It seems to have been taken for granted by all parties to the harbour dispute that Takoradi, just outside Sekondi, was the most appropriate site and here it was that the colonial government built its deep-water harbour. Certainly, as it pointed out, this was the best site technically speaking and a harbour could be constructed and maintained more cheaply here than at any other point on the coast.[39] Even in the most narrow economic terms this was a dubious criterion, since it took account only of the costs of the project and ignored the benefits that might have arisen had the harbour been located differently. If a full cost-benefit analysis had been undertaken, with the expansion of trade being the main criterion of benefit, a detailed assessment would have been made of all the possible sites; but there is no evidence of any such assessment ever having been made.

What was the real significance of the choice of Takoradi? It served expatriate mining interests more directly than if Accra had been chosen; in fact without it the new expatriate-controlled manganese industry could hardly have got started. It was, in effect if not in conscious intention, not simply a technical preference for one site as opposed to another; nor for that matter a preference for assisting mining as opposed to cocoa, which would have benefited much more had Accra been chosen: it was a decision that favoured expatriate capital as opposed to Ghanaian capital. The die was thus cast for a conflict between the colonial state and Ghanaian enterprise centring on transport that lasted throughout the twenties and thirties.

The economic dilemma created for the colonial government by the location of the harbour at Takoradi can be quickly summarised. On the one hand, the strict orthodoxy of its financial policy meant that harbour dues had to be sufficiently high to meet the interest charges and repayments of capital to the British creditors who loaned the colonial government the funds to undertake the project. On the other hand the very rationale of the harbour was to provide cheap port facilities to British mining capital. Trapped between the interests of these two factions of British capital, the colonial government had only one solution. If it could ensure full utilisation of the facilities at Takoradi it would be able to spread capital costs more thinly, lower handling costs per

[38] In fact it would probably have been cheaper to develop the Accra–Kumasi line as the Sekondi–Kumasi line was in a poor state of repair and required expensive re-alignment.

[39] 'I do not intend here to go into details of why Takoradi has been selected, but I may say briefly that a deep-water harbour can be built more cheaply here than at any other place on our coast. Secondly, that owing to the existence of a natural breakwater in Takoradi Reef and the rocky nature of the bottom there is a minimum of danger of sand and silt and no expensive upkeep of dredging.' Annual Address by the Governor, 1920, *Legislative Council Debates, 1921–2*, p. 55 below. It is interesting to note, however, that the Department of Mines believed that the exports of manganese were limited by the railway and harbour facilities at Sekondi. *Annual Report of the Department of Mines, 1920*, p. 4.

unit of throughput, and so keep dues down. But as the exports of the mines could not by themselves generate sufficient traffic to ensure full utilisation, the colonial government was forced to turn to the cocoa industry to make good the shortfall. Once again the colonial dilemma was fully represented: although built in British interests the harbour was dependent upon Ghanaian capital to discharge its aims fully. To attract cocoa into Takoradi the colonial government decided that a third railway was needed and construction work on the Central Province line started in the early twenties.[40] This new railway started in the western reaches of the main cocoa belt at Kade, some miles to the west of the eastern railway, and ran more or less parallel with the coast to join the Sekondi–Kumasi line at Tarkwa. As a result the cocoa-belt was now linked to the coast by two lines (to Accra by the eastern line and to Sekondi–Takoradi by the new one) neither of which actually traversed it. Thus the layout of the railways made a system of feeder transport necessary. By the early twenties motor lorries were being widely used for this purpose. Before many years had elapsed road transport had developed to a point where it no longer fed the railways but started to compete with them for traffic.[41] The Central Province Railway was a major casualty of this development: by the time it was completed in 1927 the roads were in full spate and it was never able to make an effective bid for traffic.

In fact it is doubtful whether the line should have been built at all if, as the colonial government intended, its main purpose was to assist the export of cocoa, for this could have been achieved more effectively and more cheaply by expanding the network of feeder roads that already existed in the main cocoa areas. Certainly the colonial government was aware of this alternative and was at pains to demonstrate the superiority of railways over roads in the colony. Roads, it argued, had their uses as tributaries to the railways and were economic over distances of up to 35 miles: over greater distances railways provided the most economic form of transport.[42]

Probably this assessment made in the early twenties was accurate for the

[40] See 'Despatch from the Governor to the Secretary of State, no. 747, 2 November 1922, on the subject of the proposed Central Province Railway', *Sessional Paper no. XIV, 1922–3*, Document 20a below.

[41] In 1920 the Annual Report of the Eastern Region remarked that 'during the year mechanical transport has become increasingly popular'. Two years later it reported, 'a minor industry has sprung up and assumed considerable proportions ... running passengers and luggage and carrying lorries between various ports'. And by the next year the industry had grown so rapidly that it was 'possible to travel all over the province' by lorry: by 1924–5 there had been established 'regular organised routes which run on schedule' covering the whole province.

[42] 'On feeder-roads to railways and ports up to a distance of about 35 miles, lorries are invaluable and will always have their uses; but on long trunk roads ... they are not a practical proposition', Despatches on the Central Province Railway, see below Document 20a, para. 36. See also Document 18, paras. 81–2 below.

time; but by the end of the decade, when lorry rates had fallen dramatically from about 2*s* 9*d* per ton mile to about 6*d*,[43] it was totally unrealistic. However, even if this fall in cost of road haulage is left out of account, the construction of the new railway was hardly justifiable even by the colonial government's own criteria, for most of the cocoa it was intended to carry was produced within 35 miles (or just slightly more) of the eastern railway on the one hand or the coast on the other. Needless to say, the 7,000 tons of cocoa which the colonial government said went unmarketed each year [44] due to inadequate transport facilities in the Central Province never materialised and Ghanaians were quite capable of getting their cocoa to ports without the new railway. So inadequate were the colonial government's transport surveys for this project, and so clearly did it contravene its own criteria of efficiency in the choice of route, that it is hard to interpret the technical and economic justifications that were put forward as anything more than attempts to rationalise what was essentially a political decision. Certainly the Central Province Railway, like the harbour at Takoradi that it was intended to serve, was dependent upon the cocoa industry for solvency, but was not suited primarily to serve the needs of the industry. The consequent refusal of Ghanaians to make use of it for shipping cocoa made it a financial liability for the colonial government; but more, it threw Takoradi into deficit when it was finally opened, as the bulk of the cocoa in the Central Provinces was shipped out through Accra or the smaller Central Province ports.[45] Not only was the attempt to reduce harbour costs for British mining interests at Takoradi thwarted, but the rapid development of cheap motor transport drew traffic away from the Accra–Kumasi line,[46] which did actually serve the cocoa industry, and spread the financial crisis to the whole of the state transport system.

[43] For estimates of rates in the early twenties, see Document 18, paras. 78–81, and Document 20a, para. 33 below: for rates at the end of the decade, see Document 22b, para. 14 below.

[44] Document 20a, para. 40 below.

[45] In the early twenties the Governor, Sir Gordon Guggisberg, gave an assurance to the inhabitants of Cape Coast and the other Central Province towns that their interests would not be injured by the construction of Takoradi Harbour or the Central Province Railway. This assurance, an attempt to cope with political opposition, proved to be critically important at the end of the twenties, when the transport authorities were eager to close the Central Province ports so as to divert traffic to Takoradi. Needless to say, political definitions dominated and the ports remained open. See the 'Report of the Central Province Trade Routes Committee appointed by His Excellency the Governor to consider and make recommendations regarding (i) Central Province Railway routes (ii) the treatment of the ports of Cape Coast and Saltpond on the opening of Takoradi', *Sessional Paper no. VI, 1928–9*, Document 21 below.

[46] Between 1923 and 1928 the volume of cocoa exported rose from 200,000 to almost 240,000 tons: in the same period the volume of cocoa carried by the eastern railway fell from 92,000 to 61,000 tons.

The issues involved in road versus rail were essentially the same as those we have discussed in connection with the location of the deep-water harbour at Takoradi, which was, after all, the keystone of the whole state transport system. On one side was the colonial government, trapped between two factions of British capital – finance and mining – seeking to reconcile its strict financial orthodoxy in the management of the state railways and harbours with the provision of cheap transport facilities for gold and manganese. On the other side was Ghanaian capital, initially concerned to lower cocoa freight costs, but rapidly developing a new sector of private enterprise – road haulage – which soon achieved its own momentum and attempted, quite successfully, to compete lucrative transport business away from the state, particularly in the eastern part of the colony. The dependence on Ghanaian traffic to make the state transport system cheap for British users led to the recurrence of the colonial dilemma, for railway charges, like harbour dues, could be kept down only if cocoa made possible a full utilisation of facilities. The almost complete failure of the Central Province Railway to attract traffic posed a direct threat to the state transport complex in the west, based on Takoradi; but hardly less important was the competitive weakness of the Accra–Kumasi line that developed in the twenties. The loss of substantial amounts of Ghanaian traffic in the east to the roads threw the whole railway system into deficit and, given the financial constraints on policy, this deficit had to be made good one way or another. The obvious solution of increasing the charges on manganese and gold was unacceptable to the colonial government, which cast around somewhat desperately for an alternative.

Two committees [47] were set up to look into the problem in the early thirties, when the depression increased the financial pressures on the colonial government and led to a greater intensity of competition in transport. Taken together these two committees had sweeping terms of reference. They made a thorough examination of colonial transport policy, examining such important questions as the basic principles of finance; whether the railways and the harbour should be expected to cover total costs, including capital and interest payments; what criteria should be exercised in the setting of rates charged on different commodities; and whether road users had an unfair competitive advantage over the railways. Generally speaking they favoured some relaxation in financial policy, arguing that it was not necessarily in the interests of the colony as a whole for the state transport system completely to cover its total costs. Had this recommendation been accepted as it stood, it would have worked to some extent in the Ghanaian interest. However, the problem of making good deficits out of general revenue would have remained and this

[47] 'Railway Retrenchment Committee Report and Recommendations 1931', *Sessional Paper no. XIII, 1931–2*; and the 'Report of the Railway Revenue Committee (road vs. rail)', *Sessional Paper no. III, 1932–3*, Document 22b below.

would undoubtedly have involved increased taxes on exports and higher import duties on goods used by Ghanaians. But the additional recommendation, to set rates on different commodities according to what the traffic would bear, set matters firmly back where they were and ensured that Ghanaian rail users, particularly those who had no alternative forms of transport available,[48] would carry the burden of the deficit and continue, in effect, to subsidise the transport costs of the mines.

Adjustment of railway rates and harbour dues did not, however, get to the heart of the matter, which was the competitive strength of the roads. The roads were believed to have unfair advantages, but neither of the committees could produce an effective solution to this problem. The difficulty that faced them was that roads fed railways, as well as competing with them, and that any attempt to redress the competitive balance by financial measures, such as higher petrol duties or increased licence fees, would not discriminate between the different types of road traffic. In the end the colonial government was forced to take direct administrative action and schedule specific stretches of road which competed with the railways, prohibiting the carriage of cocoa and various imported goods along them.[49] Such confrontation with Ghanaian interests was contrary to the normal practice of the colonial government, for reasons we have discussed above, and it is a measure of its dilemma that it was forced to act in this way. It is also a clear indication of where its allegiance ultimately lay.

Finance

So far in our discussion of policy finance has appeared mainly as an expression of the underlying colonial dilemma: how to finance agricultural diversification; how to make the transport system pay for itself, and so on. Further, there would appear, at least at first sight, to have been a possibility for the colonial government to alleviate its situation by pursuing a less rigorously conservative financial policy. As we have just seen in the case of transport, there was some discussion along these lines in the thirties. But in fact the financial constraints on the colonial government were much more than a mere expression of its dilemma, and financial policy was subject to the same set of political and economic determinants as policy in transport and agriculture. These determinants operated most forcefully over the programme of public investment.

48 This applied particularly to cocoa farmers in the area of Kumasi, see pp. 180–1 below.

49 See the 'Report of the Road–Rail Transport Committee', *Sessional Paper no. VI, 1945*, Document 23 below. There 'were even instances of the removal of road bridges over rivers . . . whether this was the intention or not it effectively discouraged the use of roads for the transport of goods', United Africa Company, *Statistical and Economic Review, no. 2*, p. 39.

The strategic importance of investment by the colonial government was much greater than its small size would suggest, and it was through its investment that it exercised the most direct and important influence on the development of the economy. Most government investment was directed into transport and communications, whose importance for the economy is obvious; for the transport system the colonial government constructed provided, in a very real sense, the physical sinews of the market, and the routes it chose and the rates it charged were important determinants of the structure of costs and prices in the colony. But the relatively low level of investment must not be left out of account, for the size of investment can influence the way in which it is financed and the method of financing in turn influences the type of project undertaken. The connection between the means of financing investment on the one hand and the choice of project and management practices on the other, was particularly close in Ghana during the colonial period.

Table II summarises the trade and financial returns of the colony for the period 1900–30 and reveals certain important facts. Firstly, during the period total expenditure amounted to over £60 million, of which something in the order of £33 million, or about 55 per cent, was allocated to non-recurrent items excluding defence: expenditure here covered the administrative, social and economic infrastructure of the colony. The last was the one that affected the development of the economy most directly, as it consisted almost entirely of expenditure on railways and harbours; it accounted for just over £13 million, or about 20 per cent of total expenditure for the period under consideration. During the same 30 years the colonial government borrowed almost exactly the same amount in London, the vast bulk of which was spent on these items. In other words the colonial government financed its expenditure on economic infrastructure, railways, and harbours, differently from that on other items: that is by borrowing rather than out of general taxation.

Secondly, it can be seen from Table II that the colonial government did not cast its fiscal net very wide, raising most of its revenue by indirect taxes on foreign trade. Yet during this period total trade amounted to over £370 million, so that economically it would have been quite possible to manage without any foreign borrowing at all, either by raising loans locally, which in fact was never considered, or by increasing taxation.[50] But what was feasible economically was impossible politically.

The colonial government freely admitted that taxation in the colony was

[50] In fact the rate of taxation in Ghana was relatively low, even when compared with other British colonies in Africa. See Frankel, *Capital investment in Africa*, p. 184.

Table II. *External trade and colonial government revenue and expenditure, 1900–29 (5 year averages) (£000s)*

	Value of trade	Colonial government revenue	Percentage of revenue from indirect taxes on external trade	Colonial government expenditure	Recurrent expenditure as a percentage of total expenditure	Development expenditure as a percentage of total expenditure
1900–4	3,202	530	67	878	46	41
1905–9	4,389	702	59	629	78	14
1910–14	8,382	1,197	60	1,093	65	18
1915–19	11,702	1,173	59	1,262	78	8
1920–4	18,796	3,392	59	3,986	56	32
1925–9	23,993	3,983	66	4,331	58	28

Sources: Tables 18, 23, 27, 29 below.

low: in fact it made the point quite forcibly at the beginning of the twenties in response to strong pressure locally, when the cry of 'over-taxation' was widely heard throughout the colony.[51] At the same time the London-appointed Committee on Trade and Taxation [52] doubted the wisdom of the expenditure projected under the Ten Year Development Programme. Nonetheless the colonial government committed itself to a low level of taxation as a cardinal principle of policy and when trade recovered after the slump of the early twenties it reduced the rate of export duty on cocoa, upon which most political opposition centred. This line of policy may in part have stemmed from an ideological commitment to *laisser-faire* [53] but it can be more realistically explained as an attempt to prevent opposition crystallising around an inflammable issue. The difficulties that can arise from taxation without representation were well known to the British and every effort was made to avoid in Ghana situations that had arisen elsewhere. In keeping with its reluctance to increase the rate of indirect taxation the colonial government was unwilling to increase direct taxation. Not only would efforts in this field have required

[51] 'The point, however, which I wish to make is that the use of the battle cries of "over-taxation" and "The Poor Native!" is unfair and not justified by facts. The 3,000,000 inhabitants of this country are taxed (indirectly) to a total of 16 shillings per capita per annum – no further comment on taxation is necessary', Despatch from the Governor to the Secretary of State dated 17 August 1922, with reference to statements on the future financial position of the colony, made in the report of the Committee on Trade and Taxation for British West Africa, *Sessional Paper no. VII, 1921–2*, Document 15 below.

[52] Report of a Committee on Trade and Taxation for British West Africa, Cmd. 1600, London 1922, Document 11 and Document 13 below.

[53] Aside from general theoretical objections to explaining real policy decisions in terms of ideas, there are strong substantive grounds for rejecting the proposition that the low level of taxation was an expression of the colonial government's commitment to *laisser-faire*. First, its policies in many other areas were frequently inconsistent with *laisser-faire* ideas. Second, *laisser-faire* itself is far from being unambiguous on this issue. While the classical exponents of *laisser-faire* considered a low level of taxation desirable politically – high taxation, they believed, reduced incentives, upset market forces, offered scope for corruption, and so on – they were much less decisive economically. It was always accepted in classical theory that the state should assume responsibility for projects that, while essential to the economy, did not yield profits to private enterprise. Given this reservation, the level of taxation becomes determined by the number and size of such projects, whose defining characteristic is heavy initial costs and low marginal costs. In other words the idea that *laisser-faire* theory suggests a low level of taxation is far too simple and needs severe modification. It could be argued that it favours the lowest possible level of taxation consistent with government meeting all its requirements: but in this form it is hardly distinctive and it constitutes a poor explanation of the behaviour of any government in particular. In addition it is interesting to reflect that as technical progress frequently increases capital intensity in the standard economic sense and reduces marginal costs relative to average costs, more projects will be categorised as suitable for government intervention as an economy develops. In other words a high level of government revenue and expenditure is quite consistent with *laisser-faire* principles. The real issue is not so much the level of taxation as its incidence.

a vastly more expensive tax administration or the creation of a class of tax farmers, but it would have further increased the monetisation of the economy which the colonial government was more interested in staunching than promoting. All the political determinants of policy in the colony converged to keep the rate of taxation down.

On the other hand, the colonial government was a willing borrower, and the details of its financial practice, as revealed through its accounting procedures,[54] show the extent to which the interests of British creditors determined, or were allowed to determine, its actions in this important field. Expenditure of borrowed funds was not consolidated into the main expenditure accounts published each year by the Treasury Department, but was recorded separately in a special 'loan works account'. Correspondingly the proceeds of borrowing were not included in the main revenue; so the main accounts fail to show the full extent of colonial government activity and give a highly inaccurate picture of its nature, since the main form of public investment, i.e. investment in transport, was almost completely left out. To add to the confusion the Treasury Department did not pursue the logic of keeping a separate loan works account to its end, for it included the repayments of debt, interest charges, and the net operating surpluses or deficits of the undertakings financed out of loans, in the main revenue and expenditure accounts – though even this was done in somewhat haphazard and inconsistent fashion. In addition, and in clear contravention of the principles of double-entry bookkeeping, it included payments into funds built up against outstanding debts as a main item of expenditure chargeable against annual revenue. This extreme caution in matters pertaining to British debts was the decisive element of financial policy and the origin of the rigid orthodoxy and conservativeness that enveloped the whole of colonial policy.[55]

The errors of accounting practice, the contravention of the principles of double-entry book-keeping, while indicative of the subordinate role technical considerations played for the colonial government when British interests were at stake, are of only secondary importance: the class practice reflected through the accounting system is more significant for understanding the political economy of colonialism. To a contemporary economist imbued with Keynesian economics and concerned with growth and planning, the Treasury Department's accounts are confusing and frustrating since they neither show budgetary surpluses or deficits, nor give a clear picture of the actual pattern

[54] An account of the colonial government's accounting practice can be found pp. 346–7 below.

[55] In 1923 the Governor, Sir Gordon Guggisberg, proposed to establish 'the nucleus of a General Reserve Fund . . . built up annually by its own interest to an amount proportional to our capital value as a country'. Governor's Annual Address, *Legislative Council Debates, 1923–4*, Document 16 below.

of expenditure. But if a different perspective is adopted the confusion evaporates and the whole point of the accounting system becomes plain: for calculating the balance between the colonial government and its British creditors it is a model of clarity. Payments due on outstanding debts are given prominence; the data on the actual allocation of resources and so on are pushed into the background. The public accounts are thus a paradigm of British colonialism in Ghana, for which the implications of policies on the local economy were of secondary importance compared with their implications for British interests.

Coupled with the limited capacity of the colonial government to raise funds locally either through taxation or through borrowing, this profound concern for the safety of British loans had repercussions far beyond the financial sector. Indeed it had a direct and significant effect on the pace and pattern of economic development in the colony through the transport system that it influenced most immediately.

Firstly, financial imperatives confirmed the official preference for railways over roads.[56] In order to guarantee the repayments of loans and interest charges the colonial government felt it necessary to make sure that the projects financed by loans themselves produced directly the revenue necessary to cover the capital costs: hence the financial preference for railways, which yielded revenue, over roads, which did not. It would have been a perfectly sound practice for the colonial government to use loans on projects which did not yield revenue directly but increased the total trade of the economy, and then to recoup the funds necessary to meet capital costs by increased general taxation. In economic terms this would have been a rational procedure, and if the aim of the colonial government had really been to maximise trade, it would have chosen projects on this criterion, and not for their capacity to produce revenue. A case for road construction could have been made in these terms. However, the colonial government was reluctant to make repayments of capital and interest charges on British loans directly dependent on taxation, which was politically volatile. In addition, of course, the railways served the mines. Thus, in the transport sector, the interests of British financial and mining capital, as well as the instinctive political caution of the colonial government, to some extent converged. It was for this reason that the challenge of Ghanaian capital through road haulage was so serious: it struck right at the economic and political roots of colonialism.

Secondly, and following directly from this, was the financial management of projects paid for out of loans, for not only was it necessary that these pro-

[56] 'Apart from the question of trade, the construction and maintenance of roads is annually becoming a greater drain on the revenue, a fact that does not attend to the reduction of taxation. Indirect revenue there may be, but, directly, money is all going out and none coming in', Document 20a, para. 36 below.

jects produce revenue directly, they also had to produce sufficient revenue to cover capital costs in addition to current running costs. This determined the level of rates charged by the state transport system, and if total revenue fell below total cost the colonial government had to meet the costs out of general taxation. The other possibility, increasing rates, disappeared when private Ghanaian road haulage competed with the state transport system in the twenties and thirties. As we have seen, the colonial government could find no financial solution to this predicament, and was forced to take administrative action against road hauliers.

It could be argued that the inflow of capital brought about by government borrowing was an advantage to the colony, as it saved scarce local capital, but against any advantages of this type must be offset the uses to which the capital was put and the consequences of these uses. In addition, it is far from clear that capital was so scarce in Ghana that a transport system could not have been built based on local sources. But, as we have seen, the colonial government was reluctant to pursue this possibility for political reasons, and so looked to London for funds. On the other hand, it showed no reluctance to borrow, and it was mainly through its borrowing that British financial interests became involved in the colonial economy, and were able to get a safe and steady return. It is beyond the scope of this work to discuss whether British financial interests forced their loans upon the colonial government in order to guarantee a rentier income, but there is nothing in the actions of the colonial government that contradicts this thesis, and it must be remembered that while money *appears* less real than gold or manganese, which are dug out of the ground, British financial interests were as real and as important in the determination of colonial political economy as British mining interests. It was through financial policy that the colonial government sought to orchestrate the interests of these two sections of British capital.

Education

Unlike policy in the areas we have discussed so far, colonial education policy did not have an immediate impact upon the economy and the interests of Ghanaian and British capital. However, education is as much a branch of political economy as agriculture, transport and finance, and colonial education policy was subject to the same set of political and economic determinants that operated in other sectors.

The autonomy enjoyed by the colonial government in the formulation of its education policy was greater than almost anywhere else. While education has a profound effect upon the development of an economy, insofar as it is responsible for the formation of the labour force, this effect makes itself felt over a period that is usually longer than the time horizons within which business forms its strategy. For this reason the colonial government escaped the close attention of capital in this sphere. British capital in particular played a largely passive role with respect to colonial education policy; firstly, because of the relatively high percentage of unskilled and illiterate labour that it employed; secondly, because the high level and professional manpower that it did employ was mostly recruited from Britain; and thirdly, because Ghanaians were willing candidates for the type of education suitable for clerical jobs, the main capacity in which British capital employed educated Ghanaian workers. In fact the main difficulties encountered by the colonial government in this sphere arose from the eagerness of Ghanaians for this type of education: official policy was to play down academic and promote technical education.[57]

The enthusiasm with which Ghanaians sought education was frequently commented upon and praised by colonial officials and visitors to the colony, although reservations about Ghanaian motives were occasionally expressed. Certainly the colonial government was unhappy with education as it developed in the colony, since it approximated more closely to Ghanaian than to official aspirations. From an early date the colonial authorities had pressed for a technical and organic structure of education, which would equip school leavers with the basic technical skills for work in agriculture and associated activities, for this type of education was central to the colonial government's desired aim of creating a 'thriving and settled peasantry'. But while the Ghanaian 'peasantry' thrived, it steadfastly refused to remain settled in the way the colonial government wished, and the development of capitalism in the countryside and its attendant transformation of social practices and perspectives had powerful repercussions on education. In fact they shaped the development of education to a much greater extent than the colonial government wished. In the early twenties the Governor declared the educational system of the colony 'rotten to the core' and proposed a series of far-reaching reforms.

The essence of colonial policy as it emerged in the twenties was an attempt to establish a two-tier or binary system of education. At the lower level education in technical skills was proposed: this was very much a continuation of existing policy, though greater emphasis was laid upon trades involving engineering skills than had previously been the case. At the apex of the system was to be an elite sector whose purpose the Governor, Sir Gordon Guggisberg, described as follows:

> ... we want to give the best men and women the opportunity of becoming leaders of their own countrymen in thought, industries and the professions. Throughout all this our aim must not be to denationalise them, but to graft skilfully on to their

[57] For a thorough discussion of the development of education in Ghana, see Philip J. Foster, *Education and social change in Ghana*, Routledge and Kegan Paul, London 1965.

national characteristics the best attributes of modern civilisation. For without preserving his national characteristics and his sympathy and touch with the great illiterate masses of his own people, no man can ever become a leader in progress whatever sort of leader he may become.[58]

These aspirations, virtually impossible to accomplish, were embodied in the most important educational undertaking of the twenties: the establishment of the Prince of Wales College at Achimota.

Whether educational policy was thought of as a far-sighted political strategy, or simply as an attempt to improve educational standards in the colony, is a debatable point. Certainly the educational criteria that informed policy corresponded more or less perfectly to the political imperatives of a colonial regime concerned to rule indirectly. Visions of the type of society that the colonial government wished to see emerge in the colony lurked just below the surface of official statements on education or were made quite explicit. On the one hand was technical training mediated with a speck of non-vocational education; on the other the elite educated to highest standards, i.e. British standards, but kept in touch with the mass of the people over whom it was to exercise political dominance. Thus the majority of school leavers were to be equipped with skills for work in agriculture, mining or the various jobs in the towns offered by the colonial government itself, while a small minority were to be inducted into the arts of politics and leadership, to assist the British while they stayed and succeed them when they left. As Guggisberg once remarked: 'Education is the corner-stone of Government's main policy.'

The successful implementation of this policy required a much greater degree of central control over education than had existed before 1920, and the efforts to establish this marked the important new departure in policy in the twenties. These efforts, it may be noted, were directed less against the various Christian missions, which had been pursuing independent work for many decades, than against the initiatives of Ghanaians in this sphere. While education differs in many important respects from cocoa production and transport, it was nonetheless an area where Ghanaian enterprise flourished and a substantial number of private 'bush' schools were established. The quality of education given in these schools was undoubtedly low, and the complaints voiced against them by the colonial government were undoubtedly valid; but it is far from evident that the closure of over 150 of them by the colonial government was a contribution to education in the colony, since their replacements had a much smaller intake: for many Ghanaian children the closing down of the 'bush' schools meant no education at all. The domination of political definitions in the formation of colonial policy is rarely more clearly illustrated.

[58] Document 37, para. 101 below.

In the development of its educational policy the colonial government acted more forcefully than in agriculture, for example, and the confidence with which it established control over education can be compared with its careful handling of cocoa farmers. No doubt this confidence arose from its having no fear of organised Ghanaian opposition, but this did not mean that Ghanaians were passive in the matter of education. In fact quite the reverse was the case and the active, though not politically united, concern of Ghanaians prevented the colonial government achieving its ends fully.

In part their educational aspirations coincided with those of the British, particularly with respect to the elite sector, for there was a section of Ghanaian society willing to accept British education in order to qualify for administrative and professional jobs within the colonial state and subsequently to provide the personnel for Africanisation in the post-independence period. But for the majority of Ghanaians such aspirations were not realistic and their educational prospects were limited to the lower levels of the system: it was here that the divergence between Ghanaian and British perspectives occurred. Ghanaians pressed for an academic type of education that would qualify them for clerical work: the British emphasised the advantages of technical training and deplored the 'glut of half-educated youths fit only for sedentary work'. While the British claim that technical education was in the long-term interests of the colony was probably valid (though it can be doubted whether the type of technical education they had in mind was the most appropriate) it was somewhat abstract: Ghanaian demands were much more in tune with the social and economic realities of the situation and the pattern of education that emerged in the lower reaches of the system reflected them quite closely. In addition it was administration that offered a way to political influence, so that an academic type of education simultaneously satisfied the ambitions of individual Ghanaians and the collective aspiration of the rising Ghanaian capitalist class. Colonial education policy failed at the lower levels, since it was an attempt to check this class and stem the development of capitalism in the countryside.

Despite this it was not a complete failure for the British. Certainly it failed to achieve its ends fully at the lower levels: that is to say it failed at the economic level. The type of technical education that the colonial government promoted for the majority of those receiving education, a minority of the population as a whole, did not correspond to the economic realities of the colony. The expansion of the colonial economy, particularly the growth of clerical and lower-administrative jobs, did not keep pace with the growth of education, and the result feared by the colonial government, large numbers of educated unemployed, ensued, providing a powerful motive force for the movement to decolonise in the years after the Second World War. Thus the economic failure was transformed into a political pressure that colonialism could not withstand. In spite of this, the colonial education policy achieved a considerable measure of political success, for the elite sector survived the change of regime and provided an important channel for British influence after the flag was hauled down. Thus it can be argued that while the education system which the British introduced ultimately failed colonialism, it succeeded posthumously.

The colonial state versus the model colony

The failure of the colonial government to maximise the trade of the colony – a goal to which it was formally committed – clearly results from its promotion of British mining interests and its corresponding neglect and discouragement of Ghanaian cocoa farmers, who, after 1920, were responsible for six or seven times more exports than the mines. However, the argument that its failure to maximise trade was due simply to this is in itself inadequate and needs some qualification; for there was present in the colony a section of British capital – namely commercial capital, represented chiefly by the United Africa Company – whose interests frequently coincided with those of Ghanaian capital. Until 1940 most of the external trade of the colony was handled by a small number of expatriate, mainly British, commercial firms, and the profitability of their investments in the colony was largely dependent upon the volume of external trade. Since this in turn was largely determined by the volume of cocoa exports, there was a strong moment of convergence in the interests of commercial and Ghanaian capital: both would have benefited from a policy of trade maximisation and both could list the same set of complaints against the colonial government.[59]

While these two sections of capital pulled the colonial government in the direction of fostering an expanded trade, the interests of the mines, along with the government's careful attitude towards British loans and its general antipathy to the rapid development of Ghanaian business, pulled it in the other direction. As it veered towards the latter and in consequence slowed the growth of trade, colonial policy, in general, can be characterised as an attempt to maintain this matrix of forces in balance. This attempt, which constitutes the political economy of colonialism, in practice consists of two antithetical elements: on the one hand, the vision of the ideal colony in the minds of the colonial administrators that informed their practice;[60] on the other, the

[59] The convergence of interests between Ghanaian and expatriate commercial capital was far from perfect. The price of cocoa was an important bone of contention and in 1937 cocoa farmers organised a hold-up of cocoa supplies, believing that the price they received from the buying firms was too low and was held down due to the formation of a ring. See pp. 240–1 and Document 33 below.

[60] Of course the vision of the ideal colony sprang out of the real situation in which the colonial administration found itself.

realities of the Ghanaian situation which stubbornly refused to conform to the colonial model.

The model colony in the imagination of the colonial administrator would appear to have possessed the following essential features. It would have an export sector firmly under the control of British capital which, when taxed lightly, would yield sufficient revenue to pay for the administration and cover the capital costs of a state-built transport system financed by loans floated in London. Most of the people would live outside this ' modern ' sector, although some of them would be involved in limited economic and social transactions with it in the capacity of petty commodity producers selling food or as workers, preferably migrant. In addition some of the people would be encouraged to produce cash crops for export, but this would be very much a subsidiary activity firmly located within the framework of existing, pre-capitalist, social and political arrangements, over which and through which the colonial state would exercise power. Any surplus balances accruing to the colonial government after the costs of administration, debt payments and interest charges had been met would be spent on social welfare programmes – health and education – to raise the ' level of civilisation '. This was the ideal profile to which the colony failed to conform.

The export sector rested in the hands of Ghanaians and the British-controlled mining industry never achieved a size where it could yield profits to investors and still cover the capital costs of the transport system vital to its operations, let alone the administrative costs of the state. At the same time the development of an indigenous capitalist class presented the colonial government with an intractable dilemma. On the one hand it provided the economic basis not only for the colonial state but also for British capital operating in the colony: through taxation it provided the funds that paid for administration and covered the loans from London which financed the transport system. On the other hand were the problems associated with taxation without representation and the political threats that Ghanaian enterprise constituted for the colonial state, both directly, if provoked, and indirectly through its erosion of the political structures through which indirect rule was exercised. The achievement of the British in Ghana was to hold this situation stable for so long, and to prevent the structural contradictions that faced them from becoming absolute.

BIBLIOGRAPHY

W. Baer and M. E. Herve, ' Employment and industrialisation in developing countries ', *Quarterly Journal of Economics*, 1966.

T. Edward Bowdich, *Mission from Cape Coast to Ashantee*, John Murray, London 1819.

A. Cardinal, *The Gold Coast, 1931*, Government Printer, Accra 1931.

K. O. Dike, *Trade and politics in the Niger Delta*, O.U.P., London 1956.
Philip J. Foster, *Education and social change in Ghana*, Routledge and Kegan Paul, London 1965.
A. G. Frank, *Capitalism and underdevelopment in Latin America*, Monthly Review Press, New York 1967.
C. R. Frank Jr, 'Urban unemployment and economic growth in Africa', *Oxford Economic Papers*, 1968.
S. H. Frankel, *Capital investment in Africa*, O.U.P., London 1938.
John Gallagher and Ronald Robinson, 'The imperialism of free trade', *Economic History Review*, 2nd Series, VI, no. 1, August 1953.
Roger Genoud, *Nationalism and economic development in Ghana*, Praeger, New York 1969.
R. H. Green and S. H. Hymer, 'Cocoa in the Gold Coast: a study in the relations between African farmers and agricultural experts', *Journal of Economic History*, XXVI, no. 3, September 1966.
W. K. Hancock, *The wealth of colonies*, Marshall Lectures, C.U.P., Cambridge 1950
R. Heussler, *Yesterday's rulers*, Syracuse University Press, New York 1962.
Polly Hill, *The migrant cocoa farmers of southern Ghana, a study in rural capitalism*, C.U.P., Cambridge 1963.
Stephen Hymer, 'The political economy of the Gold Coast and Ghana', *Center Discussion Paper, no. 73*, Economic Growth Center, Yale University, 1969.
G. E. Metcalfe, *Great Britain and Ghana: documents of Ghana history, 1807–1957*, University of Ghana (Thomas Nelson), Legon, Accra and London 1964.
R. Symonds, *The British and their successors*, Faber and Faber, London 1966.
James E. Thorold Rogers, *The economic interpretation of history*, London 1891.
United Africa Company, *Statistical and Economic Review*, no. 2.
Eric Williams, *Capitalism and Slavery*, Russell and Russell, New York 1961.

Part 2

Documents

SOURCES

The documents cited in this part have been taken with one exception from the official publications of the colonial government, the Ghana government and the British government. The main sources are Legislative Council (and Assembly) Debates, sessional papers, Colonial Office reports and reports by commissions appointed by the British government in London which relate solely or partly to Ghana. Further details of official and other publications on Ghana can be found in A. W. Cardinal, *A bibliography of the Gold Coast, 1496–1931* (issued as a companion to the census report of 1931), Government Printer, Accra 1932; and A. F. Johnson, *A bibliography of Ghana, 1930–1961*, Ghana Library Board, Longmans, Accra 1964.

1. General economic policy

It is possible to define five phases in the evolution of colonial economic policy: 1. 1898–1919: the establishment and consolidation of the physical, social and administrative infrastructure of the colonial state; 2. 1920–30: the Ten Year Development Programme; 3. 1930–45: depression, retrenchment and war; 4. 1945–50: riots and royal commissions; 5. 1950–7: terminal colonialism and the beginning of national development. While most of the documentation in this chapter is concerned with the second, fourth and fifth phases, we will survey the salient features of the whole period in these introductory remarks.

1898–1919

The construction of a railway system was the main economic activity of the colonial government during this period, which opens with the construction of the Sekondi–Kumasi line (1898–1904). Between 1909 and 1917 the second line was built, from Accra to Kumasi, and by 1920 there were 250 miles of track open in the colony. Expenditure on railways accounted for 24 per cent of total government expenditure and 88 per cent of expenditure on economic services during this period. Health and education accounted for 9.7 and 2.4 per cent respectively of total government expenditure. A rough estimate of the development of these services by 1920 is that the health service provided hospital facilities for about 0.02 per cent of the population, while one child in more than 200 had the opportunity of attending school. The most important item of government expenditure during this period was administration, which accounted for about 40 per cent of the total; the number of persons employed by the administration grew rapidly from 826 in 1900 to 2,176 in 1913 and 3,324 in 1921. The achievements of the government during this period were far from dramatic but they did provide the basis for the expansionary phase of policy in the twenties.

1920–30 : the Ten Year Development Programme

Table III gives some indication of the effects of the world-wide boom and slump that followed the First World War on the economy of Ghana. The

Table III. *Trade and central government revenue, 1918–22 (£000s)*

	Imports	Exports	Government revenue
1918	3,256	4,472	1,299
1919	7,946	10,814	2,601
1920	15,172	12,352	3,722
1921	7,661	6,942	3,016
1922	7,900	8,355	3,357

colonial government diagnosed the weakness of the economy as being due to its heavy dependence on cocoa exports. (' In 1923, 83 per cent of our exports consisted of cocoa. Again and again we have talked of " all the eggs in one basket ". Verily the truth of this has come home at last.' Document 1 below.) The solution proposed to overcome the instability of the economy was to increase its range of exports and safeguard the future of the cocoa trade by the provision of cheap transport facilities. It was with this perspective that the government launched the Ten Year Development Programme, which proposed public expenditure of £24 million on projects in transport and communications, water supply, drainage, electric power, maps, surveys, and later agriculture.

As we have noted, transportation accounted for 75 per cent of the actual expenditure under the programme and it was through transport that the colonial government had most influence on the pace and pattern of growth. In the early twenties there was considerable discussion in London as to the role that private enterprise ought to play in the development of transportation facilities in tropical Africa, and a committee was set up to look into the matter. Extracts from the report of this committee are reproduced as Document 2. The following passage from this document (p. 61 below) is an interesting illustration of the thesis we have advanced about the relationship between the colonial government and British capital. The Committee contrasted

> the meagre achievements of British enterprise in Tropical Africa... and the striking results which it shows in many parts of South America to which British capital has flowed freely... There appears to exist an impression more or less vague, but none the less real, that private enterprise is not welcome to the administrators of... [colonial] territories; that the system of Crown Colony government tends to obstruct rather than smoothen the way for the would-be concessionaire.

Although actual expenditure under the Ten Year Development Programme only reached half the level of projected expenditure, the twenties were the period of relatively rapid growth. The departure in 1927 of Guggisberg, remembered to this day as the most dynamic Governor the colony ever had,

Table IV. *Trade and central government revenue, 1928–32 (£000s)*

	Imports	Exports	Government revenue
1928	12,200	13,824	3,771
1929	10,082	12,677	3,389
1930	8,953	11,287	2,663
1931	4,813	9,300	2,278
1932	5,605	8,348	2,654

saw the formal and premature ending of the Ten Year Development Programme: the world depression of the thirties brought to an end the expansionary phase of colonialism in Ghana.

1930–45 : depression, retrenchment and war

Table IV traces the movements of the key economic indicators for the five years 1928–32 and shows the impact of the depression on the colonial economy. Between 1928 and the trough year of 1931 the value of trade dropped by 60 per cent, causing a substantial fall in government revenue. The response of the colonial government was retrenchment, and expenditure was cut back so sharply that from 1932 the government ran a budget surplus.

Table V shows how expenditure was reduced between 1928 and 1932. Ordinary expenditure was more or less maintained while the 45 per cent reduction in total expenditure was achieved at the expense of extraordinary and development expenditure. In general terms this amounted to a complete cessation of all government investment, which, in the face of the maintained level of current expenditure, had the effect of increasing the percentage of government expenditure on administration. In the early thirties administrative expenditure accounted for 41 per cent of total government expenditure as compared to about 30 per cent in the twenties. Expenditure on infrastructure for the decade averaged about 27 per cent of total expenditure as compared with 57 per cent for the twenties; the major fall coming with respect to railways and harbours, where the amount of investment was negligible.

Table V. *Central government expenditure, 1928–32 (£000s)*

	Ordinary	Extra-ordinary	Development
1928	2,397	925	1,014
1929	2,598	1,109	81
1930	2,707	751	24
1931	2,501	123	0
1932	2,349	26	0

Departments whose activities tended to be labour intensive, so that most of their expenditure was of a recurrent nature, tended to show significant percentile increases. Expenditure on agriculture, for instance, averaged 5 per cent of total expenditure in the thirties as compared with only 2 per cent in the previous decade. Expenditure on health increased from 6 per cent to 10 per cent, largely as a result of the increase in medical staff brought about by the Korle Bu hospital, built in the late twenties. The relatively high level of investment in the twenties played a key role in maintaining the level of ordinary expenditure in the thirties as the enterprises that were constructed in the phase of expansion had to be staffed during the subsequent depression. Expenditure on education repeated the pattern of expenditure on agriculture and health, rising from an average of 3 per cent of total expenditure in the twenties to 8 per cent in the thirties. Table VI shows that this sector increased in real terms as well as enjoying an increased share of government expenditure.

Table VI. *Primary and middle schools; annual average enrolment*

1920–4	31,809
1925–9	36,600
1930–4	54,819
1935–9	75,527

This expansion of education at a time of depression is significant: there are no reliable data on unemployment but it seems safe to conclude that the proportion of school leavers who got the jobs they desired decreased throughout the thirties. Complaints were heard in the Legislative Council about the failure of the 'Africanisation' policy for the civil service. In 1926 Guggisberg estimated that the number of Africans holding 'European appointments' would rise from 27, at which it then stood, to 151 by 1936, but by 1938 only 41 Africans held senior administrative appointments.

As the effects of the depression and retrenchment were increasingly felt, discontent grew, culminating in a hold-up of the cocoa crop in 1937. After the war political opposition grew sharply as a result of: low cocoa prices paid by the Cocoa Marketing Board; high import prices, resulting from the world-wide shortage of manufactured goods and shipping; and unemployment, exacerbated by the demobilisation of 47,000 soldiers of whom about 60 per cent had been abroad. The attempts by the colonial government to anticipate post-war difficulties reveal, if anything, a loss of confidence on its part. In proposing in 1944 a 'General Plan for Development in the Gold Coast' the Governor wrote to the Secretary of State as follows:

. . . So little can be counted on with confidence in the future that I put forward with some diffidence proposals which must inevitably cover a number of years. We do not know, for instance, what will be the future of Gold mining or of cocoa, the two major industries of the Colony, nor can we be sure of the response which the people of the Colony themselves will make to any plans formulated by Government.[1]

1945–50 : riots and royal commissions

The manner in which the colonial government coped with the situation that developed at the end of the war was sharply criticised by the Watson Commission which was appointed to look into the ' disturbances ' in the colony. In 1948 a colony-wide boycott developed as Africans protested against high import prices and high profit margins earned by expatriate importers. The Watson Commission (Document 3) argued that the economic situation in the colony was a reflection of conditions in the world economy at large and that such an explanation was ' absolutely meaningless to the vast majority of the inhabitants of the Gold Coast '. It criticised the foreign trading community and particularly the Association of West African Merchants (A.W.A.M.) for the manner in which it established its prices, but its sharpest criticism was reserved for the colonial government. While noting that a system of price control would have required ' an army of officials ten times the size of the staff available ' it nevertheless recorded the opinion that ' if the Government had made more robust use of its powers at an earlier stage the . . . [boycott] would never have taken place '. It particularly criticised the government for declaring its ' neutrality ' in what it chose to treat as a ' purely trading dispute ' and went on:

We cannot emphasize too strongly our view that every aspect of life in a colony, affecting the welfare of the indigenous population is a concern of the highest priority to the tutelary Government of that Colony. The people did not believe that the Government was not involved in this dispute.

The remaining part of the report that is reproduced in Document 3 is concerned with an analysis of the system of distribution and with methods of resolving conflicts that arose within it.

The Commission's views on industrialisation are presented in Document 4. Noting the widespread and ' vague ' call for industrialisation, the report states:

Apart from the possibilities of a hydro-electric scheme . . ., the establishment of any heavy industry on the Gold Coast capable of finding an export market must remain a dream. With an enervating climate in the torrid zone, lacking coal and other basic materials, the prospect is so barren that not even the greatest enthusiast could suggest to us a method of accomplishment.

[1] *Sessional Paper no. 11, 1944.*

The Commission hastens to add that this did not mean that ‘ the country is necessarily condemned to remain a dumping ground for imports ’, though it was at pains to emphasise that there were no reasons, as far as it could see, why an exporter of primary products should enjoy a standard of living less than that of an industrial economy. The Commission suggested a number of industrial projects that it thought feasible in the colony, making special mention of the distillation of spirits, the recovery and treatment of gold and the Volta River scheme. It also expressed the opinion that where industrialisation did proceed it should be on a cooperative basis, as ‘ unbridled private enterprise would at best lay the foundations for future social strife ’.

1950–7 : terminal colonialism and the beginning of national development

As a result of constitutional changes the colony achieved self-determination in 1951 and launched the same year the First Development Plan. The following year the first analysis of the colonial economy by professional economists was published in a semi-official report entitled ‘ Financial and physical problems of development in the Gold Coast ’. Extracts from the opening chapter entitled ‘ The fragile economy ’ are included as Document 5. The report argues that the structure of the economy was much more rigid than that of a developed industrial economy and that it had a tendency to exaggerate any inflationary or deflationary pressures to which it was exposed. The shortage of port and transport facilities restrained the physical volume of imports that could be handled and this played a considerable part in the price rise that followed the end of the war. The construction of Tema Harbour as part of the First Development Plan finally alleviated this problem.

1953 saw the publication of the Lewis Report on ‘ Industrialisation and the Gold Coast ’; its major conclusions and recommendations are included as Document 6. ‘ The main obstacle ’ [to industrialisation] Lewis thought, ‘ is the fact that agricultural productivity per man is stagnant ’. As a consequence the market was small, savings low and the supply of labour from the agricultural sector too slight to man a substantial industrial sector. The first priority, Lewis argued, was to improve the system of food production and to expand the infrastructure to make way for industrialisation in the future. Only industries which could be established ‘ without large or continuing subsidies’ were proposed. Among the recommendations was the suggestion that the government should ‘ give limited aid, by way of temporary protection or subsidy to newly established factories ’. It was also considered important for the government to ‘ announce its attitude to foreign enterprise, welcoming such enterprise, especially if it enters into partnership with the government or African enterprise ’. This was done by the Prime Minister, Dr Kwame Nkrumah, in a speech to the Legislative Assembly in March 1953 (Document 7) in which he made it quite clear that the government considered local capital and enterprise inadequate to meet the development requirements of the country. Foreign firms would be welcome, particularly if they trained and promoted African labour, but the government ' appreciate[d] that in industry the criterion must be that of industrial efficiency '. It was noted that foreign capital had not previously been involved in the construction and operation of public utilities and this state of affairs was expected to continue, but, with the exception of this sector, ' it is the Government's considered view that foreign capital should be free to invest in any other form of new industrial enterprise. In other words, it is hoped to see new industries which will in due course become fully self-supporting under normal competitive conditions.' The Prime Minister emphasised that the government had no plans for nationalising industry ' beyond the extent to which public utilities are already nationalised '.

Nevertheless, in order to ensure that if the nationalisation of a particular industry were to be considered essential by a successor government in the national interest, there should be suitable means for guaranteeing fair compensation. The Government intends to request the United Kingdom Government to incorporate in the Constitution appropriate provision for this purpose, following the precedents set in the Constitutions of the United States of America and of India.

To encourage and assist local industrialists, the Industrial Development Corporation was established in 1955; a statement of its policy is included as Document 8. The work of the I.D.C. was the investigation of the possibilities of new industries, which it would establish either itself (subsidiary companies) or in conjunction with reputable firms (associated companies). It was also prepared to make loans to small concerns to help them acquire machinery and so on. The Corporation also listed the types of industries that it would support: these were industries that: were new to the country; were ancillary to the development plan; used local resources and offered opportunities for the training of Africans. The policy of the I.D.C. remained fundamentally unchanged until it was disbanded in 1962.

In the course of the fifties government expenditure rose rapidly: during the five years 1945–50 annual average government expenditure was £9.6 million; this rose to £34.8 million in the period 1950–4 and to £57.9 million in the years 1955–60. The *Economic Survey* for 1955 in its review of development under the First Development Plan (Document 9) records something of the history of the plan; its initial difficulties, due to scarcities and a shortage of administrative staff; how these were overcome and how an attempt was made in 1952 to put the plan onto a five year basis as opposed to the ten year basis on which it was originally drawn up. Details are given of expenditure by project and type; the sources of finance and the achievements of the plan are assessed. The plan came to a formal end in 1956 and a two year consolidation plan was drawn up for the years 1957–9 to complete projects left outstanding. Document 10, which concludes this chapter, is a policy statement by Nkrumah on the Second Development Plan, in which the achievements of the country since 1951 are assessed and the hopes for the future stated.

1. The economy in 1920: the Governor proposes a development programme as the only way to stabilise the economy [1]

When introducing the Estimates for 1920 I congratulated Honourable Members on the fact that in 1919 we had achieved the biggest trade in the history of the Gold Coast exceeding by several millions the trade for 1918. Again, I have to congratulate Honourable Members on another record. In 1920 our total exports and imports reached £26,000,000 an increase of £8,500,000 over the figure for 1919.

The value of the imports for 1920 are about £14,000,000 as compared with the total value of about £8,000,000 for 1919, an increase of over 77 per cent. The large increase in import values is in some degree accounted for by the increased cost of commodities, but notwithstanding higher prices, there have, in numerous instances, been increased importations as regards quantities. The value of the imports of cotton goods reached nearly £4,000,000, double the 1919 imports.

Wearing apparel, perfumery, tobacco, hardware, motor vehicles, and railway plant also show considerable increases. The increased imports of high priced non-essential articles indicate that the people possessed a considerable amount of surplus wealth for disbursement during the year, and a greater wave of prosperity than the colony has ever known before. The explanation of this is to be found in a scrutiny of the export statistics relating to domestic produce. The statistics show that while over 176,000 tons of cocoa of a value of about $8\frac{1}{4}$ millions were shipped overseas in 1919, shipments for 1920 approximate over 118,000 tons of a value totalling nearly 10 millions. Although, therefore, we shipped nearly 58,000 tons less, the value was over $1\frac{1}{2}$ millions greater. Kola nuts and lumber also appreciated in value during the year, and their exports therefore considerably exceeded 1919 export values. Owing to the influence of cocoa the exports of palm kernels, palm oil and rubber have all fallen in value. The year as a whole has been one of extraordinary commercial activity and prosperity, and, taking an average throughout the year, sellers of produce have received higher prices than they ever received before.

Effect of the cocoa boom

The history of cocoa in 1920 taught several new lessons to the people of this country and emphasised one old lesson. In January the price of cocoa was £98 per ton. The rush of people to take part in the cocoa trade which had gone on in 1919 went on increasingly. In February the price reached the unprecedented figure of £122 per ton. Both Europeans and Africans were handling big cocoa business, and many of them far more money than they were used to. It was indeed apparent that a large number of the Gold Coast people had lost their heads. Members of the Professions, Clerks, Artisans practically deserted their work and took part in the great cocoa rush. It was impossible to get labour. In March there were indications of a fall. By May the price was down to £85. The wise men pulled up but the vast

[1] Governor's Annual Address, *Legislative Council Debates, 1921–2*, pp. 29–48 (extracts).

majority were unwise. They had not enough knowledge to know what was going to happen. The declining prices continued, and it soon became evident that the bottom was going to fall temporarily out of the cocoa market. By December the price had dropped to £39 per ton. Hundreds of individuals and new firms were ruined and only the older firms with sufficient capital to support them survived.

There can be no doubt that there are natives in this country who did well and permanently increased their wealth out of the great cocoa boom. But as in the case of other booms all the world over, for every one who succeeded there were a hundred failures. To begin with, hundreds of educated young Africans threw up their jobs, over a hundred in the Government Service alone, and rushed off to the cocoa fields and markets. The majority have had a severe lesson. Government appointments have naturally been closed against the return of those who deserted the service of their country, while the great decrease in the number of new firms which started business during the boom has decreased the amount of work available for their re-employment. Many young natives in fact learnt that a bird in the hand was worth two in the bush.

The unfortunate feature of so many cases was that money easily earned was easily spent. Motor cars were purchased right and left, champagne flowed freely, smoke of expensive cigars scented the air, European clothes both for men and women, at far more expensive prices than in any period of history, were purchased freely. In a few cases, as I have said, the men who made their money withdrew in time and were wise in their expenditure, but in the vast majority of cases by the end of the boom those who took part in it were far poorer than before. What made matters worse was that the farmers neglected their food crops for their cocoa and consequently the price of provisions rose to a height unprecedented in the history of the Gold Coast.

These things have occurred in other countries during booms, and the Gold Coast was by no means singular. Nonetheless, our cocoa boom afforded a fine example of the necessity for thrift. If, instead of squandering their money, they had put some by, the majority of those who took part in the cocoa boom would now be comfortably off.

When it really became apparent that we were really in for something longer than a mere temporary slump in cocoa there were two things to be considered: (1) How long was the slump going to last and what steps could be taken to deal with it? (2) What are we going to do to prevent a recurrence of a similar slump in trade?

Steps to meet the trade slump

The answer to the first question is that the slump in our two main articles of produce, cocoa and palm oil, is only temporary . . . [Events] of the past few years have shown that both these articles have become a necessity in the world. For edible oils and fats there must practically always be an unlimited demand. For cocoa there will undoubtedly be a limited demand, but this demand is very large and is increasing yearly, one of the chief reasons for the increase being the gradual growing prohibition of spirits throughout the world. Sweets, especially chocolates, are gradually taking the place of spirits.

Therefore the slump is only temporary. How long will it last? The answer to that lies undoubtedly in the unsettled condition of the world after the great war. At present practically all the markets of Central Europe are closed against us. The rates of exchange are also against us owing to the depreciated value of currency which naturally followed on the world inflation of currency and credits. We shall have to wait for the restoration of pre-war trade conditions among the nations of the world before there can be any appreciable revival in our trade. The date on which this world revival will take place is puzzling the wisest heads in Europe and America. That a general world recovery will come is certain, but unfortunately it is improbable that it will come for one or possibly two years.

It is obvious, therefore, that in forming any plans for tiding over our trade slump we should reckon on there being less demand for cocoa for twelve months. That is to say that we shall not have full sale, and that only at low prices, for our present crop.

On my return from England in October the danger that would arise from this state of affairs struck me most forcibly. The cocoa farmer, somewhat spoiled by the high prices he had received during the boom, would probably refuse to sell at the low prices obtaining in October, prices which showed signs of still further decline. Honourable Members can see the evil that would result. Either the farmer would not harvest his crop at all and would leave the pods rotting on the trees, to the subsequent deterioration of the quality of cocoa, or else he would gather and store the beans against the time when prices would recover. The latter, though preferable to the former, would have resulted in their being a glut of cocoa in the next season, that of 1921–2; and this, together with deterioration in the beans due to inadequate storage accommodation, would not only have delayed the recovery of prices, but would give Gold Coast cocoa still less reputation as a high class product in the markets of the world.

Immediate action was therefore necessary, so I personally started on propaganda tours, and in the months of October to December delivered over 50 addresses on the subject to large gatherings of Chiefs, Councillors, farmers and cocoa traders in the Eastern and Central Provinces. Copies of this address, laying down the policy to be pursued, were sent to all political officers in the Gold Coast with instructions that they should start an active campaign on similar lines. My address has been laid on the table for Honourable Members to read and has also been published in the local papers. Briefly, my advice was to sell and keep on selling, no matter how low the price got, unless they could store properly and in permanent buildings. I further pointed out to all farmers that they were trying to grow too much, that they should reduce the size of their farms to such as could be managed by themselves and their family, thus getting a bigger profit by doing away with the hired labour which had increased so very largely during the cocoa boom.

The effect of our campaign was undoubtedly good, and for some time sales were steadily maintained. In December, however, we received a severe blow by the big Combine firms stopping buying. At first this caused us some surprise in view of the large stocks of European goods held by these firms and the sale of which depended on the circulation of money. We learnt later, however, that the United Kingdom was absolutely glutted with stocks of cocoa. I am glad to say that I have now received information that the Combine firms are again beginning to buy. In the meantime we welcome the advent of a large Swiss firm of chocolate manufacturers who have made very large purchases in Ashanti and in the Western Province of the Colony.

Summing up the cocoa situation, I see no reason to doubt a steady sale at low prices during 1921. We cannot this year, or ever again, return to the high prices that were ruling last year. That being so, an absolute essential of our trade programme must be to cheapen methods of transportation both by road, railways, and improved harbour facilities for we require this cheaper transportation to encourage trade when prices are low far more than when prices are high.

Steps to prevent a recurrence of trade slumps

Dealing now with the second question. What is to be done to prevent the recurrence of a slump in our trade?

If the cocoa boom has done us harm, it will anyway have done one good thing if it has made everyone realise the danger of depending entirely on one main article of produce. In 1920, 83 per cent of our exports consisted of cocoa. Again and again we have talked of 'all the eggs in one basket'. Verily the truth of this has come home at last!

Well, what are we to do? First and foremost we have to improve our cocoa. Smaller farms, better cultivation, more attention to the advice of the agricultural officers which fell on ears deafened by the cocoa boom, all this, with better fermentation will improve our quality. And this we need urgently if we are to compete with the steadily increasing cocoa production of other parts of the world.

Necessary as that is, it is, however, the same old basket. What else can we turn to?

Undoubtedly the next best product – if not a better one than cocoa – is that of our oil palm. Neglected by everyone except that far-seeing and capable Chief Mate Kole and his Krobo farmers, our palm oil and kernel export had dwindled down to a few miserable thousand tons a year. Four things we must do:

(1) Take up again our old oil palm cultivation.
(2) Improve methods of cultivation.
(3) Run a railway and more feeder roads through the oil palm belt.
(4) Provide local centres for decortication and crushing.

For (1) we look to the Chiefs and their Councillors, for (2) to the assistance of our agricultural officer, for (3) we rely on Government activity in railway construction and on the energy of the farmers in co-operating with the Government on road construction; and for (4) we would welcome European enterprise.

I am optimistic on the recovery of our oil palm produce and fully believe that the lessons of the cocoa boom have been learnt by the Chiefs and the farmers.

Rice, copra, sisal, and sugar are all articles of produce which the Government is now encouraging, but when all is said and done, these are none of them likely to turn into huge items of export, valuable as they will prove to the farmers who grow them. We must not neglect them – indeed we must encourage both them and any other small item of export in every possible way. But what we want is something that will rival cocoa – something that will place us more firmly than ever at the top of the Crown Colony produce ladder. For we must remember that head for head, and acre for acre, we are a long way ahead of any other Crown Colony in both trade and revenue. We must maintain that position by finding something new that will compete with their steadily growing new products. Luckily we have not far to seek.

Now, Honourable Members, I have been accused of being a faddist about the Northern Territories. I plead guilty to the accusation, but if I am a faddist, I am a faddist backed up by reason – I am a faddist who has been to see what he is talking about.

And I repeat now what I said last month in this Chamber that the whole future of the Gold Coast is bound up with the development of the ground-nut and shea-butter industries of the Northern Territories.

I have been there and seen them both growing. I have seen millions of acres of country where ground-nuts are indigenous and can grow in prodigious quantities without constant labour of clearing the forest and bush of the Colony and Ashanti. And I know that the people of the northern and more inaccessible parts of the country will migrate for the farming season to the southern parts where the ground-nut grows, returning to their homes after the harvest just as they do now from the Colony and Ashanti.

With a railway there, and a deep-water harbour at the end of it, we should have 300 miles less of railway transport and 300 miles less of sea transport than Nigeria to the markets of the world.

As for the shea nut, we should be in an unrivalled position. I have seen thousands of acres of nuts rotting on the ground – thousands of acres of trees of which the nut-crops on one side have been destroyed by the annual fires – a loss easily avertible by the cultivation of surrounding belts of ground-nuts.

Honourable Members, with means of transportation – with a deep-water harbour at Takoradi and a railway from Coomassie to the neighbourhood of Tamale – we will assure the safety of Gold Coast trade. We shall have four large baskets of articles greatly in demand – cocoa and palm oil from the south – ground nuts and shea-butter from the north – together with seven little baskets of rice, copra, sisal, corn, sugar, coffee, and tobacco – little baskets, Honourable Members, but good.

And with the safety of our trade assured comes assurance of our revenue – the sinews of war for our campaign of education and progress.

Our financial state

In reviewing the history of the past year, the next point to touch on is our revenue. As I have just mentioned the fact that we attained our highest trade on record, Honourable Members will not be surprised to learn that we also attained our highest revenue.

So, for the second year in succession there has been a record in our revenue. For in 1919 we exceeded our previous highest revenue by over three-quarters of a million. Our revenue, in fact, realised £2,601,360.

Now for the year 1920. In drawing up the Estimates we anticipated a revenue of £2,389,600. Actually we have made a revenue in 1920 of £3,695,919, beating our previous record by the handsome amount of over one million pounds. These high revenues for two years in succession have not been without their effect on our accumulated balance. At the beginning of 1919 we had over three-quarters of a million in hand. By the end of 1919 this had increased to over £1,600,000. By the end of 1920 it had risen to 2½ millions.

When introducing last year's Estimates I remember congratulating Honourable Members on the fact that in our accumulated balance we had a safeguard against a slump in cocoa. Well, as we all know, that slump has come, and welcome indeed is the nest-egg to tide us over the rainy days to come.

Allowing for the expenses of the present quarter which separates 1920 from our new financial year 1921–2, we shall, on the first of April next, start with close on £2,000,000 in hand.

This means that our balance of 2½ million with which we began the year 1921 will tide us comfortably over 15 bad months, and will leave us still with a nest-egg of over one million as a reserve against a still further bad year.

So, as far as it is humanly possible to tell, we can face 2¼ years of bad trade without anxiety; we can only, however, do this by exercising the most rigid economy and by confining our chief expenditure to those items which will ultimately bring in revenue. I will, however, deal no further at present with the future, as there is much more to be said when we actually begin to discuss the Estimates for the coming year.

The Ten Year Programme

In addressing the Council on the Estimates for 1920, I gave Honourable Members a ten-year programme of development...

This programme, divides into 10 main headings [see Table 1.1].

When Honourable Members are reading this programme, I would remind them of two facts. The first, that it is at the present moment as impossible as it was a year ago to calculate the total expenditure which will be required on each item. Prices are still fluctuating in such a manner that any estimate of cost of construction involving purchase of material would require such wholesale revision as would render them useless. We have therefore not attempted during the past year to make any more accurate estimate than is shown on the printed programme. Serious as the omission may appear, in reality it is not so. Although we are mak-

Table 1.1

Item no.	Construction	Anticipated total expenditure	Expenditure based on a loan of £4m. From loan funds, first 4 years	From revenue, second 4 years	Required expenditure for second 6 years (approx.)
		(£)	(£)	(£)	(£)
I	Harbour	2,000,000	1,000,000	—	1,000,000
II	Railways	14,581,000	3,000,000	—	11,581,000
III	Roads	1,000,000	—	500,000	500,000
IV	Water supply	1,790,000	—	200,000	1,590,000
V	Drainage	1,350,000	—	200,000	1,150,000
VI	Hydro-electric works	2,000,000	—	170,000	1,830,000
VII	Public buildings	1,100,000	—	1,000,000	100,000
VIII	Town improvements	500,000	—	250,000	250,000
IX	Telegraphs and telephones	90,000	—	80,000	10,000
X	Maps, political and industrial	200,000	—	100,000	100,000
	Total	£24,611,000	£4,000,000	£2,500,000	
			£6,500,000		£18,111,000
	Grand Total	£24,611,000			£24,611,000

ing a fair start on many of these items we have not yet involved ourselves heavily in expenditure. This is partly due to lack of artisans, but still more due to our desire not to commit ourselves to the wholesale purchase of materials until prices have gone down.

The second fact to which I wish to draw the attention of Honourable Members is that, when originally submitting the programme, I pointed out that it is of such a nature that should circumstances compel us to curtail expenditure, we could easily modify the programme. That is a particularly important point in view of the present slump in trade.

I will now review briefly the progress we have made in carrying out the development programme in 1920, and when dealing with each head I will indicate briefly the work which we propose to continue or start during the coming financial year.

Transportation

In dealing with harbours, railways, and roads, I would remind Honourable Members of what I said just now – that our present system of transportation is totally inadequate to cope with any great increase in our trade. We must increase and improve the means of transportation and cheapen the cost. The former depends on the money we can spend on construction work. The latter depends on the up-to-date facilities we can provide for transhipping cargo and also on the turnover we can make in our business, in other words the more miles of railways we have open, the cheaper can be our rates.

Harbours

With regard to harbours, the Government has a definite programme, which is:

(1) The construction of a deep-water harbour at Takoradi.

(2) The improvement of the jetty accommodation and facilities for handling cargo at Accra.

(3) The maintenance of such port facilities as already exist at the various coast towns, including certain improvements at Seccondee, to facilitate the handling of manganese pending the construction of the Takoradi harbour.

I am glad to say that in the last-named item we are being considerably assisted at Seccondee by the action of the Manganese Company, and that our trade down the Volta has been greatly helped by the enterprise of the Volta River Transport Company.

I would like to mention here a subject of general interest. It became apparent about last April, that the Consulting Engineers Messrs Coode, Son, Fitzmaurice & Matthews, had completed so much of the construction of Seccondee and Accra harbours as to render the continuation of the existing system somewhat expensive. I took the opportunity when in England of consulting them in the matter. With great public spirit they agreed with my point of view and voluntarily withdrew from their connection with the Gold Coast harbours. All construction workers at Seccondee and Accra, which are now regarded as railway terminals, have therefore been placed on the railway. It is hoped that considerable economy will thereby be effected and better coordination maintained between the open lines and the two ports mentioned. Actual routine work is still carried out by the Customs Department. The latter will, in due course, probably require strengthening by the addition of one or more harbour masters but this is not contemplated at present.

The deep-water harbour

I do not intend here to go into details of why Takoradi has been selected, but I may say briefly that a deep-water harbour can be built more cheaply here than at any other place on our coast. Secondly, that owing to the existence of a natural breakwater in Takoradi Reef and the rocky nature of the bottom there is a minimum of danger of sand and silt and no expensive upkeep by dredging.

One great advantage of this harbour as planned by Messrs Stewart & McDonnell is that it can be built in instalments. The harbour, when complete, will cost £5m. and will contain ten berths alongside jetties for ocean-going steamers, including a special berth for manganese and two for coaling. Further, it is possible to extend the harbour to take as many ships as could possibly be required.

It is not, however, necessary to build the whole of this harbour now. So we have reckoned on a first instalment of six berths. This first instalment will probably cost about £3½ m., but this sum will include construction of the railway line from Seccondee to Takoradi and the complete lay-out of Takoradi township.

This is the most that I can tell Honourable Members about Takoradi Harbour this morning. As I have said before, the detailed report of the survey party will be issued for their information. A committee will shortly be assembled to consider ways and means and in due course our final proposals will be submitted to a special meeting of this Council. It is not likely that we shall be able to begin on any big scale this year, but I would remind Honourable Members that if the trade of this country is to be increased sufficiently to give us the revenue which we require for our education we must have a deep-water harbour. There is no alternative.

Accra Harbour

Improvement of harbour facilities at Accra is urgently needed. Complete plans have been prepared and work will be commenced as soon as Messrs Stewart & McDonnell have decided between the conflicting claims of the engineers and the mercantile community. Whatever this decision may be, it does not affect the removal of one of the existing jetties from its present inland site to a position a few hundred yards to the east. This work is in progress, but has been seriously delayed by the non-arrival of material required for replacements. Its completion may be expected before the next cocoa season and will considerably facilitate the handling of heavy cargo.

Railways

We have on the whole made fair progress in 1920 on our railways in spite of the shortage of labour. Our two main items of work are on the Tafo–Coomassie line and the Seccondee–Coomassie deviations. On the first named, we started work from both ends. The first twenty miles of earth-work east of Coomassie are practically finished and bridges and plate-laying are begun. At the Tafo end, bridging and plate-laying is complete almost to Bosusa station, but the earth-works and ballasting have advanced considerably beyond that point. The General Manager reports that by the end of the next financial year we shall have 50 additional miles of railway open, 25 from Coomassie and 25 from Tafo, while the earth-work and ballasting in the 90 mile gap that will then remain will be well advanced. The engineers have had to contend with the utmost difficulties in labour, especially in Ashanti, and in this respect we owe a great deal to Lieut Colonel Graham, the

Chief Railway Engineer. In Akim the keenness of the Omanhene and his people resulted in considerable progress being made.

With regard to the Seccondee–Coomassie deviations, new earth-works are practically completed up to the north of Asuasu station. The survey of the deviations has been completed to the vicinity of Opon Valley station by Mr Weller. In the first 71½ miles, 170 curves have been cut out and the radius of all curves has been doubled. The new alignment will allow a maximum gradient of 1 in 80 against imports and 1 in 100 against exports, compared with the old standard of 1 in 50. The realignment will be productive of greatly increased economy of running, and enable the railway to deal with heavier traffic.

On the much needed increase in rolling stock no engines or covered vans ordered during the war have yet arrived. Open trucks began to arrive in December. Several thousand tons of rails and sleepers for the new line and deviation have arrived.

Surveys of railway belts with the object of ascertaining the best route for new lines are being carried out by the Survey Department.

Although the subject may belong more properly to the item ‘ Roads ’, Honourable Members will be interested to hear of an experiment which I have asked the General Manager of the Railways to carry out in conjunction with the political officers and Chiefs of the Western Province. As regards transportation, the Western Province of the Colony is still far less developed than any other part of the Gold Coast, and this in spite of its having had for nearly 20 years a railway with a terminal port. At the present moment, the only roads fit for motor traffic are a few miles of the coast-line road on each side of Seccondee and about 15 miles of road from Dunkwa to Ayanfori. On the other hand, the country for from 40 to 50 miles on each side of the railway is heavily planted with cocoa. In fact, transportation has lagged hopelessly behind agricultural development. While high prices for cocoa obtained, the farmers sent a certain amount of cocoa to the railway. It is estimated that in the greater part of the area mentioned not more than a quarter of the crop was sold. Merchants established buying centres well out to the west of the railway, but nearly all these are now closed down and the activities of the farmers practically terminated by the low prices and lack of transport facilities.

It seems to me that in encouraging the people to plant cocoa and in neglecting to provide them with means of transport, Government may almost be accused of having broken faith. I do not think this is entirely the case as the presence of the goldfields has provided the local inhabitants with such means of employment as has led them to neglect road-making. However, whoever’s fault it may be, the state of affairs must be remedied.

I have therefore asked the General Manager of the Railways to peg out routes for pioneer roads in such a manner that they can afterwards be converted without deviations into first- and second-class Public Works Department roads. In selecting the routes for these roads he will confer with the political and agricultural officers and the chiefs concerned. On completion of the pegging out, the Chiefs will then have the opportunity of following the excellent example set to them by the people of the Central and Eastern Provinces of the Colony and the people of Ashanti, who have constructed pioneer roads suitable for light lorry traffic on a scale sufficient to take all their produce to the railway or the ports. On completion of these routes, the General Manager of the Railways will place on them a lorry service on commercial lines for feeding the railway, such service also being available for feeding the merchants' trading centres on the road. Naturally the amount of lorry service will depend on the existence of private enterprise on each road. Should it be found that it is not possible to run the railway lorry service on revenue earning lines, its institution will not take place.

Roads

By the end of 1920 we had approximately 812 miles of Public Works Department motor roads and 1,500 miles of Chiefs' pioneer roads suitable for light lorries open for traffic. Approximately 300 miles of each were constructed during the year under review. In spite of the shortage of labour, the Public Works Department are ahead with their five years' programme. The two chief events of the year have been the opening of motor transport between Coomassie and Tamale and the practical completion of the coastal road between Accra and Seccondee, although this latter road still requires much improvement in certain parts. It will actually be opened by the middle of next month.

With regard to the Coomassie–Tamale road, the Public Works Department, assisted in the most admirable manner by the Pioneer Company of the Gold Coast Regiment, created a record in road construction by completing over 140 miles of road between Attebubu and Tamale in the five months ending in March 1920.

With the exception of the Western Province of the Colony, too much praise cannot be given to the political officers, the Chiefs and the people of the whole of the remainder of the Gold Coast, Ashanti, and the Northern Territories for their roadmaking during 1920. The farmers of this country have realised, like the farmers of every other country in the world which is being opened up for trade, that pioneer roadmaking is part of their duty as farmers if they wish to get their produce to the market. Indifferent as many of the roads are, they serve the purpose for which they were built, and it would have been a sheer impossibility for the Public Works Department to have produced anything approaching the present amount of mileage even had staff and funds been sufficient.

I would here, however, strike a warning note. These roads, however useful they may be when prices for produce are high, are unfit to cope with low prices. The expenditure of keeping up a lorry transport service on a poor road, both in running expenses and in repairs, becomes prohibitive when prices are low. A further factor to be considered is that with poor roads only light lorries carrying light loads are possible. The better the road the heavier can be the lorry and the greater the weight it can carry, in proportion to the fuel it consumes. These points are fully recognised by the Government and in due course the Public Works Department will take up the improvement of the majority of the Chiefs' roads. But this cannot possibly be done on a wholesale scale for some considerable time. It is, however, essential, as Honourable Members will fully agree, that farmers should realise that the better they make their roads the higher the prices they will obtain for their produce.

During the past decade the necessity for opening up pioneer roads to deal with our rapidly increasing cocoa trade has, in the absence of a sufficient staff of engineers to lay them out properly, led to a large number of roads being unfortunately located by those who built them. Sharp curves and very steep gradients are everywhere noticeable and so far, when the Public Works have taken over these roads to improve them, they have had to make extensive and expensive deviations. Instructions have therefore been issued that in future no pioneer road should be undertaken until it has been pegged out by an engineer, or by a member of the Gold Coast Survey, which latter department is at present lending us very valuable assistance in this direction.

Water supply

With regard to water supply, the only actual construction work carried out in the year was the extension of well supply at Coomassie, Cape Coast, and other places, besides the extension of the Seccondee and Accra supplies. A very large amount of work has, however, been done in investigating the sources of supply for Coomassie and Winnebah. Schemes and estimates for pipe-borne supplies for both these places have been prepared while schemes for Cape Coast and Saltpond are now being investigated...

Surface drainage

With regard to surface drainage, we have made steady progress in many of the towns during the year. Owing, however, to lack of labour and staff, progress has not been all that could be desired.

Hydro-electric works

With regard to electric power and lighting, we have so far failed to discover a suitable water power station. The river Prah has been investigated and a favourable place discovered, but economic conditions at present existing do not justify the expenditure involved. The Tuno river, the streams in the neighbourhood of the Kwahu Plateau, and the Volta, are the next subjects for investigation and will be proceeded with during the coming year...

Public buildings

In dealing with the next item on the ten-year programme, i.e. public buildings, we are still faced by the difficulty of estimating their exact final cost owing to the fluctuating prices of materials. When last I alluded to this subject in addressing you on the 1920 Estimates, we were also handicapped by the cost and amount of Elder Dempster. They have reduced their homeward freight charges by 20 per cent and are contemplating lowering the outward freights in a similar manner when we can give them better harbour facilities. With regard to the amount, our chief shipping now appears to have ample cargo space and there are indications that new lines may possibly be coming into competition.

Our chief difficulty, however, remains, i.e. the cost of materials. So big are these still that we have considered it wise to cut down every possible item of permanent construction in the coming financial year. We shall practically begin no new buildings of any size in reinforced concrete. We shall carry on with those buildings which are still in hand or which had been already let out to contract. We feel it will be wiser to defer as many items as possible until prices go down.

Another factor which renders it possible to defer these big permanent buildings is the shortage and quality of labour. The cocoa boom in 1920 thoroughly upset the labour market in every direction. Not only were we short in the number of men, but those who were available could not be said to be worth 60 per cent of their value in 1914. As an example, the following is the percentage of the labour for Government work which we obtained:

Carpenters	20 per cent	of what we required
Masons	15 per cent	
Painters	15 per cent	

That is to say, we only obtained from a fifth to a seventh of the number of artisans we required. As for unskilled labour, during the greater part of the year we could only get 40 per cent, less than half what we required although the situation has improved in this respect since the end of the cocoa boom...

Town improvement

Town improvements is another item for which it has been impossible to lay down any fixed sum in the 10 year programme. As in the case of water supply, the demand is unlimited. In practically every town of any size, the necessity for improvements in sanitation brings with it the demand for considerable alterations in buildings and streets.

The main policy of the Government is to concentrate its efforts on those large towns whose rapidly growing populations cause grave dangers of epidemics through the ease with which infection spreads in congested areas. In accordance with this policy practically every large town has in the past few years received a new layout. During 1920, however, only fair progress was made in carrying out actual construction. In the first half of the year shortage of European staff, and throughout practically the whole year shortage of labour, severely handicapped progress. Although in the majority of cases the Chiefs and their people are keenly alive to the advantages and desirous of improving their towns, their efforts to provide the necessary labour have been hopeless. Again and again in large towns such as Winnebah, Cape Coast, and Seccondee, arrangements were made to start work on the Chiefs' promises to find the necessary labour – in each case only to meet with disappointment...

Telegraphs and telephones

Telegraph and telephone construction work was badly held up throughout the year by the delays experienced in obtaining material... A start has also been made on replacing our temporary lines, a step which is urgently needed owing to the expense of maintenance and the frequent breakdowns, but unfortunately revenue will not permit of much activity in this direction during the coming year.

Maps

On the last item in the 10 year programme a most excellent start has been made... Good progress has also been made with the topographical map in the Eastern Province so that it is hoped that by the end of this field season we shall be in possession of sufficient information to enable us to settle many long-standing boundary disputes and select routes for railways and roads. Similar work is also being carried out west of the Seccondee–Coomassie railway.

Among other work carried out by the survey, accurate town plans are being made...

The survey school has also been started in the old Basel Mission buildings at Odumase, kindly lent to us by the Scottish Mission, and there is no reason to doubt but that this school will soon rival the Nigerian Survey school in its result...

2. The meagre achievements of British enterprise in Tropical Africa, 1924 [1]

[The rate of railway building depends mainly on whether] the expenditure on the service of the loans can be justified by the financial resources of the colonies. The opinion was expressed both by official and non-official witnesses that in Nigeria and the Gold Coast expansion had recently been taking place as rapidly as expedient in the existing state of the resources of the countries.

There is indeed little reason to suppose that private firms will be found willing to finance, construct and operate railways unaided by Government in the present stage of development of Tropical Africa.

...nearly the whole of the railways...have been built departmentally. The reasons for this are not far to seek. The railways have not been built solely as commercial undertakings. The Uganda railway was the outcome of philanthropic and patriotic impulse on the part of the British public; and in many cases the railways were constructed in the first instance for administrative convenience as much as for commercial advantage.

The advantages of construction by the Government are found at their maximum in the case of a country like Nigeria, where a programme of construction extending over a number of years makes it possible for the colony to create and maintain in constant employment a thoroughly efficient construction staff under a first class railway engineer. Without this condition the recruitment and maintenance of such a staff would be impracticable. When, however, this condition is fulfilled, there are claimed as advantages of the State system that contractor's profits (enhanced possibly in the case of underdeveloped countries by inflated estimates to cover unknown risks) are saved; ... that plans can more easily be modified during the progress of the work as new information renders changes advisable, and that sections of the line can be brought into use as completed without incurring contractor's claims; [that delay can be avoided]; that Government can make full use of its existing railways and steamers to assist in construction work; that its political staff is in a far better position to handle indigenous labour with a minimum disturbance of the labour market than the contractor, who necessarily enters as a competitor against other employers, including the State itself; that railway construction under such conditions can be made a potent educative influence among a primitive people unused to, and timid of, service under Europeans; that the staff employed become well trained to team work in a contractor's and have greater knowledge and experience of local conditions: that so long as the railways are constructed and operated by the State all special plant raised, instead of becoming derelict on the completion of any one project, is in continuous use, whether in new construction or heavy works on existing lines.

The advantages claimed for the contract system are, in the main, that it introduces the element of competition from which, under a system of State construction, the party undertaking the work, i.e. the Government, is immune; that when a work has been put up to tender, and a tender has been accepted, the colony knows the extent of its liability, whereas there is no guarantee against any excess

[1] *Private enterprise in British Tropical Africa.* Report of the Committee appointed by the Secretary of State for the Colonies to consider and report whether, and if so what, measures could be taken to encourage private enterprise in the development of the British Dependencies in East and West Tropical Africa, with special reference to existing and projected schemes of transportation. Cmd. 2016, London 1924, pp. 5–17 (extracts). The minority report appears on p. 23.

over the estimate when the work is undertaken by the State; that firms of wide experience and reputation, whose life business is work of this kind, can carry through such projects more efficiently, more rapidly and more economically than any Government; that with such firms ready to undertake the work, the recruitment and employment of a constructional staff of its own is neither necessary nor economically sound.

Any choice between the two systems depends upon the view as to where the balance of advantage between the two systems lies. We do not think that any absolute rule can be laid down. Those who think that the balance of advantage lies with the adoption of a general policy of putting such works up to tender realise that there may be cases in which special reasons, particularly reasons connected with the labour supply, may render the introduction of an outside contraction inadvisable.

Those in favour of the contract system have been struck by what can best be described, perhaps, as a certain attitude of shyness on the part of British enterprise towards the Tropical African colonies and protectorates. A comparison has been drawn, for example, by witnesses between the meagre achievements of British enterprise in Tropical Africa on the one hand and on the other the striking results which it show in many parts of South America to which British capital has flowed freely, particularly for such enterprises as the construction of railways. Of the various reasons for apparent neglect of territories under the British flag which have been suggested to us, they note that in some quarters there appears to exist an impression more or less vague, but none the less real, that private enterprise is not welcome to the administrators of the territories concerned; that the system of Crown Colony government tends to obstruct rather than smoothen the way for the would-be concessionaire; that in any case, so far as communications are concerned, a fixed policy of departmental construction and State ownership has been deliberately decided on; that the result has been that private enterprise has passed them by, that interest in them has flagged and their potentialities have remained but little known.

[Harbours, the report suggests, should be built by private enterprise.] We think that works of this kind which require special plant and a specialised staff, are precisely the type in respect of which the maximum advantages of the contract system are to be gained....

Minority report: [Sir Edwin Stockton, M.P., a businessman, commented that] the requirements of the British public and fortunes of the colonies . . . demand the application of business methods to all colonial undertakings. There may have been reasons years ago why such a policy was undesirable, but to my mind there are none now.

3. African boycott of European firms: the Watson Commission criticises the government's handling of the situation and undertakes a close scrutiny of trading conditions, 1948 [1]

164. There can be no dispute that in the immediate post-war years many Africans in the Gold Coast had to pay prices for essential commodities that had increased more than their incomes.

[1] *Report of the Commission of enquiry into disturbances in the Gold Coast, 1948*, Colonial Office, London 1948, paras 164–258.

165. Many factors contributed to this unfortunate state of affairs. Short supplies erected black markets. The many hands through which the goods passed before reaching the ultimate consumer, added greatly to the final retail price.

166. Various measures of price control were at times attempted. We are willing to believe, that without an army of officials ten times the size of the staff available, and in the peculiar structure of Gold Coast trading, the strict enforcement of these controls was impossible. We are not satisfied, however, that in the case of textiles the Government took all steps open to it to ensure that if prices were excessive only the Africans themselves were responsible. We are of the opinion that, if the Government had made a more robust use of its powers at an earlier stage, the event with which we are about to deal would never have taken place.

167. It is plain that by the end of 1946 at latest, short supplies, maldistribution, conditional sales, pass-book customers and other devices calculated to impede fair distribution at reasonable prices had created among the mass of the population a sense of frustration and the greatest social unrest.

168. Be it remembered at the same time, that while rises in world prices, cost of production and overheads are explanations not always readily understood by masses of literate people, such factors are absolutely meaningless to the vast majority of the inhabitants of the Gold Coast.

169. It is not surprising, therefore, that by the end of 1947, there existed a well-tilled soil ready to receive the seeds of any adventure calculated to reduce prices, particularly of imported goods in short supply.

170. At that time there lived in Accra, and still does, one of the many sub-chiefs, called Nii Kwabena Bone III. This gentleman was a man of some business experience and we are prepared to believe that whatever personal ambitions he entertained, he was honestly anxious in the anti-inflation campaign which he instituted, to bring about a reduction in the prices of essential commodities in short supply for the public good. Naturally such a campaign which must add to prestige among the people made a powerful appeal to the other chiefs.

Accordingly, after a short campaign throughout the country, Nii Bone, with the support of the Chiefs, was able to impose in the Colony and Ashanti as from 26 January, 1948, a boycott on the purchase of European imported goods. We are prepared to believe that he hoped to achieve his ends by the peaceful persuasion of all Africans in the voluntary restriction of their purchases. But the cooperation of the Chiefs having been secured, the Native Administration were quick to see their opportunity in profiting from breaches of the declared boycott. A system of fines, which in our view were quite illegal, and a general intimidation of offenders against the boycott quickly grew up. The spoils to be expected from enforcement of the boycott naturally attracted many of the idle and lawless youths in the towns as voluntary enforcement officers. The difficulties of the authorities in effectively restraining this form of intimidation, which it would appear had the full approbation of some of the Chiefs, are manifest and considerable lawlessness resulted. The hostile demonstrations in Accra in the precincts of the Court at which the trial of the local chief was about to take place on charges arising out of the attempted enforcement of the boycott, showed the extent to which the importance of law and order had declined.

171. We are unable to absolve the Government of the Gold Coast at this period from the strongest criticism for its inaction. The reason may not be far to seek. Among the foreign trading community in the colony, there has long existed a conviction that the indigenous people, by reason of tribalisation and mutual dis-

trust, are unable successfully to combine effectively for any single purpose. We should have thought that the successful boycott and 'hold-up' of cocoa carried out in 1937, which resulted in the Nowell Commission, would have cured everyone of this fallacy. Unfortunately it still appeared to dominate trading circles and we think it had permeated the Administration. We say this because the first reaction of the Government to the boycott was to declare in effect that it was a purely trading dispute in which the Government, as such, must remain neutral. We cannot emphasise too strongly our view that every economic aspect of life in a colony, affecting the welfare of the indigenous population, is a concern of the highest priority to the tutelary Government of that colony. The people did not believe that the Government was not involved in this dispute. It had become known that, in place of more vigorous methods of price control for textiles, the Government had come to an agreement in 1945 with the importing firms on the retail margins which were to be charged on textiles. This was agreed at 75 per cent gross overall margin above the landed cost. Although this appears to be a high margin it will be appreciated that it was agreed on the understanding that profits on textiles were to be used to compensate for dealings in the less profitable but more essential goods.

172. There had been ample warning of impending trouble. In December 1946, the Joint Provincial Council of Chiefs had met the Chamber of Commerce in the presence of the Acting Colonial Secretary to complain about the high prices of imported goods and to ask for a fairer system of distribution. Later in the same month the Council was assured that a tentative scheme of price control had been worked out. The importing firms stated that they were placing larger quantities of goods for direct sale in the stores instead of indirectly through other distributors. No further action was taken until a year later.

173. In our view the question raised by the boycott was one calling for immediate government investigation, if need be, by public enquiry. The charge was clear: it was being alleged that importers, and particularly those associated with the hated organisation which flourished under the name of the Association of West African Merchants (A.W.A.M.) were deliberately keeping up prices of essential commodities to an outrageous extent. If that were true the Government had the power to requisition them, and it had a duty to act. But the Government took no action and the suspicion not unnaturally grew up that, at all material times, there was some private arrangement between the powerful importers (principally those represented by A.W.A.M.) and the Government whereby they were permitted to do as they pleased. We need hardly say that we are satisfied no such fantastic state of affairs ever existed, but we feel that the Government itself must be accounted responsible for the growth of this suspicion by reason of its failure to take positive steps either to clear the importers of this charge by impartial enquiry or by taking some robust positive action to prevent its continuance if true.

174. The Government indeed took no positive steps to deal with the boycott until 11 February, 1948, when a series of meetings between the Chambers of Commerce, the Nii Bone Committee and the Chiefs, under the chairmanship of the Colonial Secretary was arranged. As a result an agreement was reached whereby the gross overall profit margin to be charged by importers for cotton piece goods other than those for which maximum prices were established, was to be reduced from 75 per cent to 50 per cent for a trial period of three months. Upon this undertaking the boycott was called off.

175. We cannot help feeling that the announcement of this agreement was so framed as to lead to the greatest public disappointment. As we point out in our observations on public relations, we are dealing here with a country largely illiterate and with no objective press. We have not the slightest doubt that the way in which the agreement in question reached masses of the public was in a form calculated to suggest that the price of all the commodities affected was being reduced almost by half. The disillusionment which followed the discovery that prices were only marginally affected must have been intense. We have little doubt that it helped considerably to prepare the ground for the resentment which manifested itself in the looting and useless destruction which later took place in Accra and elsewhere.

176. We are not concerned here to discuss whether a profit margin of 50 per cent on c.i.f. prices is, or is not, reasonable. We would merely remark that the principle of a percentage margin is a pernicious one. There is no reason why a distributor's margin should vary with changes in external factors such as a rise in costs in exporting countries or a rise in transport costs. They should move with changes in distributive costs in the Gold Coast itself. A margin of 75 per cent based on costs in 1945 when supplies were very much less must have been a very liberal one when both prices and turnover were increasing.

177. This is a matter which may well right itself as and when supplies of commodities in common use substantially increase. Such increases, we are informed, may now be expected in the immediate future. We already have the satisfaction of noting that: (i) in the Gold Coast A.W.A.M. has been dissolved, and (ii) the actual prices of a large variety of commodities have to an appreciable extent been reduced. We can only express the hope that this policy will be consistently followed as and whenever conditions permit.

SUPPLIES, PRICES AND DISTRIBUTION

178. In our last chapter we dealt with the consumers' boycott arising from high prices of imported goods in short supply. But the end of the boycott in no way diminished complaints of this nature. General allegations of high prices and unfair distribution were more numerous than on any other subject. Increases in world prices and loss of normal sources of supply being meaningless to the average African, the whole of the mischief was naturally attributed to the larger importing firms. While only a long and searching examination of the books of the importers by accountants, for which we were not equipped, could afford an analytical survey in the field of costs, we are satisfied on the materials presented to us that the incidence of high prices in the Gold Coast cannot be solely attributed to the activities of importers.

179. During the war hardships were accepted cheerfully as part of the war effort but there was a general expectation that goods would become freely available again as soon as fighting was over. There is even now a widespread expectation that prices will return to their 1939 level. It is therefore not difficult to understand the disappointment in the present high prices and the impatience of controls which post-war shortages still necessitate.

180. The situation in the Gold Coast is very similar to that in so many other countries – a great shortage of consumer goods in relation to the amount of money in the hands of consumers – but many of the measures taken to protect the consumer in other countries from the ills of inflation, are, for various reasons, im-

practicable in the Gold Coast. Indeed, it is probably true to state that many features of its economic organisation actually aggravate the troubles of the ultimate consumer.

181. There is an unfortunate dearth of economic statistics in the Gold Coast which makes it impossible to assess with any degree of precision the more important factors in the present situation and their relative significance. We have, however, been able to collect a certain amount of official and unofficial data which throw some light on the reasons for the extent of the present economic malaise.

Supplies

182. Total supplies of consumer goods are undoubtedly below the level of pre-war years. There are no official estimates of the output of food crops in the Gold Coast except those destined for export. It is not possible, therefore, to discover whether the total supply of home-grown foods, which probably accounts for more than 70 per cent of wage earners' expenditures, has actually decreased or increased. Such views as were expressed to us indicate that, apart from changes in yield between one crop year and another, production was not, in the post-war years, materially different from before.

183. Imports, on the other hand, of both foodstuffs and other essential consumer goods were demonstrably lower. [Table 3.1] shows the percentage fall in the imports of commodities used widely by African consumers between 1937–8 and 1947, the last year for which complete data are available:

Table 3.1

Percentage fall		Percentage fall	
Wheat flour	37	Milk	29
Rice	98	Cotton, piece goods	25*
Sugar	46	Buckets, pails, etc.	60
Canned meat	93	Candles	70
Canned fish	95	Kerosene	45

* Imports of cotton piece goods in 1938 were abnormally low; if 1935–7 imports are taken as normal, the supplies in 1946 were 42 per cent lower.

184. Such preliminary figures as we were given indicate that supplies of one or two imported commodities had improved slightly in 1947 and were expected to improve still further in 1948, particularly cotton piece goods, but the 1946 imports are significant in that they indicate the level of supplies which was reached in the first year after the war when it was widely expected that supplies would once again be not very different from before the war. They also indicate, for durable goods, the back-log of consumers' requirements which remains to be satisfied.

Demand

185. The first factor to be considered in the post-war period is the increase in population. In 1938 the population was estimated at 3,800,000 ; preliminary results of the 1947 census indicate that it is now about 4,473,000, an increase of 18 per cent in nine years. It is also of importance for social as well as economic reasons that the increase in population was very much more evident in the towns than in

the country; whereas the total population of the four largest towns, Accra, Kumasi, Sekondi–Takoradi and Cape Coast, was about 176,000 before the war, it had risen so high as 273,000 by 1947, an increase of 55 per cent.

186. Money incomes and wages also rose rapidly during the war years, due to such factors as allied military expenditure and increased receipts for exports.

187. Here again, it is not possible to give any precise indication of the amount by which the national income has increased or the change in the amount of purchasing power left in the hands of consumers. It can only be suggested indirectly. There is no composite index of earnings but it is estimated that wages in the lowest income groups are now 2–2½ times greater than before the war. Those of clerical workers and the like have probably risen 1½ to 2 times.

188. On the other hand, the total amount of money in circulation at present, about £18 million, is about four times the pre-war amount. Against this, public revenue, derived mainly from taxation, customs and excise has not increased savings or capital accumulation. It is clear, therefore, that money demand has grown rapidly during the war and, particularly, in the post-war years, while supplies have fallen.

189. Nor would it be safe to assume that these inflationary factors have reached a peak. The farmers' receipts for cocoa, which averaged about £6 million a year before the war and about £10 million in 1946/7, may be expected to reach about £16 million in 1947/8; [2] the possibility of further increase in the farmers' price for the next cocoa crop cannot be ignored. Timber prices have doubled in the last year and exports are increasing. Values of other exports commodities are also hardening. While increased taxes, customs duties and other sources of revenue are planned for 1948/9, they will not be sufficient to offset these higher receipts. Finally, there are plans for capital developments, financed by accumulated budget surpluses or grants from the United Kingdom, which may increase inflationary tendencies, at least in the short run.

Prices

190. Under such conditions of supply and demand, it is not surprising that prices have risen greatly, particularly in the years 1946 and 1947.

191. The cost of living index based on wage earners' budgets in urban areas was 211 in December, 1947, compared with 100 in 1939. In our opinion this underestimates the real increase since imported goods are included at controlled prices where applicable, and not at the higher open, grey or black market prices.

192. Prices of home-produced goods, mainly food, have increased by more than double since pre-war years. There are, of course, wide variations between one market and another in the prices of indigenous foodstuffs, since local prices are very sensitive to local supply conditions. For example, the average price of palm oil in the market in 1947 was 19*d* per bottle, while in Koforidua it was only 9*d*. Accordingly, too great a reliance should not be placed upon general index numbers as indication of conditions in any one area. We have estimated, however, that the prices of staple foods [3] on a number of urban and country markets are probably about 2½ times the pre-war level. The retail market prices have undoubtedly risen

[2] The export value of the cocoa crop in 1947–8 is expected to total over £40 million but it is intended that about £25 million of this be held by the Cocoa Marketing Board.

[3] Cassava, cocoa-yams, corn, bananas, plantains and palm oil.

more than the prices obtained by the farmer, with the exception, of course, of cocoa.

193. The chief complaints about high prices, however, were concerned with imported goods, since those prices were expected, quite unjustifiably, to show a big decline when the war ended. Much of the criticism is of a general nature and largely based on antagonism to the large importing firms.

194. Such evidence on prices of imported goods as has been presented to us by importing firms has shown quite clearly that they have risen for reasons which are not generally appreciated in the Gold Coast. In some instances the rise is due to increased costs in the exporting countries, while in others it is due to the fact that dearer sources have had to be substituted for cheaper pre-war sources.

195. The following two examples illustrate this rise in the price of goods brought into the country[4] [Table 3.2].

Table 3.2

	1939		April 1948		
	Source	Landed cost inc. duty	Source	Landed cost inc. duty	Percentage increase
		s d		*s d*	
Billhook matchets (per doz.)	U.K.	7 3	U.K.	22 11	202
Enamel basins (per doz.)	Japan	3 7	U.K.	17 3	382
			Belgium	26 8	644
			Czecho-slovakia	28 10	705

Billhook matchets were more than three times dearer than before the war, while prices of basins, previously imported from Japan and now imported from other sources, were 5 to 8 times greater.

196. Taking a wide range of imported goods in common use in the Gold Coast we have estimated that they would cost the importing firms (including the payment of duty), about $2\frac{3}{4}$ to 3 times as much to purchase overseas and bring into the Gold Coast today as they did before the war. Some groups of commodities such as hardware and textiles have increased more than the average; others have increased less.

Index numbers of landed costs, including duty of certain classes of commodities imported into the Gold Coast, 1939 and 1948 (weighted according to 1939 quantities):

[4] We have compared some of the increases in the c.i.f prices and retail prices for the Gold Coast provided for us by importing firms with the increases in some of the f.o.b. prices for exporting countries, and, by and large, they are not materially different.

	1939	1948
Textiles	100	314
Haberdashery	100	292
Tobacco	100	155
Drinks	100	167
Hardware	100	445
Provisions	100	352
Sundries	100	283

197. This, then, is the background to the complaints of high prices of imported goods, much of the increase can therefore be attributed to factors beyond the control of the importers, to increased prices charged by exporting countries – compare the changes in the export prices of cocoa and timber from the Gold Coast – and to the disappearance of some of the pre-war cheap sources such as Japan, and the consequent need to fall back on dearer sources if supplies are to be obtained in reasonable quantity.

198. The price increases at the initial stages in the channels of distribution are, however, often greatly exceeded in the charges made to the ultimate consumer. The methods of trading in the Gold Coast, which are discussed later, afford every opportunity of adding to the price, particularly when goods are in short supply. Only one or two examples need be given. A 1lb. packet of cube sugar, which before the war sold in the retailers at 4½*d* cost 8½*d* in March, 1948 ; but this packet is usually subdivided into smaller quantities, and peddled by petty traders, the total receipts being as much as 2*s* 8*d* or 3*s*. Cotton goods, which may have been sold over the counter for 20*s* a piece, are passed from petty trader to petty trader and eventually sold for £2 or more.

199. From these examples it is apparent that the real mischief of high prices charged to ultimate consumers is attributable in large measure to the unfortunate system of wholesaling and retailing which has become an integral part of trading in the Gold Coast.

200. The evidence which we were given and some of which we have cited in this report appears to us to justify the conclusion that, for a large part of the population, prices had risen far more rapidly and to a higher extent than had many incomes or wages. Unfortunately, there are insufficient economic data to enable us to say where the shoe pinches most and where it is easiest. There is no doubt in our minds, however, that the benefits of higher export prices and the general increase in national income have not been spread evenly throughout the population. Some have benefited greatly, others have had to face a severe drop in their standard of living. The effects of these changes have been very noticeable in the last 18 months or two years.

Distribution

201. Home produced goods for local consumption, mainly foodstuffs, pottery, firewood and so on, are sold mainly either by the producer direct to the consumer through stall or market or indirectly through a middleman. The system is simple and fairly direct. As we have already stated, most of the complaints about unfair distribution were concerned with imported goods ; they related to:

(*a*) The continuation of licensing and other import controls.

(*b*) The monopolistic position of the importing firms and restriction of African enterprise.

(*c*) The basing of import quotas on past performance.

(*d*) The methods of sale employed by importing firms.

(*e*) Conditional sales.

(*f*) Excessive margins and distributive costs.

(*g*) The wide gap between the prices paid in the retail stores of the importing firms and the price paid by the African buying from a petty trader.

Licensing and import control

202. So long as goods remain in short supply and are subject to international allocation or there are shortages of specific currencies, we are of opinion that a system of import control and licences is essential. It is in practice a method of rationing between countries, similar to rationing between individuals, and makes possible a fairer distribution of essential goods than would otherwise obtain in free competition. We were impressed by the increase since 1946 in the number of commodities that can now be imported under open general licence and in the number of countries in which these are available. Unfortunately, the commodities which are still in world short supply and of which the Gold Coast is allocated a specific quantity, include those which are keenly sought in the Gold Coast such as sugar, flour, canned meats, soaps and fats.

203. In fairness to the importing firms against whom feeling has been very high in the Gold Coast we feel bound to say that we were greatly impressed by their efforts to find alternative supplies when other sources have dried up and to make up as quickly as possible, within the limits imposed by shortages and controls, for the lean years of the war. Without the extensive and intricate buying organisations of these firms, active in all main exporting countries of the world, supplies of consumer goods in the Gold Coast today would have been far less and prices would have been even higher.

204. The benefits which world-wide buying organisations can and do confer upon the territories which they serve are certainly not understood in the Gold Coast. By failing to make them known we feel that the importers have not only done themselves a great disservice but have sown the seeds of suspicion which powerful and successful enterprises normally attract.

Import monopolies

205. Concerted action by importing firms first became noticeable in the early thirties when a cocoa-buying agreement was arranged and evidence of disquiet on the part of the public is seen in the boycott of imported goods and the cocoa hold-ups in 1932 and 1937. In addition, there was the absorption or amalgamation of independent firms into the United African Company.

206. During the war force of circumstances, arising in part from shipping difficulties, made it necessary to bring the firms into closer combination under the aegis of the Association of West African Merchants, known as A.W.A.M. This was done at the instigation of the West African Governments.

207. As we have stated in the previous Chapter this association became identified after the war in the minds of the Gold Coast people as the mainspring of a conspiracy to keep prices up to an unjustifiable extent and we feel that its survival

in West Africa until April of 1948 was a cardinal blunder. There is no doubt that its origin in association with the West African Governments lent colour to the suggestion that it survived only with Government support. Even now its demise is questioned although we are satisfied that it no longer exists in West Africa.

208. With restricted supplies, allocations among the distributors were made on the basis of average annual imports in the pre-war period, 1937–41. During this period, there had been no bar to anyone entering the import trade, but, in fact, there were no African firms who were interested to any large extent.

209. The pre-war years were a period of considerable risks owing to fluctuations in the cocoa price and successful business depended on small profits and a large turnover. These importing firms maintained chains of retail and wholesale stores and sold as much as 60 per cent of their imports to African traders and re-sellers.

210. As the war period advanced, the position changed radically. The shortage of supplies coupled with a keen demand made the prospects of large profits most attractive and the desire to partake of these was widespread. Demands were made for an increased participation in the import trade, demands that were checked by the past performance policy in the allocation of quotas. This has given rise to a good deal of ill-feeling and the system was modified at the beginning of this year and more adequate provision made for newcomers. In our opinion this might well have been done earlier, even though supply conditions and prospects had not improved to such an extent as they had by the end of 1947.

211. We were pleased to be informed that some progress had been made at least for certain commodities as a result of the recent modifications [Table 3.3].

Table 3.3

	Percentage of trade by Africans	
	1937–41	1948
Sugar	1.75	21.0
Canned meats	1.0	12.4
Unmanufactured tobacco	6.5	26.0

212. The comparative failure of Africans in the larger fields of modern commerce is due to a variety of causes. The close family ties – a legacy of tribalisation – tend to destroy the fruits of individual success and prevent the saving of capital. The claims of family – in the widest conception of that word – are still very real. Further the African has no substantial security to offer upon which he can borrow capital. As we show in our Chapter dealing with land tenure he can rarely have an interest in land capable of offering any real security. These and other difficulties place him at a great disadvantage in competition with Europeans and others. Not unnaturally in these circumstances the African seeks to excuse his failure by reference to those sinister machinations of monopoly opposition. Because this has become something of an obsession and also bears on the question of high prices we feel it requires careful examination.

213. One of the more encouraging developments, however, is the further expansion of the Gold Coast Cooperative Federation which buys and imports on behalf of a number of cooperative societies. We see no reason why such an

organisation should not grow in strength and we suggest that it might develop still more rapidly by increasing its contacts with producers' or wholesale cooperative societies in other parts of the world. Its great handicap must be lack of purchasing agencies in exporting countries and such affiliations would help to overcome the weakness.

214. Added to these complaints is the fact that African importers frequently complain that they are unable to obtain certain goods when the market is otherwise free. This applies particularly to branded goods. For obvious reasons manufacturers in the United Kingdom and elsewhere adopt the policy of appointing established firms in the Gold Coast as their sole agents and distributors. It is difficult to see how this can be overcome. The mischief lies in the exclusive 'brand' consciousness among African consumers. African importers must bestir themselves to destroy this. We should have thought that with the assistance of their suppliers they were in a strong position to influence the sale of goods of equal merit under a different 'brand'.

215. Methods of distribution followed by importers also come in for serious criticism. The following figures supplied to us by one of the large importing firms shows how their trade used to be distributed:

	per cent
Sales through own retail stores	31
Sales to credit or pass-book customers	25
Sales through cash wholesales	36
Others	8
	100

216. The volume of goods offered for sale through the retail stores has now been increased, in response to popular demand and in the hope that goods may reach more quickly the ultimate consumer, at the expense of the third category of sales. It has been estimated that retail sales over the counter may now amount to about 60 per cent of the whole. But it is probable that a large part of this still finds its way into the hands of re-sellers and the pass-book customers. Many of these are women – known as 'Mammies' – forming an important link in the chain of distribution as now in use. These pass-book customers are in fact the middlemen drawing their supplies from main warehouses and stores; they are beyond control as to the price they charge on re-sale (even where a statutory price control exists).

217. In the result only the fortunate and the privileged or those able and willing to queue can acquire at retail store prices goods in short supply. The bulk of the population is compelled to buy from petty traders at prices which have attracted two or more further profits before reaching them.

218. We are satisfied that this system leads to great abuses and encourages bribery and excessive charges and should be discouraged.

219. We do not pretend that direct sales necessarily preclude the like evils. We ourselves have seen crowds of women enter a store when a consignment of goods in short supply arrived for sale over the counter. A 'tic-tac' system appears to operate outside main warehouses. Each of these women purchased a single piece of cloth at the store price and on coming out at once disposed of it to some woman trader conveniently situated round the corner. Even so we think that direct sales

on the whole would produce better results. Equally a policy of sending increased supplies to country branches might have eliminated some of the costly and unnecessary links in the chain of distribution.

220. Allegations were also made that branch managers and store-keepers employed by importers did not observe the pre-determined prices fixed by their principals. On the principle that profits cannot be hidden we were invited to observe the fine houses built by and for representatives of these classes. Even without this visual proof we are satisfied that, in a country where by general standards, gain is the important factor and the means merely incidental, practices of the kind complained of were indulged in. We accept the assurance that this was a clear breach of instructions from the principals but were unable to accede to the view that it was incurable. We are not satisfied even yet that adequate steps are being taken to ensure that such offences will not be repeated.

Conditional sales

221. General complaints were made about the evils of conditional sales. Early in 1940 conditional sales were made illegal. This Order was continued in different form in 1947.

222. The vigorous enforcement of this law is impossible without the cooperation of the public. The fact that no specific instances were cited to us speaks for itself. Much work remains to be done in the Gold Coast to convince the citizens that law enforcement is a public duty since laws are made for public protection.

Excessive costs of distribution

223. As we have already stated we are not in a position to assert that the margins claimed by the importing firms were excessive and led to undue profits, though we cannot help suspecting that they were ample. It appeared clear to us, however, that if consumers had generally been able to obtain the goods at the retail prices obtaining in these firms' stores, there would have been fewer complaints about high prices and excessive costs of distribution. We state again that much of the blame for the undeniably high prices paid by many consumers is due to the complicated traditional method by which the goods may pass through the hands of several re-sellers. The re-sellers of the Gold Coast are natural traders and they have not been slow to take advantage of the scarcity of goods and to make extortionate charges. We gain the impression, moving about the towns and countryside that there could be few of the population who were not selling and re-selling small quantities of goods, making small profits at the expense of each other. Such a system, encouraged by the custom prevailing in some parts of the country whereby the wife is expected to earn some of the expenses of housekeeping, is extravagantly wasteful of manpower and must eventually disappear if the country is to become commercially efficient.

224. One of the most paradoxical results of the distribution system is that the poorer African often has to pay more for his essential requirements, such as sugar, flour, tobacco, hardwood and so on, than the richer members of the community. For this the African trader is no less blameworthy than the importing firm. Such a situation cannot be allowed to continue since it is an obvious source of hardship and distress.

225. Various suggestions for the reduction of prices of essential goods were suggested to us: (*a*) to absorb purchasing power by increasing taxation or

increased savings; (*b*) to control prices; (*c*) to control distribution and ration the consumer; (*d*) to increase the supply of consumer goods. We spent much time in examining the complexities raised by these suggestions.

226. Taxes, both indirect and direct, have been raised recently and we are of the opinion that further increases in direct taxation, on a progressive basis, could still be undertaken without fear of the accusation that the Gold Coast was over taxed in comparison with other countries.

227. We are not over optimistic about the possibility of voluntary saving, either for personal saving or for investment, as a means of reducing the competition for consumer goods. In spite of this we think that the possibility of raising loans locally for the financing of many of the developments desired by the inhabitants of the Gold Coast should not be overlooked. There is a strong current of national feeling which might well result in a sensible response and contribution to a national loan for economic development such as that contemplated under the Volta scheme.

228. Control of prices was instituted at the beginning of the war, firstly for most locally produced foodstuffs and certain imported foodstuffs. Later it was extended to certain textiles such as bafts and shirtings and to other goods such as fishing nets, soap, tobacco and cigarettes, candles and so on. Price control of textiles other than bafts and shirtings was attempted less directly through an agreement in 1945 with importing firms to limit the average over-all gross margins on such textiles to an average of 75 per cent of the landed cost, including duty. We have given our opinion of this arrangement elsewhere in this report. Control of home-grown foodstuffs (excepting coffee and rice) was discontinued in August, 1947.

229. The whole question of price control has been referred to a Committee which was appointed in September, 1947. It would therefore be invidious to make anything more than general remarks on the subject. For any system of price control to work successfully, there appear to be at least three prerequisites: well defined channels of trade, an effective enforcing body and public conscience. Even though these are not found in the Gold Coast, we are of the opinion that some form of price control for imported essential commodities is preferable to none. It can be enforced for at least part of the supply sold to consumers and it is both psychologically and politically important to provide an indication of what may be considered a reasonable price. Further, we were not impressed by the arguments against more direct control of certain types of cotton textiles by means of fixed prices and not merely maximum prices.

230. The only other general point which we would make is on the system of fixing margins. Firstly, we think that it is probably more effective to fix only the retail price, differentiating in broad zones if it is necessary to make allowance for transport costs. Secondly, we are of the opinion that a percentage margin, though temptingly simple to administer, is unsound in principle. It makes for too high a final price, and gives excessive profits, particularly if external prices are rising or imported supplies increasing.

231. Control of the distribution of certain commodities is achieved in the Gold Coast by regulating the release for sale by the firms from wholesale stocks. In general, this is at present applied only to sugar and fats from among the imported commodities generally consumed. We are of opinion that so long as shortages exist, this is a most valuable measure to retain. It can be used to great advantage in concentrating the release of goods, of which only a small allocation has been

granted, within a short period, in preference to attempting to spread out a small quantity over a long period.

232. We explored in some detail the possibility of securing fairer distribution of goods in short supply by means of control of supplies and rationing of consumers. A number of witnesses thought that this might be possible, but the establishment of a system would require a cumbersome administrative machine, open to too many abuses. It should be undertaken only as a last resort...

234. Firstly, rationing would have to be limited to those commodities which are in common use all over the country, such as kerosene, sugar and soap. It could not include those commodities such as butter or cheese which are consumed by only a small proportion of the population, since obviously the establishment of an entitlement based on so much per head of population would be meaningless and would lead to a black market in the coupons for such a commodity or in the commodity itself.

235. Secondly, the peoples of the Gold Coast have very widely differing standards and habits of living. These variations in requirements and consumption are so great that it would require a most elaborate and flexible points system of rationing to overcome these difficulties; and such a system would be almost impossible to work in a country where almost 90 per cent are said to be illiterate.

236. Thirdly, the existing trading system offers so many opportunities for abuses that the eventual irregularities in distribution might be worse than at present.

237. Fourthly, there is not the personnel available to administer such a scheme.

238. While a precise system of rationing seems to us to be impossible to institute, we think that more could be done to achieve a better distribution of such essentials as soap, candles and sugar, of which the supply is far below minimum requirements, by arrangements with the importing firms. We believe that it would be better to release larger quantities in the country areas and let surpluses, if any, trickle back into the towns than to rely on dispersals from the towns reaching the country districts. We understand that such informal and rough rationing of kerosene led to a much fairer distribution of restricted supplies and a general reduction in the black market prices.

239. We cannot, however, over-emphasise our conclusion that the whole selling system in the Gold Coast needs reorganisation in many ways. In the first place we would like to see more African organisations participating in the import trade if they can do it as efficiently as the existing firms; we have already indicated that we think some development of cooperative organisation might be successful.

240. In the second place, we suggest that a more specialised and firmly established retail trade spread throughout the country would be preferable to the existing amorphous growth, with its multiplicity of part-time petty traders and its waste of time and effort.

241. We realise that this would call for considerable changes in social customs and therefore we are prepared to admit that such reformation must take time. We have been informed that some at least of the importing firms aim at giving up their retail activities and concentrating their attention on importing and wholesaling. This would appear to afford an opportunity for African enterprise to take over and expand either individually or cooperatively, some of the existing retail agencies. Eventually there must be some reduction in the number of petty traders, particularly in the towns, and we would welcome the introduction of a restrictive system of licensing which would result in a gradual limitation of retailing to

established shops and markets. Not only would this be of benefit economically but also in the interests of health and hygiene.

242. We considered at length whether a chain of Government-sponsored stores could be introduced in a short time to meet the present problem and reduce black market prices. There were a number of points in favour of attempting to do what had been done successfully in Ceylon, but on further reflection we were convinced that any ambitious scheme would probably not achieve its objects for the following reasons:

(*a*) The fundamental conditions are not analogous to those in Ceylon.

(*b*) Without a reasonably effective rationing system or system of tying consumers to specific retailers, there would be little or no improvement in distribution, and, as we have already stated, we consider such a rationing scheme is not practical politics at present.

(*c*) The scheme would entail a large buying and selling Government organisation, trained personnel – who are not available – the building of warehouses and stores, the acquisition of fleets of lorries with repair depots and the like.

(*d*) It is doubtful whether such a chain of shops would under present supply conditions curtail very greatly the present amount of re-selling, petty trading and breaking of the price regulations.

(*e*) It would take so long to introduce that the improvements in the supply position which may reasonably be expected in the next five years may have rendered its introduction unnecessary.

243. These are not arguments, however, for not working out some system of rationing and of allocation and distribution of a small number of important commodities, such as flour, sugar, kerosene, soap, candles and the cheaper textiles, in the event of supply conditions deteriorating. Such a worsening of the situation might call for a very drastic Government action such as requisitioning of supplies and the taking over of existing stores in some of the towns, but in the light of present circumstances and prospects, we do not recommend such an immediate course of action.

244. On the other hand, we feel that plans should be made and adopted to encourage the growth of consumers' cooperatives, both in the towns and in the country. We are the first to recognise that this will take time and will require intensive education and propaganda. We are confident that this is not only economically desirable, but also politically expedient, as a means of increasing the responsibilities of the African community and making clear the complexities and problems of modern economic life. The story of the existing truly cooperative organisations gives reason to hope that with encouragement, both financial and moral, the growth might be rapid; economic and political conditions are all in its favour at present.

245. If, as we think, the present difficulties and disquiet arising from high prices cannot be speedily and effectively alleviated by control of prices or of distribution, the only remaining practical alleviation is to increase the supply of essential imports. The relief would be immediate. We are encouraged to make this recommendation by the fact that, as we have shown, past restrictions of supplies to the Gold Coast appear to have been extremely severe. Allocations appear still to be based on minimum essential requirements estimated during the war.

246. The effect of increased supplies is clearly shown in the case of kerosene. Pre-war supplies averaged about 10,800 tons a year; the original allocation for

1947 was 7,140 tons and the black market price in Accra was 28*s* per 4 gallons against the controlled price of 11*s* 9*d*. An increased allocation in the middle of the year permitted a 10 per cent increase in releases and the black market price dropped to 13*s*. Again, as a result of fortuitous circumstances and delays in allocations, or shipments of allocations a year's supply of some commodities has been released in a shorter period, say, eight months, with beneficial effects on prices. In general, the consensus of local opinion is that an increase of supplies to the pre-war level would break the black market for most essential commodities. We are not so optimistic; we think that, in view of the increased population and the general inflationary position, the supply of some essential goods should be increased to a greater extent. It must be remembered that the value of exports from the Gold Coast has increased greatly since before the war and that a larger share of the trade is going to hard currency countries [Table 3.4]. (The visible

Table 3.4

	1938	1946
	£	£
Value of exports to British sterling area	7,674,000	11,240,000
Hard currency areas	382,000	6,748,000
Other foreign countries	3,220,000	2,154,000
Total	11,276,000	20,142,000

credit balance of trade was £3,600,000 in 1938; in 1946 it was £7,300,000.) The figures for 1947 show a further and remarkable increase in the value of exports to hard currency countries as well as in the balance of trade. From cocoa alone, the past season's export is estimated to bring in well over £15 million from Canada and the United States.

247. Increase in the allocation of certain commodities such as flour, sugar, soap, kerosene, canned meats and fish and milk to the Gold Coast which would break the black and grey markets would appear to be justified. In our opinion they are warranted to ensure the continuance of the Gold Coast trade.

248. Though prices of imported goods can never be expected to return to their pre-war levels, a reduction from their present levels would do much to restore that confidence and goodwill upon which continued production for export depends and would mitigate a very real source of political discontent.

TRADING DISCRIMINATION

249. Allegations were made before us about discrimination in the allocation of railway transport for timber export tending to discourage African traders. No specific instances capable of verification were supplied to us. Nevertheless, we pursued the matter with the General Manager of the Railways and the Shipping Companies.

250. Timber exports from the Gold Coast is a long established trade. The old established firms not only have their markets but also their shippers. Over the latter, unlike the railways, of course the Government has no control. But we understand that in this regard no difficulty arises since shipping space for the trade exceeds railway transport.

251. At present, making the best use of railway transport it is found to be

impossible to allocate freight space for more than 10,500 tons of timber for export every month.

252. At this figure 2,500 tons is allocated as a first priority for the Timber Control Board of the United Kingdom although actually the Timber Control Board requires at least 5,000 tons per month.

253. The balance of 7,500 tons of railway transport is divided in the following proportions:

(1) Established shippers having standing arrangements with the Elder Dempster Line: 40 per cent.

(2) Established shippers having standing arrangements with the Takoradi Coal and Lighterage Company Limited: 40 per cent.

(3) Shippers by the U.S.A. shipping companies: 15 per cent.

(4) Miscellaneous: 5 per cent.

254. These arrangements have been arrived at by representatives of the shipping companies, the Traffic Manager of the Railways and a Forestry Officer meeting every month. We are informed that a representative of the African exporters of timber is to be added to this informal committee.

255. The trouble appears to have arisen largely from the fact that in the last six months the number of exporters has risen from 12 to 68.

256. It is inevitable in such circumstances that the competition for the limited railway facilities is very keen. The harbour authorities cannot allow the harbour at Takoradi to become cluttered up with heavy stocks awaiting clearance. Accordingly the railways cannot accept for transport (i) timber for which shipping is not assured and (ii) timber which is not of first quality, the shipping of which will be forbidden.

257. Since banking credits play a large part in the timber export trade and every newcomer has not the experience, credit delays have undoubtedly occurred.

258. We are advised that by the spring of 1949 the acquisition of new rolling stock by the railways will enable the haul of all first class timber reasonably expected to be available for export. Until that materialises some system of allocation will continue to be necessary if existing facilities are used to procure the export of the greatest volume of timber. To ensure that such allocation is not used to defeat the efforts of the small man we suggested that the Committee of Allocation shall not only have an African representative but shall be presided over by a senior officer of the Administration whose decisions shall be final. His instructions in our opinion should be to ensure that, provided the small exporter can produce evidence (i) that his consignment is of timber of first quality and (ii) that he has completed the arrangements necessary to ensure speedy shipment, then haulage by rail should not be denied him to meet an arbitrary allocation of railway facilities to long established exporters.

4. Enervating climate and lack of raw materials give barren prospect to industrialisation : Watson Commission, 1948 [1]

Industrial development

298. At every turn we were pressed with the cry of industrialisation. We doubt very much if the authors of this cry really understood more than their vague desire for something that promised wealth and higher standards of life.

[1] *Report of the Commission of enquiry into disturbances in the Gold Coast, 1948,* Colonial Office, London 1948, paras 298–320.

299. Apart from the possibilities of a hydro-electric scheme, which we discuss later, the establishment of any heavy industry on the Gold Coast capable of finding an export market must remain a dream. With an enervating climate in the torrid zone, lacking coal and other basic minerals, the prospect is so barren that not even the greatest enthusiast could suggest to us a method of accomplishment.

300. We do not mean by this that the country is necessarily condemned to remain a dumping ground for imports. At the same time international trade is no one-way traffic. The standard of life in a country producing primary commodities need not, in an expanding world production, be materially less than in an industrial country. But while there is clearly room for many secondary industries which would enrich the country, we are unable to foresee, in any circumstances, the Gold Coast emerging as a unit of heavy industries in the world markets.

301. In the matter of secondary industries we think there is considerable scope for bold planning on imaginative lines. We may say at once, that in a country which is quickly passing to a money economy the fact ought to be faced, the intense individuality of the Africans notwithstanding, unbridled private enterprise would at least lay the foundation of future social strife. We are of the opinion therefore that in building up secondary industries an attempt should be made to run them as cooperative units. In this we are not treading new ground. Apart from the Government-sponsored Cocoa Marketing Board, which has proved so successful, we are told that in other fields Cooperative Societies, while not always maintaining the letter of their constitutions, are slowly emerging as sound units in building up economic stability in the Colony.

302. We take the view therefore that the Government, either by guarantee to the Banks or by getting up an industrial Finance Corporation, should through the Registrar of Cooperative Societies make the necessary advances to approved cooperative enterprises setting up secondary industries. The Industrial Development Corporation which has just been set up under an Ordinance of the Legislative Council might be used for the purpose. We are pleased to note that the Directorate of the corporation will have substantial African representation as likewise that of any subsidiary company formed by it. Secondary industries of the type recommended should be directed primarily to supply the needs of the home market. A few suggested to us which appear to merit consideration are: (1) fish canning; (2) utility and other furniture; (3) native cloth weaving; (4) vegetable oil refining, and soap making.

303. The suggestion that petroleum products could be obtained from cassava was also advanced. Our own enquiries do not support the proposition but the authors of the suggestion will no doubt pursue the possibility.

The distillation of spirits

304. We had it impressed on us from several quarters that among potential secondary industries in the Gold Coast was the distillation of spirits. We do not think that it was seriously suggested that such spirits would be fit for human consumption. It was suggested however that they may replace alcohol now in use for medical and commercial purposes.

305. We think that this potential use is worthy of examination and provided adequate safeguards in manufacture and distribution to prevent human consumption of the product can be devised, we see no reason why an African with the necessary capital should not be permitted to develop such a business. We would add however that we are in complete agreement with present trends in legislation

to forbid the cutting down of coconut palms for the distillation or fermentation of spirits and wine.

Recovery and treatment of gold

306. Among the complaints raised by the Trades Union Congress but also separately in two memoranda submitted on behalf of the Goldsmiths and Silversmiths of the Gold Coast was an allegation that broadly speaking the restrictions on the recovery of gold and the use thereof in manufacture had brought about a situation in which an ancient and worthy craft was in danger of extinction.

307. We have made enquiries in this regard and have been referred to the Gold Mining Products Protection Ordinance Cap. 126 of the Gold Coast Statutes.

308. We find that this Ordinance is directed to the prevention of loss of gold recovered from mining or other process in use by what may be conveniently described as European methods. But for the Ordinance we are satisfied that the loss of such gold would be very great.

309. There is no restriction under the Ordinance on the search for and recovery of gold by native methods or in the use to which such gold may be put, but a goldsmith as such must have a licence – in our view a very necessary protection.

310. The real objection appears to be that the onus of proof as to the origin of the gold is placed upon the African who is found in possession of it.

311. Notwithstanding a statement made to us in all seriousness by one witness, that after heavy rain virgin gold might be found in the street drains which it was an offence to recover (a statement we found from observation to show a gift for hyperbole) it may well be that the discovery of virgin gold has become very rare and so dried up a source of supply of the goldsmiths.

312. To meet such a situation we recommend that existing provisions which enable a goldsmith to acquire gold be extended to secure all licensed goldsmiths the right to purchase through Government a limited quantity of bullion per annum at the price at which the same is sold to the Government plus a small percentage to cover the administrative costs. We are of the opinion that such a course would meet any legitimate complaint of the goldsmiths without seriously affecting the total value of gold exported.

The Volta valley scheme

313. To harness the waters of the Volta, for the production of electrical energy and its utilisation among other things in the manufacture of aluminium alloy on the spot, we believe is a scheme which has passed the visionary stage. The bauxite deposits which lie at hand for use in the process of manufacture of aluminium doubtless hastened practical consideration of the scheme.

314. Such a scheme, apart from creating a new industry, capable so far as yet seen of very great expansion, might well enable large tracts to become fertile by irrigation. At the same time the surplus electrical energy set free could be utilised to great advantage in hundreds of ways not calling for any great imagination.

315. We are not here concerned to discuss the scheme as such nor indeed are we competent to do so. That is a matter upon which the Government must advise itself from the experts available for the task.

316. We are however very much concerned to see that in the exploitation of the natural resources of the Gold Coast the indigenous population shares to the fullest extent the advantages.

317. We realise that in so far as the execution of the project depends on the manufacture of aluminium, it is a commercial venture the success of which may well depend on world prices being maintained. If the view held by those in the trade and maintained in high places in Britain immediately after the late war is any criterion, any prediction of this nature is no sure guide. It would not be right therefore in our view, unless the scheme held prospects of paying its way independently of aluminium manufacture, for the Government of the Gold Coast to embark upon it as a national venture.

318. On the other hand while capital is entitled to a fair return measured by risk it may be proper to observe that views may differ on what is a fair return. It would be equally improper in our view to permit without adequate safeguards the investment of foreign capital. These should include a share of profits and provision for the national use of surplus water and surplus electrical energy, together with the adoption of ultimate national ownership.

319. Accordingly we recommend that, assuming the Government upon consideration, for the reasons given or other good and sufficient reason, decides not to embark on the scheme as a national enterprise, then in permitting private enterprise to carry out the scheme, such permission should be conditional on agreement on the following broad lines:

(1) The nominal share capital of the company formed to carry out the scheme should be small and the Government entitled to subscribe up to 49 per cent thereof.

(2) The bulk of the working capital should be provided by way of loan capital at a fixed rate of interest including a rate for amortisation in 50–75 years, the interest to be a first charge on the company's revenues but not otherwise secured.

(3) Upon redemption of the loan capital the Government to have an option to acquire the balance of the 51 per cent share capital at a price to be fixed, failing agreement, by arbitration.

320. We appreciate that this recommendation in this form may be quite unacceptable to foreign capital. Our intention is not to tie the hands of the Government to any fixed formulae but to indicate the kind of arrangement which in our view should be aimed at and which we think the people of the Gold Coast are entitled to expect from the exploitation of their natural heritage.

5. The fragile economy, 1952 [1]

1. If we were forced to sum up the Gold Coast economy in one word, the word we would choose would be 'fragile'...

3. The Gold Coast economy has no checks on an inflationary wave of spending.

4. Direct taxation hardly touches most people; indirect taxes are relatively light, stocks are generally very thin, virtually the only goods produced locally for consumers are foodstuffs; and the supply of these cannot be increased at short notice; imports take months to order and in any case are checked by inability of the ports and transport system to handle much more; price control is not very effective and there are few conventional restraints on profiteering; communications are too poor for goods to flow readily to areas of shortage, savings institutions are prac-

[1] *Report on the financial and physical problems of development in the Gold Coast.* Office of the Government Statistician, Accra, 1952, Ch. 1 (extracts).

tically unused by the general public; and largely, for this reason, there is no capital market in which the Government could use monetary instruments – if it had any.

5. A sudden rise in incomes can therefore rapidly out-run the supply of goods, causing people to bid for goods in short supply, forcing up prices, leading to demands for higher wages and salaries, which would in turn push prices up further. Violent inflation could rapidly develop under these conditions – and so for that matter could a depression, if income fell. Considered as an economic machine, the Gold Coast economy 'over-responds' to any acceleration, and could easily get out of control. If such an economic explosion occurred, there would be social and political disturbances, further disrupting the economy and leading to more unrest.

6. The second main economic weakness is, of course, that the earnings of foreign exchange depend mainly on one commodity – cocoa. The demand for cocoa depends on a taste-fashion, which may be temporary, and since it is a luxury, its price in the world market is highly sensitive to changes in the prosperity of a few highly industrialised countries, notably the United States and the United Kingdom. Even the other exports, minerals and timber, have markets which are similarly limited and subject to much the same influences, so that they tend to share the fortunes of the cocoa industry. Not only foreign exchange, but also the level of purchasing power inside the country, depends mainly on these commodities, and this dependence makes possible the large variations in purchasing power whose dangers have just been sketched...

The structure of national output

8. [Table 5.1] shows our estimates of the value of the output of goods and services in the Gold Coast in the three financial years before our visit.

Table 5.1

Industry	1948–9	1949–50 (Output in £m.)	1950—51
1. Cocoa farming	37	37	56
2. Forestry	4	4	5
3. Mining	7	11	13
4. Building and construction	3	4	5
5. Public enterprises (railways, etc.)	3	3	3
6. Other industries and services	38	56	63
7. Public administration	6	7	7
8. Gross territorial product	98	122	152

9. The value of cocoa output has therefore been 30 to 40 per cent of the total value of what is produced in the Gold Coast: about three-quarters of the value of exports. Taking into account other primary products altogether, nearly half the total output of the country is exported. Secondary industry on the other hand is almost negligible – virtually all manufactures except beer and furniture are imported.

10. This table in a way understates the importance of cocoa, because the prosperity of the cocoa industry really makes possible much of the other output

of the country. Much of the income earned in transport and distribution depends on handling either cocoa or the goods bought by the cocoa farmer, and taxes on cocoa, or on imports bought out of the proceeds of the sale of cocoa, are the mainstay of the administration. The whole value of Gold Coast output, which in turn determines the people's living standards and the rate of development, depends very largely therefore on one commodity.

11. It is moreover a commodity whose long-run prospects are doubtful. 'Swollen shoot' threatens the whole industry; there are doubts whether the land, particularly in the new cocoa areas of western Ashanti, will yield further crops of trees after the present ones die; and the protective forest canopy is often neglected. The maintenance of annual cocoa exports, at something near average pre-war levels (1935–8) of 270 thousand tons, is misleading; output in the best areas with long-run capacity to support cocoa is uncertain. In the short-run, however, the value of the crop depends more on its price than on its quantity.

12. This price is one of the most unstable in the world's markets. To quote one official report, it has ranged from £127 per ton (at Liverpool) in 1920 to £19 in 1933, £13 at one stage in the war, and back to around £300 in the immediate past. The price also fluctuates sharply within the season, sometimes from week to week; in the course of 1937, according to a commodity report of F.A.O., the New York price ranged between 5.1 and 13.5 cents a pound.

13. This variation in the cocoa price causes a corresponding variation in the value of national output, and a similar, though not quite parallel, fluctuation in the public's total purchasing power of which the farmer's income is the main element. In 1949–50, for example, altogether about £50 millions of purchasing power was generated in the following productive sectors: cocoa, other farming, forestry, mining and building, and of this sum half was provided by the cocoa crop. The price paid to the cocoa farmer used to vary more frequently, but since the establishment of a marketing board it has remained constant during each season. Greater stability from year to year is also now practicable, though not yet achieved. The Board's price policy over recent years has, however, muffled the internal effect of the violent increases in the world price – at the cost of rather embarrassingly large reserves. The money in the reserves might well have wrecked the economic structure, and the political structure too, if it had been passed on to the farmer; farmers' incomes would have out-run the supply of consumer goods...

Port capacity

The combination of higher consumption and greater capital development has strained the physical capacity of the country. To say which is the most serious of these strains would be hard, but a strong case can be made out for treating port capacity as the main 'bottleneck'. It certainly has been in the immediate past.

19. [Table 5.2] contains three clues indicating how severely the volume of trade was straining the ports, which were, after all, designed for a much lower level of activity. The first is the great increase since before the war in the weight of both imports and exports. The second is the slow rise in tonnage after 1949, despite the booming markets both for imports and exports. Port operations in 1950 were somewhat held up by the strike, but even 1951 did not see a great increase in trade. Exports of timber and heavy minerals have been checked by port capacity, and so have imports especially of cement. There have been only two deep-water

Table 5.2. *Tonnage handled at the main ports (000 tons)*

	Imports				Exports			
	1938	1949	1950	1951	1938	1949	1950	1951
Takoradi	299	556	586	653	470	1,319	1,280	1,421
Accra	92	273	245	326	129	65	66	64
Other	40	35	51	57	54	19	27	30
Total	431	864	881	1,036	653	1,403	1,373	1,515

Source: *A survey of some economic matters*, Ministry of Finance, February 1952, table 15. The difference between the tonnage of imports and exports is largely due to the manganese exports from Takoradi which were – post-war – over 700,000 tons: these require special ships.

berths at Takoradi for general cargo, and by 1949 these were already being used continuously, so that the remaining cargo had to be brought off by lighter or surf-boat, a process slow and expensive, involving much damage to cargoes. The third clue is in the ports used. The surf-boats at Accra have handled three times the pre-war imports, and the recourse after 1949 to the even more primitive surf-boat facilities for importing at ' other ' ports (Cape Coast, Winneba and Keta) is an indication of the pressure on capacity. Such supplementary ports are of little use for exports, except for cocoa, and the cocoa exports have been limited by imports congesting the beach.

20. So both imports and exports have been continually held up over the post-war period. Shipping delays have meant expensive demurrage charges (of the order of £1,000 a day in many cases) foreign exchange earnings have been lost and there have been recurrent shortages of various important consumer goods and building materials. Trade has also been checked by the overcrowding of the harbour areas due partly to delays in customs procedure, but mainly to lack of transport. Road access to both the main ports is limited. Rail clearance of cargo is hindered by the lack of marshalling yards, and occasionally by shortage of rolling stock, especially covered trucks. So both ports generally show giant stacks of cargo awaiting collection – and making collection more difficult.

21. Going further inland, the single track railway line from the junction at Tarkwa to Takoradi carries the bauxite of Awaso, the cocoa of the Oda and Kumasi lines, minerals from the Tarkwa area, and timber from everywhere. Meanwhile imports are struggling northward along the same pair of rails. Although two-thirds of the imports come in through Takoradi it only has (including Sekondi) 1 per cent of the population. So the great bulk of merchandise is carried further inland via Tarkwa. Since there is no rail link between the Oda line and Accra, and no proper harbour in the Eastern Province, even heavy imports for Accra that cannot be carried by surf-boat have to be taken right round by Tarkwa and Kumasi, while much heavy equipment has to be taken up to the mineral areas. Coal also has to be carried through Tarkwa to dumps throughout the system. It is not surprising that often the line from Tarkwa to Takoradi is unable to cope with the traffic particularly the timber.

22. A glance at a map shows also the more general limitations of the railway system for present economic requirements. Western Ashanti, a rapidly developing area, lacks railway facilities to shift its cocoa and timber, or to bring in imported consumer goods for which it is an increasingly important market; the Volta basin

and Togoland are heavily populated areas without rail access; and so is the three-quarters (by area) of the country stretching north of Kumasi.

23. The roads do not make up for the limitations of the rail system. Heavy road traffic cannot really use the laterite road from Tarkwa to Takoradi – though many lorries attempt to slither along it – so this road cannot take much of the strain off the most heavily burdened section of the railway. Nor can the road system further inland service the ports. The main roads i.e. those for which the P.W.D. is responsible, consist of 2,455 miles of gravel surface and 806 miles which had received (at some date) one coat of bitumen. All roads are in a poor state of repair. Since there are not even first class trunk roads between the three main towns there is no basis for a road system to carry exports and imports or even to distribute home-grown food at all widely. Considerable areas are virtually inaccessible; and, even where traffic can pass, the short life of vehicles, because of poor surfaces, raises freight rates to about 6*d* a ton-mile, even on 'good' roads. This makes the transport of goods very expensive, particularly to and from the Northern Territories, which suffer also from the costs and uncertainties of ferries, so that many of their goods are virtually excluded from the coastal markets.

24. Prices therefore often differ widely from one town to another, especially prices of foods. Poor communications not only raise freight costs; they may prevent goods reaching places where they would fetch high prices and help to bring these prices down. Traders also often do not know where there are shortages and high prices. Price quotations must be treated cautiously, because weights and measures are not standard, but such discrepancies would not explain (in a week taken at random) a cigarette tin of shelled corn costing nearly twice as much in Kumasi as in Accra (7*d* against 4*d*), 10 fingers of plantain costing 1*s* 2*d* in Takoradi and 8*d* in Kumasi, or a cigarette tin of groundnuts costing 5*d* in Accra as against 3*d* in Takoradi.

Distribution

25. Imports are distributed through the economy by a mixture of highly organised and centralised marketing as the goods enter the country, and increasing disorganisation as they reach the consumer.

26. The sea trade of the country is almost entirely carried by a shipping 'conference' which fixed identical freight rates for its component lines, and represents the lines' viewpoint on matters of common interest, such as the use by shippers of lines outside the conference.

27. Imports are largely handled by a few European firms, many of them members of a trade association, and a substantial share is in the hands of one firm, the United Africa Company, a member of the Unilever organisation. These firms are not only importers and wholesalers: they also handle some of the retail trade through branch stores, and have a number of other interests. The U.A.C., in addition to shops operating under its own name, runs the Accra Ice Company, the chains 'Kingsway' and 'Kingsway Chemists', the Gold Coast Machinery and Trading Company (the main importer of building materials) and a timber company. It undertakes vehicle sales and service, runs harbour lighters, ferries and road transport; buys cocoa as an agent of the Marketing Board; and owns two of the lines in the shipping conference.

28. Some consumer goods are also imported by small traders, which range from regular 'indent houses' to part-time traders, whose main job is often that of clerk or servant, and who are just anxious to take advantage of shortages. If the

price is still high the goods imported by such small speculators will be sold immediately they arrive – often actually on the beach. But by this time there may well no longer be any shortage, and the goods may not even be claimed from the customs sheds (where they add to the general congestion). Their sale still more depresses the price, discouraging further imports so that another shortage may develop.

29. Some of the goods brought in by European importers flow directly to the retail departments, but most are eventually sold to street traders, or 'mammies'. The mammies may buy from market dealers, who in some cases use drastic methods, – even physical violence – to maintain control of supplies. But the mammies also buy direct from the European firms as 'pass book' or 'credit' purchases. The number of such mammies is of course enormous, and turnover is often very low, perhaps only two or three transactions taking place in a day.[2] The profit margins of the street traders (and various intermediaries) may merely arise from the quantity rebate given on the 'pass book' sales, it may even be less than this rebate so that street prices are below shop price. But often goods are bought on credit and sold immediately even at a loss, in order to raise capital, a practice which will continue so long as interest rates are as high as 50 per cent a month. But sometimes the profit is more than the rebate, perhaps much more, if goods are scarce.

30. The natural question to ask is why anyone will pay a higher price to a street trader than he would pay in a shop. There appear to be a number of reasons for this. The buyer often finds the mammies more convenient; he may be ignorant of the surcharge, he can buy in smaller quantities (e.g. a penny worth of lump sugar, or ten matches and an eighth of the striking area of the box); and he may be given credit which he would not get from a shop. If the goods are scarce, as were lump sugar, kerosene and whisky at the time of our visit, the ordinary member of the public believes that he will not get served in a shop, or at least not without family connections or a 'dash', and he may well be right in this belief. Shop assistants may profiteer and refuse to serve a casual caller at the marked price whilst the manager probably finds the bulk purchases by market dealers help him achieve a high turnover, especially if he can link the scarce commodity to slower-moving lines, such as hair dressings, in 'conditional sales' – we found conclusive evidence that 'conditional sales' are made. If scarce goods are available 'over the counter', many are quickly cornered by mammies, or their agents, for resale.

31. Imported goods pass, therefore, through a shipping monopoly and an importing 'oligopoly' at one end, and at the other end, tens of thousands of street traders doing intermittent business. This structure is the source of many of the country's problems, political and economic.

32. It is possible for shipping firms to manipulate their freight charges with little fear of competitive under-cutting; and it is also possible for importing firms to exploit a shortage of goods relative to incomes. This may not even be noticeable: the invoiced prices for imports may be set so that profits are made wherever it is most convenient for the parent organisation. The suspicion aroused by these possibilities has been an important factor in recent political disturbances. There

[2] It does not follow that this system is completely uneconomic. Since there is little capital and few cottage industries, the social costs of this system are negligible. However, the point of development is to raise labour productivity until this sort of activity becomes superfluous, and mammies are drawn into more productive work.

is, for example, an almost universal belief that European firms raise their prices as soon as there is an 'award' increasing the incomes of civil servants. On the other hand, it is argued that the European firms are refraining from exerting their full trading strength, perhaps partly because of this hostility. We shall not attempt to weigh the truth in the allegations made by various parties; our point is that such a concentration of economic power increases the dangers of any situation in which consumer goods are short, relative to incomes.

33. The street traders, on the other hand, are not troubled by conventional restraints on profiteering. There are few standards of trading practice, and hence little attention is paid to the danger of losing goodwill – particularly since those traders who are creditors have in any case a hold on their customers. Nor are retail prices effectively restrained by price controls. In this confused distributive system, it would be impossible to specify 'wholesale' prices, for a consignment may be handled by ten 'wholesalers' or more. It is even difficult to decide who is the final seller or 'retailer'. In any case the public does not support price control, at least not to the extent of reporting breaches of regulations or giving evidence.

34. The 'middlemen' who handle supplies in the markets provide very few of the facilities expected of wholesalers. They do not contact food farmers, who generally take their own goods to the market; they do not inform retailers of the state of supply; and they do not carry stocks, even of durables.

35. Food prices in particular are liable to fluctuate wildly, but profits due to scarcity may be skimmed off by these middlemen – or perhaps 'middlewomen' – so that the local farmers may receive little inducement to cultivate more land or to send more to market.

36. There is little reason to believe that this unbalanced system of distribution will be improved at all rapidly by ordinary economic processes. The European companies, partly because of local opposition and partly because of reluctance to enter retailing too deeply, make little headway, and allegedly have lost a share of retail trade to the mammies over the past few years.

37. On the other hand, African enterprise is hampered by fear of family claims on capital as it accumulates. Larger premises are obvious to visiting 'brothers', but traders even fear that information about bank deposits will leak out. Pooling of capital in partnerships and firms is hindered by lack of mutual confidence, partly due to misunderstandings that continually arise over contracts many of which are due to lack of business experience, if not illiteracy. Borrowing is difficult and very expensive. Interest rates are kept high by the extensive demand for consumer credit on the one hand, and the shortage of loanable funds on the other. So it is difficult for a small trader to expand his operations greatly.

38. Consumer cooperatives are receiving official encouragement, but there seems little appreciation of the principles of consumer cooperation. There are many difficulties in making and maintaining trade contracts, and it is alleged that members use the movement as a source of scarce goods which they subsequently resell. The cooperatives have yet to capture a large share of business.

Stocks

39. Stocks of consumer goods are insufficient to prevent shortages, and check price fluctuations. There are few warehouses for storage of foodstuffs or of imports. When demand for imported merchandise, such as printed textiles, has been strong, the price has largely depended on how recently a consignment had arrived

from Europe. Flour stocks held by the main importers have been so low as a few days' supply in months when imports were low (e.g. April 1951) and sugar stocks have been less than a week's supply. The precariousness of the market for consumer goods will be perhaps more fully appreciated if one compares the rapidity of stock turnover with the fact that even under normal times the U.A.C. puts the average delay between placing an order in Britain and obtaining delivery at twelve months.

40. Stocks of other goods have also often been dangerously low. Coal has been a continuous anxiety to the railways, particularly while the transatlantic coal shipments in the 1950/1 winter were taking much of the available shipping ; and cement stocks, though improving recently, have often been less than enough for a week's building.

Domestic production

41. The limits on imported supplies and the scarcity of stocks would not matter so much if output inside the country could be suddenly increased when demand rose. There is, however, practically no manufacturing for consumers – tailoring, a little handloom weaving, some handicrafts, a brewery and furniture making. Inland of the port ' bottleneck ', only local foodstuffs are available to absorb any substantial excess of purchasing power.

42. Food production is of course determined in the short run by what has been planted, but even in the longer run deliveries of food seem sluggish. The high price for cocoa has meant that cocoa farmers have somewhat neglected food farming, and at the same time eaten more too. This may be true of many food farmers themselves – they may be prosperous enough to grow less and eat more. In addition the inflationary profits to be made in the towns, especially in distribution and building, have drawn many from productive work, such as food farming. These developments go some way to explaining the rather curious fact that although retail food prices have increased several times since before the war, there has been apparently little increase in the food sent to market. The prosperity of the country areas has if anything reduced the possibility of food supplies flowing into the towns to absorb any sudden excess purchasing power, and has thus aggravated the dangers of price inflation.

Financial institutions

43. All these economic rigidities would be less serious if there were financial institutions capable of damping the effects of fluctuations in income – an efficient tax-collecting machinery has greatly eased the post-war economic strains in the United Kingdom. In the Gold Coast, however, wide sections of the public are untouched by income tax: approximately 90 per cent is collected from companies. On income made in the year 1948–9, for example, and assessed on 31 March 1950, a total of £2.95 million of income taxes were due, of which companies were liable for £2.64 million; farmers, traders and professional people for £0.17 million ; and employees for £0.13 million, although personal income at that time was over £50 million. The personal allowance (for a married couple) was £350 ; yet only about a thousand of the self-employed are assessed to tax – and less than a dozen cocoa farmers.

44. The only effective fiscal stabiliser is the export duty. In the case of commodities other than cocoa, this is mainly a tax on undistributed profit. But the export

duty on cocoa, in its new form, with a high rate of tax once the world price exceeds £120 per ton, will make it easier for the Marketing Board to stabilise the price paid to farmers. Nevertheless, it still permits considerable fluctuations in the incomes of cocoa farmers.

45. Voluntary saving cannot be relied on to finance much investment. Habits of thrift are not widespread, partly because of the family claims on accumulation which we discussed above in a different context (as a check on the growth of a small business). In fact, a large proportion of the public lives close to the limit of what they can borrow.

46. The upshot of this discussion is as follows. Port and transport facilities impose a limit on the flow of goods from abroad into the markets of the Gold Coast, while the supply of home-produced goods, even food, cannot expand rapidly. A wave of new purchasing power, unable to expand itself on goods or to find financial outlets, can therefore swing backwards and forwards across the economy, with sharp inflationary effects . . .

6. No major programme for industrialisation justifiable at present: W. A. Lewis, 1953 [1]

252. Measures to increase the manufacture of commodities for the home market deserve support, but are not of number one priority. A small programme is justified, but a major programme in this sphere should wait until the country is better prepared to carry it. The main obstacle is the fact that agricultural productivity per man is stagnant. This has three effects. First, the market for manufactures is small, and is not expanding year by year, except to the extent of population growth; consequently it would take large subsidies to make possible the employment of a large number of people in manufacturing. Secondly it is not possible to get ever larger savings out of the farmers, year by year, to finance industrialisation, without at the same time reducing their standard of living; hence industrialisation has to depend on foreign capital and large amounts of capital for this purpose could be attracted only on unfavourable terms. And thirdly, agriculture, because it is stagnant, does not release labour year by year; there is a shortage of labour in the Gold Coast which rapid industrialisation would aggravate.

253. Number one priority is therefore a concentrated attack on the system of growing food in the Gold Coast, so as to set in motion an ever-increasing productivity. This is the way to provide the market, the capital, and the labour for industrialisation.

254. Priority number two is to improve the public services. To do this will reduce the cost of manufacturing in the Gold Coast and will thus automatically attract new industries, without the Government having to offer special favours.

255. Very many years will have elapsed before it becomes economical for the Government to transfer any large part of its resources towards industrialisation, and away from the more urgent priorities of agricultural productivity and the public services. Meanwhile, it should support such industrialisation as can be done on terms favourable to the country. That is to say, it should support industries which can be established without large or continuing subsidies, and whose proprietors are willing to train and employ Africans in senior posts. Because in-

[1] W. A. Lewis, *Report on industrialisation and the Gold Coast*, Government Printer, Accra 1953, paras 252–6.

dustrialisation is a cumulative process (the more industries you have already, the more new industries you attract) it takes time to lay the foundations of industrialisation, and it would be wrong to postpone the establishment of any industry which could flourish after a short teething period. Chapter II has suggested enough of these for a moderate programme.

256. In order to carry out such a programme the Government should:

(1) establish an Industrial Division in the Department of Commerce...

(2) Announce its willingness to give limited aid, by way of temporary protection or subsidy, to newly established factories in the industries listed as 'favourable' or 'marginal'...

(3) Announce its attitude to foreign enterprise; welcoming such enterprise, especially if it enters into partnership with the Government or with African enterprise; guaranteeing free transfer of profits and dividends, and fair compensation independently determined if nationalisation takes place; and safeguarding the employment of a proportion of Africans in senior posts...

(5) Arrange a conference of persons engaged in labour management in the Gold Coast, or interested in the subject, with a view to initiating further research and teaching...

(6) Decide to accord priority to industry over domestic consumption in the extension of public services which are in short supply...

(7) Abolish import duties on industrial raw materials...

(8) Purchase land outside Kumasi and Accra for development as industrial estates...

(9) Promote and aid the establishment of a first class hotel in Accra...

(10) Set aside funds (a) for developing industrial estates, including building factories to be leased...; (b) for lending to small African firms, under strict supervision...; (c) for lending to or investing in large scale enterprise...; (d) for operating government factories, either for pioneering purposes, or as public utilities...

(11) Increase the staff of the Industrial Development Corporation, and charge it... with the general duty of aiding African enterprise...

7. Local capital inadequate for development: foreign capital assured against the dangers of nationalisation. Nkrumah 1953 [1]

The House is well aware of the proposal to produce electricity by damming the Volta River and to construct an aluminium smelter which is now receiving detailed examination by the National Committee and the Preparatory Commission.

In addition, the Government is anxious that the economy of the country should be expanded in other directions. It has for some time been considering the possibilities of progressive industrial development in the Gold Coast and has examined the problems and difficulties which would emerge from the implementation of such a programme.

We are satisfied that there is ample scope for the establishment of many new enterprises. A start has already been made and the Government proposes to take

[1] Prime Minister's statement on foreign investment, March 1953. *Industrial Development Committee, Reports and Accounts, 1954–5*, pp. 29–31.

steps to build up and extend the industrial structure of the economy. The achievement of its objectives will take time and will require the help and assistance of all.

In formulating its policy the Government has accepted the fact that it will be many years before the Gold Coast will be in a position to find from its own resources people who can combine capital with the experience required in the development and management of new industries. It is, therefore, apparent that the Gold Coast must rely to a large extent on foreign enterprise, and the Government is anxious to give it every encouragement.

It is appreciated that foreign investors require assurances about the conditions which will apply to their investments.

First, I should like to draw attention to the importance which this Government attaches to the adoption and vigorous implementation of a policy of training African employees for eventual employment in senior technical, professional, and managerial appointments. The Government wishes to see this policy adopted in both publicly and privately owned enterprises.

It is not proposed at this stage to lay down precise limits for the numbers or percentages of Africans to be employed in senior positions as it is fully appreciated that for many years to come the number of trained staff of this calibre will be extremely limited and, in any case, circumstances vary from one industry to another but it is this Government's firm intention to pursue the policy of assuring for the future a steady increase in the number of qualified Africans in such appointments.

It should, therefore, be understood that the degree of warmth with which any enterprise is welcomed will be conditioned by the arrangement proposed for the employment, training, and promotion of Africans. The Government appreciates however that in industry the criterion must be that of industrial efficiency. It will deal with this question on a sound common-sense basis.

With this important objective in mind, and I am sure that no private management will question the wisdom or rightness of this policy, the Government proposes to encourage as much as possible the entry and investment in industry of foreign capital. The Gold Coast has reserve funds which could be made available for investment in large scale enterprises and the Government will be willing where it is approached to participate in enterprises which can be shown to be economically sound.

It is not normally proposed to regard Government participation as mandatory but rather to look upon such partnership as a natural means, in the absence of local private capital, of assisting investors to establish a new venture. There may, however, be cases in which Government participation would be calculated to serve the national interest, and the Government must reserve to itself the right to insist on partnership in such future enterprises.

Foreign capital has not hitherto been directly invested in public utilities such as railway transport, municipal omnibus services, electricity and water supply concerns, telephone and rediffusion services, and it is not expected that there will be any departure from this principle.

With this exception, it is the Government's considered view that foreign capital should be free to invest in any other form of new industrial enterprise. In other words, it is hoped to see new industries established which will in due course become fully self-supporting under normal competitive conditions.

The necessity for price control would not arise in such conditions and it is intended that control of prices should normally be restricted to industries which operate as monopolies.

It will be appreciated that under the present monetary system in operation local currency can be freely converted into sterling, and in accordance with the practice of the Sterling Area it has been the policy of the Gold Coast to permit the repatriation of non-sterling funds invested in this country since 1950 and the Government does not envisage any limitation on the present freedom to transfer without restriction profits arising from non-resident capital investment, or to repatriate foreign capital invested in the Gold Coast. It is hoped that this policy will encourage new investment and re-investment of profits.

The present Government has no plans for nationalising industry beyond the extent to which the public utilities are already nationalised, and it does not envisage any such proposals arising.

Nevertheless, in order to ensure that if the nationalisation of a particular industry were to be considered essential by a successor Government in the national interest, there should be suitable means for guaranteeing fair compensation, the Government intends to request the United Kingdom Government to incorporate in the Constitution appropriate provision for this purpose, following the precedents set in the Constitutions of the United States of America and of India.

There should be no doubt left in the minds of foreign enterprises that the Gold Coast is prepared not only to encourage the entry and investment of foreign capital but also to ensure that the interest of investors will be adequately safeguarded.

I turn now to consideration of the plans in hand for the removal of some of the technical difficulties of establishing new concerns.

The Government has been fully advised of the difficulties which face not only new enterprises but also existing enterprises, whether domestic or foreign-owned, in acquiring suitable sites for factories, offices and staff accommodation.

The Ministries responsible are at present engaged in reviewing existing sites and investigating possible new sites for factories in the principal urban centres with particular attention to the zoning of industrial areas, the ownership of land and the availability, present or planned, of communications (road and rail) services, and housing for staff and labour within a reasonable distance.

In addition proposals are under consideration for the development of industrial estates nearer the principal urban centres, on lines similar to those already contemplated at Tema. Those arrangements should benefit alike all firms which seek new premises or the use of public services.

It is not proposed to stop at this. The Government realises that to establish successfully industries, which may involve new methods of organisation, new skills and new techniques, firms may require help in getting established and some temporary financial assistance.

The new Industries Section of the Ministry of Commerce and Industry is designed to undertake the responsibility for advising both domestic and foreign capital in new ventures, for providing assistance in locating suitable sites, obtaining priorities in the supply of public services, and generally to assist in the solution of a new enterprise's problems.

The needs of each new industry in the early period of its life will also be examined. Apart from the relief from taxation provided for pioneer industries where an industry appears to suffer an unusual handicap either by reason of its initial capital outlay, or its difficulty in establishing a market, or the risks undertaken, consideration will be given to the grant of special assistance for a limited period subject to the approval of this Assembly. In suitable cases also new industries may be granted relief from import duties on specified raw materials.

These advantages and benefits will apply equally to domestic and foreign enterprise, and it is the Government's earnest wish that those with capital to invest will seek the opportunity which exists in the Gold Coast in the full confidence that they will be treated as partners in the development of the country's resources.

In conclusion, I wish to emphasise once again the importance attached to the training of Africans not only for the manual and technical skills but also for appointments to senior managerial, professional and higher technical posts. It is anticipated that private enterprise will adopt training schemes suitable to their needs, designed to provide for a steady increase in the appointment of African staff to such posts.

Expenditure on such schemes is deducted in assessing profits for income tax purposes and the existence of training posts will enable firms to qualify for an increase in their immigration quotas. I am confident that with good will and understanding, Government and private enterprise can combine to attain our objective of progressive industrial development.

8. The Industrial Development Corporation small loans scheme for local enterprise, 1955 [1]

4. With the exception of proposals to extend the existing centralised Small Loans Scheme to operate on a regional basis, the declared policy of the Board has remained largely unchanged during the period under review, and is repeated below for general information:

(i) 'The Industrial Development Corporation is charged with the statutory duty of securing the investigation, formulation and carrying out of projects for developing industries in the Gold Coast.'

(ii) 'In the performance of this duty, the Corporation will give priority of consideration to industries designed to further the development of the natural resources of the country, or to provide goods or services essential to such development. The Corporation is particularly interested in developing industries which will make use of local materials.'

(iii) 'General: its operations will normally be carried out by one or other of the following methods:

(*a*) the Corporation will itself establish new industrial undertakings, supplying the entire capital and taking full control of the management (Subsidiary Companies);

(*b*) the Corporation will be prepared to enter into agreements for the establishment of new industrial undertakings, or the expansion of existing ones, with firms of proved business capacity and financial standing on terms to be mutually agreed (Associated Companies);

(*c*) the Corporation will assist smaller industrial concerns by provision of machinery, etc. on credit terms. Such concerns must, however, be properly incorporated companies to be eligible (Loans to Companies)';

[1] *Industrial Development Committee, Reports and Accounts*, 1955–6, paras. 4–8.

(iv) 'Investments: the Corporation aims eventually to acquire an investment fund to be used to take up shares in suitable companies engaged in the development of the Gold Coast whenever opportunity offers.'

(v) 'Industrial Estates: the Corporation is actively planning for the development of an industrial estate in Accra and is preparing to extend similar facilities to other suitable areas in due course for the benefit of industries needing premises and essential services.'. . .

(vii) 'Small Loans: the Corporation has set aside an annual sum from which loans will be made to small industrial concerns, not incorporated as companies. The total amount of each individual loan is limited, adequate security must be given and a reasonable rate of interest is charged.'

5. It is again felt necessary to elucidate paragraph (2) of the above policy statement for the benefit of those wishing to put forward proposals for the establishment of industry. Such propositions, apart from appearing commercially sound, should also fulfil one or more of the following conditions:

(*a*) that the industry is a new one in the Gold Coast; (*b*) that it is ancillary to the Development Plan of the Government (e.g. provision of building materials); (*c*) that it develops or is concerned with the processing of indigenous raw materials; or (*d*) that it offers special opportunities for training Africans in the art of management.

6. With regard to Investments, the Corporation has applied to Government for a separate allocation of funds for this purpose and the matter is still under consideration. This course was adopted because it was felt that the prospect of reserving a substantial fund from profits arising from company investments was still several years ahead.

7. One important policy change that has occurred was the Board's decision in September, 1955 to establish a Regional Loans Organisation to embrace the existing Small Loans Department, with a view to providing a wider and more equitable distribution of the Corporation's available resources, in terms of financial and technical assistance, throughout the country.

8. The remaining principal functions referred to above, namely, the promotion of Companies and Industrial Estates, are also dealt with in subsequent paragraphs of this Report.

9. Review of development under the First Development Plan, 1955 [1]

290. In 1951 the Gold Coast economy had experienced one or two years in which earnings from cocoa exports had provided a substantial surplus in the balance of payments and in Government revenue. Political progress had given added impetus to the demand for both social and economic development. A general development plan had already been prepared in response to these demands and the Government which was elected in 1951 proceeded to implement these projects with every means at its disposal.

291. The Gold Coast had been administered by a small secretariat until the new Government was elected and Government services were quite inadequate for the development envisaged; apart from the mining and logging industries and the larger trading firms, more or less entirely owned by non-residents, there was little

[1] *Economic Survey*, 1955, paras 290–303.

organised private investment and the capacity of the building industry apart from the Government works services was extremely small.

292. It is not surprising therefore that the first years of development were characterised by a shortage of planning and administrative staff to implement the programme, and building capacity to execute it in the face of general post-war shortages, the high prices ruling at the time and difficulties experienced in obtaining supplies from overseas. In 1952 it was already clear that a substantial revision of the development programme was required to take these factors into account, and this revision has gone on each year in the light of progress made and inevitable changes in priorities.

293. These shortages of staff, building capacity and imported materials cannot be over-emphasised. They have been experienced in all branches of Government and in some departments the progress made under the impetus of five years of development is again being jeopardised by lack of experienced officers to replace those who have retired.

294. The original Development Plan envisaged a total expenditure of £75.1 million over ten years. In 1952 it was decided to try to complete the ten year programme in five years. At the same time a large number of new projects had already emerged beyond the stage of possibilities and some of these had already been shaped into the elements of a programme to be financed from a ' Reserve Development Fund '. Throughout this survey, these two programmes have been treated as one. The chief difference between these two sets of projects, from an economic point of view, is that the Development Plan had become primarily a five year plan in which the whole emphasis was on social and Government services, whereas the Reserve Development Fund projects had not advanced so far in planning and were essentially long-term and more national in scope.

295. The sources of finance of the development programme are shown in Table [9.1]. Out of a total of £125.4 million, revenue from cocoa duty contributed £91.5 million, contributions from the general revenue balance, arising mainly from additional cocoa duty, £19.7 million, loans from the Cocoa Marketing Board, £6.9 million, local loans £2.5 million, Colonial Development and Welfare Funds, £1.5 million and other non-recurrent items £3.2 million. Cocoa has undoubtedly been the mainstay of Gold Coast development.

296. Of a total proposed expenditure of £121.6 million upon the combined development programme, provision has been made for expenditure amounting to £108.6 million by the end of June 1957, £89.3 million on the 1951 Development Plan and £19.1 million on Reserve Development Fund projects.

297. Actual expenditure to the end of 1955 amounted to £66.5 million and it is now clear that a tremendous effort will be required to reach the target of £108.6 million by the middle of 1957. Development expenditure at the end of 1955 had reached an annual rate of £15.6 million compared with £6.4 million in 1951.

298. A summary of the projects selected for development, classified by type of service, with details of actual expenditure to the end of 1955 and provision up to the middle of 1957, is given in Table [9.2]. Communications account for 36 per cent of total expenditure to the end of 1955 and public services generally for 47 per cent, leaving a total of only 17 per cent on direct services to agriculture, industry and trade.

299. This programme has been principally determined by the obvious need to provide the minimum basic services for a modern community. The cost of maintaining these services has, however, outstripped the rate of expansion of Govern-

Table 9.1. *Amount set aside for development and expenditure on projects, 1 April 1951 to 31 December 1955 (£000s)*

	Total	Development fund	Special dev. fund	Reserve dev. fund	Second dev. fund	Reserve for 2nd dev. fund	Supplementary reserve dev. fund
Amount set aside for development							
Contribution from cocoa duty	91,463	12,577	23,465	27,133	10,608	3,536	14,144
Contribution from general revenue	19,720	19,720	—	—	—	—	—
Contribution from C.D. & W. Funds	1,532	1,439	—	93	—	—	—
Contribution from foreign operation administration	475	—	475	—	—	—	—
Contribution from U.K. Govt. towards V.R.P.P.C.	230	—	—	230	—	—	—
Net yield from investments	1,608	1,608	—	—	—	—	—
Loans from Cocoa Marketing Board	6,944	6,944	—	—	—	—	—
Local loans	2,475	2,475	—	—	—	—	—
Balance of ex-enemy assets	136	136	—	—	—	—	—
Repayment of loan to U.K. Govt.	800	800	—	—	—	—	—
Total	125,383	45,699	23,940	27,456	10,608	3,536	14,144
Expenditure on projects	66,530	36,314	22,293	7,809	114	—	—
Balance at 31 December 1955	58,853	9,385	1,647	19,647	10,494	3,536	14,144

Table 9.2. *The development programme and actual expenditure up to 31 December 1955, by type of service (£000s)*

	Original development plan 1951		Revised development programme *		Actual expenditure up to 31 Dec. 1955 *		Funds provided up to 30 June 1957 *	
	£	%	£	%	£	%	£	%
Communications	25,885	34	43,291	36	23,656	36	36,711	34
Other revenue-producing services	4,243	6	12,432	10	5,886	8	9,763	9
Services to agric., industry and trade								
Economic services	7,349	10	8,659	7	5,034	8	8,639	8
Advisory services	1,189	2	733	1	544	1	733	1
Services for law and order	3,303	4	1,599	5	3,648	5	5,599	5
Social services	25,331	34	26,345	21	18,982	28	25,458	23
Administrative and general services	7,814	10	24,545	20	8,780	14	21,658	20
Total	75,114	100	117,604	100	66,530	100	108,561	100

* Revised to 30 June 1956 and projects and expenditure financed from the Development, Special Development, Reserve Development Funds and Second Development Fund.

ment revenue other than cocoa. Current revenue excluding cocoa totalled £15.8 million in 1950–1 and £30.1 million in 1955–6, an increase of almost 100 per cent. Total expenditure, direct and on transfers, increased almost 200 per cent from £11.8 million to £34.0 million. Estimates for 1956–7, which have not yet been approved, anticipate a total of revenue, on the basis of existing rates of taxation, amounting to £30.9 million, excluding cocoa duty, and current expenditure amounting to £41.7 million.

300. It is this aspect of the development programme which tends to be overlooked. A larger part of the increase in recurrent responsibilities of Government departments has arisen from the development programme than can be directly attributed to development expenditure. Such expansion has undoubtedly benefited the country, providing an efficient and comprehensive public service. The problem remains, however, of how to provide for the cost of these services in the future and to what extent, if at all, the country can afford a further expansion of public services in the next five years.

301. Table [9.3] shows similar details of proposed and actual expenditure by type of asset and this serves again to emphasise the preponderance of investment in public buildings and social services and the relatively small investment in enterprises likely to provide an expanding source of revenue.

302. The importance of investment by private enterprise tends to be overlooked when compared with the substantial investment programme of Government but it is in many ways the more significant. Investment in publice services does not in the short-term add to the productive capacity of the economy and in the absence of increased output to sustain the rising cost of public services, these may become a burden on the country's economy.

303. If the Gold Coast is to emerge from its relatively underdeveloped condition, further capital expenditure on social and public services will have to be restricted to projects ancillary to those yielding a return in real resources. It is against this economic background that the financial implications of the Volta River Project must be reviewed.

10. Second Development Plan : policy statement, 1959 [1]

Mr Speaker,

I beg to move that this House approves the Government's Second Five-Year Development Plan for the period 1 July, 1964.

Tomorrow Ghana completes its second year of independence; therefore this is an appropriate time for me to talk to the House about future plans for the development of our country. I have frequently stated before this House and in many other places that if one sought the political kingdom all other things would be added thereto. For unless we have political independence we cannot have the means of shaping our economic, social and industrial future. Thus political independence is not an end in itself but a means to that end. Having achieved political independence our next objective is to consolidate that independence and lay the economic foundation to sustain our national independence. That is the reason why we are now embarking upon this five-year plan of development, the

[1] Speech by the Prime Minister, March 1959, on the opening of the debate on the motion approving the Second Development Plan. *Legislative Assembly Reports, 1959.*

Table 9.3. *The development programme and expenditure up to 31 December 1955, by type of assets* (*) (*£000s*)

	Development programme				Actual expenditure up to 31 Dec. 1955			
	Develop-ment fund	Second dev. fund	Reserve dev. fund	Total	Dev. fund	Second dev. fund	Reserve dev. fund	Total
Building and construction								
Housing	9,523	—	369	9,892	6,787	—	296	7,083
Roads	16,012	—	374	16,386	9,222	75	361	9,658
Railway permanent way	—	—	2,339	2,339	—	—	2,353	2,353
Harbour construction	—	—	—	—	—	—	—	—
Other building and construction	18,666	—	865	19,531	12,955	—	698	13,653
Total	44,201	—	3,947	48,148	28,964	75	3,708	32,747
Services								
Electricity	1,782	2,720	300	4,802	1,290	1	99	1,390
Water	4,911	—	1,529	6,440	3,562	—	436	3,998
Postal	2,024	—	294	2,318	1,189	—	9	1,198
Total	8,717	2,720	2,123	13,560	6,041	1	544	6,586
Other expenditure in new investment projects								
Industry and commerce	104	—	—	104	167	—	—	167
Agriculture	1,945	—	205	2,150	781	—	118	899
Preliminary surveys	1,556	—	1,082	2,638	941	—	842	1,783
Other	2,648	—	1,130	3,778	413	—	101	514

Land	290	—	75	365	124	—	30	134
Current expenditure	1,082	—	99	1,181	69	—	44	113
Total	3,650	—	196	3,846	1,253	—	82	1,335
Loans and grants								
Investment in public boards and corporations	4,678	—	900	5,578	2,737	—	—	2,737
Loans to Tema Dev. Corp.	—	—	5,925	5,925	—	—	492	492
Loans to railway and harbour administration	7,172	1,386	11,860	20,418	6,442	—	1,922	8,364
Other loans and capital grants	14,519	40	—	14,559	9,139	38	—	9,177
Current grants	900	—	—	900	1,729	—	—	1,729
Total	27,269	1,426	18,685	47,380	20,047	38	2,414	22,499
Grand total	90,090	4,146	27,368	121,604	58,607	114	7,809	66,530

* Excludes expenditure on Takoradi Harbour Extensions amounting to £6 million since 1949.

implementation and fulfilment of which will give us a solid foundation to build the welfare state. It is the aim of my Government to create the means for the good life, and create a society in which everybody in Ghana can enjoy the fruits of his labour and raise the economic and social standards of the people. This aim cannot be attained all at once but it can be realised through a series of five-year plans like the one we are about to embark upon. This Second Development Plan will, I am confident, lay the real foundations on which our economic independence can be built.

What have we accomplished so far? Although Ghana did not become politically independent until 6 March, 1957, we had been responsible for internal self-government, and for the control of economic planning and development, from the beginning of the First Development Plan. That Plan, as Honourable Members will recall, was originally intended to cover a period of ten years, but the Government, seized with the urgency of developing our natural resources, condensed the Plan into five years. Although considerable additions were made to it the First Development Plan was substantially completed by June, 1957.

In the policy statement which I made to this House on 28 May 1957, I said that the Government had decided, for good reasons, to treat the first two years of our political independence as a period of consolidation. We therefore followed the First Development Plan with a Consolidation Plan which will come to an end in a few weeks' time.

At this stage I think it appropriate to remind Honourable Members of the achievements of this Government and of the people of Ghana in developing our country during the last eight years, which, as everyone knows, have been years of tremendous political activity and full of real difficulties. Nevertheless, in every field of Government and business activity remarkable development has taken place. Honourable Members have all seen the many changes in our capital and the many fine new buildings which have been built. There have been marked changes, too, in other large towns throughout the country. New and better roads not only give us vastly improved means of communications, but also everyone can see the very large numbers of schools and hospitals and other facilities which we have provided during this period. Visitors to Ghana remark again and again about our fine system of roads. This is something of which we can justifiably be proud.

Free primary education has been introduced, the University College, Accra, and the College of Technology, Kumasi, have been established, medical services have been extended and new hospitals built. Our entire system of communication has been revolutionised for, in addition to the new roads to which I have just referred, our railways have been extended and the port of Takoradi has been developed to its maximum capacity. Many new bridges have been built, and the construction of the new port at Tema is now substantially advanced.

Members will recall that in my development policy statement in February, 1958, I emphasised that this port was the largest single project under construction in our country, and that the Government intended to keep it under constant and careful review. Members will, I am sure, be glad to learn that the rate of construction has improved appreciably during the last eighteen months, and we hope that the port will be ready to receive traffic by the end of next year. I simply select these few examples of development to remind members of the numerous and very wide range of projects on which we have embarked during the last few years and of the impressive results which have been achieved.

While all this has been happening, other forms of development have also been taking place which have not been so spectacular but which have been just as progressive, and represent solid achievement. For example, it must be remembered that during the period covered by the First and Consolidation Development Plans we progressed rapidly through the last stages of Government reform until we achieved complete political independence in 1957. These stages in our political progress necessitated an almost complete reorganisation of the administrative machinery of Government and a similar reorganisation in the sphere of local government. These major modifications have now been brought into operation.

All this has been achieved during the last eight years but what we have done in the past has only set the stage and provided a framework within which we can now go ahead and develop our economy.

Honourable Members now have before them the Government's Second Development Plan. This Plan reflects our policy for developing Ghana over the next five years. The Government has deliberately prepared the Plan so as to show the development which it believes should take place in our country in the coming years. What is the basic objective of our Plan? It is simply this. We believe that it should show what we have to do by our own hard work, by the use of our own natural resources, and by encouraging investment in Ghana – to give us a standard of living which will abolish disease, poverty, and illiteracy, give our people ample food and good housing, and let us advance confidently as a nation. We want to develop strong basic services – communications, power and water – so that we can provide a real and an effective foundation for the industrialisation of our country; and we want to ensure the continued expansion and diversification of our agriculture on which, in the final analysis, all our plans depend.

The Plan provides for expenditure up to the tremendous total of £G343 million. If £G7 million is added to this to provide for contingencies, it can be said that our total financial requirement for the Five Year Plan is some £G350 million. It will be said that this is far more than we have expended in the past and would require more capital than is at present at our disposal. In short, some people may say that our Plan is over-ambitious. As to that let me say without any hesitation that the Government is convinced that this is the very time for us to be ambitious. Without ambition nothing can be done. The Plan clearly reflects the development which we want to see take place in our country. It is up to each and every one of us to do everything in his power to see that that objective is achieved.

Within the framework of the Plan we have been realistic and prepared a carefully selected programme of development which will involve the expenditure of £G126 million. This is our immediate and minimum objective. Our achievements in the past few years have given the Government confidence to believe that, with co-operation, goodwill and hard work from everyone, we can do more than ever before. Indeed, we intend to do more, and we will do more.

It will be observed that of the £G350 million, the sum of £G100 million is set aside for hydro-electric development. I shall speak about that shortly. It is however apparent that our ability to execute this great Plan of development will largely be influenced by what we can do to obtain capital from overseas. This capital can come from two sources. First of all, there is capital provided by international institutions such as the World Bank, and by individual governments which are willing to assist the less developed nations of the world to develop their resources either by term loans or with direct grants. Secondly, capital can come from private enterprises overseas.

As to the first source, we hope that international institutions and governments which may be interested in our country will study this plan carefully and consider whether there are any individual projects with which they can help. This is one of the reasons why we have deliberately drawn up the plan on bold lines so that there can be no doubt in the minds of our friends overseas of the things which we would like to accomplish. On many occasions in the past year, representatives of several individual governments have expressed to me their interest in assisting Ghana with its development and I hope they will study this plan carefully and use it as a basis for any proposals which they may wish to make to us.

As to private investment I have made a number of statements during the past twelve months which have been quite categoric in giving assurance that capital from overseas sources is welcome in this country and the Government has introduced several measures to make conditions for capital investment attractive. We have set up an Investment Promotions Board with the sole purpose of assisting prospective investors and of reviewing investment inducements. As a further measure of assistance to overseas industrialists, the Government is taking a census of established industry in order that the present picture may be clearly seen and future opportunities more easily assessed. We have set aside in this Second Plan a large sum of money for the purpose of ensuring that adequate facilities for industrial development are available to prospective investors. We have also set aside considerable sums for direct Government participation in industry and for the pioneering of various industries directly by the Government. All these measures should make it abundantly clear that we are serious in our declared aim to develop our industrial potential to its maximum and we hope that overseas financial institutions and investors will study our plan with a view to considering in what way they can help us to realise our objectives.

In considering how overseas investment in Ghana can best be expanded we do not discriminate against any nation and we welcome to our country visits from overseas trade missions. Several have come here during the last year and we look forward to the arrival of more in the future. We hope that more of these missions and representatives of governments, private institutions, and firms will come and investigate the possibilities for investing in Ghana.

Here I should like to state quite plainly that our Government will always be ready to discuss with any government, firm or investor any sound project for development in our country and will be ready to negotiate suitable terms for such enterprises. We want industry in Ghana, and we are always ready to make reasonable arrangements with any government, institution, or individual who can bring a sound proposition to us. In short, we intend, as in the past, to follow a commonsense and practical approach to industrial development.

I now turn to our plans for hydro-electric development. I have always been convinced that an abundance of cheap electric power is the soundest base for the expansion of industry in a country such as ours. Honourable Members will be aware that after my official visit to the United States of America last year, President Eisenhower and his Government kindly agreed to share with us the cost of a reassessment of the engineering aspects of the Volta River Project and the power potential at Bui. That work was undertaken by a firm of proven ability and international renown – the Kaiser Corporation – which sent a team of engineers here in the latter part of 1958. I am happy to announce that I received the Report of the Kaiser Corporation yesterday. Their reassessment will receive the most careful consideration by the Government. I have every hope that I shall be in a position in the reasonably near future to make a detailed statement to this House on the possibilities of hydro-electric development in our country, but I wish to make this simple and basic statement forthwith, that is, that my Government is determined to develop the hydro-electric potential of Ghana to its maximum.

Mr Speaker, Honourable Members, I do not intend to discuss in detail the Second Development Plan which is now before you. I believe that Members will find that the seventeen chapters which deal with specific subjects and aspects of the problem will provide all the essential information which they desire. In addition, this debate will provide an opportunity for discussing the Plan in general terms, and also any detailed parts of it which are of particular concern to individual Members of this House.

While it is not my intention to discuss the Plan in detail, I do wish to refer briefly to certain aspects of it. As always, we recognise the paramount importance of agriculture in our economy, and we have never lost sight of the fact that cocoa represents the economic life blood of our country. We are embarking on a very large-scale campaign for spraying capsid and I regard this as probably the most vital element in our current economic development, for, if it succeeds, it can make a great difference to our total cocoa production and thus provide invaluable revenue for further development. And so, Mr Speaker, at this juncture I wish to pay tribute here to the Farmers' Council for their invaluable contribution to agricultural production and thus to the financial resources of the nation.

We are embarking on our first large-scale cattle industry in Ghana, and we are also arranging for extensive surveys of the fishing potential off our coast to be carried out.

In the industrial field we have, in recent months, made arrangements for several new enterprises to start in Ghana. Let me give Honourable Members a few examples. There is the clinker cement project which is about to start, and also the production of aluminium roofing sheets and utensils; a distillery will be built and another brewery established; another oil processing plant is being started and the Industrial Development Corporation nail factory is being expanded substantially. The match factory has just come into production. We have every intention of expanding and accelerating this programme of industrial development. In fact, negotiations for the establishment of industries include such major enterprises as motor assembly plants, a large soap factory, and flour and textile mills. Negotiations for these are virtually complete. In addition to the industries already established in Ghana, the Government hopes to see 600 new enterprises started over the next five years.

We can look forward to the completion of our great port at Tema in the relatively near future and we shall ensure that all the necessary facilities, including a new township, are provided. We are embarking on a major programme of re-equipping our Ghana National Airlines just as we shall continue to develop our own Black Star Shipping Line. Our airlines and our ships provide us with direct links with the outside world and are of special importance to us, particularly in our relations with other African countries.

In the field of communications we have also decided to go ahead as quickly as possible with modifications to the Accra Airport so that it will be able to take the most modern jet aircraft. I regard this facility as one of the highest importance, and it is directly related to our plans to build a large Conference Hall here where national, regional and international meetings can be held. Combined with this we shall ensure that sufficient first-class hotel accommodation is available in Accra, so that international and other institutions abroad may be able to arrange for conferences to be held in Ghana knowing that we have excellent facilities to offer to them. This is part of my Government's policy of encouraging and promoting tourism in the country.

We shall establish a great new broadcasting station which will carry the voice of Ghana to every corner of our continent and beyond. For some time now the Government has been considering the possibilities of introducing commercial broadcasting and television services in Ghana. The Government proposes as soon as the plans have been completed to introduce these services which we believe will help the development of the country socially and economically.

Honourable Members all know that the health of our people is very close to my heart. During this Plan I hope that we shall complete a new children's hospital, a new maternity hospital and a new tuberculosis hospital. We have engaged the finest technical advice in the world to assist us with the construction of these vital services, and I am confident that they will do much to alleviate suffering and to improve the health of many mothers and children and other citizens. Just as we shall wage war against poverty in our country, so shall we wage war against disease. We must eradicate diseases such as malaria and tuberculosis from Ghana – this is a challenge to all of us.

We have been suffering in Accra from the effects of a drought which has affected our water supply. The Government has taken energetic steps to deal with this situation and, in addition, the Rockefeller Foundation kindly provided us with the services of a recognised expert in this field. He has just reported to the Government about the measures which should be taken in the future to prevent a recurrence of the present situation and also to provide for the growing needs of our capital. The Government is determined to follow up these recommendations for it fully recognises the importance of water in our everyday life. We in Accra can claim to have one of the purest supplies of water in Africa ; we shall ensure that in the coming years there is ample for everyone, and this misfortune will never be repeated. This water shortage in Accra only highlights the urgent need for improving water supplies throughout the country, particularly in the rural areas. The plan takes these fully into account.

Education remains of paramount importance to us. We must generate a new dynamic force behind our educational policy, and ensure that it is geared to our future economic and industrial development. Amongst other things, the new plan provides for a vitally important programme of secondary education. I look forward to the establishment of a fully fledged university in Ghana not later, I hope, than 1961, which amongst many other things would enable us to pursue with confidence post-graduate work in science and technology. In addition, it is my fervent desire that during the period of the plan we shall establish a medical faculty at the University college. These plans and hopes for our university are all also related either directly or indirectly to the most important subject of research. Scientific research can play a vital part in the future development of our country, and Members will have observed that we had our first meeting of the National Research Council last week. The fact that I have assumed the Chairmanship of this Council is evidence of my deep personal interest in this subject and my intention of doing everything possible to advance scientific research in our country. One of our first tasks is to take a census of all scientists who are now working in our country – Ghanaians, other Africans, and people from overseas. The primary objective of the National Research Council is to assist, stimulate and coordinate research activities in government departments, university colleges and other educational institutes, in industry, and amongst individuals. I shall make a further announcement in the near future about our plans for the National Research Council.

I wish to emphasise that the Second Development Plan has been most carefully drawn up after many months of discussion and detailed consideration. It represents not only a programme of works, but the policy of my Government over the next five years in all fields of development activity. Hitherto, the development plans of local authorities have been included in their annual estimates. In future, it is the intention of the Government that these local plans for development shall also be drawn up on a five-year basis. The remarks which I shall now make apply equally to the Government Second Development Plan and to the schemes under the control of the local authorities.

Mr Speaker, our capital and manpower resources are limited and they must be made to go as far as possible. That is one of the reasons why we intend to take a census next year. I hope that we shall be surprised and find that our population is well over five million. We must avoid waste wherever it exists and we must ensure that our manpower is used to the greatest advantage. In addition to this we must encourage voluntary labour and exhort every person to give part of his or her services voluntarily wherever they might be most effective during the forthcoming years. In order to assist this drive for voluntary effort, the Government intends to set up Town and Village Boards to plan, coordinate and encourage voluntary schemes of development.

One of the problems facing us at the present time is the high cost of development works and I have already taken steps to seek the active cooperation of consulting engineers, architects and contracting firms to assist in the development of Ghana by keeping their cost to the minimum consistent with good work and healthy business. This assistance is not only in the interest of the country, but in the interest of the consultants and contractors themselves. We must avoid at all costs any waste or misuse of manpower, money or materials.

Our total plan for general and hydro-electric development amounts to £G350 million, and the degree to which we can attain this great plan depends not only on the Government and the Members in this House, but on the country as a whole. There is a job for every single man, woman and child, and the Government expects the maximum support of everyone in the country in order to achieve it.

This plan is not a political matter and I call on all Members of this House and all persons in Ghana, whatever their political beliefs, their creed, country or race, to make every effort during the forthcoming years to execute the Development Plan that I am now asking this House to approve. It will mean sacrifices and a very considerable increase in the amount of effort, with everyone putting his utmost into his job whatever that job might be. The time to develop Ghana and to attain our economic emancipation is now. We cannot afford to wait. The country has been liberated for the workers and farmers; they in turn must make sacrifices and work hard in the interest of our new nation.

Our full manpower resources must be mobilised towards this single effort for there is no greater loss to any country than idleness and no greater wealth than lies in its labour and resources. These must all be directed to the one common aim – the execution of the programme now before you, the people of Ghana.

I call upon the Farmers' Council, the Trades Union Congress and the Cooperative Movement to come out and stand solidly behind us in the successful implementation of the new plan. The vital task of mobilising the people of the entire nation in the struggle to fulfil this plan for the development of our country belongs to all of us.

To this end, I intend, during the next few weeks, to set up a Consultative Committee on which all political parties and workers, farmers, civil servants and other organisations which can be of help in this crusade for development will be represented. The organisations will include, of course, the Trades Union Congress, the Farmers' Council, and the Cooperative Movement. This Committee will, by all the means at our disposal, carry to the remotest towns and villages throughout the country a message calling for active support for this Plan. I call on all Honourable Members of the House to assist in this campaign by explaining the plan and the need for effort to their constituents. It is essential in doing this that all political and parochial feelings should be buried and that our constituents should be made to understand that this is a national effort. The slogan is 'Serve Ghana Now'.

To dramatise the imperative need for this national effort I ask that 1 July, 1959 be regarded as a day of dedication and for generating the enthusiasm and support required for the implementation of the plan.

I seek the active support and cooperation of the whole country in carrying out this national crusade to mobilise the goodwill and maximum effort of everyone in Ghana so that this great plan can become a reality, and bring not only satisfaction and higher standards of living to our people, but also serve as an inspiration to our brothers in other parts of this great continent who are still struggling to be free and so control their own destinies.

I beg to move!

Bibliography

1. Governor's Annual Address, *Legislative Council Debates, 1921–2*, pp. 29–48 (extracts).
2. *Private Enterprise in British Tropical Africa*, Report of the Committee appointed by the Secretary of State for the Colonies to consider and report whether, and if so what, measures could be taken to encourage private enterprise in the development of British Dependencies in East and West Tropical Africa, with special reference to existing and projected schemes of transportation, Cmd 2016, London 1924, pp. 5–17 and p. 23 (extracts).
3. *Report of the Commission of enquiry into disturbances in the Gold Coast, 1948*, Colonial Office, London 1948, paras 164–258.
4. *Report of the Commission of enquiry into disturbances in the Gold Coast, 1948*, Colonial Office, London 1948, paras 298–320.
5. D. Seers and C. R. Ross, *Report on the financial and physical problems of development in the Gold Coast*, Office of the Government Statistician, Accra 1952, ch. 1 (extracts).
6. W. A. Lewis, *Report on industrialisation and the Gold Coast*, Government Printer, Accra 1953, paras 252–6.
7. Prime Minister's statement on foreign investment, March 1953, *Industrial Development Committee, Reports and Accounts, 1954–5*, pp. 29–31.

8. *Industrial Development Committee, Reports and Accounts, 1955–6*, paras 4–8.
9. *Economic Survey, 1955*, paras 290–303.
10. Speech by the Prime Minister, March 1959, on the opening of the debate on the motion approving the Second Development Plan, *Legislative Assembly Reports, 1959*.

2. Finance

Government revenue and expenditure rose steadily during the first two years of the First World War and only showed signs of falling in the last two years, when the shortage of shipping affected the export trade of the colony. The Committee on Trade and Taxation for British West Africa stated that: 'The fall would have been much greater had not a considerable direct trade been established between the Gold Coast and the United States, and the financial situation was further saved for the Gold Coast by the imposition of an export duty on cocoa in October 1916.' (Document 11, para. 30.) Extracts from the debate in the Legislative Council on the ordinance to raise the cocoa duty are contained in Document 12. They show that while colonial government officials were in favour of an export tax on cocoa, members of the merchant community opposed the policy. This matter divided opinion in the colony for several years: while the merchant community argued that the tax was bound to harm the cocoa industry, the government contended that the continuous increases in production and exports were evidence of the fact that the tax did no damage at all. The Committee on Trade and Taxation assessed the arguments of both sides and concluded that 'it would be difficult to demonstrate that the duty has so far damaged the industry'. (Document 13.) A reduction in the rate of duty in 1922 failed to satisfy the merchant community, who continued to press for its total abolition. The argument that the tax harmed the industry and was an unfair burden on the cocoa farmer was strongly attacked by the Governor in 1924, when he attempted to show the merchants were arguing from self-interest (Document 14). Commenting on the 1922 reduction he argued that: 'the market price, as is well known to all of us, fell by an amount that corresponded to the reduction made. To the lay mind it appeared that the reduction was made use of by speculators in the cocoa trade' (Document 14, para. 47) and continued: 'At present I can see no sound reason for giving up the money we are spending for the good of our people when our experience so far has been that it will only be used for the benefit of the speculator.' (Document 14.)

The dispute over the imposition of an export duty on cocoa was part of a wider issue. The Committee on Trade and Taxation voiced the anxieties of many members of the commercial class when it declared that the financial situation at the end of the First World War was unsatisfactory, and that the colonial government would be unwise to embark on any substantial programme of capital expenditure. (Document 15a.) Referring not only to the Gold Coast but also to Nigeria and Sierra Leone, the Committee expressed the opinion that:

the abnormal and in a measure, the fictitious prosperity of these Colonies during 1919 and 1920 caused the radical change in their fiscal systems, which had been worked by the sudden decision to prohibit the importation of 'trade' spirits, to be to some extent lost sight of by the Colonial Governments; and that this has led to the work of reconstruction, which in almost every Public Department was demanded at the end of the war in the interests of efficiency, being undertaken by them on too lavish a scale and with too great rapidity.

The Governor reacted strongly to this attitude and asserted, correctly as it turned out, that the financial difficulties of the colony were essentially short term and should not be allowed to impede the Development Programme, which was anyway aimed at removing the causes of financial instability. In a despatch written in response to the report of the Committee (Document 15) he wrote: 'The point ... which I wish to make is that the use of the battle-cries of "Overtaxation" and "The poor native" is unfair and not justified by the facts. The 3,000,000 inhabitants of this country are taxed (indirectly) to a total amount of 16 shillings per capita per annum – no further comment on taxation is necessary.' In 1923 the Governor reviewed the financial arrangements of the government in an attempt to systematise practice and clarify the confusing accounting system (Document 16).[1] Guidelines for a future policy were also laid down and it is interesting to note that while the government proposed no radical departure from the ultra-conservative principles of financial policy the germs of a Keynesian-type stabilisation policy are present in this statement. As things turned out the government made no attempt to maintain its level of expenditure when revenue collapsed at the end of the twenties and the depression was met with a policy of retrenchment.

11. Revenue and expenditure maintained during the First World War [2]

29. In the Gold Coast the outbreak of war did not cause an immediate decline of revenue, the figures being as shown in [Table 11.1].

30. The fact that the imports of spirits into the Gold Coast largely consisted before the war of rum from America, the further fact that cocoa continued to find its way to continental markets until the end of 1916, and the general increase

[1] Details of the colonial accounting which clarify this document can be found in Table 23 below.

[2] *Report of a Committee on Trade and Taxation for British West Africa*, Cmd. 1600, London 1922, paras 29–31 (extracts).

Table 11.1

	Revenue (£s)
1913	1,302,000
1914	1,332,000
1915	1,456,000
1916	1,836,000
1917	1,624,000
1918	1,299,000
1919	2,601,000
1920	3,722,000

in Customs duties and in railway rates in 1915 account for the revenue of this Colony continuing steadily to increase during the first years of the war. The decline in the revenue in 1917, and the much more considerable drop in 1918, were due to lack of shipping facilities for the export of cocoa, preference being at that time given to palm oil and palm kernels. The fall would have been much greater had not a considerable direct trade been established between the Gold Coast and the United States, and the financial situation was further saved for the Gold Coast by the imposition of an export duty on cocoa in October, 1916. The increase of revenue in 1919 was in some measure due to stocks of cocoa, which had accumulated during 1918, owing to lack of facilities for shipping them, being exported during the former year. As has been noted in the case of Nigeria, the years 1919 and 1920 must be regarded as quite abnormal; yet even during the current year the Gold Coast has been able to export large quantities of cocoa in spite of the great depression in trade, and this, combined with a further increase of taxation imposed in February last, has produced a revenue during the months January to September, 1921, amounting to £1,875,270, which would give a revenue for the twelve months amounting to, say, £2,500,000, a sum which very nearly approximates to the revenue actually collected in 1919.

31. On the other hand, the ordinary recurrent expenditure of the Government of the Gold Coast has increased in the manner shown by the figures [in Table 11.2].

Table 11.2

	Recurrent Expenditure (£s)
1913	902,000
1914	1,034,000
1915	1,074,000
1916	1,139,000
1917	1,161,000
1918	1,162,000
1919	1,549,000
1920	2,249,000

12. An ordinance to raise export duties on cocoa, 1917 [1]

Colonial Secretary: I beg to move, Sir, that a Bill entitled 'An Ordinance to raise export duties on Cocoa' be read a second time . . . (I wish to present) the despatch in which the Secretary of State approved the new scheme of taxation, and with Your Excellency's permission and that of the Council I will read it now:

Downing Street,
27th June, 1916.

Sir,

I have the honour to acknowledge the receipt of your confidential despatch of the 8th of May (1916) enclosing a copy of a report of the Committee appointed by you to consider and advise the Government upon the expediency and practicability of imposing special additional taxation for the purpose of capital expenditure on railway extensions and other similar public works which would in ordinary circumstances be defrayed from loan monies.

2. In reply, I have to inform you that I approve of your recommendations to raise revenue by special additional taxation to the amount of £200,000 per annum approximately: (*a*) by the imposition of an export tax on cocoa at the rate of one farthing per pound; (*b*) by an increase of 50 per cent on the rates of cocoa carried over the Sekondi–Kumasi line; (*c*) by an increase of Court fees as recommended by the judges.

3. The Incidence of this new taxation under (*a*) and (*b*) should be very carefully watched and power should be taken to modify them at short notice if required.

4. I may add that, in view of the uncertainty of post-war conditions, you should not give absolute pledges as to the way in which the money raised by the new taxes will be spent nor should it be paid into a special fund.

5. No financial commitments on construction work should be made without my previous sanction. I have, etc.

A. Bonar Law.

. . . I will content myself with the question of principle. In the first place let me briefly remind Honourable Members that although an export duty is an innovation in this Colony this is not the first time that proposals for such duties have been mooted in the Colony. I find that so far back as the year 1906 a Committee . . . proposed a series of export duties on kola, timber, palm kernels, palm oil, rubber and cocoa, and curiously enough the duty proposed by the Committee i.e. 1/10*d* a cwt does not differ appreciably from the amount of duty we now propose to levy i.e. $\frac{1}{4}d$ per lb which works out at 2/4*d* a cwt. The Secretary of State disapproved the proposal, because, he observed, additional revenue was not necessary in the financial condition of the Colony at that time, and he added that unless they were absolutely necessary for revenue purposes he did not think export duties were a proper form of taxation. Again at the beginning of 1910, a Committee was appointed . . . to consider the question of imposing an export duty on timber, rubber and kola. For the same reason, that proposal was ultimately dropped because by the time the proposal could take shape and the Legislative Council could meet to discuss it, the financial position of the Colony had reverted to such a flourishing condition as to render further taxation unnecessary.

[1] *Legislative Council Debates, 1916–17*, pp. 82–91 (extracts).

I have some apprehension that Honourable Members may urge that a similar attitude should be adopted towards the proposed export duty now before the Council (in view of) the apparently rosy picture ... of the present financial position, but despite the fact that we expect to have a large surplus at the end of this year, I hope ... Honourable Members (will be convinced) that we have abounding services for which every penny of that surplus is urgently needed.

Secondly, I wish to assure the Council that this export duty on cocoa will not, by any means, be confined to the Gold Coast. There is already an export duty in Trinidad, Saint Lucia and Grenada, and in last October a heavy export duty was imposed in Ceylon on Tea, Cocoa, Copra, etc. The duty which was imposed on Cocoa exported from Ceylon is 2/- per 100 lbs which is almost exactly equal to the duty which we propose to levy here. In Trinidad and Tobago the duty is small, viz: 2½*d* per 100 lbs but in Saint Lucia it is 1/– to 2/– a cwt and in Grenada 7½*d* to 1/3*d* a cwt. I do not think therefore that we need fear that the exports of cocoa from this Colony will be affected on the score that no export duty is imposed on this commodity in other cocoa-growing Colonies.

There is one argument in favour of the Bill which I should like to mention because it has some bearing on the complaint that Gold Coast cocoa is very indifferently prepared and consequently fetches a comparatively low price compared with prices in other cocoa-producing countries. It is clear that with an export duty of so much per lb, the higher the price of cocoa the smaller will be the tax ad valorem so that it may possibly have the effect of producing a better quality of Gold Coast cocoa for the market. Finally we have to consider the possible effect on local prices. I am informed by a telegram received from the Crown Agents yesterday that the present price of cocoa in Liverpool and London is 56/- spot and 58/- forward, per cwt. This means of course that prices were higher last year, but even on the present figures a duty of 2/6*d* per cwt cannot be regarded as onerous on a commodity which is fetching prices of this standard.

Treasurer: I beg to second the motion; the Colonial Secretary has stated fully the objects of the Bill and the policy of the Government with regard to it, and I will therefore confine my remarks to the considerations which were before the Committee to which reference is made in the memorandum of which I was appointed by Your Excellency to be the Chairman and the members of which were gentlemen whose interests are centred in the commercial development of the Colony.

In the opinion of the Committee it would be little short of a financial disaster if the development of the cocoa industry in this Colony were arrested, or stultified by want of funds, the opinion being strongly held that to an immeasurable degree is the growth of the industry conditional upon a system of railway construction so designed as to tap the farms in the cocoa-growing districts. The Committee realised only too well the practical impossibilities of raising money for railway construction by means of a Government loan, and the only course open is to provide funds by additional taxation. They were unanimously in favour of an export tax on cocoa for the reason that this form of taxation would fall most appropriately on that section of the community which would be directly benefited by railway construction and by the improvement of feeder roads.

That the annually increasing output of cocoa in the Eastern Province of the Colony is the direct result of annually increasing railway facilities is beyond doubt. It stands to reason that the greater the facilities for handling and exporting the crops, the larger will be those crops. Experience has shown us that capital outlay on the construction of railways in this Colony has produced very handsome returns to Government and there is no reason to doubt that increased local prosperity and a very material enhancement of the public funds will follow a more vigorous policy of railway construction.

The output of cocoa during the last five years is as follows:

1911	39,726 tons
1912	38,647
1913	50,553
1914	52,888
1915	77,278

The tax which the Committee proposes is at the rate of $\frac{1}{4}d$ per lb and, based on last year's output, this would yield the sum of £180,000. This amount, together with the extra rates on cocoa railed from Kumasi to Sekondi and the additional Court fees which were approved by this Council this morning would aggregate not less than £210,000 per annum and this sum would place the Government in a position to prosecute, without undue delay, the policy of a railway construction which is so essential to the development of the Colony. With regard to that construction the Colonial Secretary (has announced) that it is proposed to extend the line at the rate of about 25 to 30 miles a year from Tafo in a northerly direction towards Kumasi and, simultaneously from Kumasi in a southerly direction to meet the Northern Extension.

The Committee fully realised that the direct effect of this tax would be felt by the cocoa planter inasmuch as he would receive so much less per load (1/3*d*) than he would otherwise receive, but it must be borne in mind that in this Colony the cocoa industry is wholly in the hands of natives. They have not such items as shareholders' dividends or the cost of European supervision to bear and, outside the actual cost of headload transport from the farms to the railway, the money they receive for their crops is a clear profit and there is no doubt as to the ability of the farmer to stand the tax. Especially is this so, when the heavy local prices which have ruled during the last two years are taken into consideration.

But, Sir, the important consideration in connection with this measure is, I venture to submit, to be found in the fact that with extended railways and feeders thereto which will enable him to save the present heavy cost of headload transport even though he has to pay the tax – the cocoa farmer will be better off than he now is without a tax and without the extended railway. I commend the Bill to the earnest consideration of Honourable Members.

Mr. Parker: I was a member of the Committee which recommended the imposition of this tax but nevertheless I propose to ask the Government to withdraw this Bill for the time being. In the first place when the Committee made this proposal it was thought that the extension of the railway and also the necessary road construction could only be carried on at the present time by means of additional taxation . . . (However it is now shown) that we are in such a strong position that railway and road construction can be carried on without this taxation. (There has now been outlined an additional) heavy building programme which the Government contemplate carrying out. In any case this is not the time for the erection of any unnecessary buildings the cost of which will be at least 30 per cent to 40 per cent more than in normal times. But what I want to point out is that the

Taxation Committee contemplate the proceeds of the cocoa tax being solely used for carrying on the construction of roads and railways and they laid great emphasis in their report on the great advantages the cocoa farmer, who everyone admits will pay the tax, will gain by better transport facilities and they point out that even after paying the tax he will be better off owing to the saving that he will effect in transport. What I wish to point out is that in recommending this tax the Committee had this special purpose in mind and that at the time it was considered that without additional taxes these works would not be carried on, more particularly the Northern Extension of the railway. It was never contemplated that this tax should be levied to enable the Government to carry out an extensive building programme.

Moreover another point which requires serious consideration is that for various reasons the cocoa market in Europe just now is very unsettled and it is quite possible that when large shipments begin to come forward from the Gold Coast there may be a very serious slump.

I am confident that if the price of cocoa falls seriously the Governor will not hesitate to use the power given to him in the Bill to vary the tax. It is quite possible however that the cocoa industry during the coming season may have to go through a very critical time, there is every indication of it, and for this reason it does not seem an opportune time to impose this tax until the outlook is more settled.

13. Cocoa duty and production, 1922 [1]

126. The rate of the duty is $\frac{1}{2}d$ per lb, or 2*s* 6*d* per load (of 60 lbs), or 4*s* 8*d* per cwt, or £4 13*s* 4*d* per ton. When first imposed in October, 1916, the rate was $\frac{1}{4}d$ per lb, or £2 6*s* 8*d* per ton, a year later it was reduced to $\frac{1}{5}d$ per lb, or £1 17*s* 4*d* per ton, but it was raised to its present figure in August 1919. At the Growers' unit of 60 lbs the rates have therefore varied as follows:

1916	1*s* 3*d*
1917	1*s* 0*d*
1919–present day	2*s* 6*d*

127. The duty is producing a large revenue, the amount collected up to the end of August 1921, from the date of its imposition in October 1916, being £1,776,000, and the proceeds of the duty during the current year will probably be at least £500,000. These large sums are collected at a negligible cost and without any friction.

128. It would be difficult to demonstrate that the duty has so far damaged the industry. Thus the exports for the four years preceding the outbreak of war and for the four years succeeding the imposition of the duty were respectively ... [Table 13.1].

This striking and rapid growth is attributable to large areas planted before the imposition of the export duty coming into bearing, especially in Ashanti. The exports from Seccondee (the bulk of which come from Ashanti) rose from 4,824 tons in 1911 to 41,318 tons in 1920.

129. The drop in the exports in 1920 may possibly be followed by a further slight drop in the current year, though the exports up to the end of August, 1921,

[1] *Report of a Committee on Trade and Taxation for British West Africa*, Cmd 1600, London 1922, paras 126–46 (extracts).

Table 13.1

		Tons
1910		22,631
1911		39,726
1912		38,647
1913		50,554
	Total	151,558
1917		90,964
1918		66,343
1919		176,176
1920		124,773
	Total	458,256

The figures for the three intervening years were as follows:

		Tons
1914		52,888
1915		77,278
1916		72,161
	Total	202,327

amounted to 84,200 tons, or at the rate of 126,300 tons for the twelve months. In this connection it may be remarked that during the present depressed state of the cocoa trade, merchants are naturally more particular as to the quality of the cocoa which they buy.

130. The export duty was opposed by all the unofficial members of the Legislative Council at the time of its original imposition, and again in 1919, when the duty was doubled, but there is at this juncture no demand by African unofficial members for its total withdrawal. They have, however, urged (in reply to a reference to them on behalf of the Committee) 'that the incidence of the export duty should vary with market prices'.

131. Mr Furley, the Secretary for Native Affairs on the Gold Coast, informed the Committee that he has never heard it put forward by the natives that the duty is unjust in its incidence. 'It is' he says, 'a form of indirect taxation to which natives do not object more than they do to any other form of indirect taxation, and they certainly do not object to indirect taxation in the way they certainly would if we replaced it with direct taxation.' (Q. 2137.)

132. In criticism of the duty it is contended, more especially by the mercantile community:

(1) That in principle any tax on produce is unsound.

(2) That at present prices the tax at its present figure is unfairly onerous, i.e. when calculated on an ad valorem basis.

(3) That the grower is taxed twice, viz on what he sells and what he buys.

(4) That the tax is impeding, or at least is likely to impede, the rate of growth of the industry in that it is so discouraging the farmer that he will cease to extend his farm and may even abandon existing farms.

(5) That competing cocoas are gradually approaching Gold Coast cocoa in price, and that, therefore, it is obviously desirable to cheapen in every way possible the cost at which cocoa can be put on board ship in the Gold Coast.

(6) That at any rate the duty should be assessed on a sliding scale, varying according to market prices.

133. As to the first of these objections, the Committee agree that a duty on the export of cocoa is in principle to be deprecated. Any factor which tends to lessen the amount which the producer obtains for his produce, must necessarily tend to restrict trade. Thus the imposition of an import duty or an increase in such a duty usually affects consumption to some degree. But although it may be conceded that all duties, and especially those on produce, must, to some extent, hamper trade, none the less some taxation is necessary, and the question for local Governments is how to get the money they require with the least disturbance, not only of trade, but of popular content.

134. As to the Second objection, viz the onerous character of the duty at the present time, figures have been produced by one of the members of the Committee which go to prove that the duty, calculated as an ad valorem one, runs up in certain cases to as much as 28.4 per cent of the price that would otherwise be paid to the farmer. (See p. 81 of the evidence.) But taking the English market price, e.g. £38 a ton, the figure works out at 12.3 per cent. Even this figure is admittedly a high one, and suggests the desirability of a sliding scale, or at least the necessity for careful and frequent scrutiny of the position. Nevertheless, the exports for 1921 would seem to show that the duty has not so far caused any appreciable diminution of the trade, and when present world trade conditions are taken into consideration, the practical maintenance of the 1920 standard of shipments is reassuring.

135. It is true that on the assumption that the cocoa grower pays the whole duty or even part of it, he is taxed more highly than other natives on the Gold Coast, who consume equal amounts of imported goods and do not sell taxable exports, but it must be borne in mind that it is impossible to make the incidence of taxation equal for everyone. It is relevant to recall in this connection that by the recent imposition of export duties on kola and timber, as well as on cocoa, the Gold Coast Government have widened the basis of taxation on produce.

136. As to the rate of growth of the industry, the figures already quoted in paragraph 3 above appear to prove indisputably that the rate has, ever since the imposition of the duty, been very remarkable. An increase in the export of Gold Coast cocoa from 72,000 tons in 1916 to 125,000 tons in 1920, is an increase of about 70 per cent in five years, or 14 per cent per annum. Of the increase of 53,000 tons about half may be attributed to the growth of the industry in Ashanti, but, even so, the rate cannot be considered otherwise than satisfactory. We have not had before us any direct evidence as to whether cocoa farms are or are not being extended as rapidly as was the case before the imposition of the duty; but it has often been urged by the Agricultural and Forestry Departments that it would be salutary if the extension of cocoa farms in the Gold Coast were slowed down to some extent, as it has in the past been considered by many to be too rapid for good cultivation.

137. The future growth of the industry is necessarily a matter of speculation. Production depends on the following main factors: (1) the areas available; (2) the population of such areas; (3) the inducements offered to growers of cocoa, i.e. prices.

As to the first of these factors, the area available and suitable for cocoa cultivation has been estimated at 24,000 square miles, or, roughly, half the area of the Colony and Ashanti, and inasmuch as probably three-quarters of the Colony are suitable for cocoa cultivation (Q.2164) the figure seems reasonably correct.[2] In any case, it is certain that there are in the Gold Coast and Ashanti large areas suitable for cocoa which are either not yet planted or not yet in bearing or not yet within a profitable zone on account of lack of transport. Examples of such areas are the hinterland of the Central Province, the rich Sefwi district of the Western Province, the Western Province of Ashanti, the Kwahu Plateau, and part of the British Mandate of Togoland.

138. The population in all the above areas is considerable. The total present population of the Gold Coast is believed to be about 2,000,000, of whom about 600,000 are in the Northern Territories, leaving, say, 1,400,000 in the Colony and Ashanti. We do not feel able to hazard any guess as to what is a reasonable or possible production of cocoa per head, but we understand that the crop in some recent years has been estimated by the agrcultural authorities at 150,000 tons. Taking into consideration the room that still exists for greatly improved transport in many of the cocoa-bearing areas, we have little doubt that the Gold Coast is capable of producing at least 200,000 tons of cocoa per annum and probably more. It may well be questioned, however, whether increase in production will take place in future as rapidly as between 1913 and 1920, though improved transport facilities revolutionise trade in that part of the Gold Coast where they are affected.

139. The ' inducements offered to the growers of cocoa ' depend on price. This price is determined by:

(*a*) The ' home price ', which in its turn depends on the balancing of the world's supply and demand.

(*b*) The cost of internal transport, e.g. rail, river, motor and head carriage.

(*c*) The cost of external transport, i.e. ocean freight (including lighterage).

(*d*) Miscellaneous charges, e.g. merchants' overhead charges, financial charges, loss in weight, etc.

(*e*) Merchants' and intermediaries' profit.

(*f*) Export duty.

None of these factors is fixed or immutable.

140. Of the above factors, the first, viz the home price, is obviously the most important. This, it is notorious, has always varied in a remarkable manner from time to time, even during the same year, as may be seen from [Table 13.2].

It will be noted that even before the war, there were variations in the same year to the extent of 13*s* 6*d* a cwt or £13 10*s* a ton, while during and since the war the fluctuations have been much more violent. The price today is appreciably lower than it was before the war.

141. An important governing factor is, of course, the stock of cocoa in the consuming countries at any given moment, and in this connection we are informed that the stock of raw cocoa in the United Kingdom on 10 October 1921, was 43,800 tons only, as compared with 63,700 tons on the corresponding date in 1920.

[2] The total areas are (according to the Colonial Office list):

Colony	24,200 square miles
Ashanti	20,000
Northern Territories	35,800

Table 13.2 *Prices for fair fermented Accra cocoa, in the United Kingdom, 1910–21* (per cwt)

	1910 *s d*	1911 *s d*	1912 *s d*	1913 *s d*	1914 *s d*	1915 *s d*	1916 *s d*	1917 *s d*	1918 *s d*	1919 *s d*	1920 *s d*	1921 *s d*
1 Jan.	46 6	48	47 6	58	54 6	68	77	52	74	65*	99† 102‡	40
1 Apr.	47	47 6	47	62 9	53 6	80	71 6	54	65*	65† 71‡	118	42
1 Jul.	45	48	57	62 9	51 6	74	57 9	53	65*	85† 93‡	76	43
1 Dec.	47 9	49	55 6	58 9	47	82	50	71 6	65*	96† 100‡	52	1 Nov. 42 6
Lowest	45	47	46 6	55	42	53	57	52	*	65	40	37
Highest	49	56	60	66	57	85	80	73	*	100	124	51

* Government controlled price from 19.3.18 to 31.1.19.
† Home trade cocoa.
‡ Exportable cocoa.

142. According to available information the world's consumption of cocoa during the last eight years has been as shown [Table 13.3].

Table 13.3

	Tons
1913	257,000
1914	259,000
1915	314,000
1916	265,000
1917	310,000
1918	310,000
1919	422,000
1920	360,000

There was thus a considerable increase in consumption even at a time when Central Europe was completely out of the market. The consumption in Germany and America during the period 1913 to 1920 was as shown in [Table 13.4].

Table 13.4

	Germany * Tons	America Tons
1913	51,000	68,000
1914	50,000	72,000
1915	45,000	85,000
1916	15,000	97,000
1917	—	157,000
1918	—	145,000
1919	20,000	172,000
1920	46,000	131,000

* Figures for Germany from 1914 inclusive onwards are estimates only.

The consumption of cocoa may be expected to increase still further as Central Europe more fully recovers its purchasing power and when Russia and Poland enter the market.

143. The second factor governing the local price, viz the cost of internal transport, is also obviously of the first importance and at present large cocoa-bearing areas are still far from any cheap means of transport. In this connection it is important to bear in mind that the remunerative yield of the cocoa duty enables Government to proceed with fair rapidity with projects for improving transport facilities, i.e. in the construction of new roads and railways.

144. As to the cost of external transport, ocean freights for cocoa per ton weight from Accra to Liverpool were 30*s* in 1913, rose to as much as 145*s* during the war and are today 60*s*.

145. Unquestionably, whatever the home price of cocoa may be, there must be geographical zones beyond which it is impossible for cocoa to be profitably grown. These zones expand or contract as the charges for internal transport, ocean freight,

export duty and other charges diminish or increase. Thus a reduction or abolition of the export duty undoubtedly extends in some degree the profitable zones, provided that the whole of the duty so remitted was eventually paid to the native producers. Even in 1920, however, much of the cocoa produced in the Sefwi district for instance was not brought to market owing to the lack of transport facilities between Sefwi and the railway.

146. As regards competition of other cocoas e.g. Guayaquil, Bahia, San Thomé, French West Africa, Nigeria, British West Indies, etc., a few years ago Bahia was the biggest producer of cocoa, but at the present time the Gold Coast is the largest producer in the world. Nevertheless Bahia is competing successfully in the American market, and the competition of the other producers also obviously requires to be very carefully watched, especially as it is reported that the difference between the price of such cocoa and Gold Coast cocoa is less today than it formerly was. It is still possible, however, to put West African cocoa on the market at a cheaper price than cocoa from other places (Question 650). It is also a fact that no difficulty is experienced at present in finding a market for Gold Coast cocoa. (Question 462). We may here observe that in so far as any remission of the duty was used to meet the competition of other countries it would fail to secure higher prices for the farmer, although in that case it would help to preserve for him a market that might otherwise be lost.

14. Reduction of cocoa duty benefits speculators not farmers: the Governor, 1924 [1]

Government opposed to reduction of export duty on cocoa

44. Willing, however, as Government is to make reductions both in import duties and in railway fares, I feel that at this period we should proceed with the utmost possible caution in considering any further reduction in the cocoa export duty. I say ‘ further reduction ’, for it will be within the memory of this Council that Government reduced the duty on cocoa by one-half in 1922. My reasons are briefly as follows.

Cocoa export duty required at present to pay for preservation of cocoa trade

45. Twelve months ago I drew the attention of Honourable Members to the fact that the rapidly increasing production of the world was tending to lower permanently the market price of cocoa, especially West African cocoa. I said: ‘In five years’ time I am firmly convinced that the market price of Gold Coast cocoa at Liverpool will seldom, if ever, exceed £35 per ton ; and it does not require very much imagination to see it falling steadily to some £30 a ton.’

As an actual fact the average price of cocoa in the last six months of 1923 was under £30 a ton. It is apparent, therefore, that the time when the cheapest possible form of transport is wanted to retain our cocoa trade is much nearer than I ventured to prophesy last year ; and we want all the money we can get to continue to build railways, harbours and roads. These public works are for the specific purpose of preserving our cocoa trade against both competition and lower prices, and it is Government’s opinion that the cost is a legitimate charge against the cocoa trade at the present moment. It is my opinion, however, that the satisfactory progress of construction of communications is steadily bringing nearer the day on

[1] Governor’s Annual Address, *Legislative Council Debates, 1924–5*, pp. 27–33.

which we can venture first to reduce, and then to abolish our present cocoa export duties.

Existence of a cocoa ring

46. It is within the bounds of possibility that increased production is not the cause of the low prices of cocoa this season for, judging from our exports, the demand appears to be brisk. It is possible that the cause may be found in speculation. In connection with this I notice that on 8 November last, at a conference with the joint West African Committee of the Chamber of Commerce, a prominent merchant affirmed that there was no such thing as a 'ring' and that the market price was governed by the supply and demand. I feel the utmost diffidence in differing from such an authority; but I would like to point out that there appears to have been such demand for our cocoa that local buying was exceedingly brisk during the first four months of this season, and that during the whole of that period the price remained excessively low.

With regard to the 'ring' I am also ignorant as to its existence; but I fancy some light is thrown on the subject of speculation by the fact that, during the period mentioned, the market price in Liverpool was less than £30 a ton, and that the price at the beginning of February was £36 a ton. The farmer had then disposed of the bulk of his crop at the lower price. If it is the case that the whole of the cocoa purchased at the lower price had not been actually sold to manufacturers in the European and American markets, someone must have made a big profit. The Gold Coast farmer, however, was not the lucky man.

Result of reduction of cocoa duty in 1922

47. Apropos of the farmer's benefit from reduction of duty, I notice that at the conference above alluded to, the same prominent merchant stated that, within twelve hours of the reduction of the duty on palm oils and kernels in Nigeria, cables went out to advance the price to be paid to the producer at once. Although the speaker gave a personal undertaking that any further reduction in the duty on cocoa would at once go to the price paid to the native, I did not observe that when we made our big reduction in 1922, any such cables, judging from the results, appeared to have been received in this country. On the other hand the market price, as is well known to all of us, fell by an amount that corresponded to the reduction made. To the lay mind it appeared that the reduction was made use of by speculators in the cocoa trade.

Harmful results of speculation in cocoa

48. Whether or not speculation in the trade of an article of human consumption is legitimate does not concern me. What does concern me is that speculation in such an article of human consumption as cocoa interferes with the legitimate course of such a trade. It not only results in an injustice to the farmer, but, I venture to think, must interfere with the business of genuine merchants. It is a thousand pities that the cocoa speculator exists – as I fear he does – for he prevents our farmer getting a fair standard price for cocoa. If this kind of speculation could be stopped, we should go a long way towards the reduction of export duties on our staple product.

At present I can see no sound reason for giving up the money that we are spending for the good of the people when our experience so far has been that it will only be utilised for the benefit of the speculator. Incidentally, I may mention here that only a few months ago, when I was anxious on account of the low price of cocoa, I conferred with my advisers both official and non-official, on the wisdom of reducing the export duty. Without one dissenting voice the decision was in the negative, the chief reason being that the adoption of such a course would tend to keep prices low rather than improve them.

Reasons against reduction of cocoa duty

49. Summarising my reasons for not looking favourably at the present moment on the reduction of the cocoa export duty, I believe that such a reduction would be an injustice to the farmer. He is not likely to get any more benefit out of a fresh reduction than he did out of the last, whereas he did get the benefit of the railways and roads constructed out of the duty. During the last cocoa season farmers brought in, by the new roads and railways, many tons of cocoa which would otherwise never have reached the market – roads and railways which it was possible for us to build owing to our revenue from the export tax on cocoa.

Price of chocolate

50. Before leaving the question of export taxes, as the chocolate manufacturers are direct buyers of our cocoa on a large scale, I will deal briefly with a subject that has been raised more than once in the home and colonial press, namely, the price charged to the consumer by the makers of chocolates. The reason why manufactured chocolate is sold at the same price, whether cocoa sells for £100 or £25 a ton, is a mystery to many of us. At the conference to which I have just alluded, it was suggested that if the makers of chocolates charged lower prices the consumption would go up. Although as I understand from the reply, the consumption in England is only a little over 10 per cent of the world's consumption it is only fair to conclude that the chocolate-maker in the United Kingdom makes a far larger profit than his rival on the continent, especially when it is remembered that the home manufacturer receives the benefit of an appreciable preference amounting to £4 3*s* 4*d* per ton in the duty paid on re-exported cocoa.

Apropos of this, *The Times* of June 12 1923, contains the following:

> Sir W. Joynson-Hicks, Financial Secretary to the Treasury (Twickenham, U.) said the results of the preference given to Empire tea was that 90 per cent of the tea imported into this country was Empire grown, and that the home consumer had his tea reduced in price by twopence per pound [Hear Hear]. In the case of the preference on cocoa, there had been no reduction, or only very little reduction, in price to the home consumer, but the imports of Empire cocoa had increased from 50 per cent of the whole imports to 90 per cent.

The wholesale price of raw cocoa is less than it was in pre-war days, while the cost to the consumer of manufactured chocolate is considerably higher even when allowance is made for increased duties and the higher cost of sugar. It goes without saying that salaries and other expenses have gone up, but when all is said and done the selling price of manufactured chocolate is so high as to interfere with consumption except by those of ample means. On the other hand the popularity of good chocolates is so great among all communities down to the very poorest, that I suggest that any possible reduction in the selling price would result in a vastly increased turnover ; but, like the gentlemen who suggest that trade would increase if I lowered the duties, I have no definite proposals to make.

15a. Financial position of the Colony unsound: Committee on Trade and Taxation: 1922 [1]

183. The Committee considers that the financial position of the British West African Colonies, with the exception of the Gambia, is far from satisfactory and that the Governments of Nigeria, the Gold Coast and Sierra Leone are today incurring expenditure in excess of the revenue which they have a reasonable prospect of obtaining from existing taxation.

184. The Committee is of opinion that the abnormal and in a measure, the fictitious prosperity of these Colonies during 1919 and 1920 caused the radical change in their fiscal systems, which had been worked by the sudden decision to prohibit the importation of 'trade' spirits, to be to some extent lost sight of by the Colonial Governments; and that this has led to the work of reconstruction, which in almost every Public Department was demanded at the end of the war in the interests of efficiency, being undertaken by them on too lavish a scale and with too great rapidity.

185. Having regard to the present state of the West African trade and to its prospects in the visible future, the Committee considers that the taxation at present in force imposes upon commerce and upon the West African producers burdens which they are ill able to bear in existing circumstances, and it is of opinion that it should be the dual object of the Governments concerned to submit their expenditure to drastic revision, and (when possible) to remit taxation.

186. The Committee recognises that many of the commitments of a Government are not susceptible of abrupt, immediate reduction, and that these Governments are under the necessity of raising sufficient revenue to cover their irreducible expenditure; but the Committee is convinced of the necessity for the utmost economy being exercised in every branch of the Public Service, and would advocate the suspension of such schemes for the execution of public works as those Governments are in a position to abandon and postpone, unless it is clear that they can be financed out of the revenues which the Governments concerned have a reasonable prospect of obtaining in existing conditions.

187. The Committee, moreover, considers that the present system whereby public works, constructed during any given year and not chargeable to loan funds, are paid for from revenue, necessitates the raising of annual funds, to defray the cost of these permanent improvements in addition to paying the recurrent expenses of administration maintenance, etc., which in the existing state of the West African trade are excessive, and which are already imposing a burden upon the commerce of those Colonies which is very serious. The Committee considers that, in existing circumstances expenditure of this description should be reduced to a minimum.

188. The committee is fully alive to the cogency of the objections which have been raised in the course of its deliberations, and in the evidence given before it, to the imposition of export duties as a means of raising revenue. It regrets that the loss of revenue occasioned by the decision to prohibit the importation of 'trade' spirits, combined with the greatly increased cost of all services and the too rapid attempt to make good during two years of abnormal prosperity the leeway lost during the war, has compelled the Governments of the West African Colonies to

[1] *Report of the Committee on Trade and Taxation for British West Africa, Sessional Paper no. VII, 1921–2*, paras 183–9.

maintain, and subsequently to increase those duties, which were originally imposed as a temporary war measure. The Committee considers that the danger of these export duties unduly handicapping West African produce, *vis-à-vis* its competitors in the world markets, is a matter which the Governments concerned must watch with great care; and that if and when, by the reduction and readjustment of expenditure, it becomes possible to diminish taxation, it should be the endeavour of these Governments to decrease and, if possible, eventually to abolish these export duties.

189. Having regard, however, to the present financial positions of these Colonies, to their existing commitments, and to the heavy fall of revenue, as compared with the receipts in 1919 and 1920, with which they are now confronted, the Committee is unable to recommend any immediate reduction of the existing export duties, or any alternative means of raising revenue which, while meeting the financial necessities of these Colonies, and proving at once adequate and stable, will be less injurious to trade and industry than are the export duties on produce.

15b. Financial position sound. Programme for expansion justified: the Governor, 1922 [1]

I believe I am right in saying that our department has recently been burdened with much additional and unnecessary work, at a time of great stress in public affairs, owing either to the wrong information in possession of the public or to the misleading use made of available information by interested persons. This is evident from newspaper articles, numerous petitions, and deputations from the Chambers of Commerce, and the questions asked by Members of Parliament at the request of their constituents. If I am correct in the above assumption, it would appear that a better understanding of the real, and very satisfactory, financial situation in the the Gold Coast by critics of Government might be beneficial.

From the local point of view I am also strongly desirous of our financial condition being appreciated at its true worth. The agitation in mercantile circles in the United Kingdom, or rather that section of it which is concerned in the Gold Coast from natural motives of self-interest, has had an echo, and an appreciable one, out here; and has been productive of discontent among the local merchants. Those, however, to whom I have recently shown actual figures have expressed themselves as satisfied with our financial condition. Indeed their only grievance now is that taxation is so high as to affect the cocoa industry, an assumption that is scarcely justified by the steadily increasing tonnage of cocoa exported.

Taxation and the financial situation

... [It is necessary to make a brief mention of taxation], for Government's critics both at home and here assert that our – erroneously termed – serious financial situation has caused such high taxation as to make the farmers sullen and disinclined to work. That such is not the case both our exports and the demeanour of the farmer thoroughly prove. There can be no doubt that trade depression has hit the merchants heavily, that the enormous profits of 1919 and 1920 no longer continue to be made, and that it would be beneficial to the merchant to do away

[1] Despatch from the Governor to the Secretary of State dated 17 August 1922, with reference to statements on the future financial position of the Colony, made in the report of the Committee on Trade and Taxation for British West Africa. *Sessional Paper no. VII, 1921–2* (extracts).

with all export duties. On the other hand it has never, until recently, been proved to my satisfaction, or that of any of my advisers, that a reduction of duty would benefit anyone but the merchant himself. When it was so proved I took, as you are aware, immediate action. The point, however, which I wish to make is that the use of the battle cries of ' Over-taxation ' and ' The Poor Native! ' is unfair and not justified by facts. The 3,000,000 inhabitants of this country are taxed (indirectly) to a total extent of 16 shillings per capita per annum – no further comment on taxation is necessary.

The vast majority of the natives, although naturally feeling the fall from the boom conditions of 1919–20, are perfectly happy, and the farmers are not only industrious but producing cocoa of a steadily improving quality.

There is, however, in this as in every other country a section of the semi-educated community which is easily led by specious and fallacious arguments. It is these people whom, for their own sakes, I am anxious to prevent being led too far astray from the path of good citizenship, where those who walk are prepared to pay moderately for the good of their country and posterity. It is these people who fail to understand that, unless the Gold Coast spends every penny it can justly afford on extending its present lamentably inadequate facilities for transport, education, and sanitation, its progress must and will be so hopelessly retarded as to give real cause for discontent, unrest, and failure to compete with other countries. As long as these people, and the public generally, remain under the impression that the financial situation is bad, they will naturally believe that the Government is spending more money than it can afford. It is therefore essential that they, and the people who are responsible for the propaganda of the ' serious financial situation ', should be told the real facts of the case, viz that the Government, in view of its large surplus balance and its steady revenue, is not only not spending what it cannot afford but is spending far less than the progress of the people of the country demands.

In concluding my remarks on this subject, I need only add that my recent request that the export duties on cocoa should be reduced is sufficient proof that neither the financial situation nor expenditure is productive of increased taxation.

The Committee's conclusion on reconstruction

I will now deal with the statement contained in the Report that ' The work of reconstruction, which in almost every public department was demanded at the end of the war in the interests of efficiency, is being undertaken on too lavish a scale and with too great rapidity. . . .'

Here I must again disagree with the Committee as far as the Gold Coast is concerned. Efficiency, as the Committee remarks, demanded reconstruction, especially in the case of communications, for the steady increase in the cocoa trade during and since the war resulted in transport and postal and telegraphic facilities falling hopelessly behind trade requirements. The wise economy exercised by Government during the war, and the large annual surpluses of 1919 and 1920, resulted, as I have shown, in such a large accumulated balance as not only to justify the policy of active development adopted with the approval of Lord Milner and your subsequent concurrence, but would have rendered this Government culpably negligent if it had followed any other course. The statistics given earlier in the despatch apparently show that the ' lavish scale ' and ' too great rapidity ' of my programme has left the country richer by £1,187,000 in accumulated balance, and in possession of such public works as add several millions to its capital value.

History of post-war reconstruction

What was the situation at the beginning of 1919? Harbours, railways, roads, telegraphs and rolling stock entirely insufficient to cope with trade; quarters for officials seriously deficient; facilities for education painfully small when compared with the demand; the country threatened with ruin through the promiscuous denuding of its forests; trade depending on a single industry with no provision for the creation of other agricultural produce on any appreciable scale; the water supplies confined to two towns; hospitals totally insufficient to deal with the demands of the people; a steadily increasing demand for the re-layout and drainage of big towns and clearing up of congested areas. In fact the arrears of work owing to the war were formidable, and, in addition, every department was hopelessly understaffed with one exception.

16. Future financial arrangements, 1923 [1]

Present system

31. I will now deal briefly with certain changes which Government proposes to make in its financial arrangements. These are to enable the financial situation to be more easily seen when Council is dealing with the budget, and to place our finance on a sounder basis.

Up to now, as reference to past estimates will show, Honourable Members have often voted recurrent and extraordinary expenditure in excess of the revenue anticipated, relying on the accumulated balance to make good the deficit. This system is not satisfactory. It clouds the financial situation, and prevents a clear financial policy being followed. It is dangerous also, as it is a hand to mouth system which may result in certain Government liabilities not being provided for. The Railway Reserves Fund is a case in point, a subject with which I will deal later.

Three principles

32. The three principles which Government proposes to adopt are as follows:

(*a*) That the annual revenue should cover both recurrent and extraordinary expenditure and a contribution to the Railway Renewals Fund, after which there should be a small annual surplus for contingencies.

(*b*) That the nucleus of a General Reserve Fund should be started, and this fund built up annually by its own interest to an amount proportional to our capital value as a country.

(*c*) That the accumulated balance, after setting aside a Reserve Fund, should be expended on the more urgent items of the development programme.

Annual recurrent expenditure

33. With regard to the first principle, annual recurrent expenditure will, as heretofore, be estimated to cover the personal emoluments and other charges for the general running and maintenance of departments, ordinary renewals of equipment, debt charges, pensions, and gratuities. The usual miscellaneous head will be continued for those items which, though they may not be strictly recurrent

[1] Governor's Annual Address, *Legislative Council Debates, 1923–4*, pp. 19–33.

in the sense that they will be repeated every year, will inevitably be replaced by other items which it is impractical to allot to any departmental head.

Very few changes will therefore be necessary in our present system of showing recurrent expenditure. Certain items hitherto shown in it as ' special expenditure ' will be reclassified as extraordinary, and freer use will be made of schedules in order to facilitate decentralisation by permitting of the easy allocation of votes. The arrangement, for example, of Head VII in the current estimates is confused in the extreme and can be made far clearer by the use of a separate schedule.

Extraordinary expenditure

34. With regard to extraordinary expenditure, it is very often difficult to differentiate between it and recurrent expenditure. In our present state of development many new works are bound to recur yearly. New roads, for example, if not wanted in one place are wanted in another, so that virtually they will be, for many years to come, recurrent extraordinary. The most satisfactory rule to adopt will be to limit extraordinary expenditure to covering such new works as the Colony can afford to pay for out of its current revenue without increasing taxation. These works should be those that are necessary for the normal development of the Colony. Up to now extraordinary expenditure has often included certain abnormal needs in capital works, obviously an unsatisfactory policy from the point of view of progress, and one not conducive to the reduction of taxation.

If we are to observe the principle that revenue should cover both recurrent and extraordinary expenditure, an important point arises in regard to the latter. What should be its maximum and minimum? In settling this point, another question has first to be answered. If the estimated revenue for any year is not sufficient to cover the estimated expenditure, which should be reduced, recurrent, or extraordinary? In considering this point one has to remember that recurrent expenditure cannot be reduced without a definite loss of efficiency, together with other disadvantages such as that of injustice to Government servants. It would therefore seem that the best course to adopt, if an insufficient revenue is in prospect, is to reduce extraordinary expenditure. This is the course that Government has decided to adopt, so that the actual amount of extraordinary expenditure in each year will depend on the surplus of revenue over recurrent expenditure.

There is, however, a limit to which extraordinary expenditure can be reduced, for there is always a certain number of small capital works that the normal progress of the country demands annually. Besides this, a certain number of new works are necessary to employ the normal staff of certain departments to their full economic working capacity. This minimum can, I consider, be fixed at £200,000 per annum. Naturally this can be further decreased in times of grave necessity, but with a loss of efficiency.

With regard to fixing a maximum for extraordinary expenditure there does not appear any urgent reason for doing this at the present time, as the amount to be spent will be automatically limited by the surplus of revenue over recurrent expenditure. For the present it is not necessary to spend more than £200,000 a year on extraordinary works, in view of the large free balance to which we can transfer any abnormal requirements. I cannot foresee the exhaustion of this free balance for very many years, but, should that occur, it would be advisable to fix a maximum for extraordinary expenditure. This might reasonably be taken as £300,000 per annum.

How shown in estimates

35. In the annual estimates separate heads will continue to be provided as heretofore for the extraordinary works of the railway, posts and telegraphs, and public works, as these are the only departments which incur expenditure on an appreciable scale.

The same system might be adopted for the extraordinary expenditure of other departments. This, however, will usually be for such minor items as initial equipment required by reorganisation or by the formation of new station or sub-department. It would therefore scarcely be worth while to have a separate head for this expenditure, which will continue to be shown as a sub-head in the recurrent estimates of the department concerned, and will be extracted in drawing up the statement of expenditure. . .

Railway Renewals Fund

36. With regard to the third item which current revenue should cover, viz a contribution to the Railway Renewals Fund, this is a subject to which Lieutenant-Colonel Hammond drew attention in his recent report on our railway system. So far this Council has voted annually any sum required by the General Manager of the Railway for the renewal of rails, locomotives, rolling stock, etc. This system has been satisfactory in so far that railway requirements have been kept up to date, but it is entirely unsound in every other way.

To begin with, under the existing system the Government has no clear idea of the liabilities it may suddenly be called on to meet in the way of replacing worn-out materials. By this I do not mean the purchase of any new locomotives or waggons that may be found necessary to deal with increased trade, for that is either extraordinary or loan expenditure that will be covered by the extra revenue earned. What I refer to is the renewal of existing stock. An excellent example is furnished by the rails laid in the last two years on the Accra–Coomassie line and on the deviation in the Secondee–Coomassie line. The life of these rails is roughly 33 years. On our present system this would mean that suddenly, in 1956, this Council might be called on to vote out of revenue over a million pounds for new rails.

A score of other examples might be given. The system is obviously unsound; the General Manager has to struggle annually for what he knows is very necessary expenditure; the Government is unprepared for its commitments and may be called on suddenly to devote a larger sum than the revenue for the year could possibly bear; and lastly it is difficult to obtain a clear profit and loss account of a business of great magnitude.

Annual contribution

37. Government is therefore recommending to the Secretary of State the formation of a Railway Renewals Fund, and Honourable Members have been asked to vote an annual contribution for the coming year. This has been fixed at approximately £100,000 but the exact amount will be subject to the advice of the railway advisers to the Colonial Office and the approval of the Secretary of State. I may add here that it is only by chance, and not by systematic organisation, that the Government finds itself in the fortunate position of there being practically no arrears to the Railway Renewals Fund. This is due to the short life of our railways, which only date from some 23 years back, and to the amounts voted annually

for Railway Capital Works. The date on which the most expensive items of equipment of the railway become exhausted has not yet arrived and we are fortunately not too late to start a renewals fund that will cover our liabilities when the time comes.

Other renewals funds

38. It would appear sound for Government to take similar action with regard to other departments. The annual contributions required will, in comparison with the railway, be small, and the subject is one that will be fully enquired into during the coming year.

Summary of first principle

39. Summing up the first principle enunciated, if it is found at any time that the estimated revenue for the coming year is not sufficient to cover recurrent and extraordinary expenditure, plus a contribution to the Railway Renewals Fund, Government will have to reduce first extraordinary expenditure, and secondly recurrent expenditure, in that order. If on the other hand, it is estimated that there will be an appreciable surplus of revenue over the forms of expenditure mentioned, Government is in a strong position for considering any reduction of taxation or railway rates that may be considered advisable.

Second principle : Reserve Fund

40. The second principle adopted by Government is the maintenance of a sufficient Reserve Fund. Here we are in an exceptionally favourable situation in having an accumulated balance of over two million pounds. As regards this, I may say here that I am not satisfied that the balance sheet... is of a sufficiently clear nature... It appears somewhat difficult to see from it what exactly is our position with regard to reserve funds, investments, liquid balance, etc. I have therefore asked my financial advisers to produce a clear statement that will, at the same time, be in accordance with the requirements of the Secretary of State.

Present disposal of balance

41. Speaking generally, our accumulated balance of over two million pounds is disposed of as follows: (1) Partly invested at remunerative rates of interest in war loan and other securities by the Crown Agents. (2) Partly invested at small interest and at short notice. (3) Partly used for immediate necessities in connection with cash payments from month to month. (4) Partly locked up in unallocated stores.

Proposed arrangement of accumulated balance

42. In the above distribution the Reserve Fund is included under the first subhead. I do not propose to go into the details of the proposed adjustment of our present accumulated balance, as that is a subject which Honourable Members will consider with the Colonial Secretary in Select Committee. Generally speaking it should be considered in future under four heads: (1) A General Reserve Fund. (2) Unallocated Stores. (3) Cash for immediate requirements. (4) Free balance.

As an example our present accumulated balance might be considered as distributed as follows:—

	(£s)
General Reserve Fund	500,000
Unallocated stores	290,000
Cash requirements	100,000
Free balance	1,210,000
Total accumulated balance	£2,100,000

General Reserve Fund

43. With regard to the above division, the maintenance of a sufficient reserve fund is the first essential of sound finance. The Secretary of State has already approved of the amount being fixed at £500,000 and has given instructions that it should not be touched without reference to him. The principle should be strictly observed that no request should be made to expend this fund except under such totally unusual conditions as the temporary and complete failure of trade; and in any case not until the greatest possible reduction has been effected in special, extraordinary, and recurrent expenditure in the order named. This reserve fund should be increased annually by the interest derived from its investment, but when the total reaches two millions it might well be retained at that figure and the resulting interest used to benefit general revenue.

Unallocated stores

44. The unallocated stores of departments should not exceed £250,000 and it is probable that the cash requirements will seldom exceed £100,000.

45. I have not included the Railway Renewals Fund in the accumulated balance as this fund is formed by an annual contribution from revenue and is a separate fund. Naturally it will add to the general assets of the country, and will be invested, but it will be an asset that is earmarked for providing for railway renewals.

Free balance

46. I now come to an item in our accumulated balance which is of the utmost importance to us at the present time, viz the free or liquid balance which remains after providing for the items just mentioned. This free balance amounts to approximately £1,210,000.

The question arises, what is the most profitable use to make of this large sum? Are we to lock it up and merely draw the interest from it, or are we to use a part of it for capital works with the object of reducing extraordinary expenditure and possibly of reducing taxation?

Free balance and taxation

47. Before dealing with this question I should like to allude to a suggestion that has been strongly made in some quarters, viz that we should at once reduce duties or railway rates and use the free balance to make good our loss. The principle does not appear to me to be sound. To reduce taxation means to reduce revenue, and to reduce revenue for two or three years by parting permanently with our savings would not be good finance. It is equivalent to living on capital. Supporters of this scheme contend that reduction of taxation will not mean reduction of revenue; they say trade would benefit, and that its increase will automatically make up the loss. They say that this has been proved by the results of reducing the cocoa duty

in the past year. The likelihood of this fortunate result being repeated with any certainty if we make further reductions in taxation is, to my mind, problematical. I consider the chances are very much modified by five circumstances:

(1) That you can overdo reduction. We have already reduced and must mark time to see what its ultimate effects really are going to be.

(2) This year's revenue benefited by the late date on which the reduction took place.

(3) We have now, in the interest of good finance, added a Railway Reserve Fund to our annual expenditure.

(4) Most important of all, our transport facilities are still not far enough advanced to permit of a sufficiently increased export of cocoa to make up the loss caused by a reduction of duties.

(5) Finally it is not my opinion that our taxation is oppressive in view both of what the people of the country are getting for it and of the fact that it is far less than that of any other country.

48. Nor, in view of the fact that we have an ample reserve fund, would it be sound finance in the present state of the Colony to lock up our free balance. It would be far more advisable to expend carefully a portion of it on capital works that are urgently required.

Special expenditure out of free balance

At the present moment the Gold Coast is urgently in need of new roads, water supplies, buildings, etc. If the current revenue has to cover all the expenditure involved, taxation would not only require to be increased but any question of reducing it would be manifestly impossible. If the country did not possess a large free balance it would only be possible to construct a totally inadequate – in view of our necessities – number of those urgently required public works. Fortunately, as I have shown, we have a free balance of £1,210,000. By deliberately earmarking a portion of this free balance to certain public works, under a head entitled 'Special expenditure out of free balance', the country will be able to undertake the more urgently required works. Some of these are at present being carried out under 'extraordinary expenditure', with the result as I have already pointed out, of inflating that head to such an extent that the revenue has to maintain too high or an annual deficit to be reckoned with. Consequently in the estimates for the coming year I have asked Honourable Members to vote certain sums under the heading of 'Special expenditure out of free balance.'

49. The special expenditure to which I have referred can be divided into two classes, viz revenue-producing works and non-revenue-producing works.

Revenue-producing works

Revenue-producing works are in every way thoroughly justifiable so long as the resulting revenue covers the cost of running, maintenance and renewals, and the payment of interest on the capital outlay. The works constructed would be of the nature of electric lighting, pipe-borne water supplies, road rails, tramways, etc.

Loans to municipal councils

50. This class of revenue-producing expenditure can also conveniently include any loans or advance made to municipal councils or similar authorities (on the payment of interest and sinking fund) for the construction of local works. This

form of expenditure by Government of its free balance can be justified by the necessity for keeping the larger trade centres, and especially the sea ports on which all our trade depends, in a thoroughly sanitary condition to prevent loss of trade through long periods of quarantine. The very small rate of interest charged on these loans can be considered as a fair charge against the local inhabitants in return for the great benefits they receive from local improvements. The share of the country at large in the maintenance of any particular sea port would continue to be represented by an annual grant under extraordinary expenditure.

Non-revenue-producing works

51. With regard to the second form of Special expenditure, viz on non-revenue-producing works, it is possible that some Honourable Members may raise objections. The circumstances in which we find ourselves are, however, of a special nature as I shall endeavour to show.

There are certain works which, although they will not return direct revenue, are urgently required by the advance of civilisation and the general progress of the country. They are works which the country has not been able to afford in the past owing to lack of funds, or which it could not afford to undertake in the future without either a loan or increased taxation.

Arrears of works

52. The long spell of enforced economy during the war and the subsequent period of trade depression prevented the construction of many urgently needed works. Concurrently, however, the cocoa trade advanced at a phenomenal rate, from an export of 52,000 tons in 1914 to 160,000 tons in 1921–2. The resulting accession of prosperity vastly and justifiably increased the needs of the population, both in such material directions as transportation, and in such other directions as increased facilities for education, sanitation, medicine, and water supplies. In addition to these necessities of the general population, the requirements of Government itself have largely increased. Prisons, court-houses and quarters have all become deficient in accommodation.

The size of our accumulated balance indicates that more might have been spent in these directions in the last few years. On the other hand the trade outlook warranted caution being observed when we met to draw up the estimates every year. The result has been that we now have a free balance of £1,210,000. Government proposes to spend part of this, as I have already explained, on revenue-producing works, and in addition to expend part on some of the works that are greatly in arrears.

Programme of special works

53. Unless a definite programme of expenditure on special works is definitely laid down there will be great difficulty in differentiating between the works to be constructed under special and extraordinary expenditure respectively.

The programme of special expenditure for the coming year is shown in the estimates, and it will be seen that the non-revenue-producing items are three in number, viz:

(1) Hospital. The completion of the great central medical institution known as the Gold Coast Hospital, to which I have referred earlier in my address. About £130,000 has already been spent on this hospital under extraordinary expenditure, and its completion requires a sum of £47,450 in the coming financial year.

(2) Secondary school. The construction of the great central training institution known as the Gold Coast Secondary School, to which also I have referred in my remarks on education. Preliminary expenditure on this school to the extent of some £20,000 has already been incurred under extraordinary expenditure.

(3) Arrears of quarters. The third and last item of the special programme is the completion of the arrears of quarters for Government officials. At present in the whole country there are some 200 officials either doubled up in single quarters or living in temporary bush huts of mud and wattle. This insanitary and uncomfortable method of living has a serious effect on efficiency, an effect which has been accentuated by the lengthened tour of service recently introduced, and which renders it both advisable and paying for the Government to provide healthy and adequate quarters. In addition to this, Government is annually paying a fairly large sum for rental and doubling-up and bush-hut allowances. Approximately eighty quarters are required and there appears no sound reason, with such a fluid balance as we possess, for spreading construction over ten or fifteen years, as would be necessary if the work were to be undertaken out of current revenue. In addition to this, if the actual work of construction is concentrated in two to three years, economy will be effected in supervision.

Revenue from special expenditure

54. While it has been comparatively easy to draw up the above programme for the construction of non-revenue-earning works, it has been somewhat more difficult to do so in the case of revenue-earning works. I do not propose to enter into details of the proposed programme here, as the various items are included in the development programme given at the end of the printed copy of my address, and can be fully discussed in Select Committee. In some cases it is doubtful whether the revenue resulting from some of the works will do more than cover maintenance, renewals, and interest on the capital outlay. In other cases, such as the Accra electric light and power, the new trunk telephones, the agricultural plantations, and the forestry sawmills, the revenue resulting will add annually to general revenue a further sum equivalent to a generous sinking fund. In the case of water supplies the question is complicated by the fact that the system of rates has not yet been fully organised; this is now under consideration by a special committee.

Water rates

I may here say that Government does not propose to install expensive pipe-borne water-supplies unless there is a reasonable prospect that the revenue from the rates will pay for maintenance, renewals, and interest. The same principle will apply to the wholesale extension of any existing pipe-borne supply to a new village or a new quarter of a town. Minor extensions will, for the present, continue to be an extraordinary charge.

Development programme

55. When examining those items in the Development programme which it is proposed to charge against special expenditure, Honourable Members should note three points. (1) . . . The expenditure that the free balance will permit in the ten years 1920–30. (2) . . . What we have already spent on the various items. Previous expenditure has, of course, been under the head ' extraordinary '. To arrive at the total amount that we propose to expend in the next seven years it is therefore necessary to deduct the figures in the second column from those in the first.

(3) I would ask Honourable Members to bear clearly in mind that the figures given are merely proposals showing how we can, as we are at present situated, carry out a definite programme. Should at any time we encounter a period of revenue depression we can postpone a large number of items.

Total special expenditure

56. Altogether Government proposes to spend on special works:

Revenue-producing works	£606,000
Non-revenue-producing works	£340,000
	£946,000

The above amount is what Government proposes to spend out of its free balance of £1,200,000. This expenditure will extend over seven years and in the meantime the general revenue will directly benefit by the returns received. This eventually will be directly conducive to the reduction of taxation.

Advantages of special expenditure

57. Summing up, the advantages of the proposed special expenditure are as follows:

(1) It will provide the water supplies, sanitary improvements, lighting, telegraphic communications, and new agricultural industries demanded by the general progress of the country; and at the same time produce a revenue that will cover outlay, maintain renewals and interest on the capital.

(2) It will provide a medical institution necessary for the training of the large African staff required for efficiently carrying out the Government's duty in improving the conditions of health and sanitation of the people.

(3) It will provide the great secondary school without which no real intellectual, material, or industrial advance can be made by the people of this country.

(4) It will provide those arrears of quarters which are demanded by the Government in the interests of the health and efficiency of its officials.

In concluding my remarks on this new form of expenditure I can only record my deep conviction that it is the only way by which we can carry out at a reasonably early date the developments so urgently required in the cause of progress and at the same time hope from the revenue received therefrom to reduce present taxation.

Bibliography

11. *Report of a Committee on Trade and Taxation for British West Africa*, Cmd 1600, London 1922, paras 29–31 (extracts).
12. *Legislative Council Debates, 1916–17*, pp. 82–91 (extracts).
13. *Report of a Committee on Trade and Taxation for British West Africa*, Cmd 1600, London 1922, paras 126–46 (extracts).
14. Governor's Annual Address, *Legislative Council Debates, 1924–5*, pp. 27–33.
15. Despatch from the Governor to the Secretary of State dated 17 August 1922, with reference to statements on the future financial position of the Colony, made in the report of the Committee on Trade and Taxation for British West Africa, *Sessional Paper no. VII, 1921–2* (extracts).
16. Governor's Annual Address, *Legislative Council Debates, 1923–4*, pp. 19–33.

3. Transport

It was through its transport policy that the colonial government exercised most direct influence over the economy and it was transport, particularly railways and harbours, which got the lion's share of government resources during the expansionary phase of colonialism in the twenties. This chapter is primarily concerned with policies of this period, both those that were implemented and those that never got beyond the stage of proposal, and with how the government at a later date sought to deal with the consequences of development during the decade. The documents presented here can be grouped under four heads: 1. general surveys of the transport system and transport policy; 2. rates to be charged by government transport facilities; 3. new railway routes, built, and proposed but not built; 4. road versus rail.

Ormsby-Gore's survey of the transport system and government policy (Document 17) anticipates issues dealt with more fully in subsequent documents. In addition to surveying port and railway facilities and outlining proposals for expansion, he also touched upon the matter of railway rates, giving figures to show that the rates paid on cocoa were relatively high and that it was ' cocoa and cocoa alone, [that] at present enables the railway to pay its way '. In 1926 the road–rail competition had not yet matured into a serious problem for the colonial government and Ormsby-Gore's comments on roads (' The Gold Coast has the best and most developed system of motorable roads in British Tropical Africa ') carry no forecast of the problems that arose so soon after he had visited the country. He does, however, conclude his remarks on road transport on a note that was to be repeated many times when Ghanaian lorry owners had started to compete effectively with the government railways; ' while fully recognizing the great part played by motor transport in the recent development of the Gold Coast ', he wrote, ' one cannot help feeling that the business has yet to be brought on to a sound commercial basis '.

In the colonial view of the development of transport in the twenties, railways had first priority and road transport was allocated a subordinate role. This view was presented somewhat dramatically by the Governor in his annual address to the Legislative Council in 1923 (Document 18). ' With more railways ', he said, ' we shall be safe for all time – without them our future is not only imperilled, it is doomed.' The limited importance and value of roads was stated as follows:

> The only advantage at present gained by using motor transport is that it is less costly than head carriage, and more economical in man power. On feeder roads to railways and ports, lorries are invaluable up to a distance of about 35 miles and will always have their uses; but on long trunk roads . . . they are not a practical proposition. It is obvious that motor lorries can only be regarded as temporary and inadequate measures in meeting the general demands for trade in this country.[1]

In his annual address for the following year the Governor turned his attention to the question of railway rates (Document 19), which were being disputed by various elements of the commercial community as part of the issue of the level of taxation. The Governor put the government's case as follows:

> The rates on a railway that has a correct financial policy should not be considered as taxation. The correct financial policy of a government railway is, in my opinion, that its annual earnings should cover its maintenance and running costs, its annual debt and pension charges and an annual contribution to its renewals funds, which last-named item is nothing more or less than maintenance. I consider that these are sound business principles. They would not apply to a privately owned railway system, for the latter must have shareholders and shareholders must have dividends. Under normal conditions a Government railway which makes a profit may be fairly considered as a means of taxation.[2]

Document 20a presents the government's reasons for building the Central Province Railway which, as we have noted (p. 23 above), was an essential adjunct to the decision to locate the deep-water harbour at Takoradi in the west of the country. In addition to the arguments that the future of the cocoa trade was dependent upon the provision of cheap rail transport and that lorries were uneconomic over distances of 35 miles, an additional one was put forward, to the effect that railways were preferable to roads since they produced revenue directly. While the government emphasised that the most important purpose of the line was to assist the cocoa industry, it went to great pains to show how it would help the export of other crops. We have argued that by the colonial government's own criteria this line was not rationally located and that it was of no assistance at all to the cocoa industry. The other lines which the government planned but never constructed in the twenties were not directed towards the main cocoa-growing areas at all and the interests of the cocoa industry figured only as a marginal consideration, if they were considered at all, in the choice of routes (Documents 20a and 20b). The proposed Western Province line was to run from Tarkwa to Bibiani, a route chosen for two reasons: 1. The likely development in the near future of the bauxite deposits in the Sefwi-Bekwai district. 2. The re-opening under the

[1] Document 18, para. 81.
[2] Document 19, para. 25.

control of the Ashanti Goldfields Corporation of the gold mine at Bibiani which had been shut down for a number of years. The proposed Northern Territories line, promoted by the United Africa Company, was primarily concerned with shea-nuts. No serious consideration was given to the possibility of building a line to Trans-Volta, through the area which was an important supplier of food.

The expansion of road transport was greatest in and around the cocoa belt and the first victim of reduced charges on lorries was the Central Province Railway. The intention of the colonial government in building this line was to move cocoa westwards across the country and ship it overseas through Takoradi, but farmers and merchants found it cheaper to move their cocoa down to the coast by road and then overseas through the Central Province ports of Cape Coast and Saltpond. The general manager of the railways argued that if these ports remained open the Central Province Railway 'would practically be a financial failure for some years'. Strong opposition to this position developed and a committee was set up in 1928 by the Governor to examine the whole question of 'trade routes' in the Central Province (Document 21). The debate on whether to close the ports was finally settled in favour of local interests against their closure, who were able to produce assurances from the previous governor in 1922 that the construction of the new railway would not 'injure' local interests 'nor after the opening of Takoradi would Cape Coast or Saltpond become sufferance wharves'.

Road competition affected not only the Central Province Railway but also drew traffic away from the southern stretch of the Accra–Koforidua line, which ran into the cocoa areas. This section of the railway system was the most productive of all and yielded considerable revenue to the government; competition from Ghanaian road transport enterprises threw the whole government transport system into deficit. In 1928 the Governor gave a strong hint of the likely direction of government policy when he quoted an extract from a policy statement of a Colonial Office conference:

> It should be borne in mind that Colonial Governments have very heavy commitments in their railways . . . It is difficult to see how they could afford to let their railways become unremunerative. In order to prevent such a misfortune without unduly crippling road motor development it is imperative that roads should be planned wherever possible in such a way as to cooperate and feed, rather than compete with the railways.

But, of course, by 1928 it was impossible in Ghana to prevent the competition occurring; the problem of the colonial government was how to handle it after it had already reached an advanced stage. The depression worsened the situation as far as the solvency of the railways was concerned and the colonial government set up two committees, in 1931 the Railway Retrenchment Committee, and in 1932 the Railway Revenue Committee (Documents 22a and 22b), to examine the financial policy of the railways in the face of competition from road transport. Among the many issues discussed by the committees the most important were the financial principles that should govern the setting of rates on the railway and whether the road transport benefited from ' unfair ' advantages. While the logic of the arguments produced in the reports of these committees is at times tortuous, three conclusions emerge quite clearly: 1. they favoured the railways against the roads; 2. they favoured European enterprise in mining against Ghanaian enterprise in cocoa; and 3. they were unable to find a fiscal solution for the problem of the railway deficits.

The consequence was that the colonial government took administrative action against road transport in the *Carriage of Goods Road Ordinance* (1936), which provided ' not for the licensing but for the prohibition of specified goods over scheduled roads '. In 1945 the Road–Rail Transport Committee (Document 23) was set up to consider whether this ordinance should remain in effect and ' what form of Government control of road services should be introduced so as to assist the development of cheap and efficient road transport, due regard being had to the public interest in the railway '. And it concluded:

We think . . . that in present circumstances the answer to the road-rail issue can be simply expressed as the removal of all prohibitions at present in force except that applying to cocoa which should also be abolished as soon as the cocoa traffic is definitely assured to the Railway by its own marketing system or by any other means.

This statement must be understood in the light of earlier ones in which railways were seen as the means of ensuring the future of the cocoa industry. The conclusion to which the documentation in this chapter points is quite the contrary; that the cocoa industry was the means of ensuring the future of the railways.

17. ' Cocoa and cocoa alone enables the railway to pay its way ': Ormsby-Gore, 1926 [1]

Ports and harbours

The tonnage and value of sea-borne trade handled at Gold Coast ports has been expanding very rapidly, as may be seen from . . . [Table 17.1].

The main increase in the tonnage of sea-borne trade in the Gold Coast has been due to the rapid increase in the output of manganese ore from 7,195 tons in 1921 to 340,000 tons in 1925. Of the total tonnage handled in 1925, no less than 559,058 tons passed through the port of Sekondi ; and it is interesting to recall that . . . an estimate made in 1924 gave only 420,000 tons as the figure which would be reached in 1927.

[1] *Report by the Honourable W. G. A. Ormsby-Gore on his visit to West Africa during the year 1926*, Cmd 2744, London, 1926, pp. 48–55 (extracts).

Table 17.1

	Total tonnage	Value (£s)
1921	378,000	12,419,000
1922	542,807	13,219,000
1923	637,540	15,306,000
1924	785,653	15,961,000
1925	920,000	17,788,000

Accra is the second most important port of the Gold Coast, being the capital of the country and the terminus of the Eastern railway, and from the point of view of value – but not tonnage – the trade of Accra is still approximately equal to that of Sekondi. It is apparent that quite apart from the question of Takoradi, the main development of the future will be at the western rather than at the eastern port, because of the development of the mining industries, the opening of the Central Province Railway (which connects with Sekondi) and the extension of the cocoa output of Ashanti and the Western Province, as against the probable decline of tonnage of cocoa produced in the Eastern Province. In addition to the two main ports there are the subsidiary surf-boat ports, of which Winneba (which ranks third), Cape Coast and Saltpond are the most important.

The inadequacy of all the existing Gold Coast ports, and the loss and damage to goods, as well as the danger and inconvenience to passengers, has already been alluded to. The capacity of Sekondi to handle existing traffic is being strained to breaking point, and it is only thanks to the very remarkable efforts, the long hours worked, and the great skill in organisation, that there has not been a serious breakdown already.

It is no part of my duty to reopen the various controversies that have ranged round the construction of a harbour at Takoradi some five miles from Sekondi. The decision to construct this harbour was taken by the late Lord Milner, who appointed Messrs Stewart and McDonnell both as consulting and constructional engineers. In 1924 this firm resigned, and a contract for the work was placed with Messrs McAlpine, the firm of Rendel, Palmer and Tritton acting as consulting engineers. Much is due to Messrs Stewart and McDonnell for the way in which they carried out the investigation and the preliminary work at the harbour. One of the chief difficulties lay in the development of the only available granite quarry in the neighbourhood. Today progress is most satisfactory. We visited the works on 9 April, and were much struck with the energy with which the work is being pressed forward.

The length of the main breakwater – the biggest work and most essential feature of the whole scheme – is to be 2,534 lineal yards. Of these, 1,700 had been completed by 9 April, leaving 834 further yards to be constructed. Including the concrete wall on the top of the breakwater there had been deposited 385,100 cubic yards of material by 9 April, of which no less than 103,400 had been put in place since 1 January 1926. This main breakwater is being built 30 feet wide at the top, with a height of 15 feet above low water. The sea face is protected by large granite blocks. I was particularly struck by the large size of the blocks now being delivered from the quarry, and it is quite clear that only by means of material on such a scale will the breakwater be enabled to stand the very heavy surf. With the recent rapid advance of the main breakwater, it has also been possible to make progress with the lee breakwater, and the construction of the lighter wharves and reclamation in the base of the harbour are also proceeding satisfactorily.

The bottle-neck all along has been the quarry, both as regards the quantity and size of the granite extracted. The present methods of exploiting the quarry seemed to be admirable, and the output of the quarry by April averaged 12,000 cubic yards a week. The rate of progress of the work can best be judged from ... [Table 17.2] of the monthly output of granite. These figures are taken not from wagon returns, but from actual measurements of stone in breakwaters and dykes.

Table 17.2

	Granite (cubic yds)
April 1925	8,631
May 1925	12,768
June 1925	12,806
July 1925	15,440
August 1925	16,896
September 1925	23,951
October 1925	27,155
November 1925	25,214
December 1925	34,199
January 1926	45,285
February 1926	43,871
March 1926	50,122

Although this rate of progress is satisfactory, it must be remembered that the estimated quantity of granite required for the main breakwater alone is over one million cubic yards.

The contract date for the final completion of the harbour is 31 December 1928, but it is now anticipated that the harbour will be partially open for commercial use before that date. The two breakwaters when completed will enclose an area of 220 acres available for anchorage. The deep-water berths for ocean-going steamers will be located along the inner side of the lee breakwater, and provide berths for two large general cargo steamers and one berth for manganese ore export, affording a depth alongside of from 25 to 32 feet at low-water. The lee breakwater can be utilised for the construction of three more berths as and when required, while for the more distant future a central pier would be constructed into the middle of the harbour to a length which would provide anything up to eight further berths.

Along the foreshore at the base of the harbour a continuous wharf is being constructed 2,000 feet in length, with low-water depths of 5 to 10 feet for the northern half, while the southern will form a timber wharf for floating mahogany and other logs out to vessels anchored in the harbour. Adjacent to the latter is a slipway for carrying out repairs, etc. to lighters and tugs.

The two general cargo berths on the lee breakwater will each be equipped with transit sheds 400 feet long and 30 feet wide, with both road and rail access, and electric cranes. At the back of the manganese wharf there is to be an open space

450 feet long and 150 wide for dumping ore. A further transit shed, as well as sites for cocoa warehouses, will be provided behind the lighter wharf. The one million-gallon service reservoir and water tower are already practically completed.

The total cost of Takoradi Harbour and port works is estimated at between £3,000,000 and £3,250,000. Over and above this there will be the cost of the lay-outs, roads, drains, new Government buildings, etc. of Takoradi town. These will involve a further expenditure of not less than £500,000. Considerable progress has already been made in the construction of roads of access and in the lay-out of the main thoroughfares of the town. A town plan of modern design has been drawn up and approved. The European and native hospitals erected by Messrs Stewart and McDonnell in connection with their work are of a permanent character, and are already in use.

At Accra there is a short breakwater, the effect of which has been to cause the silting up of the beach immediately behind it, and it would appear impossible to improve further the protection without the expenditure of a large sum of money which would not be justified.

Railways

The Gold Coast railway consists of 495 miles of line based on the seaports of Sekondi and Accra, meeting at Kumasi, the capital of Ashanti. Of this, 100 miles (the branch line from the western line at Huni Valley to Kade in the Central Province) is nearing completion and will be open for through traffic by the end of this year.

In 1924 investigation was directed by the Government into the possibility of branch lines in the Western Province of the Colony. Detailed economic and traffic surveys were obtained and made the subject of a full report by the general manager of the railways in June 1925, which established that the population and prospects of the country west of the line between Sekondi and Kumasi were far too scanty (short of any further outstanding mineral discovery) to warrant the construction of a railway. It would seem, therefore, that any project for a western branch would have to be made from Kumasi in a northwesterly direction through an area where cocoa is developing. But at present there has been no detailed investigation of this area, and any project in this direction would be affected by the route to be taken by any railway to the Northern Territories if and when that is constructed.

The Northern Territories railway is the chief problem before the Gold Coast Railway Department. The distance in a direct line from Takoradi due north to the northern frontier is roughly 440 miles. At present the railway only goes as far north as Kumasi, 168 miles by rail from the coast. Consequently the greater part of the Territory is outside the economic radius of the railway. The whole of the Northern Territories with an estimated population of half a million is quite outside its reach. The density of this population, very sparse in the neighbourhood of the Ashanti boundary, increases as the northern frontier is approached, while immediately to the north of British Territory lies the most densely populated part of the whole of French West Africa. This district of the Haute Volta contains a population of 3,000,000 with an average density of 9.3 per square kilometre. The total population of French West Africa is a little over twelve millions, with an average density of 2.6 persons per square kilometre. This Haute Volta area is not at present served by any of the French railway systems.

The Northern Territories of the Gold Coast approximate in climate and conditions to much of Northern Nigeria, and may be suitable for the cultivation of ground-nuts and American cotton. The bulk of the area is free of tsetse fly, and cattle are fairly numerous. The meat supply of the Gold Coast Colony is obtained from the Northern Territories and French territory beyond them. The present wastage of cattle driven down on the hoof is at least 50 per cent.

Consequently the Gold Coast cannot be said to have been fully developed until the railway to the Northern Territories has been constructed. That it is the duty of Government to construct such a railway as soon as the financial situation permits, is, I think, clear. It would increase the variety as well as the total of the economic products of the country, would improve and cheapen the supply of locally-grown food, especially meat, and would increase the supply and mobility of labour. All authorities are agreed that if and when the railway is constructed, it would be of no real value unless it were carried right through to Navoro, the principal trade centre in the extreme north. Alternative routes are now being surveyed, and the Engineer in charge informed me that the route from Kumasi via Tamale appeared likely to be the cheapest and most satisfactory. The chief obstacle – the Volta river – would require a bridge costing not more than £100,000. I feel that a decision cannot be arrived at until the present investigations and reconnaissance surveys are completed, and this will not be before the spring of 1928. In any case I do not think construction should be commenced before 1929, when Takoradi is complete and open. Only then can the financial position of the Colony be fully appreciated and the practicability of raising another large loan for so long an extension (approximately 380 miles) be decided.

On the existing main lines the carrying capacity of the bridges and culverts between Sekondi and Kumasi (168 miles) and Kumasi–Tafo (126 miles) is a 16-ton axle load; on the new Central Province railway the capacity is 12½ tons. On the Eastern line 12 tons from Tafo to Mangoase (26 miles) and 10 tons from Mangoase to Accra (39 miles). The heaviest rail is on the Sekondi–Obuasi (124 miles) section of the Western line, which is 80 lb per yard, and the lightest 45 lb between Accra and Mangoase. The maximum grades are 1 per cent against exports except on the Accra–Mangoase section where the ruling grade is 1 in 80, and 1 in 80 throughout against imports. The maximum curves are of 1 per cent radius. The short Prestea branch (18 miles) has a capacity of only 6½ tons axle loads, 1.40 grades, and 330 feet radius for curves.

The heaviest engines and trains now in use are those engaged in the manganese ore traffic from Insuta (mile 36) to Sekondi. These engines have 13-ton axle loads and haul trains of 750 tons gross representing 500 tons of ore. Manganese ore and wood (firewood and timber props) for the gold mines constitute over 50 per cent of the total tonnage hauled by the railway. Unfortunately these are all ' short hauls '. The approximate average rate charged by the railway on both categories of goods is 5*d* per ton mile. Coal is carried to the mines at an even lower rate, namely 3*d* per ton mile. At the present scale of rates the railway is just paying – that is to say, after defraying all proper charges on railway account. In the Gold Coast the form of presenting the railway accounts for the financial year 1925/6 will show a true separation of Colonial and railway finance for the first time. The result is estimated to produce a small profit of about £18,000 on a gross revenue of about £1,000,000. It would appear that unless there is an increase in the tonnage carried over the longer hauls, and unless the railway system expands so as to secure more economical working, there is no possibility of further reductions in railway rates.

Cocoa, and cocoa alone, at present enables the railway to pay its way, and the rate on this commodity varies from *9d* to *5d* per ton mile. In the neighbourhood of Accra fierce competition obtains between the railway and motor transport for the carriage of cocoa and of the more expensive articles of import. Any further attempt of the railway to meet this competition by special local reduction of rates would to my mind, be undesirable. If motor transport in this particular area can beat the railway, let it. The present railway revenue from cocoa is over £400,000 a year, and no appreciable reduction of the rates now in force would be possible without throwing upon the general taxpayer the necessity of subsidising the cocoa rate. This, I think, would be quite unjustifiable. The actual tonnage of cocoa carried by the railway was 119,114 tons in the calendar year 1921, and 156,148 tons in the financial year 1924/5.

The new railway workshops at Sekondi – the headquarters of the Gold Coast railways – are nearing completion, and when completed will provide an up-to-date and economical means of dealing with all requirements. Altogether, I was much impressed by the progress and efficiency achieved by the Gold Coast railway management, bearing in mind the remarkable development of trade during the last five years.

Roads

The Gold Coast has the best and most developed system of motorable roads in British Tropical Africa. The total mileage is now 4,734 of which no less than 3,434 have been constructed in the last six years. The work is still going steadily on. A new and comprehensive system of feeder roads to the new Central Province railway is being undertaken. Most of these, together with some additional roads in the Eastern province and Southern Ashanti, are being carried out by a special temporary Roads Department personnel seconded from the Royal Engineers. Both the Public Works Department and native authorities are also engaged in extending in each year the road system in North Western Ashanti, the Western Province, and Southern Togoland. It is in the Northern Territories, however, that some of the greatest feats of road building have been accomplished. The 'great northern road' from Kumasi to Tamale, a distance of 240 miles, is a really first class motor road. Mr Flood made a complete circuit by motor of the Northern Territories from Kumasi, visiting Tamale, Yendi, Navoro, Wa, Bole, Kintampo back to Kumasi, a distance of 1,140 miles in 14 days. During a recent traffic census it was recorded that in six months 1,500 motor vehicles, and 600 trailers crossed the Volta ferry at Yeji between Kumasi and Tamale.

I should especially like to mention the construction of a new road by the two Konors (Paramount Chiefs) of Kroboland (Eastern Province) over the Akwapim hills from Odumase. I had the personal privilege of opening this new road constructed by the Chiefs and their people entirely on their own initiative through very difficult but very rich forest country. The achievement reflects the greatest credit on all concerned.

I have already alluded to the special Tarmet roads of the Gold Coast and the strain put upon the roads by the rapid expansion of motor transport. Undoubtedly the wear and tear to the roads, especially in the height of the cocoa season, is very great, and as is perhaps not unnatural in a country where there are many competing native private owners, as well as European transport companies, there has been a tendency to overload and overdrive all forms of motor transport. Limitations of weight and speed for different types of vehicle have necessarily been imposed with a view to reducing the cost of road maintenance. The police have undoubtedly had a hard task in endeavouring to enforce the law and in proportion as they have succeeded there have been complaints regarding the interference of the State in this matter. It would be impossible for the Government to leave the matter without any restrictions – if only in the interest of life and property – and there are limits to what the Gold Coast can afford on annual road maintenance.

Further there has been a good deal of cut-throat competition between the lorry owners during the last two years, and rates have been cut so low that in many cases no allowance has been made for depreciation, and some transport concerns have been carried on quite uneconomically. Under these circumstances people must expect to lose money, and if the speed regulations operate as a further steadying influence it will not be at all a bad thing. While fully recognising the great part played by motor transport in the recent development of the Gold Coast, one cannot help feeling that the business has yet to be brought on to a sound commercial basis.

18. 'With more railways we shall be safe for all time: without them our future is not only imperilled, it is doomed': the Governor, 1923 [1]

Importance of transport

77. I will now turn to what is, without any doubt whatever, by far the most important subject in this country, the question of transport. If we are to increase our trade to secure the necessary funds for progress we must cheapen and extend our means of transport. More than that, and I say this with all the emphasis at my command, the future existence of our trade is seriously imperilled unless we can cheapen and extend our transport systems.

I have dealt exhaustively with the conditions and cost of transport in this country, and have gathered information as the result of long and close personal investigation of the problem by myself and by my transport and agricultural officers. I ask Honourable Members to make a close study of the facts, and I appeal to all classes of the community to put on one side all personal and local considerations and to give their valuable assistance to the Government in averting the great danger that undoubtedly threatens the Gold Coast if we do not by every means in our power cheapen and extend our transport facilities.

Present cost

78. Careful and patient enquiries show that the following are the costs of transport per ton mile by our different systems:

Transport by:

Head	5*s* to 6*s*
Lorry	2*s* 9*d*
Road-rail	1*s*
Railways	first 50 miles, 7½*d*; second 50 6*d* third 50, 4½*d*; fourth 50, 3*d*

[1] Governor's Annual Address, *Legislative Council Debates, 1923–4*, pp. 42–55 (extracts).

Head transport

79. With regard to head transport, a ton of cocoa equals 33⅓ headloads at 60 lbs; a day's journey is approximately 15 miles; the cost of a carrier is 1*s* 6*d* per day, which I may say is a very moderate estimate for the cocoa season, and 6*d* per day for the return journey if without a load. Mr Batty, in his evidence before the Trade and Taxation Committee, gives 6*s* 3*d* per head ton mile as his estimate; this is more likely to be correct than my 5*s* to 6*s*. In any case the high cost affects trade, and with low market prices the effect cannot but be injurious to the sale of cocoa.

Lorry costs

80. With regard to lorry transport, by far the majority of our motor roads are not capable of taking heavier loads than 15 cwt and about 10 cwt in a trailer. Heavy rains often result in temporary closing of roads, causing considerable inconvenience and expense to merchants. I have found some difficulty in obtaining from local transport companies a satisfactory estimate of the cost per lorry ton mile. This is due to the varying nature of the roads in different localities, and to the fact that at least 50 per cent of the return journeys are made empty except for a few passengers. The fact that transport companies are often part of a large commercial concern is in itself not conducive to eliciting reliable information. Mr Batty, in the tables which he laid before the Trade and Taxation Committee, estimates the cost of motor transport at figures varying between 3*s* 2*d* and 3*s* 4*d* per ton mile. This is probably fairly correct, and is well confirmed by the reliable statistics that we have recently produced in the reorganised Government motor transport service. Mr Batty evidently goes on the sound principle of including overhead charges in calculating rates, whereas locally I find that there is a strong disinclination to adopt this course. Someone, obviously, has to pay these.

My final conclusion is that, allowing generously for casual passengers on the return journey, the average cost per ton mile of lorry transport is 2*s* 9*d*. Companies that form part of a general commercial business undoubtedly reduced this rate, but in the end the full rate of 2*s* 9*d* is borne indirectly by the consumer of imports and the farmer. If, for example, a company carries cocoa for 1*s* 6*d* a ton mile it is obvious that it must make good the loss of the other 1*s* 3*d* in some way or another. Presumably this is done by charging more for imported goods or giving less for cocoa; in any case it is the consumer or the producer that pays.

Economic limits of lorries

81. It is obvious from the figures I have given that head-transport should be replaced by motor lorries as rapidly as possible; it is wasteful of the manpower required for cocoa-producing, and particularly wasteful in view of our limited population; it is ruinously expensive, especially in the cocoa season.

Although lorry transport is cheaper than head-carriage, it must however be borne in mind that there are distinct economic limits beyond which it is not a satisfactorily paying proposition. This distance depends chiefly on the weights which we can build our roads to carry, and also on the market price of cocoa. Take for example, the case of Oda (Nsuaem). The cost of transporting by lorry a ton of cocoa to the nearest port, Saltpond, a distance of 63 miles is £8 13*s* 0*d* whether the price of cocoa at home is £30 a ton or £50 a ton. If the home price is

£42 a ton the farmer would receive 8*s* 6*d* a load; if it is £35 a ton he would receive 4*s* 8*d*.

Numerous other examples will be found in the despatch to which I have referred. Apart, however, from the question of trade, the construction and maintenance of even our light roads is annually becoming a greater drain on the revenue. This is a fact that does not tend to the reduction of taxation. Indirect revenue there may be, but, directly, money is all going out and none coming in. The only advantage at present gained by using motor transport is that it is less costly than head-carriage, and more economical in manpower. On feeder roads to railways and ports, lorries are invaluable up to a distance of about 35 miles and will always have their uses; but on long trunk roads of the nature of those running from Winnebah and Saltpond to Nsuaem and from Cape Coast to Prahsu, they are not a practicable proposition. It is obvious that motor lorries can only be regarded as temporary and inadequate measures in meeting the general demands of trade in this country. Both the cocoa and kola trades are seriously handicapped by long distances run, and the price of imported goods in the interior is kept at a high level.

Value of railways to trade

82. In view of the comparison just made between the cost of transport by rail and by lorry, it seems useless to labour the question further. I ask Honourable Members, however, to consider seriously if it is not better for the Government to provide railways where motor-roads have gone beyond their economical limits. A railway is the cheapest form of transport, and in addition it covers all the expenses of maintenance and capital cost. Lorry roads, on the other hand, though useful up to a range of 35 miles, do not actually recover the cost of construction and maintenance, which it must be remembered, is eventually paid by the trader and the farmer. Undoubtedly motor-roads bring an indirect return from increased trade, but so does a railway and to a far greater extent.

Transport and competition

83. I now come to the most important aspect of the situation. Even if our transport facilities are adequate to deal with our present trade, which I venture to say very few people can assert, are they sufficiently cheap to enable us to maintain it against the competition of other countries? If there is no likelihood of this competition increasing, it is possible that a moderate annual outlay on communications might in due course even increase our trade.

But what is the situation? As Honourable Members are aware, the Gold Coast at present produces more cocoa than any other country in the world. We are responsible for more than one-third of the world's production. The nearest country to us is Brazil, with only one-quarter of our crop. Even during the present period, when several European markets are closed, the world's consumption apparently exceeds the supply. With the restoration of normal trade, we ought therefore to be thoroughly satisfied with our position.

This happy state of affairs, is, however, not going to continue indefinitely. There is a small cloud on the horizon, a very small storm cloud that promises to grow steadily and steadily until the whole sky is overcast. Like wise traders who are compelled to sell their goods in the open, we must put up our awnings against the coming rain. These awnings are railways.

Cocoa competition with Nigeria

84. To see the nature of this little cloud I must draw the attention of Honourable Members to certain activities in neighbouring colonies. Other countries in the world have been attracted by our success with cocoa. Among those locally are Nigeria, the Cameroons, Sierra Leone, and I believe both Dahomey and the Ivory Coast. All these countries have been for some time past, and are still, engaged in planting cocoa. Notable among them are Nigeria and the Cameroons. Nigeria with her extensive waterways, her active programme of railway construction, exported 19,000 tons from 1907–13. In the six years 1914–20 she exported 92,000 tons. I have not got the figures for the Cameroons, but judging from our own and French activity in the mandated areas, she also is likely to become at no distant date, a serious rival.

Increased annual production

In ten years Nigeria has multiplied her production by six, the Gold Coast by four. There is no reason whatever, from what I hear, why in five years' time Nigeria should not be exporting 40,000 tons a year, and in ten years' time 100,000 tons. I hope, and feel confident, that in the two corresponding periods we will have increased our exports of cocoa to 200,000 tons respectively. This, I may add, we can only do if we increase our railways. The final result will be that in 1927 Nigeria and the Gold Coast alone will have added about 80,000 tons to the world's production and in 1932 about 160,000.

World's cocoa consumption

85. The question arises, can the world absorb this additional production of Nigeria and the Gold Coast, as well as the increase probable in other countries? In discussing this question I have been told that all will be well when Germany, Russia and Austria recover from the war, and when French trade again becomes normal. In answering, I will first draw Honourable Members' attention to the [following] figures [Table 18.1], showing the approximate consumption of certain countries in 1913 and in 1921.

Table 18.1

	1913	1921
United States of America	67,000	124,000
Germany	51,000	102,000
Great Britain	27,000	47,000
France	27,000	33,000
Holland	30,000	28,000
Switzerland	10,000	6,000
Spain	6,000	8,000
Canada	2,000	6,000
Italy	2,000	4,000
Belgium	6,000	8,000
Norway	1,000	3,000
Austria	6,000	3,000
Russia	5,000	Nil.
Other countries omitted	—	—
Totals	251,000	390,000

Will peace increase demand

86. In the case of Germany the figures are baffling. She apparently consumed twice as much cocoa in 1921 as in 1913. French consumption went up but she took 18,000 less than she did in 1919. Taking France and Germany together, they consumed 57,000 more tons in 1921 than they did in 1913. I am unable to find out whether this increase is likely to be maintained.

If the figures concerning Russia and Austria are correct, I cannot see that we have very great hopes of the restoration of their trade conditions bringing in a greatly increased demand for cocoa. Their combined consumption in 1913 was 11,000 tons. In 1921 it was 3,000. It seems likely that the revival of trade in those countries will bring a certain increased demand but apparently not a very great one.

In view of the figures which I have just given I find it difficult to believe that the restoration of normal conditions in Europe is going to increase consumption to such an extent that it will absorb the great additional production that is certain. I sincerely trust that it may be so, and also that the yearly increasing demand for cocoa-fat may do something towards meeting the increased production.

Production v. consumption

87. Even, however, if this proves to be the case, I think that no observant person can deny that at the present moment production is rapidly catching up consumption. Restoration of economic conditions in Europe is not going to be effected in a brief period, and in the interval production is going on steadily increasing. A moment must arrive, if indeed it has not already done so, when the cocoa-bearing countries of the world are over-producing. The price of every commodity in the world is subject to the law of supply and demand. Putting aside the high prices of the boom year, the present price of cocoa is low compared with other years. There is and must be a limit to what the world can consume. Within reason, there is no limit to what the world can produce. The more the world produces the lower will fall the price of cocoa.

Lesson from rubber

88. I would remind Honourable Members of the great rubber boom of a few years back, a boom that corresponds strikingly to our great cocoa boom. There was a universal demand for rubber far exceeding the supply, and the price rose to half a crown a pound. Fortunes were made, rubber plantations increased, everywhere there was great local prosperity. Then came the reaction, there was over-supply, and last year the price was 10½*d*. I wonder, Honourable Members, if the Legislative Councils of rubber colonies in their prosperous days ever felt alarmed about over-production? Did they see it coming, and did they strain every nerve to improve their communications and cheapen their transport so as to compete with their rivals?

Urgency for more railways

89. Honourable Members, we have our rivals, and, to use a hackneyed expression, no uncertain ones. I would have no uneasiness if they were sitting still and not building communications; but this is not the case, everywhere an active development policy is being adopted. It is essential that the Gold Coast shall not

be behindhand. Our first step to meet the coming competition has already been taken, Takoradi Harbour. The next step is to build more railways.

In five years' time I am firmly convinced that the market price of Gold Coast cocoa at Liverpool will seldom, if ever, exceed £35 a ton; and it does not require very much imagination to see it falling steadily to some £30 a ton. What the effect of this on the farmer and the merchants will be if we do not cheapen our transport I leave to the imagination. Not only are railways required but they are required now; as soon as it is possible to build them. Nothing is to be gained, everything is to be lost by deferring their construction until competition becomes intense. This intensity will first begin to be felt towards the end of 1926. By that date therefore we should have more railways. Any postponement will lead to our being beaten in the world's cocoa market. Should that occur the Gold Coast will inevitably, for a period at any rate, be in a bankrupt condition. With more railways we shall be safe for all time – without them our future is not only imperilled; it is doomed.

New line constructed

90. With regard to the work of the past year, we have made satisfactory progress with the three main items. We now have 354 miles of open lines and the completion of the last 36 miles of the Accra–Coomassie line is anticipated in June. The sections opened up to date have resulted in a steadily increasing revenue, and there is no fear but that this line, like any other line we may build in the country, will easily earn enough to more than cover expenditure on maintenance, capital outlay, and renewals. During the year I was obliged to divorce railway construction on this line from open lines, as experience has shown this to be the better system.

Deviations

91. Good progress has been made with deviations. The new line has been opened as far as Tarquah for some time, and we have been able to secure greatly increased economy by running heavier trains. This, however, is entirely due to Takoradi Harbour Works having lent the railway their new heavy engines; the delivery of our own engines was so greatly delayed by the engineers' strike in England that they are not yet erected. It is anticipated that the new line will be through to Dunkwa, 101 miles from Seccondee, before the next cocoa season; of this distance 60 miles have been relaid with 80-lb. rail. The work on deviations is being carried out by the Railway Department.

Survey, Central Province Railway

92. Good progress has been made with the survey of the Central Province Railway. We should have been severely handicapped in this survey owing to Mr Weller's retirement after long and good service, had we not available an experienced railway locator in the person of Major Silcox, whom we have fortunately been able to second from our Harbour Works staff. For the first time in the history of the Gold Coast Railway, location has been expedited by the contoured map of the Survey Department. It is possible on this map to pick out several alternative general routes, and on one of those routes Major Silcox has already located a line which, up to date, is better in gradients and curves, and will prove cheaper to construct, than in the case of any other line hitherto built.

Route of Central Province Railway

93. With regard to the route of the Central Province Railway, I held a preliminary conference on the subject with the merchants on 29 June at Accra, and between 26 August and 13 September I visited Seccondee, Cape Coast, Saltpond and Winnebah. At these places I held nine conferences with the various Chambers of Commerce, chiefs, and citizens. In each case the meeting was of a protracted nature. Throughout the conferences, the Chambers of Commerce strongly opposed the construction of any railways whatever, as they considered they would increase taxation.

Railways reduce taxation

This is a misapprehension which it is difficult to understand, for, in the past and for many years to come, it is not likely that any railway constructed in this country will cause increased taxation. On the contrary, in view of the increased trade caused by cheaper transport, new railways are directly conducive to reduction of taxation.

Effect of Central Railway on Central Province ports

94. Naturally in Cape Coast the local inhabitants were desirous of the railway starting from that town. Unfortunately this is not practicable owing to the greatly increased cost that would result both in capital outlay and in maintenance. The chief fear of the Cape Coast people is that the Central Province Railway will destroy the trade of their town. That this will not be the case I endeavoured to prove to them with, I fear, but little success. For reasons which Honourable Members will find in my despatch no. 747 I am still of the opinion that the proposed Central Province Railway will not injure the future trade of Cape Coast, Saltpond, or Winnebah. On the other hand if a railway were taken to any of these ports it would inevitably destroy the other two. Much as I sympathise with the inhabitants of Cape Coast in their desire for their town to be a railway terminal, Government is bound to provide the cheapest line for dealing with the exports of the hinterland of the Central Province. That line cannot be economically run to any other place but Secondee, and eventually Takoradi.

Procedure and cost

95. When the route for the railway has been decided on, and the Secretary of State has approved in principle of the undertaking, I propose to lay the whole question before this Council. I am glad to be able to inform Honourable Members that we have been able to reduce the cost of railway construction to the neighbourhood of £11,000 per mile. This includes rolling stock, telegraphs, and everything necessary for running the railway.

Central Railway progress 1922–3

96. Railway revenue in 1922 was £834,640, an increase of £128,000 on 1921, and earnings in January last rose to the record monthly figure of £119,000. Highly satisfactory economies have been effected in maintenance, chiefly owing to the excellent work of our new Chief Mechanical Engineer, Mr Sells, and his assistants, foremost among whom were Mr R. A. Buchanan. Other officers whose work has been specially commendable are Mr W. E. Lewis at Accra and Mr W. D. Frost at Secondee.

Railway inspection

97. I am glad to be able to inform Honourable Members that a most satisfactory inspection of the railway was carried out during the year by Lieutenant-Colonel F. D. Hammond, D.S.O., R.E. Colonel Hammond's report has been laid on the table and has proved of the utmost value in reducing expenditure. Government appreciates very highly the tact and efficiency with which he carried out his work, the successful result of which, however, is also due to the courtesy and complete cooperation of the General Manager of Railways and all his officers. To my mind the inspection was just what such an inspection ought to be, conducted on principles of constructive criticism, conference and cooperation.

P.W.D. roads

98. With regard to roads, we have maintained steady progress during the past year. The work of the Public Works Department in this respect has shown a great advance, especially in the Central and Eastern Provinces of the Colony, and, in view of the absence of metalling and of the heavy traffic during the cocoa season, must be regarded as most creditable to all concerned. The number of miles of Public Works Department road is now 1,033 and another 143 miles will be taken over next year. In addition about 230 miles of new roads have been surveyed and pegged out.

Tarmet system

Experiments in the 'Tarmet' system have proved so successful that in the coming year we are making a start in applying it to country roads. The advantages of this system are heavier loads and economy in maintenance. The cost of converting an ordinary country road to this system varies according to the distance away of metalling and water. It varies from about £800 to £1,500 a mile, according to locality. The Director of Public Works considers that £1,000 per mile may be taken as the average cost of conversion of all the roads in the country. Naturally it will be many years before we can complete all the roads in this system. In the meantime we propose to deal with those which have the heaviest traffic.

Pioneer motor-roads

99. Excellent work has been done throughout the year by the Political Officers and Chiefs in pioneer motor-road construction. The result has been an increase of trade in the several outlying cocoa districts. Approximately 200 miles of motorable pioneer roads were opened during the year, bringing the total of pioneer roads to 2,417 miles, and of all motor-roads to 3,450 miles. Good progress was made in converting wood culverts to concrete, about 300 having been dealt with in the last 12 months by cooperation between the Public Works Department, Chiefs, and Political Officers.

Expenditure 1923–4

100. In the coming year I am asking Honourable Members to vote £84,300 for all classes of new motor-road construction, an increase of nearly £22,000 on this year's expenditure, and also a further vote amounting in all to £91,500 for road maintenance.

Road committee

101. As usual the Chiefs and people have shown their appreciation of the value of motor-roads by the work they have done on them. At the request of the Honourable Nana Ofori Atta I have recently appointed a Committee in the Eastern Province to examine and report on the conditions of road-making and maintenance, especially in the case of pioneer roads. I hope that the report of this committee will contain valuable suggestions.

Road-rails

102. In view of the annually increasing cost of maintenance I am glad to inform Honourable Members that I have now received such satisfactory reports of the success of the road-rail system of transport as to justify its inclusion in our expenditure. I am now in communication on the subject with the Secretary of State with a view to obtaining his approval in principle. Pending his reply I now bring the question before this Council. Honourable Members will find that they are asked to provide £35,000 out of our free balance for the construction of a road-rail between Soadru and Winnebah. From the Government point of view the revenue from this road-rail will cover all maintenance and renewal charges, and pay 5 per cent on capital outlay. If the first idea with regard to this road, which was to convert it to the Tarmet system, is carried out, the cost will be close on £25,000, without cheapening transport materially, and without paying any interest on the capital outlay. From the merchant's point of view the road-rail will reduce his transport from 2*s* 9*d* to 1*s* per ton mile ; in other words he will save 27*s* 3*d* on every ton of cocoa or of imports between Winnebah and Soadru. Reckoning that 14,000 tons of trade pass along this road, the merchant will save £18,000 per annum on his transport. It has been represented to me that it will cost the merchant some £10,000 to move his garages from Winnebah to Soadru. Without venturing to challenge the accuracy of this estimate, I consider that even then he will make a substantial gain.

From the point of view of the Chief and people of Winnebah, the road-rail will provide a cheap form of passenger traffic and will greatly facilitate the trade in fish and foodstuffs between Winnebah and the interior.

Western Province roads

103. I am glad to be able to report that far better progress is being made with feeder roads to the railway in the Western Province of the Colony. Honourable Members will remember my criticising severely the absence of roads in the Western Province two years ago. Thanks to the energy of Mr Popham, the Provincial Commissioner, and Mr Hall, the Provincial Engineer, a good start has been made on the work.

Ashanti roads

104. By far the majority of roads in the Western Province and in Ashanti have not yet reached their economic limit, but they are steadily doing so, and the necessity for a railway is already becoming apparent. With regard to Ashanti, owing to the progress made by the Accra–Coomassie line, the most urgent requirement of the moment in feeder roads is between Nkawkaw and Juaso. I have therefore given the Chief Commissioner funds for this purpose.

Takoradi harbour

105. With regard to harbours, excellent progress has been made on the preliminary work at Takoradi. A very large amount of work of this nature is necessary in all harbour works. I have been very much impressed with the efficiency of organisation and the energy of the Harbour Works staff. In spite of being seriously handicapped by the non-delivery of materials owing to the engineers' strike in England, they hope to make up for time lost thereby. At present it is considered that the date of completion will be March 1925, a delay of three months on the original date, which Messrs Stewart and McDonnell believe they will be able to make up if no further strikes occur.

In connection with the construction of this harbour it is interesting to note that we are using the biggest steam shovel ever built in Great Britain. It would well repay Honourable Members, if they have the opportunity of visiting Takoradi, to see this shovel at work in the various operations of the harbour engineers.

Harbour Advisory Committee

106. During the year with the approval of the Secretary of State I appointed an advisory committee to examine the monthly progress reports rendered by the Chief Harbour Engineer. The Committee consists of two engineers in the persons of the General Manager of Railways and the Honourable Director of Public Works, and of a finance member in the person of the Deputy Treasurer. Up to date the reports have been satisfactory.

Accra port

107. Excellent progress, though again delayed by the engineers' strike, has been made by Messrs Stewart and McDonnell on the improvements to Accra beach. The import sheds should shortly be completed, and the general layout of the beach with sidings and roads has been taken in hand. Major Craig, the Engineer-in-Chief, has succeeded in effecting economies amounting to £10,000 on the original estimate of £100,000 and I have directed that part of this saving should be devoted to the reconstruction of the Accra Light, concerning which Honourable Members will remember that we have had many and serious complaints.

19. Railway rates not taxation : the Governor, 1924 [1]

25. So much has been said about the iniquity of our customs duties and railway rates that I feel it is incumbent on me to state clearly Government's views on this so-called taxation.

To begin with, I consider that railway rates should be left out of the question. The rates on a railway that has a correct financial policy should not be considered as taxation. The correct financial policy of a Government railway is, in my opinion, that its annual earnings should cover its maintenance and running, its annual debt and pension charges, and an annual contribution to its renewals fund, which last-named item is nothing more nor less than maintenance. I consider that

[1] Governor's Annual Address, *Legislative Council Debates, 1924–5*, pp. 18–21.

these are sound business principles. They would not apply to a privately-owned railway system, for the latter must have shareholders and the shareholders must have dividends. Under normal conditions a Government railway that makes a profit may fairly be considered as a means of taxation.

Reduction of rates effected in 1923

In point of fact our own Government railway is just paying its way. A few months ago we considered it advisable to help the cocoa trade by making reductions in rates on the Accra line. We took off the 15 per cent surcharge on cocoa and reduced the rate on petrol. By these, and other reductions, we invited a loss of some thirty to forty thousand pounds. I took this risk because the local merchants proved, to my satisfaction at any rate, that the exports of rail-borne cocoa at Accra were going to exceed our estimate. I did that as an earnest of Government's intentions with regard to the reduction of railway rates and I am prepared to consider the subject still further when the representatives of trade in this country prove to the satisfaction of me and my advisors that there is going to be an increase in our rail-borne exports. I do not see eye to eye with any expert, whatever his position may be, who advocates that a Government railway should be run at a loss. To adopt such a course would not help trade, for the loss would have to be borne by trade in some other form.

Economy in working as a factor in railway fares

26. The reduction of railway rates chiefly depends on the economical administration of the railway. Speaking generally, the cost of running per mile can be reduced in two directions. First, in the very careful organisation and administration of all branches of the railway service. Every detail demands the most careful consideration, for it affects the cost per mile. To mention a few things at random, the strength of the staff must be the lowest possible consistent with efficient running. The internal organisation of workshops for repairs must be carried out so as to secure rapidity, efficiency, and convenience in the repair and overhaul of locomotives and rolling stock. The traffic branch must be run in such a manner as to secure a convenient train service, a rapid turnover of rolling stock and a minimum of light running. The Engineering Branch, although its functions are chiefly confined to spending money, takes a very large share in the economical running of any railway, for if its work on the maintenance of the permanent way and the bridges is neglected, delays in running ensue and costs go up, while if extravagantly conducted, costs of running are again increased.

Economies effected in 1923

27. Appreciable economies have been effected in the Government railway since Colonel Hammond's visit in 1922–3, owing to the admirably willing manner in which the General Manager and the whole of his staff cooperated with him and have followed up his investigations. In a railway system such as ours, that adds between 50 and 100 miles to its open lines every year, it is difficult to see the effect of economies in staff and general expenses, for every new section means new expenditure. As, however, railway revenue increases accordingly, reliable judgment on the economical working of the line can be formed on the cost per open mile under normal conditions. In recent years this cost has not shown the reduc-

tion that might have been anticipated from the addition of new line, but the conditions have been distinctly abnormal.

Present abnormal conditions are against economical working

For one thing there was a very large increase in salaries in 1920; and to-day the railway is working under very difficult conditions indeed with regard to the repair and overhaul of locomotives and rolling stock. This will be readily understood when I say that the locomotive mileage in 1918, the year in which the present workshops were opened, was 610,000; and in 1923 had increased to 1,042,000. Steps have been taken to remedy this, and Honourable Members will notice that in the proposed loan there is an item for the improvement of terminal facilities which are bound to result in greatly improved speed and economy of working in the shops. When they are completed we may confidently anticipate reduction in the cost of running.

Congestion of railway termini

28. Another obstacle to economical railway running at the present moment lies in the confined and highly congested railway area at the port of Secondee, resulting in the long detention of covered vans by the lighterage companies and in uneconomical shunting operations. When it is considered that the tonnage handled at Secondee rose from 107,000 tons in 1911 to 340,000 tons in 1923; that the estimate for 1924 is 400,000; and that even in 1919 the cramped nature of the space available for railway working at Secondee was the subject of adverse criticism, it becomes apparent at once that the increase of over 200,000 tons since the last named date has completely swamped traffic facilities at Secondee and added greatly to the cost of running. There is, unfortunately, no remedy for the existing state of affairs until the opening of Takoradi harbour.

Turnover and overhead charges are factors in rates

29. Another factor on which railway rates depend is overhead charges. The greater the length of open lines – provided always that traffic is available and economical running is maintained – the less per mile will be the distribution of overhead charges. This is a fact which I have brought before now to the notice of Honourable Members, namely that the greater the turnover on the railway the less will be the rates. We are, I believe, just at the stage where every additional mile of new line opened is going to have a reducing effect on railway rates, and I anticipate confidently that by the time the Central Province railway is handed over to open lines an appreciable reduction will be possible.

Government is sympathetic on reduction rates

30. I have dealt somewhat fully with the subject as I felt that it was essential that, in view of the general impression that our railway rates are a form of taxation, I should enlighten Honourable Members as far as I can. I can only repeat here that any proposal that is backed by sound and well-considered arguments, and that will not result in the railway suffering a heavy loss in the coming year, will receive the sympathetic consideration of Government. I will go so far as to say that I am prepared to risk a slight loss at this particular period . . .

20a. New railways 1920–30 : (a) The Central Province Railway [1]

15. [Two witnesses] were both evidently under the impression when they gave their evidence to the Committee that cocoa duties were retarding the development of the cocoa areas. No proof whatever of this is yet evident nor is it likely to be in view of our recent reduction of the duty. What has retarded cocoa production has been the absence of sufficient communications. The farmer, with the example before his eyes of unmarketed cocoa in areas far from railways and motor-roads, is certainly not going to extend his farms until he knows that the Government is going to provide communications. Once the fact becomes certain that a railway is going to any particular neighbourhood, cocoa farms will begin to increase in number. Already, owing to the rumour that a Central Province Railway will be built into West Akim, farmers in the neighbourhood of Nsuaem, Akim Soadru, and Akyeases are appreciably increasing their planting.

From the foregoing remarks ... two points are perfectly clear: (i) that any tendency that may at present exist to stop planting is due not to the cocoa duty but to the cost of transport; (2) that definite encouragement to increase planting be given by cheapening transport facilities.

16. I now turn to a most important factor in increased rate of production, i.e. prospects of immigration into the cocoa-bearing areas of natives from the non-cocoa districts. [One witness] in his evidence before the Committee on Trade and Taxation (paragraph 676) alludes to the possibility of natives of the Northern Territories coming down to help in the cultivation of cocoa. Later, in paragraph 2,275, (the) Secretary for Native affairs deprecated any suggestion to develop the cocoa industry by an immigrant population, and agrees that Government should not take any direct steps to introduce such immigration. I am, however, strongly of opinion that such will come naturally. Ownership of the land and family and tribal ties are no doubt obstacles to immigration at present, but are not obstacles to the natural development of the system which are either insuperable or which are not now overcome. Mankind will, by natural laws, go to where food is plentiful and a profitable living is to be made ; instances of this have constantly occurred in the past in the history of Europe, and are still occurring, and it must be remembered that family and tribal ties were as strong there in the past as they are at present in the Gold Coast. Locally we have many examples of migration from the Krobo, Akwepim, and Krepi countries into neighbouring areas to take part in the cocoa industry ... Among the floating population in the Gold Coast and Ashanti that comes from the Northern Territories and neighbouring countries, a population that includes Dagombas, Gonhas, so-called Hausa, Yorubas, Lagosians, Mendis, Timinis and many other races, there are many who stay to settle. The majority of them are doubtless engaged in trade and in transport work, but there are many who are engaged in actual work in the cocoa-farms, and of these there are certainly some, a small number at present it is true, who are now coming into actual possession of plantations. Natural laws, in fact, have begun to take effect. In addition to this, the constant famines that occur in the Northern Territories must have an appreciable effect which cannot but be greatly for the good of the Gold Coast generally, for the races of the Northern Territories are

[1] Despatch from the Governor to the Secretary of State, no. 747, 2 November 1922, on the subject of the proposed Central Province Railway, *Sessional Paper no. XIV, 1922–3*, paras 15–42 (extracts). This line was constructed.

strong and virile, with barely enough food to maintain themselves throughout the year and certainly no opportunity for making a profitable living.

Summarising the question of immigration, I am strongly of the opinion that, whatever attitude Government adopts in the matter, natural laws are resulting, and will continue to result increasingly, in immigration into the cocoa-bearing areas in the Gold Coast from less productive parts of the country.

17. The last factor to be considered in estimating increased production is the accuracy of the last Census. One of the chief criticisms levelled at Government in connection with its development schemes is the inadequacy of population, doubts in particular being thrown on the 1921 Census which, it is said was over-estimated. The boot is on the other leg. If anything the population was under-estimated, and it is my opinion, and that of many officers whose duties carry them into all parts of the country, that it was considerably under-estimated. In a country of this nature no really satisfactory census can be taken in the rural areas unless (the political officer is well acquainted with) every town, village, and farm hamlet in his district. As your Grace is aware, the small staff of Political Officers that we were able to afford in the past led to their being shifted constantly from district to district. Affairs in this respect have now been placed on a more satisfactory footing and permanence in district service is gradually taking effect. The older officers, however, are still suffering from the numerous transfers of the past, and the new officers who compose the vast majority of the staff had not, by 1921, attained the personal knowledge of their areas that is necessary to ensure a satisfactory census ...

Incidentally I may here mention that the latest revised figures show a population of 2,297,283, including the British Mandate of Togoland...

Other trade of the Central Province area

26. Besides cocoa, the products of the Central Province area which should be considered in connection with the railway are palm-oil and kernels, kola, and timber.

With regard to the first, any railway that would help the palm-oil industry at present would have to be taken through country which is south of the cocoa-belt. If anything should happen to cocoa, however, it should not be forgotten that the cocoa-belt is equally suitable for the oil-palms, and that the clearing of old cocoa-farms could then be utilised for planting.

With regard to kola, it is difficult to estimate the exact production; I have asked for the information to be included in the report of the Agriculture Department... The nearest road-heads are at Nsuaem and Aiyinabrem, and, as the freight per ton to the nearest port from these towns is £8 13*s* 3*d* and £6 1*s* 0*d* respectively, it is obvious that the kola trade is seriously hampered by cost of transport. During the past few years cultivation has greatly increased, but the trade depression in Northern Nigeria, and the Nigerian import duties on kola threaten a serious check in exports.

I interviewed the Hausa chiefs at Saltpond and Cape Coast on the subject and was informed that the above-mentioned causes, combined with the cost of local transport, are handicapping them severely. Not being affected by the intense parochialism which naturally posssesses the inhabitants of the Central Ports, they received my announcement of the proposed route of the Central Province railway with unfeigned satisfaction. They consider that the saving produced by railway transport will enable them to continue their competition with Nigeria and to extend their energies. As Your Grace will doubtless remember, the Hausas (or so-called Hausas) have practically the whole of the kola trade between us and Nigeria.

With regard to timber, the valuable woods of the Central Province have practically not been touched with the exception of a very small area near the river Prah. The opening of the new railway, together with the facilities for rapid shipment at Takoradi, will undoubtedly lead to a large export. By the time the railway is completed the Forestry Department will be in thorough working order and will be able to safeguard the interests of the native owners of the forests; thus the lamentable effects of the wholesale destruction without re-afforestation of valuable timber forests in the Western Province will be avoided.

27. With regard to the imports of the Central Province area, the average of the past five years shows an annual total tonnage of some 20,000 tons landed at Winneba, Saltpond, and Cape Coast. The majority of these imports find their way by the motor-roads into the interior. By the time imports reach road-head the cost of transport has added greatly to their selling price, and naturally from road-heads onwards head-carriage does not decrease this price. The import trade of the Central Province area is therefore at present limited by the range of transport, and is certainly far under the size which it could attain.

Although it is certain that some of the import trade will be taken away from the Central Province ports by the new railway, they will continue to supply the area south of the railway zone... The import trade of the railway zone itself cannot fail to be greatly increased by the new railway. In addition to the fact that the terminus, Takoradi Harbour, will admit of cheaper ocean freights and cheaper handling, railway transport itself will immensely decrease to the merchant the cost of delivery of goods up-country. The increased spending power of the natives that will follow the anticipated extension of the cocoa industry, together with the cheaper process of imported goods, will lead to a very appreciable increase in the import trade. This is analysed later in paragraphs 32ff.

29. The object of the proposed railway is to cheapen cost of transport and thereby: (*a*) to permit of the export of cocoa at present unmarketed at low prices; (*b*) to increase cocoa production; (*c*) to save the kola trade; (*d*) to open up the timber trade; (*e*) to increase the import trade; (*f*) to facilitate competition in trade; (*g*) lastly and most important of all, to ensure the future of the cocoa trade...

31. The chief trade routes (i.e. roads) from the hinterland of the Central Province to the Central Province ports vary in quality: the majority are not capable of taking heavier traffic than light lorries with a 15 cwt load and about 10 cwt in a trailer. Heavy rains result in the temporary closing of these roads, a fact which often causes considerable inconvenience and expense to merchants when the arrival of a cargo-boat at one of the ports necessitates rapid handling of produce from up-country. Owing to the difficulty and expense of obtaining suitable metalling, and the shortage of labour caused by the population being entirely devoted to agriculture, the upkeep and construction of the roads in such a manner as to permit the use of heavy lorries (and thereby to cheapen transport) is prohibitive. It is true that the Director of Public Works has evolved a method of road construction (locally known as 'Tarmet') which is suitable to the country and will enable the roads to take lorries of a total weight (with load) of from four to five tons, but the average cost of converting existing lorry roads to this system is £1,000 per mile. Consequently, in view of the necessity for extending our present

light-road system, it will not be possible to convert more than about 40 miles per annum. This means that for many years the majority of the motor roads will only be suitable for light loads and that lorry transport will continue to be a costly business.

32. I have found some difficulty in obtaining from local transport companies a satisfactory estimate of the cost per lorry ton mile; this is understandable for it depends on the type of lorry (i.e. its possible load) and on the nature of the various roads in the district. At all the Central Province ports the tenders for lorry hire made by local companies to Government was 2*s* 6*d* per ton mile with . . . , lorries that can carry rather more than a ton if the road is in good condition. Transport for Government is, however, generally outwards from the ports and not inwards, the companies rely on bringing produce in on the return journey. The tender to Government is therefore probably not a fair indication of the actual cost. At any rate the amount of Government hire is small compared with general traffic. The private company that carries cocoa at 2*s* 6*d* per ton mile from road-head to the port must, in about 33 per cent of the cases, return empty up-country to get a further load. If this is correct, the cost of transport to the company would therefore be 3*s* 4*d* per ton mile. There are, however, certain factors that compensate to a limited extent, e.g. the carriage of passengers, and, allowing for the margin of profit, the real cost to the [haulage] company of running must be somewhere between 2*s* 9*d* and 3*s* per ton mile.

The above mentioned estimate of empty journeys is based on the trade of the Central Province ports. In the last four years this was:

Exports	122,000 tons	(say 30,000 annually)
Imports	78,000 „	(say 20,000 annually)

The whole of the exports were by lorry from up-country. With regard to the imports their disposal is approximately as follows:

Consumed by Government and the population of and around the ports	5,000
Consumed by the population south of the line Akoraso–Aiyinabrem	10,000
Consumed north of above line	5,000
	20,000

While therefore, 30,000 tons come down by lorry, only 15,000 tons go up, namely, 50 per cent empty journeys. Allowing, generously, for passengers, it is reasonable to assume that 33 per cent of the lorry journeys are made empty.

The managers of transport companies are naturally loth to give to Government too many details concerning their charges. From answers to my questions I deduce that 2*s* 6*d* a ton mile is not a paying proposition under present conditions. . .

Further, you will notice that, in paragraph 10 of the report on motor transport attached to my despatch No. 452 of 14 July [it was] reckoned at that time that the cost per ton mile by autocar was 2*s* 7*d* but that allowing for one way empty it was 5*s* 2*d*. This amount strengthens my conviction that the half-crown rate of the merchants is a false estimate of cost, as it depends on a full return load. My final conclusion therefore is that 2*s* 9*d* per ton mile is the minimum cost of lorry transport that is borne by the consumer of imports, for, though 2*s* 6*d* may be the rate of hire, he must pay the other 3*d* indirectly, probably in the selling cost of imported goods, for the merchant must make up his loss somewhere.

33. Lorry transport, however, is only available at road-head; beyond that point

the cost of head-transport has to be considered. The disadvantages of this are: (1) it is wasteful of manpower in cocoa production in view of the limited population; (2) it is ruinously expensive, especially in the cocoa season. With regard to cost, the following figures are illuminating: (*a*) One ton equals 37 loads at 60 lbs and therefore requires, say, 37 carriers. (*b*) A day's journey is approximately 15 miles. (*c*) Cost of carrier 1*s* 6*d* per day (a moderate estimate for the cocoa season) and 6*d* per day for the return journey if empty. Total 2*s*. (*d*) Therefore cost per ton £3 14*s* 6*d*, or per ton mile 5*s*.

[One witness] in his evidence before the Committee on Trade and Taxation, gives 6*s* 3*d* as his estimate. This is more likely to be correct: in any case, the high cost affects trade, and when competition brings lower market-prices the effect cannot but be injurious.

If the farmer does not carry his produce to the lorry himself, he has to pay a carrier out of the price received from the buyer; if the merchant pays the carrier, the farmer gets less for his cocoa. In any case the farmer suffers, and the cost of head-transport becomes a compelling reason for the growth of population and cultivation in the neighbourhood of motor-roads and railways.

34. If the rates at present in force on the Secondee–Coomassie line are adopted for the Central Province Railway, the comparison between the cost of railway, motor and head-transport is as . . . [Table 20 (a) 1].

Table 20 (a) 1

Transport (per ton mile)		
Head		5*s* to 6*s*
Lorry		2*s* 9*d*
Rail	first 50 miles	7½*d*
	second 50	6*d*
	third 50	4½*d*
	fourth 50	3*d*

35. An example of the deterrent effect of head-transport on the marketing of cocoa in the Kade area is [realised easily when it is] seen that the cost of transport of a ton of cocoa to the nearest port is £11 5*s* 9*d* of which 50 per cent is lorry (41 miles), 40 per cent is carrier(15 miles), 10 per cent is railway (26½ miles).

36. Apart from the question of trade, the construction and maintenance of roads is annually becoming a greater drain on the revenue, a fact that does not tend to the reduction of taxation. Indirect revenue there may be, but, directly, money is all going out and none coming in. The only advantage at present gained by the use of motor transport is that it is less costly than head-carriage and more economical in manpower. On feeder-roads to railway and ports up to a distance of about 35 miles, lorries are invaluable and will always have their users; but on long trunk roads like those running from Winneba and Saltpond to Nsuaem, and from Cape Coast to Prahsu, they are not a practicable proposition.

37. In the minutes of evidence of the Trade and Taxation Committee, pages 78ff. some interesting tables are given . . . in support of [the] contention that the export duty was killing the cocoa trade. I do not propose entering into the controversy further than to say that [this] contention has not hitherto been supported

by facts, and that the longer the Government pays the greater cost of maintaining lengthy road communications in preference to railways, the further distant becomes the time when rates and duties can be lowered.

In reading the evidence given before the Committee, however, one cannot help being impressed by the fact that, in their anxiety to induce the Government to lower export duties, the merchants paid insufficient attention to the great cost of transport. Now that the export duty on cocoa has been halved, motor charges form an increased percentage of the merchant's expenses.

I give . . . a table [20 (a) 2] in which I . . . deal rather more clearly with the question of profit. The table shows the cost to the merchant of transport and charges per ton of cocoa from a farm six miles from Akoraso to Europe via the port of Winneba. If the first item, head-transport, is paid by the farmer it may be presumed that he gets a correspondingly better price for his load.

Table 20 (a) 2. *Analysis of charges and profits on one ton of cocoa*

Farm	Six miles from Akoraso
Buying station	Akoraso
Port	Winnebah, 37 miles from Akoraso
Home market price	£42 a ton

	£	*s*	*d*
Coast and home charges	7	4	4
Steamer and lighterage	3	11	4
Head transport	1	16	0
Lorry transport	5	1	8
Export duty	2	6	8
Total charges	£20	0	0

The home market price is £42, so there is £22 to be divided between the merchant and the farmer. On the supposition that the farmer received 10*s* per load, he gets £18 13*s* 4*d* and the merchant gets £3 6*s* 8*d*. The farmer therefore makes a profit of 7*s* 6*d* a load, or £14 a ton . . . This is 300 per centum on his outlay. Looked at from another point of view, the farmer's profit is 33⅓ per cent of the home market price. The merchant's profit is 7.9 per cent of the home market price and 8.6 per cent of his outlay.

[As many people are] evidently labouring under the curious delusion that the Government is bleeding the people, the following comparison of 'profits' on the above-mentioned ton of Akoraso cocoa is enlightening:

Farmer gets £18 13*s* 4*d* out of which he has to pay for any labour he may employ.

Merchant gets £3 6*s* 8*d* clear profit.

Government gets £2 6*s* 8*d* which it spends on the Agricultural Department, roads, railways, education and other things for the people.

40. Having, I trust, proved that the only successful way to reduce the cost of transport in the Central Province area is to build a railway, it is now advisable to enquire how far the results mentioned in paragraph 29 above will be attained by its construction.

(*a*) The export of hitherto unmarketed cocoa.

(*b*) The increase of cocoa cultivation. [Certain areas in the Central Provinces] are producing some 7,000 tons of cocoa per annum which do not come to market. These areas will be trapped by the new railway, and the natural sequence will be motor feeder-roads starting from the chief stations into the country as in the case of the Accra–Coomassie Railway. The result will be the marketing of all produce as well as the steady and systematic growth of the new plantations until eventually ... some 42,000 tons of cocoa in 1926 and over 50,000 tons in 1930 should be exported from the Central Province area, an increase over present marketed crops of about 16,000 and 26,000 tons respectively, nearly all of which increase will be due to the railway.

(*c*) Saving the kola trade. The new railway will certainly go far towards saving our kola trade with Nigeria especially as its terminus will be at Takoradi, for it is a well known fact that rapidity of transport and protection from the weather in port handling prevents a great wastage of this export. In this contention I am strongly supported by the Hausa Chiefs ... Anything that can be saved by the kola trade in transport and handling charges in this country will go far to balance the import duties in Nigeria. The kola trade is at present brisk but has not increased during the past 18 months owing to the lack of purchasing power in our chief market, Northern Nigeria. It has, however, held its own in spite of this disadvantage and there can be no increased doubt that it will increase with the return of normal conditions and the arrival of the railway in or near areas ... which are all favourable to the growth of this crop and contain an annually increasing number of Hausas engaged in the local kola trade.

(*d*) Timber trade. The new railway will penetrate a forest rich in mahogany and valuable timbers especially in the two belts lying between Nsuaem and Foso and Opon Valley ...

(*e*) Import trade. The railway will cheapen the transport of imports, and therefore selling prices, with a consequent appreciable increase in the volume of trade of the railway zone (see paragraph 32).

(*f*) Trade competition. At present all merchants and firms who are independent of the 'Combine' are severely handicapped in their Central Province trade by two things, firstly, the practical monopoly of lighterage by two firms, one of which belongs to the 'Combine'; and secondly the practical monopoly of motor transport by one firm, also in the 'Combine'; Takoradi harbour and the railway therefrom will remove the first named obstacle to the enterprise of the independent merchant in most of the Central Province area, and the railway will remove the second obstacle. Whether or not there is any chance of the Gold Coast suffering from a trade monopoly exercised by one combination of firms, the fact remains that at present this chance exists; the danger therefore cannot be ignored; and it is all-important that the way should be made easier for the independent merchant.

41. I have left until the last the most important reason for the construction of the railway: its absolute necessity to the preservation of our cocoa trade; indeed to all our trade. As your Grace is aware, the Gold Coast at present produces more cocoa than any other country in the world; it exports annually between one-third and one-half of the world's production. Even during the present period, when several European markets are closed, the demands of the world exceed the supply; with the restoration of normal trade conditions demands will increase and the Gold Coast, in company with other cocoa-growing countries, will be in the satisfactory position of not being able to supply all that the world wants.

This state of affairs is, however, not going to continue indefinitely; in fact the end is within sight. Other countries have been attracted by our success, and among those locally are Nigeria, the Cameroons, Sierra Leone, Liberia and, I believe, both Dahomey and the Ivory Coast. All these countries have been and are engaged in planting cocoa, notably Nigeria, which is, in view of her extensive waterways and still-water harbours, our most formidable rival, as will be seen by the following figures:

Cocoa exports from Nigeria

1907–13	18,884 tons
1914–20	91,527

The Cameroons is likely to be another very serious rival judging from our own activities in the mandated area and those of the French. I understand that cocoa farms in the Cameroons to the extent of some two or three thousand tons of cocoa have been recently destroyed by volcanic eruption. Either this year or next that cocoa would have come into the market in competition with ours, and the amount destroyed is, I understand, small compared to what is already growing.

Not only the West African colonies are concerned. South America, the West Indies and, I understand, both Ceylon and the Malay states, are growing cocoa. The slump in rubber renders the Malayan states a formidable rival in the cocoa field. This slump has been so recent that cocoa production is at present limited, but the next few years should see very heavy crops put on the markets.

Altogether when present activities in cocoa-growing in Africa, America and Asia are considered, it is easy to see that there is going to be a very big competition in cocoa, followed by over-production. The history of rubber will be well within Your Grace's memory; briefly when the demand exceeded the supply the price was half-a-crown a pound; today with over-supply the price is $10\frac{1}{2}d$. I can without difficulty imagine the Government of 'rubber' colonies in their prosperous days writing in very much the same strain as I do now on the necessity of improving their communications and cheapening the transport of rubber to the coast in view of coming competition.

I would have no uneasiness if the countries I have mentioned were sitting still and not building communications. But this is not the case: everywhere an active development policy has been adopted in the British colonies; it is essential that the Gold Coast should not be behindhand. We have already taken steps to meet the coming competition in building Takoradi harbour. The Harbour Committee which sat last year foresaw the danger of the coming competition so clearly that the first factor they considered when enquiring into the necessity for improving existing transport facilities was competition . . . With regard to competition, the Committee makes the following remark: 'It clearly behoves us to take any steps that are possible to put our products and especially our chief product on the world's market at the smallest possible cost and in the best possible condition.' Further, the committee says: 'It is agreed on all hands that some steps must be taken forthwith to improve our harbour facilities in a drastic degree if we are to retain our existing trade.'

Naturally the Committee were primarily dealing with the harbour, *vis-à-vis* trade, but their remarks apply with equal force to railway and trade. I am strongly of the opinion that in five years' time the market-price for Gold Coast cocoa at Liverpool will seldom, if ever, exceed £35 a ton; and it does not require very much imagination to see it falling steadily in ensuing years to some £30 a ton.

The effect of this on the profits of the farmer and the merchant can easily be seen if a study is made of paragraph 37 and of the tables mentioned in paragraph 39, the figures in which may require minor alterations but give a reasonable idea of present profits with market prices at £42 and £35. What the profit to the farmer and merchant will be when the price falls to £30 and no railway exists, can easily be deduced.

42. I have, I trust, said enough to show that the cocoa-growing areas of the Gold Coast require more railways. Had we the money and the labour we should be thoroughly justified in building at least two more lines – into the Western Provinces of the Colony and Ashanti respectively – but these will have to wait the completion of the Central Province railway which, owing to population and great productive capacity, should take precedence of all other proposed lines.

Not only is the railway required, but *it is required now*; as soon as it is possible to build it. *Nothing is to be gained, everything is to be lost, by deferring its construction until competition becomes intense.* I am firmly convinced that *the intensity will first begin to be felt towards the end of 1926. The date of completion of the railway should therefore lie in that year.* Any postponements will lead to our being beaten in the world's cocoa markets by other countries. Should that occur the Gold Coast will inevitably, for a period, be in a bankrupt condition. *The more the situation is considered the more important becomes the construction of the Central Province Railway.*

20 (b). The Northern Territories Railway [1]

Products and trade

31. In the Northern parts, millet and guinea corn are the chief products and form the staple food of the district. These commodities are only grown for local consumption. Other products are shea butter, ground nuts, cotton, benni-seed, neri or neale seed, fibre, kapok, skins and hides.

32. In Ashanti, the principal products are cocoa, kola, yams, maize, rice and the usual foodstuffs.

33. From the Traffic Survey report, . . . [Table 20 (b) 1] is the estimated tonnage . . . between Kumasi and Navongro.

34. This is a small amount of traffic for a railway 350 miles in length, but at least two-thirds of this distance is through an undeveloped country, where the possibilities are great when transport facilities are improved and an outlet to the markets is found for their products . . .

8. Shea butter. The distribution of the tree is widespread throughout the Protectorate, being most prevalent in well drained, fairly open soil, but rarely found in marsh land. The collecting of the nuts is entirely in the hands of the women and at present the kernels are used for local consumption and export to Ashanti and the Gold Coast. It is chiefly used for cooking, for burning in lamps and medicinally. The shea butter season is from the middle of June to the end of September . . .

11. The price presently offered for the raw commodity does not tend to make the native take any active part in the industry, and until such time as a reasonable

[1] Papers relating to a project for the construction of a railway between Kumasi and the Northern Territories of the Gold Coast. *Sessional Paper no. XIII, 1927–8* (extracts). This line was never built.

Table 20 (b) 1

Downward traffic	
Fowls	189,080
Cattle	36,775
Sheep and goats	47,387
	Tons
Shea butter	1,050
Ground nuts	4,000
Cotton	180
Benni-seed	100
Yams	100
Cocoa	9,700
Miscellaneous	70
With 6,620 cattle and 9,453 sheep and goats at Nkoranza.	
Upward traffic	
	Tons
Kola	14,000
Cloth and blankets	200
Salt	200
Miscellaneous	200

price is paid this industry will never become a commercial proposition and the male population will not take part in it. Very wide areas have often to be searched before a kerosene oil tin of kernels can be obtained and I have walked through areas of shea nut trees for miles without seeing any fruit. I am unable to account for this but it is probable that the natives set fire to the bush too late in the season and so destroy the flowers and buds on the trees.

18. Cotton. This commodity is now in the experimental stage and cotton seeds are being distributed by Government to the Chiefs and it is expected that the venture will eventually be a success. Small quantities of cotton are now grown and manufactured locally. The British Cotton Growing Association were established in the Northern Territories a number of years ago, but they were forced to close down owing to the lack of transport. The export of cotton is given as 180 tons.

20. Of the other commodities, very little export would be obtained but it is said that the harvests are increasing yearly. Rice, tobacco, and maize are largely grown, as well as yams, in the southern part of the Northern Territories.

(Despatch from the Governor to the Secretary of State, no. 414, 4 June 1929.) [2]

25. In conclusion I wish to make it clear that the proposed postponement of a Northern Territories Railway as a project of the near future will by no means mean a postponement of the development of the Protectorate. The extent to which the Northern Territories is served by excellent motor-roads cannot be realised by anyone who has not travelled round the Protectorate. There are now

[2] Despatches relating to the construction of a railway between Kumasi and the Northern Territories of the Gold Coast. *Sessional Paper no. XIV, 1929–30* (extracts).

2,124 miles of such roads and it is safe to say that no town village of any importance is without good motor communication. Moreover there are three trunk roads running due north and south: (1) Navrongo–Tamale–Kumasi, (2) Lawra–Bole–Kintampo–Kumasi, (3) Djereponi–Yendi–Kete–Krachi.

My policy is to develop these roads as follows:

(i) To make the Navongro–Tamale road an all-weather road by replacing the 'drifts' at Nasia, Pwalagu, etc. by bridges or ferries (see item 258, Head 29 Estimates for 1929–30). (The consolidation of the Tamale–Kumasi section with permanent bridges and culverts will be complete in 1930.)

(ii) To extend the Lawra–Bole–Bamboi road direct to Wenchi...

(iii) To extend the Yendi–Krachi road to link up with the old German road from Kpandu to Wurupon. (The section Krachi–Akrosu has already been re-opened with temporary bridges.)

To make these three main arteries of traffic capable of carrying lorries at all times of the year, and at the same time to improve the cattle routes (a work which is in hand), will involve expenditure amounting to only a fraction of the cost of a railway. Yet, official opinion is unanimous that such arteries will be adequate to deal with the trade of the Protectorate (including international trade over the frontiers) for many years to come...

A. R. Slater, Governor.

(Despatch from the Secretary of State to the Governor, no. 728, 14 August, 1929.)

I have the honour to acknowledge the receipt of your despatch no. 414 of 4 June, on the subject of the proposed construction of a railway to the Northern Territories. I have read your full and clear view of the case with great interest and after careful consideration, I cannot but agree with you that circumstances at present do not justify the construction of such a railway which must accordingly be postponed and need no longer be regarded as a project to be taken up in the near future. I agree that it ought to be sufficient for the present to improve communications in the Northern Territories by means of further construction and improvement of roads on the lines [laid down]... in your despatch. I have no objection to the publication of your despatch as a Sessional Paper.

3. I enclose a copy of a correspondence with the United Africa Company Limited, in which the Company press for the construction of a railway to the Northern Territories. I shall be glad to have your comments on their letter in due course. I have etc.

Passfield.

Africa House,
Kingsway, London, W.C.2,
26th June, 1929.

The Rt. Hon. the Secretary of State for the Colonies, Downing Street, S.W.1.

Sir,

British West African Territories

We have the honour to call your attention to an opportunity of development in the Gold Coast Colony which exists at the present time and which we venture to submit is ripe for immediate consideration, as it will make possible the export from that country of valuable products now being entirely wasted and corresponding import of manufactured goods from this country.

The Gold Coast depends almost exclusively upon the cocoa crop for its prosperity, which is obviously a dangerous economic position. As a result of a careful survey which has been made, it has been found that there exists in the Northern Territory of the Gold Coast very large quantities of the wild tree on which grows the shea nut – one of the most valuable nuts known to the trade. Owing to the lack of transport facilities this large crop is never gathered and the country's wealth in this important direction is thus entirely thrown away. The effect of this is that a corresponding import into the Colony of manufactured goods from this country is lost. Investigations and reports made by the Gold Coast Government have disclosed the existence of this large forest of shea nut trees and we have ascertained that, if these nuts could be gathered and marketed, we could find an almost unlimited market for them in this country, on the Continent of Europe and in America. The shea nut has been described as the finest oil seed in the world, but all attempts made by merchant houses to collect and market these nuts from the Gold Coast have ended in failure, owing to the cost of carriage by the primitive methods available in the absence of modern transport.

Some years ago the Gold Coast Government made a survey, plans and estimates for a railway to continue the present Takoradi–Kumasi Railway into the Northern Territories through the shea nut area, but no further steps have been taken for its construction and the crop remains ungathered each year and is burned up by the sun and wasted.

The Gold Coast territories at present depend for their prosperity almost wholly upon the production and price of cocoa and the recent fall in the value of this article has had a most serious effect upon the Colony's revenue, upon the prosperity of the inhabitants and upon the exports of manufactured goods from the United Kingdom to the Colony. It is obvious that new sources of revenue and of prosperity must be found, if the trade with the Colony is to expand. The present export tax upon cocoa presses heavily upon the producer, who, as the most valuable asset the Colony now possesses, should surely be taxed as lightly as possible and it is evident that nothing could be more damaging to the interests of the Colony in its present state than to add in any way to the burden already borne by this sole main source of the country's wealth.

This railway having been fully surveyed, its construction could be undertaken immediately. If this were done and the service of the necessary loan were provided by imposing some direct taxation upon the inhabitants of the area, in the form either of a hut tax or a poll tax, so that they would derive immediate benefit from the expenditure incurred on their behalf, they would be encouraged to abandon the present practice of leaving the shea nuts to rot upon the trees, and would not merely gather this wild crop but could probably engage in the agricultural production of ground nuts, which could readily be cultivated in this area. It is believed that within a reasonable time the new railway would earn interest on its capital and prove a profitable investment in itself; but apart from this, it is clear that the construction of the railway would immediately broaden the bases of the whole wealth of the Colony and of its power to import the products of British labour.

Railway communications have been confined to the cocoa-producing districts; other districts have been left largely unprovided not only with railways but even with good motor roads. Although some roads exist in the Colony they are of such light construction as to be unsuitable for the carriage of goods on an economic scale. It is believed that, in addition to the construction of this line of about 200 miles of railway extension from Kumasi to the Northern areas of the Gold Coast, great advantage to the Colony would accrue if better roads could be constructed to feed the line, so that goods might be brought from considerable areas to the Central Trunk line and thence to the Coast.

The construction of a second railway to connect up with the Takoradi railway, and in the direction of the Western frontier of the Gold Coast Colony, is also an essential work before the Western Province products can be effectively developed and marketed. The greater portion of this province consists of an area suitable for the production of cocoa and other tropical produce. Considerable quantities of cocoa are, in fact, grown there, but its development has been retarded owing to lack of transport and when the future policy for the development of the Gold Coast is considered this matter should undoubtedly be taken into account. This project would, however, be much slower in bringing any large additional prosperity to the country compared with the exceptional opportunity which seems to be presented by the project of the Northern railway from Kumasi; indeed there can be few instances existing in the Empire at the present time where the construction of so comparatively simple and short a line or railway would open up such a large and immediate source of revenue and prosperity.

Our attention has been drawn to the matter partly by the demand which we have found to exist throughout the world for these shea nuts and partly by the falling off in the exports of manufactured goods from this country to the Gold Coast which has followed from the reduction in the price of cocoa. In our view, the opening up of this rich additional territory in the Gold Coast, which will enable a large additional population to acquire wealth and come into the orbit of civilisation, will result in the immediate demand for goods produced in this country and add considerably to the volume of our exports and to the employment which they provide.

Should you require further information upon this important subject, we shall be pleased to hold ourselves at your disposal. We have etc.,

for the United Africa Company Limited
Robert Waley Cohen, Chairman.

20 (c). The Western Province Railway [1]

HISTORY

In his Despatch no. 218, dated 14 March 1924, to the Secretary of State for the Colonies, His Excellency the Governor stated that on the completion of the survey of the Central Province Railway he proposed to survey the route for the Western Province Railway. On 27 October 1924, His Excellency ordered that a traffic survey should be made by an experienced Traffic Officer in company with the Political and Agricultural officers concerned. In December 1924, I was instructed by you to make an estimate from the topographical maps available. The traffic

[1] Correspondence relating to the proposed Western Province Railway from Tarkwa to Babeaneha, 114 miles. *Sessional Paper no. X, 1930–1* (extracts from Enclosure A). This line was not built.

and agricultural survey was commenced on 23 January 1925, at Ankobra Junction and completed on 23 April 1925 at Nkoranza.

On 20 June 1925, you submitted to the Honourable the Colonial Secretary your report on the Western Province Railway, including the results of the traffic survey, the report of Sir (then Major) Albert Kitson, Director, Geological Survey, on the mineral prospects of the country to be traversed, and also an estimate of the financial results of the first year's working.

This report was laid before His Excellency the Governor, and in his Despatch no. 521, dated 15 July 1925, to the Secretary of State for the Colonies he stated that for the present he had abandoned the idea of railway development in this direction and favoured the survey of a railway to the Northern Territories.

The preliminary survey of the Northern Territories Railway was completed in July 1927, and on the return of the Railway Survey Branch from leave, in November 1927, the subject of the Western Province Railway was again brought up. The chief reasons for the re-opening of the question of this survey were: (1) The likely development in the near future of the large bauxite deposits in the Sefwi-Bekwai district. (2) The re-opening under the control of the Ashanti Goldfields Corporation of the gold mine at Babiani which has been shut down for a number of years.

At the conference held at Accra on 8 December 1927, His Excellency the Governor discussed this subject with the Honourable the Colonial Secretary and yourself, and a decision was arrived at that the Railway Survey Branch should make a preliminary survey from Tarkwa to Babeaneha (Bebieani) via Prestea and Asankrangwa and prepare an estimate of the cost of construction.

At the same time other departments interested should also make a report upon the territory proposed to be served by this railway. The preliminary survey was started on 21 December 1927, and the field work completed by 25 July 1928. Sufficient data was obtained to make a close estimate of the cost of construction . . .

L. E. Silcox, Engineer in Charge, Surveys.

ECONOMIC CONSIDERATIONS

41. Gold

In the Bibiani locality railway freight depends very largely on the future of the mine. The Ashanti Goldfields Corporation is now investigating its possibilities. At present we do not know what values will be found in depth.

42. If it prove itself a great mine, it will give a great fillip to gold-mining in the neighbourhood. On the other hand, if Bibiani be a failure, the gold-mining industry in the area will cease.

43. Bauxite

Enormous quantities of bauxite are awaiting development but 125 miles and 160 miles are very long hauls to the coast for a low-priced mineral. It is doubtful whether it would pay to ship it for many years to come. If some metallurgical treatment were undertaken with a view to shipping a higher-priced product, ore freights would be reduced but other traffic would be increased owing to the larger plant and personnel employed.

44. The essential point is that this freight should not be relied on until shipments are guaranteed.

45. Manganese ore

This is bound up with the bauxite question. In summing up from a mineral point of view, I feel that I cannot recommend the construction of the railway beyond Asankrawgwa at present, or until freights are guaranteed by the mining companies contemplating operation in this area.

46. From the point of view of capital cost the mineral deposits would be more cheaply served by a branch line from Dunkwa, following roughly the route of the present motor road . . .

W. G. G. Cooper, Geologist.

PROPOSED WESTERN RAILWAY

Agricultural survey of part of Western Province

I beg to submit the attached report relating to all that part of Western Province likely to be affected by the projected Western Railway, i.e. Ankobra, Sefwi, Aowin and the N.W. portion of Tarkwa districts.

Cocoa being the only crop of sufficient importance to provide railway freight presently, careful attention has been given to ascertaining the approximate quantity available and the local distribution thereof, together with areas of young trees and the probable increase in output during the next few years.

Coffee appears likely to become a minor industry of some importance, and is worthy of attention and encouragement. It should be maintained and extended in addition to cocoa. Otherwise there is a real danger of the crop being abandoned in favour of cocoa, should the value of the latter increase as the result of improved transport facilities.

Kola cannot be regarded as of any potential value. Wild trees are sparsely distributed throughout the area, and crop yields are small.

Coconut cultivation should be given encouragement, as the difficulties of drying copra might be overcome by the use of artificial driers, these latter being established and utilised on cooperative principles.

Oil palms are not referred to, since in general the area dealt with is too densely afforested to permit of natural establishment. In the northern part of the Tarkwa district around the mining and firewood areas where vast clearings have been made there is a high percentage of oil palms in the natural secondary growth the utilisation of which is worthy of attention, if only to supply the demand for culinary purposes within easy reach of the railway.

Food crops are always in demand for the mining towns and the acute shortage has been responsible for the high cost of living which has obtained for many years. It seems likely that the area between Asankrangwa and Prestea would lend itself to development for the cultivation of such crops.

Necessity for development of road systems

[This] is commented on and should be further emphasised by those acquainted with the province. North of the Aowin district and west of the Tano is a vast tract of potentially rich forest land, favoured with a well distributed rainfall, which is as yet untouched. The area is sparsely populated but no development is possible until the country is opened up by roads, and made accessible to people living in less favoured localities. The arterial road suggested . . . would mean extending the Dunkwa–Wioso road for another forty odd miles beyond the latter town. The total length from Dunkwa would then be over one hundred miles, but even so it would be a sound economic proposition, as has been proved in Western Ashanti. Apart from the appalling waste of man power, head transport is extremely costly amounting to at least 5*s* 3*d* per ton mile, whereas the maximum cost of motor transport is 1*s* 3*d*. Thus it will be seen the cocoa farmer would at once receive an additional 4*s* per load; sufficient to induce him to harvest the whole crop. The roads suggested in the report are essential for development of the area and in no way dependent on railway construction.

Cocoa tonnage for projected railway

The survey and census serves to show that some 10,000 tons of cocoa will be available as freight. Little of this can be regarded as new freight since approximately 80 per cent has in the past been going to the Kumasi–Sekondi railway, and will be a loss to that section if the proposed line is put through. On the other hand, the increased value of crops will arouse interest and annual increases in tonnage may be expected.

In conclusion, I would like to express appreciation of a very good report supported by valuable data. The survey party have been out in the field throughout the whole rainy season and have had to contend with difficulties and hardships such as can be understood only by those acquainted with the country.

A. C. Miles, Officer-in-Charge, Div. of Statistics and Surveys.

21. A move by the transport authorities to have the Central Province ports closed is successfully resisted, 1928 [1]

Report of the Central Province Trade Routes Committee, appointed by His Excellency the Governor to consider and make recommendations regarding (i) Central Province Railway rates; (ii) the treatment of the ports of Cape Coast and Saltpond on the opening of Takoradi. To give similar advice in the event of Cape Coast and Saltpond being closed as ports of entry and made sufferance wharves . . . [Presented here are] a few outstanding considerations and the final recommendations of the General Manager of the Railways.

23. A governing factor is the present and probable future cost per ton mile of the conveyance of goods by motor lorries, and as to this the Committee was confronted with what appeared at first to be seriously conflicting statements. On the one hand it was stated that goods had been transported recently from Anyinam to Accra, a distance of 83 miles for 36*s* a ton or nearer 5*d* than 6*d* per ton mile . . . On the other hand, [one witness] speaking from intimate knowledge of the conditions on the roads in the Central Province, actually competing with the Central Province Railway, stated that he did not see how transport could be effected at less than 10*d* per ton mile, e.g. at a cost of 43*s* 4*d* per ton for the journey from Fosu to Cape Coast . . .

24. [A further witness from one of the major transport firms] expressed the opinion that it is not an economic proposition to run motor transport at less than

[1] Report of the Central Province Trade Routes Committee appointed by His Excellency the Governor to consider and make recommendations regarding (i) Central Province Railway routes; (ii) the treatment of the ports of Cape Coast and Saltpond on the opening of Takoradi. *Sessional Paper no. VI, 1928–9*, paras 23–44 (extracts).

the present 10*d* per ton mile, unless some new form of transport is introduced, such as road trains. He indicated that this 10*d* often has to cover the return journey as well, because one may get no load back. He estimated that return loads were obtained probably for less than 50 per cent of Journeys, and thought that 10*d* per ton mile was about a good fair average. [He] considered that ' pirates ' (i.e. private owners of single lorries) did not interfere much with the large transport firms on long hauls. They are unable to carry as much as the firms.

25. With regard to the possibility of road trains this witness stated that his firm was not contemplating their introduction. He did not consider the present roads suitable for them, except where tarmetted, and even then in many cases gradients were not suitable. The only likely stretch in fact seemed to be between Swedru and Winneba. Moreover the firm could not count on sufficient big loads. [He] did not think it would be possible to run at 6*d* per ton mile under 5-ton loads. Even then it would not in his opinion be an economic proposition. The Director of Public Works stated that he would be opposed to the introduction of road trains because of the curves.

26. [This witness] concluded by stating that he did not anticipate further reduction in the cost of motor transport. It might possibly come down to $9\frac{1}{2}d$ but he would not like that. As far as he was concerned he thought the railway could look on 10*d* as a more or less fixed fair figure.

27. ... The Committee [was encouraged] to take into consideration not what was an economic rate, but what was the ruling rate which is set by private owners, the ' local standard rate '. [The Committee was given] the following figures:

The ruling rate varies in different districts.

Between Oda and Saltpond	8*d*
Between Fosu and Saltpond	8*d*
Between Yankumase and Cape Coast	9*d*

In some parts it is much lower. Native owners run between Suhum and Nsawam for 5.6*d* per ton mile. The average rate (charged by native owners) throughout the Colony is 7.29*d*.

A large proportion of the lorries are owned by small cocoa brokers and it often pays them to lose money on their transport in order to take advantage of the price of cocoa. Their transport is subsidised by their cocoa. Messrs Elder's Road Transport have to come down to these rates. Otherwise they would have their fleet idle ... Messrs Elder's rate between Fosu and Saltpond and between Oda and Saltpond is 9*d*. They can get loads at present at that rate. In Ashanti the rate varies from $10\frac{2}{3}d$ to $5\frac{5}{8}d$. Between Oda and Winneba they are running at $7\frac{1}{4}d$; the native rate is even lower, say 7*d*. [The opinion was expressed] that the railway would never compete unless it brought its rates down to the equivalent of 3*d* per ton mile of the distance by road: [this] was the only rate that would freeze out the two roads in competition with the Central Province Railway. [It was estimated] that 60 per cent of European-owned cocoa comes down in native-owned vehicles. [It was] thought that the number of European vehicles was more in proportion to native-owned in the Central Province than in the Eastern Province.

28. [Some evidence suggested] that the Government would have to reckon with the possibility of a motor transport rate of 6*d* per ton mile. Lorries get bigger every year. Maintenance costs are coming down. Running costs are not appreciably higher. The recent increase in the petrol duty was a mere flea-bite. A

moderate rise in the licence fees on vehicles would not in his opinion affect the cost of running perceptibly.

Another important factor with regard to the traffic that may eventually be expected to use the Central Province Railway was indicated . . . that a great deal is at present coming down the roads that might use the railway because merchants have not yet established depots at Fosu and Oda.

29. They were waiting to see if it was worth their while. Building involved a large expenditure and they could not know for a few years whether such expenditure would be justifiable. [One view] thought it a mistake extending the railway terminus to Kade through virgin forest instead of stopping at Oda, to which place cocoa from all that neighbourhood could be brought. The merchants would prefer to await developments, as they had suffered before from building prematurely at places on a new line of railway, particularly at Tafo.

30. The capital cost of the Central Province Railway was £1,216,890. A sum of £71,225 per annum is required to pay interest and sinking fund on the loan. The railway would require to earn £150,000 per annum in order to pay. At the present time it is not paying . . .

31. The General Manager of the railways expressed the opinion that the Central Province Railway will probably in say ten years' time pay its way, even if the ports of Cape Coast and Saltpond remain open. On the other hand if the ports were closed, the railway could do more now to reduce its loss. With regard to the suggestion made by those interested in the Central Province ports that a decision should be deferred and the actual effect on Takoradi and the Central Province Railway of the ports remaining open be observed over a certain period, the difficulty is that if Cape Coast and Saltpond remain open, very low rates will have to be charged on the Central Province Railway and the railway would find it very difficult to raise them, as the position would warrant, if it was ultimately decided to close the ports. Rates, once reduced, have a tendency to become permanent.

32. The basis of calculation, said the General Manager of the railways, if the ports remained open, must be what is the probable cost of road transport per mile, looking forward a year or two, in order that some stable terms may be arranged for railway carriage . . . In the event of Cape Coast and Saltpond remaining open he was of opinion that in order to attract traffic from areas north of the railway line nothing higher than Class III net rates should be charged on all through traffic to and from Takoradi and Sekondi (with the exception of spirits). The freights from Fosu to Takoradi (106 miles) would be 41*s* 3*d* per ton and from Oda to Takoradi (132 miles) 48*s* 9*d*, which compare favourably with the lorry freight from Fosu to Cape Coast (52 miles), 43*s* 4*d*, and from Oda to Saltpond (55 miles), 45*s* 10*d*, at 10*d* per ton mile . . .

The Director of Public Works was of opinion that, as a question of general policy, looking at the interest of the Colony as a whole the ports of Cape Coast and Saltpond ought to be closed . . . If they remain as sufferance wharves, some steamship companies will call with cargo, and for cargo, and if any company does so, others in competition will have to do likewise. The result would be that the ports would continue to be served as they are now and no practical benefit would ensue from the closing of them as ports of entry. Certainly there would be no advantage for steamship companies ; rather the reverse . . .

37. . . . The General Manager of the railways said that in his opinion, if Cape Coast and Saltpond remained ports of entry, the Central Province Railway would practically be a financial failure for some years. Apart from the loan charges it

would not even pay its running cost, and this would mean a burden on the revenue.

38. On the other hand, ... those members who represented the Central Provinces and the towns of Cape Coast and Saltpond – the Acting Commissioner of the Central Province, Captain Stickings, Mr Van Hiem and Mr Korsah – brought forward various reasons why the ports should not be closed, and Mr Isherwood, on behalf of the Accra Chamber of Commerce, expressed himself as entirely in agreement with the case put forward by the representatives of the Central Province.

39. It was pointed out that the closing of the two ports would affect the interests of about 200,000 people, practically the whole of the Fante tribe; that these people would have to pay £3 per ton additional on all their imports if these had to be brought from Takoradi by road, on a 10*d* per ton mile basis, and that from a political point of view it was a serious matter that it was Fanties, and practically only Fanties, who would thus be penalised.

40. [One witness] expressed the opinion that Takoradi harbour would be amply remunerative without sacrificing Cape Coast and Saltpond to contribute to it. Let Takoradi go on for two or three years and see if it fails to pay owing to the competition of Cape Coast and Saltpond. Do not be in a hurry to close them on the strength of a mere estimate and anticipation. If Government closes these ports and after a time reopens them, because it is realised that Takoradi can pay its way without inflicting this hardship on Cape Coast and Saltpond the towns will have been ruined and the reopening will be of no avail, because emigration will already have taken place, the people will have been scattered, the trade shattered and it will be impossible to restore the former prosperity. The closing of the two ports will result in:

(*a*) Diminution of population.

(*b*) Reduction of cocoa price paid to the farmers, owing to the heavy charges. The farmers will be discouraged, production will decrease and quality worsen.

(*c*) Reduction of imports and exports owing to decreased population and difficulties of transportation.

(*d*) Depreciation of property in Cape Coast and Saltpond. There will be a consequent difficulty in paying rates in Cape Coast and a serious situation will be created.

(*e*) The embitterment of about 200,000 people, mostly Fanties and the creation in them of a permanently dissatisfied attitude.

41. [One witness], on behalf of his own Corporation and the merchants generally, protested very strongly against the closing of the two ports because they have valuable interests in both towns, which will undoubtedly be jeopardized. Trade in both centres has been steadily increasing for the last ten years. He thought it would result in a loss of revenue if the ports were closed. The growing trade of these ports should be nursed. If the merchants are compelled to use motor transport to supply these places, it will be at an increased cost to the inhabitants. The cost of imports and the cost of native foodstuffs will alike rise. The interests of the Banks will be affected. There will be a serious depreciation on all properties. Government is spending £155,000 on a pipe-borne water supply for Cape Coast and is spending money on other works. Properties are being re-assessed on an upward grade to pay for these improvements.

The numerous schools in Cape Coast (boarding establishments) will be much affected. The road from Cape Coast and Saltpond to Takoradi is not in a fit state for heavy traffic. It is often closed. Heavy motor traffic will have to be used and great difficulty will be experienced in dealing with it at the ferry. Trade at Elmina is growing and [the town is to be developed] as a separate centre instead of [being run] from Cape Coast.

About 1,000 tons of cocoa is expected for shipment from Elmina this season. Trade in kernels is also being developed. All the villages in the neighbourhood have roads to Elmina. [It was argued that] the eight or nine thousand pounds expected for Takoradi from the closing of Cape Coast and Saltpond should come out of general revenue, if it is needed. [It was] considered a serious point that it was only Fanties who were going to be taxed and affected like this. The position of Saltpond was peculiar. Trade would be driven to Winneba, and Takoradi would not benefit. The palm products trade might stop altogether again owing to low prices.

42. The Acting Commissioner of the Central Province emphasised that the closing of the ports would result in the migration of many of the people. There is not sufficient local food-supply to support the population. He thought that intense bitterness would be caused. He was very strongly in agreement that the ports should not hastily be closed but that the effect of Takoradi and the Central Province Railway in operation should be observed over a fairly long period and that the people's minds should be prepared.

43. Mr Korsah, on behalf of the people of Saltpond, supported the view expressed by [the merchants from Cape Coast]. He pointed out that Saltpond was 17 miles from Cape Coast, 60 miles from Winneba and 72 miles from Takoradi, and that people could not afford to pay the increased prices entailed by road transport. Mr Korsah gave examples of the onerous increases that would be caused in the cost of importing commodities in common use. With regard to produce for export, the production of palm oil kernels was being developed and the merchants were supporting the farmers and producers. With the additional cost of transport to Takoradi or Winneba the price that would be paid for these commodities would not even pay for the cost of production, and production would cease entirely. This would be trade lost to the Colony.

44. But what changed the equilibrium of opinion and has made it possible for us to submit an almost unanimous recommendation on this most important term of reference was the evidence given . . . regarding the Conference on the subject of the Central Province Railway held by the late Governor, Sir Frederick Gordon Guggisberg, at Cape Coast on 7 September 1922 . . .

The report was evidently adopted officially and a copy furnished to the Secretary for Native Affairs by the Governor's private secretary . . . [It contains] the most definite assurances given by the late Governor that Cape Coast would not be injured by the Central Province Railway, and that neither after the building of the Central Province Railway, nor after the opening of Takoradi harbour, would Cape Coast or Saltpond become sufferance wharves . . .

[Letter from the General Manager of the Railway, 26 May 1925.[2]]

Proposed Central Province Railway rates

1. I have the honour to address you on the subject of the principles to be adopted in the fixation of railway rates on the Central Province Railway, the section of which up to Fosu is due to be open about September of this year.

[2] Appendix IV.

2. It will be recollected that at the time of the inception of the proposed railway the cost of motor lorry transport was in the vicinity of 2*s* 6*d* to 2*s* 9*d* per ton mile, at which rates our existing railway rates would for almost all classes of goods have secured to the railway the traffic originating along its course. At the present time the traffic of the principal towns along the route: Fosu, Achiasi, Oda, Wanchi and Kade, is carried by lorry at the rate of 1*s* per ton mile, the reduction in cost being due to better roads, cheaper petrol, better and more powerful lorries and better transport organisation of the motor transport companies.

3. The Central Province Railway is therefore up against established competition both for exports and imports and the traffic will continue to be carried by motor lorries so long as the roads remain, unless railway transport to Sekondi is made sufficiently advantageous over motor transport. It is further believed that motor transport is capable of a slight reduction on the existing rates of 1*s* a ton mile at present charged by the motor transport companies.

4. The above considerations entirely preclude, if the Central Province Railway is to carry any of such goods to and from Sekondi, the higher rates now charged by the railway on the more expensive types of goods, however easily these goods may be able to bear the existing rates of railway freight. The attached table [Table 21.1] . . . shows this clearly.

Table 21.1. *Comparison between existing railway rates to Sekondi jetty and existing motor lorry rates to Coast ports* *

	Fosu (106 miles)		Oda (136 miles)		Kade (153 miles)	
	Existing railway rates	Motor rates to Cape Coast	Existing railway rates	Motor rates to Saltpond	Existing railway rates	Motor rates to Accra via Nsawam
	s d	*s d*	*s d*	*s d*	*s d*	*s d*
Cocoa	58 6		69 9		75 9	
Class III	39 0		46 6		50 6	
Class II	69 2		81 8		88 3	
Class I	117 0	47 0	139 6	55 0	151 6	70 0
Class B	190 10		228 4		248 4	
Class A	249 6		309 6		342 9	
Cement	19 6		23 3		25 3	

* On the basis of lorry rates at 1*s* per ton mile.

22. Committees unable to find a practical solution to the problem of 'unfair' competition to which the railways are subjected by the roads. (a) The Railway Retrenchment Committee, 1931 [1]

53. In the course of the Committee's deliberations questions relating to the rates and dues charged by the railway and harbour administrations came frequently under discussion and led eventually to consideration of the financial policy according to which these charges are framed. The same point of policy was raised

[1] Railway Retrenchment Committee Report and Recommendations, 1931. *Sessional Paper no. XIII, 1931–2*, paras 53–77, financial policy (extracts).

directly by the President of the Chamber of Mines both in his written and oral evidence.

54. The Committee understood that the basis upon which railway rates and harbour dues are founded is that the total revenue of each system shall cover all its working expenses and extraordinary expenditure together with all the fixed capital charges which relate to that system. Where a profit over and above these expenses is made it is paid into general revenue although, according to the Committee's information, rates and dues are not framed with a view to such a contribution to the colony's surplus.

55. It was not denied by the General Manager that, as compared with other African railways, certain rates charged on the railway are high and Mr Millar made similar assertions with harbour dues on manganese ore at Takoradi in comparison with those charged at a South African port. On the other hand rates over the portions of the railway are driven to a relatively very low point by the strong competition of competitive road users, while Takoradi revenue suffers from the cheapness with which cargoes can be placed aboard or landed at neighbouring ports both British and French.

The issues arising out of these facts were: Firstly: whether the policy of framing rates and dues so as to cover all charges, both working and capital, is in the best interests of the Gold Coast; and secondly: what measures, if any, should be taken to reduce the force of competition from motor lorries and cheaper ports.

56. The total cost of a transportation system may be classified as follows: Recurrent: (a) working expenses; (b) pensions and gratuities; (c) renewals fund contributions; (d) interest on loans; (e) sinking fund contributions.

Extraordinary: capital works.

57. The Committee considers that there can be no dispute upon the point that the system's revenue must at the very minimum be calculated to cover (a) (b) and (c) above.

In connection with the liability of the railways to find the whole of the capital charges incurred on its account, the President of the Chamber of Mines (Mr Millar) took the view in his evidence that the railway should be made to pay its way but that its liability in respect of both interest and sinking fund should first be largely reduced . . .

58. The issue which presented itself to the Committee was, however, anterior to Mr Millar's point and raised the question whether it is essentially necessary for a State-owned railway to aim at producing sufficient revenue to cover all the capital charges which would properly be debited against a railway conducted on commercial lines.

59. The Committee desires to point out that railway receipts form only one of several channels through which revenue flows to Government as a result of increased wealth on the part of the community. Most of the heads of revenue appearing in the Gold Coast budget but particularly customs, licenses and internal revenue, tend to rise or fall *pari passu* with the quantity of and the prices paid for the raw products exported from the dependency. It does not follow, therefore, of necessity that the country loses as a whole because certain commodities are moved by its transportation systems at rates which are unremunerative to those systems when capital charges are taken into account, for the revenues flowing back indirectly from their production and sale may be such that it is better for the country as a whole to move such commodities at a loss than to insist on rates

which, though sufficient on paper to cover transportation expenses, in practice would tend to diminish or to eliminate their production.

60. The corollary of this is that, if the railway is to be required for the benefit of the country to charge rates in certain instances which, though reimbursing it for working expenses do not fully cover the cost of transportation inclusive of capital charges, the country must be prepared to carry a portion of these latter charges. If it were possible to determine the relation between the value of exports and the indirect revenue received by Government which is created by that value it might also be possible to fix formulae for the relative liabilities of the railway and Takoradi harbour on the one hand and of the colony on the other for the capital charges of those systems. The Committee doubts whether such a determination is possible – it is certainly beyond its own competency – but does not hesitate to come to the general conclusion that, having regard to the facts that the local transportation systems were built partly for administrative and defensive objects and that from the commercial point of view these systems are only two of several channels through which the Gold Coast derives revenue from the producer's efforts, general revenue may properly be called on to bear a portion of the capital charges arising from the construction and equipment of those systems.

61. The Committee considers that this question, which is fundamental to the financial policy of the railway and of Takoradi harbour, could profitably be examined by an expert economist and commends that suggestion to Government's consideration. As they view the matter, they are not prepared to recommend an arbitrary allocation of capital expenditure, such as that suggested by Mr Millar: indeed, if and for so long as rates and dues can be devised which, without injurious reactions upon industry, will produce revenue sufficient to cover interest charges on the loan money spent on the Dependency's transportation systems, they consider it reasonable that those charges should be so borne. Their contention is that the determining factor in the fixation of rates and dues should be the ability of commodities to bear the rates charged for their carriage rather than the principle that each transportation system must be made to pay its whole way in working expenses and interest.

62. The case of sinking fund charges on the railway loans is, in the opinion of the Committee, essentially different. They should be borne by the general revenue of the Dependency in view of the fact that when the loans have been completely amortized the Gold Coast will come into possession of a free railway system and a free harbour. The Committee noted that the sinking fund contributions account of Takoradi harbour is borne by the colony.

63. A further point connected with the financial policy of the transportation systems ... was whether railway profits, when any, should continue to be paid over to general revenue which would also bear the system's losses or whether they should be funded as a reserve in order to cover losses in leaner years. In this connection Mr Millar made the further suggestions (1) that all payments of surplus earnings from the railway made to the consolidated (i.e. general) revenue since 1 January 1921 should be deducted from the capital expenditure on which the railway should pay interest and sinking fund and (2) that rates should be adjusted so that surplus earnings do not exceed 2½ per cent on the capital invested. The Committee presumes that Mr Millar intended to suggest a similar policy in respect of Takoradi harbour.

64. ... In the Committee's view such a fund would have the obvious advantage of the colony that its estimates would cease to be liable to sudden violent

dislocation as has occurred recently when an anticipated revenue item in the colony's estimates of £50,440 has been replaced by an unforeseen expenditure item of £187,000. Moreover, in thus achieving a greater independence of considerations affecting the general revenue, the General Manager [of the railways] should be in a better position to lay down and maintain rate scales drawn on a scientific basis.

65. The Committee therefore commends the suggestion to Government's consideration. As regards Mr Millar's two riders above mentioned, the Committee is of the opinion that other factors, such as the losses borne by general revenue over the period, would have to be taken into account: they are also doubtful whether any good purpose would be served by attempting to lay down a maximum profit, at any rate at this stage.

66. The second issue [mentioned in paragraph 55 above] was what measures, if any, should be taken to reduce the competition which the railways suffer from road-using transport, and Takoradi harbour from neighbouring and cheaper ports. As regards the road versus rail problem the Committee did not disregard the argument that Government would not be justified in placing even the smallest handicap upon road-borne traffic, with the object of relieving the railway of some of the stress of competition, in as much as any such measure must raise the cost of production and thereby react unfavourably upon Gold Coast trade. This argument, however, disregards the fact that, making all allowance for administrative objections, much of the greater part of the capital expenditure on the railway and the whole of that on Takoradi harbour have had the development of production as their aim and, secondly, that whether or not the railways and the harbour are used in the marketing of the colony's produce, the capital charges thus created, to say nothing of maintenance expenses, have to be met from the wealth produced in the colony. If the revenue of the two systems is inadequate to meet such capital charges as are considered to be their proper liability the general taxpayer must make good the deficiency. That in itself would constitute a hardship on the taxpayer. If, further, the latter has to bear the current cost of a road system – also designed largely for the producer's benefit – while the latter escapes from any greater share of both burdens than would descend upon him in his capacity of general taxpayer, the hardship develops into inequity.

67. The Committee devoted considerable thought to the search for a practicable remedy for the unfair competition to which the railway is subjected by the roads and they greatly regret their inability to discover one. The members were inclined to support a heavy increase in licence fees from motor lorries but after discussion it was recognised that such a measure, if effective at all, would tend to restrict the area within which cocoa can be grown and transported by such vehicles to the railway.

The problem is essentially one the solution of which must not affect roads feeding the railway: it follows that no general measure arriving at an increase of the cost of road transportation will serve.

68. Another suggestion put forward was the periodical closing of certain roads to heavy traffic: this was discarded as impracticable. The taxation of heavy traffic using the competitive roads was also proposed; Mr Millar suggested the lease of their transport rights to firms at specified freight rates and the ordinary toll-gate system also came under discussion.

69. Although by either of these latter measures it would be possible to discriminate between non-competitive and competitive roads and although no other

method of achieving that result was suggested, nevertheless the Committee do not recommend the adoption of either. It was felt that Mr Millar's proposal might lead to highly invidious situations, and the Committee feel that the institution of toll-gates would fail to meet general acceptance. Apart from the delay to traffic which would affect all road users and the practical difficulties of selecting positions which would attain the object sought by the measure, an elaborate and expensive inspectorate system would be necessary unless evasion and speculation were to become rife; lastly, any such institution would be and would remain the object of general dislike. The most that the Committee can say for it is that in principle it is the best solution in sight; they are too doubtful of its success in practice to recommend its employment.

Railway rates and harbour dues

70. Certain specific points relating to railway rates and harbour dues fell to be considered by the Committee.

(1) Passenger rates – 3rd class. Passenger fares are at present one penny a mile plus 15 per cent and this form of traffic is suffering heavily under road competition. The General Manager who brought the matter before the Committee expressed the belief that no reduction which did not decrease the fare to a figure in the region of three farthings a mile would have any appreciable effect in obtaining for the railway a greater share of this traffic. He was inclined to favour such a reduction. The Committee saw no objection to that course and in the circumstances assumed that the General Manager would submit his considered proposal to Government for consideration.

(2) Rates on manganese ore from Nsuta. The Committee was informed that the African Manganese Company had already applied to Government for a lower rate on manganese ore from mine to Takoradi, representing that owing to high local transportation costs it is not possible for the Company to quote successfully against the competitors whom it has to meet today in a greatly restricted market. The importance to the Gold Coast of the continuance of this industry is, in the opinion of the Committee, too obvious to require to be stressed by them: a very considerable revenue must flow into the Treasury as a result of the Company's wage payments and the money spent by its employees. It was no part of the Committee's duty to endeavour to ascertain what in the circumstances is the right economic rate to charge on this traffic.

(3) Rates charged on cocoa exported from Ashanti. [It was] stated that the total inward and outward goods traffic receipts during 1930–1 would be classified as to origin as follows:

Ashanti: Dunkwa–Kwahu Prahsu inclusive	£487,764
Nsuta	154,761
	£642,525

out of a total goods traffic of approximately £756,548. It would therefore be seen that that part of the railway system mentioned above contributed no less than 84.9 per cent of the total. Ashanti itself was responsible for 64.4 per cent of the total. This does not take into account passenger traffic, the receipts from which for Ashanti must represent a big percentage of the total earned in this department. He asserted that at existing rates all Ashanti Traffic to and from the port of Takoradi would travel by road if that form of transportation were possible, a conclusion which proved that existing rates were of penalising proportions where such could be imposed.

The General Manager did not deny that as a rate on raw produce exported in bulk, the rate on cocoa from Kumasi to Takoradi (81*s* 9*d*) was high. He stated, however, that he would be unable to replace by railway earnings the loss which would accrue from even a small reduction of railway rates on cocoa from Ashanti. In the circumstances the Committee can make no recommendation for such a reduction at the present time.

(4) Rates on cocoa consigned from Kwahu Prahsu–Konongo section of the railway to Takoradi. The attention of the Committee was directed specifically towards the cocoa rate from certain stations in Ashanti on the Accra line to Takoradi. The stations and the rates per ton concerned are the following:

	s	*d*
Akwasiho	70	0
Kwahu Prasu	74	0
Bompata	85	10
Juaso	90	11
Konongo	92	11

The rate from Nkawkaw to Accra is 51*s* 6*d* a ton and the effect of the disparity between it and the other rates named is to encourage the transport of cocoa by road from Konongo, Juaso, etc., to Nkawkaw whence it is railed to Accra at a comparatively cheap rate, thus diverting business from the Kumasi–Takoradi line and from Takoradi harbour which under other circumstances the latter might legitimately hope to secure. Cocoa shipped at Takoradi has in addition to bear harbour dues amounting to 3*s* 3*d* a ton.

As has been stated above no reduction of the rate for cocoa from Kumasi to Takoradi (81*s* 9*d* a ton) can be recommended in present circumstances; but after discussion the Committee agreed that, anomalous though it may appear at first sight, a flat rate of 75*s* a ton from all stations between Konongo and Kwahu Prasu inclusive to Takoradi should be introduced, the Kumasi rate being left unchanged. Mr Lewis assured the Committee that, although the Kumasi Chamber of Commerce objected on principle to the present high freight rate from Kumasi and would continue to press for its reduction, they would readily appreciate the motive governing the suggested reduction in the rates for cocoa consigned from Konongo–Kwahu Prasu to Takoradi and would not use it as a lever for securing a decrease in the rate from Kumasi.

(5) Cocoa rates – Tafo–Nsawam to Accra. A possible anomaly in the rates from stations between Tafo and Nsawam to Accra was also mentioned. After discussion the Committee decided to leave the point to the consideration of the General Manager.

71. The terminal charge (1*s* 6*d* a ton) at Takoradi was criticised and explained as representing the cost of shunting wagons and facilities for this service. The Committee were informed that a similar charge is levied on all British railways and that at Apapa, Nigeria it is 2*s* 6*d* a ton. The General Manager strongly opposed the abolition of this terminal charge and the Committee accepted his view.

Takoradi harbour dues

72. The president of the Gold Coast Chamber of Mines informed the Committee that in his opinion the harbour dues are too high and in support of his argument quoted figures to show that the port charges on 8,000 tons of manganese ore exported at a South African port amounted to £244 10*s* whereas the corresponding figure at Takoradi was £1,549 9*s* 1*d*. In the absence of details as to how they are made up the Committee was not in a position to make a comparative analysis of these figures.

73. It was alleged that excessive charges had the effect of diverting traffic, both imports and exports, to other ports in the Colony. The Committee noted that Takoradi harbour dues were settled in 1927 by a Committee representative of Government after full consultation with and approval of the mercantile and shipping interests, but they were based on the assumption that Sekondi, Cape Coast and Saltpond would be closed as ports of entry which assumption has not been realised except in the case of Sekondi. If Cape Coast and Saltpond had ceased to be ports the resulting increase in the trade of Takoradi would in all reasonable probability have permitted the harbour to pay its working expenses and fixed charges. It could not hope at existing charges to compete successfully with surf ports at which no port charges are levied and the expectation that the economic value of the convenience, speed and safety of handling cargo alongside wharves in smooth water would automatically attract most of the trade of Saltpond and Cape Coast had proved by no means fully justified. In this connection it was noted that the shipping companies made no differentiation in their rates for cocoa freight on account of this factor.

74. In the Committee's view the problem at Takoradi harbour is fundamentally similar to that presented by the railway, namely, that the port charges were calculated with the object of covering the cost of all the working expenses and fixed charges arising on account of its construction, inclusive of sinking fund charges. The Committee is not in a position to state definitely that the Gold Coast as a whole would benefit were the Takoradi harbour charges to be reduced substantially at the loss of direct harbour revenue ; in their opinion this again is a question which requires reference to an expert economist and they commend this suggestion to Government's consideration.

Transhipment charges

75. [One witness] raised the question of transhipment charges, at present 3*s* 3*d* per ton for transhipment between ship and ship and 6*s* 6*d* per ton when cargo has to be put ashore and reshipped. He stated that the effect of this high charge was to exclude business which would accrue profitably were the rate lowered. The General Manager admitted that the point was worthy of full consideration and undertook to investigate it and to report his conclusions to Government. The committee welcomed this assurance.

Railway renewals fund

76. In the estimates for 1931–2 the sum of £108,854 was provided for renewals, but as an emergency measure in the present crisis payment has been suspended. The corresponding figure for 1932–3 is calculated to be £126,892 and the question has arisen whether provision should be deferred for the second year in succession. The General Manager pointed out that the fund had only come into

existence in 1923–4 while some of the wasting assets of the railway had been in use for more than 25 years and would inevitably require replacement at an early date. The fund was therefore not solvent and every deferment enhanced its unsound position. Renewals could not be postponed indefinitely without grave risk to life and property or without creating an uneconomic burden on the future. The Committee were impressed with the gravity of a second suspension of contributions but were not in a position to say whether the financial prospects of the Gold Coast for 1932–3 are grave enough to justify what in normal circumstances would be an indefensibly imprudent step.

Possible conversion of six per cent loan

77. The question was raised whether it was advisable to endeavour to obtain the conversion of the 6 per cent loan to a lower interest figure. This was a matter beyond the competency of the Committee, who, however, desire it to be recorded for the consideration of Government.

22(b). The Railway Revenue Committee, 1932 [1]

Railway competition with motor transport

Although it was definitely stated in the terms of reference that the decline in the railway revenue was attributable, in the main, to competition from road transport, we considered it advisable to ascertain from those of the witnesses who had a special knowledge of the subject, their views as to the accuracy or fallacy of this statement. This we did and with the exception of [one witness], who was inclined to ascribe the railway's failure to attract sufficient traffic to lack of enterprise on the part of the management, they were all emphatic in their assertion that the whole system of motor transport in the Gold Coast – if, indeed, one can be said to exist – rests at present on such an uneconomical basis that it is impossible for the railway or other properly organised and regulated transport service to compete successfully with the owners of a few small lorries for the traffic from areas which are served by both road and rail. We will examine this contention in detail in a latter part of our report . . .

Sinking Fund and Contributions to Renewals Fund

5. In the course of our examination of the railway's financial position, two questions of interest were raised, the one relating to the Sinking Fund, as to whether it was a fair charge to place against the railway, and the other to the payments made by the railway to General Revenue in past years. Both of these questions received the consideration of the Railway Retrenchment Committee and in regard to the first the members unanimously recommended that the Sinking Fund charges should be borne by the General Revenue of the Colony. This at first appeared to us to be a reasonable and sound recommendation, as on the amortisation of the loans the Colony will obtain possession of a free fully equipped railway. But this opinion we altered when we learnt from the Treasurer that the total contributions paid in respect of Sinking Fund charges and Renewals was in fact equivalent to, but did not exceed, the amount which it would pay to a Renewals Fund alone if it were a commercial concern. He explained that if the

[1] Report of the Railway Revenue Committee (road v. rail), *Sessional Paper no. III, 1932–3*, paras. 3–22 (extracts).

railway were a commercial concern, it would have to pay working expenses, superannuation charges (corresponding to pension charges); contribute in full to Renewals, make provision for an adequate reserve fund; possibly provide for the redemption of debentures and lastly pay a dividend on share capital. He added that the railway dues as at present constituted, meet these charges but that there was a peculiarity as regards the allocation of the annual contribution to the Renewals Fund which, however, was properly assessed upon the basis of the rate of depreciation of the wasting assets. The peculiarity lies in the fact that only two-thirds of the amount thus arrived at is credited to the Renewals Fund, the remaining one-third being regarded as a contribution toward a Sinking Fund to liquidate that proportion of the Colony's debt incurred in the construction and improvement of the railway. While we agree with the General Manager, that to maintain the Renewals Fund at an economic level it should be credited in full with the annual contribution and the reduction of one-third from it tends to render the fund insolvent, we are, at the same time, satisfied from the Treasurer's explanation, that the user of the railway is not paying more than he should (the Retrenchment Committee suggests that he is) as the total annual contributions to the Sinking and Renewals Funds do not exceed the amount due in respect of the latter fund if calculated on a proper basis. We agree with the Treasurer that the allocation of the contributions is the concern of Government which in its relation to the railway stands in the position of a guarantor.

Balance of amounts paid by the railway to general revenue in past years

6. As it had been suggested that of the surplus balances paid over by the railway to General Revenue in past years there still remain, after the loss for 1930–1 had been met, approximately, £500,000 to the credit of the railway and that this amount should be regarded as being available to finance the railway during the present period of trade depression, we requested the Treasurer to assist us in determining, as far as it is possible to do so, the position between Government or general revenue on the one hand and the railway on the other. He submitted the following statement:

	(£s)
Net railway revenue handed over to General Revenue between 1 April 1922, and 31 March 1930	2,767,912
From this have to be subtracted the following amounts:	
(*a*) Loss in railway in 1930–1	120,013
(*b*) Estimated loss in 1931–2	139,000
(*c*) Charges borne by General Revenue in respect of railway loans from 1 April 1922 to 31 March 1927	1,832,255
(*d*) Pensions paid from General Revenue in respect of railway servants for the same period	62,900
(*e*) Amount expended from surplus balances on capital works between 1 April 1922 and 31 March 1931	536,942
(*f*) Estimated expenditure on capital works 1931–2	3,060

These deductions total £2,694,170 and when subtracted from £2,767,912 leave a balance in favour of railway of £73,742. But as the Treasurer pointed out, this credit of £73,742 would become a heavy deficit if payment were made of the contributions to the Renewals Fund. It will be seen from items (*e*) and (*f*) of the Treasurer's statement that the cost of capital works has been or will be charged to revenue and not to capital account. The correctness of this may be questioned by those who hold the view that interest only on the amount expended on capital works should be so charged: but the fact remains that of the surplus balances paid by the railway to general revenue only £73,742 may be considered as standing to the credit of the railway and that this would be converted into a debit if the contributions to renewals fund were paid.

Extent to which deficit may be attributed to competition of motor transport

8. We will now examine the extent to which this deficit of £246,426 may be attributed to competition from motor transport which for the time being we will assume to be fair. On studying the map of the Colony it will be seen that the road system in Ashanti and the Western Province was developed with due regard for the interests of the railway which there preceded the roads. In both of these Administrations the roads are complementary to, and not competitive with, the railway and the result of this system, which does not provide direct access to Takoradi by road, is that of a total revenue of £756,548 obtained from goods traffic in 1930–1 no less than £487,766 or 64.4 per cent was derived from traffic either forwarded from or received at stations on the section of line between Kwahu Prahsu and Dunkwa where, as has been indicated, there is little competition between road and rail.

History of road and railway construction in the Eastern and Central Provinces

9. In the Eastern and Central Provinces, on the other hand, the history of road and railway construction is different. For various reasons the Accra–Kumasi railway was built in comparatively short sections, a considerable period elapsing between the completion of one section and the commencement of another. Nsawam, Mangoase, Koforidua, Tafo and Anyinam became in their turn railheads, and from each of these towns were constructed feeder roads. In many cases (i.e. the Koforidua–Nkawkaw road) these roads run parallel to the railway and, not having been abandoned with the extension of the line but on the contrary improved, they now provide for the transport by road direct to and from Accra of cocoa and other freight which were formerly carried by the railway.

Figures showing decline in cocoa and general goods traffic

10. . . . Comparing the figures for 1924–5, when the effect of road competition first began to be felt, with those for 1930–1 it will be seen that there has been a decrease of 46,006 tons in the quantity of goods forwarded with a resultant loss in revenue of £116,952. The number of passengers carried has also fallen from 486,015 in 1924–5 to 374,825 in 1930–1 and the revenue derived from that source from £68,840 to £49,297. Illustrative though these figures are of the effect of road competition in the traffic and revenue of the railway, it is the tonnage of cocoa railed which provides the most accurate test for measuring the extent of that competition. The exports of cocoa from Accra for the past five years were as follows:

	Tons
1927	97,868
1928	91,403
1929	100,136
1930	80,251
1931	112,272

These figures show that, excepting 1930 when owing to a hold-up by the farmers there was a sudden drop of some 20,000 tons, which was shipped in the following year, the quantity of cocoa exported annually does not fluctuate to any appreciable extent and may be placed at an average of 96,500 tons. Of this amount the railway in 1924–5 carried 91,643 tons, representing approximately 95 per cent, as compared with 51,139 tons or 53 per cent in 1930–1. Thus in six years there has been a fall of over 40,000 tons in cocoa freights alone as the result of road competition, the effect of which will be further manifested by comparing the tonnage for 1927–8 with that for the following year. Between 1924–5 and 1927–8 the cocoa traffic decreased from 91,643 to 51,780 tons. Then the Nsawam–Accra road was closed for reconstruction. This brought about an immediate increase in tonnage which rose by 25,578 tons to 77,358 tons, but on the road being re-opened it quickly receded to 50,139 tons in 1930–1 and returns from various stations indicate that even that low figure will not be reached during the current year.

Fall in passenger traffic

11. That passenger traffic also has been adversely affected by road competition will be seen from the following figures [Table 22 (b) 1] which are for the whole railway system including the Central Province section:

Table 22 (b) 1

	Passengers carried	Passenger receipts (£s)	Passenger train miles
1923–4	1,334,756	187,664	253,747
1924–5	1,347,916	187,571	276,450
1925–6	1,450,325*	195,969	293,174
1926–7	1,452,915*	202,404	347,043
1927–8	1,728,493*	244,616	411,418
1928–9	1,875,002*	258,340	495,896
1929–30	1,846,564*	245,750	525,949
1930–1	1,336,489*	174,522	490,141

* Excludes extraordinary traffic in Achimota workmen.

The important fact which . . . table [22 (b) 1] discloses is that for the conveyance of practically the same number of passengers the railway in 1930–1 ran services either by sentinel steam coaches or ordinary trains involving 336,394 train miles more than in 1923–4 without of course obtaining any additional revenue therefrom, compelling the railway to augment the local services in order to maintain its passenger traffic at the level of 1923–4, when such services did not exist, and thus of reducing its net earnings from this service.

The closing of the Nsawam–Accra road (the road which has unquestionably caused greater loss to the railway than any other) coincided with the introduction of a local service on that section of the line. The result, which must be attributed principally to the closing of the road, was that in 1928–9 the number of passengers booked at Nsawam rose to 195,000 but began to fall as soon as the road was reopened to motor traffic, and it reached the low figure of 106,000 in 1930–1. No better proof of the effect of road competition on the railway passenger traffic can, in our opinion, be required than that afforded by these figures, which become all the more convincing if account is taken of the increased facilities provided in the way of more frequent services and reduced fares.

Conditions in the Central Province

12. Turning to the Central Province we find that the Cape Coast–Foso, Saltpond, Oda and a considerable portion of the Winneba–Oda roads were in existence before the construction of the Central Province Railway. Subsequently the Cape Coast–Foso road was extended to Brofoyedru in Ashanti and new roads to the north of Oda and Kade were built for the purpose of feeding the Central Province Railway and thus allowing the produce from these hitherto undeveloped areas to be transported to Takoradi at rates which left a fair margin of profit for the farmers. But far from fulfilling the object for which they were built, these roads have merely served to divert to the Central Province ports cocoa which prior to their construction was head-loaded either to Obuasi or Anyinam and carried thence by rail to Sekondi or Accra. They certainly enabled the farmers to obtain a better price for their produce but they have not brought traffic to the railway. The Central Province produced on an average 46,000 tons of cocoa a year. Mr Miles of the Department of Agriculture stated in his evidence before us that the most economical outlet for one-third of this produce is through Takoradi via the Central Province Railway; but the returns for 1930–1 show that, despite drastic reductions in rates, only 2,264 tons out of 4,026 tons railed were forwarded to Takoradi, the other 1,762 tons being carried for short distances only and unloaded at stations which are connected by road with the Central Province ports. If Mr Miles's estimate is accepted as correct, then the Central Province railway is losing yearly some 12,000 tons of cocoa traffic (i.e. the difference between one-third of the total output and the amount transported by rail to Takoradi) as the result of road competition, which cannot however be said to have affected the passenger traffic, which is negligible except between stations in the Central Province. The people have long-established connections with Cape Coast, Saltpond and Winneba and, whatever may be the facilities for travelling afforded them on the railway they will not abandon their visits to those towns in favour of Sekondi which is more than three times the distance from their homes. The competition between road and the rail, in so far as the Central Province is concerned, is confined, therefore, to not more than 12,000 tons of cocoa. But this figure does not include cocoa from Asuom, Otumi, Apiramang, and other towns which are linked up with Kade by motor roads.

. . .

Railway rates reduced to a figure below that at which motor transport can be run economically

14. In the course of his statement before us [one witness] said that the lowest inclusive cost at which a lorry of 15 cwt carrying capacity could be run was 3.83*d* per running mile which is equivalent to a little more than 5*d* per ton mile. And he added that it is only by persistent over-loading that a lorry of 15 cwt capacity (this equals 12 bags of cocoa) can be made to pay on the Accra–Nsawam road as strict adherence to the provisions of the Motor Traffic Ordinance would leave the owners no profit with running costs at the figure given above. This statement served to support the conclusion, which we had already reached, namely, that with petrol at its present price, motor transport cannot be run economically at less

than 6*d* per ton mile. The following table which gives the rates charged on spirits and cocoa between Accra and the more important stations on the line to Kumasi in 1923 and 1931, disproves the suggestion that the Railway Authorities have not brought down the rates to a figure which should allow, provided road transport is run on an economic basis, of their obtaining the greater part of the goods traffic from the area in the Eastern Province which the railway serves [Table 22 (b) 2]:

Table 22 (b) 2

Station	Distance (miles)	Rate per ton 1923 *s d*	1929 *s d*	1931 *s d*	Rate per ton mile (pence)
		Spirits			
Nkawkaw	110	195 10	62 6	50 0	5.45
Anyinam	86	170 0	53 0	35 0	4.88
Tafo	65	125 0	37 11	25 0	4.62
Koforidua	52	103 4	30 4	18 6	4.27
Nsawam	27	54 0	15 9	8 0	3.55

Station	Distance (miles)	Rate per ton 1923 *s d*	1927 *s d*	1931 *s d*	Rate per ton mile (pence)
		Cocoa			
Nkawkaw	110	76 8	65 0	50 0	5.45
Anyinam	86	61 6	41 0	35 0	4.88
Tafo	65	47 6	35 6	25 0	4.62
Koforidua	52	38 10	27 0	18 6	4.27
Nsawam	27	15 0	9 0	8 0	3.55

The present rates on the Accra–Kumasi railway, which are applicable to all traffic, including petrol but excluding dangerous goods, are therefore lower than those at which motor transport can be run economically even if allowance is made for the double handling at Accra. The reductions made on the Central Province Railway have been even more drastic and are now considerably below 3*d* per ton mile, the figure to which the Central Province Trade Routes Committee stated that they would have to come down in order to attract traffic to the railway . . . [Table 22 (b) 3].

These rates are decidedly competitive and should, but do not, ensure for the railway the greater part, if not the whole of the cocoa from the country to the north of the line and within five miles of it on the south. To take Oda for example: this town which, apart from Swedru, is the most important cocoa-buying centre in the Central Province, is situated 52 miles distant from both Saltpond and Winneba, and the cost of transporting a ton of cocoa thence to either of these ports by motor lorry should not be less than 26*s* if running costs are to be fully covered. The lighterage at Winneba and Saltpond is 7*s* a ton, so the total cost of

Table 22 (b) 3

Stations	Distance (miles)	Cocoa per ton (shillings)	Cocoa per ton mile (pence)	Ordinary goods per ton (shillings)	Ordinary goods per ton mile (pence)
Kade	156	28	2.0	30	2.3
Oda	138	20	1.73	22	1.9
Achiasi	133	18	1.62	20	1.8
Foso	108	18	2.0	20	2.2
Twifu	87	18	2.5	20	2.75

shipping a ton of cocoa from Oda through these ports is 33*s*. The freight on the railway from Oda to Takoradi is 20*s* a ton. To this must be added 3*s* 3*d* harbour dues and 5*s* lighterage, making a total of 28*s* 3*d* a ton as compared with 33*s*, if either Winneba or Saltpond is used as the port of export. But despite this saving of 4*s* 9*d* a ton and the superior facilities for loading which it affords, only 2,264 tons of cocoa were shipped through Takoradi in 1930–1 from the areas through which the Central Province Railway runs.

Economies already effected by railway authorities . . .

15. Although a wide interpretation of our terms of reference did not preclude our inquiry into the cost of running the railway, we decided not to do so but to accept, for the purpose of our report, the finding of the Railway Retrenchment Committee that 'failing a general reduction in the scale of personal emoluments, no further appreciable reduction in working expenditure can be effected immediately without a dangerous sacrifice of efficiency.' The General Manager informed us that 40 Europeans and 89 African posts had been, or were to be, abolished, and that these represented 23.7 and 13.2 per cent respectively of the staff as it was in 1930–1. He gave us . . . figures to show the reduction in expenditure between 1930–1 and 1932–3 [Table 22 (b) 4]:

Table 22 (b) 4

	1930–1 (£s)	1931–2 (£s)	1932–3 (£s)
Maintenance of track, etc.	115,971	107,113	90,884
Locomotive and carriage	283,577	247,840	189,365
Traffic expenses	92,931	88,675	72,968
Accounting stores and management	47,209	45,031	39,135
Charges by other departments	35,681	34,762	29,132
Totals	575,369	523,421	421,484

We express no opinion as to whether further economies could be made – we do not consider ourselves competent to do so – but, apart from this question we are satisfied that short of running its own motor transport, a course which we do not recommend, the Railway Management has taken all steps possible to secure its proper share of passenger and goods traffic and that it would have succeeded in doing so had it merely to compete with properly organised motor transport services run on an economic basis and carrying the overhead charges which such services must bear. We will now examine the nature of the road competition with which the railway has to contend to see if, as we have assumed, it is fair in its incidence.

Proceeds of motor taxation less than one-third of expenditure on roads

16.... It is clear, therefore, that the conditions as regards the respective tracks on which the two competing systems of transport operate, have hitherto favoured road transport enormously. On the one hand is a railway, completely State-owned, and therefore under the necessity, if conducted on a strictly commercial basis, of fixing its freight and passenger rates at such a level that all charges on account of the capital expended on the construction of its track, together with all charges in respect of the maintenance of the track, are covered by such rates; and on the other hand a road transport service, privately owned, but operating on State-owned roads, towards the construction and maintenance of which, such road transport services have contributed, during the last ten years, less than one-third of the total cost. As has been stated above, £2,444,810 is the amount by which the general taxpayer has relieved road transport services during that period of charges which should, on a strictly commercial basis, be borne by such services. This represents the measure of advantage which has, in consequence, accrued to road transport in its competition with the railway. It cannot but be regarded as an anomaly that the taxpayer should have been called upon to subsidise to such an extent a form of transport which, along many routes, runs in direct competition with the form of transport which he himself owns. And here it must be remembered that as no other form of vehicular traffic uses the roads in this colony no ground exists for contending that motor transport should not bear the whole cost of the construction and maintenance of roads.

Further consideration of the expenditure on roads

18. We have, however, so far only dealt with the question on the basis of the figures of the last ten years, and it may no doubt be argued that on the basis of the 1931–2 figures, road transport services do in fact bear the full cost of all road works. This, at first sight, appears to be a valid argument, for the estimated cost of road works in 1931–2 is £199,080 whereas total motor taxation if maintained at the 1930–1 level will amount to £271,222 a figure which we hasten to add is unlikely to be realised as the importations of petrol have decreased from 8,000,000 gallons in 1929 to 5,000,000 gallons in 1931; and there are indications that they will fall still lower in 1932. But taking the figures... it must be pointed out that they show the position in the most favourable light in so far as motor transport is concerned, for, in the first place, they represent only the actual disbursements by the Central Government, no allowance being made for the value of communal labour used on the construction and maintenance of roads under the Roads Ordinance. That the value of this labour cannot lightly be disregarded will be realised if we mention that to maintain these roads by means of labour paid at the current rates would, it is estimated, involve additional annual expenditure of £150,000. Further, the cost of constructing many important roads (e.g. Adawso–Mampong, Adawso–Mamfe, Apedwa–Kibi and Nkawkaw–Mprawso) has been borne by the Native Administrations and is not included in the figures...

Again, although a reduction in the estimated expenditure on trade roads has been achieved in the current estimates, this should not be regarded as anything more than a temporary respite. Owing to a large expenditure during the last two years on the reconditioning of the tarmet roads, it has been possible temporarily to reduce maintenance charges, but the previous standard of maintenance must be restored in due course, if a most serious deterioration of the road surface is to be avoided.

Furthermore, motor transport services have hitherto been entirely relieved by the general taxpayer of the entire cost of the construction of new roads, and of improvements to existing roads. It is true that such works must have now been almost completely suspended owing to the financial depression, and it is possible that some years will elapse before this country is again in a position to undertake further capital expenditure of this nature, but these considerations do not relieve motor transport services, if they are to be treated on a strictly commercial basis, of the obligation to make some return to the general taxpayer on account of the large expenditure which has already been made.

Amount that motor transport services may justifiably be called upon to pay

19. . . . No less than £1,900,113 has been expended on capital road work during the last decade; so making due allowance for the money and the value of labour expended by the people on the construction of pioneer roads and for expenditure incurred previous to 1921–2, it would scarcely be an exaggeration to assess the present total expenditure on these services at £2,500,000. We are, therefore, of the opinion that calculating interest on this amount at 5 per cent but entirely ignoring the Sinking Fund it would not be inequitable to require of motor transport services that they should make annual payments of £125,000 for some years to come on account of past expenditure on capital works.

Financial aspect of the road versus rail competition

20. Briefly stated, the financial aspect of the road *versus* rail competition, in so far as the former is concerned, is that, if motor transport services are to be treated on exactly the same basis as the railway, motor taxation should for the next few years at least cover the following estimated charges:

	(£s)
(a) Maintenance of trade roads	130,000
(b) Maintenance of town roads	25,000
(c) Maintenance of political roads	150,000
(d) Reimbursement to general taxpayer on account of capital works	125,000
	430,000

In paragraph 18 above we mentioned that, unless a marked revival in trade occurs, a decrease in the revenue from duty on petrol must be anticipated. This being so, it will not be wise to count on obtaining from motor taxation more than £260,000 to meet charges of £430,000 which in our opinion may correctly be debited to road users. Thus there remains a gap of £170,000 to be bridged. We do not suggest that it will be possible or expedient completely to bridge this gap by motor taxation, but we contend that the figures do quite conclusively prove that motor transport has in the past been accorded, and will, on the present basis of taxation, continue to hold a privileged position as compared with the railway, in respect of the charges incurred on providing and maintaining the track on which it operates. We are fully conscious of the difficulty of placing a monetary value in terms of running miles on this advantage, but assuming that the number of motor vehicles on the register is 7,000 (excluding motor cycles and trailers) and that each vehicle runs 12,000 miles a year, it may be taken, on a rough calculation, that motor transport is subsidised by the general taxpayer to the extent of 0.56*d* per running mile. If 30 cwt is accepted as the average pay load carried by commercial vehicles, the advantage works out at approximately 0.37*d* per ton mile.

Export duty on cocoa should not be taken into consideration

21. In commenting on the argument advanced in the preceding paragraph one member of the Committee observed that the export duty on cocoa was first imposed for the expressed purpose of providing funds to defray the cost of the construction and improvement of roads and that if account were to be taken of the revenue derived from that tax there would be no amount owing on account of capital works. This statement is only partially correct for although feeder roads to the railway are mentioned in the report of the Committee which was appointed in 1926 to devise means of raising additional revenue, the terms of the report make it clear that the principal object of the tax was to finance the extension of the Accra–Kumasi railway, work on which had then been suspended. But even assuming the statement to be correct, the fact that a tax on cocoa, which falls principally on those who have no direct interest in motor transport, was imposed to meet the cost of roads would not affect the contention that of the expenditure incurred on their construction and improvement, the users of roads, as distinct from the general taxpayers, have not contributed an amount proportionate to the advantages and benefits which they have derived therefrom, on the contrary it would support the argument that the taxpayers have subsidised motor transport to the extent of the amount realised from the export duty on cocoa and have thus placed the railway, which they themselves own, at a disadvantage in the competition for passenger and loads traffic in the areas where both forms of transport exist.

Comparison of the incidence of motor taxation

22. Before leaving the question of motor traffic taxation, we would mention that we have been able to compare the incidence of such taxation in the Gold Coast with that in certain other Colonies for the quinquennial period 1926–30. The . . . percentages [Table 22 (b) 5] represent the proportion which total motor taxation bears to total expenditure on roads for that period in each of the Colonies named:

Table 22 (b) 5

Colony	per cent
Gold Coast	33.1
Nyasaland	38.2
British Somaliland	39.1
Cyprus	42.9

Table 22 (b) 5—*continued*

Colony	per cent
Jamaica	46.8
Nigeria	54.1
Hong Kong	54.5
Gibraltar	66.6
Grenada	80.5
Kenya	89.3
Ceylon	91.3
British Guiana	125.0
Palestine	130.7

The value of the above figures may be affected by local considerations of which we are unaware, but even so they must be regarded as affording definite proof of the correctness of our contention that motor transport in this Colony is unreasonably favoured in the matter of taxation.

23. Prohibitions on the movement of cocoa by road should be abolished as soon as the cocoa traffic is definitely assured to the railway, 1945 [1]

Your Excellency,

We were appointed in April last a Committee to consider and report:

(*a*) whether in view of the importance of securing cheap and efficient rail and road transport services for both passengers and goods, the existing system by which restrictions are placed on road transport by the Carriage of Goods Ordinance, 1936, should continue;

(*b*) as to what form of Government control over road services should be introduced so as to assist the development of cheap and efficient road transport, due regard being had to the public interest in the railway;

and to make recommendations . . .

The local road–rail issue

3. We do not consider it necessary to set out again the whole complex problem of coordinating railway and road transport; the comparative disabilities of a railway as a common carrier, with fixed rates, unable to carry from door to door, vulnerable to destructive competition from road transport, but yet an essential means of transport that must be paid for by its users; or the proper advantages of road transport for short haul traffic, providing flexible and convenient services for both passengers and goods and giving a large amount of direct and indirect employment. These general principles of the problem have been set out often enough. The inevitable general conclusion that the development and operation of railway and road transport services should be controlled by a common representative body in the interests of the users of both is found, on examination, to be idealistic to the extent that account has to be taken of actual local conditions and has for this reason to be whittled down to what is necessary and practicable

[1] Report of the Road–Rail Transport Committee. *Sessional Paper no. VI, 1945*, paras 1–23 (extracts).

under these conditions. The local situation in the Gold Coast is that as a result of the rapid expansion of road transport in the period following the first war and after examination of the problem by a Committee appointed in 1932 to consider what steps should be taken in view of the serious losses suffered by the railway during recent years mainly owing to road competition, the Carriage of Goods Road Ordinance was passed in 1936. This ordinance provides not for licensing but for the prohibition of the carriage of specified goods over scheduled roads. It has been applied so as to prohibit the carriage of cocoa to the coast by road and the carriage of imported goods and beer by road from the coast into Ashanti. There are 16 sections of road to which these prohibitions apply. They are equipped with barriers at which vehicles passing through are inspected and recorded by the Police. This system has now been in use for nearly ten years and in spite of the objections that can be raised to it in principle, in fact it works and is generally understood – and for that reason accepted.

4. During the war two developments have taken place that require mention. First, on account of the general shortage of vehicles, tyres and petrol, road transport has been placed under strict control and reduced in volume. The census taken in January 1945, showed 3,800 lorries licensed as compared with 5,000 in 1930. Nearly two thirds of the present total are of pre-war manufacture. 2,850 were licensed in the Colony and 950 in Ashanti and the Northern Territories. The purposes for which the lorries are used are:

Passengers and goods	2,533
Goods only	388
Logging	78
Contracting	71
Mining	54
Government and town councils	360
Miscellaneous and insufficient information	316

In addition there are 79 ' buses ', 41 of which are owned by town councils and 38 are owned privately.

It will be seen from the above that about two thirds of the total number of lorries in the country are used for the general transport of passengers and goods. The gross weights are:

Below 50 cwt	180
50 cwt	1,411
51–99 cwt	572
100–110 cwt	1,291
Over 110 cwt	66
Insufficient information	280

5. The second development that has taken place is the standardization of cocoa buying prices at all rail points and Senchi ferry. This system has been introduced as a part of the war-time machinery for the purchase of cocoa by the West African Produce Control Board. Since the producer thus gets the same price for his cocoa at up-country railway stations as he gets for it delivered to the port, there is no inducement to send it by road to the coast. The operation of this scheme by which the purchasing agency pays the transport differentials is not only of considerable benefit to the up-country producer; it also assures to the railway the transport of the cocoa crop.

6. The cocoa crop is of vital importance to the railway, as is shown by the ... statement of goods revenue for 1943–4 [Table 23.1].

Table 23.1

	(£s)
Bauxite	90,900
Manganese	149,405
Cocoa	391,517
Timber	50,208
Native produce	58,500
Petrol and oil	62,500
U.S.A. traffic	58,800
General goods	276,850
Livestock	10,225
Total	1,148,905

The total railway revenue for 1943–4, including coaching (£402,400) and miscellaneous (£39,760) amounted to £1,590,975, of which total 25 per cent was goods revenue on cocoa. This percentage is likely to increase as passenger and other goods traffic is lost to road transport in the post-war period – a loss estimated by the railway management to amount to not less than £350,000 annually.

7. With the exception of certain areas in the vicinity of the ports, including the surf ports of Cape Coast and Winneba which the Government for its part has said that it is willing to operate if the shipping companies have the inducement to use them, there can be no justification for transporting cocoa by road to any destination other than the nearest rail point. We assume that the present system of standardised cocoa prices will continue, whatever form of controlled marketing is adopted, and if and when it is established for certain that it will continue, it would be possible, without risk of loss to the railway, to remove the present prohibition of the carriage of cocoa over the scheduled road sections. But that state of certainty has not yet been reached and until it is we recommend that the prohibition should remain.

8. We see no reason, however, to retain the existing prohibition on the carriage of imported goods or beer over the ten road sections to which such a restriction at present applied. No one is likely to wish to transport beer over these sections to any appreciable extent. But the present prohibition is absolute except with the permission of the Governor in Council. It may often prove desirable to use road transport for imported goods on these routes, and there is little reason to believe that this would cause any appreciable financial loss to the railway, so long as there are no cocoa-lorries returning empty to pick them up. Such prohibitions are obsolete and unnecessary restrictions in present conditions, and we therefore recommend that in respect of the carriage of imported goods and beer they should be abolished.

9. The policy whereby in the past gaps were deliberately left in the system of road communications, so as to prevent competition with the railway, has been abandoned.

10. In the case of a Government railway such as the Gold Coast railway, we hold the view that the well-known principle of rating according to 'what the

traffic can bear ' must give way to the importance, in the public interest, of charging the lowest possible rate consistent with efficient transport and the avoidance of subsidy from taxation. The railway rates in the Gold Coast are distinctly high, and the aim should be to reduce them, but we recognize that the possibility of reduction depends mainly on the securing of the cocoa traffic for carriage by rail. It is, moreover, impossible to estimate now with accuracy what the post-war losses of revenue on passengers and other goods traffic will amount to.

11. We do not consider that the railway should attempt to operate road services, and should prefer to see these left to private enterprise. Nor do traffic demands justify in our view any further railway construction. We think, therefore, that in present circumstances the answer to the road–rail issue, paragraph (*a*) of our terms of reference, can be simply expressed as the removal of all the prohibitions at present in force except that applying to cocoa, which should also be abolished as soon as the cocoa traffic is definitely assured to the railway by its own marketing system or by any other means.

Road transport

12. The Gold Coast is well equipped with road communications, in comparison with other African Territories, and the African has not been slow to develop the owner-driver single lorry transport business as an attractive and remunerative occupation. But the standard of transport provided at present is generally deplorable. The number of passengers carried is governed in practice not by the licensed carrying capacity of the vehicle or by safety regulations but merely by the physical limits of the space into which the passengers, together with the planks on which they sit and the goods and livestock which accompany them, can be squeezed. Passenger transport cannot be separated from goods transport; the reason why most people want to travel is to accompany their goods and so personally supervise their disposal. There is a very large unsatisfied demand for road transport, both on the main routes and from village to village. As soon as vehicles are available, there will be few villages of any size in the country without at least one African lorry-owner available for hire. This is essentially the small man's industry and any system of licensing the road services that he may operate would involve at once the consideration of several thousands of individual cases and routes and the task, impossible at present, of enforcing the conditions of the licences. An even greater practical objection to attempting to place the whole country under a system of road service licensing is the pronounced seasonal factor whereby the lorries transporting cocoa during the six months' main crop buying season are not needed for that purpose for the remaining half of the year. An illustration of the difficulty of matching licensed road services to the economic needs of a route under local conditions is provided by the case where during the main fishing season a large catch is landed at a small place ordinarily requiring practically no transport. Such an event produces a cry of ' send lorries ', and unless the lorries are immediately available (not being delayed by the need for some special permit) the fish are not fit to transport.

13. We consider that the practical difficulties involved in applying any general route licensing system in the Gold Coast would be so great as to outweigh considerably any real advantage that such control would confer.

14. These difficulties do not, however, apply to the main long-distance routes on which services for the carriage of goods and passengers are regularly operated and on which road services are the essential (because the only) means of trans-

port. The standards of efficiency and public safety at present observed on these routes are very low, and they are not likely to be improved so long as the operators who try to improve them (in respect of maintenance and reliability of the vehicles, suitability of accommodation, time-tables, fares and freight rates) are subject to unlimited competition from private vehicles, generally bought on hire-purchase and run to death in a short time. Such competition ultimately generally tends to raise transport costs. The benefits of control of road transport services on a main route have been amply proved by experience. They have not yet been seen in the Gold Coast, because the system has not been tried. It would in our view be a very desirable experiment to make, with a view to demonstrating the benefits and to producing results on which would depend the decision as to how far it should be applied progressively to other routes. The purpose of controlling the selected experimental routes would not be to create any sort of exclusive licence or monopoly. Any person prepared to fulfill the conditions laid down by the licensing authority would be eligible for a licence; the time when the traffic offering is less than the capacity of the licensed services is a long way ahead.

15. We suggest that two routes be taken for this purpose: Accra–Sekondi and Kumasi–Tamale. Both are important main routes carrying considerable traffic, especially in the carriages of passengers-*cum*-goods, they do not compete with the railway (apart from the small stretch between Accra–Nsawam), and there can therefore, be no ground for suggesting that licensing is being introduced as a medium to drive traffic to the railway.

Road costs and road taxation

23. It may be of interest (if not of practical value) to set out the position regarding expenditure on roads and the revenue derived directly from road transport for the years 1936–44. The expenditure figures, which are the amounts expended under Road Votes plus 20 per cent for overheads and excluding any provisions on account of capital cost before 1936 [Table 23.2] (see p. 198).
So expressed, revenues exceeded expenditure over the eight years by some £750,000 but the annual capital charge (which the 1932 Committee put at £125,000) would if included, produce a deficit. We have not thought it necessary to pursue this matter of road costing, but give the figures as they stand for general information.

Bibliography

17. *Report by the Honourable W. G. A. Ormsby-Gore on his visit to West Africa during the year 1926*, Cmd 2744, London 1926, pp. 48–55 (extracts).
18. Governor's Annual Address, *Legislative Council Debates, 1923–4*, pp. 42–55 (extracts).
19. Governor's Annual Address, *Legislative Council Debates, 1924–5*, pp. 18–21.
20. (a) Despatch from the Governor to the Secretary of State, no. 747, 2 November, 1922, on the subject of the proposed Central Province Railway, *Sessional Paper no. XIV, 1922–3*, paras 15–42 (extracts).

    (b) Papers relating to a project for the construction of a railway between Kumasi and the Northern Territories of the Gold Coast, *Sessional Paper no. XIII, 1927–8* (extracts); and Despatches relating to a project for the construction of a railway between Kumasi and the Northern Territories of the Gold Coast, *Sessional Paper no. XIV, 1929–30* (extracts).

Table 23.2

Expenditure on roads (£s)	
1936–7	305,000
1937–8	353,000
1938–9	334,000
1939–40	274,000
1940–1	241,000
1941–2	234,000
1942–3	240,000
1943–4	252,000

Revenue derived directly from road transport (£s)

Year	Motor licences	Drivers' licences	Import duties on petrol and oil	Ferry tolls and rents	Total
1936–7	65,842	2,610	285,626	6,507	360,585
1937–8	75,028	2,593	379,304	3,769	460,694
1938–9	77,792	3,045	329,683	10,168	420,688
1939–40	69,513	3,050	347,752	7,374	427,689
1940–1	74,930	2,581	220,767	4,505	302,783
1941–2	75,841	2,617	232,184	9,475	320,117
1942–3	73,527	2,650	288,640	6,207	371,024
1943–4	73,723	2,731	232,194	10,256	318,904

(c) Correspondence relating to the proposed Western Province Railway from Tarkwa to Babeaneha, *Sessional Paper no. X, 1930–1* (extracts from Enclosure A).

21. Report of the Central Province Trade Routes Committee appointed by His Excellency the Governor to consider and make recommendations regarding (i) Central Province Railway routes; (ii) the treatment of the ports of Cape Coast and Saltpond on the opening of Takoradi, *Sessional Paper no. VI, 1928–9*, paras 23–44 (extracts).
22. (a) Railway Retrenchment Committee Report and Recommendations, 1931, *Sessional Paper no. XIII, 1931–2*, part 3, paras 53–77, financial policy (extracts).
    (b) Report of the Railway Revenue Committee (road *v.* rail), *Sessional Paper no. III, 1932–3*, paras 3–22 (extracts).
23. Report of the Road–Rail Transport Committee, *Sessional Paper no. VI, 1945*, paras 1–23 (extracts).

4. Agriculture: General

The Committee on Agriculture Policy and Organisation,[1] which reported in 1928, identified four phases in the history of the Department of Agriculture. The first phase (1889–1905), characterised as the ' botanic garden era ' was a time when ' agricultural policy was limited to the importation of plants and (the study of) their behaviour under local conditions '. The result was a ' lasting confusion in the minds of the public between horticulture and agriculture '. The second phase (1905–15) saw the addition of instructional and demonstrational work to the duties of the department [2]: during this phase the structure of the staff of the department changed and most of the agricultural stations and sub-stations that existed in the twenties were established. The third phase (1915–22) saw ' marked changes of function and organisation. During this period instructional work was organised on a provincial basis and a staff of specialists was provided '.

Most of the documents presented in this section refer to the fourth phase, the period after 1922, which the Committee described as one of twofold transition.

On the one hand, the Government has definitely passed from the stage of a limited policy of protection of existing industries to a full acceptance of responsibility for a policy of development of local agricultural resources. On the other hand, the Department of Agriculture is ceasing to be an institution limited to demonstrational and instructional work and is becoming the recognised machine by which a policy of progressive development must be formulated and put into effect.

Agriculture was belatedly included, in 1923, in the Ten Year Development Programme and accounted for just over 1 per cent of actual expenditure under the programme, slightly more than was anticipated. Table VII gives a breakdown of anticipated and actual expenditure.

In his speech to the Legislative Council in 1923, the Governor surveyed these schemes and developments in other fields and concluded that ' the

[1] *Report of the Committee on Agricultural Policy and Organisation, Sessional Paper no. XVII, 1927–8.*

[2] The activities of the Department of Agriculture with respect to the cocoa industry are discussed in Ch. 5 below.

Table VII. *Anticipated and actual expenditure on agriculture and forestry under the Ten Year Development Programme* (£,000)

	Anticipated	Actual
Sisal plantation	47.8	47.8
Copra development	31.6	16.3
Firewood reserve (Achimota)	17.0	5.6
Rice development	5.3	5.3
Plant sanitation	100.0	51.5
Forests reserve survey	20.0	9.1
Cotton development	30.0	15.0
Total	251.7	150.6

Department [of Agriculture] has made excellent progress both in dealing with the cocoa industry and in encouraging new products ' (Document 24). A more comprehensive survey was undertaken in 1926 by Ormsby-Gore (Document 25) who argued strongly in favour of greater importance being attached to agricultural development.

In the past the status of the Director of Agriculture and his department has been too low. In some cases the Director of Agriculture has not been a member of the Legislative Council. It must now be recognized that the heads of the Agricultural Department are quite as important as the heads of any other Departments.

Emphasising the difference between the Gold Coast and Nigeria, Ormsby-Gore noted that:

With the exception of the Northern Territories, there is no large area where a new economic crop could be introduced, nor is there any considerable extent of country with rich natural resources like the oil-palm belt of South Eastern Nigeria still untapped. Practically all the Colony and Ashanti are in the economic radius of road or railway, and in places where that is not so the population is sparse. I do not say that the maximum of production has been reached, but that there is not room for any startling development of new economic crops.

Nonetheless the 1920s saw attempts, none of which survived the depression of the thirties, to encourage crops other than cocoa as part of the diversification programme.

In addition to the projects included in the Ten Year Development Programme, the colonial government sought to stimulate the cultivation of oil palms, described by Guggisberg as ' the next-best product – if not a better one than cocoa '. Before the First World War the colonial government introduced a Palm Oil Bill, the aim of which was to revive the old-established industry ' by encouraging capitalists to erect modern machinery for the expression of oil from the pericarp of palm fruits '.[3] It was the colonial government's belief

[3] G. E. Metcalfe, *Great Britain and Ghana : documents of Ghana History*, University of Ghana, Nelson, Accra and London, 1964, pp. 540–4.

that the establishment of perennial markets would encourage local production and that compulsion would be unnecessary to ensure deliveries since 'experience shows that the native farmers of the Gold Coast are sufficiently alive to their commercial interests to take their produce to the most accessible market at which they can obtain fair prices'. The venture was a failure and in 1923 Guggisberg described the industry as 'practically dead in spite of our great productive area' (Document 24). Undismayed, the colonial government proposed a new scheme for the revival of the industry, which differed significantly from the pre-war scheme in that it did not rely on private capital. In fact, quite the contrary:

Economic conditions have changed in the Gold Coast largely as a result of the successful development of the cocoa industry. The average farmer instead of being as formerly a labourer himself has now become an employer of labour.

Likewise, cocoa has been responsible for the development of the individualistic spirit in production as against the communal co-operative system under which palm oil was produced in former days. This no doubt has its advantages and also its disadvantages . . . but it is unlikely that the people will return to the old-time laborious methods of preparing palm oil and kernels under existing conditions; and if these products are to be successfully developed as they obviously should, central power-driven factories equipped with labour-saving machinery and a communal or co-operative production of fruits require to be instituted and developed.[4]

This scheme also failed to produce the desired results and a later one, proposed in 1929, reverted back to the idea of capitalist development; the colonial government proposed to subsidise the Niger Company which had developed a 'small type of unit factory' (Document 26b). Yet throughout the schemes of the twenties runs the idea of communal or cooperative development,[5] and the Department of Agriculture was always somewhat distrustful of foreign capital. Witness the following statement on a series of trials on the processing of shea nuts in the Northern Territories:

I have very little doubt that further trials are justified and still less doubt that these trials should be carried out by Government and not by private individuals or firms. Results of trials will have a very direct bearing on the question of developing the Northern Territories, and without them we cannot even know the difficulties which have to be cleared away before a profitable industry can be built up. Where the risks of failure are so great and the benefits resulting from success so general to the whole colony, it seems to me that, not only is Government justified in accepting the responsibility but the matter should not be left to private enterprise.[6]

[4] Document 26a, para 8.

[5] One initiative was the attempt to establish a communally organised coconut industry. For details of the scheme, see Report on communal coconut plantations, *Sessional Paper no. X, 1921–2.*

[6] Document 27, p. 226 below.

The difficulties of starting a profitable export trade in shea nuts in the Northern Territories were in part due to heavy transport costs. The colonial government attempted to find a way round this problem by processing the nuts locally and so reducing them in weight. The correspondence relating to the trials undertaken and the decision to spend £600 on further trials is reproduced in full in Document 27, in order to give some insight into the nature of colonial administrative practice.

In 1939, the semi-official West Africa Commission (Document 28a) wrote a critical survey of the work of the Department of Agriculture, criticising particularly its research stations. Given the importance of the cocoa industry, it expressed surprise that no research station was established in the cocoa belt until 1937 and that the one then set up at New Tofo was in an area not typical of conditions in the cocoa belt. The same point was made about other research stations, none of which was typical of the country it was intended to serve. This chapter concludes with the comments of the Watson Commission, 1948, on agricultural development (Document 28b). Representations were made to the Commission of five subjects, which it discussed at length: 1. The absence of any alternative crops to cocoa. 2. The lack of close contact between the Department of Agriculture and the farmer. 3. The weakness of agricultural education, experimentation and demonstration. 4. The excessive attention to the problems of export crops in comparison with crops for home consumption. 5. The absence of plans for future development. In criticising the work of the Department of Agriculture the Commission laid the blame on the colonial government and not on the staff of the department.

The Gold Coast has never been provided with the machinery in the form of staff, buildings and experimental stations to provide for the basic needs of its agriculture.

Ample evidence is available to confirm this view; firstly, in the small annual expenditure, over a period of many years, on agriculture relative to the revenue of the country and to the value of the agricultural exports, secondly, in the almost complete disregard of agriculture in the more advanced stages of education and in the award of scholarships for study abroad; and thirdly in the lack of interest in technical problems shown by many members of the Administration.[7]

24. Agricultural development: cautious optimism by the Governor, 1923[1]

Sisal and copra

71. The Accra Sisal Plantation and the three provincial coconut plantations near Labadi, Cape Coast, and Beyin have made excellent progress during the year. The success of the sisal production, which comes into bearing in 1925, has warranted the establishment of the necessary machinery and tramways. Provision for this is made in the Special Expenditure of the coming year. With regard to

[7] Document 28b, paras 324–5.

[1] Governor's Annual Address, *Legislative Council Debates, 1923–4*, pp. 36–9. This statement is representative of others made by the Governor during the period.

the coconut plantations, the progress made has been so good as to confirm the opinion that they will result in large copra industries in three parts of the Colony which are unsuitable for either cocoa or the oil palm. Especially we have a faith in the Cape Coast plantation giving that populous area an opportunity of a large and thriving industry in a few years' time.

Rice

72. We are now establishing a central power-driven factory for the Appolonia rice plantation, and provision for this is made in the Special Expenditure of the coming year.

Shea and groundnuts

73. As Honourable Members are well aware, I have, since my first arrival in this Colony, been deeply impressed by the potential value of our shea and groundnut industries in the Northern Territories, provided that at some future time we can supply the necessary railway transport. A most valuable report by Mr McLeod, the Conservator of Forests, has been published in Sessional Paper no. VIII and the foreword of that report details the steps Government have taken in the matter. Briefly, after personal inspection, our experienced Conservator of Forests reckons that there are roughly 192 million shea trees in the Northern Territories capable of producing over 250,000 tons of shea butter annually. This figure is naturally based on the number of trees, but careful and systematic steps are in progress to ascertain the productive capacity of the population. When to the presence of this great indigenous product is added the natural capacity possessed by the Northern Territories for groundnut production, it cannot be doubted that there is a great potential trade in the Northern Territories, trade eagerly awaited by over 500,000 inhabitants whose desire for manufactured articles is daily whetted by labourers returning from the south.

Although we cannot anticipate any appreciable development of the shea and groundnut industries until a railway is constructed, it is gratifying to learn that Major-General Grey is making plans to open up trading centres in the Northern Territories, and proposes to export a certain amount of shea and groundnuts. In order to encourage the new industry the Government has reduced its railway rates on shea nuts and groundnuts for export to £1 per ton from Coomassie.

Palm oil

74. With regard to the palm oil industry, at present practically dead in spite of our great productive area, I have carried out much correspondence during the year. Valuable as the palm oil and kernel industry may prove to us in the event of anything happening to cocoa, we shall not be able to compete with other palm oil countries unless we adopt the latest system of cultivation. I have therefore approached the Governors of other West African colonies with a view to our uniting in sending an agricultural officer to the East to ascertain the latest lessons and methods.

Kola

75. The extension of the kola plantations to which I alluded last year made steady progress in several parts of the country, but the industry, especially in the northern part of the Central Province and in the southern part of Ashanti, is

seriously handicapped by lack of railway transport. The progress made in kola cultivation in the French territories surrounding us, and in Nigeria, is such as to promise to kill our trade in the future unless we can provide the cheapest form of transport – railways.

Tobacco

The progress of tobacco cultivation during the past year has been negligible, and does not promise to be any greater in the future. Incidentally I may mention that I had the pleasure of smoking several excellent cigars made from the tobacco grown in the Juaso plantation by the indefatigable and enterprising Mr Martinson of the Agricultural Department. With regard to cotton, Major Jackson, the Honourable Provincial Commissioner of the Eastern Province, and Mr Knowles, the Provincial Superintendent of Agriculture, have displayed the most praiseworthy keenness in developing cultivation, and it seems that we may indulge in a little mild optimism on the possible results.

General results, 1922–3

76. Summing up the agricultural situation, the Department has made excellent progress both in dealing with the cocoa industry and in encouraging new products during the past year, and I have strong hopes that the new officers, who have picked up the work with unusual rapidity, have acquired such experience that the country can safely leave the safeguarding of agriculture in their hands. The agriculture school at Coomassie which was started during the year has proved an undoubted success, and should in due course help to reinforce with a gradually increasing African staff the over-worked European officers.

25. Agricultural policy: comprehensive survey by Ormsby-Gore, 1926 [1]

The Agricultural Departments in British West Africa have been considerably augmented and reorganised in the last few years since the war. A sound Agricultural Department must contain three essential elements. First, a scientific staff at headquarters working directly under the Director of Agriculture at the problems set by him. This staff will consist of agricultural chemists, botanists, entomologists and mycologists. Bio-chemists would also be a help. As far as possible this scientific staff should be at one station working in one group of laboratories: such research should be centralised. Further, it should be coordinated – not merely between the four West African Colonies – but with the similar research which is to be carried on in Trinidad and at Amani in East Africa. Such agricultural research centres should preferably be situated at the same place as the principal model or experimental farm, and, further, should be connected with any agricultural college or training centre for native assistants for the Agricultural Department's staff.

This arrangement is now in being at Ibadan in Nigeria, and, further, it is proposed that both at Ibadan and at the corresponding station at Njala in Sierra Leone the principal training college for teachers in the rural schools should also be contiguous. Such a concentration is of the highest importance to the future economic development of the African Dependencies.

[1] *Report by the Honourable W. G. A. Ormsby-Gore on his visit to West Africa during the year 1926*, Cmd 2744, London 1926, pp. 139–53 (extracts).

In addition to this central organisation there are two further requirements. First, where the country is very varied in soil and climate as in the case of Nigeria, and where agriculture is to be used on direct native production, a whole network of model and experimental farms is essential – not only for the study of the economic crops of each locality, but also for the study and development of food crops. Experimental work in the field is the principal function of this section. Secondly, there should be a section of the Agricultural Department devoted to maintaining contact between the research workers and the native producer. The exact relations of these officers with officers of other departments and, where they exist, with the native administrations, are not easy to define – and yet it is on the agricultural officers in the field that success will depend. Cooperation between agricultural and administrative officers is most important. Agriculture plays such an all-important role in the life of the African that every provincial and district officer should take a keen interest in the agricultural progress of the people who look to him, as the principal representative of Government, in all matters. As it is the duty of the agricultural officer to work as far as possible with and through the District Officer, so the District Officer must be active in understanding and helping forward the work of the Agricultural Department.

In the past the status of the Director of Agriculture and his Department has been too low. In some cases the Director of Agriculture has not been a member of the Legislative Council. It must now be recognised that the heads of the Agricultural Department are quite as important as the heads of many other Departments. If we are to develop our tropical possessions we have got to realise the value of the scientific staff both in the laboratory and in the field, and we must provide careers in the Agricultural Departments in the Colonies which will attract personnel possessed not only of high technical qualifications but of capacity for leadership and ability to inspire others.

There is one matter connected with the Agricultural Departments – and in this connection I include the Veterinary Departments also – and that is the character of the agricultural bulletins and the annual reports of Agricultural Departments. They are, at present inclined to be too technical. If close co-operation between the Agricultural and Veterinary Departments on the one hand and the administrative staff or the farmer on the other is to be secured, it is necessary that the work done by the scientific staff should be brought to the knowledge of the non-technical officer in an easily understandable form. At the present time the agricultural bulletins and reports are of a highly technical character, and though they contain much of great scientific and general interest it is presented in a form which is over the head of the ordinary reader. It was suggested to me that the four Colonies might combine for the purpose of issuing a quarterly agricultural review the articles in which would be of such a character that they could be readily followed by officers of the administrative and other Departments, and by educated Africans. Such a publication would prove a means of circulating information and of letting research officers of the different Colonies know what is going on in neighbouring territories. Veterinary work should, of course, be included, as well as items of interest to British West Africa regarding, for example, what is being done in French West Africa or by the Imperial College of Tropical Agriculture in Trinidad. I think the suggestion is a good one and might be examined at the coming conference of representatives of the Agricultural Departments of the four Colonies due to take place in Nigeria next December.

I hope that it may be possible to arrange for such agricultural conferences to be held regularly every three years in one or other of the Colonies – preferably in a different one from the last. It might also be considered whether such conferences should be attended from time to time by acknowledged experts from outside the West African staffs, which would effect a personal liaison between agricultural research work in the tropics and those who study the whole field of analogous work throughout the Empire.

Primary production and its organisation in the Gold Coast

The task of the Agricultural Department in the Gold Coast is in some respects different from that in Nigeria. With the exception of the Northern Territories, there is no large area where a new economic crop could be introduced, nor is there any considerable extent of country with rich natural products like the oil palm belt of South-Eastern Nigeria still untapped. Practically all the Colony and Ashanti are in the economic radius of road or railway, and in places where that is not so the population is sparse. I do not say that the maximum of production has been reached, but that there is not room for any startling development of new economic crops – such as is happening with cotton in the north of Nigeria or seems likely to occur with cocoa in the south-west of that country. The Northern Territories are, however, as yet undeveloped but, until they are brought into economic radius of road and railway, development is not possible. The immediate task of the Department is therefore to consolidate the present position.

The activities of the Department are bound to centre on cocoa. Nearly 80 per cent of the value of the total exports of the Colony is derived from cocoa, and it is obvious that the protection, improvement, and development of this staple product must be its first care. Reliance on a single crop brings certain dangers with it. In the event of the spread of disease, a partial failure of the crop, or even a comparatively small fall in price, the economic position of the Colony would be seriously affected.

...The prices of food-stuffs, in the various towns seem unduly high, and it is equally important that the cultivation of locally grown food-stuffs should be stimulated in order to avoid the necessity for importation.

Cocoa

The most important action recently taken in regard to the cocoa industry has been the campaign of plant sanitation instituted last year. The cocoa-growing country has been divided into several areas and three or four officers specially appointed for the purpose have been allotted to each, to work through it giving advice to the farmers in regard to the care of the trees and the treatment of the various diseases to which they are subject. It will take two or three years before the effects of this campaign can be fully felt.

The real problem, however, of the cocoa industry in the future is how far the soil has been depleted of the necessary mineral content by the very heavy crops which have been borne in the past ten to twenty years. There are, I understand, already signs of falling-off in the yield in areas which have been under cultivation for some time. Not only is there danger to this crop from the impoverishment of the soil, but also from the deforestation which has become serious in certain parts of the Colony. I shall be dealing with this question later in connection with the work of the Forestry Department.

Palm oil

Formerly the oil palm industry in the Gold Coast was considerable. The exports from this industry some forty years ago were worth about £1,000,000, but they are now only about one-tenth that sum. There has been a slight revival in this trade in the last two years, due mainly to the extension of the road system. The decline of the oil palm trade is entirely due to the success of the cocoa, in which the labour is less arduous and the returns greater. Indigenous palms are found over considerable areas in well-defined belts, the thickest belt being in the Western Province on the edge of the high forest, and this belt is said to be extending inland as the forest recedes.

The industry is and always will be important for local domestic purposes. Steps have been taken to remedy the damage done by the felling of trees for palm-wine by giving demonstrations in tapping the living palm, but the people still prefer the more wasteful method of felling the tree.

Groundnuts

A considerable quantity of groundnuts are grown in various parts of the Colony for local use, but the amount is not sufficient for local consumption, and there is even some importation from Nigeria. This is obviously a point where the native should be encouraged to grow more in order to reduce the price of foodstuffs. However, apart from the Northern Territories where, as I have said, it may be possible in time to develop an export trade, there is no large area of the country where the groundnut industry might be developed.

Kola

There is a considerable export trade in kola nuts, averaging approximately 14,000,000 lbs for the last four or five years. This figure is exclusive of the large number which are exported overland to French territory and Northern Nigeria, of which it is impossible to form an accurate estimate. It may, however, be expected that there will be an attempt to grow this crop in the Colonies in question in order to avoid importations. The future of the Gold Coast kola nut industry is therefore by no means assured.

Cotton

During the last few years considerable attention has been given to the possibility of introducing the growing of cotton, chiefly in Togoland and the adjacent parts of the Colony. The result has been to increase the output from 7,700 lbs of seed cotton in 1922–3 to 450,000 lbs in 1924–5. In spite of this satisfactory increase, I am rather sceptical as to whether it will be possible to make any very great expansion except in the Northern Territories, which must, of course, await the construction of a railway.

Shea nuts

There is a shea nut belt in the Northern Territories corresponding to that in Nigeria. The difficulty in the development of this industry lies in the cost of transport to Kumasi for transhipment by the railway, and in the lack of population in the area. The 240-mile run from Tamale to Kumasi at present involves a cost of 1*s* 6*d* per ton mile by motor transport.

Rice

A certain amount of rice is grown in various parts of the Colony, but chiefly in the Western Province. As rice is imported in considerable quantities, every possible encouragement should be given to the growers of this crop with the object of reducing the cost of local foodstuffs. The Government have installed a small rice-mill not far from Axim in the Western Province, and there is a farm near it where different varieties of rice are being tried. These experiments should be carefully watched.

Sisal

A government sisal plantation was commenced in 1920 near Accra with the object of introducing a crop which could be grown on the barren and unproductive area between the sea and the forest. An area of 3,000 acres, subsequently reduced to 1,000 was lent to the Government by Accra Chiefs for the purpose. The sisal plants on the whole have grown well. Catch-cropping between the aloes was tried, but it has had a distinctly adverse effect on the yield. Labour has been a serious difficulty at times, but this has been overcome by the use of contract labour from the Northern Territories.

The factory – some three miles from Accra – is connected with the railway by a branch line, and is provided with Robey sisal hemp machinery of the most modern pattern. Leaves are brought into the factory on trucks on portable lines and pulled by a light tractor. The fibre is reported on as being of good average strength, but insufficiently washed and with defects in brushing and baling due to certain faults in some of the machines. These defects are now being remedied. The capital cost of the undertaking was about £35,000. The yield of fibre to green leaf is about 3¼ per cent, and the yield per acre varies from 9 to 20 cwts. It is estimated that when everything is favourable and labour sufficient the local production cost is about £20 per ton. Some further £7 is required to cover freight and shipment. The value of sisal in European and American markets today is approximately £40 to £45 per ton.

It must be remembered that the establishment of this plantation, being of an experimental nature, costs considerably more than is usually reckoned as necessary to establish sisal in places where it is a recognised industry, and the plantation has to pay interest upon a much larger sum than would be necessary to establish a similar area at the present time.

It is considered that the plantation and the factory have shown the possibilities of the industry. The Government were, in my opinion, quite right in making the experiment, which may possibly lay the foundation for the introduction of a new economic crop in a dry area unsuitable for any other alternative crop. The further development of this industry must, however, lie with private enterprise. Sisal is essentially a plantation crop requiring considerable capital and skilled management. It is doubtful whether it can ever succeed as a native peasant industry.

Coconuts

There is a small but flourishing export of copra in the Keta–Ada areas, and the Government is endeavouring to encourage the extension of planting in various places along the coast. Until the demonstration plots begin to bear, however, there is not likely to be much prospect of the natives displaying much initiative in the extension of this crop. There can be no doubt that there is room for the further development of the coconut industry in the coastal belt.

Limes

Messrs Rose and Company have undertaken to erect a mill for pressing limes when 300 acres of mature limes are available, and upward of 500 acres have now been planted near Abrakampa on the Accra–Cape Coast road.

Bananas

Several varieties of bananas are grown by natives for local consumption, and it is possible that this industry could be developed.

The question of the organisation of the Agricultural Department is one which demands careful attention. At the present moment there are about twenty small agricultural stations scattered throughout the Colony and Ashanti. These stations are in charge of junior members of the staff supervised by the senior officer of the district in which the station is situated. For the development of more scientific agriculture small scattered stations seldom provide proper facilities, and I understand that proposals are being considered for handing over some of the small stations to Chiefs to be run as local nurseries, while stations of a larger size are to be established in each of the main producing areas.

The work of training the African staff of the Department is carried out at a Training Centre recently established at Kumasi. The building in which the school is housed has been provided out of a generous gift by Messrs Cadbury for the purpose of improving agricultural education. Over and above the cost of the building there is a sum of money available from the gift for the creation of agricultural scholarships at the Kumasi Training Centre.

The research offices of the Agricultural Department are accommodated at Aburi, some twenty miles from Accra. The existing laboratories are inadequate, and I understand that the reorganisation of the Research branch is under consideration. It is clearly essential that there should be no overlapping between the work at Aburi and that at Cadbury Hall, Kumasi.

The activities of the Veterinary Department are at present mainly confined to the Northern Territories. There is a considerable live-stock trade with French territory to the north of the Northern Territories, and there is a large demand for cattle, sheep and goats in Ashanti and the Colony, owing to the fact that none are reared there. The cattle are detained at veterinary quarantine stations on the frontier, and then proceed by definite live-stock routes to the southern markets. There are indigenous non-humped cattle in the Northern Territories which kill better than the imported cattle, and also stand a journey better. The owners, however, are as a rule unwilling to trade, as cattle constitute the currency for procuring wives and for other purposes.

The Department is trying to increase the production of cattle, and also to improve the strain by the introduction of English bulls and also Zebu bulls. Model stock-farms have been established at two places besides Tamale, and live-stock shows have also been held.

There is a veterinary school at Tamale for training Africans in the practice and theory of veterinary science with a view to employment in Government service. I understand that the work of the school is somewhat hampered by the lack of a proper laboratory.

I should also like to call attention to the existence of the small herds of cattle in the coastal area in the Colony, which though small in size are healthy and immune from fly. It would be interesting if it were possible for experiments to be made with these cattle, as it would seem that they might in the future form the course of meat supply for the coast towns. I understand that at present they are largely used for dowry purposes.

Minerals

The territory is rich in minerals, and the Government have been and are actively engaged in examining its resources. The Geological Survey Department have discovered bauxite, manganese and diamonds in recent years, and are now engaged in surveying the Northern Territories.

As its name implies the existence of gold in the Colony was the first reason for its connection with European trade. Gold has been exported from the Gold Coast since the discovery of the country in the fifteenth century, though the industry was in the hands of the natives until the latter part of the nineteenth century. In 1879 a company commenced mining operations near Tarkwa, and from that year there was a rapid increase in the export. The disturbances in Ashanti in 1900 checked the progress of the industry, but the construction of the railway and the improvement in methods of transport gave it a fresh impetus.

Gold is widely diffused throughout the Colony, Ashanti, and certain places in the Northern Territories, in quartz and alluvial deposits. In 1925 the value of gold and gold-dust exported was over £875,000 which is about the average annual amount for the past few years. The mines are mainly situated in Tarkwa district. The Ashanti Gold Fields Corporation have a concession at Obuasi, and there is also mining in progress at Akim Abuakwa. Prospecting for gold still continues, though slowly and with difficulty. The tropical conditions, the heavy jungle through which paths have to be cut, and the high cost of transport make the work of prospecting slow and arduous. The improvement of communications is, however, facilitating this work.

Some of the reefs are very rich, in particular that at Obuasi, though there have been difficulties in extracting the gold owing to the presence of a high percentage of graphite in the ore.

Apart from gold there are important manganese and bauxite deposits. There has been a phenomenal increase in the export of the former, which was discovered during the war in the Western Province of the Colony. In 1916, 4,000 tons were exported, while in 1925 the amount had risen to 340,000 tons. It is estimated that the capacity of output of the mines at Nsuta can be increased to 360,000 or 400,000 tons per annum. The mines are fortunately situated close to the Sekondi–Kumasi Railway, and the carry to the coast is not large.

There are important bauxite deposits at Mount Ejuanema in the Eastern Province, over which the Government have obtained a concession from the native chiefs. It is not, however, likely that these deposits can be economically worked until, at any rate, Takoradi Harbour is complete.

Diamonds were found a few years ago in the Eastern Province near Kibbi, and there are several companies now interested in the industry. The export of diamonds has increased from £365 in 1920 to £184,000 in 1925.

The development of the Colony in the past owed a great deal to the enterprise of the mining companies, who did much pioneer work. Indeed, the original construction of the Sekondi–Kumasi railway owed its inception to their initiative, and in the case of the Tarkwa-Prestea branch they guaranteed the working costs. They have also formed a useful training ground for mechanics.

Forestry

The forests of the Gold Coast are a rich asset to the country. Apart from their value both for the export trade and for internal use, the security of the cocoa crop depends on adequate forest protection. The establishment of a Forestry Department in the Gold Coast was comparatively recent, dating only from 1908. A Forestry Ordinance, submitted to the Legislative Council in 1910, met with such opposition that it was withdrawn and another less satisfactory Ordinance substituted which, however, though passed, was never brought into effect. In 1919 the Forestry Department was reorganised, and arrangements were made for its expansion.

Before the war its policy had been largely directed towards the productive side of forestry. It, however, became apparent that deforestation was becoming a serious problem, due not only to the spread of cultivation, but also to the steady advance of the open savannah area of the coastal belt. There has, however, been great difficulty in persuading chiefs to set aside reserves. It is almost impossible to persuade the native that it is essential for the future of the crops and water supply of his country that certain forest areas should be maintained. Practical difficulties arise from the unsettled state of the tribal administration, due to the frequent destoolment and deaths of the chiefs, and also to inter-tribal friction, and the complexity of the land problem.

In 1923 a campaign for the establishment of adequate forestry reserves for protective purposes was launched. In that year there were two reserves covering 111 square miles, and there are now 12 reserves occupying approximately 450 square miles, though this represents less than half of the total required. Twelve further reserves have already been selected, and negotiations for their protection are being undertaken. There still, however, remain certain important directions in which further action is essential. For example, certain reserves should be set aside without delay against the encroachment of the coastal savannah, which threatens the cocoa in some of the richest areas of the Colony. In order to deal with this serious problem it is to my mind essential in the interests of the natives themselves that new forestry legislation should be undertaken. The importance of this subject has not been sufficiently appreciated by the people of either the country or the coast towns.

Full warning has been given to all concerned that if reserves were not voluntarily set aside, new legislation would have to be undertaken. In the Governor's speeches on the Estimates in 1924, 1925 and 1926 this warning was clearly repeated. I think the time has now come when legislation can no longer be safely postponed, and I strongly recommend that it should be put in hand forthwith.

As far as the productive aspects of forestry are concerned, exports for 1925 amounted to 2,200,000 cubic feet, valued at £286,000. There is an export duty of 2*d* per cubic foot, which is at present the only direct source of revenue from the forests. The main export is mahogany, and the proper exploitation of the marketable timber is controlled by Government. The supply of mahogany in the accessible parts of the forests is being gradually worked out and adequate protection of the young growth of the species is difficult except in the reserves.

Considerable use is made of local timber in the construction of buildings and furniture, but from the fact that unmanufactured timber to the value of over

£50,000 was imported in 1924 it would seem that it is worth investigating whether more local timber could not be made use of. I understand that there has never been a full and detailed investigation into the various types and uses of tree, and the addition of a sylviculturist or an officer who has taken a course in that subject to the staff of the Department is clearly desirable.

Land tenure

The state of affairs brought about by the existing system of land tenure in the Colony presents the most important problem which the administration has to face. The essential principle is that all land, including waste or unoccupied land, is community land at the disposal of the chiefs and elders of the stool, and is allocated for farming by them under native customary law. The idea of ownership in the sense in which we use the term is unknown to native customary law. It has been Government policy to recognise this, and there is no considerable area of the land of the Colony at the disposal of the Government.

There is only a limited amount of land held by the Government either as a result of acquisition by treaty or concession, as in the case of the forts on the coast, or under special Ordinances where it has been acquired for the public service or for other such purposes.

I am convinced that any radical alteration in the general policy of the Government in regard to the land is neither practicable nor desirable, but when I say that I do not wish to be understood to mean that the present position is satisfactory. At present litigation about land is a curse to the country. It arises from disputes not only over boundaries between tribes and chiefdoms, but also between families and individuals who have acquired claims to land in certain places. Boundary disputes have become increasingly frequent, and the result is that many of the stools have been seriously impoverished, while some have been reduced to a condition of bankruptcy. The subjects of the stools are submitted to heavy levies to pay lawyers' fees, and this is one of the chief causes of discontent among the poorer peasantry.

The whole question is in great confusion. For instance, when the Government started the sisal plantation near Accra on ground at that time unoccupied and unused, no fewer than four chiefs claimed the same land. In another case I was told that two deeds were registered under the Registry Ordinance on the same day, each purporting to record a separate transaction but each relating to the same plot. This is a state of affairs which clearly demands amelioration.

Further the introduction of the concepts of English law frequently at variance with native custom is producing a modification if not an elimination of transactions under native custom. The first cause of this is economic, namely the introduction of permanent crops on agricultural land and the growth of land values in urban areas. The second cause is the direct and indirect influence of members of the legal profession trained in the English law of real property. The absence of any codification of the native law and its nebulous and contradictory state renders action of lawyers in this respect more or less inevitable. I was informed that a very large proportion of land theoretically still held under native customary law is being dealt with by methods approximating to English law. I think we are bound to recognise that matters have gone so far that the clock cannot be put back.

We have further to consider how far by general legislation or by legislation dealing with one or more aspects of the problem the existing chaos can be put in order.

There is no legislation applying the statute of limitations, which is an important feature of the law of real property in England, to suits respecting land in the Gold Coast, with the result that there is no finality to any decision given in the Courts, and a dispute may be reopened after a lapse of many years. I regard the introduction of legislation of this nature in the Colony as an essential change.

To refer to a second point. The existing Land Registry Ordinance merely provides for the registration of instruments. That is to say, it does not and it cannot convey a little of any land described in such instruments nor does it assure that other documents dealing with the same property do not exist. It is clear that there is a vital distinction between a system of the registration of deeds now in existence and that of a registration of title based on the compulsory production of all relevant documents and evidence. I consider that as far as is possible we should endeavour to build up such a system forthwith.

Obviously this can only be done where title has been proved to the satisfaction of the Courts, and therefore the register such as I contemplate can only be made as and when the decisions of the Courts are given either during current litigation or by special declaration for the particular purpose. It is obvious that any system of registration of title can only be an adjunct of the general law of real property, and it seems clear that where that law is uncertain no system of registration can materially help or be effective.

The question next arises whether any modification can be made in the procedure of existing tribunals who deal with land. I may explain that the Court of first instance in land cases is the native tribunal, from which cases can be taken before the Provincial Commissioner's Court, from whom appeals lie to the Supreme Court sitting either as a Divisional Court or as a Full Court.

Under this system an ever-increasing expenditure is involved, but although this alone is causing serious hardship to those involved in any such litigation it is only one aspect of the present difficulties. The moment a land case is taken beyond the Divisional Court the whole dispute is dealt with far away from the scene of the case, in a wholly artificial atmosphere. The essential thing is to secure that the facts of the case should be decided *in situ*, and that only questions of law should be taken to the higher Courts and heard. I should again like to emphasise the importance of imparting the maximum degree of finality to the decisions of the Courts.

In a very large number of cases the principal object must be to secure the demarcation of the boundary. Further, it is above all necessary that decisions should not be given by the Courts as to abstract rights as to land, the boundaries and position of which have not been adequately determined. This should not now be so difficult, as accurate surveys of all important areas have been made.

It has been suggested to me that a Lands Board or Local Court could be constituted by ordinance to deal with any case not settled by the native tribunal. No case should come before the Divisional Court before it has been considered by the Land Court. The function of the Land Court would be to determine the facts *in situ*. No appeal against its decision on the facts should be allowed, but only on points of law. The result of this would be that the points to be dealt with in the Superior Courts would be clearly defined and, as the facts would already be established, arguments only would be called for and not fresh evidence. There can be little doubt that the new law of real property in England, which came into force in January this year, will and should have a direct bearing upon the local problem in the Gold Coast.

I will not go further into the complexities of this problem, but I am fully satisfied that the time has come for definite action by the Gold Coast Government in these matters. There is ample evidence in existence regarding the lines upon which legislation could be based, and in my opinion there is no necessity to wait for any further commissions or enquiries. The importance of regularising the position of affairs in the Colony is the more urgent, owing to the threatened development of analogous problems in Ashanti.

Before leaving this subject I should like to remark that there appears to be some necessity for a central authority in the municipal areas for dealing with land. It has been found necessary for the relief of congested areas and the prevention of haphazard extension of the rapidly growing urban areas to set up a Town Planning Board for the Colony with corresponding committees on the Municipal Councils. One of the results of the new legislation has been the establishment of a number of minor authorities who tend to overlap each other without central control. As an example, it came to my notice that the following functions were being or would shortly be carried out simultaneously in Accra:

(*a*) Ascertainment of ownership and valuation of property by the assessment committee for the purpose of collecting rates.

(*b*) Ascertainment of ownership, survey and valuation by the Town Planning Board for the purpose of compensating evicted persons from congested or insanitary areas.

(*c*) Collection of returns showing ownership and value of properties transferred *inter vivos* for taxes on the transfer of property.

(*d*) The registration of deeds affecting ownership and transfer of land by the Registrar of the High Court.

(*e*) The location and record of ownership of land by the Lands Branch of the Survey Department.

The authorities engaged in the various branches of the work each do it in a limited manner to suit their own special requirements, and therefore in a way that is not generally useful to each other.

26. Attempts to develop oil palm industry : (a) by co-operatives, 1924 [1]

6. It is not suggested that the people should abandon or neglect their cocoa plantations and revert to the exploitation of the oil palms. Cocoa has brought great prosperity to this country and I see no reason to anticipate that it will not continue to be a successful crop if it is given the necessary care and attention. It is doubtful, however, if it would be wise policy to extend the already large area under this crop, necessitating the destruction of more jungle or bush when already the dangers of extensive clearings are becoming apparent in a reduced humidity affecting the health of the cocoa trees, and the rainfall in this country is so near the minimum necessary for the successful growth of cocoa. It is however recommended that the surplus energy of the people should rather be devoted to the development of other products (such as those of the oil palm) and thus ensure to

[1] Correspondence relating to the development of the oil palm industry, *Sessional Paper no. IV, 1924–5*, paras 6–18 (extracts).

the producers a more constant return than cocoa upon which they are so dependent today and which is suffering from a lack of demand at the present time.

7. The collection of palm fruits and the preparation of the products by ordinary native hand methods entails such hard work; also the products prepared in bulk by such methods are not of the best quality and only fetch a relatively low price. One need not wonder therefore that the people turned their attention to cocoa which offered them a much better return for the labour required. It would be foolish however to think of abandoning the oil palms, which are indigenous to this country and therefore less addicted to pests and diseases, and of which extensive areas have been built up in past years and are an asset of great potential value. Attention obviously requires to be directed to labour-saving appliances and means by which the wealth they represent can be made available for the benefit of the native owners and the general progress of the colony; the object I have in view in writing this is to show briefly how this may be done.

8. Economic conditions have changed in the Gold Coast largely as a result of the successful development of the cocoa industry. The average farmer instead of being as formerly a labourer himself has now become an employer of labour. Likewise cocoa has been responsible for the development of the individualistic spirit in production as against the communal co-operative system under which palm oil was produced in former days. This no doubt has its advantages and also its disadvantages (which, however, it is unnecessary for me to discuss here), but it is unlikely that the people will return to the old-time laborious methods of preparing palm oil and kernels under existing conditions; and if these products are to be successfully developed as they obviously should central power-driven factories equipped with labour-saving machinery and a communal or co-operative production of fruits require to be instituted and developed.

9. Few local individuals have the initiative to instal the necessary machinery; and, even if they have, there are not many affluent enough to purchase the machinery themselves, or have a sufficiently large area of palms to justify them doing so.

10. It is proposed therefore that groups of farmers, who own oil palm land and are prepared to supply fruits to a factory, should form themselves into associations or co-operative societies, for the purpose. They should subscribe to a fund to purchase machinery and to provide the necessary buildings for a factory. Money so subscribed should be credited to each individual or family and his or their share in the factory will be in proportion to the amount subscribed and they will receive interest on it annually.

16. A European manager and engineer will be necessary to see that the machinery is kept running in good order, and to regulate the supplies of fruits and sales of oil and kernels produced, to ensure that all the members of the association get equal justice; and the factory staff as far as possible should be natives of the district. A management committee of the members would be appointed to deal with important matters as they arise and to keep all the members closely interested and fully acquainted with the progress being made.

17. A factory of this kind would confer a great boon on the local people, it would ensure for them a steady income from their oil palms and would be a distinctly progressive step in agricultural practice in this colony. The people will be relieved from the laborious methods hitherto practised in the preparation of palm products; loss or waste that is going on today would be avoided and the

people would be assured of all the profits in the undertaking, which could not fail to increase their individual wealth.

18. If the local people however are not able at present to finance schemes on the lines here suggested, an alternative scheme could be adopted. Independent companies should be encouraged to erect similar factories and run them themselves, the growers or owners of the palms entering into an agreement to supply fresh palm fruits to the factory at a price agreed upon. Under such a scheme of course the native producers will have no further interest in the factory but the option could be retained of taking over the factory at a subsequent date as a going concern for the community on the lines previously suggested. Until such a time therefore as the members of the community are affluent enough to advance the capital required, this procedure is recommended for adoption; and until the co-operative spirit is more fully developed it is perhaps the one in which rapid progress could be made.

Under either scheme a ready market would be assured for all the fruits the people could supply, and this would mean to the people an important income which today is being lost.

26 (b). By subsidising the Niger Company, 1929 [1]

From the Governor to the Secretary of State, 6 September 1929, no. 665.

My Lord,

I have the honour to address Your Lordship on the subject of the oil palm industry in this colony and to seek your approval of a scheme whereunder the United Africa Company propose, with the help of a Government subsidy, to make an experiment in developing that industry on modern lines.

3. . . . In my address to the Legislative Council in March last, I made the following reference to the subject:

> During the past year much consideration has been given to the question of devising some means of stimulating the declining oil palm industry of the Colony. This decline is, of course, primarily due to the increase of the cultivated area of the more profitable cocoa crop, the supply of labour will not generally admit of the co-existence of two great local industries. There are, however, certain areas, e.g. in the Krobo plantations and in the oil palm belt north of Appam, where the energies of the population are not entirely absorbed by cocoa farming, and I believe that attention can profitably be given, either by private enterprise or by Government, to developing the oil palm industry at those places.
>
> In these days of competition from the East no development of this industry would be worth undertaking which did not include the provision of power mills for the extraction of the oil. There is no intention, however, of considering the erection of large factories, as it appears in the highest degree improbable that a highly capitalised factor could be supported entirely on fruit purchased from farmers and there are obvious objections to establishing in the Gold Coast plantations on the eastern model. The Niger Company have, however, devised a small type of unit factory and there is some reason to believe that

[1] Despatch from the Governor to the Secretary of State, 6 September 1929, *Sessional Paper no. III, 1930–1*, no. 665.

one or more units of this kind might well prove profitable in the areas I have mentioned. The Niger Company have asked that the Government should assist them in making an experiment by granting a small subsidy in the early years of the enterprise and this request is receiving careful consideration. You are no doubt aware that the Nigerian Government offers such subsidies.

16. The subsidy proposed is admittedly a liberal one, but it is less than originally suggested by the company, and is not in itself very large even in the extremely unlikely event of the Government having to pay the maximum rate. As the Director of Agriculture observes, while it is improbable that a large palm oil industry can be established coincidentally with our present cocoa industry, some arrangement should be made by which the Government and public may learn how to handle oil palm produce efficiently and profitably. It is within the bounds of possibility that our oil palm resources may have to be tapped in the future, and at present we have no reliable information as to the method likely to be successful under local conditions of labour and economics. Although the proposed scheme is experimental, its justification lies in the fact that the problem is one of general importance to the country, and if the conduct of the experiment is to be entrusted to private enterprise – which in my opinion is a preferable course to its conduct by Government – the assistance afforded by the Government should be reasonably generous in order to ensure a full and fair trial.

27. Government spends £600 to 'Enquire into the possibilities of the Shea Nut Industry', 1929 [1]

From the acting Governor to the Secretary of State. No. 490.

Government House,
Accra,
3rd July, 1928.

Dear Sir,

I have the honour to report that I have authorised the issue of a Special Warrant for £600 to augment the provision made under Head 21 item 57 'Agricultural Development' with special reference to the shea nut industry.

2. From time to time during the past ten years references have been made to the potentialities of this industry in reports by political officers, agricultural officers, and others; and statements that the late Governor recorded on pages 28–9 of his Address to the Legislative Council dated February 1925, that a total of over 43,000 tons of kernels is harvested annually in the Northern Territories and that there is a prospect of an export trade amounting to 53,000 tons of kernels or 26,000 tons of shea butter per annum ... It has been estimated that the available exports by the Northern Territories railway might amount to 41,000 tons of kernels per annum, but that owing to the paucity of population not more than 4,200 tons might be carried in the first year. [It has been estimated that if] the tonnage to be so carried is put at 5,000 the revenue therefrom will be £22,850.

[1] Despatches relating to the shea-nut industry of the Northern Territories, 1929, *Sessional Paper no. XI, 1929–30*. These despatches are presented in an almost complete form: all that has been omitted are certain references to the estimates and earlier correspondence.

3. In all the correspondence there appear to be no figures which have been obtained by exact and systematic experiment and therefore I asked the Acting Director of Agriculture to furnish a report on the industry, with definite recommendations as to the steps to be taken and the expenditure to be incurred.

I pointed out that, while there was no doubt a vast number of trees in the Northern Territories, our problems were, first, to ascertain whether from them can be derived any marketable products ... in sufficient quantity. Shortly afterwards I went to Tamale and Yendi and as the result of what I saw and of my conversations with Captain Coull, Superintendent of Agriculture, I asked Mr Auchinleck to visit the Northern Territories himself.

4. In the report which he submitted on his return, Mr Auchinleck wrote as follows:

With regard to the possibility of establishing a profitable export industry in shea kernels or fat, I have pointed out certain difficulties to the Government. They are as follows:

(*a*) no factory method for pressing shea kernels locally has been devised;

(*b*) the fat is admittedly defective, from the point of view of the manufacturer, because of unsaponifiable matter;

(*c*) purification of that fat for edible purposes has not yet been effected or perfected;

(*d*) the present limits of market demands in Europe and America are not known;

(*e*) the trees are scattered and profitable centralisation appears impossible under present conditions;

(*f*) transport costs are heavy or even prohibitive;

(*g*) prices of shea fat are lower than those of coconut oil or palm oil;

(*h*) yields are extremely low per tree;

(*i*) the tree is an extremely slow grower and increasing the density per acre or establishing new areas would take probably not less than ten years.

We have no exact information on any of these points excepting yield records, and the only attitude which the department should adopt and adhere to is that reliable information must be obtained by investigation and trial. It is not easy to measure the harm that has been done by unwise propaganda and unsound calculations regarding this crop locally, nor will it be easy to prevent more harm being done. I can see no earthly use in associating the name and reputation of this department with unsound propositions of this kind. We are here to supply exact information not to join in a general popular chorus of unsound propaganda.

Outside of the trials at Yendi, the limit to which I am prepared at present to go in the matter of shea development is as follows:

(*a*) to recommend the Government to make a trial of a limited scheme of purchase in a prescribed area and up to a fixed maximum cost;

(*b*) to recommend a shipment of 100 tons of kernels by the department to the London market;

(*c*) to purchase a steam-heated case for the cotton hydraulic press at Tamale and make trials of the possibility of expressing the fat locally at a profit.

The purchase scheme might be centralised at the Yendi plot, but you should advise in this matter. In any event it should be near Tamale or Yendi, for transport reasons.

In making these recommendations, I am fully aware that the financial results of the scheme are likely to involve a loss to Government. The gross cost would be about £2,000, the net loss probably not more than £500. The information obtained would certainly be worth £500, even if it had no other result than to put a stop to unsound propaganda.

Subsequently, in view of the almost certain loss, he revised his recommendations and stated that it would be advisable only to ship twenty tons to England during this season. He estimated the cost of a ton of kernels to be £26 landed in London whereas the market price was then £12 15*s*, to £13 a ton.

5. It is to be hoped that the results of this shipment will show whether kernels or fat are likely to be a marketable commodity and will afford some guide as to the provision which should be made for experiments in 1929–30. In any event, having regard to the extent to which the development of this industry must affect a decision as to the construction of the Northern Territories railway, it is desirable that the Agricultural Department should be placed in a position to give definite advice on the subject. I have, etc.,

T. S. Thomas ; Acting Governor.

The Right Honourable L. S. Amery, M.P., etc.

From the Secretary of State to the Governor. No. 697.

Downing Street,
13th August 1928.

Sir,

I have the honour to acknowledge the receipt of your despatch no. 490 of the 3rd of July, and to convey to you my approval of your issue of a Special Warrant for £600, to augment the provision . . . ' Agricultural Development ' of the current Estimates, in order to cover the cost of an enquiry into the potentialities of the shea nut industry.

2. I shall be glad to learn in due course the results of the enquiry. I have, etc.,

L. S. Amery.

The officer administering the Government of the Gold Coast.

From the Governor to the Secretary of State. No. 49.

Government House,
Accra
23rd January 1929.

Sir,

With reference to your despatch no. 697 dated the 13th August 1928 approving the issue of a Special Warrant for £600 to augment the provision made under ' Agricultural Development ' of the Estimates for the current financial year for the purpose of covering the cost of an enquiry into the potentialities of the shea-nut industry I have the honour to inform you that in October last a trial shipment of shea nuts was despatched to England.

2. The cost per ton of the consignment landed in England worked out at approximately £25 and the price realised was only about £10 per ton.

3. It is obvious, therefore, that it is an uneconomic proposition to export shea nuts as such to England. I am advised, however, that the expression of the fat from the nut reduces the weight by about 55 per cent and I have approved of a further trial shipment being made in 1929–30 of the fat only, so that the transport costs may be reduced to a minimum.

4. To express the fat locally a special press will be required and I propose to detail Mr J. E. Symond, Superintendent of Agriculture, during his forthcoming leave of absence to visit various firms in England with a view to his selecting a suitable press and obtaining the same through the Crown Agents.

5. I also propose that Mr Symond should visit Belgium to obtain information regarding the methods of extraction adopted by manufacturers, as I understand that there is no demand in the United Kingdom for shea kernels.

6. If you approve I shall be glad if the necessary arrangements can be made for Mr Symond to undertake these enquiries. It is at present proposed that he should proceed on leave in March next, and I recommend that he be granted the usual allowance whilst making his investigations. I have, etc.

A. R. Slater, Governor.

The Right Honourable L. S. Amery, M.P., etc.

From the Secretary of State to the Governor. No. 289. [Re] Governor's despatch no. 49 of 23 January.

Downing Street,
6th April 1929.

Sir,

I have the honour to transmit to you, for your information copies of the papers noted below on the subject of the shea nut industry in the Northern Territories. I have, etc.,

L. S. Amery.

The officer administering the Government of the Gold Coast.

Downing Street,
22nd February 1929.

Sir,

I am directed by Mr Secretary Amery to transmit to you copies of the correspondence on the subject of enquiries which are being undertaken by the Government of the Gold Coast regarding the shea nut industry in the Northern Territories.

2. It will be observed from the Governor's despatch of 23rd January that a trial shipment of shea nuts has resulted in a loss, partly owing to high transport expenses and that the Governor proposes to make a further trial shipment of the fat expressed from the nuts only, with a view to reducing the cost of transport to England. He recommends that Mr J. E. Symond, Superintendent of Agriculture should visit various firms in England in order to select a suitable press for extracting the fat from shea nuts, and should also visit Belgium to obtain information regarding the methods of extraction adopted by manufacturers there.

3. Mr Amery would be glad to receive any advice on that subject, and in particular to receive suggestions as to the firms that Mr Symond should visit. I am, etc.

John A. Calder.

The Secretary, Imperial Institute.

Imperial Institute,
London, S.W.7.
22nd March 1929.

Sir,

With reference to your letter no. 6332/29 of the 22nd February last, with enclosures, I now send you the following observations relating to the enquiries which are being undertaken by the Government of the Gold Coast regarding the shea nut industry in the Northern Territories.

2. The principal firms in this country who make oil-expressing plant are: Messrs Rose, Downs and Thompson, Ltd, Old Foundry, Hull (London Office, 28 Victoria Street, S.W.1); Messrs Greenwood and Batley, Ltd, Albion Works, Leeds (London Office, 16 Great George Street, S.W.1); Messrs Manlove, Alliott and Co., Ltd, Bloomsgrove Works, Nottingham (London Office, 41/42, Parliament Street, S.W.1).

3. It is suggested that Mr J. E. Symond should consult these firms as to the plant they recommend for crushing shea kernels. In this connection it may be mentioned that in November last the Imperial Institute received a letter from the Director of Agriculture in the Gold Coast asking to be put in touch with a firm who could supply a box-head to be used with hydraulic baling press for the experimental preparation of shea fat. At the request of the Imperial Institute Messrs Rose, Downs and Thompson undertook to do what they could to assist and the Director of Agriculture was advised to communicate with them.

As regards the suggestion that Mr Symond should visit Belgium in order to obtain information regarding the methods of extraction adopted by manufacturers in that country, the only firm in Belgium known here to be dealing with shea nuts and fat is the Raffinerie du Congo Belge who have a factory at Baesrode near Termonde. This Company (formerly operating in the United Kingdom as Messrs De Bruyn, Limited) is associated with the Niger Company and thus with Messrs Lever Brothers Limited. They have devoted much attention to the extraction and refining of shea butter and it is to be anticipated that they may not be very willing to supply much information regarding their methods. You may however consider it desirable to approach Messrs Lever Brothers or the Niger Company on the subject.

5. The extraction and refining of shea fat has also been undertaken recently by a firm at Aarhus in Denmark (probably the Aarhus Olisfabrik) but the Imperial Institute has no further information at present.

6. With reference to the general question of the development of the demand for shea nuts and butter from West Africa, I may say that this question has been under consideration for some time by the Imperial Institute Oils and Oilseeds Committee with a view to finding an increased market for the butter in this country or elsewhere, particularly for edible purposes. Prejudice has existed in certain quarters against shea butter as an edible fat on account of the amount and nature of the unsaponifiable matter present in it, and the Committee decided that it would be advantageous if this aspect of the question could be investigated with a view to arriving at a definite and authoritative conclusion.

7. At the request of the Imperial Institute, Professor J. C. Drummond of University College, London kindly undertook this work and feeding trials and other experiments are now in progress. The full results will however, not be available for some months yet.

8. It was stated by the trade representatives on the Committee that commercial consignments of shea nuts differing in shape had been found to yield fats containing different percentages of unsaponifiable matter and that this fact suggested a possible means of selecting nuts with a low percentage of this constituent. The Committee were of opinion that this point was worth further investigation and at the request the Imperial Institute suggested to the Governors of Nigeria and the Gold Coast that the Departments of Agriculture should cooperate in an enquiry to ascertain definitely whether distinct varieties of the shea trees occur in either country or whether there are well-marked differences in the size, shape, etc. of the nuts which would enable them to be easily differentiated. It was suggested that a series of botanical specimens of the trees from different localities, together with corresponding samples of nuts, should be collected for examination respectively at the Royal Botanic Gardens, Kew, and at the Imperial Institute.

9. A series of specimens has recently been received from Nigeria in response to this request and is now under examination.

10. In considering the question of installing machinery in the Gold Coast for the preparation of shea butter it will be desirable to ensure in advance that a remunerative market can be found for the quantity of fat to be produced. The refining of shea butter presents technical difficulties and so far as is known only two or three firms are at present engaged in it. This fact reduces competition for the butter for edible use, and, failing its disposal for this purpose, it would have to be sold for soap-making.

11. We shall be glad to discuss the whole subject with Mr Symond and to give him every possible assistance in his enquiries. I am, etc.,

W. Furse, Director (Lt Gen. Sir William Furse).

The Under Secretary of State, Colonial Office, S.W.1.

8th April 1929.

Sir,

I am directed by Mr Secretary Amery to acknowledge the receipt of your letter of 22nd of March, regarding the enquiries which are being undertaken by the Government of the Gold Coast in connection with the shea nut industry in the Northern Territories, and to thank you for your offer to discuss the matter with Mr J. E. Symond.

Mr Symond will be instructed to communicate with you when he arrives in this country. I am, etc.,

J. E. W. Flood.

The Secretary, Imperial Institute.

From the Secretary of State to the Governor. No. 691.

Downing Street,
20th July 1929.

Sir,

With reference to my predecessor's despatch no. 289 of the 8th of April, I have the honour to transmit to you a copy of a report by Mr J. E. Symond as to the prospects of the shea-nut industry in the Northern Territories together with a copy of a letter from Mr Auchinleck commenting on the report.

2. I shall be glad if you will inform me by telegram whether an order should be placed for machinery as recommended by Mr Auchinleck or Mr Symonds. I have, etc.,

Passfield.

Governor Sir A. R. Slater, K.C.M.G., C.B.E., etc.

From J. E. Symond, Supt Agric. Gold Coast.

101 Ullet Road,
Liverpool,
1st July 1929.

Shea nut industry in Northern Territories

Sir,

I have the honour to forward my report on enquiries in connection with the shea nut industry in the Northern Territories of the Gold Coast, and to request that you will be good enough to submit it to the Honourable Director of Agriculture, who is in this country, for his consideration. In accordance with instructions, I have consulted the Imperial Institute, various manufacturers of oil-expressing machinery, and commercial authorities on marketing conditions and prospects.

Market prospects

The demand for shea kernels and fat is at present centered almost exclusively on the continent in Belgium, and as few firms are engaged on the product, the market is not steady. I am informed that there is no shortage of supply for such demand as exists. The fat, however, has properties which are useful in connection with the making of margarine, certain kinds of pastry, ointments, and of course soap-making; and I learnt that there is a possibility of the demand extending to America. This is not definite owing to the possible imposition of an import tax.

Small quantities would not readily be saleable if offered as isolated lots, and might have to wait some time for a market unless regularity of supply could be guaranteed. The price of shea fat at 1 March 1929, was given as £32 per ton with kernels at £13, but I am advised that £30 per ton for fat is nearer the mark as a constant price. The percentage of free fatty acid in the fat is an item affecting the price, and that quoted above is for good quality.

Production and costs

The question of refining shea butter need not be considered, as I am told that this is a process too technical, and requiring too expensive a plant, to be considered locally. In connection with suitable machinery for expression I have consulted the following firms:

Messrs Rose, Downs and Thompson, Hull; Messrs Greenwood and Batley, Leeds; Messrs Manlove Alliott, Nottingham. The last named firm had supplied the plant for Messrs de Bruyn (now the Raffinerie du Congo Belge) who are probably the largest users of shea kernels, and their representative whom I interviewed had seen the plant at work.

The kernels are too large to go direct to crushing rolls in the same way as small oil seeds such as groundnuts, and must be reduced first by means of a disintegrator. After being reduced in the rolls to meal, the product is steam heated and slightly moistened, and finally pressed in what is known as a cage press. I am advised that it is impossible to avoid a certain amount of vegetable matter in suspension in the expressed oil, and for this reason the use of a filter press is also recommended. Commercial people with whom I discussed this point did not regard filtering as necessary, as the oil would in all probability be filtered in any case by the consumer. But as the additional cost of a filter press is not great I consider it would be as well to produce oil of as high a standard of purity as possible. The percentage of free fatty acid can be reduced by pressing the kernels in as fresh a state as possible and by careful attention to proper storage, avoiding damp and consequent heating.

The cost of machinery as outlined above, capable of dealing with half a ton of nuts a day, would be approximately £600 f.o.b. England. No portion of the Tamale cotton ginnery plant could economically be converted for any process; though the engine there can be used as the motive power, and the plant driven from existing shafting. The figure of £600 given is therefore for machinery without the engine. I estimate a further charge for freight and erection in Tamale of some £400.

The provision of suitable containers in which to export expressed fat is a difficult question. The high transport costs in the Northern Territories absolutely prohibit the idea of taking barrels or metal containers, up empty. The only solution is the use of the four gallon petrol tin. While sufficient of these could be collected locally in Tamale for a trial shipment of a few tons, there are not sufficient to supply a large and constant demand.

Possible profit

Assuming a market price of £30 per ton, I am of the opinion that it is definitely not possible to export shea fat from the Northern Territories at a profit under existing conditions of transport. Sufficient kernels to provide a ton of oil would cost approximately £14 at Tamale, and the transport cost to England totals a further £13 per ton (£10 of which is involved by the lorry carriage between Tamale and Kumasi). This leaves only three pounds per ton for working costs and overhead charges, a figure which I am confident is insufficient. The advent of a railway would, I estimate, reduce the transport charge by £8 per ton and make the export a profitable one.

It is probable that some profit, however, could be realised by sale within the Colony. There is a small but steady demand for it in Ashanti and the Colony proper, and it is constantly retailed in Kumasi at prices approximating £80 per ton. In this connection it is significant that there is a small annual import of shea fat from Nigeria to the Gold Coast. In 1927, 33 tons were imported.

Conclusions

It will be seen from the foregoing that in view of the limited quantities which it would be feasible to export as an experiment, and the doubtful market conditions, it is improbable that Government would recoup any of its expenditure in installing machinery, until such time as transport conditions improve.

In the event of it being considered that the information to be gained warrants the expenditure involved in installing a plant, several complementary lines of investigation, which could simultaneously be worked out, suggest themselves, such as: 1. factors affecting and controlling percentage of free fatty acid; 2. disadvantages or otherwise of germination in the kernel; 3. effect of long storage on kernels under varying conditions; 4. quality of fat from possible different botanical varieties.

In addition such machinery would be suitable for dealing with groundnuts, a crop suited to large areas of the Northern Territories and of probable future importance, which also has the advantage of maturing at a different season to shea nuts.

I recommend, if machinery is to be installed that a plant as outlined (by) Messrs Manlove Alliott and Company should be ordered without delay. To this estimate must be added the necessary belting and a sufficient supply of press and filter cloths to deal with twenty tons of nuts. The machinery must be adjusted to run from the existing shafting, and must include very full and detailed instructions as to installation and running. . . I have, etc.,

J. E. Symond, Supt of Agriculture

The Under Secretary of State

St Mary's,
Westbrooke,
Worthing,
15th July 1929.

Sir,

I have been through the papers attached to your letter of 13th July, concerning machinery for extraction of shea fat in the Gold Coast, and in addition had the opportunity of discussing the question with Mr J. E. Symond at Rothamsted about a fortnight ago.

2. Mr Symond's report clears up the technical question of extraction in a satisfactory manner, and it is evident that no insuperable difficulties stand in the way of erecting machinery and making experiments in expression of fat. With the figures and plant now available, a trial factory can be built.

3. The Imperial Institute has been of great assistance in this matter. It is evident from Sir William Furse's letter that market facilities in the United Kingdom will have to be explored very carefully before any large shipments can be risked. Quite clearly, too, steps would have to be taken to introduce shea fat to English dealers and manufacturers before it can become recognised as an ordinary staple, comparable with palm-oil or coconut-oil. Towards this end continued cooperation and investigations by the Imperial Institute will be necessary.

4. In considering the advisability of erecting trial-machinery at Tamale out of public funds, I naturally must be influenced by questions of ultimate supply, labour facilities and transport, as well as by technical and marketing questions on this side. It is because the industry is a potential and not an actual one, and because its development will be attended with considerable risk, that the Government is justified in assuming responsibility for carrying out investigations and trials.

5. There is no doubt regarding the amplitude of the supply of nuts occurring in the Northern Territories. The Department of Agriculture . . . estimates an annual crop of 151,846 tons, a figure probably under the mark. In terms of oil, this means about 60,000 tons annually, of a gross value of about £1,500,000 (at £25 to £30). This means very little, however, as a guide to advising as to the possibility of developing the industry, since the trees are scattered over an area of 29,313 square

miles. In addition, the Department's trials show that, even where the trees are massed together so as to form a 'full stand' per acre, the yield per acre, is very, very low. The yield ranges from 49 to 103 pounds of kernels (say 20 to 50 pounds of oil) per acre... The difficulties of centralisation of the crop are enormous where transport is undeveloped, the population sparse, the trees scattered, and the gross monetary return only about 5 to 12 shillings per acre per year.

6. [It has been] estimated that about 50,000 tons of kernels can be collected by the present population. This is probably approximately correct, so far as the collecting capacity of the population is concerned, but it is the figure for the whole of the Northern Territories. Naturally, one railroad, say from Tamale to Kumasi could not tap the whole supply. I doubt whether half would be tapped, but no reliable estimates are at present available.

7. The possibility of handling shea as a plantation-crop, that is of establishing 'full-stands' similar to cacao farms or coconut groves, along a railway line or road has to be considered. The present distribution of population does not make the outlook very hopeful, and the growth of the trees is terribly slow, to judge from our figures: indications go to show that 18 to 20 years are probably necessary for bringing trees to fruiting-maturity, from seed... There is always a possibility, of course, that if prices were fair and steady, the people might plant seed in their farms, growing food crops between until the sheas covered over. For a 50-mile radius round Tamale the population is fairly thick and likely to increase, and the people have practically no export-crop to bring them in regular money.

8. When all the difficulties and disadvantages have been given full weight, we have, I think, still some grounds for recommending further moderate expenditure in making certain experiments. The mere existence of a potential, large supply of unused fat will always lead the public to demand active investigations regarding development: it has become a perennial question in the Gold Coast. Criticism is naturally all the more acute because every one realises that an export product is necessary if the Northern Territories are to progress. Then, too, the potential value of shea fat is always emphasised when the necessity for railway development is being pressed on government.

9. I have very little doubt that further trials are justified, and still less doubt that these trials should be carried out by Government and not by private individuals or firms. Results of trials will have a very direct bearing on the question of developing the Northern Territories, and without them we cannot even know the difficulties which have to be cleared away before a profitable industry can be built up. Where the risks of failure are so great, and the benefits resulting from success so general to the whole Colony, it seems to me that, not only is Government justified in accepting the responsibility, but the matter should not be left to private enterprise. I may add that reliable facts and figures will be necessary throughout, since the economics of labour and transport are the ruling factors and are capable of adjustment by Government, and there is no hope of securing, far less of publishing reliable figures from private firms.

10. I recommend, therefore, that the erection of a trial mill at Tamale be sanctioned, to be operated by the Department of Agriculture for the purpose of obtaining facts and figures for publication concerning the possibility of developing a shea industry. It should be regarded frankly as an experiment, and criticised accordingly. Its immediate object would be to ascertain the cost of extracting shea fat locally and of shipping it to the United Kingdom. From the information so gained, the Government will get the material for deciding whether possible

adjustments of labour and transport can be effected so as to establish a profitable industry.

11. The capital cost would be about £1,000 as shown by Mr Symond's figures and Messrs Manlove Alliott's estimate. Annual expenditure could be limited to £1,000 which sum would suffice for preparation and shipment of about 30 tons of fat, and the trial is limited to a provisional period of three years (say 1930–1–2). Naturally, if early shipments proved a complete failure through irremovable difficulties, the trial could be stopped at once. Simultaneously with the trials, market investigations would be carried out by the Imperial Institute and the Gold Coast Bureau and chemical questions on quality by the Imperial Institute and the local department. I have, etc.,

G. Auchinleck, Director of Agriculture, Gold Coast.

Telegram from Governor, Accra, to Secretary of State, London, dated 20th August 1929: With reference to your despatch no. 691 of 30th July, please place order for shea-nut machinery as recommended by Auchinleck. Slater.

28. Criticisms of Agricultural policy : (a) by the West Africa Commission, 1943 [1]

140. Before reviewing the work accomplished by the Department of Agriculture and offering suggestions for future consideration, it will be convenient to trace some of the principal stages in the official approach to the development of colonial agriculture.

Types of development in tropical agriculture

141. A brief survey of the tropical dependencies of the British Empire shows that they can be divided into four main categories. In the first group of countries with no significant native population, agricultural development depended on settlers from Europe employing imported labour for the performance of the actual field work. This group included most of the colonies in the Caribbean region, Bermuda, Mauritius and the Seychelles. The second group with a native population, whose needs were easily met by a restricted form of agriculture, consisted of Malaya, Sarawak, North Borneo, Fiji and the Mandated Territories of New Guinea, Papua, Samoa and other islands in the Pacific. In these countries there was generally scope both for European planting, often with imported labour, as well as for developing native agriculture as the needs of the people increased. Thirdly, there were territories with a well developed native agriculture and a native population, which was already dense or increasing rapidly through settled conditions of administration or large-scale irrigation schemes. With the exception of Ceylon and Cyprus these were in continental areas, and included, in addition to India and Burma, the British dependencies in Tropical Africa and the Condominium of the Anglo–Egyptian Sudan. In many of these countries, but not in West Africa, there was scope for European planting and farming in areas at high elevations, where for climatic reasons there was either no native population or only hill or forest tribes with little interest in cultivating land. Examples of such areas were the tea districts of India and Ceylon, and the highlands of Kenya,

[1] The West Africa Commission, 1938–9, *Technical Reports*, Leverhulme Trust, London 1943, paras 140–94 (extracts).

Tanganyika, and Nyasaland. The fourth group, of little agricultural importance, consisted of small and usually isolated regions held for strategic reasons along the principal sea trade routes, e.g. Gibraltar, Malta, Aden, Singapore and Hong Kong.

The West Indian model

142. The older colonies belong to the first group and lie in the Caribbean region. They were started in the time of the Stuarts, when some of the islands in the West Indies were granted as concessions to people having influence at the English Court. Here plantations were started for sugar cane, tobacco, cotton, cocoa and coffee, the labour being supplied by slaves from West Africa and by bondsmen deported from England for either political or criminal offences. In these early days, when the European demand for these commodities far exceeded the supply, plantation enterprise yielded very great profits, and little attention was paid to the local production of food-stuffs for the labour force. Certainly the slaves were allowed to grow their own ' provision crops ' such as yams, coco-yams, tannias, sweet potatoes and spinach plants, and seed of a few African food crops, such as guinea corn, pigeon pea, cowpeas and beniseed. It is a striking commentary on the shortcomings of the food ration that the African of the West Indies acquired a wide knowledge of flora of these islands, particularly of species useful for greens, soups, ' tea ' and medicinal purposes. The bulk of the food was imported, and even at the present day there exists a prejudice against locally produced food-stuffs. In British Honduras, for example, the ration laid down by the Government for feeding labourers in mahogany camps consists of salt pork and white flour, while locally produced food-stuffs, such as maize, rice, and sugar, are looked upon as inferior to similar products imported from abroad. It is not so long since it was a criminal offence to grow rice in British Guiana, as it was thought that its cultivation would interfere with the work on the sugar plantations. Rice with which to feed East Indian indentured labour was imported all the way from India and Burma.

143. As time went on the West Indian Colonies lost their virtual monopoly, especially for sugar, which had become, and still is, the most important crop in most islands. Sugar had not only to compete with other parts of the tropics, but also with the bounty-fed beet sugar on the continent of Europe.

144. Some of the island governments had for a long time maintained botanic gardens, to which promising economic plants were introduced from other parts of the tropics and distributed to plantation owners. In this way the nutmeg industry of Grenada, and the lime industry of Montserrat, Dominica and St Lucia were started. It was felt, however, that something more was required to help the West Indian planter. An Imperial Department of Agriculture for the West Indies was therefore started for the smaller colonies, while the larger colonies, such as Jamaica, Barbados, British Guiana, and Trinidad, established their own Departments of Agriculture. European officers of high standing were appointed, including entomologists and mycologists, to attend to plant diseases, which were rife in introduced crops owing to the scanty attention which these often received. Chemists were appointed to analyse soils and suggest manurial treatment, to investigate processing, and to analyse the juice of new seedling canes. Very scant attention, however, was paid to the production of local food-stuffs, and to peasant agriculture. The West Indies still imports the bulk of its food, and endeavours on this costly system to compete with other parts of the tropics. It is only fair to say, however, that within recent years considerably more attention has been paid to

local or maintenance agriculture. Rice, for example, has become the second most important crop in British Guiana, which can produce the whole of her requirements, with a surplus for export. Peasant agriculture now plays a prominent part in the work of many Island Departments of Agriculture.

145. Conditions in West Africa are very different from those which existed formerly in the West Indies. It belongs to the third category mentioned above. There exists an industrious agricultural population, who live on the crops they grow. There is at times a scarcity of food through climatic reasons and the improvidence of the people in not maintaining a reserve of food from one season to the next. The production of crops for export is therefore a secondary consideration, except where an appetite for luxuries has been whetted by easily earned money, e.g. from West African cocoa.

The Indian model

146. There are many parallels between West Africa and India, and a short description of what has taken place in India, and its bearing on West African and especially Nigerian conditions, will not come amiss.

147. Europeans originally went to India, as to West Africa, for purposes of trade. Trading stations, generally forts, were established all along the coast by Portuguese, Dutch, British, and French companies. The East India Company held its charter from the Crown, and so did the French East India Company. The rivalry between the different trading companies, especially when the British were often at war with the French, led to frequent clashes between the troops employed by these companies, often supplemented by regular troops from Europe and by those of the Indian rulers. Some Indian territories were conquered and the rulers of others were rewarded as allies of the British. The overthrow of the Delhi kingdom, which through its viceroys ruled the greater part of peninsular India, meant taking over the administration of large parts of the conquered country. To provide the necessary funds the land revenue system of the Delhi dynasty was maintained, and was put on to a cash basis. The ownership of land was recognised, and it was soon laid down that no land in the settled districts was to be alienated to Europeans. Except in parts of Bihar, no land on the plains of British India has ever been so alienated. All planting enterprise has been in the hills. For such enterprises, as in the West Indies, labour had to be introduced, but this was a simple matter in India, where supplies of paid labour could always be obtained from the more congested parts of the country.

148. Even in the early days of the East India Company great interest was taken not only in the local crops but also in industries and manufactures, e.g. cotton goods woven in the country and often dyed and printed, sugar, pepper, etc. Government botanists were appointed to identify and study economic plants. Roxburgh's name is well known for his botanical research, and Buchanan Hamilton, also a botanist, is chiefly remembered at the present day for his very detailed economic survey of Mysore, South Canara and Malabar, which was carried out under the orders of the Company at the beginning of last century. The Company also expended large sums of money on agricultural enterprise. A spice garden was started in Malabar, with the object of breaking the Dutch monopoly. Seed of Bourbon cotton, for example, was imported freshly each year for a considerable time, and distributed to native farmers to grow. Some of it survives to the present day. Experienced American cotton growers were engaged and large farms were opened, both in Bombay and Madras, in an endeavour to improve the yield

and quality of the cotton crop. Dharwar American cotton is the survival of this effort. The Company was interested in the possibility of growing tea in the northern hills; it introduced seed from China, and tried out wild tea discovered in the Assam hills. The Royal Botanic Gardens at Calcutta were also established by the East India Company, as well as the gardens at Saharanpur.

149. After the Mutiny, when the administration of the country was taken over by the British Government from the East India Company, trade was separated from administration, the former becoming to a great extent a matter for the trading firms themselves. In the early days the Indian Government took the initiative in introducing various species of cinchona to combat the scourge of malaria, and a successful industry was established under Government control. It then financed the introduction of rubber-producing plants from the New World, and it was due to the enterprise of the Indian Government that the rubber industry of Malaya and Ceylon was founded. It will be seen that the attitude towards agriculture, both of the East India Company and the Indian Government, was very much the same as in the colonies.

150. With settled administration the population rapidly increased, and during the latter part of last century parts of the country were subject to severe famines. To relieve the situation fresh areas of land were made available for more intensive agricultural settlement by large irrigation projects, but it was then realised that something more should be done to improve indigenous agriculture. Agricultural colleges were started in some provinces and placed in the charge of qualified European officers, but it was only in Bombay that any real attempt was made to study Indian agriculture. This was done by Mr Mollison, the Director of Agriculture, who realised its importance from seeing the dire results of successive famines in that presidency. Elsewhere the farms attached to the agricultural colleges tended to adopt European methods of farming, rather than to study those which were indigenous to the country.

151. During this period the Royal Botanic Gardens and the Museum at Calcutta made a botanical study of many of the Indian crops and investigated local industries and crafts connected either directly or indirectly with Indian agriculture. Such information was published in the Indian Agricultural Ledger, which had a series devoted to agricultural crops and practices.

152. It was not, however, till early in the present century, when Lord Curzon was Viceroy, that a really determined effort was made to improve Indian agriculture. An Indian Agricultural Service was established, and a nucleus staff, consisting of two agricultural officers, a botanist, a chemist, and a principal of a newly organised Agricultural College and Research Institute, was appointed to each province, while an Imperial Research Institute staffed with specialist officers was started at Pusa. The provincial staffs were subsequently increased, as need arose, by the addition of more agricultural officers and of other technical officers, such as entomologists, mycologists, and, later, crop specialists. The duties of the agricultural officers were in the first place to make detailed tours in the districts, to survey existing agricultural practices, and, where it was considered necessary, to initiate agricultural stations where local practices could be investigated, and to improve existing agricultural crops by selection.

153. This new outlook on tropical agriculture was a definite break from previous policy. The Indian Provincial Departments of Agriculture, as newly constituted under Lord Curzon's viceroyalty, were not directly concerned with plantation crops, except in so far as these were indigenous to the country and to

peasant agriculture. Planters' Associations had their own scientific services, usually financed by an acreage cess, and Provincial Governments sometimes assisted by grants and by seconding officers of the Agricultural Service. It is interesting to note that the Ceylon Department of Agriculture, which for many years had concentrated on plantation crops, also handed over this work to research institutes in order to be free to give its own undivided attention to indigenous agriculture . . .

The Gold Coast Department of Agriculture

184. The work of this department has to a great extent been subordinated to the marketing of the cocoa crop. The Government shared in the prosperity which cocoa brought to this dependency. It imposed an export tax on cocoa, and its customs revenue from imports increased enormously. The money was spent almost as quickly as it came in. Railways and all-weather roads were constructed for the rapid movement of the cocoa crop from the producing areas to inland markets, and then to the ports. An excellent harbour was constructed at Takoradi and connected with the terminus of the railway from Kumasi to Secondee. Large sums were spent on survey, education and health services, and the administrative service was greatly enlarged. Recurring expenditure rose rapidly, and, as Government income was so directly dependent on the cocoa crop, it was but natural that the Department of Agriculture should devote much time and energy to this crop.

185. It is therefore all the more extraordinary that until 1937 there was no single agricultural station in the cocoa belt proper at which research could be carried out on the requirements of the crop. It is difficult to see how any officer of the Department could be expected to offer correct advice on cultural or other treatments, as he had had no opportunity to acquire knowledge under the local conditions. Thus when diseases and pests became serious, the technical officers of the Department had no means of knowing how any remedial measures they might suggest would affect the general health of the trees. At one stage they suggested cutting out diseased parts of the trees, but this opened the canopy, with disastrous results.

186. Much of the work of the Department has been devoted to setting up standards for marketed cocoa, and a special Produce Inspection Branch was established. Their work has not been backed up by appreciable price bonuses for better quality.

187. The agricultural officers have devoted a large part of their time to building up cooperative societies for marketing cocoa. Some of these societies also carry out the fermentation and drying of the beans. In future, the work put into the organisation of these cooperative societies, and the contacts established, should prove useful to the district agricultural officers when they are in a position to pass on reliable information about the cultural requirements of the cocoa crop. Now that the Government has at last opened a Cocoa Research Station at New Tafo it is to be hoped that such knowledge will be forthcoming. The station has been well equipped with laboratories and houses, but it would have been better if a site with a more regular stand of cocoa had been selected in the first instance.

188. Realising the danger of the Gold Coast becoming a one-crop country, the Department has devoted some attention to alternative export crops. A successful though small industry in limes has been established in the neighbourhood of Cape Coast as a result of the work of the nearby agricultural station of Asuansi. There has also been a considerable expansion in coconut planting along the coast west

of Axim ; and within the last five years a small export trade in bananas has been established, chiefly in the Western Province, with financial assistance from the Government.

189. The Department of Agriculture has been singularly unfortunate in its legacy of agricultural stations. Except in the Northern Territories, none of them appears to be typical of the country which it is intended to serve. The station at Kpeve in British Togoland is situated in a rich pocket of soil, surrounded by hills carrying scrub bush. It was originally intended for investigational work on cocoa, but as it lies outside the region of evergreen forest its value for such work is more than doubtful. At the present time such cocoa as still exists has a hard struggle to maintain itself against adverse climatic conditions. There is no difficulty in growing annual crops on this station, but it is difficult to see what assistance such work can be to the surrounding hilly country. The station at Asuansi, again, is not typical of the coastal region. It is situated on an area of land where the Ashanti hordes used to camp when they raided the coast. Judging by the large amount of broken pottery and other signs of permanent occupation, the area was an old village site, and is much more fertile than the surrounding country. The station at Kumasi is attached to Cadbury Hall, which for many years has been used for instructional purposes for the training of the African subordinate staff of the Department of Agriculture. It is of little value now owing to soil erosion and to the encroachment of the town of Kumasi on to the site.

190. It is only within the last two or three years that any attention has been paid by the agricultural staff of the Department to increasing the local production of food-stuffs. Up till that time the policy of the colony (apart from the Northern Territories) has been that which for so long has ruled in the Caribbean region, namely, the production of crops for export. Recently a series of demonstration ‘ food farms ’, of a size considered suitable for a family, have been opened up in various parts of the coastal region and in the cocoa belt. These farms are divided into four equal portions, so that a rotation of crops can be adopted. One portion is laid down to a temporary pasture of Centrosema (*Centrosema plumieri* (Turp. Benth.)) and is folded with sheep, which not only enrich the area on which they graze, but supply manure for the remaining fields and some income from the meat produced. It was not possible for us to draw any conclusions, as the only farm we saw was situated on the unusually rich dark soil of an old village site. Provided the rains were sufficient its success might be taken as a foregone conclusion. In commenting on what to us seemed an unhappy choice of centres for these experimental and demonstration farms, we more than once evoked the reply that the choice of abnormally rich soils had been made deliberately in order that the outstanding success of the crops might arouse interest. We are of the opinion – one which has been many times commented upon in different parts of Tropical Africa – that the African farmer is an excellent judge of soils and that he would naturally be inclined to discount the value of an easy success on a good rich soil.

191. The idea of utilising Centrosema as a pasture plant for sheep has been worked out at the Asuansi agricultural station, and it seems a pity that agricultural officers carrying out this work should not have had more knowledge, based on experimental work on the treatment of the other crops which are being grown in rotation with these pastures.

192. Work in the Northern Territories has been much closer to native agriculture than has that of the south. Some thirty miles north of Kumasi the evergreen forest region is left behind, and deciduous open forest replaces it. This country

south of the Black Volta is somewhat similar to the middle belt of Nigeria. The country is only sparsely populated, and large areas are shown on the map as being uninhabited. Tamale, the headquarters of the Northern Territories, is about 250 miles north of Kumasi by road. This road passes through sparsely inhabited country most of its distance, and without a more detailed knowledge of the country lying to the east of this road, which seems to be much more densely populated, it is not possible to assess the agricultural possibilities of the southern part of this region. North of Tamale, in the Dagomba country, one sees excellent yam cultivation and a certain amount of pennisetum millets, but it is not until the granite country of the Mamprusi Division is reached that one comes across a really dense population with a well developed and intensive subsistence agriculture. The Department of Agriculture has a large agricultural station near Tamale, which one infers was started at a time when there was talk of extending the railway northwards and it was necessary to ascertain the possibilities of providing adequate freight for the railway. The feasibility of growing cotton on a more extensive scale was explored, but, though the economic botanist has selected strains and has carried out trials with cottons introduced from other parts of West Africa, little material progress has been made. With the abandonment of the idea of a railway the question of other export products which could stand the cost of road transport was investigated. Trials were carried out to see whether shea butter could be extracted from the nut by modern machinery, but the costs were found to be prohibitive. The agricultural station at Tamale has therefore turned towards the improvement of existing methods of subsistence agriculture, while the economic botanist has devoted much time to selection work on native cereals.

193. The most successful work has, however, been carried out by the agricultural officer in the Mamprusi district. It is one of the few areas in West Africa where a really sound agricultural survey has been carried out as a basis for agricultural improvement. The result has been that considerable success has been achieved within a comparatively short time, and the confidence of the population has been obtained. Details of this work have been published by the Department in one of its bulletins. Mixed farming is the basis of improvement; it is mainly a modification and systematisation of existing native practice.

194. Tribal life in this area is in danger of breaking up at the present time owing to the absence of room for expansion, but by more intense methods of farming the younger generation may be induced to stay at home instead of wandering off south to seek work and perhaps remaining there as labourers. It has already been possible to secure local support for prohibiting grass fires in order to conserve grass for bedding cattle. The Native Administrations are now working very keenly, and may be trusted to support other sound measures.

28(b). By the Watson Commission, 1948 [1]

321. We do not intend to describe in any detail the agricultural systems found in the Gold Coast. This is readily available in other publications. We merely wish to emphasise a few points which we think important in considering past policy

[1] *Report of the Commission of enquiry into disturbances in the Gold Coast, 1948*, Colonial Office, London 1948, paras 321–36 (extracts).

and future development. The Gold Coast is predominantly an agricultural country. The great majority of its people are dependent, directly or indirectly, on agricultural production, for their day-to-day food, for the payment of imports, and for the revenue which has to provide such social services as they enjoy. There are four further factors which must influence very greatly potential developments. Farms are small and almost entirely in the hands of African peasant farmers. The system of land tenure in the Colony and Ashanti is largely one of tribal ownership, the individual farmer filling the role of tenant. Insecurity of tenure militates at every turn against the better utilization of the land. In the Northern Territories, the system is different and there is greater control in the use of land vested in the Government. There was, and still is, a heavy burden of indebtedness and the present system of credit does not meet the requirements of the farmers. Finally, there is a considerable amount of absentee landlordism, particularly in the cocoa belt. All of these have undoubtedly handicapped progress.

322. Suggestions for improvements in the system of land tenure and for the solution of many of the present problems are embodied in the report of a special enquiry which was held in 1947 and we do not propose to deal specifically with this question, except to emphasise its importance for the future well-being of the colony.

323. Apart from questions specifically dealing with cocoa production, a number of representations were made concerning the Department of Agriculture and the agricultural policy of the country. The relevant ones may be considered in five groups: (*a*) the absence of any alternative crops to cocoa; (*b*) the lack of close contact between the Department and the farmer; (*c*) the weakness of agricultural education experimentation and demonstration; (*d*) the excessive attention to the problems of export crops in comparison with crops for home consumption; (*e*) the absence of plans for future development.

324. Before dealing with these points, we wish to make one or two general observations about the work of the Department, though we do so with reservations as we may not have received a full picture of its work in the short time at our disposal. We did not receive any serious complaints about the efficiency or quality of the staff; the main source of trouble was, rather, the limited scope of its activities. This is no reflection on the staff but rather on the Administration's agricultural policy. Agriculture appears to have been the Cinderella Department – before as well as since the war. The Gold Coast has never been provided with the machinery in the form of staff, buildings, and experimental stations to provide for the basic needs of its agriculture.

325. Ample evidence is available to confirm this view; firstly, in the small annual expenditure, over a period of many years, on agriculture relative to the revenue of the country and to the value of the agricultural exports; secondly, in the almost complete disregard of agriculture in the more advanced stages of education and in the award of scholarships for study abroad; and thirdly in the lack of interest in technical problems shown by many members of the Administration.

326. This neglect is eloquently reflected in the following paragraph taken from the report of the Director of Agriculture for the year 1945–6:

> The Department's sole laboratory accommodation was handed over to the West African Cocoa Research Institute in 1944; since then no laboratory facilities have been available save in the citrus research building at Asuansi.

Over the same period the Department has had the services of only one entomologist and one chemist. There has also been a shortage of locally trained African staff. Cadbury Hall, at Kumasi, which was run as a Departmental Training School, and gave an excellent training for junior staff, was closed down in 1939 and no effective alternative was substituted. It is now proposed to enlarge Cadbury Hall as an interim measure but an Agricultural School on a larger scale is to be built on the new Agricultural station at Kumasi. The Agricultural School in Nigeria has recently trained three of our young men.

327. The question of alternative cash or export crops in the place of cocoa was evidently exercising many minds and a number of suggestions were put forward. On many occasions, we challenged witnesses to name for us economic substitutes for cocoa, but no real alternative was forthcoming. It must be admitted that there is no other crop which would yield such returns on the world market. If the Gold Coast fails to save its cocoa industry, it is throwing away the advantages which Providence has given to it in natural conditions for cocoa production which are without parallel in the rest of the world. These unique natural conditions have enabled the Cocoa Marketing Board to obtain what is practically a monopoly price somewhere about eight times the pre-war price level.

328. Many of the crops suggested were better suited to conditions outside the cocoa belt, such as rice, cotton, soya beans, sunflower, castor seed and so on. We understand that a small amount of experimental work has been done in past years on the production of alternative crops but the complaint is that it has not been systematic or continuous and that the results, if any, have not been brought adequately to the notice of the farmer. Whether this is a fair criticism or not, we would recommend a more intensive search for possible substitutes as a partial insurance in anticipation of the disaster that would occur if wiser counsels do not prevail and the cocoa industry dies. Some of the large reserve funds in the hands of the Cocoa Marketing Board might be used for this purpose since the work would be of direct benefit to the cocoa farmer himself.

329. Criticisms were also made of the lack of contact between the Department's staff and the farmers. So far as we could ascertain, this was not deliberate policy on the part of the Department but is merely a reflection of the understaffing that has occurred. We do, however, feel that, if the number of personnel can be increased some of the functions of the Department can be decentralised to some extent, especially those of the more senior officials. There appears to be too much reference back to Accra.

330. There is no need for us to elaborate on the inadequacy of research and experimental stations. The dearth is obvious and has been evident for many years. Experience in other parts of the world has shown conclusively the dependence of agricultural progress on adequate scientific research and the application of its results in practice for farmers to see. The lack of this essential link in agricultural development for so long a time merely accentuates the urgency of remedying it. We are well aware of the shortage of trained scientific personnel at the present time, a shortage that may become more acute if conditions of service in the colonies become less attractive, but this confirms us in our view that more active measures should be taken to develop agricultural education facilities, particularly in the training of scientific research workers. The lack of appreciation of the importance of this aspect of the work is seen in the fact that though large numbers of Government Scholarships for University education have been awarded

this is the first year in which any have been made available for agriculture; three have now been granted.

331. There is also need for more demonstration work if the results of research and experiment are to be adopted in practice. Here again, shortages of staff and equipment seem to be the limiting factors. We were told of some of the good work being carried out by the Department in its experiments and observation trials and in developing systems of mixed farming in the Northern Territories. The only complaint brought to us was that there was not more of it.

332. Possibly the most serious criticism was the greater interest displayed in the export crops at the expense of the crops grown for home consumption. This is undoubtedly a difficult balance to strike; it cannot be denied that the export crops provide most of the revenue upon which depends the maintenance of law and order, the provision of education and health services and so on; expenditure on research and development can easily be shown to produce dividends. Fundamentally however the life of the colony depends on its food supply.

333. The two existing research institutes in the Gold Coast are concerned with cocoa and limes, both of them commercial export crops, and a large part of the Department's staff is devoting most of their time to those two crops, and possibly a third, coconuts – also of export interest.

334. By way of contrast with the apathy towards food crops, we were told of the war-time agricultural developments, when a phenomenal increase in vegetable production and the development of a bacon industry were quickly achieved to meet the requirements of the Services. We agree that this indicated that results can be achieved under pressure.

335. We would like to see a great intensification of the efforts to improve the yields and quality of home grown foodstuffs. Two lines of development appear to us to be necessary; to improve the existing systems and to modify them so as to meet the demands of an expanding and commercialised economy. There are ample opportunities in both directions. We would place a high priority on the first; we believe that the days when local production was adequate for local needs are past; the population is increasing rapidly and their purchasing power has risen; there is no superabundance of food today in relation to the needs of the people. Levels of food consumption have been low in the past and we are prepared to accept the argument that nutritional levels must be improved if the level of output – mental and material – is to be raised and production costs brought more closely into line with world prices. There is therefore, in our opinion, a strong case for a higher priority for work on food crops; it should certainly take precedence over – or at least rank on a par with – any further development in export crops.

336. We should like to emphasise once again that, though we are critical of the Administration, we would not wish to cast any aspersions on those in the Agricultural Department or the Research Institutes. We saw work of the highest quality being carried on under difficult conditions; there is evidence of drive and initiative which, we think, may have been lacking in the past. The agricultural problems are well known to the experts and we are confident of their solution. But they must have more help. We have seen the plans for the future development of agricultural production. They seem admirably directed to meet many of the criticisms which were brought to us. Our only comment on them is that they might well be more ambitious in the light of the issues at stake.

Bibliography

24. Governor's Annual Address, *Legislative Council Debates, 1923–4*, pp. 36–9.
25. *Report by the Honourable W. G. A. Ormsby-Gore on his visit to West Africa, during the year 1926*, Cmd 2744, London 1926, pp. 139–53 (extracts).
26. (a) Correspondence relating to the development of the oil palm industry, *Sessional Paper no. IV, 1924–5*, paras 6–18 (extracts).
(b) Despatch from the Governor to the Secretary of State, 6 September 1929, *Sessional Paper no. III, 1930–1*, no. 665.
27. Despatches relating to the shea-nut industry of the Northern Territories, 1929, *Sessional Paper no. XI, 1929–30*.
28. (a) The West Africa Commission, 1938–9, *Technical Reports*, Leverhulme Trust, London 1943, paras 140–94 (extracts).
(b) *Report of the Commission of Enquiry into disturbances in the Gold Coast, 1948*, Colonial Office, London 1948, paras 321–36 (extracts).

5. Agriculture: Cocoa

Despite its great success the cocoa industry was a source of continuous anxiety to the colonial government. The emphasis of government policy on the industry shifted as circumstances changed, but, as we have argued above, the industry never received direct and sustained economic or technical assistance from the government. The documents in this section illustrate the point by concentrating on the three most important areas of government policy: 1. The concern with the methods of cultivation of the cocoa farmers and the quality of the final product. 2. Marketing. 3. The treatment of diseased cocoa trees.

1. The concern of the colonial government with the methods of cultivation and the quality of cocoa reached its peak in the years after 1910, when the cocoa industry became the largest export industry in the colony. The Department of Agriculture started a crusade against the industry, predicting disaster and calling for firm measures of control to be taken. The following extracts from a despatch from the Director of Agriculture in 1915 illustrate clearly the position the department took as regards the industry.

I live in constant dread of disaster overtaking the industry through the careless or negligent practices employed by natives and I have constantly advocated an increase of the European staff of my Department and legislation to control the anomalies . . .

I have long ago abandoned the idea that friendly persuasion will accomplish all that is necessary and in the interests of the people themselves and the future of the industry, I am strongly of the opinion that a system of more complete inspection and supervision of cocoa farmers should not be longer delayed . . .

Personally I see no objection to powers being given to European officers in the Agricultural Department to enforce legislation in the matter of farm sanitation . . . Experience in this colony, I think, shows that the more power a man has, the more he is respected and obeyed.[1]

The Deputy Director of Agriculture carried on the attack in the same vein. In a letter later that year he sought to explain why cocoa produced in Ghana fetched lower prices than cocoa produced in the West Indies. He did not seek an explanation in terms of the fact that the products of the areas were

[1] Papers relating to the cocoa industry, *Sessional Papers no. II, 1916–17.*

essentially dissimilar and not comparable in terms of price and quality. Rather he argued:

> it is necessary to take into consideration the fact that whereas the producers of West Indian cocoa are either Europeans, of European extraction or are sufficiently intelligent to use European methods, the producers of cocoa in this Colony and Ashanti are natives in a most elementary state of civilisation, whose sole aim, as yet, appears to be the attainment of a maximum amount of money with a minimum expenditure of energy – however uneconomical the system – and whose lack of foresight for the future welfare of the industry – and consequently of themselves – has not yet been compensated by adequate legislative measures.[2]

The views of the Department of Agriculture were most fully developed in a survey of the industry undertaken by the Director during the First World War and published in two parts in 1918 and 1919. Document 29 contains extracts from these reports which urge control of both production and marketing arrangements, as methods of preventing plant disease and improving the quality of cocoa. The Governor of the colony at that time (Clifford) did not doubt the expertise of the Department of Agriculture, but was concerned with the political implications of the department's proposals. In 1915 he endorsed the fears of the Commissioner of the Eastern Province that the proposed legislation 'will result not in improving cultivation but in bringing the Agricultural Department into collision with the native population and thereby impairing its usefulness'.[3] The following year he stated the position even more sharply: 'I am, however, quite convinced that the somewhat primitive methods of dealing with this matter which have been suggested by the Director of Agriculture would not only fail of their intended effect but would prove highly injurious.'[4] And again: '[There] are political considerations, without the province of the Director of Agriculture, which the latter cannot be expected to take into account, but which the Government cannot afford to ignore or neglect.' This latter statement is taken from a despatch from the Governor, which was read to the Legislative Council in 1917 by the Colonial Secretary, in answer to a question on whether the government intended to introduce legislation 'to enforce the proper cultivation of cocoa in this colony to stop the spread of disease' (Document 30). It can be seen that the Governor was aiming to placate the Department of Agriculture by permitting legislation, but at the same time was preventing the Department from obtaining the blanket measures it sought and which, he feared, would lead to a serious political confrontation between the administration and the cocoa farmers.

[2] Papers relating to the cocoa industry, *Sessional Papers no. II, 1916–17.*

[3] *Ibid.*

[4] *Ibid.*

The issue, however, did not end here. When Clifford's successor, Guggisberg, reviewed the progress of the cocoa industry in 1923 (Document 31), he found it necessary to refute reports that the colonial government intended to restrict cocoa cultivation.

I have recently read that the policy of the Gold Coast Government is to limit [cocoa] production. No more absurd and incorrect statement could have been made. The policy of this Government is to increase cocoa production up to the full working capacity of the population. In view of the right of every man to grow as much as his land can produce I do not see what other policy this Government could adopt.[5]

The method by which the government aimed to increase cocoa production was via the expansion of transport facilities, particularly railways, although these, as we have noted, were of minimal assistance to the industry. In the 1920s government policy moved away from direct attacks on the industry to attempts to reduce its significance via neglect and diversification. The last statement included on this issue is by a Ghanaian member of the Legislative Council, Nana Ofori Atta, who in 1926 refuted the charge that the cocoa farmer was 'lazy and so careless doing things he does not care whether he earns his livelihood or not'. It is interesting to note that Ofori Atta supported the Governor in opposition to the Department of Agriculture and made explicit the position taken up by both Clifford and Guggisberg that what was at stake was not merely a technical issue but a political one.

2. Documents 33 and 34 deal with marketing arrangements, which by the end of the thirties had become the most important issue concerning the cocoa industry and one to which the colonial government was forced to turn its attention. The Commission on the marketing of West African cocoa (1938) (Document 33) described the events of 1937 which led to its being set up as follows:

The introduction of a Buying Agreement combining twelve firms, which normally purchase most of the crop, led to a hold-up of cocoa, which remained fairly effective for over five months and was accompanied by a boycott of most European goods. We formed the conclusion that the hold-up, although supported by the use of various illegal forms of pressure, began and remained an essentially popular movement. It arose chiefly out of the African's fear of monopoly, intensified by the suddenness with which the Agreement was introduced, by a lack of frankness about its provisions, and by a fall in prices that occurred simultaneously with, although not as a result of, it.[6]

This last point was certainly not accepted by Ghanaian cocoa farmers whose main cause for protest was the monopolistic conditions, which they felt were driving low prices even lower. The Commission made recommendations

[5] Document 31, para. 65.
[6] Document 33, para. 466.

which aimed to make the state appear as an impartial arbiter between the two parties – Ghanaian producers and European buyers – while effectively coming down on the side of one – European buyers. It openly attacked the Ghanaian middlemen, partly because it suspected they were politically isolated and weak and partly because it believed that producers were strongly indebted to them, in the way that Indian producers were in debt to local money lenders. Indebtedness of the Indian variety was not a feature of the Ghanaian cocoa industry, which this commission did not really understand and about which it brought out all the old platitudes about 'casual methods of production' and so on. The Commission studied various proposals for reforming marketing and eventually proposed the establishment of a statutory body, consisting of 'recognised leaders of the Africans', representatives of the firms and public officials. We have argued that the main impact of the proposal was to prevent the consolidation of the organisation of cocoa farmers which had begun spontaneously in the hold-up of 1937. There is considerable evidence in its report to suggest that the commission was quite clear about this as an aim of policy and was well aware of the political strategy underlying its organisational proposals.

The outbreak of war obliged the government to intervene more directly in the marketing of the crop than was envisaged by the Commission. The *Report on cocoa control in West Africa, 1939–43* described the procedures adopted during the war and made recommendations for the post-war period. Of these the most important was the proposal 'to break the direct link between the producers and world market prices' which led to the establishment of the Cocoa Marketing Board, whose practices and the disputes they engendered lie beyond the scope of this work.

3. This Chapter concludes with an extract from the *Report of the Commission of enquiry into disturbances in the Gold Coast, 1948* on the cutting-out of diseased cocoa trees (Document 35). At the time cutting-out was the only method of dealing with disease but the Commission did not see this as a criticism of the government, which had been forecasting disaster for many years but was completely unprepared when it actually overtook the industry. The Commission did criticise the colonial government, not for the policy of cutting-out as such, but for the manner in which the policy was implemented. It reported widespread political opposition and a belief quite widely held that the government was deliberately attempting to destroy the industry. While the fear that the government did intend the destruction of the industry was almost certainly invalid, what is clear is that the cocoa farmers' mistrust of the government was so great that it must have had a real basis: this real basis can be found in the systematic opposition of the colonial government to the progress of the cocoa industry over a period of forty years.

29. Director of Agriculture concerned about the future of the cocoa industry: measures of control proposed, 1918 [1]

1. The first export of cocoa from this country was in 1891, viz. 80 lbs weight. Production steadily increased until in 1911 it eclipsed that of any other single country in the world. Since then even more rapid progress in production has continued and the annual cocoa crop is now estimated at considerably over 100,000 tons, approximately half the total production of the world...

2. We have been wont to congratulate ourselves on the rapid development of such a large and valuable industry and there is undoubtedly some occasion for our pride by reason of the fact that cocoa is an introduced crop, and rarely, if ever in the history of the world can a similar instance be given of an industry of such magnitude and value being developed in so comparatively short a time by native races. It has been the most important factor in the development of this country and of its inhabitants, but it is realised that the industry is getting beyond control and various aspects of it require more attention, and if necessary regulation, to place it on a satisfactory basis. Already there are signs of overproduction with a consequent lowering of values; manufacturers in England have made representations regarding the unsatisfactory nature of the general quality of the product – presumably due to a radical defect in our commercial system; a wholesale practice of cheating is reputed to be engaged in by native buyers which is and must have a demoralising effect on the general community; and the careless or slovenly methods of cultivation and consequent increases of diseases in the plantations – due for the most part to the extension of farms beyond reasonable limits by the native owners in their haste to make money quickly – are all causing anxiety as to the stability and future progress of the industry...

19. The whole subject resolves itself into two main considerations: (*a*) the steps which may be necessary to secure the continued successful cultivation or production of cocoa in this Colony and (*b*) the steps which may be necessary to regulate the trade in cocoa generally with a view to secure more just dealing and to effect a general improvement in the quality of the cocoa produced...

The steps which may be necessary to secure the continued successful cultivation or production of cocoa in this Colony

20. The rapid development of cocoa cultivation conclusively proves that it has been found to be very lucrative. Prior to the introduction of cocoa the natives were content to exploit the indigenous products such as palm oil and kernels, rubber and kola, but at no time did the total value of these products exported in any one year approximate to more than one-fourth the annual value now of the cocoa crop. And although other crops have been introduced and brought to their notice, notably coffee in pre-cocoa days and latterly rubber, etc., their cultivation has never been seriously considered; and they have latterly also, to a large extent, neglected the exploitation of the indigenous products in many cases even neglecting to grow food crops in favour of imported European foods.

21. Cocoa suits local conditions of soil and climate to a remarkable degree and at normal values I doubt if any other crop can or could be grown by the natives with such lucrative results. Having thus far been so very successful with this crop,

[1] W. S. D. Tudhope (Director of Agriculture), Enquiry into the Gold Coast cocoa industry, *Sessional Papers nos. II and IV, 1918–19*, paras 1–2 and 19–45 (extracts).

and having due regard to the state of misery to which the people themselves would be reduced, the stagnation of trade with its serious losses alike to the mercantile community and Government, should conditions be rendered either unfit for cocoa to survive or the plantations be wiped out by diseases or pests – not impossible or indeed improbable contingencies – it behoves us not to shut our eyes to the danger but to do everything we can, by regulation if necessary, to guard against them.

22. Hitherto no restrictions whatever have been put on the destruction of forests or in the extension or maintenance of farms and it is here a danger lies. Enormous areas of forest land have everywhere been cut down for cocoa and when one considers that it is undoubtedly due to the huge extent of forest and its concomitant humidity more than to anything else that cocoa can be successfully grown in this country, since we have the lowest rainfall of any cocoa-growing country in the world, it seems to me of vital importance that regulations restricting destruction of forests should be introduced before it is too late.

It may be recounted that the enlightened Omanhene of Akim Abuakwa (Honourable Ofori Atta, C.P.E.) did introduce some regulations enforcing reservation of certain areas in his division a few years ago, and certain Headchiefs in Ashanti have also done likewise, but a much wider application of the principle is necessary all over the country and I think ought to be enforced in the general interest of the community as a whole. At the rate of destruction indulged in during the past twenty years it is unpleasant to conjecture what may happen within the next few decades. The object I think could be attained by prohibiting further destruction of forests by [restricting the] planting cocoa within certain defined limits.

23. The fear has been expressed that the production of cocoa is already approaching the world's requirements, so, even if the dangers referred to in the preceding paragraph were not apparent, a continued extension of output might cause a serious lowering in the value of the commodity to such an extent that it would be no longer profitable to the producers, and it is worthy of serious consideration whether restriction is not necessary from this point of view alone. I have frequently pointed out to the farmers that they are much better with say £1 a load for 50 loads of cocoa, than with half the amount or less for 100 loads.

24. The present seems an opportune time for the introduction of such legislation. Extension of plantations which went on uninterruptedly right up to the recent crisis in trade, is now temporarily suspended (although it will no doubt be renewed on the return of normal conditions) and the people are in the mood to see reason in what at other times they might ignorantly call undue interference. It would also presumably have the effect of securing more attention to existing farms which, both in cultivation and sanitation, require more persistent effort to secure continuous and better results and to prevent and overcome diseases and pests.

25. The objectionable and dangerous practice of abandoning or semi-abandoning a farm when it is attacked by diseases or pests or when it becomes less lucrative for want of proper cultural attention should be prohibited. A fruitful field for the dissemination of diseases and pests is introduced, fraught with danger to the better tended farms and the whole industry, and this practice is all too common.

Speaking generally the cocoa plantations, once established, are treated like ordinary native indigenous products and the bulk of the cultivation they receive is associated with the collection of the crop. The industry is still of comparatively recent birth and the people are not alive to possibilities of disaster overtaking their farms. The warnings and advice of agricultural officers have done much to educate them not only with regard to proper methods of cultivation but also in the preparation of the product, but something more is required and this many of the more enlightened farmers themselves realise. If present methods are not improved it may well be that established farms will become increasingly less productive, should they not be killed out altogether. During my enquiry I have listened to many complaints that the older farms are now giving less crop and I have seen for myself the destruction that is being wrought by pests and diseases and cannot but view with alarm the prospect of their more rapid development in future, aided as they have been through the increased inattention given plantations during the past three years . . .

27. Prevention is better than cure and example better than precept. These principles can be seen applied on any of the agricultural stations on all of which diseases and pests have been kept under control and efficient cultivation maintained whereby the yields are kept up, and it is especially with regard to the former that I suggest action should be taken. More efficient cultural attention is at the root of the whole matter and it is with regard to this that I consider a form of compulsion is necessary . . .

The steps which may be necessary to regulate the trade in cocoa . . .

30. Evidence collected goes to show that with only a few exceptions the mercantile community generally do not show any appreciable desire to help in this worthy object, and many valuable opportunities, I believe, have been literally thrown away in past years. It is not perhaps altogether fair to blame them; the cocoa is brought in to them in small quantities and the amount of work entailed in selecting and grading it must be very considerable; and I am assured that the difference in price they stand to receive – stated to be somewhere about 2*s* to 3*s* per hundredweight – does not compensate them for the additional time and labour required. Most of the larger buyers therefore have adopted the principle on their own admission of only buying and selling on a basis of one grade only and at one price. This is discouraging to say the least of it to those farmers who have benefited by instruction and who succeed in producing better quality material, as they get the same price for it as their neighbour who has not taken the same care in its preparation. This is a very general complaint of the farmers.

31. It appears to me that it is very much a matter of local market conditions. Most of the cocoa is bought by native buyers, many of whom have no special qualifications as judges of cocoa, their main qualification being that they understand weights and scales (which they are frequently able to manipulate to their own advantage). Some of them visit farms in the bush and buy direct from the farmers and many of the latter complain that they are coerced into selling. Be that as it may the latter are relieved of the transporting of their produce to the nearest trading centre and are frequently only too glad to sell at their farms on these conditions. The result however is that the bulk of the cocoa when it arrives at the depot of the exporter is indiscriminately mixed . . .

34. It was with a view to discussion of this subject that the question of adopting fixed markets or buying centres for cocoa, a system of licensing buyers and substituting measures of capacity instead of weights were brought forward in connection with this enquiry. The suggestion of fixed buying centres has been generally rather adversely received (*a*) by several of the mercantile firms, pre-

sumably because they resent Government interference of any kind; (*b*) by most of the buyers, presumably because they fear they would not be able to have the same opportunities for exploiting the illiterate producer; and (*c*) to some extent by the producers because they fail to appreciate the advantages it would bring and fear it might cause them more inconvenience. The licensing of buyers has also, probably for the same reasons, not received very favourable consideration; and except for the illiterate producers, who are most anxious for its introduction, the compulsory use of definite standard measures does not receive very much support. After giving the matter careful consideration however I do think some form of control is necessary in the best interests of the industry.

35. [There are a] large number of semi-educated and irresponsible individuals who are now engaged in buying cocoa and a (considerable) amount of cheating is reputed to be going on. On my tour I had numerous complaints from farmers of being cheated. I also found buyers operating with scales that were obviously tinkered with so that they would register extra weight, many of which were spring balances which I understand are not legal, and I am thoroughly convinced that the farmers' complaint is justified and that wholesale cheating is being indulged in . . .

36. In consideration of all the facts I have therefore come to the conclusion that Government supervision is necessary even if for no other reason than to counteract the demoralising influence of the practices referred to. The magnitude of the industry offers plenty of scope for honest individual enterprise and the honest man – both European and native – has nothing to fear from control, rather he will be benefited by protection against the unscrupulous individuals, as the object ought to be to eliminate the latter altogether. I therefore suggest the following: (*a*) *buying centres* arranged by the District Commissioners with the assistance of the local chiefs and approved by the Government, should be fixed and no selling or buying allowed outside these centres, i.e. all buying on farms and all roadside buying prohibited; (*b*) *buyers should be licensed* as well as their premises (this principle applies in the case of rum selling, and cocoa is of infinitely greater importance); (*c*) *the provision of the Weights and Measures Ordinance should be more rigidly enforced* . . .

37. These measures would to my mind do much to instil a healthy life into the industry. Buying would then perforce have to be done openly and it may be assumed that this would do much to reduce the irregularities already referred to, and if buyers stood a chance of having their licences forfeited this would make them more careful. A much better opportunity would be afforded for the inspection of the product and general supervision of the buying, which would give those desirous of grading the cocoa an opportunity for doing so – by general assent most difficult at the present time. Farmers in some instances might be put to a little inconvenience but this would be more than compensated for, I anticipate, by results. They would be within little more than one day's journey away from these centres however – and in early days many of them were in the habit of transporting their produce up to seven days' journey and even more. But even if it did have the results of retarding extension of cocoa farms or output in the very remote districts, this might be a blessing in disguise. A large number of inspectors might not be necessary as the local Chief or Headman of each selected centre should be given a sort of controlling interest and he would report any irregularities to the District Commissioner or the Inspector, and the buyers' licenses should be granted by the local District Commissioner for all operating within his district. The fee to

be charged for a licence is a matter for consideration but I think the object would be served without making it too high . . .

44. There is just one other matter I wish to refer to in connection with this enquiry and it is the great necessity which exists for more internal transport. Further extension of roads suitable for motor transport is very necessary, but the first and greater need is the extension of the railway system. Motor transport, to judge by the prevailing charges, is much more costly and it is obvious that its place is merely as a feeder to the railways. I am aware that the linking up of the Coomassie and Akwapim railways has already been approved and is only in abeyance owing to temporary financial considerations. Its completion will no doubt alleviate matters and should be proceeded with at the earliest possible moment; and the central part of the Colony, now producing large quantities of produce, should receive similar attention as early as possible.

45. In conclusion I have to add that although I have had necessarily to refer to several disquieting features regarding the industry in this report I am by no means a pessimist. During the ten and a half years I have been associated with it in my official capacity I have witnessed much development and some considerable progress. Rapid development, as was only to be expected, brings with it pitfalls and dangers, and new features which have to be carefully watched. The responsibility of Government is correspondingly increased. I have dealt with some of the more important features that appear to me to call for regulation, and I trust the suggestions I have brought forward will receive the consideration they deserve, and that the discussion of the subject will result in a substantial improvement of the industry, the future success of which means so much to the people of this country.

30. Legislation on cocoa diseases : political caution by the Governor, 1916 [1]

Colonial Secretary: With the Governor's permission I will read an extract from a despatch [2] which His Excellency has recently addressed to the Secretary of State on this among other agricultural subjects:

Recently a draft Bill has been drawn up, and circulated to the Paramount Chiefs in the principal cocoa-producing districts for their consideration and comments, the object of which is to provide the machinery for coercive and punitive measures directed against persistent neglect by cocoa-farmers of reasonable sanitary precautions calculated to check or to eliminate insect and fungoid-bred diseases.

This Bill proposes that, from time to time, certain areas, in which disease due to neglect is specially prevalent, should be proclaimed, and should thereupon be placed under the immediate control of the Agricultural Department. Thereafter, so long as the area in question continues to be ' proclaimed ', all cocoa-farmers who possess gardens within its boundaries, will be compelled, under pain of fine and imprisonment, to cultivate and tend their trees under expert supervision and in the manner prescribed by the Director of Agriculture.

Having regard to the fact that a farm upon which disease is prevalent is in theory at any rate to be regarded as a plague-spot, from which infection may

[1] *Legislative Council Debates, 1916–17*, pp. 82–91.

[2] Papers Relating to the Cocoa Industry, 1916–17.

spread in all directions to the destruction of neighbouring estates, such an Ordinance would appear to be reasonable enough. The peculiarities of local circumstances, however, render the policy of its application open to certain objections, if the matter be judged from the native point of view, which cannot, I think, be wisely neglected, and which may be conveniently summarised as follows:

(*a*) In the Gold Coast and Ashanti, where the area under cocoa is today of enormous extent, it is not possible to pass a law of universal application which will be of any practical effect, or which, if the attempt were made to apply it forthwith to all cocoa-farmers, would not be at once capricious and oppressive in its operation.

This I should perhaps explain, is due to the fact that neglected gardens are so numerous in practically every cocoa district – properly cultivated patches being, indeed, the rare exceptions – that the vast majority of cocoa-farmers would forthwith be converted by such a Bill into persistent law-breakers, who would be liable to fine and to imprisonment in default of payment. The Government being clearly unable to punish the bulk of the agricultural population with any approach to even-handed justice, the Bill would have either to remain inoperative or to be used as an instrument for the infliction of penalties upon a few offenders, chosen at random, who had had the misfortune to attract attention, while their neighbours escaped scot free. I need hardly say that I am, on principle, opposed to the practice of placing upon our statute book any law which is obliged to be at once wholly inoperative in the case of the majority of those who fail to comply with its provisions and very partial and capricious in the detection of the individuals marked out for punishment under its penal sections. In the present instance, moreover, I am convinced that the majority of the natives concerned would elect to take their chance of escaping prosecution – for each individual would feel that the law of average was in his favour – if the only alternative were to be the performance at stated intervals of some additional uncongenial work.

(*b*) The operation of the law having, in these circumstances, to be applied to certain selected areas, in which the carrying out of its provisions could be made immediately and practically effective, and the number and extent of these chosen areas being limited by the supervisory staff at the disposal of the Agricultural Department, the partial and capricious operations of the law would now affect, not individuals, but groups of farmers whose cocoa-gardens chanced to be situated in certain ill-fated localities.

In this connection I would venture to remind you that the only homogeneity which the Gold Coast Colony and Ashanti today possess is conferred upon their inhabitants by the existence of the British Colonial Government. The native races inhabiting this part of West Africa are divided up among themselves into a very large number of petty states, each self-contained and complete in itself... Many of these small states fall within the cocoa-growing area; and speaking generally, the unsatisfactory agricultural methods, which it is our desire to discourage, are common to them all. In these circumstances, therefore, it will be realised that the task of singling out some particular area for supervisory and for coercive or punitive measures would be one of great delicacy. It would be impossible, in my opinion, to pick out any one particular Paramount Chief's division which would be fairly accounted an awful example, deserving peculiar treatment that was not merited in an equal degree by most, if not by all, of its immediate neighbours. Accordingly, though the law would possess the advantage of being practically operative, at any rate in a few specially selected areas, its application would inevitably be as partial and capricious as ever, while the sense of grievance which this would very naturally engender, would be felt not by certain individuals, but by certain individual tribes or parts of tribes.

I think that there is a certain probability that the cocoa-farmers in the immediate vicinity of the areas selected for supervision and coercion would be likely to profit by the example to some extent; but I do not think that this effect would be very wide-spread while there can, in my opinion, be no doubt that the action taken by the Government would occasion a great deal of resentment and would tend to quicken inter-tribal jealousies and animosities. These are political considerations, without the province of the Director of Agriculture which the latter cannot be expected to take into account, but which the Government cannot afford to ignore or to neglect.

(*c*) Where practically all cocoa-farmers are offenders against approved methods of cultivation, the argument that punitive measures are necessary in the common interests loses much of its effect, since the gardens owned by the people whose division was singled out for treatment would in many cases be constantly exposed to infection owing to their proximity to other non-treated areas, the carelessness of whose owners would be temporarily immune from punishment. In fact, it is only in localities where the neglected garden is the exception, not the rule, that this argument can be regarded as having any real force, at any rate in the opinion of the people directly concerned.

(*d*) Cocoa diseases are not new phenomena in the Gold Coast. On the contrary, they have long been familiar to native cultivators. The latter have learned by experience that when these diseases become very prevalent, it is expedient to let the garden so affected lie fallow for a year or two and that as Gold Coast cocoa is of a sturdy forest variety, a return to natural conditions almost invariably leads to more or less complete recovery. The native farmers, therefore, look upon this temporary or periodical abandonment of particular pest-ridden farms as the obvious and natural remedy which lies ready to their hands; and the officers of the Agricultural Department while deploring the wastefulness of a process which, if only due care were exercised by the people, should not be necessary, very generally admit that recovery usually results, and the farmer loses only through interruption of continuous production. This is of no great moment, however, to the natives concerned, for it is a very general practice nowadays for a farmer and his family to own several cocoa-gardens. Moreover to a people who, until very recently, had never attempted to cultivate any particular plot of land permanently or continually, and who even today do so almost exclusively where cocoa has been planted, the temporary or periodical abandonment of a cocoa-garden is viewed with perfect equanimity, and in their estimation is a far more natural process than is the cultivation, year after year, of the same piece of ground.

For all these reasons, therefore, I consider that it will be very difficult to convince many even of the most intelligent of the cocoa-farmers, whose property we desire to improve and to preserve, that the action suggested is advisable – far less that it is necessary. In spite of this, however, were I fully persuaded that the effect, which it is our object to produce, would actually be attained by the introduction of a Bill, such as that here discussed, I should not hesitate to urge the Legislative Council to adopt it. As matters stand at present, however, I am by no means sure that it would prove to be very efficacious, while the discontent and unrest which putting it into operation in certain selected areas would inevitably cause, make me reluctant to embark upon a coercive policy if it can be avoided.

31. The Governor affirms the right of every man to grow as much as his land can produce, 1923 [1]

Cocoa, our mainstay, has again done well; there has been no falling off in the demand. Last financial year we exported close on 160,000 tons, and this year our records up to date show that we shall again reach this figure, an amount of 20,000 in excess of what Honourable Members estimated last March. For the coming year we estimate an export of 155,000 tons, a conservative estimate.

Potential cocoa production

65. Last year I informed Honourable Members that I believed that the Gold Coast was then producing some 170,000 tons of cocoa annually, and was capable of producing at least 200,000 tons. I notice that the last-named figure was the opinion of the members of the Trade and Taxation Committee! This amount, 200,000 tons, is based on the population of the cocoa-growing areas; the potential production based on the soil is far greater, for at present far less than one-seventh of the cocoa-bearing area is actually under cultivation. As our production depends on our population, there can be little fear of the Gold Coast itself overflooding the world's markets.

With regard to this, I have recently read that the policy of the Gold Coast Government is to limit production. No more absurd and incorrect statement could have been made. The policy of this Government is to increase cocoa production up to the full working capacity of the population. In view of the right of every man to grow as much as his land can produce I do not see what other policy this Government could adopt.

Agricultural map

66. The Agricultural Department is at present compiling maps showing the actual and potential production of the various districts based on the population. The information given will include palm-oil, copra, and other products, and should prove valuable in planning the development of transport. Due allowance will naturally be made for the labour required for the production of foodstuffs. Pending the completion of this map as many steps have been taken as possible to ascertain present and potential productivity. The whole subject is dealt with exhaustively in my despatch no. 747 of 2 November 1922, which has been published as a Sessional Paper and laid on the table.

Unmarketed cocoa

67. Briefly I am convinced from the evidence before me that in the Central Province alone there are at present about 7,000 tons of cocoa which are unmarketed owing to the lack of railway transport. These figures are based on the evidence of political and agricultural officers of long experience in the area in question. When the cost of motor transport from, say, Oda (Nsuaem) to Saltpond, viz. £8 13*s* 0*d* per ton, is considered; and when it is further considered that the cocoa has to be carried over long distances by head load to the motor-road, it is obvious that the cost of transport must be heavily handicapping the cocoa trade at anything but high prices.

[1] Governor's Annual Address, *Legislative Council Debates, 1923–4*, pp. 39–42.

Improvement in preparation of cocoa

68. I am glad to say that there has been a notable improvement during the past year in the methods by which cocoa has been prepared for the market. Perfection has by no means been reached, but the steps taken by some of the chiefs to discourage the sale of badly fermented cocoa have, in certain districts been successful. The work being done in this respect by the Farmers' Union, and by the Agricultural and Commercial Society of the Gold Coast, as well as by the agricultural officers, has been most valuable. It has been a long and weary row for Mr Tudhope and his officers to hoe, but I consider that they should be greatly encouraged even if they are not wholly satisfied by the improvement of the marketed bean. It is most disheartening, however, for all these officers and chiefs to find that their strenuous efforts to improve the preparation of the bean have been to a great degree neutralised by the thorough wetting which the cocoa so often gets in the surf. Anyone who has seen the dripping bags that are so often slung into the holds of the steamers, and the resulting masses of mouldy cocoa that are craned on to the Liverpool wharf, must have been impressed by the necessity of improving our antediluvian methods. Various suggestions have been made in the past year for Government inspection of cocoa, but as at present advised I do not feel that the time is ripe for us to undertake this duty. The subject, however, is still under consideration.

Cocoa farmers

69. Valuable progress has been made during the year by all the agricultural officers, and especially by the Research branch, in investigating cocoa diseases, and Mr Patterson, the Government Entomologist, is now on a visit to St Thome to obtain the latest lessons from that place. With regard to the instruction of the cocoa farmer in methods of cultivation and of avoiding black pod and other diseases, the agricultural officers have done very hard work and made definite if entirely inadequate progress. They have received valuable assistance from the Gold Coast Agricultural and Commercial Society, whose exhibitions at various provincial towns and villages have been of the utmost value. In giving praise to this society I include not only those citizens and merchants who sacrificed their leisure to its work, but also the officers of the Agricultural Department who form the bulk of its working members. The thanks of Government are also due to the political officers at whose centres the exhibitions were held. I believe these small shows to be of far more value than a centralised one on a large scale. They get at the actual farmer far more, and I trust that the Agricultural and Commercial Society will continue on this principle. Big central shows should, in my opinion be chiefly held for the purpose of exhibiting implements of agriculture; in short, they should give manufacturers a chance of exhibiting their goods and ascertaining the needs of the local farmer; and should give the latter the opportunity of seeing what he can buy to help him in his farming. In concluding my remarks on the Agricultural and Commercial Society I would convey the gratitude of Government to Mr Bard, the late Honorary Secretary, to whose initiative and energy the society practically owes its origin and success.

Cocoa diseases

70. Promising, however, as has been the advance made by a few farmers in methods of cultivation and in avoiding disease, general progress is very far indeed

from being thoroughly satisfactory. There can be no doubt that up to date the willingness of the farmer to adopt better methods of keeping his farm has had serious effects on many plantations. So far, the ill effects are not permanent as regards the country at large. Present methods, however, cannot go on indefinitely; and Government has now arrived at the conclusion that active steps must be taken to prevent the possible spread of disease. The subject is receiving the immediate and careful attention of the Director of Agriculture, and I hope to be able to inform Honourable Members in a short time of Government's proposals for dealing with disease.

32. Ghanaian support for the Governor against the Department of Agriculture, 1925 [1]

Nana Ofori Atta: ... My conviction is that the cocoa farmer, speaking with all due respects to all responsible people who hold a contrary opinion, is not guilty of the charge of being so lazy and so careless doing things that he does not care whether he earns his livelihood or not. I desire to take this opportunity of recording most emphatically our deepest resentment at the idea which seems to prevail in certain quarters that the native farmer is, and can be, content with any price that is offered him for his commodity. The price that is suggested is so preposterous, so indefensible in itself that I would rather not waste time on it. As I have said, it is, to me, utterly inconceivable that the cocoa farmer as a human being should be so blind to his own interest as not to carry on a work which him alone it benefits in the end.

It must be granted, Sir, that no person can do an impossibility, and I think that this Council should accept the fact that it is unreasonable to expect the farmer to do what is impossible for him to do. Though it is generally known that the native farmer employs the services of his family in making and looking after his farms, it must be admitted that the farmer has extended his activities to such an extent that it is absolutely impossible for him and his family alone to maintain his farms in a satisfactory condition. With the prospects which the cocoa industry in the country has ever had before it, I question whether any person more enlightened would not be doing the same thing by adding to his farms almost every year. The situation is therefore such that the farmer naturally relies upon outside labour, for which he has got to pay, to maintain his farms in good condition. So if the price of cocoa comes down so miserably as has been the case for some years past, the farmer is hopelessly beaten. There is no doubt that during the current financial year, the farmers, generally speaking, have, during the first three months of the season, received a fair price for their produce, and I cannot conceive why, if such a state of affairs continues, the farmer cannot spend money to keep his farm in a satisfactory condition.

It is necessary perhaps to recall attention to what Your Excellency said in your message last year. You said: 'I notice that certain home journals connected with the trade still continue to advocate that the policy of the Gold Coast Government should be to limit production. Again I characterize this as an indefensible suggestion. In view of the right of every man to grow as much as his land can produce, the policy of this Government is to encourage cocoa production up to the full working capacity of the population.'

[1] *Legislative Council Debates, 1925–6*, pp. 290–2.

If the Director of Agriculture is not going to show sympathy with a farmer who, not because of vain greed, but because of reasonable demands, has extended his cocoa farms to such an extent that, without expending a fairly large sum of money on outside assistance, he cannot attend to all at once, I can only say that statements made as to drastic operations forming no part of the Scheme in respect of the Insect Pests Ordinance can only be regarded as statements merely made to invoke sympathy in connection with the passage of the Ordinance when the Bill was under discussion at the second reading stage. I do sincerely hope that the Director of Agriculture who a short while ago showed a good deal of energy as a Provincial Superintendent in Eastern Province will, when the inspecting staff commence their duties, issue such instructions as will sympathetically deal with the situation I have referred to. As I have already said, if the prospects of the cocoa business be as good as it has been a few months ago, I am positive, Sir, that the farmers will be enabled to attend to their farms satisfactorily without any compunction.

Now a word about the local pride. It must have been known to Your Excellency that during the year under review, the farming community, Chiefs and people in the Eastern Province, have been struggling very hard with a view to find a fair deal for their produce. The Honourable Colonial Secretary has made very important remarks regarding cocoa prices. This shows how very important it is from every point of view that good prices should be obtained for cocoa. For that reason I am suggesting that should it occur at any time in our anxiety to effect improvements, any party or parties should take a line of action which may not be wholly to the advantage of the farmers commonly, you should, as a father, say a word to enlighten us in order that the country may escape what in the end may prove an embarrassing and perhaps an irreparable position . . .

33. Cocoa hold-up, 1937 : statutory marketing scheme proposed [1]

462. We found in the Gold Coast an agricultural industry that perhaps has no parallel in the world. Within about forty years, cocoa farming has developed from nothing until it now occupies a dominant position in the country's economy – cocoa being virtually the only commercial crop – and provides two-fifths of the world's requirements. Yet the industry began and remains in the hands of small independent native farmers. In spite of casual methods of production the Gold Coast industry shows signs of great vitality and should maintain its pre-eminence for a long time to come.

463. The development of this valuable permanent crop has strongly influenced the economic life of the country. It has caused a great access of wealth; it has altered and is still altering the attitude towards land and thereby the system of land tenure; multiple and absentee landlords are now common; and labour consisting largely of immigrants, is almost universally employed. Under these conditions, violent price fluctuations have serious effects and are a major cause of indebtedness.

464. The system of marketing cocoa, which is at once crude and complex, is the result partly of the unwillingness of the farmers to deliver their own cocoa and partly of the intense competition among European buying firms. There are large

[1] *Report of the Commission on the Marketing of West African Cocoa.* Cmd 5845, London 1938 (extracts from paras 462–545).

numbers of commission buyers of all degrees of importance, whose purchases are financed by considerable sums advanced by the buying firms before and during the season. The buying firms are either merchants, combining produce-buying with sales of goods, or manufacturers. Overhead expenses are heavy and competition has thinned the ranks of the firms until thirteen now buy practically the entire crop. Of these, one is responsible for about half.

465. Efforts have been made to develop the cooperative societies as an alternative channel of marketing. Under difficult conditions they have not gained a strong footing, and there is disillusionment about their advantages, as a means of marketing. As banks they have been much more successful. An undue proportion of the time of agricultural officers and of the funds voted to the Department of Agriculture has been spent in detailed supervision of societies.

466. The introduction of a Buying Agreement combining twelve firms, which normally purchase most of the crop led to a hold-up of cocoa, which remained fairly effective for over five months and was accompanied by a boycott of most European goods. We formed the conclusion that the hold-up, although supported by the use of various illegal forms of pressure, began and remained an essentially popular movement. It arose chiefly out of the Africans' fear of monopoly, intensified by the suddenness with which the Agreement was introduced, by a lack of frankness about its provisions, and by a fall in prices that occurred simultaneously with, although not as a result of it.

467. We found little ground for criticising the handling of the difficult situation by the local Government.

468. The hold-up and boycott were suspended at the end of April by a truce lasting until the 1st of October, 1938, under which the operation of the Buying Agreement was also suspended; a system of export control was introduced by Ordinance for the period of the truce . . .

CHAPTER XV

Recommendations

Introductory

490. We have reached the conclusion that the continuance of the Buying Agreements introduced in the Gold Coast and Nigeria in 1937 is undesirable, but at the same time that the present conditions of cocoa marketing in these countries are unsatisfactory to the firms and to producers alike. It is essential in our opinion that any scheme of reform, alternative to the Buying Agreements, must, if it is to be really satisfactory, provide for certain requirements. These are as follows:

(i) The removal in the interests both of producers and of shippers of various undesirable features of the marketing system, which have been described in our Report.

(ii) The strengthening of the economic position and morale of producers in relation to the buyers, both European and African.

(iii) The recognition of the legitimate interests of both the African community and the shippers.

(iv) The maintenance of free competition in the purchase of the cocoa crop.

(v) The avoidance of any unnecessary expense in marketing.

Possible solutions considered

491. Various proposals which have been made for dealing with the situation have been considered by us and are discussed briefly below.

A trade practices agreement

492. . . . In view of the attitude of the firms and their Coast agents [a trade practices agreement] is unlikely to have much success without the support of a Buying Agreement.

The fixing of market centres and the licensing of buyers and middlemen

493. In several African dependencies the principle of compulsory licensing of buying firms and middlemen has been applied to the marketing of certain native crops; in some the further step has been taken of prohibiting the sale of certain commodities except at approved market centres and under conditions prescribed by Ordinance.

494. We think that the licensing of buyers might be of value under Coast conditions as elsewhere. It might be used to prevent any further expansion of the numbers of middlemen, which are probably already excessive. A system of licensing buying stations might also be used to prevent these from being unduly increased in numbers or extended too far into the bush, with the possible consequence of increasing the already heavy overhead expenses. Further, it might be possible by means of a licensing system, and in consultation with the firms, middlemen and native authorities, to eliminate some at least of the undesirable practices which at present exist in cocoa marketing.

495. The institution of market centres coupled with the prohibition of sales of cocoa elsewhere would apparently be welcomed by some at least of the firms; but we have been impressed by certain adverse arguments brought forward. If it were proposed merely to prohibit sales of cocoa at the farm and to require it to be sold in small village centres, it seems unlikely that so far as the firms are concerned the system of buying would be much altered; they would still have to rely on commission buyers and would probably continue to make advances. It may be doubted also whether sales in the bush could be effectively prohibited . . .

496. If, on the other hand, the object were to prescribe markets in which the European firms would have their own buying stations and to prohibit sales elsewhere, a more radical alteration of present arrangements and habits would be involved. It would be necessary to license buyers and buying stations. Producers would have to bring in their cocoa to markets, which in many cases would be at a considerable distance from their farms, unless they were prepared to entrust someone both to transport and to sell it. We are informed that farmers would object to leaving their farms on journeys of this kind. Moreover, the cost of a passenger's fare might have to be added to the cost of transporting even small quantities of cocoa. It was also suggested to us by a senior Coast representative of one of the firms that this system would probably entail additions to the already numerous stations of the firms and a further increase in European staff.

497. For the various reasons given, we consider that it would be unwise to attempt to enforce in West Africa the concentration of cocoa buying and selling in large central markets. There might be certain advantages in restricting sales to local village markets, but we do not believe that these would be sufficient to justify the general introduction of a compulsory system or that it could be strictly

enforced without the active support of the middlemen. The licensing of buyers and the institution of central markets would do nothing to give producers the feeling of security which is greatly needed.

Export quotas

498. A principal of one of the Agreement firms proposed the continuance of the system of export control used during the truce . . . for a period of, say, ten years. His view was that, under more stable conditions, it would be possible to rationalise the purchase of cocoa on the Coast 'by eliminating all forms of redundancy such as overlapping buying stations, as well as reducing supervisory and other costs'; there would thus be savings in overheads, 'the benefits of which would be passed on automatically to the producer'. He suggested that, with a Buying Agreement unsupported by quotas, there was the risk that shippers not parties to it, or new entrants to the trade, could upset by aggressive competition the member firms' efforts to regularise marketing. Export quotas would give the necessary stability. Some provision on a more generous basis than under the truce would require to be made for possible newcomers to the trade. 'A representative committee consisting of Government – representing the Africans – merchants, and manufacturers, sitting in London, should formulate the technical details of the scheme.' A plan of this kind, it was suggested, would allow for a gradual improvement of the trade in easy stages.

499. Although it is possible that this plan might help to reduce overheads, which is obviously desirable, it is open to serious objections. Even the temporary quota arrangements under the truce aroused strong dissatisfaction among the Africans and others; this would be redoubled if there were any prospect of their permanent adoption. Moreover, it is undesirable in principle that definite shares of the cocoa trade should be vested for any prolonged period in particular firms, to the exclusion of effective competition. Finally, it was admitted to us that a Buying Agreement would probably be a necessary complement of the scheme. We cannot recommend the adoption of this plan.

'*Cocoa Union Limited*'

500. A more elaborate and ambitious scheme was put forward on his personal responsibility by a principal of another Agreement firm. His proposals were briefly as follows: A company, to be called Cocoa Union Limited, should be formed in England with capital subscribed by cocoa exporters established in the Gold Coast and/or Nigeria in proportion to their shipments in 1935–6 and 1936–7. The Board of Directors would consist of representatives of the British Government and one representative each of the Gold Coast and of the Nigerian producers. The Governments of the two countries should prohibit exports for five years except under licence, and grant licences solely to the Company, which would undertake to market the entire crop on behalf of the African producers. A system of price-fixing should be adopted which would secure (*a*) to the producer a basic price determined with regard to the previous season's price level; and (*b*) to the Company a fixed rate of commission, and also interest at prescribed rates on money used in the financing of marketing. The actual purchase and the disposal of the crop in the consuming markets would be done on behalf of the Company by the shareholders, who would receive an agreed schedule of expenses for their services. Any profits after deduction of the basic price, commission,

interest and schedule of expenses would be shared between the producers and the Company on a basis which secured to the producers a proportion increasing as the amount of profit increased. The Company would be entitled to carry forward any loss as a first charge on the profit of the subsequent season.

501. The author of the scheme maintained that, from the point of view of the producers, it would ensure that the profits of the shipper, i.e. the Company, would be both known and shared; while from the point of view of exporters the danger of losses through over payment and over declaration would be eliminated. Centralised selling should enable the Company to obtain a rather higher price in the world market; and centralised collection should permit of savings in overheads.[1] The gains realised in these ways would benefit both producers and buyers.

502. We have considered this scheme carefully. Obviously much would depend on points of detail such as the rate of commission, the manner in which the basic price was to be determined, the precise basis of profit-sharing, etc.; and certain additional safeguards, including modifications of the proposed directorate, would also appear to be needed. Supposing that these points could be satisfactorily met, that the Africans could be persuaded to accept the scheme and that Government were willing to provide the necessary legislation we agree that there is much in favour of these proposals. The objections to them however are so serious, in our opinion, as to outweigh the advantages. A monopoly backed by statute and dominated by the Agreement firms, whose operations are already suspected as aiming at monopoly, would simply not be acceptable to African opinion. Moreover, we believe that official participation would do more to weaken the prestige of the Colonial Government than to allay the apprehension of the Africans, even though there were one or two native representatives on the Board.

503. If at some future date producers were sufficiently organised to place them on a more equal business footing with the firms, and if the scheme could be made more elastic by giving some scope for newcomers to the trade and for adjustments among existing buyers, we think that this plan should then be reconsidered. Under present conditions, however, we do not regard it as desirable or as practical politics.

Gold Coast Cocoa Farmers' Federation, Limited

504. This Society was formed and registered as a limited liability company during the hold-up. In evidence the Chairman, Sir Ofori Atta, explained that it was intended to meet the desire of the Chiefs and farmers to be more effectively organised. The Society would act as a sort of marketing board which would place farmers in contact with persons of market experience in the Gold Coast and abroad, who would advise them how to sell their cocoa to the best advantage. It was intended to provide members with financial backing, but not to restrict their freedom of sale. The promoters include a number of Chiefs and Head farmers; the capital is to be £50,000 in £1 shares. The directors may not exceed 300, and one-third of them are to retire at each annual general meeting. Membership is open to individual farmers, to associations or groups for the marketing of cocoa, and also to other persons at the discretion of the directors. Farmers or corporate shareholders must pledge themselves to deliver their supplies to the Society and may only resign from it after six months' notice. The Society, which

[1] The witness, however, did not contemplate any ambitious scheme of rationalisation on the Coast, holding the view that the firms are not at present over-established.

is to have numerous local branches, may itself take delivery of cocoa and sell it for its members, and is then bound to make prompt payment of the proceeds less transport costs and a levy not exceeding 6*d* per load. An advance not exceeding three-quarters of the value of the cocoa may be made when the funds of the Society permit. It may also authorise persons to act as its agents, and may not normally refuse to appoint anyone to whom a member wishes to sell his cocoa.

505. This scheme is evidently an attempt to build on the farmers' groups developed in the Gold Coast during the hold-up, and is a natural development of a spontaneous form of organisation. Its provisions as regards marketing appear somewhat vague. There is a danger that middlemen might acquire a disproportionate influence on the directorate and that business efficiency might suffer from the multiplicity of directors, unless a competent manager were appointed with wide powers. We doubt whether as a marketing or as a credit organisation it would greatly assist producers. There is no indication that it would do anything to remove the abuses complained of by the firms. Nevertheless, this scheme goes some way to meet the need for a representative organisation of producers; and the idea of federating local groups is of value.

Price-fixing by Government

(i) *Stabilisation of prices*

506. A number of African witnesses have suggested that cocoa prices to producers should be stabilised at a level considerably above that of the past season. Apart from vague reference to Government action, no indication has been given as to how this object could be achieved. In the absence of any international control scheme, Governments could not assume responsibility for guaranteeing the price of a commodity subject to such speculative influences as cocoa without incurring grave risks. The share of the Gold Coast and Nigeria in the total world supply of cocoa, viz. about half, would be insufficient to enable them to dictate the world price level of cocoa, even if on general grounds this were desirable. In dismissing this proposal, however, we would not exclude the possibility of measures for reducing to some extent the local incidence of fluctuations in the world market.

(ii) *Determination of minimum prices*

507. It has been suggested that Government should participate, whether directly, or in a supervisory capacity, in ascertaining and fixing a minimum price for cocoa based on world prices. The suggestion was, of course, made in connection with the Buying Agreement; but the possibility of prescribing minimum prices in fixed market centres has also been mentioned. In either case the conditions of the local and world markets for cocoa make the system unsuitable in our opinion for application to the Gold Coast and Nigeria. Unlike the case of Uganda cotton, for example, the output of these countries is so large as to have an important influence on world prices; the bulk of the crop is purchased by three or four firms; and finally there is a strong feeling among the natives against any limitation of competition, a result that commonly follows from the fixing of minimum prices.

(iii) *Form of organisation recommended*

508. Each of the alternatives discussed so far falls short in one or more respects of the conditions that we considered to be necessary in order to place the marketing of cocoa in West Africa on a sound and secure footing. After consulting many opinions and after prolonged thought, we see no other way of meeting these conditions than by the general application of the system already exemplified on a small scale by the Cooperative Societies of the Gold Coast and Nigeria; the association of producers for the collective marketing of their produce, and for the representation of their joint interests.

509. To be successful, any scheme of this kind must, we consider, include certain essential features, which are as follows:

(i) The nature and functions of the organisation adopted should be acceptable to the agricultural community.

(ii) Producers should be associated throughout the cocoa areas in a system of local marketing groups.

(iii) Cocoa should be collected for joint sale at depots operated by such groups.

(iv) The cocoa so assembled should be offered in bulk lots freely and without discrimination to buyers already established and any newcomers to the trade.

(v) The possibility of direct export for sale should be provided.

(vi) Africans should be employed wherever possible.

(vii) Buyers should be given definite guarantees of quality and suitable incentives should be offered to producers to maintain quality.

510. The application of these general ideas to the particular circumstances of the Gold Coast . . . is considered below.

GOLD COAST

511. The need for reorganising the marketing of the cocoa crop is more immediately urgent in the Gold Coast than in Nigeria. The cocoa industry is much larger and is far more important to the economic life of the country; the abuses complained of by the firms appear to have taken deeper root; and feeling about the position of cocoa farmers in relation to the buying firms was and remains more intense and more widespread. Under these conditions it seemed to us essential to find a plan that could be introduced and would take effect rapidly.

512. We have considered carefully the possibilities of developing the existing Cooperative Societies. These might have provided a nucleus for the organisation which we desire to see made general throughout the country. We do not, however, regard the prospects of their rapid development as encouraging. At present the Societies market less than 3 per cent of the crop; there is considerable disillusionment about their benefits as a means of marketing cocoa. Their credit and banking facilities are now regarded as their chief attractions.

513. It would be preferable, other things being equal, that a plan of reorganisation should be built and operated on an entirely voluntary basis; but we feel that in the circumstances this is impracticable. We therefore recommend, instead, the adoption of the expedient which in recent years has been increasingly used in the United Kingdom, in the Dominions and in foreign countries, namely, the association of the whole body of producers of a commodity within a statutory marketing scheme.

514. We should have preferred to recommend a detailed plan without reservations, but we do not feel in a position to do so. We are unable to discuss the subject with the African leaders, whose support we consider essential, since we did not hear an important section of the evidence until our return to London. We felt that it would be inappropriate under these conditions to open discussions with the firms. Our recommendations are therefore expressed in the following broad terms:

1. That the principle of the association of all cocoa producers on a statutory basis for the marketing of their produce should be accepted by Government;

2. that the recognised leaders of the Africans should be incited by the Gold Coast Government to participate, either personally or by representatives, in a drafting committee appointed to elaborate the details of a statutory scheme providing for the essential features enumerated in paragraph 509;

3. that the collaboration of the representatives of the firms be sought by the drafting committee; and

4. that to assist its deliberations the committee should use, as a general basis of discussion, a draft scheme framed by ourselves.

515. The following is a summary of the essential features of the scheme, which we tentatively worked out in some detail in order to test its possibilities:

(i) Under an Ordinance establishing the scheme, all cocoa farmers in the Gold Coast Colony and Ashanti would become members of a Cocoa Farmers Association.

(ii) The main functions of the Association would be to represent the interests of producers and to assemble and sell on their behalf the entire cocoa crop of the Gold Coast. In all normal circumstances the bulk of the crop would be sold, on a free competitive basis, to firms or individuals established in the Gold Coast, including any newcomers to the trade, but the Association should none the less be free, whenever and so far as it might appear desirable in the interests of producers, to ship direct to world markets.

(iii) The Association would be governed by a Board, including African representatives, official representatives (one of whom would act as Chairman) and possibly one or two independent co-opted members.

(iv) For the purposes both of representation and of marketing all producers would be organised in a system of local Groups, of which there might be some 500. The Groups' areas would be defined with a view to convenience in the collection of cocoa, but as far as possible they would be based on political sub-divisions. Every farmer would participate in the Association through being a member of the local Group covering the area in which his farm was situated. Each Group would be supervised by a committee, appointed in a manner consistent with tribal custom, and also by a general meeting. The organisation and working of the Groups would be supervised by a number of Group Supervisors employed by the Association.

(v) For the purposes of marketing, the Groups would be organised by Regions, i.e. six to ten large areas surrounding the main buying centres. There would be Regional Committees, including representatives of the Groups, of local Chiefs and of Government.

(vi) Marketing would be conducted by permanent salaried employees of the Association, who would be responsible to the Board through the General Manager. This staff should include Europeans only so far as was found to be necessary in the interests of business efficiency and should to a large extent consist of

Africans. The General Manager should be a European of considerable business ability and experience, and should be paid a salary commensurate with those paid in business posts entailing similar responsibilities. Apart from the General Manager and the assistants attached to him at the Board's Headquarters, the marketing staff would consist of Regional Managers; District Managers in sub-divisions of the regions; and salaried Group Secretaries.

(vii) Each Group would be responsible for operating its own depot, i.e. a substantial store capable of holding a fair proportion of the crop produced within the Group's area. The depot would be the assembly point for all the cocoa produced in the Group area. The Groups should progressively organise their own collection, employing collectors and possibly operating their own lorries. In the early stages it would probably be impracticable to prohibit the operations of independent minor buyers operating between farms and Group depots.

(viii) It should be made an offence for a shipper to buy cocoa except from the Association.

(ix) Regional Managers, acting on broad directions from the General Manager, would offer cocoa for sale at the comparatively small number of main buying centres, where all or most of the existing buying firms have establishments with European staff in charge. Regional Managers would be kept informed through District Managers, and these by the Group Secretaries, of the supplies available.

(x) The Groups, in reporting their stocks of cocoa, and the Regional Managers, in offering cocoa, for sale, would describe it in accordance with agreed specifications. Any disputes as to the quality supplied would be referred to arbitrators.

(xi) The bulk of the crop would, in normal circumstances, be delivered to buyers' stations. The Regional and District Managers would give instructions for the delivery of cocoa from Group depots. It would be a matter of convenience whether the Association or the buyer arranged the transport.

(xii) Payments for cocoa purchased would be made to the Association's account. Groups would be paid for their cocoa on the basis of an average price, calculated by (*a*) pooling the proceeds of all cocoa sales during an appropriate period, (*b*) deducting a levy for operating expenses, reserve, etc. and (*c*) dividing the remaining sum by the number of tons sold. It would be a matter of expediency whether short or long pool periods were used. If short periods of two or three weeks were used it would be possible to dispense with payments on account; but for long periods a system of advance payments, with a final settlement, would be needed. From the average or pool price suitable deductions for transport costs would be made in order to arrive at the price to be paid to the Groups for distribution to producers.

(xiii) In order to encourage a generally satisfactory standard of quality, a guaranteed premium of an appropriate amount would be payable to Groups, and through them to producers, for cocoa tendered and accepted as high-grade. The funds for this, in so far as they were not provided by premiums received from buyers, would be met out of the levy. Cocoa of quality inferior to the ordinary standard would be paid for at a rate lower than the pool price.

(xiv) The Association would be free to export cocoa for sale through brokers in London or elsewhere. It would be free to make forward sales in anticipation of the crop season.

(xv) The Association should attempt to secure the participation of the buying firms in a Joint Committee, in which current problems of cocoa producing and marketing could be discussed.

(xvi) Apart from its representatives and marketing functions the Association's organisation would be available and should be used, for the agricultural and economic education of producers, for assisting in the preparation of crop estimates, and for cooperating in the promotion of approved schemes for agricultural credit facilities.

516. Reform on these lines would involve radical changes in the conditions of cocoa marketing in the Gold Coast, the more so since its farmers, although producing the largest cocoa crop in the world, are the least organised of cocoa growers. In Brazil and Venezuela there are now important organisations representative of producers, and in Trinidad the planters have for some years marketed a large part of the crop through the Cocoa Planters Association. Under the conditions suggested the Gold Coast farmers would acquire an organisation for marketing and the representation of their interests which would be even more comprehensive than these.

517. We are aware that no parallel case is to be found in the Colonial Empire of the combination of an entire body of primary producers in a statutory organisation. We consider nevertheless that provided various practical difficulties can be met a reorganisation of the Gold Coast cocoa industry on these general lines is both justifiable and desirable in view of

(i) the supreme importance of the industry to the agricultural community and to the country as a whole;

(ii) the special commercial and political conditions of the Gold Coast, which underlie the whole situation that we were appointed to investigate;

(iii) the absence, so far as we ourselves can discover, of any satisfactory and less drastic alternative;

(iv) the precedents afforded by the agricultural policy of Great Britain and the Dominions.

518. In Great Britain the policy followed under the Agricultural Marketing Acts by successive Governments for the past seven years has enabled farmers to combine effectively and to reorganise the marketing of several of the more important agricultural products. In Australia and New Zealand producers of various export commodities have had similar advantages for an even longer period. The 300,000 cocoa farmers of the Gold Coast certainly stand in no less need of organisation, and we see no reasons in principle why they should not be given the same facilities for combination as farmers in other parts of the Empire. The hold-up has proved the existence of remarkable capacities among the mass of farmers for joint action, and among their leaders for organisation.

519. It might be objected that the Marketing Acts in Great Britain provide for essentially democratic methods of organisation and procedure. These would certainly be inappropriate in the Gold Coast, where the ballot-box is not a commonplace of public life; and we do not envisage that either the question of initiating a scheme or matters involved in its operation should be put to the general vote of producers. We have nevertheless recognised the principle that public support is necessary in recommending that African leaders be invited to assist in the drafting of a scheme; and, in our own tentative plan, by providing for African representation in central and local bodies. Others are more qualified to indicate what form of representation would best suit West African customs, but it is evident that the collaboration of the Chiefs must be secured.

520. A fully developed scheme embodying the ideas we have indicated, would, in our opinion, provide the following advantages:

To producers

It would maintain free competition among buyers and ensure as far as possible the payment of the best price justified by supply and demand conditions. Losses through false weighing would be minimised. A premium would be paid for good quality cocoa, to the benefit of the careful producer. A means of collective representation and negotiation would be afforded and producers would be placed on a more equal footing with the buying firms. Cocoa could be exported to world markets for sale on behalf of producers.

To the firms

The abuses resulting from indirect forms of competition and especially those connected with declarations would be eliminated. Advances would not be necessary. Delivery would be made in convenient bulk lots. The general level of quality should be raised, and, it is to be hoped, standards of quality would be guaranteed. The number of buying points could be reduced. It would be possible to cover forward sales made before the season by means of forward purchases from the producers' organisation. In general, cocoa buying would be rendered less speculative, expensive and laborious.

General

Through the provision of a recognised channel for collective bargaining, the country should be spared a recurrence of the recent dislocation of its economic life. An effective instrument for the education of producers in agricultural and economic matters would be provided. The preparation of agricultural statistics, especially crop estimates, might also be facilitated. New opportunities of steady and constructive employment would be available to literate Africans. If at any time the idea of an international control scheme for cocoa should take more definite shape, the Gold Coast would be in a far better position to play its part than if producers remained unorganised. Short of this, if some means of utilising surplus cocoa locally could be found, a producers' organisation would make it possible to share the lower price realised for it equitably among producers.

521. We fully realise that changes of the character we propose will not be accepted without searching criticism. Apart from the question already mentioned of the suitability of our proposals to colonial conditions, it seems desirable to anticipate certain objections that may be raised regarding their expediency, their effects on sectional interests, and certain practical difficulties of their application.

522. Critics may cite the case of the Zanzibar clove industry to illustrate the difficulties of attempting a comprehensive organisation of producers under statute. A scheme was recently adopted which gave to the Zanzibar Clove Growers' Association a monopoly of the local marketing of cloves. Difficulties arose from the opposition of middlemen, and it was ultimately found necessary to modify the scheme by reserving to them the purchases of one-half of the crop. Conditions in Zanzibar, however, are essentially different from those in the Gold Coast. The middlemen are Indians and form a racial and social community distinct from that of the farmers. They were supported in their opposition to the proposed scheme by a boycott of Zanzibar cloves in India, which normally consumes about one-third of the crop. As a result large stocks of unsold cloves accumulated to the acute financial embarrassment of the Association, which as part of its policy was obliged to buy all cloves offered.

523. One effect of our proposals, fully applied, would be to deprive the middle and larger brokers of their function in the marketing of cocoa, and opposition from them is to be expected. It should, however, be modified by the fact that under the scheme numerous salaried posts would be available which literate brokers would be qualified to fill; moreover, most brokers have their own farms and many engage in merchandise trading. Assuming that the brokers resist our proposals with all the influence in their power, they will at most persuade the agricultural community not to accept them; but once a scheme on the lines suggested were adopted brokers would not be in a position to hamper its operation by any form of direct action.

524. Some of the Chiefs might have the same misgivings about a statutory producers' scheme as they have about the farmers' groups which came into existence during the hold-up; namely, that it might weaken their authority. The drafting procedure and general type of representation that we suggest should make such fears groundless. Some sections of African opinion on the other hand may object to Government participation in the direction of a scheme, although farmers may welcome it, recalling the unfortunate history of certain previous cocoa marketing ventures, managed by persons deficient in experience or integrity. We are convinced, in any case, that the industry is too closely linked with the economic welfare of the country for Government to refrain from active participation in, and ultimate responsibility for, a statutory marketing scheme.

525. In general our proposals are designed to draw out African criticism in advance, so that it can be used constructively in forming a scheme that is acceptable and will command the positive support both of the rank and file and of the recognised leaders. It will be the duty of the latter, if they accept our proposals in principle, not only to assist in framing a suitable scheme, but also to collaborate in explaining it and securing that it is operated as intended.

526. It is to be hoped that the collaboration of the firms will be sought, and willingly given, both in the preparation of a detailed scheme and, through a joint committee, in its actual operation. We are encouraged to believe that some at least of the firms will be attracted by the advantages of our proposals, since several of their witnesses spoke favourably of collective sale by producers. Nevertheless, some opposition may be expected. The main objections from established firms, whether explicitly formulated or not, will probably be first, that an effective and official recognised form of combination among African producers is undesirable – a view with which we have expressed our disagreement; secondly, that our general proposals would make it easier for new competitors to establish themselves on the Coast; if this is true, we do not consider it to be an objection from the standpoint of the interests of the Colony as a whole.

527. Various practical difficulties are likely to be raised as objections by the firms and others. We refer briefly to some of the more important problems involved.

Finance

528. Very tentative estimates made by us, on which we have taken independent opinion, suggest that a capital outlay of about £300,000 might be required to put our detailed plan into full operation. The annual cost is still more difficult to estimate, as it would depend largely on the salaries paid. It should not, however, exceed £250,000 or about 6*d* a load. A large part of the initial capital expense

would be required for the construction of depot stores, although in some areas it should be possible to rent or acquire stores from the firms or brokers.

529. We recommend that an initial grant towards capital expenses from Government funds, or from the Colonial Development Fund, be considered. Failing this, a Government loan should be made, at a reduced rate of interest. It might also be considered whether a part of the export tax through which, as we have pointed out in paragraph 55, the cocoa industry contributes materially to the revenue of the country, could be earmarked as a contribution towards the annual expenses of the scheme.

Staff

530. We attach great importance to our recommendation that Africans should be employed wherever possible; good opportunities of a career would thus be provided for literate Africans of business capacity. It is even more important in the interests of farmers, however, that efficiency should be maintained. In making appointments the requirements of business should not be outweighed by racial interests and sympathies, and when suitable African candidates did not present themselves, Europeans should be appointed. The question of finding suitable staff admittedly presents difficulties; experienced opinion indicates, however, that these should not prove unsurmountable. The position of General Manager, in a fully-developed scheme such as we advocate, would be very important, and should undoubtedly be filled by a European. We desire to emphasise that it would be false economy not to offer for this responsible post a salary sufficient to attract a man of real commercial and organising ability.

Method of introducing a scheme

531. A considerable effort of organisation would be needed in order to introduce a fully-developed scheme, and it might be desired to proceed by stages. We think it would be unwise to attempt to operate the new system of marketing side by side with the old in the same districts; resistance and even obstruction might then be encouraged from interests opposed to the general adoption of the scheme. If, therefore, a gradual development is desired, we recommend that at least the proposed ground-work of organisation, namely the system of local groups, should be introduced generally throughout a considerable area. Ashanti would seem to provide the most favourable starting point, owing to the homogeneous character of the people and of the political structure. It would probably be expedient, however, to introduce the same arrangement simultaneously in a defined area within the Colony and Togoland. An alternative method of development would be to begin by introducing the Groups system throughout the cocoa areas as the foundation on which to build the more complete forms of organisation required. Development policy would obviously be governed largely by the attitude of the various parties concerned.

532. We recommend (i) that the Ordinance providing for a scheme should be sufficiently comprehensive to permit of the development of a complete scheme; (ii) that it should be of an enabling character and that the application of the scheme to prescribed areas should be determined by proclamation; (iii) that the scheme should be generally applied and developed to its complete form as quickly as circumstances and considerations of efficiency permit.

Selling and pooling policy

533. The system of pooling must depend on how fully the scheme is developed, on selling policy and on the credit facilities available. A scheme consisting of local groups, united under a purely supervisory body, would operate with short-period pools on lines similar to those followed by the present Cooperative Societies. Under a more developed scheme, in which selling was coordinated by regional or even central control, a longer pool period would be needed and part payments in advance might become necessary. Provided such payments are made there is much to be said in favour of the long pool period, which would even out the effects of price fluctuations on producers' returns.

534. It would also be advantageous from the point of view of accounting and effective control to concentrate the administration of pooling as much as possible; any plan of centralised selling should therefore be accompanied by centralised pooling.

535. The selling policy of the Board of a centralised scheme would have to take into account many complex and changing factors which cannot at this stage be evaluated. We suggest that it would be unwise to restrict its powers by hard and fast rules. The character and ability of the General Manager and the ultimate responsibility of Government should be sufficient to ensure that a reasonably cautious policy is pursued.

536. We anticipate that the established shippers will continue to be the normal channel of sales for the bulk of the crop; it is to be hoped that they will be prepared to cooperate with the Board through a Joint Committee in establishing a better industry. At the same time we consider that the export of a part of the crop by the producers' organisation is desirable even in normal circumstances, since Africans attach great importance to having direct access to world markets. Published statements of the results of direct exports should help to convince Africans that the possibilities of realising better prices in this way are strictly limited.

537. In the light of experience gained, the Board might find advantage in following, with due caution, a policy of spreading the period of sale by forward selling in advance of the season and possibly even by prolonging the marketing period for some weeks. If forward contracts were offered they should certainly be open to firms established on the Coast.

538. The possibility must be faced that in certain circumstances shippers might abdicate the merchants' function of carrying stocks and thus leave the burden to the producers' organisation. A Board such as we advocate would not have powers to buy cocoa outright from producers. It would be essentially a selling agency, and its policy should be, subject to the exceptions suggested in the preceding paragraphs, to sell cocoa as it was delivered by producers. We have explained however that, if the pooling period were longer than a few weeks, it would be necessary for the Board in the ordinary course of business to make a part payment against cocoa supplied, with a final settlement at the end of the pool period. Bank advances would probably be required for prepayments, and to this extent the Board would be financially committed. It should be the Board's policy to restrict such commitments. If there were difficulties in selling current supplies to the Coast firms, it would be necessary for the Board to sell freely in world markets. It goes without saying that, if conditions demand, prepayments would be reduced or even temporarily suspended.

539. In any case there is no obvious reason for supposing that the shippers' present policy of buying cocoa as it is offered would be altered. The knowledge that a restriction of purchases by the Coast firms would justify, and even necessitate, more extensive direct exports to world markets would act as a deterrent. Considerations of prestige will presumably continue to influence shippers, since producers organised in Groups will be no less influenced than separate individuals by the fact that XYZ Limited or Messrs. M and N had bought their cocoa. Shippers will still need to spread their overhead costs and to have a convenient means of transferring funds from the Coast, and they will still know that if the cocoa is not sold in one way or another the purchasing power of their African customers will be dammed at its source.

Cooperative Societies and credit facilities

540. So far we have not explained the part that would fall to the cooperative movement under the proposed system of marketing. The Groups would duplicate, on a larger scale, the function now performed by Cooperative Societies. In these circumstances the continuance of the latter as marketing units would hardly be justified. Members might find some consolation in the knowledge that their societies had pointed the way to collective sale under a generally applied system. We consider, however, that the Gold Coast cooperative movement should concentrate in future on the vital functions of accepting deposits and providing credit in which it has achieved distinct success.

541. At present credit is available to farmers chiefly through money-lenders and brokers. The effect of transferring the brokers' functions to Groups would be to withdraw one existing supply of credit, namely, the advances made by the firms – and especially those made before the season – which are distributed by brokers to growers. The personal funds of money-lenders and brokers might remain available, but brokers would have no incentive to make loans on easy terms or even without interest, as they occasionally do at present in order to secure an option on crops.

542. In these ways a producers' marketing scheme would tend to restrict the credit available to producers, and to limit the possibilities of cheap credit. On the other hand, it seems likely that at present producers are often tempted to accept credit or to make forward sales against their own interests. Whatever might be the net effect on credit of a producers' marketing, thrift and credit would be of great value as a means of reducing indebtedness.

543. Professor Shephard and Sir Frank Stockdale have both expressed the view that cooperative credit facilities should be linked with cooperative marketing. The reasons, we understand are (i) that a marketing society affords information of the character and income of prospective borrowers, and (ii) that marketing, as a more tangible function, is more likely to attract support in the initial stages of a cooperative movement. At the same time, other authorities contend that it is sounder policy to separate the functions of marketing and banking ; in support of this view they adduce the experience of cooperation in Europe and elsewhere.[1]

544. We suggest that the cooperative credit movement in the Gold Coast has now taken firm enough root to be able to develop on its own merits – in fact its

[1] See e.g. ' Cooperation in China ' by W. K. H. Campbell, Cooperative Adviser to the Government of China under the Auspices of the League of Nations in *Year-Book of Agricultural Cooperation*, 1938, p. 463.

development may have been handicapped of late by the disappointing results of cooperative marketing. Moreover the institution of compulsory marketing through Groups would give credit societies additional security.

545. Our recommendations regarding credit and cooperation are as follows:

(i) that the Cooperative Societies should surrender their functions of cocoa marketing as the system of marketing through groups is developed;

(ii) that Government should adopt a definite policy of promoting cooperative thrift and credit societies;

(iii) that all Africans residing within the neighbourhood of a society should be considered eligible to become members; it might be desirable however to confine the issue of credit to farmers, while the deposit facilities should be available to all. Under these conditions the problem of indebtedness would be attacked from two directions: the farmer would not need to borrow from individuals with capital available and the latter would be encouraged to deposit their capital at a low but assured rate of interest;

(iv) that special provisions should be made as regards loans for the redemption of mortgages. It is undesirable that small societies in which deposits must be available on demand should have a large part of their funds locked up in this way;

(v) that the societies should be federated in district unions and that district co-operative banks should be established to act as clearing houses between local societies. Then handling of mortgages credit might suitably be referred to such banks;

(vi) that a separate Department of Cooperation should be formed which should, however, work in close contact with the Department of Agriculture. The Registrar should have special knowledge of cooperative credit, and the staff should receive special training; and

(vii) that the cooperative credit movement should be developed in harmony with the proposed marketing organisation; and the officers of the latter should assist in propaganda for cooperative credit. Societies should have the legal right to secure payment of overdue loans or interest from the Group to which a defaulting member is attached, out of money due to him for his cocoa. They should also be able to demand that a defaulter should be required to supply his cocoa direct to the Group.

34. Wartime experience of cocoa marketing and proposals for stabilising domestic price, 1944 [1]

1. From the outbreak of war, His Majesty's Government has guaranteed the purchase of the total cocoa production of the British West African Colonies. In fulfilling this guarantee His Majesty's Government has undertaken on the one hand to bear any eventual loss on resale, and on the other hand to invite Parliament to vote a sum equivalent to any agreement with the Colonial Governments concerned, for expenditure on objects of benefit to them. The object of this report is to indicate the reasons for this policy and to describe the means adopted in carrying it out, up to and including the season of 1942–3.

[1] *Report on cocoa control in West Africa and statements on future policy*, Cmd 6554, London 1944, paras 1–39 (extracts).

Background

2. Since British West Africa normally produces for export about half of the world's supplies of cocoa beans, its importance as a world supplier is obvious. Although the production of the Western Province of Nigeria is substantial, by far the greater part is produced in the Gold Coast, and the importance of the cocoa industry to West Africa as a whole, and to the Gold Coast in particular, is very considerable. Cocoa is the mainstay of thousands upon thousands of peasant farmers (cocoa is not produced in British West Africa on European-run plantations) and provides a livelihood for countless numbers of wage-labourers who are employed by the farmers in the maintenance of their farms and the harvesting of the crops. Cocoa is the great provider of external purchasing power, and, in the case of the Gold Coast, the budgetary position of the Government depends to a very large degree on the prosperity of the cocoa industry.

3. As cocoa is a seasonal crop, the merchant firms will normally purchase the whole crops only if they can be sure of reselling them over the year. The outbreak of war cut off at one blow access to some of the more important markets in which West African cocoa had normally been resold, and, as a result, the merchant firms were unlikely to purchase any more cocoa than that for which they could find an immediate outlet. The requirements of the United Kingdom fall far short of the output of West Africa, and there was no prospect that in the ordinary course alternative markets could be found to take the place of those cut off by the blockade, and of those others diminished by the need to conserve shipping space for essential requirements. Clearly, since the merchant firms were unable, in view of the uncertainty of disposal, to undertake the risk involved in purchasing the entire crops, there was no alternative but for His Majesty's Government itself to undertake this risk and to purchase the crops of the Gold Coast and Nigeria. The merchant firms themselves realised the necessity for this action on the part of His Majesty's Government, and their cooperation assisted in the smooth working of the scheme.

4. In the first place the purchase was carried out by the Ministry of Food, and subsequently by the West African Cocoa Control Board (now the West African Produce Control Board) an organisation established by and operated under the authority of the Secretary of State for the Colonies . . .

The West Africa Cocoa Control Board (now the West African Produce Control Board)

22. In describing the actual working of the Board, it is not possible to draw precise lines between its functions and those of the many other authorities upon whom its work directly or indirectly impinges. The fixing of prices, production policy, the working of the quota system, all these are in practice considered by the Board in full consultation with the Colonial Governments concerned, the Resident Minister in West Africa who has certain special coordinating functions in regard to produce, the Ministry of Food as a chief customer, the Treasury, the British Colonies Supply mission, a liaison with the United States authorities, and the Colonial Office itself. The actual day-to-day affairs are handled by the Marketing Director, who has a small staff in London, and by Controllers in West Africa, who are at the same time the officers in whom are vested the powers of control under local legislation, and also the local representatives of the Board. Matters of principle and importance, such as the periodical review of price policy,

are the subject of preliminary correspondence with the Governments and Departments concerned, and are considered and reported on by the Cocoa Sub-Committee before final submission to the Board, which normally meets once a month, or as business dictates.

23. The Board has proved its value as a means of steering the West African cocoa industry through a potentially very difficult period, and it has also arrived at a means of handling the produce of West Africa, by a combination of the existing commercial machinery with the coordination and simplification essential in war-time, which has greatly facilitated the orderly disposal of produce and the economical use of shipping and manpower. It has removed uncertainty from the minds of the producers, and the profits accruing from its operations promise to be substantial. Moreover, His Majesty's Government has promised that Parliament will be invited in due course to vote a sum equivalent to any profit realised on the transactions of the Board, whether for return to the cocoa producers or for expenditure on objects of benefit to them.

The quota system

24. . . . It was arranged from the first that the actual task of purchasing and exporting cocoa should be shared out among those already engaged in the trade in accordance with previous performance. This principle is one which has been widely followed in other connections, and it has merits of rough justice and practicability which need no elaboration. The system is open to the criticism that it 'freezes' the trade in proportions determined by conditions which become increasingly remote in time. At the end of the first year of control it was, however, arranged that the small shippers in the Gold Coast should, as a group, receive an increased share of the trade and, at the end of the second year, the export quotas of the Cooperative Societies were increased so as to include the tonnage previously handed over by them to other exporting firms. Apart from this, the Board has been obliged to set its face against completely new entrants into the trade, since once an exception was made it would have been virtually impossible to discriminate between the very numerous actual and potential claimants. Trade conditions under control are, moreover, so radically different from those of normal times that the ability to handle a quota under control would be no guide to ability to survive in competitive conditions. The problem is undoubtedly a difficult one, and the Board felt, during the period under review, that, until some major decision had been taken regarding the continuance or otherwise of control as a permanent feature of the trade in West African produce, no change of principle in the quota system would be justified. The system has therefore continued from year to year with but minor modifications.

Price policy (purchases)

25. . . . The Board was charged, as a primary responsibility, with maintaining the West African cocoa industry at a time when the normal operations of the market would undoubtedly have ruined it. This task is performed by fixing a 'floor' for prices, the decision in each year being taken after consultation with the local Governments regarding the needs of the industry. The Board was, however, also obliged to be mindful of the fact that it was operating with funds provided by the United Kingdom taxpayer, who would have to meet any eventual

deficit on the Board's working. That is now happily a very remote contingency, but, as indicated in Section II of this paper, the likelihood more than once seemed very real. Prices were, therefore, generally fixed at a low level, against which must, however, be set certain other considerations. In the first place the prices, if low, were certain, and the producer was secure in the knowledge of what his produce would fetch. Secondly, in the Gold Coast, a system of price 'flattening' has been introduced, so that the up-country producer is much less at a disadvantage than previously, as compared with the producer near the port of shipment. In the third place – particularly after the outbreak of war with Japan – other West African commodities, notably oilseeds, palm oil and rubber, sprang into prominence, and it was important not to divert effort from their production to that of a commodity which was for long in surplus supply. The demand for labour for military works has already been mentioned. Finally and increasingly, a most careful watch has been necessary on the danger of inflation, which arises from heavy purchases of West African produce and full employment in West Africa at a time when the supply of consumer goods is necessarily very limited.

26. In pursuing a low-price policy, the Board was also mindful of the fact that His Majesty's Government has undertaken to invite Parliament in due course to return either to the West African cocoa producers, or, in agreement with the colonial governments concerned, towards expenditure on purposes designed to be of benefit to these producers, the equivalent of any profits made during the period of cocoa control. The basic principle of the division of such profits between the various territories (British and French) is that the sum should be divided in proportion to the cocoa actually purchased during the period of control, due account being taken of any disparity in buying prices not covered by quality differentials.

Price policy (sales)

27. The prices received by the Board varied from year to year, and according to destination. In nearly all cases, the price realised represented a substantial profit per ton over the purchase price although ... in some years total receipts fell short of total outgoings. The price received in the United Kingdom during the first year of control was a free market price since at that time the Ministry of Food had not assumed control of the sale and distribution of cocoa in this country. Thereafter, it was agreed that the Board should sell to the Ministry at the free market price current in the United Kingdom at the date of the assumption of internal control by the Ministry. The price received elsewhere, on the other hand, was determined by the market, and tended increasingly to exceed that received from the Ministry of Food. This situation appeared increasingly anomalous, but it did not seem equitable that the Ministry of Food price should be solely determined by, say, that received from the United States, i.e. by market conditions peculiar to New York. A formula was consequently evolved, and brought into operation as from the 1942–3 season, under which the price received by the Board from the Ministry in any one season was to be the average price received by the Board in the previous season for *all* sales, including those to the Ministry of Food. This enabled the Ministry of Food price to follow general trends, and allowed an influence to outside market prices proportionate to the quantities involved. . .

Proposals as to future policy (marketing)

33. For some time past consideration has been given, in consultation with the Resident Minister in West Africa (Viscount Swinton) and the Governors of the Gold Coast and Nigeria, to the whole question of the post-war organisation for the purchase and export of British West African cocoa, having regard both to the Report of the Commission on the Marketing of West African Cocoa (Command Paper 5845 of 1938) and to the experience gained during wartime control.

34. It is evident that it would not be in the genuine interests of either producers or consumers to revert after the war to pre-war conditions, with excessive price fluctuation and the other undesirable features to which attention was drawn in the report of the 1938 Commission. War experience has added weight to the view that a prime need of the cocoa industry, if it is to attain prosperity and efficiency, is a reasonably stable price basis, by which is meant not necessarily prices fixed over periods of several years, but the avoidance of short-term fluctuations. To achieve this result it is necessary to break the direct link between the producers' price and world market prices, the existence of which in the past has caused the local purchase prices to reflect every vagary of speculation on the world's produce markets. Careful consideration of this problem has led to the conclusion that the means best adapted to this end in the circumstances of the West African cocoa industry would be the continuance in essence of the present system whereby all cocoa would be bought at uniform prices, fixed at any rate seasonally, and sold to the world markets by special organisations created for that purpose, which would operate as regards both purchase and disposal either direct or through such agents as it might seem expedient to employ.

35. It is therefore proposed that there should be established in the Gold Coast and Nigeria, as from the beginning of the 1945–6 season (i.e. in October 1945), organisations empowered by law to purchase the total production of cocoa, to prescribe the prices to be paid to the producers, and to be responsible for the disposal of the cocoa. These organisations would be established by, and responsible to, the Colonial Governments, and would be required to act as trustees for the producers.

36. In the Gold Coast it is intended that the organisation to be set up should be presided over by a senior Government Officer, and should have an official majority. The other members will include Africans and representatives of other interests. The Government majority will represent the interests of the producers and will act as trustees for them until such time as the producers' Cooperative Societies have developed sufficiently to enable them effectively to provide their own representation. It is contemplated that representatives of the producers should eventually constitute the majority in the proposed organisation.

37. In the case of Nigeria, it is proposed that the functions in question should be entrusted in the first instance to the Supply Branch of the Nigerian Administration or whatever post-war organisation may be created to succeed it, and that there should be an Advisory Committee presided over by a senior Government Officer and representative of the producers and other interests concerned.

38. At this point it is appropriate to emphasise four important considerations. In the first place, these proposals do not in any way represent a departure from the policy of fostering and of developing the cooperative movement among West African producers. The development of this movement remains a cardinal object of Government policy, and indeed it is felt that the growth of the movement may

be greatly strengthened and accelerated through the operation of the scheme that is now proposed. Secondly, the constitution and composition of the proposed local organisation are not to be regarded as final or permanent. Quite apart from such variations in the proposals set out above as may on further consideration seem appropriate before the scheme is brought into being in 1945, the organisations may be expected to change and to develop with experience, both in the direction of increased and more direct representation of the producers themselves, and in the light of the development of the general international commodity policy. Thirdly, the scheme, while designed to meet the special circumstances of the West African cocoa industry, can be fitted in without difficulty as a part of any wider international scheme that may later be established. Should it be deemed desirable to institute some international organisation for dealing with the problems of the world production or marketing of cocoa, His Majesty's Government would be willing to participate in such an organisation, and it is considered that its operation would not be incompatible with the existence of producers' marketing agencies such as those now proposed for British West Africa. Finally, the proposals involve no change whatever in the arrangements whereby the entire British West African output of cocoa is now available for allocation by the Combined Food Board in Washington, and the decisions of that body will continue to be put into effect as hitherto.

39. In order that the local organisations may be in a position to maintain a steady purchase price policy whatever short-term fluctuations may occur on world markets, it will be necessary for them, with the necessary funds, to place at their disposal, in pursuance of the undertaking referred to in paragraphs 1 and 26 above, a substantial proportion of the profits already realised on the Board's cocoa account over the period 1939–43. Appendix V [to this report] shows that the net excess of receipts over expenditure on this account over the period in question is £3,676,253, and the results of the season 1943–4 are indeed likely to result in a substantial addition to this profit. This it is considered would be the best and most appropriate way of carrying out the undertakings to which reference has been made, the more particularly since it would not be practicable to attempt to return to each producer his precise share of the profits, proportionately to his production, for the reason that in the West African Colonies cocoa is normally produced and marketed in small quantities by many thousands of small farmers, and the detailed records necessary for such a division of products do not exist.

35. Cutting out diseased cocoa trees meets strong political opposition, 1948 [1]

259. The prosperity today of the Gold Coast depends on cocoa. The menace to that prosperity is 'Swollen shoot'. Upon cocoa, so far as yet seen, depend the plans for a better country – better education, better medical attention, better housing and all those things which spell social improvement and which the people long for.

260. In the five pre-war years, the export of cocoa brought into the Gold Coast about £5,300,000 a year. This represented about 98 per cent of the value of its agricultural exports and not less than 63 per cent by value of the total exports. In spite of a heavy reduction in the quantity marketed since then the export value of

[1] *Report of the Commission of enquiry into disturbances in the Gold Coast, 1948*, Colonial Office, London 1948, paras 259–77.

the cocoa crop had risen in 1946/7 to £9,500,000 while in 1947/8, as a result of the phenomenal increase in world prices, the total export value of cocoa had risen to approximately £41,000,000.

261. The output has, however, shown a marked decline from the peak of 300,000 tons in 1936/7, to a post-war figure averaging about 200,000 tons (representing purchases from the farmer). Many reasons are given for this alarming decline such as the low prices obtained during the war years with consequent lack of attention to cultivation and harvesting, particularly unfavourable climatic conditions, loss of soil fertility and ageing of the trees. We are satisfied that the main contributing cause of the decline in production is the spread of 'Swollen shoot' disease.

262. This disease, first identified as such in 1936 (though noticed in various parts of the cocoa belt in earlier years) is now known to be caused by a virus carried from tree to tree by a mealy-bug which has fed on the sap of an infected tree. A diseased tree cannot recover, it dies within 16 to 24 months. The life of the virus is limited to not more than 36 hours in the mealy-bug and not more than 48 hours in the tree after it has been cut.

263. Work carried out at the West African Cocoa Research Institute, subsequently confirmed by observation on other cocoa farms in the Eastern Provinces, shows that the spread of the disease is very rapid. One experiment in an area of 4,636 trees, where the disease was allowed to spread unchecked, gave the following results:

	No. of diseased trees	Total yield of cocoa pods
August 1945	1,450	41,771
August 1946	2,131	33,716
August 1947	2,976	24,569

There are some 400 million cocoa trees in the Gold Coast and it is estimated that nearly 50 million of them are at present infected. Competent authorities estimate that the present rate of spread is about 15 million trees a year and that, if unchecked, the cocoa industry will have practically disappeared in 20 years.

264. The only remedy for the disease is to cut down the infected tree. This opinion has been arrived at after intensive research by the expert scientists of the Research Institute based not alone on their experience but drawing upon experience in other parts of the world. No scientific evidence to confute this claim was presented to us. There is no known cure for any virus disease in any plant anywhere in the world and varieties of cocoa trees which might be immune to this virus disease have not yet been found.

265. At first, the cutting out of diseased trees was left to voluntary effort by the farmers, but the response was inadequate to counter the increasing spread of the disease. Accordingly the Government started in January 1947 to use existing compulsory powers to enable the Department of Agriculture to cut out diseased trees without the consent of the owner. No complaints about the methods used were received until late in the summer and it was not until January 1948 that serious opposition arose. In our view this opposition was to a great extent politically inspired. Between August 1945 when cutting out by Government labour with individual farmer's approval was begun and December 1947, some 2½ million

diseased trees had been cut out, without physical opposition. During the next three months there were numerous instances of violence and the compulsory cutting out of diseased trees was suspended in April 1948. Farmers in the Gold Coast like most farmers throughout the world tend to an innate conservatism.

266. There were, in our opinion, certain weaknesses in the administration of the cutting-out campaign due to urgency on the part of the Agricultural Department to deal expeditiously with a disease that threatened to upset the whole economy of the country. Various criticisms were made:

(i) It is said that the propaganda designed to tell the farmer about the disease, its nature, rate of spread and probable effect was inadequate. There is no doubt that there is a genuine confusion in the minds of many cocoa farmers, between previously experienced ills of the cocoa tree, such as Sahlbergell, Heliothrips and Drought Die-back, and the present Swollen shoot virus. This confusion is accompanied by a failure to recognise that what may cure one disease is useless to cure another.

(ii) Diseased trees – and, in the earlier stages of infection it often takes a trained eye to detect the symptoms – should have been clearly marked by trained personnel before the cutting-out squads went to work.

(iii) The system whereby labourers were paid on the basis of the number of trees cut out led to indiscriminate cutting of healthy and diseased trees.

(iv) Farmers were not notified of the probable arrival of the cutting-out squads and the work was sometimes carried out without their knowledge.

(v) Some farmers forestalled, by bribes, the cutting out of their diseased trees.

(vi) Cutting out of cocoa trees is not a complete cure since the virus can exist in trees other than cocoa and the mealy-bug is also found in other trees and plants. This is true, but it is not an argument against reducing the sources of infection to a minimum and reducing the risk of infection to a comparatively negligible factor.

267. While constrained to admit that in some cases these criticisms can be justified and that both the propaganda and methods of administration could have been better than they were, it is equally clear to us in the light of the number of trees successfully and peacefully cut out between 1945 and 1947, that much of the later hostility to cutting out has been deliberately stimulated. We consider that the natural reluctance of the farmer to cut out a tree which may produce one further, though smaller, crop has been exploited for political reasons. We are confirmed in this by Dr Danqah, who told us that the Government's scheme for eradication of the disease is scientifically sound but politically inexpedient.

268. In addition we were told by some farmers of the most fantastic and malicious stories current throughout the cocoa belt which have poisoned the mind of the cocoa farmer and created a distrust which will take time to eradicate. Two examples, only, need be given to illustrate these rumours: (i) Britain intends to sell the Gold Coast to the United States but wishes to ensure the death of the cocoa industry to avoid subsequent competition; (ii) the large importing firms such as the United Africa Company, are starting big plantations in the Far East or in East Africa, and are anxious to reduce West African production.

269. The fear of exploitation, which we found to be very real, is a fertile soil for any evilly disposed person to sow the seeds of suspicion, however unreal or fantastic. While ordinarily such rumours would appear to call for no action, so seriously do we regard the need for removing suspicion that we feel a widely

publicised declaration by the Secretary of State nailing them as mischievous lies is called for.

270. As we have said, no scientific cure other than cutting out was suggested to us. Instead we were treated to the following alternative policies: (*a*) let nature take its course and the disease will cure itself; (*b*) replanting should be started after the land has been rested for a year or two; (*c*) science will find some other remedy; (*d*) cocoa production should be allowed to decline and alternative crops introduced.

271. These suggestions are merely counsels of despair and can only lead to disaster. The cures for the less complex troubles of the industry which have been experienced in the past, such as soil exhaustion, lack of shade trees, abuse of pruning and so on, will not answer for Swollen shoot. Experiences of virus diseases in other plants and other countries does not yield any hope that their severity will decrease. The development of immune varieties is the only known counter-attack. So far these have not been evolved. Even if a resistant type were discovered tomorrow, it would take at least five years to test whether this resistance was likely to last, and a further ten or fifteen years to assess the yielding capacity of such trees and to supply farmers with worthwhile quantities of seed. We cannot see that any other investment of the £3,000,000 (which the cutting out of diseased trees and rehabilitation of the cocoa are estimated to cost) would bring the same return to either the farmer or the Gold Coast. We are confident, in the absence of any scientific evidence to the contrary, that cutting out is the only possible method of control and that replanting with cocoa is the only economic course to be followed in the Gold Coast. Many witnesses were asked to suggest alternative crops which would maintain financial returns in any way comparable to cocoa, but no satisfactory answers were received.

272. It is, of course, possible that this misrepresentation of the Government's aims and the deliberate confusion of the issues involved have reached such a pitch that in the interests of ordered progress an interval of 'marking time' may be necessary. But we are not prepared to believe that the last word has been spoken. We cannot believe that those political leaders among the farmers themselves, who wish to achieve self-government in the near future and who are ambitious for the continued progress of the Gold Coast, are prepared to sit back and watch the ebb of its life's blood. This indeed would be the negation of political responsibility.

273. We suggest that the first step must be to establish or restore confidence in the scientists' claim that cutting out is the only sure remedy. We recognise, with regret, that present feeling makes it unlikely that further British scientific advice will be accepted as impartial. We therefore recommend that a small panel of three plant pathologists, of high repute, drawn from countries not commercially interested in cocoa, should be appointed to study the incidence and nature of the disease and to report on the means of its speedy eradication. Should it put forward some sound alternative, so much the better. In the event of their confirmation that cutting out is the only remedy, we recommend that that policy be followed subject to certain changes in administration and procedure. We envisage the following procedure:

(i) That, whenever possible, the owner of the diseased trees or his agent should be given clear notice of the visit of the Agricultural Department's representative.

(ii) That diseased trees should be clearly marked or branded by trained staff before being cut out.

(iii) That an order should be served on the farmer to cut out the diseased trees within, say, thirty days of the date of the order.

(iv) That an opportunity be afforded to the farmer to make representations and to appeal if, in his opinion, non-infected trees have been marked.

(v) That if the trees have not been cut out by the farmer himself within a specified time, they should be cut out by the Department's agents at the farmer's expense.

(vi) That the rehabilitation grant to those farmers who agree to the cutting out of their diseased trees be increased from its present level of £12 per acre to, say, £24 or £30 for an initial period of, say, two years and subsequently reduced progressively to its former level.

274. We suggest, also, that as soon as compulsory cutting out is resumed, it should commence in the Ashanti part of the cocoa belt, in which the disease is not as yet widespread and where the chances of agreement with the farmer would appear to be better, particularly if the rehabilitation payments were enhanced during the earlier stages of the treatment. Of the estimated 40 million diseased trees in the Gold Coast, only some 400,000 were to be found in Ashanti and of these 300,000 had already been cut out before the opposition grew in February and March 1948. The Ashanti farmer is more likely to accept, if the implications of the spread of the disease were made clearer to him, the cutting out of a very small proportion of trees – possibly as low as one in a thousand – than to see his industry disappear, as it has already disappeared in certain parts of the Colony. As Ashanti at present produces about one-half of the total output, the saving of the Ashanti crop would be no small achievement. Moreover, there is a convenient natural gap between the main cocoa areas in the Colony and in Ashanti which runs, north-east to south-west, from Kwahu to Dunkwa practically along the common provincial boundary, and which would afford a fair quarantine area between the two provinces. The campaign might be carried into the Colony as soon as conditions permit.

275. As further encouragement, and to enable the work of cutting out to proceed by agreement, we suggest that the Cocoa Marketing Board, out of the funds at its disposal, offers a bonus during the next five years, based on the number of trees or cocoa sales, to all farmers producing a certificate from the Department of Agriculture showing that as from a predetermined date their farms are free from trees suffering from the disease.

276. We would urge that the Government invite at the earliest opportunity the cooperation of African political leaders to overcome the hostility which only manifested itself in the past few months.

277. This cocoa problem is not a sectional, nor merely a farmer's problem; it is a national problem since the economic life of the Colony is at stake. The Swollen shoot issue is really the prime test of the ability of African leaders to shoulder political responsibility.

Bibliography

29. W. S. D. Tudhope (Director of Agriculture), Enquiry into the Gold Coast cocoa industry, *Sessional Papers nos. II and IV, 1918–19*, paras 1–2 and 19–45 (extracts).

30. *Legislative Council Debates, 1916–17*, pp. 82–91.

31. Governor's Annual Address, *Legislative Council Debates, 1923–4*, pp. 39–42.
32. *Legislative Council Debates, 1925–6*, pp. 290–2.
33. *Report of the Commission on the marketing of West African cocoa,* Cmd 5845, London 1938, paras 462–545 (extracts).
34. *Report on cocoa control in West Africa and statements on future policy,* Cmd 6554, London 1944, paras 1–39 (extracts).
35. *Report of the Commission of Enquiry into Disturbances in the Gold Coast, 1948*, Colonial Office, London 1948, paras 259–77.

6. Education

The Watson Commission began its survey of education in 1948 (Document 38, para 358) as follows: ' Nothing impressed us more than the interest of the people of the Gold Coast in education. Practically every African who sent in a memorandum or appeared in person before us, sooner or later started to discuss education. This interest, in our opinion, is as deep-rooted as it is widespread.' These words echo those of Ormsby-Gore, who surveyed education in the colony in 1926 (Document 36) and began by commenting that ' even to the most casual visitor the demand for education by the people of the Gold Coast is most striking '. He continued: ' The urgent needs of the present situation have been recognised by the Government and provision is now being made both in regard to the provision of schools and the training of teachers on a larger scale than anywhere else in Tropical Africa.'

Ormsby-Gore outlines some of the measures taken by the colonial government in the twenties, while Document 37, which is an extract from the Governor's annual address to the Legislative Council in 1925, contains the main official policy statement on the subject in the twenties and is perhaps one of the fullest statements on colonial education policy ever made by a colonial administrator.

The Governor starts by stating that education is ' the cornerstone of Government's main policy ' and then proceeds to criticise the existing educational system as ' rotten at the core '.

Not only is it inadequate in not going far enough, but it has proved inefficient in its results. Inadequate because it fails to provide facilities for that secondary and higher education which is essential if the African is to become an efficient citizen and is to qualify himself for leadership in the affairs of this country under the conditions attending the advent of modern civilization. Inefficient, because the character-training necessary to citizenship and leadership has been largely omitted in the present system.[1]

The single most important fault of the system was that it was not geared to the employment requirements of the colony. Education emphasised the literary skills and the Governor estimated that ' our schools were turning out annually

[1] Document 37, para 89.

some four thousand to five thousand boys, the vast majority of whom, owing to the nature of their education, were only suitable for clerical work' at a time when 'I doubt very much whether five hundred clerks per annum are required to replace the normal wastage throughout the country'. Only a thorough reorganisation of the educational system could overcome this defect. On the one hand, the Governor thought it necessary to promote character-training so that 'the young African in Africa, like the young Englishman in England, understands that manual work does not disgrace an educated man'; on the other hand a full reform of the educational structure, teaching methods and syllabuses was required.

The objects of education were summarised as follows:

We want to give all Africans the opportunity of both moral and material progress by opening for them the benefits and delights that come from literature and by equipping them with the knowledge necessary to success in their occupations, no matter how humble. We want to give those who wish it an opportunity of qualifying themselves to enter any trade or profession. And finally, we want to give the best men and women the opportunity of becoming leaders of their own countrymen in thought, industries and the professions. Throughout all this, our aim must be not to denationalize them, but to graft skilfully on to their national characteristics the best attributes of modern civilisation. For without preserving his national characteristics and his sympathy and touch with the great illiterate masses of his own people, no man can ever become a leader in progress, whatever other sort of leader he may become.[2]

The achievement of these objects was seen as requiring the reconstruction of the educational system on the basis of the following fifteen principles of education.

1. Primary education must be thorough and be from the bottom to the top.
2. The provision of secondary schools with an educational standard that will fit young men and women to enter a university.
3. The provision of a university.
4. Equal opportunities to those given to boys should be provided for the education of girls.
5. Co-education is desirable during certain stages of education.
6. The staff of teachers must be of the highest possible quality.
7. Character-training must take an important place in education.
8. Religious teaching should form part of education.
9. Organised games should form part of school life.
10. The course in every school should include special reference to the health, welfare and industries of the locality.
11. A sufficient staff of efficient African inspectors of schools must be trained and maintained.

[2] See p. 288 below.

12. Whilst an English education must be given, it must be based solidly on the vernacular.

13. Education cannot be compulsory nor free.

14. There should be cooperation between the government and the missions, and the latter should be subsidised for educational purposes.

15. The government must have the ultimate control of education throughout the Gold Coast.

An idea of the extent to which the reforms of the twenties succeeded in terms of the colonial government's own ends, and of the extent to which official thinking on education remained more or less unchanged over a period of twenty years, can be had by comparing what the Watson Commission had to say on education (Document 38) with the policy statement of the twenties which we have just summarised.

The success of the colonial government in changing the pattern of education so as to reduce the number of unemployed school-leavers seeking clerical work was far from complete and the Watson Commission spoke of the problem in terms almost identical to those of the Governor twenty years before.

It is realised that literary education alone is doing great harm in the Gold Coast. It is creating a gulf between town and country. It is producing a youthful hooligan element in the towns as boys emerge from school to find a glut of clerks and to find themselves disinterested in, or not equipped for, other occupations. It is creating a false sense of values in which the dignity of labour is lost sight of. There must be an immediate expansion of craft, technical and vocational training throughout the entire structure.[3]

This recommended expansion, however, was to take place within the existing, pyramidal structure of the educational system as it existed. Expansion was to occur but it was to be cautious: 'The pushing ahead of too ambitious schemes for the rapid expansion of primary education may do incalculable harm both to the structure of the whole educational system and to the economy of the country as a whole.'[4] In other words, the fear of the Watson Commission was that the pyramidal structure of education would be threatened if the base was expanded too rapidly and so it emphasised 'the need for an increase in the number of secondary schools and for the provision of part-time education for those who cannot find places in senior primary and secondary schools'. It continues:

We fully appreciate the pressure that has emanated from the indigenous desire for mass literacy; but if the peoples of the Gold Coast wish to achieve a progressively greater measure of self-government within a reasonably short time and if they wish to model its economic organisation on those of the more industrialised and commercialised countries in the world, it will be achieved only by a soundly balanced system of education. If the material is limited, the alternatives are to build a narrower ladder, that, while tapering, reaches its objective, or to build so

[3] Document 38, para 374.

[4] *Ibid.* para 371.

broad a ladder that it fails to reach anywhere. The former seems to us the only possible alternative.[5]

It was the latter alternative that was opted for by the independent government, for the issue at stake was not educational but political and what the colonial government was attempting was the creation of an elite trained, on the one hand to a level comparable with that of the educated minority anywhere in the world (i.e. Britain), and on the other hand in touch with the great mass of people who were to remain illiterate. The Watson Commission in the forties reiterates this position, that was stated so emphatically in the twenties, and the unchanging nature of colonial thinking on education is an important indication of how fundamental it was to the whole political strategy of colonialism in Ghana.

36. Education provided on a larger scale in Ghana than anywhere else in Tropical Africa : Ormsby-Gore, 1926 [1]

Even to the casual visitor the general demand for education by the people of the Gold Coast is most striking. This demand is not new. As long ago as the year 1900 the number of children at school in the Gold Coast Colony was estimated at 12,000. Today there are over 35,000 in regular attendance at recognised schools. Such an expansion has placed a very great strain on both Government and missionary societies, and I heard it stated that the rapid extension of the school system has outrun the provision of the supply of properly trained European and native staff. As a result it is even said that the quality of the education given has in some respects deteriorated and that the quality of teaching was better twenty years ago than it is now.

The urgent needs of the present situation have been recognised by the Government and provision is now being made both in regard to the provision of schools and the training of teachers on a larger scale than anywhere else in Tropical Africa. A new Education Ordinance has just been passed and under it a strong and representative board of education has been set up, on which the missionary societies and the native community each have four representatives. The Ordinance aims at improving the quality of the teaching throughout the country by raising the status and technical qualifications of the teachers, who in the future will have to be registered. Classes for all the standards are being prepared and increasing provision is being made by way of grants for missionary and private schools and for an increased inspectorate.

The most important step, however, that the Government of the Gold Coast has taken to deal with the question of education has been the foundation of the Prince of Wales College and School at Achimota. While it is true that this institution is designed to provide education of a higher form than secondary, its main object is to set standards for all types of education throughout the colony. It will include instruction from the kindergarten upwards to University standards.

[5] *Ibid.* para 373.

[1] *Report by the Honourable W. G. A. Ormsby-Gore on his visit to West Africa during the year 1926*, Cmd 2744, London 1926, pp. 84–7 (extracts).

The whole system which is being instituted at Achimota rests on adapting education to native mentality, traditions and needs. The vernacular as well as English will be maintained throughout. Much depends in the future on the success or failure of the education given there. It is new of its kind in the history of education in West Africa and is therefore an experiment. I am sure that the Government have done wisely in doing their best to secure the best possible staff for this work and to furnish the institution throughout with the most up-to-date equipment.

The actual buildings lie on rising ground eight miles from Accra. They are far enough advanced to allow the Principal and the greater part of his staff to live there, and the infant school has already been opened. The grounds include large playing fields and an experimental farm. By January 1927 it is hoped that construction will be far enough advanced to enable the lower primary school to be opened. The construction of the Prince of Wales College should be sufficiently complete to enable the boys' upper primary school, the secondary school and certain classes of more advanced education to be started in January 1928.

The total cost of the buildings and equipment is estimated in the neighbourhood of half a million pounds, and from this it will be seen that we are taking the most ambitious step that has yet been taken in British Tropical Africa. A European staff of over twenty is already in the colony and their early arrival has enabled them to become acquainted with the life and language of the people of the country before undertaking their duties as instructors.

Achimota is a boarding school and in addition to it there are already large Government day schools in the principal towns. There is also in Accra a first-class technical school for older boys where advanced instruction in wood, cement and metal work is provided. I had the privilege of laying the foundation stone of a new day school in Kumasi which will provide accommodation for 800 pupils.

Most interesting are the four Junior Trade Schools, two in the colony, one at Mampong in Ashanti, and one at Yendi in that part of Togoland attached to the Northern Territories. These schools are rural in their surroundings and are residential in type. Each is under a European headmaster and students from considerable distances are admitted for a three or four years' course. In these schools while much of the instruction is in common, boys undertake one line of special instruction. These special courses can be either agriculture, building and masonry, carpentry and woodwork, or metal work. They are in every way admirable institutions, and quite apart from the high quality of the instruction given in the several arts, I was much struck by the discipline and character training given at those which I visited. They are to be regarded as a very promising feature in the scheme of education in the colony. I should like to add that in such schools the personality of the headmaster plays a very great part. He has to have a knowledge of craftsmanship as well as character and enthusiasm, and without such men, who are hard to find, this type of school cannot succeed.

The education of girls is receiving increasing attention and there is a very good school for girls under a European Headmistress at Accra.

Instruction of native teachers has hitherto been given at a special training college in Accra, shortly to be transferred to Achimota. Other native teachers are also trained by the various missions, while a large grant has been made to the Scottish Mission by the Government for building a new training college for their teachers.

Conditions and educational requirements in the Northern Territories are very different from those which obtain in the colony and Ashanti. The life of the native communities there has not yet been affected to any considerable extent by outside influence, and it would be inadvisable at this moment to introduce a system of education designed for the southern areas. The Government has, therefore, decided to establish a separate Education Department for this part of the Territory, and its personnel are being carefully selected.

37. Fundamental principles of education policy, 1925 [1]

PREPARATORY PERIOD IN THE WORK OF EDUCATIONAL REFORM

87. I will now turn to what is uppermost in the thoughts of all Africans – the corner-stone of Government's main policy, namely education. I have spoken so many times on this subject that the unofficial Members of this Council must be fully aware that Government has long been deeply engrossed in planning the educational reforms which we believe to be necessary, and in considering the expenditure involved. I have noticed, however, that there has lately been some anxiety as to when we are going to stop talking and get to work. This anxiety is natural, but the delay which has occurred in taking action is equally natural. The recommendations of the Educationalists Committee, 1920 were so far-reaching and costly that it would have been unwise if we had accepted them without making searching enquiries into their soundness and obtaining the best advice possible.

It was evident that a ' preparatory period ' was necessary, in which to carry out the following work:

(i) Investigation of local educational requirements by committees.

(ii) Ascertaining the experience of other countries with similar educational problems.

(iii) Formulating definite principles to guide us permanently in the reconstruction and extension of our present system of education.

(iv) Planning in detail the steps required to give effect to those principles.

88. Thanks to the progress made in the last twelve months, we have completed the first two items of work ; and today I shall inform Council of the principles of education which we propose to adopt, and which, after consideration by the Board of Education, will complete the third task before the end of this month. The Board will then be in a position to begin work on the last item of the preparatory period. Indeed this last item has so far advanced that we have been able to start the construction of that great institution at Achimota which will form the model for all education in this country.

GENERAL DEFECTS IN OUR PRESENT SYSTEM

Failure of primary education

89. As the remedies which Government proposes to adopt will cause increased expenditure on education, I will here inform this council of what we have found

[1] Governor's Annual Address, *Legislative Council Debates, 1925–6*, pp. 59–104 (extracts). This represents the most complete statement on education during the inter-war period.

wrong in our present system. It will be within the recollection of Honourable Members that I have constantly repeated in the last few years that, in my opinion, the system of education in this country is rotten at the core. Not only is it inadequate in not going far enough, but it has proved inefficient in its results. Inadequate, because it fails to provide facilities for that secondary and higher education which is essential if the African is to become an efficient citizen and is to qualify himself for leadership in the affairs of this country under the conditions attending the advent of modern civilisation. Inefficient, because the character-training necessary to citizenship and leadership has been largely omitted in the existing system; and because the actual primary education imparted at our schools has seriously failed to give good results except in comparatively few instances.

. . .

Field of employment for educated Africans

91. One serious result of the failure to pass the Civil Service Examination due to our present system is unemployment. Last year I remarked that our schools were turning out annually some four thousand to five thousand boys, the vast majority of whom, owing to the nature of their education, were only suitable for clerical work. Even if they were all fitted to be good clerks, this number is far in excess of what is required in this country. There was a period when a clerk of any sort was greatly in demand – indeed the same remark applies to good clerks today – but those conditions no longer exist; I doubt very much whether five hundred clerks per annum are required to replace the normal wastage throughout the country. What employment is open to the remainder, roughly four thousand able-bodied and intelligent but wrongly educated youths who failed to find clerical work? Cocoa-brokers? There is a limit to this field of employment, indeed I am not certain that it is not decreasing. Storekeepers? Judging from the number of small stores already existing all over the country, and from the fact that every African whether educated or not is a small trader, there is not room for more than a small increase in this field of employment. In such Government services as the General Police, the Printing Office, the Sanitary Department, etc., there is a certain but limited field of employment; but here again a good education is usually essential to promotion to the higher grades and ranks.

Field of manual labour

92. So much for the field of employment in which a good education is essential. I confess that the outlook there is most depressing. What about that other field in which the education backs up the work of the hand – the field of manual labour? Here there are ample opportunities for the educated product of our primary schools. Mechanics, carpentering, motor-driving, engine-driving, and other skilled trades are all employment in which educated artisans can do superior and better-paid work than the illiterate. A certain number of young men take up this work by apprenticing themselves to various Departments and private firms, or by joining the technical school; but the vast majority of the educated youths who have failed to pass the Civil Service Examination consider that it is below their dignity to take up any profession which involves manual labour. If this can be said with regard to the skilled artisans whom I have mentioned, how much more can it be said with regard to other and less skilled forms of manual labour, labour in road building, house building, agriculture? Yet this is the only field in which the

majority of boys who leave school early are in future going to find employment. A very few have sunk their false pride and have relieved their families of the cost of keeping them. The majority still use the word 'labourer' as a term of contempt, and prefer to be supported by their families rather than earn their daily food by doing a day's honest manual work

Necessity for abandoning contempt of manual labour : attitude of parents

93. Until the education and the spirit in our primary schools have been so altered that the young African in Africa, like the young Englishman in England understands that manual work does not disgrace an educated man, our list of educated unemployment in this country will mount up steadily year by year. Not only the spirit of the schools, however, but the spirit of parents who send their children there has to change if we are to keep down unemployment. I give all parents the credit of sending their children to school with the good intention of enabling them to progress towards a higher state of civilisation ; but, at the same time, they expect that those children will get such a good education as will enable them to take up a lucrative appointment in return for the money spent on them. Parents are beginning to find that the kind of education given to their boys has not resulted in any reward for the sacrifice they have made in sending them to school. What I want them to realise is that schools must teach thoroughness – which at present they do not – and that however much we may improve our system of education, the field of employment is limited unless the majority of those educated take up manual work. The sooner the parents realise this the better for them.

Changed conditions necessitate educated boys taking up manual labour

94. I will conclude my remarks on this subject of unemployment by referring to certain facts that came to light in our enquiry into the petition against the application of the Municipal Corporations Ordinance to Accra. The petitioners assert that in Accra from five hundred to six hundred boys leave school per annum and can find no employment. Referring to this the Special Commissioner appointed to enquire into the petition remarked as follows:

> Another point which is usually lost sight of is the impossibility of either Government or the European trading community giving employment to all those who annually pass through the schools of the Colony. In the past, owing to the small number of schools and the insignificant proportion of the youth of the country which attended them, there was a chronic insufficiency of clerks available for the Public Service and the mercantile community – an insufficiency which resulted in the services of every boy who had passed the Seventh Standard being eagerly competed for. Nowadays things are very different. A few statistics will make this clear. In 1903 there were in the Gold Coast and Ashanti 139 Government and Mission Schools on the Assisted list with 13,955 pupils. In 1923 the corresponding figures were 299 schools and 33,110 pupils. The annual surplus in the supply of educated youths can only be absorbed by private enterprise either in the form of trade or of manual labour. That the dignity of labour is gradually being recognised can already be seen in the Keta-Ada district where many fishermen, weavers and farmers although literate are nevertheless not too proud to make their living in the same way as their fathers did before them.

Neglect of character-training

95. At first sight it would appear as if this contempt of manual labour is a cause of unemployment rather than a defect in our system of education. Nevertheless it is a defect, for it reveals a very serious failing in such character-training as is imparted in our primary schools. Any character-training that does not dispel in a boy's mind the idea that manual work is contemptible must be poor indeed. As a matter of fact, character-training is practically non-existent in the vast majority of schools in this country. That, at any rate, is one of the defects brought to light by this question of unemployment.

Defects in actual education

96. What, however, are the chief causes of the defects in our actual education itself? As Honourable Members are aware, both the Government and its technical advisers have long arrived at the conclusion that the quality of our African teachers required raising. Steps to do this have been taken by lengthening the period spent at the Training College, but this in itself is not going to produce a better teacher unless the system of training is good, and unless the student has received a thorough and sound primary education before entering. I think that a brief description of our ' vicious circle ' of education will give Honourable Members a pretty clear idea of the defects of the present system.

The primary education of the African teacher

To begin with, before entering the Training College for Teaching a boy has to pass standard VII in one of the existing primary schools. In acquiring the necessary knowledge to obtain this certificate he is taught by one of those very teachers who, in nine cases out of ten, we recognise are inefficient. He is taught more subjects than the English boy in a corresponding English school; but also the African boy is taught in what is to him a foreign language by teachers who are imperfectly acquainted with that language, while the English boy is taught in his own language by one to whom the language belongs. Moreover, in this country the value of the standard VII certificate varies so greatly in the different schools as to be an extremely unreliable index of the boy's attainments.

The training of the African teacher

The would-be teacher, armed with his certificate, enters the Training School College. Here, often for the first time in his school career, he gets a little character-training, beginning however at a period when any such training is little likely to leave a permanent mark. He has comfortable and clean living and feeding quarters. He is looked after by a Housemaster who is only too anxious to gain his confidence; he takes part in games to the great benefit of his physique and character, and generally enjoys himself. So far so good. The black side of the picture is that this unfortunate young African is taught – in a foreign language which he speaks imperfectly and in which he cannot think at all – about twice the number of subjects which are in the curriculum of similar schools in England, where moreover the boy learns in his own language. I said that the African boy at the Training College is taught: I should have said crammed; crammed until his head is bursting. It is no fault of the Training College Staff: it is the fault of the general system of education.

And then he leaves the Training College and goes out to some school in the country where he has to teach a number of children generally far in excess of the number with which he can reasonably be expected to deal properly, children whose eager and intelligent faces show that they want to learn. But the poor teacher, his head crammed with all the subjects which they poured into it at the Training College, is, in nine cases out of ten, only able to pour it undigested into the heads of his pupils – into their heads, not into their brains. He is, in fact, employed in doing to them what his teacher at his primary school formerly did to him – telling his pupils what he knows and not teaching them. And that, Honourable Members, is the root reason for our defective system of education. Half-educated boys are put through a forcing process which results in their being crammed to teach and not trained to teach.

Other faults in our present system of education

97. There are many other faults in our present system, some arising out of the reason just stated, others due to the nature of the system itself. These I will allude to when dealing with the remedies. There are some Africans who hold that our standard of education has deteriorated. There is no proof of that. What has probably happened is that the standard of thought and living of people has risen, and the standard of education has not kept pace with it. They say that the dearth of inspections is responsible for this falling off. That may be so ; indeed, Government is fully aware that its inspectorate staff is short and has taken steps to increase it, but not to increase it to the number that is required to carry out the inspection of the present system of education. For no matter how many inspectors we engage they would not make a success of a system which is itself so defective as to be unable to produce efficient teachers.

REASONS FOR PRESENT SYSTEM

98. Here I must pause for one moment to consider the reasons why education in the country has not been improved before now. Let no teacher in this country think that I am throwing stones at him personally. He is, as a rule, an earnest hard-working man, in many cases entirely devoted to his work. It is not the teacher that I am criticising – it is the system which has produced him. Nor am I throwing stones at the Education Staff. They are thoroughly conscientious men who have worked hard for many years to make a success of a system which had been established long before their arrival. . . Indeed there is no one to blame for the defects of our present system, for when this system was started the past governments of this country were working in the dark. How true this is can be realised when it is considered that even in England, with all her modern civilisation, the system of primary education has been so much criticised in recent years that it has been, and is being, drastically re-organised. The education of the peoples in the Empire who have depended on us has been based – and often unsuitably – on principles which mainly apply to conditions in England and not to actual local conditions. Until quite recently everyone has been working in the dark as to the best system of education required to enable our tropical dependencies to absorb modern civilisation with the greatest benefit to themselves and the least disturbance of their racial characteristics. . .

OBJECTS OF EDUCATION

101. Summarised, Government's objects are as follows: We want to give all Africans the opportunity of both moral and material progress by opening for them the benefits and delights that come from literature and by equipping them with the knowledge necessary to success in their occupations, no matter how humble. We want to give those who wish it an opportunity of qualifying themselves to enter any trade or profession. And finally, we want to give the best men and women the opportunity of becoming leaders of their own countrymen in thought, industries, and the professions. Throughout all this, our aim must be not to denationalise them, but to graft skilfully on to their national characteristics the best attributes of modern civilisation. For without preserving his national characteristics and his sympathy and touch with the great illiterate masses of his own people, no man can ever become a leader in progress whatever other sort of leader he may become.

FIFTEEN PRINCIPLES OF EDUCATION

102. I will now deal *seriatim* with fifteen principles on which we must base our system of education in order to gain the objects just mentioned. In each case I will refer generally to the steps we shall have to carry out to give effect to the principle.

First principle – primary education must be thorough and be from the bottom to the top

103. This will necessitate drastic alterations in our present system. The most valuable period in a child's life from the point of view of education is the kindergarten period, for this is the only period during which it is possible to lay skilfully and thoroughly the foundations of character and of education. It therefore follows that only the best and most suitable teachers must be employed in the kindergartens. The salaries of these teachers should usually be at least as high as those of masters employed in far less important work in the upper standards.

...

107. Another step that we shall have to take to make elementary education more thorough is the adoption of a uniform standard VII throughout all the schools. At present it varies in the different schools and in none is it equal to the seventh standard in the Empire as a whole. Unless the subjects taught in our seventh grade are drastically overhauled, and a fixed standard adopted for all schools, a false impression of its value will be given to employers and pupils alike and to the teachers of the work done...

109. With regard to missions, I do not foresee any greater difficulties than those which we shall ourselves experience, except on the financial side. Here Government should be prepared to give greater assistance than in the past, provided that it is clearly understood that the ultimate control of primary education throughout the country remains in our hands. Judging by the keenness of the two missions which undertake the greater part of educational endeavour in this country, by their loyal cooperation with us in the past, by their desire for improvements in education, and by their anxiety concerning financial resources, I feel that my invitation to cooperate with us in this great and essential work will receive a hearty response. When our model school is working it should prove a valuable

example to their schools, and both raise and unify our whole system of primary education.

Second principle – the provision of secondary schools with an educational standard that will fit young men and women to enter a university

110. Government has already started the construction of a secondary school at Achimota. On the success of this school, the local support that is likely to be forthcoming, the financial situation at the time, and on the progress made in training teachers, will depend the extension of Government secondary schools to other parts of the country. It is hoped that the method of working and the standard adopted at Achimota will be beneficial in raising the standard of education in non-Government secondary schools.

Third principle – the provision of a university

111. This is a principle to which full effect cannot be given until sufficient boys and girls have received a thorough secondary education, and until it is apparent that there is a widespread demand. Unless these two conditions are fulfilled it would obviously be useless to start a university. At any rate this cannot be done until the secondary school at Achimota turns out thoroughly educated candidates who are anxious to enter a university.

In the meantime Government proposes, when sufficiently educated students become available, to establish advanced classes at Achimota in such advanced education as will take them to what is practically the second year of university training: viz. the intermediate study for the degrees of B.A., B.E., etc., grading to scholarships at English universities for competition among those doing well until the time for forming our own university arrives. It is in these advanced classes that candidates for the medical profession will receive special instruction in Chemistry, Physics and Biology, thus qualifying them to enter our medical school at the Gold Coast Hospital. Here also the candidates for the engineering profession should be able to complete the theoretical side of their studies; with regard to the practical side I regret to say that I am advised that at present, and for many years to come, local facilities for instruction in engineering will not permit of a candidate securing a full engineering degree, or becoming a member of the Institute of Civil Engineers, without further study and practical experience in England.

Fourth principle – equal opportunities to those given to boys should be provided for the education of girls

112. It is satisfactory to see that the people of this country are at least alive to the fact that, if they wish to advance in civilisation the women must be as well educated as the men. This principle will involve considerable expenditure by both Government and missions, so it is not expected that the new buildings necessary for the great increase in primary education involved can be provided at once. It is expected, however, that in those places where there is a demand for the education of girls, any expansion of present facilities should be for them and not for boys...

With regard to the standard of girls' education, the existing girls' schools throughout the country have the same defects as those which I have described in my remarks on primary education; similar remedies will therefore be necessary.

It is also desirable that great improvement in our present method of preparing girls both for earning their living and for their domestic duties should be made.

Sixth principle – the staff of teachers must be of the highest possible quality

114. Whatever difference of opinion may exist on any of our principles there is one on which everyone is agreed: only the best men and women should be entrusted with the education and character-training of the rising generation. When I say the best I mean men and women who have received a secondary education and a sound training in teaching, who have high characters and sympathy with children, and who are prepared to devote their lives to what should be the most important work in the world.

115. It is on the African, however, that we shall have to depend for ninety-nine per cent of our teaching staff. Here the state of affairs beggars description. I have paid tribute to the many good qualities of our present teachers, but these qualities, no matter how excellent they may be, fall lamentably short of what is required as far as ability to teach is concerned. Why this is so I have shown in my remarks on the ' vicious circle ' (paragraph 96). We have plenty of material out of which to make good teachers, for there is no race that has greater love of children than the African, but hitherto our machine for converting him into an efficient teacher has been woefully deficient; its defects must be remedied.

Government has therefore placed the provision of good teachers as the first and most urgent item of work in carrying out the reforms in our present system of education. We have always been alive to the importance of the subject, as Honourable Members are aware. We have endeavoured with the material at our disposal, to raise the standard in the Training College. In this a certain measure of success has been achieved, but the task of the staff has been an impossible one owing to the ' vicious circle ' in which for ever revolve the ill-educated school-boy and the over-crammed teacher . . .

The majority of the missions are as much impressed as we are with the importance of employing efficient teachers. They can help the general cause by refusing to open new schools until their old schools are properly staffed, and by cooperating with Government in improving such seminaries as they now have. In doing this they will receive willing help in funds.

116. With Government and the missions working together and in full agreement on the importance of the subject, there is no reason why, in due course, there should not be more than one really sound institution for the training of teachers in this country. That, however, is by no means all that is required. We want people of the best type and of the highest character that the country can produce to take up the profession of teaching. Such character-training as we intend to develop in our educational system will help, but neither that nor the finest training institution in the world will secure for us the men we require unless we raise the status of a teacher until it is worthy of the importance of the post which he fills. A Teacher's Certificate should be the most valuable document issued in this country.

Fortunately Government is in a position to take immediate steps in raising the status of the teacher. The first will be that of raising salaries. Money will not make good teachers – it is devotion to the work that counts – but if we want the best men, and if we want to get the best out of them, we must free them from harassing distractions by placing them out of reach of poverty, and giving them the opportunity of steady advancement. To begin with, initial salaries must be raised until a teacher starts his service on a higher grade than a clerk does. In other words the four years' training as a teacher which he requires – beyond the date when his primary education would have enabled him to obtain a clerkship – must be made up for by making his initial salary higher than that of a clerk in his fifth year.

117. The course which Government favours is the creation of a 'Register of teachers' in the Director of Education's office. This book will contain the name of every teacher in possession of a standard or temporary certificate. All teachers whose names are on the Register will be known as registered teachers, and will be the only teachers recognised by Government. The Register will form a valuable safeguard to missions and others when engaging new teachers and will help good teachers to secure good posts.

...

We consider that it is of the highest importance that the efficiency of a teacher should be maintained, and here the best guide is the efficiency of the school he is teaching. In order to encourage teachers to improve themselves we are prepared to give them opportunities which, if taken advantage of, will lead to increased salaries. We are therefore drawing up a scheme of giving further training to the best teachers in every sixth year of their service, paying them their salaries during their course of instruction. Only the best teachers will be selected for these courses at the conclusion of which they will rise to higher grades in their profession. This process should be repeated in their twelfth and eighteenth years of service. In addition short 'refresher courses' should be held at various training centres in the country to enable teachers to maintain their efficiency.

118. No effort to raise the status of the African teacher will meet with complete success if we allow thoroughly unqualified men to masquerade as teachers. There are, unfortunately, a large number of men of this description scattered through the country, usually out of sight in bush villages, but by no means unknown in the large towns. These inefficient teachers – and naturally, inefficient schools – are increasing in number.

There are several reasons for this; I will deal with two here. In the first place, both Government and Mission schools are full to overflowing and quite unable to admit all those desiring education. Secondly the demand for education is increasing at a rapid pace throughout the whole country. The result is that the country is full of small 'bush-schools,' often started by boys who have only passed the third or fourth standard of education. Beyond the merest smattering of English, and a very elementary knowledge of reading, writing, and arithmetic, these 'bush-teachers' have no education; as for ability to teach, that is non-existent. These teachers and their schools would not take in an educated African parent: he would soon see through them. But by far the majority of parents are illiterate, and know nothing about education or how it should be given. They are anxious to educate their children, and, as the recognised schools are too crowded to admit their children, they send them to the nearest 'bush-school', or get a boy, such as the one I have just described, to start one. They pay a few shillings a month to the teacher and firmly believe that their children are being educated. Naturally they are entirely deceived; their children may be learning a little 'pidgin-English', but practically nothing else.

In many of these bush-schools, however, there is a far worse side. The children receive little or no education in them, but are deprived of healthy play and exercise, and of the education in village lore and usefulness which comes to those who live in and run about the village and its fields. The children are not only not educated, but they are being taught habits and given ideas that are entirely unsuitable to their surroundings. The tendency, in fact, when they have learnt a little 'pidgin-English' is for them to be contemptuous of their illiterate relations and of manual labour, for their ill-educated teacher comes from the very class of primary school-boy who holds manual labour most in contempt.

For the sake of the parents, for the good of the children, and for the honour of the professional teacher, these unqualified 'bush-teachers' must be abolished – an end must be put to the harm which many of them are at present undoubtedly doing to the young children.

I regret to say that many of these 'bush-schools', with inefficient teachers like those I have just described, were started in past times by the missions in their anxiety to spread Christianity. These schools still exist, for, as usual, it is harder to destroy an evil than to prevent it. While it is obvious that no moral harm is being done to the children in this case, yet a great deal of harm is being done to their education; for they are at the very age when its foundations should be skilfully laid. While sympathising deeply with the Christianising work of the missions, and appreciating fully the benefits of Christianity which they confer on the people, I cannot agree that there is justification for allowing any school to be run by an unqualified and ignorant 'bush-teacher', however good a Christian that teacher may be. Religion should take a leading place in any scheme of education in this country; but, though a school should include religion in its teaching, it should also include real education. No school should teach the usual subjects with a view to giving this religious teaching. Every subject should be taught purely in the interest of the pupil. And religious teaching itself should be given in the same spirit, not in the interests of one or another religious body, but reverently in the interests of the pupils themselves.

Seventh principle – character-training must take an important place in education

119. We feel that the adoption of this principle is essential if our education is going to produce good citizens and leaders in thought, industries, and the professions among Africans. No doubt it is far more difficult to carry out character-training efficiently at day-schools than at boarding-schools, but when we consider Dr Jesse Jones's definition it is evident that we can do a good deal of useful work at the former.

Eighth principle – religious teaching should form part of education

120. The manner in which this principle is applied will naturally differ greatly in Government and mission schools. Government schools cater for the population generally, irrespective of sect, and therefore the religious training in them must be entirely non-sectarian. We feel that this is essential in all Government schools; while, in any residential school that we start, we feel certain that the introduction of hostels managed by representatives of the various religious denominations would seriously interfere with the practical working and spirit of the school. 'Religious teaching' in Government schools means the teaching of religion, not of the dogmas of any particular denomination; if this does not satisfy parents, they always have the alternative of sending their children to the boarding-schools run by their own mission. Government must cater for the people generally, irrespective of social class or religious sect.

Ninth principle – organised games should form part of school life

121. The great benefit to the health and physique of children which has resulted from the introduction of organised games into certain schools is full justification for the inclusion of this principle in our educational policy. Most striking examples of this are furnished by the Training College, the Technical Schools, and the Trade Schools, in all of which organised games are rendered easier by their residential nature. For the above reasons, and owing to the opportunities which games afford of developing self-control and initiative, Government is strongly of the opinion that organised games should form part of the life of every school. We also consider that they should not be carried to excess . . .

Tenth principle – the course in every school should include special reference to the health, welfare, and industries of the locality

122. I dealt just now with the serious unemployment among the literate classes in this country, and showed that the chief cause is the contempt for manual labour which has existed for many years past in the mind of boys in our primary schools. This contempt really arises from the fact that our curriculum of education, with the exception of a certain amount of hygiene, bears no relation whatever to the conditions of life existing in this country. In certain cases, so few as to be negligible, an attempt has been made to correlate Western education and local life; if these attempts are not made by all schools we shall continue to create an annually increasing mass of unemployed literate men and, to a less extent, women.

123. Western education is a necessity for African people if they are to absorb without harmful results the Western civilisation that is now advancing steadily inland from the sea, and that must eventually swamp the whole country. If we allow that Western education to continue to deal exclusively with the conditions existing in the country in which it originated, if we do not make it deal directly with actual conditions out here, we shall condemn the great mass of educated Africans to the same sad fate that has befallen hundreds of thousands of educated persons in the Eastern races of the Empire. More than that we shall destroy exactly what we want to preserve, national character and national life.

124. It is therefore essential that in every school we should include work that deals with the life, welfare, and pursuits of the town or village in which it lies. More than that, the school should take an active part in the life surrounding it. All this can be done without interfering with the giving of a thorough primary education. It will be of immense benefit to every child to learn to apply the education which he or she is receiving to the conditions of life around the school, and not to the conditions depicted in the illustrated primers and readers . . .

Eleventh principle – a sufficient staff of efficient African inspectors of schools must be trained and maintained

126. Efficient inspection is one of the secrets of success in education. At present our Inspection Staff consists entirely of Europeans, each of whom owing to his passage and his long leave, costs approximately twice as much as an African. We cannot afford to employ enough to deal adequately with the present number of schools, much less to deal with them under a more thorough system of education. It is essential that we should train African inspectors of the same type and character as our teachers, with, if anything, higher educational qualifications.

Naturally it will be some time before the necessary number of fully qualified African school inspectors will become available.

Twelfth principle – whilst an English education must be given, it must be based solidly on the vernacular

127. Education must be in English because there are several languages, some with several dialects, spoken in this country; in none of them do suitable text-books exist. Any idea that a thorough education can be carried out in the vernacular may therefore be dismissed as unpractical.

Probably the most important recommendation of the 1920 committee was that English should be a subject, and the vernacular the medium of instruction. Now, the teaching of English is the very thing in which our present system of education has failed most. There is no necessity to dwell on the results of this failure; they are visible in the work of the majority of clerks and in the results of the Civil Service Examination to which I have already referred, for one of the most searching tests in these examinations is knowledge of the English language. No wonder that the rest of our primary education has failed, for how can people learn the many subjects taught them in standards I to VII when they have a mere superficial knowledge of reading, writing, and understanding the language in which these subjects must largely be taught?

The reason why English has been so imperfectly learned is that it has usually been taught in English and not in the vernacular. A language cannot be taught to a child by making him repeat by memory certain sounds the meaning of which he does not understand, yet this is the system which has generally prevailed and has laid the foundations of the parrot-like knowledge that is such a strong characteristic of the boys and girls turned out by our primary schools. Children cannot be interested and cannot learn unless they understand what they are doing and what is being said to them.

It is in the kindergarten that the acquisition of a language is most easy, and Government has therefore determined that the vernacular shall be used to lay a thorough foundation for English in all infant schools, and that its use shall be continued to the utmost extent possible and practicable during the whole of primary education.

The adoption of this principle will necessitate all Europeans employed in education speaking the vernacular. More than that, without this knowledge of the local language a European cannot get an insight into the mind of the teachers and their pupils, a most important consideration in view of the fact that the African and European have different lines of thought and methods of expressing themselves. Experience has shown that a knowledge of the vernacular unconsciously produces a change in the psychology of the European himself which gives him a far better understanding of the African with whom he is dealing and obtains from him greater confidence and affection.

Government therefore insists that all Europeans whom we are employing in our educational system shall learn the vernacular. In adopting this course we shall encounter serious difficulties, for I believe that I am correct in saying that there are no less than nine different vernaculars in this country. We shall have to adopt the expedient of selecting, with the advice of the Board of Education, the two or three languages which cover the largest ground.

Thirteenth principle – education cannot be compulsory nor free

128. The adoption of compulsory education in this country at the present time is manifestly impossible. Many years must elapse before we have sufficient teachers and sufficient funds for building purposes. Compulsory education may come in due course, but the time is so unripe as to make any further discussion of the subject useless.

Nor can education be free of charge. To have free without compulsory education would lead to such invidious distinctions as to render impossible the satisfactory administration of any system that could be devised. The question of school revenue must also be considered: what Government itself receives is small enough to have very little effect, but we could not afford to do without it, far less to increase our schools without it; while as for the missions, the revenue they receive from fees is an essential factor in the existence of most of their schools.

Generally speaking, we can adopt the principle of low charges during primary education and of higher fees for secondary and more advanced education. From certain remarks which I have read in the local press it appears that in some quarters the view is held that the Government's secondary schools should practically be free of charge. That is quite impossible. We intend to charge as low fees as possible, but both now and for many years to come those desirous of secondary or higher education will have to pay for it. The scale of fees at Achimota has not yet been decided on. They will at least cover the cost of the students' maintenance; and even if they go further and include instructional fees, as in my opinion they certainly should, they will be less than a third of the expenses now borne by a family sending a boy or girl to school in Europe to get an education which is in no way superior to that which will be provided locally...

Fourteenth principle – there should be cooperation between the Government and the missions, and the latter should be subsidised for educational purposes

130. This is not a new principle in the Gold Coast. For many years we have made grants for education to, and cooperated with, the larger and more important missions. It is a tribute to Mr Oman, the Rev. A. W. Wilkie, and the Rev. H. Webster that cooperation has increased so much during the post-war period that the Government and these missions are now working in perfect harmony.

I have noticed from time to time both in this Council and out of it that there has been some tendency to underrate the value of the educational effort of the missions in this country. A moment's consideration will show that this is an entirely mistaken view to take. It probably arose from a really bad educational fault that was common among nearly all missions in the past, namely their starting schools far in excess of the number of properly qualified teachers available, the outcome of their very natural desire to extend the benefits of Christianity to as many people as possible. To begin with, the result was not serious as far as education was concerned. As time passed, however, the demand for education steadily increased and parents hastened to send their children to the nearest available school. With missions of several denominations in the field the result can be imagined; if a mission could obtain boys and girls for religious teaching of its denominational nature by starting a school it naturally did so. For several years in this and other countries a serious competition arose between the missions of the various denominations to increase their schools. They did great work for

Christianity, but not for education, because they tried to do too much with inefficient tools. We are feeling the effects of this today . . .

Fifteenth principle – the Government must have the ultimate control of education throughout the Gold Coast

131. By 'ultimate control' is not meant the control of details but the control necessary to ensure that school buildings are healthy, that properly qualified teachers are employed, and that a fixed and common standard of primary education is maintained throughout the country. At the present moment there is no controlling body of education in this country; as in all cases of divided control, the results have been bad. There is no single person in this country who can claim justly that our system of education is either efficient or goes far enough. Parents and families are making sacrifices for their children in the blind hope that they are benefiting them; in reality, as I have pointed out, they are in many cases seriously harming them.

This state of affairs will continue until there is one controlling hand on education in this country. In our present state of development, material and intellectual, the hand can only be that of Government. It is the Government which is responsible for providing the country with a sound system of education: that responsibility cannot be transferred to any other body, however much or however advantageous it may be to entrust the execution of details to others. Indeed, we consider that it is better to devolve the actual work of education. For one thing, religion is an important detail in education and can be better imparted in Mission schools. Also we have no desire to discourage experiments, which we should undoubtedly do if we do not devolve some of the work of education to Missions and private enterprise. Experiments should be welcomed so long as thoroughness and efficiency is maintained in education. By retaining the ultimate control of education Government could help financially deserving experiments while it could put a stop to those which appear dangerous to the children . . .

Full discussion of principles

132. In laying down the fifteen principles with which I have just dealt we have made a great step forward, such a step, I venture to think, as has not been surpassed by any African country. We now have a definite line to guide us from the kindergarten to the university. Government is going to adopt these principles in no autocratic manner, for the steps necessary to carry them out will be fully discussed by the Board of Education. In due course the amendments required in our Education Ordinance will come before this Council, before which, as some will be of a far-reaching nature, ample opportunity will be given for their consideration by Honourable Members.

Growing cost of education

133. And what about the cost entailed by our principles of education? I have consistently warned Honourable Members that if we are to have an efficient system in this country we must expect to have to pay far more than we have done in the past. Two years ago I warned them that it might eventually reach £500,000 per annum; last year I likened our growing expenditure on education to a snowball that was constantly increasing in size as it rolled along, and one Honourable Member warned me that it might grow into an avalanche. Well, we do not want

an avalanche of a financial nature to overwhelm this country, so I took the Honourable Member's caution to heart and have done my best during the past year to work out what I think education will ultimately cost this country.

Expenditure on buildings

Expenditure on education can be classified under two heads, the first of which is the construction and equipment of new schools, and adding to existing ones. I make out roughly that, including the expenditure already made on Achimota, we shall have to spend about £400,000 on buildings and equipment during the next five years. This sum can comfortably be provided out of surplus revenue. Should that be exhausted by 1930, any additions thereafter can be provided under Extraordinary Expenditure. The buildings therefore are comfortably within our reach.

Annual cost

With regard to the Recurrent Expenditure, I make out roughly that this will increase steadily from £123,000 (Education Department, plus Achimota, less Extraordinary Expenditure) which Honourable Members are being asked to vote for 1925–6, to close on £400,000 in 1935. However much this may alarm some Honourable Members it does not cause me any particular anxiety, for I am confident that by that time we shall be in possession of a revenue of four million pounds per annum, even if we reduce certain Customs duties. My belief is based on the fact that by 1930 we shall have completed those harbours, railways and roads that will increase trade to such an extent as to bring in a revenue of four million pounds.

Ability to meet cost

Whatever criticism any Honourable Member may make of the principles of education adopted by Government – a criticism, I may add, that will receive full consideration – I do not believe that there is a single member of this Council that will grudge Government's expenditure of one-tenth of its revenue on education, or, if we can afford it, to increase that proportion to one-eighth. Government's critics will, no doubt, point out the fact that our annual expenditure in connection with other Departments has grown and makes a great demand on the revenue. That is true but on the other hand, certain of the technical Departments will begin to decrease, first, when the new scale has reached its full height, and secondly, when Africans are sufficiently educated and trained under our new system to replace Europeans.

No reduction in education

In the meantime, should we encounter a lean year, or should any anticipation of a revenue of four million pounds prove over-optimistic, I consider that Government's firm policy should be, first of all, to decrease Extraordinary Expenditure to some £150,000 per annum ; and if further reductions are needed, to effect them in any other Department but that of education. These reductions can quite easily be effected ; naturally there will be a certain loss of efficiency ; but so long as this loss of efficiency is not in education no serious and permanent ill-effects can ensue.

Good work of Education Department

134. In concluding my remarks on education, I desire to bring to the notice of Council the strenuous and good work of the Director of Education and his staff of Inspectors during the past five years. Mr Oman has, throughout, taken a leading part in the task of considering the reforms necessary, while his staff have been shorthanded and overworked. The interim period between the old and new systems of education is naturally a very trying time for those charged with the administration of education. This period is not yet at an end, but the staff of the Education Department should be encouraged by the additions which we are making to their number and by the thought that the next few years will see the remedies applied to those defects in our existing system of which they themselves are only too keenly aware. When the new system comes into force their work should be both lightened and more satisfactory.

38. Rapid expansion of primary education at the expense of secondary education may do incalculable harm both to the structure of the educational system and to the economy of the country as a whole, 1948 [1]

358. Nothing impressed us more than the interest of the peoples of the Gold Coast in education. Practically every African, who sent in a memorandum or appeared in person before us sooner or later started to discuss education. This interest, in our opinion, is as deep-rooted as it is widespread. It does not spring solely from any mercenary assessment of material benefits but from some genuine desire for learning itself.

359. The initial impetus was provided by the missions and missionary schools. The seeds which they have sown have produced a crop that must have far exceeded their expectations – a crop which is not without its embarrassments for those who have to meet today's demands.

360. The following figures give the approximate numbers of children in primary and secondary schools last year [Table 38.1].

Table 38.1

	No. of schools	Enrolment
Primary		
Government and Government-assisted schools	578	87,531
Approved senior primary	157	13,661
Non-assisted (including 'designated')	2,018	97,219
Secondary		
Assisted	10	2,209
Non-assisted	18	1,851

Though the enrolment represents only about 4½ per cent of the population, it indicates a very rapid rate of increase. Between 1926 and 1946 the numbers in the

[1] *Report of the Commission of enquiry into disturbances in the Gold Coast, 1948*, Colonial Office, London 1948, paras 358–80 (extracts).

Government and Government-assisted schools rose from 33,000 to 90,000 while the numbers in the non-assisted schools had risen from 25,000 to 99,000.

361. Primary education normally commences at the age of about six and consists of three stages, covering ten years, though the majority of pupils at present pass through only the first two stages: Infant primary (classes 1–3), junior primary (standards I–III), senior primary (standards IV–VII). Secondary education covers about four years. Of the ten assisted schools, five are for boys, four for girls, and one (at Achimota) is co-educational.

362. There is one Government technical school.

363. The non-assisted schools which are often assisted by Native Administrations are, unfortunately, not comparable with the Government and assisted schools. They are often ill-housed, ill-equipped and staffed by untrained teachers. Their existence and their very rapid expansion, however, does give a very clear indication of the unsatisfied demand for education.

364. In addition to the schools, there are post-primary teaching colleges, designed to turn out two categories of teachers, those with Certificate A and those with Certificate B, the former is obtained after passing a four-year post-primary or two-year post-secondary course, while the latter is obtained after a two-year post-primary course. The Certificate A courses are given at two co-educational institutions, and at seven assisted mission or church institutions. The Certificate B course which qualifies holders for work in infant and junior schools only is given in eight institutions. The total enrolment at the end of 1947 was 1,266, an increase of almost 300 over 1946 and more than 900 above the pre-war figures. There are also specialist courses for trained teachers in domestic science and in arts and crafts at Achimota.

365. Educational courses are also provided by the Departments of Agriculture, Survey, Forestry, Police, Posts and Telegraphs and so on, for their employees.

366. Finally, the higher education facilities in the Gold Coast consist of Intermediate Courses in engineering, science, arts and commerce centred at Achimota, with an enrolment of about 100. There are also said to be some 200 Gold Coast students in the United Kingdom. In October 1948, the University College at Achimota will start its work, completing the educational ladder in the Gold Coast to a university degree level.

367. We think that it would be useful at this stage to give an indication of what recent developments have meant in terms of money. In 1938–9 the Government expenditure on education was about £213,000. The following figures show the actual expenditure in 1946–7 and estimates for 1947–8:

	1946–7	*1947–8 estimates*
Government 'ordinary' expenditure	£467,000	£835,000
Government 'development' expenditure	£223,000	£320,000
Native Administration (approx.)	£130,000	£200,000

368. These expenditures show a very large increase over the pre-war years and it is important to relate them to the revenues of the country [Table 38.2]. In 1938–9, the amount spent by the Government on education represented 5.7 per cent of its revenue; the estimates for 1947–8 show that the proportion had risen to so high as 11.3 per cent. The Native Authorities' proportions are higher as might be expected, but show a similar increase. The burden of education on both

Table 38.2

	Gold Coast Government's revenues (including extraordinary and development revenues)	Native authorities' revenues
1938–9	£3,780,000	—
1946–7	£7,568,000	£778,000
1947–8	£10,236,000	£945,000

national and local revenues is already about twice as great as in the United Kingdom.

369. It is, in our opinion, important to bear in mind these facts when considering the criticisms of the educational system which were brought before us. Our impression is one of almost mushroom growth, which has been even more stimulated in the post-war years [putting pressure on the] finances of the country and on the administrative staff of the Education Department, neither of which has increased in proportion to the development in education.

370. The complaints can be grouped into four main headings: (*a*) educational facilities are too few and the rate of increase is too slow; (*b*) the development has been ill-balanced; (*c*) the curricula are not adapted to the needs of the country; (*d*) the method of teaching is not as effective as it might be.

371. It is, of course, true that the educational facilities are inadequate in relation to the number of children to be educated and we are told that the full development of universal primary education would take at least twenty years to achieve if finance and other factors are taken into consideration. This, however, appears to us to represent a minimum time, since at the end of only ten years there are expected to be at least 750,000 children of primary school age (450,000 children of infant-junior age and some 300,000 of senior primary age). It took twenty years for the school population to double itself between 1906 and 1926, and another twenty years almost to treble itself between 1926 and 1946. Can it more than quadruple itself in the next twenty years and yet maintain even the present standards? Do the trends in national wealth and public revenue and the economic prospects of the country warrant such optimism? We feel that it would be more realistic, so far as primary education is concerned, to base plans for the future on a longer period than twenty years. The pushing ahead of too ambitious schemes for the rapid expansion of primary education at the expense of secondary and higher education may do incalculable harm both to the structure of the whole educational system and to the economy of the country as a whole.

372. At present only a small proportion of the boys and girls who enter school at six years pass into the senior primary school from standard III, at twelve years of age. In comparison with the 200,000 children at primary schools there are only some 4,000 places at secondary schools. We think, therefore, that the need for an increase in the number of secondary schools and for the provision of part-time education for those who cannot find places in senior primary or secondary schools should have the highest priority in the extension of educational facilities.

373. We fully appreciate the pressure that has emanated from the indigenous desire for mass literacy; but if the peoples of the Gold Coast wish to achieve a progressively greater measure of self-government within a reasonably short time and if they wish to model its economic organisation on those of the more indus-

trialised and commercialised countries in the world, it will be achieved only by a soundly balanced system of education. If the material is limited, the alternatives are to build a narrower ladder that, while tapering, reaches the objective, or to build so broad a ladder that it fails to reach anywhere. The former seems to us to be the only possible alternative.

374. Turning now to the criticism that the curricula are not adapted to the needs of the country, the general complaint appears to be that the education provided in the schools actively discourages pupils from turning to trades and crafts. It is possibly true that in the past there was a tendency on the part of Africans to decry technical or craft training but certainly this tendency has disappeared; there was everywhere a demand for education of the hand as well as the head. It is realised that literary education alone is doing great harm in the Gold Coast. It is creating a gulf between town and country. It is producing a youthful hooligan element in the towns as boys emerge from school to find a glut of clerks and to find themselves disinterested in, or not equipped for, other occupations. It is creating a false sense of values in which the dignity of labour is lost sight of. There must be an immediate expansion of craft, technical and vocational training throughout the entire structure.

375. The method of education also came in for criticism. It is said that there is an almost complete absence of questions and answers or exercises which involve deduction from, and application of, principles learned. There is an undue reliance on memorisation. We ourselves observed among the younger people a tendency to repetition and lack of critical thought. This is a menace to the pupils themselves as well as to the community, for a literate man so educated is susceptible to propaganda and rumour of the crudest absurdity.

376. It was alleged that in the Department of Education there was an excessive centralisation and a lack of contact or understanding between those administering and those teaching. We are satisfied that, if these exist, only understaffing and pressure of work account for them.

377. Bearing in mind all the difficulties which we have indicated, we suggest certain practical modifications and alterations in the present system which we think would meet some of the valid criticisms. We recommend:

(i) That greater emphasis should be placed on senior primary and secondary education, and that the present educational policy should be reconsidered urgently with a view to continuing to a higher level the education of a greater number than at present. We think that this will bring better results to the Gold Coast in the long run.

(ii) That the standard VII year at the senior primary school might well be abandoned entirely. We were advised on several occasions that this would not entail any decrease in efficiency but would be a positive improvement. Much of the work in this year is mechanical revision for the purposes of a Primary School Leaving Certificate which could, with advantage, be taken in standard VI if its form was altered somewhat. In addition the elimination of this wasted year would release some some 200 trained and certificated teachers.

(iii) That the teachers released by this modification and the 300 which are expected to be turned out annually from the teacher training colleges should be used for the following purposes:

(*a*) To increase the numbers of secondary schools and senior primary schools.

(*b*) To train pupil-teachers. The pupil-teacher system is a well-tried expedient, but it is efficient only if the best trained teachers can supervise this work.

(*c*) To organise continuation classes for the majority of children who leave school at twelve years after standard III. The tragedy of the present system is the large number of children who are turned out of school at this age with a mere smattering of unrelated knowledge and unprepared for the environment into which they come to live.

(*d*) To improve the teaching in the 2,000 non-assisted infant-junior primary schools of which 760 have been ' designated ' as ripe for improvement.

(iv) That measures should also be taken to increase the amount of technical and vocational training in schools. A class of politicians, administrators and clerks on the one hand and a large population of labourers and semi-skilled operatives on the other are not sufficient to produce a highly developed country. Industrial, agricultural and commercial efficiency and progress are dependent on an extensive skilled class who can work with their hands and their brains. In addition to craft and technical training in schools, trade centres and technical schools or institutes will be required for further education. We believe that the insistent demand from Africans for such facilities are an indication that the false value placed on a clerical ' clean-hand ' job will be more easily dissipated than many people believe.

(*a*) In infant-junior schools. At present time is allotted in infant-junior schools for handiwork but we are informed that this is not used seriously or to full advantage. Too frequently work of this nature is regarded as being so unimportant as to be completely neglected. We should like to see the establishment of school gardens, a most successful development in many other countries, taken up seriously and energetically.

(*b*) In continuation classes. The continuation courses which we have recommended above should be associated with a parallel vocational training in an apprenticeship system outside school. We suggest that on two or three afternoons or evenings per week, such pupils should attend school for a continuation of their education in arithmetic, English and, say general knowledge. Such pupils should be permitted to take examinations open to pupils who have remained at school and, more particularly, the examinations or tests leading to trade and technical schools. Part-time paid teachers such as local literates and community leaders should be employed to supplement the fully trained teachers.

The system of apprenticeship should be sponsored and regularised by the Department for those attending the continuation classes mentioned previously. Carpenters, masons, blacksmiths, fishermen, painters, printers, weavers, and many other tradesmen and craftsmen should be encouraged to accept apprentices. We are aware of many apparent difficulties in organising this work but we are imbued with a deep sense of the urgency of this problem. Much help might be obtained from the technical branches and persons employed by the various Departments, Education, Agriculture, Forestry, Public Works and so on, workshop managers, commercial firms and from the tradesmen and craftsmen throughout the country. The Army, with its various trades and workshops, could also help. This is a national problem calling for attention. 'The devil finds work for idle hands to do ' is no platitude in the Gold Coast.

The establishment of such a system would involve:

(1) The acceleration of the opening of the three or four technical institutes proposed in the Ten-year Development Plan.

(2) The accordance of the highest priority to the provision of accommodation, equipment and materials for use in instruction.

(3) The recruitment of further trained staff from outside the Gold Coast.

(4) The assistance of the Labour and other Departments, in surveying the field of unemployment and the demand for different types of labour and in enlisting the interest and cooperation of employers.

(*c*) In senior primary schools. Vigorous efforts should be made to introduce one or more trade or craft teacher into every senior primary school, for too long the only work deemed suitable for such schools has been carpentry and for too long the idea has prevailed that teachers of this work should have a special training. This is no doubt desirable but the need is too great at present to worry about such refinements. Use should be made of skilled tradesmen and craftsmen, even if they are illiterate. The problem of increasing the number of trained technical teachers should be tackled with as much energy as has the training of non-technical teachers.

(v) That the content of education in the schools should be reconsidered. In our opinion it is at present too ' bookish ' and the books on which it is based have, for the most part, been written for use in countries very different from the Gold Coast. In particular, the subjects of geography, history, nature study, and civics, which are taught academically even in junior primary schools, should be reduced in favour of a body of general knowledge, taught in relation to the child's environment. Similarly the teaching of basic subjects such as arithmetic, reading and writing must be more closely related to the child's surroundings and to the practical work which we wish to see in every school. There is a great need for schemes of work and for special textbooks, suited to West African conditions, written by educationists experienced in the schools of the country.

378. With regard to further education we think that the potentialities of continuation courses should be further examined. Some witnesses said that there was no demand for such facilities; others stated that the demand would arise if the facilities were present. We consider that the time is ripe for experiments in mass education, possibly in two urban and two rural areas as a start. We feel that in this direction may lie a more rapid and more effective attainment of the goal than through the present policy. Each mass education unit would be given the task of carrying out a well-defined project designed to improve the life of the community and the general conception of citizenship. Their programme of work would include not only the development of, say, social services but also of recreational activities. Literacy would be included in the target. Each unit would require a trained mass education officer to plan and coordinate the work, to train the personnel in techniques and to supervise their work. In addition specialists in the subjects included in the projects chosen for the area in which the team is working would be required.

379. In concluding our observations on education, two matters, we feel, call for special mention. We do not think that the pioneer work of the Churches and Missions has been mainly responsible for inculcating the desire for education; they have made possible the rapid development to the present stage. The process now envisaged must affect to some extent the autonomy of their schools and

teacher-training colleges; it may not be easy for many to limit denominational interest in favour of purely educational aims or to accept an intrusion of technical and vocational training into a more literary curriculum. But, from the views that were expressed to us by various leaders, we are hopeful that these difficulties will be bridged and that the cooperation of the missions will continue as successfully as in the past.

380. Our second comment refers to the disorders and strikes that occurred in some schools and in Achimota during the recent disturbances. A number of more thoughtful Africans were whole-hearted in their condemnation of this action by pupils and students, but we were not convinced that the dangers of such occurrences are sufficiently widely appreciated. We have seen similar situations arise in other countries – initially, perhaps, as the result of some trivial, non-academic grievance. But such actions are insidious; before long, the strike becomes a common occurrence and academic standards are affected. We have known strikes of students because they objected to the subjects contained in the degree course, or because the examinations were considered too difficult, or even because the examiners have 'failed' a popular student. These may, at present, seem foolish and inexcusable to the students of the Gold Coast and they may aver that they could never happen there. But the virus is an infectious one and spreads rapidly. Education is still a privilege for the few and the time available to the average students is woefully short in relation to what there is to learn. Time wasted can never be regained and the intrusion of politics into schools and colleges must inevitably affect standards of both teaching and learning. It is because we wish to see the new University College hold its own among the universities of the world and to see its teachers and its students freely interchanging with those from other institutions that we are prompted to give this word of advice. We have evidence that trouble among the students and schoolchildren was stirred up for political ends. We condemn unreservedly the unscrupulous selfishness of those who caused this trouble while we suggest to students that, however strongly they may feel on any issue, they should resist the temptation to take such action as must interfere with and eventually degrade academic standards.

Bibliography

36. *Report by the Honourable W. G. A. Ormsby-Gore on his visit to West Africa during the year 1926*, Cmd 2744, London 1926, pp. 84–7 (extracts).

37. Governor's Annual Address, *Legislative Council Debates, 1925–6*, pp. 59–104 (extracts).

38. *Report of the Commission of Enquiry into Disturbances in the Gold Coast, 1948*, Colonial Office, London 1948, paras 358–80 (extracts).

Part 3

Statistical Abstract

in conjunction with Stephen Hymer

There are cases in the following tables where the totals do not add up exactly. This is generally due to the fact that extensive rounding has taken place. In addition many of the entries in these tables are themselves the sums of a considerable number of figures so that given the sheer volume of the calculations involved, in conjunction with the scope and nature of the material, it has not appeared worth our while to eradicate small discrepancies.

Throughout the tables '—' equals 'not applicable' and '..' equals 'not available'.

Statistical Abstract: Introductory Note

Three considerations have governed the collection and presentation of these statistical tables.

1. The desire to follow as closely as possible the original sources in the mode of presentation, as the way a government presents its figures, is an important indicator of what it thinks significant. Modifications of a quite extensive nature have been made in two areas: trade and government finance. In the first this was necessary because the colonial government did not aggregate trade into commodity groups, which meant particularly in the case of imports a number of different categories far too large to be presented here. Reclassification of the government's public accounts was necessary due to the peculiarities of the colonial accounting system. Wherever the data presented here have in some way been processed so that they differ from how they were originally published by the colonial government full details are presented. Thus for instance there is included in the relevant section an account of the colonial system of public accounting.

2. We have attempted insofar as it has been possible and consistent with 1. above to present tables in such a way that they link with the *Statistical Abstracts* and other sources published in the 1960s.

3. We have borne in mind that the statistics might prove of interest to economists and others whose main interest is not in Ghana as such but in the statistical analysis of the process of economic change. This has affected the way in which certain tables have been presented. For instance we have presented a résumé of the five development plans launched at one time or another in the country despite the fact that the last fell outside our period altogether and was discontinued long before its allotted time. We have also calculated wage indices from the data that were available although this was something not attempted by the colonial authorities and the data we used for this purpose were far from ideal.

It is quite clear that these different aims often contradict each other and we have been well aware of this. Often the difficulties have presented themselves in the form of deciding how extensive a table should be, how many different categories should be presented and whether the figures should be presented on an annual basis. These issues have mostly been resolved on an ad hoc basis and no doubt there will be more details here than interest some and too little for others. Where possible we have presented tables on an annual basis: back-up tables which give a detailed breakdown of material presented on an annual basis we have presented on the basis of five year averages. Where it has proved impossible to get data for series which ideally we would have wished to present on an annual basis we have chosen selected years. Where necessary we have made interpolations but have limited this practice to the minimum essential.

The printed table is a curious phenomenon: it carries all the appearance of authority and accuracy and yet is an object of considerable mistrust. The question arises, how accurate are these statistics?—and it is virtually unanswerable as we have no way of checking them independently. In part accuracy is not absolute but dependent upon the uses to which the material is to be put and this material gives a perfectly adequate picture of the colonial economy, the relative magnitudes of trade, of government expenditure and revenue, of transport and communications and education, and of wages and how these changed during the period 1900 to 1960. Whether it is sufficiently accurate to form the raw material of elegant econometric models is another question: nothing we will say here will in any case prevent the wilful econometrician from pursuing his inspiration. A word or two, however, on the general validity of the data is in order. A first glance at the titles of the tables and sections indicates the limited range of their coverage. With one or two very limited exceptions, all the data presented here have been gathered from official publications and so are restricted by the range of the colonial government's statistical gathering. For instance, the data on foreign trade are almost certainly an accurate record of what passed in and out of the country through the chief seaports but are probably hopelessly inaccurate concerning overland trade with surrounding countries. In addition where this trade did pass through official frontier posts the accuracy of the records is also subject to question as it is likely that the frontier official did not literally distinguish between sheep and goats to take but one example. How important this is in quantifiable terms it is almost impossible to say. Probably with respect to imports our categories are so highly aggregated for it to make no substantial difference with respect to the pattern of trade, but even this vague degree of assurance with respect to the quantity of trade is probably too much, particularly for the early part of our period. Suffice it to say that the sea-borne trade ultimately proved decisive in the development of the economy and the data presented here are a reasonably accurate record of it. Another section where the accuracy of the data must be called into question is that which covers population. Table 1 which shows the different estimates of population, differing in some instances by as much as 30 per cent for total population, show the type of inaccuracies that these data are heir to. Data on such things as government finance, data, that is, on the activities of the colonial government or activities that came under direct colonial supervision such as rail transport and postal communications, are not subject to this type of error and are in all probability accurate to a fault.

Next it is worth noting the omissions, of which the most important is the absence of data on agricultural production. Of this the colonial government had very little idea and in fact, as noted in the discussion of colonial agricultural policy above,[1] official ignorance played an important part in the formulation of decisions. On the whole these statistics are a record of the activities of the colonial government itself and of those economic activities in which it was perforce involved. The justification for presenting them is not that they reveal a complete picture of the economy of Ghana during the period 1900 to 1960, but that they present a reasonably accurate picture of a part of it whose importance need not be argued.

SOURCES

The main sources for the statistics presented in this part are official publications of the colonial government of the Gold Coast. The most important are the annual *Blue Book* of the Colony; the annual reports of the administrative departments – Customs, Education, Medical, Mines, Police, Prisons, Posts and Telegraphs, Public Works, Railways and Harbours; plus Colonial, Trade, and Municipal reports all published annually. The data on demography were taken from the censuses conducted in 1891, 1901, 1911, 1921, 1931, 1948 and 1960, supplemented by R. R. Kuczynski, *A demographic survey of the British Colonial Empire*, Oxford University Press for the Royal Institute of International Affairs, 1948. For the period after independence in 1957 data were taken from the main statistical publications of the Government of Ghana: *Economic Surveys* published annually and the *Statistical Yearbooks*, 1961 and 1962. A wide range of material is presented in W. A. Cardinal, *The Gold Coast, 1931*, Government Printer, Accra 1932. Secondary sources include S. La Anyane, *Ghana Agriculture*, Oxford University Press, Accra and London 1963; and R. Furse, *Aucuparius, recollections of a recruiting officer*, Oxford University Press, London 1962. Details of sources are given for each table.

[1] See p. 12 above.

7. Population

Table 1. Population of Ghana by region, 1891–1960 (census years) (000s)

Year	Total	Colony	Ashanti	Northern Terr.	Togoland included as follows: Colony	N. Terr.
1891	—	765	—	—	—	—
1901	1,894	1,095	364	435	67	77
	(1,550)	(896)	(346)	(308)		
1911	2,104	1,227	346	531	77	89
	(1,504)	(854)	(288)	(362)		
1921	2,538	1,396	448	694	96	111
	(2,298)	(1,283)	(407)	(606)	(87)	(101)
1931	3,160	1,715	585	861	126	168
1948	4,876	2,637	962	1,277	208	250
	(4,118)	(2,246)	(826)	(1,039)	(173)	(210)
1960	6,727	3,741	1,697	1,289	..	..

NOTES

Original data (those in parentheses where different from final figures) are taken from *Statistical Yearbook, 1962*. ' Colony ' includes the Western, Central, Accra, Eastern and Volta regions. ' Ashanti ' includes Ashanti and Brong-Ahafo. ' Northern Territory ' includes the Northern and Upper regions.

Togoland was divided, part given to the Northern Territory, part given to the Colony. The original figures for Togoland (those in parentheses where different) are taken from the *Census of Population, 1948*, Tables 2, 3 for years 1921, 1931 and 1948. Figures for years 1901 and 1911 are estimated by projecting backward the growth rate of Togoland from 1921–48.

The original data were corrected following Kuczynski's estimate of Ghana's population (see Kuczynski, *Demographic Survey*). The corrections were as follows:

a. 1901: Kuczynski estimates the total (not including Togoland) at not less than 1,750,000 (see p. 419). The figures for each region have been increased in the same proportion as Kuczynski's estimate. The projected figure for Togoland is then added to give a total of 1,894,000.

b. 1911: Kuczynski (p. 413) estimates the colony at 1,150,000 (excluding Togoland). Ashanti is increased in this same proportion. Kuczynski also adds 80,000 to Northern Territories because females were undercounted (pp. 398–9). The projected figures for Togoland are then added to the Northern Territory and to the Colony in order to bring the total to 2,104,000.

c. 1921: Kuczynski sets the colony figure at 1,300,000. All other regions including Togoland are therefore increased proportionately.

Regional figures and the total for the year 1948 are increased proportionately to bring the total population in line with the revealed rate of growth between 1931 and 1960. This increases regional figures by 0.18%.

Table 2. Population growth rates* (in percentage/years)

Years	Total	Colony	Ashanti	Northern Terr.	Togoland Colony	Togoland N. Terr.
1901–11	1.1	1.2	- 0.5	2.2	1.5	1.5
1911–21	2.1	1.4	2.9	3.1	2.5	2.5
1921–31	2.4	2.3	3.0	2.4	2.1	5.1
1931–48	3.2	3.1	3.8	2.8	3.8	2.9
1948–60	3.1	3.5	6.4	0.1	—	—
1901–60	2.4	2.3	3.1	2.1	—	—

NOTES

* Simple growth rate obtained by dividing growth rate for period by number of years.

This table indicates a steady increase in the rate of growth, in part due to improvement in the efficiency of census technique. The most reliable conclusions that can be drawn from the data are:

1. Present population growth rate is 2.5% or better.
2. The rate of growth was much lower, probably close to zero, around 1900. The original census estimates show an increase of 134,000 in the Colony between 1891 and 1901, which could easily be accounted for by the increased census accuracy.
3. It is not possible to date exactly when between 1900 and 1930 the change to more rapid growth rates occurred.
4. There is little significant difference between regions. Notable exceptions are:
   a. The very high (6.4%) average annual growth rate in Ashanti between 1948 and 1960.
   b. The very low (0.1%) average annual growth rate in the Northern Territory, also in 1948–60.

Table 3a. Percentage of population under 15 by region, 1921–60 (census years)

Year	Total	Colony	Ashanti	N. Terr.	Togoland
1921	—	39.8	37.0	—	—
1931	39.7	38.7	40.1	40.5	42.2
1948	39.3	38.0	39.7	43.7	36.7
1960	44.5	44.6	46.0	42.8	—

NOTES

Sources: 1921, *Census Report, 1921*; 1931, Kuczynski, *Demographic Survey*, p. 435 (see Table 1 above); 1948, *Census of Population, 1948*, Report and Tables 6 and 11; see also Table 1 above; 1960, *Population Census, 1960*.

Table 3b. Age distribution of population, 1948 and 1960 (percentage)

Age	1948	1960
Under 15	39.3	44.5
15–24		16.8
	43.3*	
25–44		26.2
45–64		9.3
	13.7*	
65 and over		3.2

NOTES

* Note that the 1948 categories consisted of 0–15, 16–45, 45 and over. For this reason the combined figure * is not correct.

Figures for 1948 are taken from *Census of Population, 1948*. 1960 data are taken from *Statistical Yearbook, 1962*.

Table 4. Foreign Africans in Ghana, by origin, 1921–60 (census years) (000s)

Country	1921	1931	1948	1960
Dahomey	..	..	..	31.6
Ivory Coast	..	..	..	54.4
Liberia	12.6	6.8	..	8.7
Mali	..	—	..	19.4
Niger	..	—	..	24.9
Nigeria	21.2	67.7	..	190.8
Togo	..	—	..	280.6
Upper Volta	..	—	..	194.6
Other West African	14.5	199.1	..	6.0
Other African	..	15.6	..	0.7
Total	48.6	289.2	174.1*	811.7

NOTES

* A partial explanation of why the 1948 total is lower than 1931 is a difference in enumeration technique: 1931 figures were based on country of origin (the child of foreign nationals who was born in Ghana was still considered a foreigner); in 1948 foreigners were defined as born outside of Ghana.

Source: *Statistical Yearbook, 1962*.

Table 5a. European population in Ghana by nationality, 1921–60 (census years)

Nationality	1921	1931	1948	1960
British	1,609	1,825	4,211	7,420
French	79	153	180	..
German	2	76	8	..
Italian	59	103	14	4,500
Swiss	80	141	221	..
Other	54	87	392	..
Total	1,883	2,385	5,026	11,920

Table 5b. European population in Ghana by region, 1921–60 (census years)

Year	Colony	Ashanti	Northern Terr.	Togoland	Total
1921	..	..	..	..	1,883
1931	1,819	425	98	43	2,385
1948	4,078	757	191	..	5,026
1960	5,990	1,200	230	..	7,420

NOTES

Togoland is incorporated in Colony and Ashanti figures in the 1948 and 1960 data.

1921 and 1931 figures from Kuczynski, *Demographic Survey*, pp. 441–2.

1948 figures from *Census of Population, 1948*.

1960 figures from *Population Census, 1960* and *Statistical Yearbook, 1962*. For 1960, British-only figures are given; further breakdown is not available.

Table 6a. Population by origin and place of enumeration, 1931 (000s)

Place of birth	Area of enumeration: Colony	Ashanti	Northern Terr.	Togoland	Total
Colony	1,415.9	20.3	1.1	4.9	1,442.2
Ashanti	15.4	471.5	1.7	0.3	488.9
Northern Terr.	19.7	22.7	628.8	1.6	672.8
Togoland=Volta	11.2	1.2	—	253.1	265.5
Other Africans	125.0	68.8	61.3	34.1	289.2
Others (Europeans)	1.8	0.5	0.1	—	2.4
Total	1,589.0	585.0	693.0	294.0	3,161.0

NOTES

Source: Cardinal, *The Gold Coast*, p. 55. See also Table 1 above and Table 8 below.

Table 6b. Population by region of birth and region of enumeration, 1960 (000s – percentiles of population remaining and migrating by region, in parentheses)

Place of birth	Region of enumeration			
	Colony*	Ashanti†	Northern Terr.	Total born in region
Colony	3,263.8	152.2	20.0	3,436.0
	(95.0)	(4.4)	(0.6)	(100.0)
Ashanti	92.6	1,285.1	12.0	1,389.7
	(6.7)	(92.5)	(0.8)	(100.0)
Northern Terr.	82.8	106.3	1,183.1	1,372.2
	(6.0)	(7.7)	(86.3)	(100.0)

NOTES

* Colony=Western+Accra+Eastern+Volta.

† Ashanti=Ashanti+Brong Ahafa.

Source: *Population Census, 1960*, Table 13.

Table 7. Persons living in urban areas – by size of town, 1921–60 (census years) (000s – figures in parentheses are percentage)

Year	Under 5,000		5–10,000		10,000 and over	
1921	2,411.1*	(95.0)	47.2	(1.9)	79.7	(3.1)
1931	2,864.8*	(90.7)	192.6	(4.1)	165.6	(5.2)
1948	4,436.3*	(91.0)	133.4	(2.7)	306.3	(6.3)
1960	5,175.9*	(76.9)	406.6	(6.6)	1,114.5	(17.1)

NOTES

* Figures for towns under 5,000 calculated by subtracting figures over 5,000 from total given in Table 1 above.

Sources: 1921 and 1931 data for towns of over 5,000 are from Cardinal, *The Gold Coast*, pp. 158–9. 1948 data are from *Census of Population, 1948*, Table 8. 1960 figures are from *Statistical Yearbook, 1962*.

Table 8. Population of main towns 1921–60 (census years) (various years – 000s)

Town	1921	1931	1948	1960
Towns over 10,000 population in 1960				
Accra	41.1	60.7	133.2	337.8
Kumasi	23.7	35.8	58.6	180.6
Cape Coast	14.9	17.7	23.2	41.2
Takoradi	—	—	17.3	40.9
Tamale	3.9	12.9	16.1	40.4
Koforidua	5.4	10.5	17.7	34.9
Sekondi	9.5	16.9	26.4	34.5
Winneba	7.0	10.9	15.1	25.4
Obuan	3.9	7.6	15.7	22.8
Nsawam	6.1	8.9	8.6	20.2
Tishie*	7.6	5.7	5.3	19.8
Oda	..	..	8.4	19.7
Agona Swedru	..	..	10.9	18.3
Keta	9.8	6.4	11.4	16.7
Asamankese	5.4	5.9	8.8	16.7
Uendi	..	..	7.7	16.1
Nkawakaw	..	..	5.0	15.6
Tema	—	—	1.9	14.9
Ho	..	..	5.8	14.5
Wa	2.8	5.3	5.2	14.3
Tookwa	..	..	7.7	13.5
Wyakrom	6.3	6.4	7.8	13.5
Prestea	..	..	6.3	13.2
Bibiani	..	..	7.2	12.9
Bawku	..	..	6.9	12.7
Dunkwa	..	..	6.8	12.7
Akwatia	..	..	4.5	12.6
Sunyani	..	..	4.6	12.2
Berekum	..	..	5.4	11.1
Anloga	..	..	4.3	11.0
Old Toto	..	..	2.6	10.9
Konongo	..	..	6.5	10.8
Wenchi	5.0	5.3	3.8	10.7
New Tato	..	..	3.2	10.6
Agogo	..	..	4.7	10.7
Suhum	..	..	5.1	10.2
Towns over 5,000 population in 1931				
Apam	2.9	8.6	4.0	8.7
Nungua	..	7.9	1.1	7.1
Marec	4.8	7.3	7.3	7.6
Mumford	..	7.3	4.0	8.7
Atsiavi Agblegbo	..	6.7	4.3	<5.0
Aboso	..	6.6	10.0	5.1
Saltpond	6.3	6.4	7.1	9.9
Berracoe	3.0	5.5	..	<5.0
Abetiti	3.9	5.4	4.0	<5.0
Osodse	5.6	5.2	3.9	5.8

NOTES

*Gradual *drop* in population up to 1948.

Sources: 1921 and 1931 from Cardinal, *The Gold Coast*; 1948 figures from *Census of Population, 1948*, Tables 8 and 9; 1960 figures from *Statistical Yearbook, 1962*; 1948 figures are African population only.

Table 9. Population employed in selected occupations, 1891–1960 (census years)

Occupation	1891	1901	1911	1921	1931	1948	1960
Professional and technical	..	..	214	1,066	2,064	4,160	33,880
Doctors	..	..	17	468	201	596	5,250
Lawyers	..	..	27	50	50	..	..
Pharmacists	..	..	13	23	..	231	490
Surveyors	..	..	6	48	149	210	1,180
Teachers	..	..	151	477	1,664	3,123	26,960
Administrative	..	..	..	..	..	..	13,100
Clerical	1,376	1,400	2,349	15,174	6,693	6,555	43,180
Civil services	..	..	219	763	4,843	6,232	20,340
Police	..	..	219	763	1,736	2,937	9,020
Other	..	..	..	..	3,107	3,295	11,320
Commercial	4,795*	9,400*	10,929	17,767	48,388	93,204	346,350
Traders	..	..	3,670	4,998	10,698	..	..
Hawkers	..	..	683	895	..	91,501†	..
Sellers (fish)	..	..	..	4,732	..	..	..
Storekeepers	..	..	161	1,739	..	1,703	..
Market traders	..	..	6,415	5,403	37,690	..	..
Fishery and farming, etc.	20,103	10,310	..	30,794	76,122	77,595	1,541,230
Fishermen	16,593	5,930	..	9,502	8,429	13,521	56,060
Hunters	..	..	..	..	..	211	1,380
Farmers	3,510	4,380	..	21,292	67,693	63,863	1,483,790
Mining	..	..	..	..	..	19,281	33,840
Transportation and communication	..	..	87	590	4,260	11,650	46,290
Road transport	..	..	87	590	4,260	7,979	40,060
Rail transport	..	..	..	..	..	1,644	2,300
Water transport	..	..	..	..	..	1,338	3,020
Air transport	..	..	..	..	..	55	70
Communications	..	..	..	..	..	634	840
Services	2,795	2,665	..	3,569	16,430	10,010	27,970
Domestics, etc.	2,795	2,665	..	3,569	16,430	10,010	27,970
Blue collar	3,095	..	3,745	18,588	43,641	44,979	304,720
Construction	..	..	18	136	236	323	..
Blacksmiths	..	..	298	728	1,179	1,779	8,620
Masons	..	..	557	1,024	2,673	3,431	31,940
Butchers	..	..	280	294	..	1,133	6,020
Carpenters	..	..	1,445	1,944	5,616	5,015	49,940
Mechanics	3,095*	..	80	228	1,593	..	..
Goldsmiths	..	..	575	692	1,807	3,683	7,440
Shoemakers	..	..	73	295	985	2,531	5,530
Tailors	..	..	419	1,085	3,245	6,243	29,790
Bakers	..	..	..	2,155	5,264	1,723	19,250
Washermen	..	..	..	637	..	1,922	..
Dressmakers	..	..	..	1,676	1,597	2,546	47,300
Weavers	..	..	..	308	607	710	12,180
Labourers	..	..	..	7,396	18,381	13,150	80,840
Painters	..	..	..	..	458	790	5,870

NOTES

* For 1891 and 1901, figures are for top *cities* only. All those not classified as clerical, fishing, farming, services, or 'mechanics' were deemed 'commercial'.

† 1948 figures for the commercial group lump traders, hawkers and fishsellers under one heading: 'hawkers'.

Source: *Census of Population* (for census years).

Table 10. Selected occupational groupings as a percentage of total population, 1891–1960 (census years)

Occupation	1891	1901	1911	1921	1931	1948	1960
(Total population)	265,000	1,894,000	2,104,000	2,538,000	3,160,000	4,876,000	6,727,000
Professional and technical	..	..	..	0.04	0.07	0.09	0.50
Administrative	..	..	..	..	..	..	0.19
Clerical	0.18	0.07	0.11	0.60	0.21	0.13	0.64
Civil service	..	..	..	0.03	0.15	0.13	0.30
Commercial	0.63	0.50	0.52	0.70	1.53	1.91	5.15
Fishing and farming, etc.	2.63	0.54	..	1.21	2.40	1.59	22.94
Mining	..	..	..	..	..	0.40	0.50
Transportation and communication	..	..	..	0.02	0.13	0.24	0.68
Services (domestic)	0.37	0.14	..	0.14	0.52	0.21	0.42
Blue collar	0.40	..	0.18	0.73	1.38	0.92	4.53

NOTES

Source: Tables 1 and 9 above.

Table 11. European population by occupation, 1902–48

	Government	Commerce	Mining	Missionary	Total
1902–9	361	397	945	103	1,806
1910–19	619	788	747	120	2,274
1920–9	995	1,594	475	117	3,181
1930–9	949	1,560	1,080	279	3,868
1940–4	868	..	1,280*	..	3,601
1948	493	2,233	698	194	3,618

NOTES

* 1941 only.

Sources: 1902–44, Kuczynski, *Demographic Survey*, p. 445; 1948, *Census of Population, 1948* (refers to male non-Africans).

Comparable figures for the period 1956–9 (average) are as follows:

	1956–9
Agriculture, forestry and fishing	195
Mining and quarrying	866
Manufacturing	478
Construction	656
Electricity, water and sanitary services	83
Commerce	1,718
Transport, storage and communications	255
Services (including government and missionary)	1,382
Total	5,633

Source: *Labour Statistics*.

8. Wages

Table 12. Wage index for selected occupational groups, 1900–38 (1921 = 100)

	Domestic servants		Carpenters			Masons			Blacksmiths			Painters			Fitters			Labourers		
Period	Min.	Max.	Period	Min.	Max.	Period	Min.	Max.	Period	Min.	Max.	Period	Min.	Max.	Period	Min.	Max.	Period	Min.	Max.*
1900–15	33	66	1900–1	43	45	1900–1	43	45	1900–1	43	45	1900–2	40	30	1900–6	—	—	1900–3	38	50
			1902	43	50	1902–4	43	55	1902–15	43	50	1903	40	35	1905–15	66	55	1904–6	38	63
			1903–4	43	55	1905–10	57	55				1904–5	40	40				1907	38	75
			1905–10	57	55	1911–15	57	64				1906	40	30				1908–10	38	63
			1911–15	57	64							1907–15	60	40				1911–15	38	63
(1916–19: Not available)																				
1920–4	100	100	1920	100	91	1920	100	91	1920	100	91	1920	100	80	1920	117	91	1920	—	100
1925–30	100	—	1921–2	100	100	1921–2	100	100	1921–2	100	100	1921–4	100	100	1921	100	100	1921	100	—
1931–5	—	—	1923–4	129	109	1923–4	129	109	1923–4	143	100	1923–4	90	115	1925–30	117	91	1922–6	75	—
1936–8	83	78	1925–30	129	91	1925–30	129	91	1925–8	86	86	1925–30	90	60	1931	110	—	1925/8	75	125
			1931	114	82	1931	114	82	1929–30	86	91	1931	80	52	1932–3	117	82	1929–30	75	150
			1932–4	100	82	1932–4	100	82	1931	74	80	1932–3	70	55	1934–5	117	86	1931	65	100
			1935–8	100	86	1935–8	—	—	1932–4	100	73	1934–8	70	60	1936–8	110	—	1932–8	75	125
									1935–8	100	86									

NOTES

*As no maximum wage rate is available for 1921, the index is calculated on the base 1920 = 100.

The actual money wages recorded in the base year 1921 are as follows:

	Min. £	Min. s	Min. d	Max. £	Max. s	Max. d	
Domestic servants	34	0	0	36	0	0	per annum
Carpenters		3	6		5	6	per day
Masons		3	6		5	6	per day
Blacksmiths		3	6		5	6	per day
Painters		2	6		5	0	per day
Fitters		3	0		5	6	per day
Labourers		2	0		..		per day

Except for domestic servants the wage index is based on payments to workers employed by the P.W.D. In some cases domestic servants received food and clothing and housing in addition to money wages.

Source: *Blue Books.*

Table 13. Earnings index for selected government employees, 1900–38 (1921 = 100)

Year	Doctors		1st class dispensers		2nd class dispensers		Nursing sisters (senior nurses)		1st class nurses		2nd class nurses		1st class teachers		2nd class teachers		1st class clerks		2nd class clerks	
	Wage	No. in sample	Wage	No. in sample	Wage	No. in sample	Wage	No. in sample	Wage	No. in sample	Wage	No. in sample	Wage	No. in sample	Wage	No. in sample	Wage	No. in sample	Wage	No. in sample
1900	42	38	51	2	54	8	35	4	22	9	22	24	46	4	—	—	70	28	45	118
1901	44	35	56	2	59	13	34	4	21	6	22	14	52	4	45	2	71	25	49	115
1902	44	28	70	2	61	13	34	4	23	9	17	22	36	1	62	2	84	10	83	111
1903	49	39	75	2	59	13	35	5	23	7	23	22	52	3	68	3	93	12	85	127
1904	51	41	79	2	65	13	35	5	23	8	22	29	68	4	75	5	89	16	86	141
1905	52	39	84	2	64	15	35	5	23	7	24	24	70	3	79	5	81	12	90	121
1906	52	47	89	2	78	10	37	5	22	7	23	26	67	4	81	8	94	15	93	144
1907	51	46	93	2	82	9	36	7	24	9	23	32	68	3	100	7	97	18	94	150
1908	53	53	82	2	83	8	37	6	25	10	26	28	80	3	87	7	100	16	94	153
1909	51	58	84	2	87	8	38	6	26	7	27	20	81	4	83	7	100	16	94	149
1910	51	60	86	2	91	8	38	7	29	8	26	27	84	4	81	10	100	17	94	173
1911	48	54	78	3	90	8	38	9	28	9	24	29	94	2	86	12	79	7	88	189
1912	53	62	84	2	87	8	39	7	30	10	25	33	98	3	86	16	80	23	77	335
1913	53	71	78	3	75	19	39	10	32	8	31	38	93	3	83	22	83	25	86	302
1914	54	66	78	4	74	20	42	10	..	..	49	33	98	3	66	52	82	49	71	543
1915	52	41	83	4	79	20	44	11	..	..	52	33	..	..	75	53	79	21	76	267
1916	59	60	88	4	83	22	75	3	..	..	55	33	97	1	77	60	81	49	74	678
(Data not available for 1917–20)																				
1921	100	51	100	6	100	25	100	17	100	2	100	15	100	9	100	96	100	91	100	698
1922	100	58	114	8	110	33	101	16	126	3	110	21	117	8	107	156	114	95	124	679
1923	98	54	118	6	117	31	97	21	128	3	119	21	121	6	110	149	116	100	116	843
1924	96	59	121	6	120	34	96	23	132	3	99	42	126	9	123	171	118	105	119	852
1925	90	73	125	6	118	36	89	26	139	3	92	58	133	9	126	192	119	110	120	715

Table 13. Earnings index for selected government employees, 1900–38 (1921 = 100)—*continued*

Year	Doctors		1st class dispensers		2nd class dispensers		Nursing sisters (senior nurses)		1st class nurses		2nd class nurses		1st class teachers		2nd class teachers		1st class clerks		2nd class clerks	
	Wage	No. in sample	Wage	No. in sample	Wage	No. in sample	Wage	No. in sample	Wage	No. in sample	Wage	No. in sample	Wage	No. in sample	Wage	No. in sample	Wage	No. in sample	Wage	No. in sample
1926	90	74	125	6	123	35	86	23	133	5	92	67	135	9	127	217	117	119	128	829
1927	85	82	124	7	118	45	131	26	131	5	95	70	138	9	132	220	120	116	124	948
1928	85	92	119	7	116	47	126	43	134	5	96	81	128	18	132	242	119	131	125	1,053
1929	86	95	115	7	118	47	129	36	130	9	94	97	128	17	134	256	119	135	122	1,108
1930	88	96	113	6	117	53	137	36	128	8	97	104	130	19	138	253	118	141	122	1,184
1931	92	86	116	7	117	56	139	36	134	8	89	159	130	22	140	297	118	127	127	1,148
1932	95	78	120	6	114	67	139	36	134	8	99	137	135	17	142	284	120	119	131	1,118
1933	85	35	..	..	..	..	130	26	..	..	..	..	..	..	..	..	..	..	..	..
1934	88	35	..	..	..	..	130	27	..	..	..	..	..	..	..	..	..	..	..	..
1935	89	33	118	6	103	88	136	26	142	5	85	185	142	15	153	238	116	49	140	522
1936	86	41	120	6	106	85	139	29	144	6	86	190	143	15	160	234	124	40	142	412
1937	88	40	120	6	112	81	140	28	134	6	86	207	140	14	174	234	128	54	141	476
1938	89	39	116	9	119	79	139	31	138	6	83	257	139	15	167	238	127	50	147	467

Table 13. Earnings index for selected government employees, 1900–38 (1921 = 100)—*continued*

NOTES

After 1921 the year ran from 1 April to 31 March. The data here have been kept on a calendar basis for convenience.

Doctors.

Category unchanged throughout the whole period – mainly European. The sharp fall in the numbers in the 30s is reflected in the fall of total appointments to the Medical Service for the whole Colonial Empire. See R. Furse, *Aucuparius*, pp. 314–31.

1st Class dispensers.

Category unchanged throughout the whole period.

2nd class dispensers.

Until 1921 this category includes 3rd class dispensers. As a category this group ceased to exist in 1921 from which year only two classes of dispensers were categorised.

Nursing sisters.

Category unchanged throughout the whole period – mainly European.

1st class nurses.

1914–16: no employment in this category.

2nd class nurses.

Until 1921 3rd class nurses are included in this category. After 1921, 2nd and 3rd class nurses were included together.

1st class teachers.

1901 and 1910–14: 1st class and principal teachers.
1901–2: 1st class teachers only.
1903–9 and 1916: principal teachers only.
After 1921: 1st class teachers only – category of principal teachers dropped and consolidated with 1st class teachers.

2nd class teachers.

1900: nobody employed in category.
1901–3: 2nd and 3rd class teachers.
1904–5: 4th class teachers.
1906–9: 3rd and 4th class teachers.
1910–13: 2nd, 3rd and 4th class teachers.
1914–16: 2nd and 3rd class teachers.
1921: 2nd, 3rd and 4th class teachers.
1922: 2nd class teachers.

1st class clerks.

Includes principal/chief clerks. 1935–9 covers only staff of Political Administration and Department of Posts and Telegraphs. Their departments were the largest employers of clerical labour and give a reasonably representative structure of wages.

2nd class clerks.

1900–1: 2nd, 3rd and 4th class clerks.
1902–16: 2nd, 3rd, 4th and 5th class clerks.
1921–2: 2nd, 3rd and 4th class clerks.
After 1922 an insignificant number of clerks only were employed below the 2nd class level and the data here refers only to 2nd class clerks.
1935–9 restricted sample, see note above, 1st class clerks.

Source: *Blue Books* until 1932–3: the data for the later years were gathered from the annual reports in the Civil Administration. This was published in two volumes, one for European, one for African employees. Unfortunately copies dealing with African employees proved too difficult to get for 1933 and 1934.

Method: The salaries of each employee in the categories listed (subject to qualifications in the footnotes) were added together and divided by the number employed in each category to give the average wage. In some instances the movement of the index is not independent of the change in the numbers employed. Each employee received an annual increment subject to an upper limit. If the number of employees remained constant over a number of years the average wage would seem to rise as a result of individuals moving up the incremental scale. A large increase in the numbers employed would appear to bring down the average wage as a result of the new employees coming in at the bottom end of the scale. Reductions in numbers employed have an unpredictable effect on the average as an employee might have left from either end of the scale. As the certain movements of the index are structural to it we have presented the numbers included in the sample as the main structural factor affecting movements of the index. The index is only presented as useful for tracing long-term movements in Civil Service Wage rates – it is completely unreliable for short-term fluctuations.

9. Development plans

Table 14. Expenditure by sector under five development plans (£000s)

	Ten year* 1920–7	1st development 1951–7	Consolidation 1957–9	2nd development 1959–63†	Seven year‡ 1963–70
Productive**	151	7,933	5,682	38,071	177,300
Industry and mining	—	3,091	3,456	27,454	109,300
Agriculture, forestry and fishing	151	4,842	2,226	10,617	68,000
Social services	1,977	28,494	9,982	47,686	150,300
Education	—	12,331	4,131	16,545	64,000
Health and sanitation	—	4,644	681	9,497	31,100
Other social services	—	579	—	1,050	10,500
Housing	—	5,182	1,447	11,647	20,000
Public administration	—	3,033	2,861	3,840	19,000
Public buildings	1,512	—	—	—	—
Police and prisons	—	1,981	686	2,729	5,700
Broadcasting	—	744	176	2,378	—
Town improvement and surface draining	465	—	—	—	—
Infrastructure	10,143	43,910	22,055	48,584	89,200
Roads	1,223	14,822	3,456	—	26,400
Railways and inland waterways	5,621	8,006	3,641	—	8,700
Ports and harbours	2,264	—	—	—	5,500
Tema Harbour	—	8,200	7,894	40,027	—
Airports and airplanes	—	153	521	—	1,500
Shipping	—	—	—	—	2,000
Other transport	—	183	13	—	—
Posts and telecommunications	276	1,643	596	—	9,600
Electricity	188	2,123	1,173	4,448	11,100
Water and sewerage	204	5,359	1,520	4,109	24,400
Takoradi township	189	—	3,241	—	—
Tema township	—	3,421	—	—	—
Maps and surveys	178	—	—	—	—
Other					
Volta††	—	1,558	373	20,453	33,700
Defence	—	2,689	498	16,479	—
Miscellaneous contingencies	156	9,099	4,147	14,134	25,000
Total	12,427	93,683	42,737	185,407	475,500

NOTES

* This was initially a ten year development plan, but it ceased to be effective after Guggisberg's departure from Ghana.

† Initially, a five year plan was superseded in 1963–4 by the Seven Year Development Plan.

‡ These estimates cover only planned government expenditure. The Seven Year Development Plan was discontinued by the military government in 1966.

**Classification system based on the one used in the Seven Year Development Plan. See *Seven Year Development Plan*, Government Printer, Accra 1963, p. 34.

††From Reserve Development Fund separate from First and Consolidation Plans.

Sources: *Legislative Council debates; Treasury Reports; Development Estimates; Gazettes; Digests of Statistics; Seven Year Development Plan.*

Table 15. The Ten Year Development Programme, 1920–30. Estimates and actual expenditure (£000s)

	1920–4		1920–30	
	Estimates	Expenditure	Estimates	Expenditure
Agriculture*	—	64	216	151
Public buildings	1,000	618	1,100	1,512
Town improvements	420	211	1,850†	465
Surface drainage	—	—	—	—
Roads	500	364	1,000	1,223
Railways	3,000	4,139	14,581	5,821
Ports and harbours	1,000	467	2,000	2,264
Posts and telegraphs	80	244	90	276
Electricity	170	58	2,000	188
Water supplies	200	854	1,790	204
Takoradi townships‡	—	—	669	189
Maps and surveys	100	105	200	178
Miscellaneous§	—	227	440	156
Total	6,470	7,351	25,936	12,627

NOTES

* First introduced in 1923–4.

† Initially separated into two heads: town improvements 1350, surface draining 500.

‡ First introduced in 1927–8.

§ First introduced in 1922–3.

Source: *Legislative Council Debates.*

Table 16. First, Second and Consolidated Development Plans. Estimates and actual expenditure (£000s)

	First Development Plan		Consolidation Plan		Second Development Plan	
	Estimates	Expenditure	Estimates	Expenditure	Estimates	Expenditure
Industry and mining	3,246	3,091	1,736	3,456	25,331	27,454
Agriculture, forestry, fishing	5,876	4,842	2,758	2,226	24,668	10,617
Education	12,628	12,231	5,064	4,131	27,852	16,545
Health and sanitation	5,271	4,644	1,736	681	23,500	9,497
Other social services	579	579	—	—	5,000	1,050
Housing	5,225	5,182	1,481	1,447	17,000	11,647
Public administration	3,374	3,033	2,052	2,861	13,852	3,840
Police and prisons	2,674	1,981	964	686	7,677	2,729
Broadcasting	693	744	425	176	2,677	2,378
Roads	11,698	14,822	4,759	3,456	25,212	—
Railways and inland waterways	8,422	8,006	2,074	3,640	13,657	—
Tema Harbour	—	8,200	7,850	7,894	2,500	40,027
Airports and airplanes	195	153	344	521	4,004	—
Shopping	77	—	—	—	1,265	—
Other transport	118	183	11	13	1,611	—
Posts and telecommunications	1,718	1,643	806	596	4,761	—
Electricity	1,916	2,123	2,377	1,173	8,765	—
Water and sewerage	5,907	3,421	1,806	1,520	20,150	4,448
Tema township	—	—	6,932	3,241	—	4,109
Volta	—	1,558	104	373	100	20,453
Defence	2,826	2,689	425	498	—	10,479
Miscellaneous	10,540	9,099	4,130	4,147	13,584	14,134
Total	82,983	88,224	47,834	42,736	243,166	179,407

NOTES

See footnotes, Table 14.

Table 17. Seven Year Development Plan. Planned and projected structure of investment (£000s)

By economic sector	Total state and private investment
Agriculture	176.6
Industry	206.4
Mining	41.7
Transport	62.9
Housing	76.2
Infrastructure	109.4
Social services	127.9
Other	75.2
Depreciation	140.2
Total	1,016.5

NOTES

Source: *Seven Year Development Plan*, p. 271.

10. External trade

Table 18. Imports, exports and the balance of visible trade, 1900–60 (£000s)

Year	Imports	Exports	Balance of visible trade (−equals deficit)
1900	1,283	885	−398
1901	1,795	560	−1,235
1902	2,120	774	−1,346
1903	2,082	980	−1,102
1904	2,001	1,340	−661
1905	1,486	1,646	160
1906	2,058	1,996	−62
1907	2,366	2,641	275
1908	2,029	2,525	496
1909	2,394	2,655	261
1910	3,439	2,697	−742
1911	3,874	3,792	−82
1912	4,023	4,307	284
1913	4,952	5,427	475
1914	4,456	4,942	486
1915	4,509	5,943	1,434
1916	5,999	5,816	−183
1917	3,386	6,364	2,978
1918	3,256	4,472	1,216
1919	7,946	10,814	2,868
1920	15,152	12,352	−2,800
1921	7,661	6,942	−719
1922	7,900	8,335	435
1923	8,448	8,959	511
1924	8,315	9,914	1,599
1925	9,782	10,890	1,108
1926	10,285	12,104	1,819
1927	13,770	14,350	580
1928	12,200	13,824	1,624
1929	10,082	12,677	2,595
1930	8,953	11,287	2,334
1931	4,803	9,300	4,497
1932	5,605	8,348	2,743
1933	5,543	8,048	2,505
1934	4,848	8,117	3,269
1935	7,956	9,971	2,015
1936	11,656	12,636	980
1937	19,228	16,218	−3,010
1938	10,380	15,425	5,045
1939	10,626	16,235	5,609

Table 18. Imports, exports and the balance of visible trade, 1900–60 (£000s)—*continued*

Year	Imports	Exports	Balance of visible trade (−equals deficit)
1940	7,631	14,323	6,692
1941	6,268	13,548	7,280
1942	9,877	12,550	2,673
1943	10,167	12,631	2,464
1944	9,828	12,314	2,486
1945	10,954	15,743	4,789
1946	13,220	20,303	7,083
1947	22,590	27,415	4,825
1948	31,378	56,115	24,737
1949	45,416	49,927	4,511
1950	48,129	77,407	29,278
1951	63,793	91,990	28,197
1952	66,610	86,377	19,767
1953	73,803	89,943	16,140
1954	71,050	114,594	43,544
1955	87,877	95,661	7,784
1956	88,920	86,599	−2,321
1957	96,685	91,602	−5,083
1958	84,593	104,558	19,965
1959	113,024	113,359	335
1960	129,617	115,989	−13,628

NOTES

Sources: *Blue Books* and *Statistical Yearbooks.*

Table 19. Balance of payments estimates, 1950–60 (£m.)

	Current account			Capital account			
	Credit	Debit	Balance	Credit	Debit	Balance	Total
1950	93	73	20	7	33	−26	106
1951	112	92	20	10	30	−20	122
1952	108	96	12	5	12	−7	113
1953	115	110	5	9	17	−8	127
1954	142	101	41	12	46	−34	154
1955	122	120	2	21	26	−5	146
1956	113	126	−13	22	4	18	135
1957	123	137	−14	18	8	10	145
1958	138	127	11	2	11	−9	140
1959	146	157	−11	27	17	10	174
1960	150	177	−27	34	10	24	187

NOTES

Sources: *Statistical Yearbook, 1962* and *Economic Survey, 1957.* Discrepancies are due to errors and omissions.

Table 20a. Value of imports by commodity group, 1900–60 (£000s)

	Food drinks and tobacco	Clothing leather and textiles	Other consumer goods	Construction	Fuel	Other	Machinery	Transport equipment	Total
1900	249,428	143,506	148,544	38,377	12,943	19,271	33,023	31,537	676,629
1901	161,370	111,060	72,091	40,365	45,402	16,765	15,953	17,225	480,231
1902	193,741	62,502	76,433	31,158	24,195	19,990	13,998	16,779	438,796
1903	123,881	61,296	71,929	29,893	20,715	19,033	14,626	15,127	356,500
1904	150,055	65,943	73,766	29,432	19,896	17,946	15,308	16,005	388,351
1905	141,349	66,381	65,316	53,735	17,494	16,757	30,744	16,155	407,931
1906	133,582	66,319	67,690	54,416	14,174	17,674	31,030	16,250	401,135
1907	122,048	70,347	77,787	58,356	62,764	20,581	31,409	57,735	501,027
1908	147,347	77,121	74,953	53,618	11,358	19,755	29,031	54,911	468,094
1909	115,948	66,915	71,557	53,507	13,272	18,036	30,595	57,975	427,805
1910	135,524	70,020	93,217	52,312	15,725	20,091	29,807	55,500	472,196
1911	161,990	73,408	103,382	52,303	14,432	19,156	29,502	54,754	508,927
1912	173,168	75,571	107,614	54,927	13,404	18,197	31,191	57,465	531,537
1913	191,911	71,394	105,096	57,346	12,709	18,748	32,649	60,163	550,016
1914	244,392	75,812	106,647	55,109	16,559	17,578	29,957	50,990	597,044
1915	223,359	66,560	98,880	61,951	16,690	20,083	34,382	59,995	581,900
1916	199,544	89,537	123,515	87,911	23,231	26,815	44,460	80,407	675,420
1917	215,452	117,621	135,707	100,950	35,345	42,150	54,664	99,475	801,364
1918	288,114	165,746	159,556	122,447	46,580	65,617	68,304	129,408	1,045,772
1919	359,290	233,915	177,781	139,780	55,833	60,923	68,521	125,699	1,221,742
1920	419,867	304,606	220,984	155,626	82,406	65,108	73,286	132,073	1,453,956
1921	326,359	312,256	166,374	127,022	96,681	41,682	68,301	125,832	1,264,507
1922	243,192	211,122	127,870	76,032	69,114	37,198	35,335	61,446	861,309
1923	258,908	234,202	110,185	76,861	58,433	55,116	37,471	59,538	890,714
1924	237,268	266,137	113,016	78,381	50,997	53,514	40,255	62,595	902,163

Table 20a. Value of imports by commodity group, 1900–60 (£000s)—*continued*

	Food drinks and tobacco	Clothing leather and textiles	Other consumer goods	Construction	Fuel	Other	Machinery	Transport equipment	Total
1925	237,929	247,978	108,945	74,350	50,295	59,336	39,707	60,700	879,240
1926	212,130	233,490	106,970	74,810	50,430	55,680	39,250	61,090	833,850
1927	226,072	385,880	111,100	73,441	46,713	50,730	38,971	61,794	994,701
1928	219,415	245,543	107,504	68,385	45,278	49,204	38,238	60,040	833,607
1929	213,859	239,468	105,126	68,096	46,374	46,307	38,786	62,025	820,041
1930	205,759	213,982	99,247	65,879	39,914	42,472	38,695	63,966	769,914
1931	196,692	143,428	94,312	62,731	37,896	37,412	39,062	66,458	677,991
1932	200,375	124,514	100,324	62,092	38,546	36,199	36,955	62,698	661,703
1933	190,530	19,104	96,027	60,776	35,285	33,658	37,568	64,277	537,225
1934	184,424	144,636	88,733	55,496	26,531	32,772	38,334	66,907	637,833
1935	181,876	123,042	90,150	55,133	26,563	32,564	38,138	65,135	612,601
1936	176,352	123,415	91,710	58,450	26,669	31,327	39,463	67,056	614,442
1937	184,919	177,041	96,256	73,787	27,708	32,078	57,984	120,707	770,480
1938	186,208	158,512	98,717	81,718	23,779	34,644	61,961	129,337	774,876
1939	181,798	147,585	94,668	67,723	24,383	35,198	63,585	132,675	747,615
1940	248,145	184,411	131,314	87,602	31,254	46,958	72,537	148,802	951,023
1941	302,979	193,329	153,056	97,951	37,529	48,853	82,534	170,787	1,087,018
1942	335,110	299,034	186,910	109,569	41,934	51,676	94,033	194,894	1,313,160
1943	440,180	395,316	226,272	108,433	53,194	105,776	101,882	211,125	1,642,178
1944	354,380	462,737	268,401	96,315	48,870	101,963	127,501	268,301	1,728,468
1945	385,660	457,816	432,305	88,480	45,621	84,395	102,854	208,538	1,805,669
1946	394,173	506,197	227,610	119,236	36,487	71,253	113,329	231,275	1,699,560
1947	462,079	681,793	294,718	165,630	39,636	95,103	167,581	352,703	2,259,243
1948	464,425	663,791	377,157	227,336	52,098	103,487	202,593	473,356	2,564,243
1949	592,831	646,188	333,085	224,051	58,745	126,185	212,154	499,034	2,602,273

[illegible]	[illegible]	[illegible]	[illegible]	[illegible]	60,041	122,356	233,357	538,983	2,727,163
1951	650,177	883,850	407,066	295,806	67,326	180,534	277,063	590,329	3,352,151
1952	670,860	841,250	441,058	317,166	92,232	148,453	295,619	654,691	3,461,329
1953	660,109	710,826	455,927	292,901	72,668	109,342	320,166	775,265	3,397,204
1954	639,406	508,120	420,636	265,016	65,587	80,941	183,424	812,533	2,975,663
1955	623,033	486,424	430,684	271,285	77,581	85,764	180,844	881,079	3,036,694
1956	625,939	510,623	434,055	247,638	87,541	86,028	170,995	512,342	2,675,161
1957	642,237	479,936	450,142	268,261	90,968	90,918	176,189	504,883	2,703,534
1958	643,076	515,529	444,413	262,445	86,704	86,185	183,332	531,097	2,752,781
1959	631,699	498,760	436,036	237,874	83,226	84,306	190,608	555,356	2,717,865
1960	652,205	503,655	455,951	241,712	82,623	89,217	197,014	565,227	2,787,604

NOTES

This table is calculated on the basis of current prices and the volume of imports in 1926 (i.e. $P_t\ q_{26}$).
Source: *Blue Books*.

Table 20b. Volume of imports by commodity group, 1900–60 (1953=100)

	Food drinks and tobacco	Clothing leather and textiles	Other consumer goods	Construction	Fuel	Other	Machinery	Transport equipment
1900	11	7	7	5	3	5	5	4
1901	14	11	11	12	1	4	12	11
1902	17	11	11	8	—	4	21	10
1903	16	10	12	9	1	4	28	6
1904	15	9	13	8	—	4	18	2
1905	12	9	11	6	1	5	10	1
1906	13	9	13	7	2	5	18	3
1907	16	10	13	7	—	6	16	2
1908	14	10	15	8	1	6	17	3
1909	15	10	14	8	1	7	15	2
1910	17	11	22	10	1	7	24	3
1911	19	13	26	14	3	10	22	3
1912	22	14	26	14	3	13	23	4
1913	25	15	27	13	3	13	17	6
1914	23	7	26	15	4	12	15	6
1915	19	12	22	13	3	17	11	6
1916	26	13	33	17	4	19	12	17
1917	12	10	19	12	5	12	10	8
1918	9	4	14	10	2	12	8	4
1919	20	5	26	15	4	38	8	18
1920	23	12	47	28	6	22	19	67
1921	18	10	27	11	4	11	17	71
1922	22	6	30	16	5	20	22	91
1923	23	32	27	25	6	31	33	55
1924	27	20	27	24	8	35	29	50
1925	29	32	31	29	10	35	31	66
1926	32	31	30	24	13	41	33	55
1927	42	36	42	43	15	47	36	83
1928	46	42	44	42	17	41	47	68
[illegible]	[illegible]	[illegible]	39	37	19	45	35	59

[illegible]	[illegible]	[illegible]	[illegible]	[illegible]	21	39	31	52
1931	24	25	25	14	21	33	13	21
1932	20	47	23	18	16	38	28	19
1933	25	26	25	19	14	42	26	17
1934	19	33	24	20	18	33	46	17
1935	29	60	37	35	27	52	80	35
1936	36	68	40	44	33	49	88	42
1937	52	69	61	57	49	59	122	65
1938	36	33	27	36	58	40	103	39
1939	36	35	26	42	66	43	80	32
1940	25	26	22	28	56	53	65	14
1941	22	28	16	21	61	37	31	8
1942	24	34	17	21	87	41	26	11
1943	24	28	15	14	76	29	23	8
1944	23	24	16	13	70	24	23	9
1945	25	28	21	22	58	39	32	45
1946	28	31	28	35	63	42	49	29
1947	39	36	41	44	69	56	52	53
1948	41	53	40	50	54	71	66	78
1949	68	90	61	76	61	58	80	96
1950	78	72	68	73	71	73	92	99
1951	88	71	76	94	83	86	86	100
1952	86	70	82	98	100	110	90	100
1953	100	100	100	100	100	100	100	100
1954	92	88	94	90	149	291	56	114
1955	114	108	127	116	205	250	72	122
1956	116	83	126	116	161	299	81	233
1957	136	101	127	109	184	319	74	200
1958	126	73	124	96	206	302	72	151
1959	178	108	152	143	205	409	104	273
1960	185	133	184	161	228	413	125	308

NOTES

This table is calculated on the basis of current volumes and 1926 prices (i.e. $q_t\ P_{26}$).

Table 20c. Price of imports by commodity groups, 1900–60 (1953=100)

	Food drink and tobacco	Clothing leather and textiles	Other consumer goods	Construction	Fuel	Other	Machinery	Transport equipment	Total
1900	14	9	16	12	52	15	6	2	11
1901	24	16	16	14	63	15	5	2	14
1902	29	9	17	11	33	18	4	2	13
1903	19	9	16	10	28	17	5	2	11
1904	23	9	16	10	27	16	5	2	12
1905	22	9	14	18	24	15	10	2	12
1906	20	9	15	19	19	16	10	2	12
1907	19	10	17	20	86	19	10	7	15
1908	22	11	16	18	16	18	9	7	14
1909	24	10	16	18	18	16	10	7	14
1910	21	10	20	18	22	18	9	7	14
1911	24	10	23	18	20	17	9	7	15
1912	26	11	24	19	19	17	10	7	16
1913	29	10	23	20	17	17	10	8	16
1914	37	11	23	19	23	16	9	7	18
1915	34	10	22	21	23	18	11	8	17
1916	30	13	27	30	32	24	14	10	20
1917	33	16	30	34	49	39	17	13	24
1918	44	23	35	42	64	60	21	17	31
1919	54	33	39	48	77	56	21	16	36
1920	63	43	49	53	113	60	23	17	43
1921	50	44	37	43	133	38	21	16	37
1922	37	30	28	26	95	34	11	8	25
1923	39	33	24	26	81	51	13	8	26
1924	36	38	25	27	70	49	12	8	27
1925	36	35	24	25	69	55	12	8	26
1926	32	33	23	26	69	51	12	8	25
1927	34	54	24	25	65	46	12	8	29
[illegible]	[illegible]	[illegible]	23	23	63	45	12	8	25
[illegible]	[illegible]	[illegible]	[illegible]	[illegible]	[illegible]	[illegible]	[illegible]	[illegible]	24

[illegible]					[illegible]	[illegible]	12	8	23
1931	30	20	21	21	52	34	12	9	20
1932	30	17	22	21	53	33	12	8	19
1933	29	27	21	21	49	31	12	8	21
1934	28	20	19	19	37	30	12	9	19
1935	28	17	20	19	37	30	12	8	18
1936	27	17	20	20	37	29	12	9	18
1937	28	25	21	25	38	30	18	16	23
1938	28	22	22	28	33	32	19	17	23
1939	27	21	21	23	33	32	20	17	22
1940	38	26	29	30	43	43	23	19	28
1941	46	27	34	33	51	45	26	22	32
1942	51	42	41	37	58	47	29	25	39
1943	67	56	50	37	73	97	32	27	48
1944	54	65	59	33	67	93	40	35	51
1945	59	64	95	30	63	78	32	27	53
1946	60	71	50	41	50	65	35	30	50
1947	70	96	65	56	55	87	52	45	67
1948	70	93	83	78	72	95	63	61	76
1949	76	91	73	76	81	116	66	64	77
1950	86	90	76	74	83	112	73	70	80
1951	98	125	89	100	93	165	86	76	99
1952	102	118	97	108	127	136	92	84	102
1953	100	100	100	100	100	100	100	100	100
1954	97	72	92	90	90	74	57	105	88
1955	95	68	95	93	107	79	56	114	89
1956	95	72	95	84	121	79	53	66	79
1957	97	68	99	92	125	83	55	65	80
1958	97	73	97	90	119	79	57	68	81
1959	96	70	96	81	114	77	60	72	80
1960	99	71	100	82	114	82	61	73	82

NOTES

This table is calculated on the basis of Laspeyre's Price Index i.e. $\left(\frac{P_t \; Q_{26}}{P_{26} \; Q_{26}}\right)$

Table 21a. Value of major exports, 1900–60 (£000s)

Year	Gold	Diamonds	Manganese	Cocoa	Rubber	Palm oil	Palm kernels	Kola	Timber Logs	Timber Sawn	Total
1900	38	—	—	27	328	239	97	..	68	—	797
1901	22	—	—	43	104	178	90	..	55	—	492
1902	97	—	—	95	89	235	132	44	22	—	714
1903	255	—	—	86	196	146	105	..	49	—	837
1904	346	—	—	200	361	129	86	..	54	—	1,176
1905	596	—	—	187	324	88	77	..	84	—	1,358
1906	822	—	—	336	334	125	81	..	80	—	1,778
1907	1,131	—	—	515	333	119	102	78	169	—	2,447
1908	1,122	—	—	541	168	129	78	..	158	—	2,196
1909	982	—	—	755	264	121	112	..	83	—	2,317
1910	790	—	—	866	359	161	185	..	148	—	2,509
1911	1,058	—	—	1,613	219	129	176	..	139	—	3,334
1912	1,439	—	—	1,643	169	113	205	118	229	—	3,916
1913	1,626	—	—	2,489	88	66	159	..	366	—	4,794
1914	1,659	—	—	2,194	22	38	89	142	241	—	4,385
1915	1,755	—	—	3,657	25	26	50	139	91	—	5,743
1916	1,201	—	6	3,848	79	38	86	130	94	—	5,482
1917	1,718	—	50	3,147	110	25	75	239	69	—	5,433
1918	1,365	—	56	1,797	57	84	153	262	137	—	3,911
1919	1,404	—	72	8,278	34	40	253	350	103	—	10,534
1920	889	—	68	10,056	27	114	222	452	342	—	12,170
1921	855	—	12	4,764	7	8	31	463	206	—	6,346
1922	889	—	106	5,841	5	20	46	311	254	—	7,472
1923	851	—	327	6,567	9	37	57	320	150	—	8,318
1924	875	85	526	7,250	9	36	111	401	..	—	9,293
1925	840	99	681	8,222	34	44	115	283	..	—	10,318
1926	850	363	685	9,181	53	52	125	259	..	—	11,568
1927	727	512	683	11,727	31	30	107	191	..	—	14,008
1928	685	584	610	11,229	26	13	104	179	139	—	13,569
[1929]	[illegible]	[illegible]	[illegible]	[illegible]	[illegible]	[illegible]	[illegible]	127	160	—	12,155

[illegible]	[illegible]	[illegible]	[illegible]	[illegible]	22	11	69	138	100	—	9,848
1931	1,069	441	389	5,493	5	5	37	38	62	—	7,539
1932	1,692	537	124	5,511	3	11	60	7	37	—	7,982
1933	1,842	518	357	4,971	8	0	23	4	30	—	7,753
1934	2,421	757	481	4,041	5	1	19	1	69	—	7,795
1935	2,635	546	612	5,204	14	7	43	81	110	—	9,252
1936	3,047	585	613	7,660	24	6	107	94	106	—	12,242
1937	3,911	648	1,025	9,989	33	11	104	91	130	—	15,942
1938	4,842	548	908	4,541	30	10	40	88	77	—	11,084
1939	6,178	464	790	5,101	33	5	27	101	55	—	12,754
1940	7,208	338	1,087	4,495	50	10	41	111	109	—	13,449
1941	6,851	629	1,015	4,007	38	10	21	91	136	—	12,798
1942	6,603	613	1,264	2,385	144	17	20	89	155	—	11,290
1943	5,295	721	1,188	3,493	347	12	92	153	238	—	11,539
1944	4,485	659	1,423	3,890	188	11	148	137	278	—	11,219
1945	4,084	479	1,976	7,144	175	8	100	130	463	—	14,559
1946	5,568	622	2,265	9,488	106	4	74	169	879	—	19,175
1947	4,896	746	2,233	16,634	35	8	65	309	1,318	—	26,244
1948	5,754	1,280	2,699	42,166	39	3	165	265	1,987	—	54,358
1949	6,414	1,480	4,006	34,019	33	24	69	271	1,511	—	47,827
1950	8,719	2,678	5,007	54,604	26	22	131	321	2,758	1,127	75,393
1951	8,562	6,417	7,217	60,310	49	26	115	489	3,179	1,798	88,162
1952	9,238	5,400	8,333	52,533	49	30	362	412	2,282	1,875	80,514
1953	9,458	3,925	8,722	56,143	37	26	410	388	3,238	2,642	84,989
1954	9,828	4,272	5,112	84,599	26	50	516	273	3,641	3,067	111,344
1955	9,048	5,532	5,196	65,559	26	—	339	186	4,438	3,690	94,014
1956	7,488	7,920	7,044	51,062	37	—	525	233	5,169	4,345	83,823
1957	9,792	8,976	8,988	50,873	44	—	276	175	5,386	4,853	89,363
1958	10,596	8,664	8,640	62,318	48	—	335	383	6,221	5,056	102,261
1959	11,196	8,664	6,780	68,779	64	—	116	762	7,971	5,380	109,712
1960	11,088	9,840	6,384	66,434	67	—	138	1,200	10,425	5,832	111,408

Table 21b. Volume of major exports, 1900–60

Year	Gold (000 oz.)	Diamonds (carats)	Manganese (000 tons)	Cocoa (000 tons beans)	Rubber (000 tons)	Palm oil (000 tons)	Palm kernels (000 tons)	Kola (000 tons)	Timber logs (000,000)	Timber sawn (000 cu. ft)
1900	10	—	—	0.5	1.5	17.0	12.8	..	0.9	—
1901	6	—	—	1.0	0.7	12.6	12.8	..	0.9	—
1902	27	—	—	2.4	0.7	17.0	17.0	..	0.3	—
1903	71	—	—	2.3	1.0	10.4	13.2	..	0.9	—
1904	93	—	—	5.2	1.8	9.0	11.0	..	2.0	—
1905	159	—	—	5.1	1.6	6.4	9.8	..	1.1	—
1906	217	—	—	9.1	1.6	8.6	9.3	..	1.0	—
1907	292	—	—	9.5	1.6	7.5	9.7	1.5	2.3	—
1908	288	—	—	12.9	0.8	9.1	8.9	..	2.4	—
1909	254	—	—	20.5	1.2	8.1	11.6	..	1.2	—
1910	205	—	—	23.0	1.4	8.2	14.2	..	1.9	—
1911	280	—	—	40.3	1.2	6.5	13.2	..	1.8	—
1912	378	—	—	39.2	0.9	5.8	14.6	2.9	3.0	—
1913	423	—	—	51.3	0.6	3.4	9.7	..	4.8	—
1914	429	—	—	52.9	0.3	2.0	5.6	3.6	3.1	—
1915	462	—	—	77.3	0.3	1.3	4.1	3.7	1.2	—
1916	316	—	4	72.2	1.0	1.8	5.8	3.1	1.3	—
1917	448	—	29	91.0	1.3	0.8	4.8	5.4	1.5	—
1918	354	—	31	66.3	0.6	2.7	8.9	6.0	1.9	—
1919	360	—	33	176.2	0.3	3.8	9.9	7.4	1.3	—
1920	230	—	43	124.8	0.1	2.5	7.7	7.3	2.7	—
1921	221	—	7	133.2	0.05	0.3	1.6	6.2	1.8	—
1922	228	—	61	159.3	0.007	0.8	3.1	5.4	3.1	—
1923	225	—	136	200.6	0.1	1.4	3.7	6.2	2.1	—
1924	232	70	233	223.3	0.2	1.3	6.6	7.9	2.6	—
1925	218	80	339	218.1	0.5	1.4	6.6	6.2	2.6	—
1926	220	300	345	230.8	0.6	1.7	7.6	5.6	2.4	—
1927	189	460	369	210.0	0.3	1.1	6.5	5.2	1.6	—
1928	179	700	324	225.1	0.2	0.5	6.2	5.0	2.0	—
[illegible]	[illegible]	[illegible]	[illegible]	[illegible]	0.3	0.6	6.6	3.1	1.9	—

[illegible]	[illegible]	[illegible]	417	190.6	0.2	0.5	5.4	4.0	0.5	—
1931	273	880	247	244.1	0.1	0.3	4.0	1.3	0.8	—
1932	286	840	51	233.7	0.01	0.7	7.0	0.4	0.4	—
1933	294	800	265	236.1	0.02	0.02	3.0	0.2	0.3	—
1934	351	2,390	340	230.3	0.1	0.06	3.4	0.2	0.8	—
1935	371	1,350	399	268.9	0.3	0.4	6.5	3.6	1.4	—
1936	434	1,410	411	311.1	0.4	0.5	11.3	4.3	1.2	—
1937	558	1,580	527	236.2	0.5	0.5	8.5	4.3	1.5	—
1938	677	1,300	324	263.2	0.5	0.6	5.2	4.1	0.9	—
1939	793	1,090	336	280.7	0.7	0.4	4.1	4.7	0.7	—
1940	858	570	477	223.9	0.9	0.5	5.9	5.0	1.3	—
1941	815	1,080	429	218.9	0.7	0.4	3.3	4.5	1.5	—
1942	786	1,050	483	123.9	1.9	0.4	2.8	3.3	1.9	—
1943	630	1,320	423	187.3	3.2	0.5	8.4	4.4	2.8	—
1944	534	1,160	504	202.8	1.7	0.5	12.6	5.3	3.2	—
1945	475	810	702	232.2	1.5	0.4	8.0	6.1	3.2	—
1946	646	810	765	236.3	1.0	0.2	5.9	6.2	5.2	—
1947	568	750	589	180.2	0.4	0.2	3.7	8.5	6.6	—
1948	671	1,030	630	214.3	0.4	0.04	7.1	5.8	7.9	—
1949	656	930	741	263.6	0.4	0.2	2.9	5.9	7.8	—
1950	705	1,140	711	267.4	0.3	0.2	4.1	5.4	10.4	2.1
1951	692	1,760	806	229.5	0.3	0.2	2.4	5.7	9.1	2.7
1952	704	2,130	794	212.0	0.3	0.2	6.3	5.5	7.5	3.0
1953	733	2,160	746	236.6	0.3	0.4	7.0	5.7	10.4	4.7
1954	788	2,120	447	214.1	0.3	0.5	8.7	4.7	12.6	5.3
1955	723	2,280	540	205.9	0.2	—	9.6	3.5	16.9	6.5
1956	598	2,520	636	234.4	0.3	—	11.5	4.0	19.6	7.4
1957	788	2,930	640	260.2	0.3	—	6.9	2.9	24.5	7.8
1958	852	3,280	5.3	197.3	0.4	—	7.9	6.2	27.0	7.8
1959	902	3,120	526	250.2	0.6	—	2.8	8.6	28.0	8.0
1960	892	3,280	547	302.8	0.8	—	3.0	11.6	29.0	8.3

Table 21c. Price of major exports, 1900–60 (1953=100)

Year	Gold	Diamonds	Manganese	Cocoa	Rubber	Palm oil	Palm kernels	Kola	Timber logs	Timber sawn	Export price index
1900	28	—	—	21	191	22	13	..	24	—	32
1901	28	—	—	18	138	22	12	..	19	—	22
1902	28	—	—	17	112	22	13	..	23	—	23
1903	28	—	—	16	175	22	14	..	17	—	25
1904	28	—	—	16	181	23	13	..	9	—	26
1905	28	—	—	15	177	22	14	..	24	—	28
1906	29	—	—	16	185	23	15	..	26	—	27
1907	30	—	—	23	189	25	18	74	23	—	30
1908	30	—	—	18	191	23	15	..	21	—	25
1909	30	—	—	16	192	24	16	..	22	—	24
1910	30	—	—	16	224	31	22	..	25	—	25
1911	29	—	—	17	166	32	23	..	25	—	22
1912	29	—	—	18	171	31	24	59	24	—	27
1913	30	—	—	21	134	30	28	..	24	—	24
1914	30	—	—	17	67	30	27	57	25	—	22
1915	37	—	—	20	78	31	21	55	24	—	23
1916	29	—	13	22	72	34	25	61	23	—	24
1917	30	—	14	14	75	50	27	65	15	—	19
1918	30	—	15	11	89	50	29	64	23	—	17
1919	30	—	19	20	94	59	44	69	25	—	22
1920	30	—	14	34	183	72	50	90	40	—	35
1921	30	—	15	15	132	45	32	109	37	—	18
1922	30	—	15	15	59	38	25	84	26	—	17
1923	29	—	21	14	59	42	26	75	23	—	15
[illegible]	[illegible]	[illegible]	[illegible]	14	66	42	29	74	—	—	15

			[illegible]	[illegible]	[illegible]	49	30	67	—	—	17
1926	30	67	17	17	76	48	28	67	—	—	18
1927	30	61	16	23	87	44	28	54	—	—	24
1928	29	46	16	21	93	43	28	52	22	—	22
1929	24	49	15	17	88	45	25	60	27	—	18
1930	30	42	17	15	82	37	21	50	64	—	18
1931	30	28	13	9	45	24	16	43	25	—	11
1932	46	35	21	10	26	24	15	25	30	—	13
1933	48	35	11	9	30	18	13	29	32	—	12
1934	53	18	12	7	39	17	10	7	28	—	11
1935	55	22	13	8	43	26	11	33	25	—	12
1936	54	23	13	10	50	20	16	32	28	—	14
1937	53	23	17	18	52	34	21	31	28	—	22
1938	55	23	24	7	49	24	13	31	27	—	14
1939	60	24	20	8	44	20	11	31	25	—	15
1940	65	32	21	8	47	29	12	32	27	—	19
1941	65	32	20	8	47	39	11	29	29	—	18
1942	65	32	22	8	69	62	12	39	26	—	23
1943	65	30	24	8	96	41	19	51	27	—	19
1944	65	31	24	8	96	35	20	38	28	—	17
1945	45	32	36	13	100	34	21	31	46	—	20
1946	67	42	25	17	92	39	21	39	54	—	25
1947	67	55	33	39	85	67	30	53	64	—	43
1948	66	68	37	83	78	136	39	67	80	—	75
1949	76	88	46	54	76	149	41	67	62	—	57
1950	95	130	75	86	89	141	54	87	85	95	86
1951	95	200	77	111	134	185	80	125	112	118	109
1952	101	140	90	104	149	204	98	109	97	111	104
1953	100	100	100	100	100	100	100	100	100	100	100
1954	96	111	98	166	87	147	101	84	92	103	143

Table 21c. Price of major exports, 1900–60 (1953 = 100)—*continued*

Year	Gold	Diamonds	Manganese	Cocoa	Rubber	Palm oil	Palm kernels	Kola	Timber logs	Timber sawn	Export price index
1955	97	134	83	134	95	—	60	77	84	101	120
1956	97	173	95	92	103	—	78	84	84	104	97
1957	96	169	121	82	119	—	68	88	70	111	92
1958	96	146	145	133	101	—	72	90	74	115	123
1959	96	153	110	116	100	—	70	130	91	120	113
1960	96	166	100	92	77	—	77	151	115	125	101

NOTES

Sources for Tables 21 a, b and c are as follows: Value and quantity data were taken from *Statistics of external trade and shipping and aircraft movement 1935–1953*, Central Bureau of Statistics, Accra 1954, pp. 29–36.
Prices of cocoa, rubber, palm kernels, palm oil and kola units were taken from: S. La Anyane, *Ghana agriculture*, pp. 203–15.

Gold: prior to 1932, the quantity of gold exported was measured in bullion ounces.

Cocoa: quantity data for the period 1893–1935 was multiplied by 0.453 to make up for the differences in units used for measuring (lbs *v* tons).

Rubber: after 1942 there is a further classification into 'wild' and 'plantation' rubber. These are combined in this table. Quantity data for the period 1886–1935 was multiplied by 0.453 to make up for the difference in units used for measuring (lbs *v*. tons).

Kola nuts: a five-year average was used for the period 1900–13 as no annual data was available (also taken from La Anyane). Quantity data for the period 1914–27 was multiplied by 0.453, and for the period 1928–44 by 50.7 to make up for the difference in units used for measuring. The figures for 1931–5 do not include a reference to kola nuts exported from the Northern Territories (including the Northern Section of Togoland under British Mandate) direct to French Territory.

Lumber: Data for the period 1948–60 was taken from the *Quarterly Digest of Statistics*, and for the years 1961–2 from the *Statistical Yearbook*, 1962. Logs data for 1946 and before was multiplied by 127.33 to make up for the differences in units used to measure logs. Quantity data for the period 1900–20 was divided by 10 to reconcile the different units used before and after 1920 in measuring logs.

Year	U.S.A. and Canada	Central and S. America	United Kingdom	Other C'wealth	W. Europe	E. Europe and China	Japan	Rest of World
1900	70	—	602	128	512	—	—	39
1901	124	—	1,579	161	490	—	—	5
1902	106	—	1,894	206	687	—	—	6
1903	84	—	2,034	214	618	—	—	114
1904	52	—	2,300	161	703	—	—	123
1905	30	—	2,222	195	595	—	—	91
1906	47	—	3,113	203	596	—	—	96
1907	61	—	3,713	304	827	—	—	104
1908	57	—	3,428	189	714	—	—	165
1909	49	—	3,576	303	945	—	—	177
1910	60	—	4,341	232	1,239	—	—	190
1911	157	—	5,297	351	1,464	—	—	148
1912	302	—	5,304	670	1,720	—	—	335
1913	353	—	6,981	688	1,790	—	—	568
1914	263	—	6,412	587	1,693	—	—	344
1915	679	—	7,545	776	1,211	—	—	243
1916	1,355	—	7,978	551	1,670	—	—	263
1917	1,728	—	5,898	373	804	—	—	113
1918	1,589	—	5,053	736	86	—	—	266
1919	4,978	—	11,007	562	1,653	—	—	562
1920	4,784	—	17,691	754	2,134	—	—	2,141
1921	1,996	—	9,044	646	1,727	—	—	1,191
1922	2,836	—	9,509	757	2,636	—	—	498
1923	3,191	—	8,907	600	3,941	—	—	769
1924	2,735	—	8,292	714	5,640	—	—	849
1925	3,444	—	9,737	667	5,786	—	—	1,041
1926	4,108	—	8,689	1,580	6,124	—	—	1,290
1927	5,118	—	12,275	1,197	7,817	—	—	1,715
1928	4,425	—	10,617	907	8,145	—	—	1,922
1929	5,269	—	8,374	816	6,296	—	—	2,006
1930	2,901	—	8,782	725	5,935	—	—	1,898
1931	2,164	—	6,989	396	3,457	—	—	1,098
1932	2,359	—	7,161	364	2,991	—	—	1,081
1933	1,958	—	6,703	500	3,030	—	—	1,401
1934	1,711	—	7,245	514	2,058	—	—	1,439
1935	2,215	80	9,383	796	3,442	244	234	689
1936	29,292	101	10,687	890	4,425	319	307	818
1937	5,000	128	13,713	1,290	6,632	574	503	931
1938	2,116	49	11,794	758	3,266	275	285	1,002
1939	2,645	65	13,273	773	2,477	217	213	1,459
1940	3,927	88	9,876	4,986	830	39	130	1,098
1941	2,593	18	7,641	8,053	35	9	12	1,035
1942	1,989	39	14,603	2,636	49	7	1	1,523
1943	2,650	113	14,571	1,985	129	55	2	1,835
1944	4,378	118	12,460	2,103	181	263	..	1,605
1945	6,756	31	13,838	2,441	898	..	..	2,048
1946	6,783	17	18,918	3,081	2,017	511	..	2,196
1947	13,890	21	22,994	3,853	5,003	1,177	131	2,934
1948	19,125	10	37,486	8,190	12,644	3,928	25	5,282
1949	16,719	25	46,501	7,032	15,510	3,382	1,748	3,378

Table 22a. Direction of trade, 1900–60 (Total trade: £000s)—*continued*

Year	U.S.A. and Canada	Central and S. America	United Kingdom	Other C'wealth	W. Europe	E. Europe and China	Japan	Rest of World
1950	25,705	294	58,547	8,177	21,062	2,478	2,512	6,482
1951	31,899	385	72,187	9,237	27,438	4,189	4,012	6,073
1952	29,512	606	72,785	7,207	27,492	4,763	2,845	7,221
1953	28,437	515	80,216	7,917	31,870	4,373	3,984	5,065
1954	23,900	2,700	80,700	10,600	49,700	8,500	5,300	4,300
1955	21,900	2,700	80,100	12,700	48,000	5,800	8,900	3,500
1956	21,100	2,800	71,600	12,600	50,700	3,800	9,000	3,900
1957	21,000	4,300	74,900	11,200	52,400	9,200	10,300	5,000
1958	25,000	3,600	74,400	12,400	57,800	3,000	6,800	5,600
1959	30,400	3,700	80,200	11,600	76,700	5,700	9,200	8,900
1960	27,700	3,600	83,900	12,880	80,700	13,250	11,700	12,000

NOTES

'U.S.A. and Canada' includes Canada since 1954. Before that Canada is included in 'Other Commonwealth'.

Table 22b. Direction of trade: Imports, 1900–60 (5 year averages and selected years) (£000s)

Year	U.S.A. and Canada	Central and S. America	U.K.	Other C'wealth	W. Europe	E. Europe and China	Japan	Rest of World
1900–4	*67*	—	*1,169*	*110*	*298*	—	—	*51*
1905–9	*25*	—	*1,530*	*71*	*332*	—	—	*109*
1910–14	*189*	—	*2,908*	*211*	*526*	—	—	*261*
1915–19	*791*	—	*3,672*	*250*	*149*	—	—	*158*
1919	1,514	—	6,056	180	45	—	—	152
1920	2,230	—	11,826	224	213	—	—	659
1920–4	*1,136*	—	*6,979*	*267*	*665*	—	—	*448*
1925–9	*1,409*	—	*6,139*	*413*	*2,127*	—	—	*813*
1929	1,602	—	4,758	399	2,275	—	—	1,049
1930	1,324	—	4,395	297	1,947	—	—	991
1930–4	*806*	—	*3,188*	*265*	*935*	—	—	*770*
1934	560	—	2,698	327	429	—	—	889
1935–9	*890*	*85*	*4,663*	*545*	*1,562*	*262*	*307*	*610*
1940–4	*1,004*	*75*	*4,335*	*1,268*	*94*	—	—	*1,202*
1945–9	*2,140*	*18*	*13,911*	*2,249*	*3,340*	—	—	*1,767*
1950–4	*3,763*	*881*	*35,191*	*4,322*	*11,278*	*802*	*3,730*	*4,505*
1955	4,100	2,700	41,600	7,300	18,900	1,700	8,900	2,700
1956	4,300	2,700	41,700	7,300	18,800	1,700	9,000	3,400
1957	5,600	4,200	40,700	7,700	20,900	2,800	10,300	4,500
1958	5,000	3,600	36,600	6,900	18,400	2,600	6,800	4,700
1959	8,000	3,700	45,300	7,100	28,700	3,500	8,600	8,100
1960	9,300	3,800	47,600	6,400	37,000	5,100	10,800	9,800

Table 22c. Direction of trade: exports, 1900–60 (5 year averages and selected years) (£000s)

Year	U.S.A. and Canada	Central and S. America	U.K.	Other C'wealth	W. Europe	E. Europe and China	Japan	Rest of World
1900–4	*20*	—	*513*	*64*	*304*	—	—	—
1905–9	—	—	*1,680*	*168*	*403*	—	—	*18*
1910–14	*70*	—	*2,759*	*287*	*1,055*	—	—	*56*
1915–19	*1,275*	—	*3,824*	*350*	*936*	—	—	*131*
1919	3,464	—	4,951	382	1,608	—	—	410
1920	2,554	—	5,865	530	1,921	—	—	1,482
1920–4	*1,972*	—	*3,710*	*428*	*2,551*	—	—	*641*
1925–9	*3,064*	—	*3,800*	*420*	*4,702*	—	—	*782*
1929	3,667	—	3,616	417	4,021	—	—	957
1930	1,577	—	4,387	428	3,988	—	—	907
1930–4	*1,426*	—	*4,188*	*234*	*2,572*	—	—	*614*
1934	1,205	—	4,547	187	1,629	—	—	550
1935–9	*7,363*	—	*7,107*	*356*	*2,486*	*63*	—	*369*
1940–4	*2,103*	—	*7,495*	*2,670*	*151*	—	—	*217*
1945–9	*10,514*	—	*14,026*	*2,670*	*3,875*	—	—	*1,401*
1950–4	*24,122*	—	*37,696*	*4,305*	*20,235*	*4,059*	—	*1,323*
1955	17,800	—	38,500	5,400	29,100	4,100	—	800
1956	16,800	100	29,900	5,300	31,900	2,100	—	500
1957	15,400	100	34,200	3,500	31,500	6,400	—	500
1958	20,600	—	37,800	5,500	39,400	400	—	900
1959	22,400	—	34,900	4,500	48,000	2,200	600	800
1960	18,400	—	36,300	6,400	43,700	8,100	900	2,200

NOTES

Sources: 1935–53, *Blue Books*; 1954–60, *Statistical Yearbook, 1961*.

11. Public finance

Table 23. Government revenue and expenditure; surpluses and deficits; allocation of surpluses and financing of deficits, 1900–60 (£000s)

Year	Revenue	Expenditure	Surplus + Deficit −	Foreign loans	Domestic loans	Appreciation + Depreciation − of investments	Contribution to sinking funds	Repayment of loans	Changes in surplus balances
	(1)	(2)	(3)	(4)	(5)	(6)	(7)	(8)	(9)
1900	382	903	−521	202	—	—	—	—	−319
1901	495	849	−354	197	—	—	—	—	−157
1902	510	1,179	−669	915	—	—	—	−25	221
1903	511	923	−412	56	—	—	—	—	−356
1904	533	538	−5	—	—	—	—	—	−5
1905	454	508	−54	—	—	—	−5	−20	−79
1906	511	544	−33	—	—	—	−11	−27	−71
1907	537	531	+6	—	—	—	−11	−15	−20
1908	599	656	−57	—	—	—	−11	−20	−88
1909	594	906	−312	965	—	—	−11	−25	617
1910	755	941	−186	—	—	—	−11	−149	−346
1911	815	895	−80	—	—	—	−11	−25	−116
1912	899	975	−76	—	—	—	−16	−20	112
1913	942	1,193	−251	—	—	—	−21	−20	−292
1914	984	1,464	−480	994	—	—	−21	−20	473
1915	1,011	1,394	−383	—	—	—	−21	−20	−424
1916	1,378	1,217	+161	—	—	—	−21	−20	120
1917	1,128	1,145	−17	—	—	—	−27	−15	−59
1918	845	1.086	−241	—	—	—	−32	−20	−293
1919	1,935	1,471	+464	—	—	—	−32	−25	407
1920*	2,985	3,189	−204	3,900	—	—	−32	−20	3,644
1921	2,220	5,704	−3,484	—	—	—	−32	−20	−3,536
1922	2,462	3,493	−1,031	—	—	—	−32	−20	−1,083
1923	2,828	2,696	+132	—	—	—	−57	−20	55
[illegible]	[illegible]	[illegible]	−1,951	—	—	—	−57	−20	−2,028

[illegible]	[illegible]	[illegible]	−1,480	4,330	—	—	−57	−96	2,717
1926	3,200	4,642	−1,442	—	—	—	−134	—	−1,576
1927	3,987	4,472	−485	—	—	—	−54	—	−539
1928	3,771†	4,286	−515	—	—	—	−49	—	−564
1929	3,389	3,789	−400	—	—	—	−52	—	−452
1930	2,663	3,482	−819	—	—	—	−28	—	−847
1931	2,278	2,622	−344	1,130	—	—	−9	—	777
1932	2,654	2,375	+279	—	—	—	−24	—	255
1933	2,654	2,168	+486	—	—	—	−33	—	453
1934	2,760	2,204	+556	—	—	—	−38	—	518
1935	32,31	2,401	+830	—	—	—	−498	—	332
1936	3,733	2,845	+888	—	—	—	−841	—	47
1937	3,748	3,194	+554	—	—	−21	−320	—	213
1938	3,717	3,340	+377	—	—	−125	−145	—	107
1939	3,704	3,581	+123	—	—	−73	−42	—	8
1940	3.844	3,859‡	−15	—	—	−4	−39	—	−58
1941	4,118	3,547§	+571	—	—	−27	−39	—	505
1942	4,135	4,093	+42	—	—	+34	−39	—	37
1943	4,286	4,504	−218	—	—	+8	−39	—	−249
1944	5,418	4,452	+966	—	—	+10	−83	—	893
1945	7,145	5,957	+1,188	—	—	+26	−83	—	1,131
1946	7,535	6,546	+989	—	—	+27	−84	—	932
1947	10,209	9,902	+307	—	—	−71	−1,084	—	−848
1948	11,601	11,404	+197	—	—	+58	−84	—	171
1949	18,058	14,059	+3,999	—	—	−222	−84	—	3,693
1950	20,840	17,750	+3,090	—	600	+8	−84	—	3,614
1951	38,929	23,076	+15,853	—	1,700	−541	−1,584	−89	15,339
1952	42,965¶	38,444	+4,521	—	3,520	+367	−84	−159	8,165
1953	48,428	48,052	+376	—	4,515	+186	−1,409	−384	3,284
1954	80,587	46,681	+33,906	—	4,381	−2,164	−97	−853	35,173

Table 23. Government revenue and expenditure; surpluses and deficits; allocation of surpluses and financing of deficits, 1900–60 (£000s)—*continued*

Year	Revenue	Expenditure	Surplus+ Deficit−	Foreign loans	Domestic loans	Appreciation+ Depreciation− of investments	Contribution to sinking funds	Repayment of loans	Changes in surplus balances
	(1)	(2)	(3)	(4)	(5)	(6)	(7)	(8)	(9)
1955*	64,099	70,314	−6,215	—	6,500	−4,942	−248	−600	−5,505
1956	49,502	59,171	−9,669	151‖	2,970	+646	−447	−550	−6,899
1957	59,922	57,731	+2,191	—	—	+1,470	−447	−3,874	−660
1958	66,719	75,742	−9,023	4,030	—	+1,339	−405	−594	−4,653
1959	70,231	87,118	−16,887	—	22,281	−1,724	−291	−597	2,782
1960	83,413	111,834	−28,421	7,094	5,963	+218	−434	−1,304	−16,884

*Covers 15 months

Source: Treasury Department *Annual Reports.*

NOTES

†Includes £305,000 transferred from reserves.

‡Includes £500,000 interest-free loan granted to the Imperial Government.

§Includes £300,000 interest-free loan granted to the Imperial Government.

¶Includes repayment of £800,000 loans by Imperial Government.

‖Relates to advances from the Joint Consolidated Fund London.

Sources: *Annual Reports of the Treasury Department;* also *Blue Books;* and *Annual Reports of the Accountant General.*

A Note on the Colonial Accounting System.

The data presented in this table and subsequent tables in this section have been gathered from accounts kept by the colonial government but extensive reclassification and reorganisation have been undertaken. This was done for two reasons. First, the manner in which the colonial government organised and presented its accounts differs in many important ways from that recommended by the United Nations and currently used by most countries including Ghana. Reclassification on the United Nations basis thus makes comparison with contemporary data possible. Second, the colonial accounting system contains many idiosyncrasies which make them of little value to economists as they stand. Some of these have been discussed already.

Table 23 which shows the colonial government's annual surplus or deficit is the main summary table: Tables 24–30 are breakdowns of the various columns of Table 23. Thus Table 24 gives details of government revenue: Tables 25–9 details of government expenditure; and Table 30 of public debts, etc. In many cases detailed breakdowns of these tables are presented in supplementary tables: thus for instance Tables 24 b and c provide some further breakdown of the main revenue data presented in Table 24a. By working across the columns of

Table 23 we can systematically cover most of the tables in this section. Where an important point arises which is specific to one of the back-up tables but is not of general importance it is dealt with in a footnote to that table.

First a word on Table 23 itself. The colonial government did not summarise its own accounts in this form and in fact made no real estimate of its budgetary surpluses and deficits. The construction of this table therefore required extensive reclassification which is the subject of this note.

Column 1: *Revenue*. The number of heads under which the colonial government gathered revenue were sufficiently few as to pose no serious problems of reclassification: this, of course, reflects the limited scope of its fiscal policy. However, the data presented in column 1 does not completely coincide with the totals of Table 24a as the latter includes current revenue from railways and harbours for various years. In detail column 1 of Table 23 equals the total of Table 24a minus the following: railway revenue for the years 1903–28, 1938 and 1941–4; light harbour dues 1900–50; and revenue from harbours 1942–4. Current expenditure on railways and harbours has been excluded from all expenditure data so as to maintain consistency.

Column 2: *Expenditure*. Here the reorganisation of data has been most extensive. As regards the economic classification the colonial category, ordinary or recurrent expenditure, presented few difficulties as it concides more or less completely with the United Nations' one of current expenditure. But matters are quite different with respect to the capital account or extra-ordinary expenditure and expenditure on loan works as it appears in the colonial accounts. Not the least of the difficulties is to discover what was actually spent here, for the colonial government fused the two categories together in a most confusing fashion and did not enter actual expenditure on loan works into the main accounts at all.

Loan works was the designation given to projects financed out of foreign borrowings from London but on occasions the colonial government found that it was committed to an actual expenditure on one of these projects before borrowed funds were received. When this happened it advanced itself the necessary funds which it entered as an extra-ordinary expenditure under the head 'expenditure on loan works'. Later, when the loan was realised it would pay itself back and enter a negative amount under the same head so that over a period of years it appears that no expenditure on loan works actually took place. To complicate the issue further the repayment of the debt and payments into funds held against the debts was treated as an expenditure and entered accordingly. Properly speaking the latter is no expenditure at all and we have omitted all contributions to funds from the expenditure accounts. We have also omitted the former and in its place included the actual expenditures undertaken, information on which is to be found in a cumulative form in a separate loan works account that appears in *Treasury Department Reports*.

The difficulties presented by reconciling the two systems of functional classification presented less serious problems. One particular problem does however deserve attention. In the U.N. system of classification railways are treated as an economic service while roads are treated as a community service. Generally speaking such a distinction would seem difficult to justify, especially is this so in the case of Ghana. Yet in practice it has been impossible for us to include roads as an economic service with railways for it is virtually impossible to get an accurate annual estimate of colonial government expenditure on roads. This is because roads were built by the Public Works Department (P.W.D.) and separating out this department's road expenditure from expenditure on other items did not prove feasible. (Table 43 below gives a breakdown of P.W.D. expenditure for selected years.)

The accounts as we present them are on the basis of the United Nations functional classification and the colonial economic classification: in particular we have retained the category of extra-ordinary expenditure and included expenditure on loan works as development expenditure.

Columns 3–9: *Surpluses*, *Deficits*, *Allocation of Surpluses and Financing of Deficits*. These data presented much fewer difficulties. Column 3 is calculated from columns 1 and 2; the data in columns 4–8 are taken from various parts of the consolidated accounts and the *Treasury Department Reports*; and column 9 is calculated residually.

Table 24a. Government revenue by source, 1900–60 (£000s)

Year	Total revenue	Indirect taxes: Import duties (1)	Indirect taxes: Export duties (2)	Indirect taxes: Other taxes (3)	Direct taxes: Income tax (4)	Direct taxes: Profit tax (5)	Direct taxes: Mineral duty (6)
1900	383	281	—	—	—	—	—
1901	496	351	—	—	—	—	—
1902	512	382	—	—	—	—	—
1903	578	370	—	—	—	—	—
1904	682	384	—	—	—	—	—
1905	586	334	—	—	—	—	—
1906	683	386	—	—	—	—	—
1907	709	414	—	—	—	—	—
1908	752	490	—	—	—	—	—
1909	779	459	—	—	—	—	—
1910	1,007	611	—	—	—	—	—
1911	1,112	663	—	—	—	—	—
1912	1,231	736	—	—	—	—	—
1913	1,302	780	—	—	—	—	—
1914	1,332	769	—	—	—	—	—
1915	1,456	828	—	—	—	—	—
1916	1,886	1,150	32	—	—	—	—
1917	1,624	683	211	—	—	—	—
1918	1,299	489	131	—	—	—	—
1919	2,601	1,253	419	—	—	—	—
1920	3,722	1,711	571	—	—	—	—
1921	3,016	979	798	—	—	—	—
1922	3,357	1,494	541	—	—	—	—
1923	3,743	1,682	473	—	—	—	—
1924	3,971	2,000	283	—	—	—	—
1925	4,116	2,165	274	—	—	—	—
1926	4,365	2,075	318	16	—	—	—
1927	4,122	2,890	272	19	—	—	—
1928	3,914	2,264	321	18	—	—	—
1929	3,397	2,185	284	21	—	—	—

[illegible]	[illegible]	[illegible]	[illegible]	12	—	—	—
1931	2,284	1,166	300	7	—	—	—
1932	2,671	1,362	279	6	—	—	—
1933	2,685	1,366	439	19	—	14	—
1934	2,778	1,393	481	32	—	17	—
1935	3,268	1,858	539	38	—	26	—
1936	3,775	2,332	589	35	—	38	—
1937	3,792	2,288	463	42	—	36	—
1938	3,780	1,856	810	29	—	53	—
1939	3,734	1,679	911	30	—	68	—
1940	3,869	1,208	1,328	31	—	62	—
1941	4,142	1,525	1,327	46	—	35	—
1942	4,332	1,553	1,014	50	—	69	—
1943	4,720	1,592	1,014	47	—	37	—
1944	5,867	1,482	959	44	1,231	29	—
1945	7,172	1,860	1,421	50	1,472	104	—
1946	7,568	2,461	975	53	1,819	38	—
1947	10,246	3,595	856	67	3,011	47	—
1948	11,639	4,295	1,236	85	2,959	—	11
1949	18,106	7,516	3,454	99	3,441	4	182
1950	20,861	7,222	4,949	112	4,239	3	211
1951	38,929	9,732	19,576	128	4,766	—	412
1952	42,965	9,545	16,827	106	6,773	—	1,581
1953	48,428	12,010	18,570	783	5,685	—	2,232
1954	80,587	12,944	49,271	173	5,977	—	1,207
1955	64,099	18,280	24,690	307	6,148	—	1,357
1956	49,502	16,364	12,586	799	5,221	—	2,010
1957	59,922	14,983	22,734	1,999	5,443	—	2,330
1958	66,719	16,109	25,757	2,991	6,016	—	1,759
1959	70,231	18,900	22,358	3,027	5,643	—	1,508
1960	83,413	25,862	16,158	3,165	6,578	—	2,036

Table 24a. Government revenue by source, 1900–60 (£000s)—*continued*

Year	Interest on investments and loans (7)	Share of profits W.A. Currency Board (8)	Rents of government lands and buildings (9)	Royalties (10)	Investment appreciation Profits on invest. sale (11)	Share of profits Bank of Ghana (12)
1900	1	—	—	1	—	—
1901	1	—	—	7	—	—
1902	4	—	1	3	—	—
1903	1	—	1	2	—	—
1904	1	—	2	5	—	—
1905	1	—	2	—	—	—
1906	1	—	3	9	—	—
1907	1	—	3	18	—	—
1908	1	—	3	15	—	—
1909	2	—	4	22	—	—
1910	2	—	3	18	—	—
1911	1	—	4	25	—	—
1912	3	—	4	28	—	—
1913	3	—	4	25	—	—
1914	9	—	4	24	—	—
1915	9	—	5	26	—	—
1916	16	—	5	17	—	—
1917	33	—	6	24	—	—
1918	29	—	6	28	—	—
1919	39	—	7	21	—	—
1920	332	—	8	23	—	—
1921	157	—	10	22	—	—
1922	72	—	10	24	—	—
1923	49	112	9	20	—	—
1924	26	110	11	18	—	—
1925	30	107	9	23	—	—
1926	177	119	17	41	—	—
1927	116	140	18	31	—	—
1928	121	156	18	41	—	—
[illegible]	110	194	22	38	—	—

[illegible]	[illegible]	[illegible]	[illegible]	72	—	—
1931	88	72	30	69	—	—
1932	89	115	25	62	174	—
1933	74	199	22	27	—	—
1934	78	105	20	95	35	—
1935	88	86	24	72	38	—
1936	104	42	32	36	2	—
1937	153	40	32	114	2	—
1938	148	—	23	84	2	—
1939	145	—	26	49	3	—
1940	142	148	26	122	—	—
1941	148	46	32	107	1	—
1942	149	46	34	108	1	—
1943	138	43	30	95	4	—
1944	108	101	46	82	2	—
1945	441	187	32	116	—	—
1946	467	202	56	46	1	—
1947	471	100	125	115	4	—
1948	501	154	90	76	1	—
1949	515	130	112	43	—	—
1950	599	283	152	111	1	—
1951	864	324	172	117	19	—
1952	1,546	—	191	168	1	—
1953	1,919	309	225	118	65	—
1954	2,319	354	400	121	3	—
1955	2,680	404	515	112	—	—
1956	2,312	399	436	138	10	—
1957	2,146	780	433	172	—	—
1958	2,260	1,564	471	186	—	5
1959	2,098	581	589	212	14	285
1960	6,342	—	642	—	—	—

Table 24a. Government revenue by source, 1900–60 (£000s)—*continued*

Year	Revenue from Ashanti (13)	Revenue from N. Terr. (14)	Licences (15)	Light/ harbour dues (16)	Repayment of loans (17)	Grants, imperial govt. (18)	Grants, local sources (19)	Other receipts (20)
1900	3	8	14	2	—	50	—	3
1901	19	7	20	2	—	25	—	7
1902	16	9	20	2	—	20	—	6
1903	12	12	21	2	—	23	—	12
1904	12	13	29	2	—	32	—	4
1905	12	13	26	2	—	14	—	7
1906	20	14	22	2	—	10	—	2
1907	13	18	24	2	—	5	—	4
1908	10	11	27	2	—	—	—	3
1909	8	2	29	2	—	—	—	13
1910	13	2	31	2	—	—	—	12
1911	18	2	39	2	—	—	—	3
1912	16	3	46	2	—	—	—	3
1913	16	4	43	3	—	—	—	4
1914	18	4	48	3	—	—	—	7
1915	18	4	45	2	—	—	—	7
1916	19	4	54	2	—	—	—	6
1917	—	—	64	2	—	—	—	18
1918	—	—	45	1	—	—	—	12
1919	—	—	42	2	—	—	—	15
1920	—	—	61	3	—	—	—	98
1921	—	—	65	3	—	—	—	15
1922	—	—	78	3	—	—	—	27
1923	—	—	88	4	—	—	—	82
1924	—	—	90	4	1	—	—	141
1925	—	—	115	5	9	—	—	21
1926	—	—	145	7	2	—	—	31
1927	—	—	184	8	2	—	—	12
1928	—	—	190	8	6	—	—	317
[illegible]	[illegible]	[illegible]	178	8	3	—	—	10

[illegible]	[illegible]	[illegible]	132	8	1	17	—	19
1931	—	—	120	6	11	57	—	26
1932	—	—	137	17	11	13	—	84
1933	—	—	140	31	1	2	—	67
1934	—	—	155	28	1	1	—	21
1935	—	—	159	38	1	2	—	4
1936	—	—	181	42	1	1	—	6
1937	—	—	190	44	1	1	—	8
1938	—	—	172	40	2	54	—	50
1939	—	—	146	31	6	185	—	13
1940	—	—	143	25	3	26	—	10
1941	—	—	141	24	2	2	—	48
1942	—	—	145	21	4	2	—	60
1943	—	—	159	24	4	9	—	67
1944	—	—	166	20	20	18	—	73
1945	—	—	169	26	—	142	—	147
1946	—	—	220	33	—	120	—	84
1947	—	—	254	37	—	188	—	104
1948	—	—	357	38	—	220	266	99
1949	—	—	404	48	1	356	381	104
1950	—	—	512	21	1	172	706	134
1951	—	—	548	—	18	144	38	83
1952	—	—	604	—	821	72	2,434	162
1953	—	—	683	—	145	440	2,098	284
1954	—	—	709	—	387	483	3,052	115
1955	—	—	914	—	99	742	3,241	232
1956	—	—	907	—	87	987	3,018	116
1957	—	—	886	—	92	36	3,034	91
1958	—	—	970	—	98	—	2,326	456
1959	—	—	1,068	—	95	27	6,668	345
1960	—	—	996	—	186	84	12,395	750

Table 24a. Government revenue by source, 1900–60 (£000s)—*continued*

Year	Railways (21)	Railway electr. supply (22)	Harbours (23)	Posts and telegraphs (24)	Electricity (25)	Other (26)
1900	—	—	—	1	—	21
1901	—	—	—	1	—	58
1902	—	—	—	1	—	48
1903	65	—	—	2	—	56
1904	147	—	—	4	—	50
1905	130	—	—	8	—	39
1906	172	—	—	7	—	37
1907	168	—	—	8	—	31
1908	150	—	—	9	—	31
1909	182	—	—	10	—	47
1910	249	—	—	14	—	50
1911	295	—	—	13	—	46
1912	329	—	—	13	—	48
1913	357	—	—	14	—	50
1914	381	—	—	14	—	54
1915	446	—	—	24	—	44
1916	506	—	—	29	—	48
1917	494	—	—	30	—	60
1918	453	—	—	33	—	72
1919	664	—	—	50	—	91
1920	736	—	—	63	—	117
1921	796	—	—	68	—	103
1922	892	—	—	69	1	148
1923	1,012	—	—	74	1	139
1924	1,073	—	—	76	2	137
1925	1,106	—	—	86	10	156
1926	1,156	—	—	94	8	156
1927	134	—	—	114	14	165
1928	134	—	—	126	22	172
[illegible]	[illegible]	—	—	128	25	192

				120	28	208
1931	—	—	—	106	29	199
1932	—	—	—	94	26	178
1933	—	—	—	91	26	167
1934	—	—	—	98	25	162
1935	—	—	—	101	26	171
1936	—	—	—	109	29	197
1937	—	—	—	135	35	210
1938	23	—	—	133	35	266
1939	—	—	—	131	35	276
1940	—	—	—	116	38	440
1941	7	—	—	141	45	465
1942	170	9	6	176	57	659
1943	328	13	86	212	75	742
1944	357	13	72	218	84	743
1945	—	—	—	248	100	657
1946	—	—	—	290	91	612
1947	—	182	—	304	184	601
1948	—	—	—	386	195	670
1949	—	—	—	408	225	684
1950	—	—	—	451	279	704
1951	—	—	—	598	408	984
1952	—	—	—	671	397	1,067
1953	—	—	—	825	655	1,382
1954	—	—	—	875	735	1,463
1955	—	—	—	1,200	1,054	2,123
1956	—	—	—	1,171	1,052	1,888
1957	—	—	—	1,456	1,357	1,950
1958	—	—	—	1,808	1,546	2,397
1959	—	—	—	1,834	1,849	2,130
1960	—	—	—	2,041	2,451	3,465

 Table 24a. Government revenue by source, 1900–1960 (£000s)— *continued*

NOTES

Source: All years except 1900/1, 1940/1, and 1943/4, Treasury Department, *Annual Reports*. 1900/1, *Blue Books*. Figures for the years 1940/1 and 1943/4 are obtained from the actual comparative columns of 1942/3 and 1945/6 Budget Estimates.

The data exclude receipts from borrowing and transfers from loan fund, but 1928/9 includes transfer from reserve fund. Prior to 1927/8 railway gross receipts are included in the revenue, and thereafter net receipts, until April 1945, when the railway and Takoradi Harbour accounts were completely separated from the accounts of the central government.

Although the treasury revenue figures by major items seem to be consistent over the years, the grouping of most of the sub items under the main items follows an inconsistent pattern. For example, before 1917, royalties were partly classified under Ashanti and partly in miscellaneous, 1917–1925/6 under miscellaneous, 1926/7–1944/5 under licences and other internal revenue, 1945/6–1959/60 under direct taxes, and in 1960/1 under miscellaneous taxes on production and expenditure.

In order to minimise some of these irregularities a few adjustments were made, and in some cases items which are of importance have been shown separately through the years. The arrangement of the revenue items in the table is therefore slightly different from that of the treasury. However, the sub items can be regrouped into any other form of classification.

Other adjustments which are necessary in order to avoid overstatement of the revenue by mere bookkeeping transactions were also made. For example, reimbursement from loan fund of amounts advanced and spent on loan works. Also from 1953/4 to 1958/9 public works overhead charges and public works annually recurrent expenditure chargeable to the road fund were deducted from revenue as well as in expenditure. From 1951/2 direct receipts, other than loans and interfund transfers to the development funds, are included in revenue. (See attached statement.)

'Import duties' relate to specific and *ad valorem* duties and collections made by the Post Office on parcels.

'Export duties' relate mainly to duties on cocoa, timber, kola nuts and minerals. Export duty on minerals other than diamonds won by African diamond diggers ceased in 1952 and was replaced by minerals duty under the Minerals Duty Ordinance 1952. No export duties were collected before 1916.

Other indirect taxes represent customs miscellaneous receipts: overtime fees, warehouse rents, penalties, forfeitures and seizures; excise duty on beer and cigarettes are included from 1934/5 and 1956/7 respectively: local duty on cocoa processed locally included from 1953/4; included also is betting tax from 1955/6.

'Income tax' relates to taxes on company profits and personal incomes. No income tax was collected before 1944/5; included also is betting tax from 1955/6.

'Profits tax' relates to tax paid on profits by mining companies operating under the concessions ordinance. Figures not given separately from 1951/2.

'Minerals duty' relates to gold duty from 1948/9 to 1951/2 and thereafter duty on all minerals except diamonds won by African diamond diggers. Minerals refer to gold, diamonds, manganese, and bauxite.

Interest on investments and loans comprises interest on surplus and reserve funds invested in foreign securities, loans to local authorities and other bodies. Interest paid by railways and harbour administration on capital loans are included from 1945/6.

'Share of profits from West African Board' relates to the country's share of interest earned on investments by the West African Currency Board. No figures were reported before 1924/5.

Railways: gross revenue from 1903–1926/7 and net revenue from 1927/8 to 1944/5. Railway accounts entirely separated from central government accounts as from April 1945.

Takoradi Harbour: net revenue from 1928/9 to 1943/4.

Posts and telegraphs: 1901–3 figures relate to receipts from postal services in the colony. From 1904 figures for Ashanti and Northern Territories are included.

Electricity: sale of electric power was not available until 1922/3; figures from 1947/8 include charges for other services performed for other government departments and private consumers.

Other sales: fees and earnings relate mainly to receipts from sales of goods and services by other government departments; stamp duty is included to 1925/6. Included also are contributions of civil servants to widow and orphans pension scheme from 1914 to 1950/1.

Licences and fines: 1900–16, figures represent receipts from licences and fines in the colony: 1917–1959/60, they include collections in Ashanti and Northern Territories. Stamp duty included from 1926/7.

Light and harbour dues: only light dues from 1900, Accra Harbour dues are included from 1932/3. The Accra Harbour and other ports were taken over by the Railway Takoradi Harbour Administration in 1950/1 fiscal year.

Revenue from Ashanti: revenue for the years 1900–3 represents unadjusted revenue for Ashanti; 1904–16, figures exclude earnings by posts and telegraphs department, rents of government lands and buildings and royalties. From 1917 the Ashanti revenue items were distributed to their corresponding revenue items in the colony.

Revenue from Northern Territories (see note on revenue from Ashanti).

'Repayment of loans' relates to repayment of loans granted from revenue or surplus funds.

Grants from the imperial government: 1900–7, grants from the British Government towards cost of administration of Northern Territories; 1908–1929/30, no grants, included also from 1953/4 to 1957/8 are contributions by H.M. Government towards cost of Volta River Project Preparatory Commission.

Grants from local sources: mainly grants from the Cocoa Marketing Board, 1959/60 figures include voluntary contributions by cocoa farmers for development purposes.

Unclassified covers overpayments in previous years recovered, unclaimed monies, and other unspecified receipts, and includes land sales which relate to premia on government leases.

Table 24b. Import duties by major commodity group, 1900–60 (£000s)

	Dairy, fish and meat	Cereal (Rice, flour and meal)	Sugar	Alcoholic beverages beer, spirits, etc.	Tobacco	Oil products	Cosmetics drugs and medicine	Explosives	Textiles and clothing	Footwear	Metal manuf.	Parcel post	Mis-cellaneous	Total*
1900–4	—	—	—	—	—	—	—	—	—	—	—	—	—	—
1905–9	—	—	—	279	—	—	—	—	—	—	—	—	—	279
1910–14	—	11	3	466	46	13	7	—	72	—	8	12	17	655
1915–19	—	7	—	424	104	18	15	—	160	—	—	26	—	754
1919	3	3	3	382	183	36	26	4	396	4	24	49	6	1,119
1920	3	6	4	548	140	18	66	5	778	13	80	107	4	1,772
1920–4	15	16	13	565	179	51	38	4	396	6	39	—	10	1,332
1925–9	19	—	33	1,253	257	157	28	—	291	7	22	—	15	2,102
1929	—	—	36	1,044	186	230	28	—	211	6	18	—	17	1,776
1930	—	—	34	728	330	326	29	1	209	5	17	—	17	1,696
1930–4	16	—	29	320	319	246	27	19	186	—	16	—	20	1,198
1934	24	18	25	185	310	218	26	23	204	—	16	—	21	1,070
1935–9	44	—	—	309	418	405	40	41	343	—	41	—	26	1,667
1940–5	15	11	—	156	480	321	38	34	224	—	11	—	23	1,313
1945–9	—	16	—	477	1,253	559	143	64	585	—	110	—	44	3,251
1950–4	—	—	—	1,510	2,856	1,343	424	112	1,818	—	289	—	301	8,653
1955	42	55	62	2,766	3,485	2,333	698	138	2,811	148	630	231	1,490	14,889
1956	49	71	66	2,560	3,279	2,501	804	111	2,911	192	613	265	1,677	15,099
1957	68	74	91	2,681	2,115	3,098	893	107	4,358	261	647	285	1,887	16,562
1958	67	73	62	2,419	1,530	3,500	796	127	3,405	179	692	243	1,696	14,789
1959	74	92	91	2,656	1,582	3,825	947	151	3,896	313	867	277	2,444	17,215
1960	69	111	107	2,947	2,075	3,943	1,011	146	6,106	427	1,453	331	3,181	21,907

NOTES

*Totals do not reconcile with data for import duties in Table 24a since here the figures refer to calendar years and there to financial years.

Sources: *Customs Departmental Reports: Trade Reports: Digest of Statistics.*

Table 24c. Export duties by commodity (£000s)

	Cocoa	Diamonds	Gold	Manganese	Wood and timber	Kola nuts	Palm kernel	Total*
1900–4	—	—	—	—	—	—	—	—
1905–9	—	—	—	—	—	—	—	—
1910–14	—	—	—	—	—	—	—	—
1915–19	159	—	—	—	—	—	—	159
1919	419	—	—	—	—	—	—	419
1920	580	—	—	—	—	—	2	582
1920–4	535	1	—	—	12	6	1	555
1925–9	262	20	—	—	14	—	—	296
1929	278	28	—	—	12	—	—	318
1930	222	31	—	—	5	—	—	259
1930–4	265	29	44	—	3	5	—	344
1934	269	40	146	—	3	7	—	464
1935–9	320	35	265	—	3	10	—	633
1940–4	412	39	681	31	12	11	—	1,188
1945–9	702	53	394†	91	44	14	—	1,298
1950–4	17,084	271	—	204‡	101	15	—	17,675
1955	28,785	270	—	—	135	10	—	29,200
1956	13,851	390	—	—	188	11	—	14,440
1957	12,511	453	—	—	172	8	—	13,144
1958	26,812	450	—	—	213	17	—	27,492
1959	23,976	437	—	—	296	24	—	24,733
1960	18,077	380	—	—	478	32	—	18,967

NOTES

*Totals do not reconcile with data for export duties in Table 24a since here the figures refer to calendar years and there to financial years.

† Four year average 1945–8. From October 1948, the export duty on gold was replaced by a duty on gold production.

‡ Three year average 1950–1. The *Mineral Ordinance 1952* replaced the existing export duties on diamonds and manganese by a duty on manganese iron. This ordinance, however, does not apply to diamonds won by small diggers which continue to be subject to export duties.

No export duties were collected on commodities exported out of the country before 1916.

Sources: *Customs Departmental Reports; Trade Reports* and *Digest of Statistics*.

Table 25. Government expenditure (economic breakdown), 1900–60 (£000s)

Year	Ordinary	Extraordinary	Development	Personal emoluments as % of total	Total
1900	252.1	263.3	387.7	19	902.9
1901	330.5	138.4	379.8	23	849.3
1902	440.4	80.8	658.1	17	1,179.4
1903	499.7	52.7	370.6	30	923.0
1904	491.1	38.9	10.6	46	537.5
1905	471.0	46.9	—	50	508.0
1906	462.0	40.0	41.7	46	543.5
1907	470.0	26.9	34.0	49	530.9
1908	507.4	68.0	80.8	41	656.2
1909	530.6	82.2	292.6	31	906.3
1910	590.0	80.0	271.0	31	941.1
1911	636.3	114.2	144.4	36	894.9
1912	701.9	158.8	116.4	36	975.3
1913	741.2	223.8	228.1	31	1,193.3
1914	857.6	357.4	249.1	29	1,463.9
1915	947.3	293.8	152.5	30	1,394.0
1916	891.8	212.6	112.1	37	1,216.5
1917	905.2	190.8	48.6	40	1,144.6
1918	922.9	131.0	31.6	43	1,085.5
1919	1,261.4	71.8	138.1	48	1,471.2
1920	1,844.9	570.7	774.1	26	3,189.7
1921	2,906.8	739.8	2,057.0	21	5,703.6
1922	2,132.0	376.4	984.4	28	3,492.8
1923	2,095.7	205.1	395.5	35	2,696.3
1924	2,271.4	354.2	2,221.8	23	4,847.4
1925	2,594.6	391.1	1,499.0	25	4,484.6
1926	2,567.6	287.8	1,786.5	23	4,641.9
1927	2,330.0	412.8	1,729.3	25	4,472.2
1928	2,396.5	925.3	1,013.9	28	4,286.3
1929	2,597.8	1,109.5	81.3	35	3,769.7
1930	2,707.2	751.0	23.8	37	3,482.0
1931	2,501.4	122.6	—	47	2,622.0
1932	2,349.3	25.7	—	47	2,375.2
1933	2,157.6	11.0	—	48	2,167.6
1934	2,183.0	20.8	—	49	2,204.1
1935	2,238.2	163.4	—	46	2,401.4
1936	2,471.1	373.9	—	40	2,844.6
1937	2,729.5	463.8	—	37	3,193.8
1938	2,793.9	548.8	—	36	3,339.6
1939	3,027.5	551.6	—	32	3,581.4
1940	3,613.0	230.2	—	31	3,859.4
1941	3,413.1	138.1	—	32	3,547.0
1942	3,886.5	207.0	—	29	4,093.4
1943	4,076.2	437.2	—	27	4,503.9
1944	3,719.0	729.9	—	28	4,451.5

Table 25. Government expenditure (economic breakdown), 1900–60 (£000s)—*continued*

Year	Ordinary	Extraordinary	Development	Personal emoluments as % of total	Total
1945	4,424.3	1,042.7	490.1	22	5,957.0
1946	5,156.8	560.1	829.5	22	6,546.0
1947	7.774.4	1,045.8	1,081.6	21	9,901.5
1948	9,263.8	1,238.1	901.9	21	11,403.8
1949	10,677.4	1,994.1	1,387.8	22	14,059.2
1950	12,253.3	3,282.2	2,215.4	17	17,749.8
1951	14,134.8	2,520.6	6,456.8	15	23,076.3
1952	22,282.2	2,245.8	13,915.2	13	38,443.6
1953	28,144.9	4,372.3	15,591.0	12	48,051.5
1954	26,788.9	1,451.5	17,538.2	13	46,681.0
1955	38,438.1	3,165.8	28,581.7	12	70,313.6
1956	36,617.4	2,076.9	20,477.0	15	59,171.4
1957	37,593.2	—	19,688.1	18	57,281.3
1958	46,122.0	—	29,620.1	15	75,742.3
1959	58,501.1	—	28,617.0	13	87,117.6
1960	68,687.2	—	43,146.3	18	111,833.5

NOTES

The year 1921 relates to the period 1 January 1921 to 31 March 1922. The years after 1921 relate to the period starting on 1 April of the same year and ending on 31 March of the year after.

Sources: *Treasury Department Reports*; *Blue Books*; *Statistical Abstracts, 1961.*

Table 26a. Government expenditure (functional breakdown), 1900–60 (£000s)

Year	General services	Community services	Social services	Economic services	Misc. services	Public debt charges	Total exp.
1900	395	44	25	418	20	0	903
1901	326	41	33	423	11	15	850
1902	247	100	35	755	13	29	1,179
1903	251	113	43	460	11	45	923
1904	237	94	46	93	10	57	537
1905	236	89	46	75	9	51	508
1906	265	81	45	87	6	59	543
1907	274	55	46	91	8	56	531
1908	278	101	53	140	30	55	656
1909	286	134	57	358	10	61	906
1910	307	211	71	263	18	70	941
1911	330	242	90	151	12	70	895
1912	350	313	105	123	14	69	975
1913	371	441	119	182	10	70	1,193
1914	485	521	129	222	16	90	1,464
1915	446	306	146	372	10	113	1,394
1916	492	252	146	205	11	110	1,216
1917	463	253	149	148	21	110	1,145
1918	416	205	134	181	38	111	1,085
1919	464	181	138	305	268	112	1,471
1920	625	871	279	1,020	163	231	3,190
1921	904	1,182	398	2,606	121	493	5,704
1922	715	715	322	1,291	99	351	3,493
1923	740	792	331	418	64	351	2,696
1924	777	1,167	379	2,076	96	352	4,847
1925	789	1,456	412	1,222	124	481	4,484
1926	863	1,368	392	1,425	34	560	4,642
1927	886	1,313	457	1,600	43	173	4,472
1928	958	1,399	537	1,027	344	21	4,286
1929	941	1,596	632	508	79	13	3,770
1930	944	1,117	676	527	175	40	3,479
1931	944	566	578	335	152	47	2,622
1932	981	441	529	287	82	55	2,375
1933	912	356	488	279	72	60	2,168
1934	901	377	504	293	67	62	2,204
1935	910	445	523	327	136	60	2,401
1936	944	610	553	471	207	59	2,845
1937	1,025	817	614	486	193	59	3,194
1938	1,150	826	637	556	112	59	3,340
1939	1,433	872	638	497	94	46	3,581
1940	1,806	845	673	421	80	34	3,859
1941	1,569	712	718	414	100	34	3,547
1942	1,753	970	693	520	124	34	4,093
1943	1,733	1,028	806	761	142	34	4,504
1944	1,722	1,012	896	774	13	34	4,451

Table 26a. Government expenditure (functional breakdown), 1900–60 (£000s)—*continued*

Year	General services	Community services	Social services	Economic services	Misc. services	Public debt charges	Total exp.
1945	1,958	1,229	1,223	1,159	45	342	5,957
1946	1,800	1,436	1,618	864	486	342	6,546
1947	2,236	2,302	2,207	1,066	1,728	364	9,901
1948	3,695	2,659	2,248	1,505	940	356	11,403
1949	3,918	3,017	2,726	2,432	1,621	346	14,059
1950	5,539	3,252	3,052	3,346	2,215	345	17,750
1951	6,911	5,831	5,162	4,198	631	343	23,076
1952	8,791	9,287	10,811	8,933	125	495	38,444
1953	10,921	10,733	13,317	12,290	—	790	48,051
1954	10,141	12,208	12,076	9,612	—	1,383	45,681
1955	16,037	18,296	16,450	18,100	482	949	70,314
1956	16,754	14,870	13,041	13,274	362	871	59,171
1957	15,668	11,361	13,983	15,040	377	851	57,280
1958	19,199	14,172	15,147	22,338	4,054	831	75,742
1959	21,443	18,989	18,066	22,441	5,316	862	87,118
1960	31,372	23,186	23,968	30,699	588	1,516	111,331

NOTES

See note to Table 24a.

Table 26b. Government expenditure; general services, 1900–60 (5 year averages and selected years) (£000s)

Year	Organs of State		Financial admin-istration	Tax admin-istration	General economics regulations	Defence and foreign affairs	Justice and Police	Other general services	Total
	Central	Regional							
1900–4	*10*	*35*	*9*	*32*	—	*155*	*39*	*10*	*291*
1905–9	*11*	*60*	*13*	*37*	—	*82*	*48*	*17*	*268*
1910–14	*14*	*101*	*15*	*55*	—	*81*	*66*	*36*	*369*
1915–19	*19*	*90*	*22*	*51*	—	*131*	*101*	*42*	*456*
1919	22	75	24	48	—	127	113	54	463
1920	38	112	40	74	—	116	168	78	626
*1920–4**	*40*	*130*	*41*	*85*	—	*117*	*193*	*112*	*716*
1925–9	*45*	*171*	*42*	*101*	—	*117*	*244*	*165*	*887*
1929	52	155	39	109	—	107	278	200	940
1930	47	148	40	98	—	102	290	219	944
1930–4	*41*	*126*	*37*	*90*	—	*94*	*273*	*274*	*936*
1934	37	115	34	90	—	88	269	267	900
1935–9	*38*	*135*	*34*	*140*	—	*165*	*279*	*300*	*1,092*
1940–4	*44*	*142*	*53*	*199*	—	*612*	*312*	*354*	*1,717*
1945–9	*145*	*484*	*77*	*390*	—	*414*	*595*	*617*	*2,721*
1950–4	*300*	*2,083*	*1,075*	*346*	*9*	*1,032*	*1,640*	*1,976*	*8,461*
1955–60†	*639*	*4,510*	*1,955*	*421*	*48*	*5,123*	*3,393*	*3,122*	*19,209*
1955	405	4,465	1,519	451	24	2,328	2,979	3,864	16,035
1956	250	4,883	2,395	325	65	3,442	2,337	3,109	16,754
1957	328	4,635	1,363	371	61	3,638	3,270	1,999	16,665
1958	753	4,551	3,210	424	101	3,495	4,253	2,410	19,197
1959	1,100	3,203	1,954	492	38	6,573	3,740	4,343	21,443
1960	1,176	6,563	1,812	577	63	12,674	4,713	3,794	31,373

NOTES

* Includes 5¼ years and is averaged accordingly.

† Includes 6¼ years and is averaged accordingly.

Table 26c. Government expenditure; community and social services, 1900–60 (5 year averages and selected years) (£000s)

	Community services				Social services			
Year	Construction	Fuel & power*	Roads*	Scientific services	Education	Health	General social services	Total
1900–4	59	—	—	19	7	28	1	115
1905–9	83	—	—	9	11	38	0	141
1910–14	334	—	—	12	22	81	0	448
1915–19	239	—	—	1	25	117	0	382
1919	180	—	—	3	16	122	—	321
1920	828	—	—	43	56	223	—	1,150
1920–4†	848	—	—	53	95	230	0	1,226
1925–9	1,331	—	—	73	196	290	0	1,892
1929	1,512	—	—	84	268	363	—	2,227
1930	1,036	—	—	81	305	371	—	1,793
1930–4	537	—	—	57	247	308	0	1,149
1934	330	—	—	47	220	284	—	881
1935–9	663	—	—	51	250	343	1	1,307
1940–4	863	—	—	50	332	417	8	1,671
1945–9	1,157	452	435	84	971	752	281	4,133
1950–4	3,739	954	3,315	254	5,517	2,198	1,169	17,146
1955–60‡	6,780	2,795	5,954	611	10,368	4,030	1,708	32,245
1955	7,993	2,187	7,538	577	9,828	4,108	2,513	34,744
1956	6,257	1,889	6,381	343	7,496	3,324	2,222	27,912
1957	3,997	1,558	3,442	365	9,098	3,341	1,544	23,345
1958	5,118	2,536	6,008	511	9,364	3,854	1,930	29,321
1959	8,589	3,619	5,978	803	12,830	4,485	751	37,055
1960	10,422	5,677	5,868	1,219	16,187	6,066	1,714	47,173

NOTES

* Expenditure under these heads was not separated out from expenditure by the Public Works Department until 1945 which is contained within Construction.

† Covers 5¼ years and is averaged accordingly.
‡ Covers 6¼ years and is averaged accordingly.

Table 26d. Government expenditure; economic services, 1900–60 (5 year averages and selected years) (£000s)

Year	Agriculture	Mines	Manu-facturing and commerce	Railways	Harbours	Transport and communi-cations	Other economic services	Total
1900–4	3	0	—	361	0	65	—	430
1905–9	7	1	—	60	29	52	—	150
1910–14	17	3	—	71	55	42	—	188
1915–19	33	4	—	115	24	68	—	242
1919	58	4	—	162	9	72	—	305
1920	40	8	—	786	64	122	—	1,020
1920–4*	78	13	—	915	249	156	—	1,412
1925–9	124	22	—	323	470	218	—	1,156
1929	133	26	—	29	69	253	—	510
1930	137	13	—	125	17	203	—	495
1930–4	123	11	—	25	3	181	—	344
1934	123	10	—	0	—	159	—	292
1935–9	162	16	—	63	—	224	—	464
1940–4	270	15	—	4	10	278	—	578
1945–9	694	24	10	76	—	601	—	1,405
1950–4	3,922	87	327	1,384	365	1,580	11	7,676
1955–60†	7,894	141	1,638	140	4,301	4,450	939	19,503
1955	8,098	186	610	—	5,533	3,673	—	18,100
1956	6,898	140	911	190	2,080	3,054	—	13,273
1957	6,637	137	1,636	—	3,685	2,954	—	15,049
1958	7,295	102	2,356	—	7,850	4,202	528	22,333
1959	8,198	123	1,683	—	3,907	5,558	2,971	22,440
1960	12,214	191	3,024	685	3,823	8,376	2,369	30,682

NOTES

* Covers $5\frac{1}{4}$ years and is averaged accordingly.

† Covers $6\frac{1}{4}$ years and is averaged accordingly.

Table 27a. Government recurrent expenditure (functional breakdown), 1900–60 (£000s)

Year	General services	Community services	Social services	Economic services	Misc. services	Public debt charges	Total exp.
1900	151	25	25	31	20	6	252
1901	202	27	33	42	11	15	330
1902	213	56	35	94	13	29	440
1903	237	75	43	89	11	45	500
1904	232	63	46	83	10	57	491
1905	236	54	46	73	9	51	471
1906	265	42	45	44	6	59	462
1907	274	33	46	52	8	56	470
1908	278	35	53	56	30	55	507
1909	286	55	57	61	10	61	531
1910	307	74	71	49	19	70	590
1911	330	89	90	46	12	70	636
1912	350	109	105	54	14	69	702
1913	371	108	119	63	10	70	741
1914	428	129	129	64	16	90	858
1915	400	108	146	171	10	113	947
1916	423	113	146	88	11	110	892
1917	415	127	149	83	21	110	905
1918	396	122	134	122	38	111	923
1919	459	151	138	133	268	112	1,261
1920	585	444	279	142	163	231	1,845
1921	904	739	398	251	121	493	2,907
1922	715	415	322	231	99	351	2,132
1923	740	384	331	226	64	351	2,096
1924	777	429	379	238	96	352	2,271
1925	789	449	412	239	224	481	2,595
1926	863	448	392	270	34	560	2,568
1927	886	482	457	288	43	173	2,330
1928	958	502	537	330	48	21	2,396
1929	940	592	623	350	79	13	2,598
1930	942	567	676	352	131	40	2,707
1931	944	506	577	320	107	47	2,501
1932	981	421	529	286	76	55	2,349
1933	912	348	488	278	71	60	2,158
1934	901	359	504	291	66	62	2,183
1935	907	371	523	300	78	60	2,238
1936	939	402	545	319	206	59	2,471
1937	1,023	480	603	372	193	59	2,729
1938	1,135	476	624	389	112	59	2,794
1939	1,399	477	630	389	91	46	3,027
1940	1,781	684	662	375	77	34	3,613
1941	1,561	630	707	382	98	34	3,413
1942	1,742	861	684	441	124	34	3,886
1943	1,719	834	790	550	149	34	4,076
1944	1,475	785	864	547	13	34	3,719

 Table 27a. Government recurrent expenditure (functional breakdown), 1900–60 (£000s)—*continued*

Year	General services	Community services	Social services	Economic services	Misc. services	Public debt charges	Total exp.
1945	1,542	948	950	596	45	342	4,424
1946	1,507	965	1,110	747	486	342	5,157
1947	2,104	1,138	1,466	975	1,728	364	7,774
1948	3,246	1,669	1,704	1,347	940	356	9,264
1949	3,482	1,654	1,894	1,680	1,621	346	10,677
1950	4,110	1,618	2,160	1,805	2,215	345	12,253
1951	4,935	2,580	2,960	2,649	631	343	14,135
1952	6,302	4,329	6,058	4,973	125	495	22,282
1953	8,768	3,895	9,013	5,671	—	790	28,145
1954	8,317	2,965	7,726	6,398	—	1,383	26,789
1955	12,419	5,214	11,007	8,850	—	949	38,438
1956	13,333	4,221	9,828	8,363	2	871	36,617
1957	12,900	3,604	10,923	8,938	377	851	37,593
1958	15,190	4,771	11,797	9,478	4,054	831	46,122
1959	16,757	10,830	12,758	11,977	5,316	862	58,501
1960	21,232	12,877	17,592	14,882	588	1,516	68,687

Table 27b. Government recurrent expenditure; general services, 1900–60 (5 year averages and selected years) (£000s)

Year	Organs of state: Central	Organs of state: Regional	Financial administration	Tax administration	General economic regulations	Defence and foreign affairs	Justice and police	Other general services	Total
1900–4	*10*	*35*	*9*	*32*	—	*71*	*39*	*10*	*207*
1905–9	*11*	*60*	*13*	*37*	—	*82*	*48*	*17*	*268*
1910–14	*14*	*92*	*15*	*55*	—	*79*	*66*	*36*	*357*
1915–19	*19*	*87*	*22*	*51*	—	*96*	*101*	*42*	*419*
1919	22	75	24	48	—	122	113	54	458
1920	38	112	40	74	—	76	168	78	586
*1920–4**	*38*	*130*	*41*	*85*	—	*109*	*193*	*112*	*709*
1925–9	*45*	*171*	*42*	*101*	—	*117*	*244*	*165*	*887*
1929	52	155	39	109	—	107	278	199	939
1930	47	148	40	98	—	102	290	217	942
1930–4	*40*	*126*	*37*	*90*	—	*94*	*273*	*274*	*936*
1934	35	115	34	90	—	88	269	267	898
1935–9	*38*	*135*	*34*	*140*	—	*155*	*279*	*298*	*1,079*
1940–4	*44*	*135*	*53*	*198*	—	*561*	*311*	*354*	*1,656*
1945–9	*142*	*285*	*74*	*387*	—	*312*	*569*	*604*	*2,376*
1950–4	*287*	*1,394*	*666*	*343*	*9*	*688*	*1,314*	*1,784*	*6,486*
1955–60†	*416*	*2,399*	*1,751*	*433*	*30*	*3,882*	*2,737*	*3,077*	*14,727*
1955	354	2,334	1,444	520	24	1,657	2,375	3,710	12,418
1956	215	2,285	2,393	323	13	3,029	2,071	3,004	13,333
1957	283	2,536	1,293	371	27	3,503	2,886	1,999	12,893
1958	269	2,101	3,185	424	26	3,313	3,468	2,403	15,189
1959	361	2,485	1,185	492	35	5,073	2,784	4,343	16,758
1960	907	3,250	1,445	577	63	7,687	3,521	3,771	21,221

NOTES

* Covers 5¼ years and is averaged accordingly.

† Covers 6¼ years and is averaged accordingly.

Table 27c. Government recurrent expenditure; community and social services, 1900–60 (5 year averages and selected years) (£000s)

	Community services				Social services			
Year	Construction	Fuel and power*	Roads*	Scientific services	Education	Health	General social services	Total
1900–4	*30*	—	—	*19*	*7*	*28*	*1*	*86*
1905–9	*33*	—	—	*9*	*11*	*38*	*1*	*93*
1910–14	*90*	—	—	*12*	*22*	*81*	—	*204*
1915–19	*124*	—	—	*1*	*25*	*117*	—	*267*
1919	148	—	—	3	16	122	—	289
1920	401	—	—	43	56	223	—	723
1920–4†	*408*	—	—	*53*	*95*	*230*	—	*785*
1925–9	*438*	—	—	*56*	*196*	*289*	—	*979*
1929	508	—	—	84	266	358	—	1,216
1930	486	—	—	81	304	369	—	1,240
1930–4	*382*	—	—	*57*	*247*	*307*	—	*995*
1934	311	—	—	47	220	284	—	862
1935–9	*390*	—	—	*51*	*249*	*335*	*1*	*1,026*
1940–4	*709*	—	—	*50*	*328*	*405*	*8*	*1,500*
1945–9	*686*	*203*	*302*	*84*	*703*	*657*	*64*	*2,699*
1950–4	*1,599*	*465*	*821*	*192*	*3,683*	*1,544*	*356*	*8,661*
1955–60‡	*3,865*	*1,226*	*1,160*	*392*	*7,625*	*3,281*	*919*	*18,468*
1955	3,571	1,288	—	355	7,048	2,924	1,035	16,221
1956	2,925	985	—	311	6,492	2,526	810	14,049
1957	3,310	930	—	364	6,897	3,059	967	14,527
1958	2,858	1,487	—	426	7,435	3,449	912	16,567
1959	5,157	1,586	3,379	707	8,255	3,867	636	23,587
1960	7,338	1,386	3,868	284	11,529	4,682	1,382	30,469

NOTES

* Expenditure under these heads was not separated out from expenditure by the Public Works Department which until 1945 is contained within Construction.

† Covers 5¼ years and is averaged accordingly.

‡ Covers 6¼ years and is averaged accordingly.

Table 27d. Government recurrent expenditure; economic services, 1900–60* (5 year averages and selected years) (£000s)

Year	Agriculture	Mines	Manuf. & commerce	Transport & communication	Other econ. services	Total
1900–4	3	—	—	64	—	68
1905–9	7	1	—	49	—	57
1910–14	17	3	—	36	—	55
1915–19	43	4	—	72	—	119
1919	58	4	—	70	—	132
1920	40	8	—	94	—	142
1920–4†	73	13	—	122	—	207
1925–9	104	22	—	170	—	295
1929	133	26	—	191	—	350
1930	137	13	—	203	—	353
1930–4	123	11	—	172	—	305
1934	122	10	—	158	—	290
1935–9	147	13	—	193	—	354
1940–4	186	13	—	260	—	459
1945–9	509	23	10	527	—	1,069
1950–4	2,920	58	58	1,252	11	4,299
1955–60‡	6,420	115	276	2,801	386	9,998
1955	6,324	109	—	2,417	—	8,850
1956	5,537	95	578	2,153	—	8,363
1957	5,942	98	425	2,474	—	8,939
1958	5,721	102	321	2,933	400	9,477
1959	6,199	123	126	3,629	1,900	11,977
1960	10,401	191	277	3,898	115	14,882

NOTES

* Railways and harbours are excluded from this table, since current expenditure under these heads has not been included in the accounts as presented here.

† Includes 5¼ years and is averaged accordingly.

‡ Includes 6¼ years and is averaged accordingly.

Table 28. Government extraordinary expenditure (functional breakdown), 1900–56 (£000s)

Year	General services	Community services	Social services	Economic services	Misc. services	Total	By P.W.D.	Posts & telegraphs
1900	243	19	—	—	—	263	19	—
1901	124	14	—	—	—	138	14	—
1902	34	43	—	2	—	80	43	2
1903	14	37	—	—	—	51	37	—
1904	5	31	—	2	—	38	31	2
1905	4	34	—	2	—	40	34	2
1906	—	38	—	1	—	40	38	1
1907	—	21	—	5	—	26	21	5
1908	—	65	—	2	—	68	65	2
1909	—	78	—	3	—	82	78	3
1910	—	73	—	6	—	80	73	3
1911	—	108	—	5	—	114	108	1
1912	—	152	—	4	—	156	152	2
1913	—	212	—	10	—	223	196	10
1914	56	286	—	14	—	357	272	14
1915	46	173	—	73	—	293	167	12
1916	69	119	—	23	—	212	119	3
1917	47	106	—	36	—	190	106	7
1918	20	67	—	43	—	131	67	2
1919	5	29	—	37	—	71	29	—
1920	40	405	—	124	—	570	405	27
1921*	—	443	—	296	—	739	443	94
1922	—	300	—	75	—	376	300	7
1923	—	178	—	26	—	205	178	16
1924	—	305	—	48	—	354	305	3
1925	—	324	—	66	—	391	324	—
1926	—	236	—	51	—	287	236	10
1927	—	320	—	92	—	412	320	9
1928	305	503	—	117	—	925	503	27
1929	—	1,004	8	96	—	1,109	1,004	61
1930	2	548	2	152	44	751	548	32
1931	—	60	—	16	44	122	60	12
1932	—	19	—	—	5	25	19	—
1933	—	8	—	1	1	11	8	—
1934	—	18	—	1	1	20	18	1
1935	3	74	—	17	68	163	74	—
1936	4	207	8	152	—	373	207	2
1937	1	336	11	114	—	463	336	42
1938	17	350	13	167	—	548	350	34
1939	37	395	8	108	2	551	395	22
1940	8	160	11	45	3	230	160	13
1941	11	81	11	31	1	138	81	8
1942	10	108	8	78	—	207	108	14
1943	16	194	16	210	—	437	194	13
1944	245	226	31	226	—	729	226	28

Table 28. Government extraordinary expenditure (functional breakdown), 1900–56 (£000s)—*continued*

Year	General services	Community services	Social services	Economic services	Misc. services	Total	By P.W.D.	Posts & telegraphs
1945	365	131	18	527	—	1,042	228	13
1946	206	282	37	33	—	560	277	3
1947	25	946	35	38	—	1,045	398	5
1948	449	513	204	71	—	1,238	513	13
1949	435	560	384	613	—	1,994	530	9
1950	1,400	716	206	959	—	3,282	709	48
1951	1,206	710	48	555	—	2,520	695	21
1952	1,095	492	44	613	—	2,245	485	21
1953	1,414	2,419	61	466	—	4,372	400	49
1954	581	132	218	518	—	1,451	128	128
1955	508	128	732	1,316	—	2,658	124	167
1956	651	164	225	675	360	2,076	139	151

NOTES

* Includes 15 months.

Financial services are excluded because the items contained under that head – loan repayments and transfers to funds – cannot be considered as real expenditure. Most of the extraordinary expenditure under this head before 1945 was on defence.

Extraordinary expenditure was ceased as a budgetary classification in 1957. See Notes to Table 24a above.

Table 29. Government development expenditure (functional breakdown), 1900–60 (£000s)

Year	General services	Community services	Social services	Economic services	Total
1900	—	—	—	388	388
1901	—	—	—	380	380
1902	—	—	—	658	658
1903	—	—	—	371	371
1904	—	—	—	11	11
1905	—	—	—	—	—
1906	—	—	—	42	42
1907	—	—	—	34	34
1908	—	—	—	81	81
1909	—	—	—	293	293
1910	—	63	—	207	271
1911	—	45	—	99	144
1912	—	52	—	64	116
1913	—	120	—	108	228
1914	—	106	—	143	249
1915	—	24	—	128	152
1916	—	19	—	93	112
1917	—	20	—	29	49
1918	—	16	—	16	32
1919	—	3	—	135	138
1920	—	21	—	753	774
1921	—	—	—	2,057	2,057
1922	—	—	—	984	984
1923	—	229	—	166	395
1924	—	432	—	1,790	2,222
1925	—	683	—	816	1,599
1926	—	684	—	1,103	1,786
1927	—	510	—	1,219	1,729
1928	—	294	—	739	1,014
1929	—	—	—	81	81
1930	—	—	—	23	139
1931	—	—	—	—	—
1932	—	—	—	—	—
1933	—	—	—	—	—
1934	—	—	—	—	—
1935	—	—	—	—	—
1936	—	—	—	—	—
1937	—	—	—	—	—
1938	—	—	—	—	—
1939	—	—	—	—	—
1940	—	—	—	—	—
1941	—	—	—	—	—
1942	—	—	—	—	—
1943	—	—	—	—	—
1944	—	—	—	—	—
1945	51	149	255	35	490
1946	87	188	470	83	829
1947	106	218	705	52	1,082
1948	—	476	340	86	902
1949	—	802	447	139	1,388

Table 29. Government development expenditure (functional breakdown), 1900–60 (£000s)—*continued*

Year	General services	Community services	Social services	Economic services	Total
1950	29	918	686	582	2,215
1951	769	2,540	2,154	994	6,457
1952	1,394	4,466	4,708	3,347	13,915
1953	739	4,411	4,287	6,153	15,591
1954	1,152	9,110	4,131	3,145	17,538
1955	3,109	12,785	4,720	7,969	28,582
1956	2,769	10,480	2,988	4,240	20,477
1957	2,768	7,757	3,061	6,102	19,688
1958	4,058	9,401	3,351	12,732	29,620
1959	7,687	8,159	4,237	6,392	28,617
1960	10,151	10,309	8,637	14,049	43,146

NOTES

Development expenditure in the period 1900–31 was termed by the colonial government 'expenditure on loan works'; see notes to Table 23 above. Expenditure on loan works was limited to railways, harbours and waterworks. The following table shows how funds were allocated between these different projects.

Loan works expenditure, 1900–30 (*£000s*)

	Railways	Harbours	Waterworks
1900–4	362	—	—
1905–9	60	30	—
1910–14	74	51	77
1915–19	56	24	17
1920–4	835	249	—
1925–9	264	413	—

During the 1920s government investment was financed out of accumulated balances. We have added this expenditure into the main accounts by including it with extraordinary expenditure which was the practice followed by the government. The following table gives a breakdown of 'special' expenditure for the six years in which it took place.

Special departmental works from accumulated balances (*£000s*)

	Surveys	Agriculture	Forestry	Posts & telegraphs	P.W.D.	Takoradi*	Other†	Total
1923	—	18	—	10	189	—	40	257
1924	7	10	1	24	354	—	71	467
1925	19	31	4	25	561	—	3	642
1926	25	32	4	59	583	—	76	779
1927	19	17	5	24	430	276	61	832
1928	21	4	3	26	333	167	31	584

* Included in main accounts as harbours.

† Included in main accounts as P.W.D.

Further details of government capital investment and development expenditure can be had from Tables 14–16 above which deal with the various development plans.

Table 30a. Public debt, 1900–60 (£000s)

	Nominal debt outstanding			Sinking funds			Interest	
Year ending	External debt*	Internal debt	Total	Held in foreign securities†	Net debt outstanding	Year	Earned on sinking funds‡	Paid on debt out-standing§
Dec. 1900	345.5	—	345.5	—	345.5	1900	—	—
Dec. 1901	1,330.1	—	1,330.1	—	1,330.1	1901	—	15.2
Dec. 1902	2,082.7	—	2,082.7	—	2,082.7	1902	—	28.8
Dec. 1903	2,253.0	—	2,253.0	—	2,253.0	1903	—	44.6
Dec. 1904	2,272.5	—	2,272.5	—	2,272.5	1904	—	56.5
Dec. 1905	2,248.2	—	2,248.2	—	2,248.2	1905	—	51.1
Dec. 1906	2,252.7	—	2,252.7	18.7	2,234.0	1906	2.9	58.5
Dec. 1907	2,207.0	—	2,207.0	30.1	2,176.9	1907	1.0	55.8
Dec. 1908	2,207.2	—	2,207.2	43.2	2,164.0	1908	1.5	54.5
Dec. 1909	2,663.5	—	2,663.5	56.5	2,607.0	1909	2.4	60.8
Dec. 1910	2,514.1	—	2,514.1	69.9	2,444.2	1910	2.4	70.3
Dec. 1911	2,489.1	—	2,489.1	84.0	2,405.1	1911	3.2	69.5
Dec. 1912	2,469.1	—	2,469.1	102.7	2,366.4	1912	3.1	69.2
Dec. 1913	2,449.1	—	2,449.1	128.2	2,320.9	1913	4.2	70.0
Dec. 1914	3,464.1	—	3,464.1	154.6	3,309.5	1914	5.1	90.0
Dec. 1915	3,444.1	—	3,444.1	182.1	3,262.0	1915	6.1	112.6
Dec. 1916	3,424.1	—	3,424.1	210.9	3,213.2	1916	17.4	110.2
Dec. 1917	3,409.1	—	3,409.1	246.1	3,163.0	1917	8.8	110.1
Dec. 1918	3,389.1	—	3,389.1	288.1	3,101.0	1918	10.4	110.8
Dec. 1919	3,364.1	—	3,364.1	332.5	3,031.6	1919	12.8	111.8
Dec. 1920	7,344.1	—	7,344.1	379.6	6,964.5	1920	15.4	230.3
Mar. 1922	7,319.1	—	7,319.1	437.3	6,881.8	1921	18.7	350.5
Mar. 1923	7,299.1	—	7,299.1	490.7	6,808.4	1922	21.8	350.1
Mar. 1924	7,279.1	—	7,279.1	578.1	6,701.0	1923	30.8	350.1
Mar. 1925	7,259.1	—	7,259.1	664.7	6,594.4	1924	30.0	351.2

Mar. 1926	11,791.0	—	11,791.0	756.9	11,034.1	1925	35.6	350.4
Mar. 1927	11,791.0	—	11,791.0	930.0	10,861.0	1926	38.7	558.6
Mar. 1928	11,791.0	—	11,791.0	1,112.5	10,678.5	1927	41.9	548.3
Mar. 1929	11,791.0	—	11,791.0	1,303.3	10,487.7	1928	50.0	548.3
Mar. 1930	11,791.0	—	11,791.0	1,505.4	10,285.6	1929	56.6	548.3
Mar. 1931	11,791.0	—	11,791.0	1,680.1	10,110.9	1930	67.8	548.3
Mar. 1932	12,961.0	—	12,961.0	1,813.0	11,148.0	1931	75.6	548.3
Mar. 1933	12,961.0	—	12,961.0	2,017.9	10.943.1	1932	81.3	601.0
Mar. 1934	12,961.0	—	12,961.0	2,485.2	10,475.8	1933	90.8	601.0
Mar. 1935	11,863.0	—	11,863.0	1,705.8	10,157.2	1934	110.4	568.1
Mar. 1936	11,435.0	—	11,435.0	1,801.6	9,633.4	1935	75.9	560.1
Mar. 1937	11,435.0	—	11,435.0	2,696.6	8,738.4	1936	81.4	550.0
Mar. 1938	11,435.0	—	11,435.0	3,149.1	8,285.9	1937	124.1	550.0
Mar. 1939	11,435.0	—	11,435.0	3,208.2	8,226.8	1938	142.2	550.0
Mar. 1940	10,400.0	—	10,400.0	2,460.7	7,939.3	1939	148.9	550.0
Mar. 1941	10,400.0	—	10,400.0	2,608.2	7,791.8	1940	109.3	519.0
Mar. 1942	10,400.0	—	10,400.0	2,747.4	7,652.6	1941	—	519.0
Mar. 1943	10,400.0	—	10,400.0	2,980.5	7,419.5	1942	124.7	519.0
Mar. 1944	10,400.0	—	10,400.0	3,142.6	7,257.4	1943	133.1	519.0
Mar. 1945	8,410.0	—	8,410.0	1,358.3	7,051.7	1944	—	519.0
Mar. 1946	8,410.0	—	8,410.0	1,505.8	6,904.2	1945	60.8	341.2
Mar. 1947	8,410.0	—	8,410.0	1,674.5	6,735.5	1946	67.2	340.4
Mar. 1948	8,410.0	—	8,410.0	2,778.9	5,631.1	1947	74.1	342.5
Mar. 1949	8,410.0	—	8,410.0	2,993.5	5,416.5	1948	127.3	355.1
Mar. 1950	8,410.0	—	8,410.0	3,028.7	5,381.3	1949	133.0	344.9
Mar. 1951	8,410.0	600.0	9,010.0	3,271.5	5,738.5	1950	142.1	344.2
Mar. 1952	8,410.0	2,242.3	10,652.3	4,658.8	5,993.5	1951	147.3	342.2
Mar. 1953	8,410.0	5,663.7	14,073.7	5,193.1	8,880.6	1952	224.3	492.8
Mar. 1954	8,410.0	9,979.8	18,389.8	6,802.1	11,587.7	1953	228.6	788.6
Mar. 1955	8,410.0	14,034.3	22,444.3	6,933.7	15,510.6	1954	302.2	1,381.7

Table 30a. Public debt, 1900–60 (£000s)—*continued*

	Nominal debt outstanding			Sinking funds			Interest	
Year ending	External debt*	Internal debt	Total	Held in foreign securities†	Net debt outstanding	Year	Earned on sinking funds‡	Paid on debt outstanding§
Jan. 1956	3,180.0	19,470.4	22,650.4	2,392.1	20,258.3	1955	317.3	943.6
Jan. 1957	3,331.0	21,941.1	25,272.1	2,949.2	22,322.9	1956	110.0	869.6
Jan. 1958	3,180.0	18,391.5	21,571.5	3,358.2	18,213.3	1957	132.5	849.3
Jan. 1959	7,210.0	16,820.7	24,030.7	3,830.0	20,200.7	1958	158.8	830.9
Jan. 1960	3,180.0	38,578.1	41,758.1	4,230.1	37,528.0	1959	170.1	861.6
Jan. 1961	10,274.0	43,962.7	54,236.7	4,834.2	49,402.5	1960	193.0	1,516.0

NOTES

* Excludes suppliers' credit.

† Figures from 1906 to 1933 relate to book value, whereas figures from 1934 relate to market value. No funds throughout the period were held in the form of domestic securities.

‡ Figures to 1927 represent actual interest earned on sinking funds invested. From 1928 the figures are estimates calculated at an average rate of $4\frac{1}{2}$% on book values at the beginning of each fiscal year.

§ All years except 1928–45 represent actual interest paid on loans outstanding. Figures for the years 1928 to 1945 were according to the rates given for each loan.

Details of the most important colonial borrowings are as follows: during 1902 a loan of £1,035,000 was raised at 3 per cent. £915,000 of this sum was realised and spent on loan works. The following year a further £63,000 was raised of which £56,300 was realised and spent. Both loans were made at 3 per cent and redeemed in March 1935 from the proceeds of the loan sinking fund and the supplementary sinking fund. The amount available from these funds was £1,028,235 leaving a deficiency of £69,765 which was paid from advances from the colony's surplus funds. This amount was made good during the next financial year.

A loan of £1,030,000 was raised at 3.5 per cent in 1909 and redeemed in May 1935 by a 3 per cent conversion stock of £602,000 and the amount in the relevant sinking fund. £965,000 of this loan was realised and spent on loan works.

During 1914 a loan of £1,035,000 was raised at 4 per cent and redeemed in 1939 out of the relevant sinking fund and part of the supplementary sinking fund. The amount realised on this loan was £993,800.

In 1920 the colonial government borrowed £4,000,000 at 6 per cent. This was redeemed in fiscal year 1944 partly by conversion into a 3 per cent loan of £2,010,000 redeemed in 1963, and partly by payments from the relevant sinking fund and the supplementary sinking fund. The amount realised and spent was £3,900,200.

In 1926 a loan of £4,628,000 was floated to cover expenditures already undertaken. The amount realised was £4,350,300.

Source: *Treasury Department Reports.*

Year	2,300.0† Loan from Cocoa Marketing Board	3,520.0 Loan from Cocoa Marketing Board	4,015.4 Loan from Cocoa Marketing Board	2,408.0 Loan from Cocoa Marketing Board	2,000.0 Loan from Cocoa Marketing Board	Total amount paid during the financial year	Loan ou tstanding at end of year
1950	—	—	—	—	—	—	600.0
1951	57.7	—	—	—	—	57.7	2,242.3
1952	89.1	9.6	—	—	—	98.7	5,663.7
1953	91.5	107.7	—	—	—	199.2	9,479.8
1954	94.0	122.1	137.5	—	—	353.6	11,534.2
1955	121.6	159.6	179.2	103.5	—	563.9	12,970.3
1956	100.1	133.6	149.5	86.4	59.7	529.3	12,441.0
1957	102.9	139.0	155.2	89.7	62.8	549.6	11,891.5
1958	105.8	144.7	161.2	93.1	66.0	570.8	11,320.7
1959	108.7	150.6	167.3	96.6	69.4	592.6	10,728.1
1960	111.8	156.7	173.7	100.3	72.9	615.4	10,112.7

NOTES

* This table excludes Local Treasury Bills and Advances from the Joint Consolidated Fund – Crown Agents

† £600,000 of the approved loan of £2,300,000 was paid to the Government in 1950–1 and the balance of £1,700,000 paid in 1951–2.

Source: *Treasury Department Reports.*

Table 31a. Revenue and expenditure of municipal authorities, 1900–60 (£000s)

	Accra			Sekondi			Cape Coast			Kumasi			Total – all councils		
Year	Rev.	Exp.	Surp./ Def.	Rev.	Exp.	Surp./ Def.	Rev.	Exp.	Surp./ Def.	Rev.	Exp.	Surp./ Def.	Rev.	Exp.	Surp./ Def.
1900	3.2	3.8	—0.6	—	—	—	—	—	—	—	—	—	3.2	3.8	—0.6
1901	3.9	4.2	—0.3	—	—	—	—	—	—	—	—	—	3.9	4.2	—0.3
1902	3.5	3.2	0.3	—	—	—	—	—	—	—	—	—	3.5	3.2	0.3
1903	5.2	5.2	0.0	—	—	—	—	—	—	—	—	—	5.2	5.2	0.0
1904	5.3	5.8	—0.5	—	—	—	—	—	—	—	—	—	5.3	5.8	—0.5
1905	5.2	4.9	0.3	2.1	1.6	0.5	—	—	—	—	—	—	7.3	6.5	0.8
1906	5.1	4.8	0.3	2.8	2.7	0.1	2.1	1.2	0.9	—	—	—	10.0	8.7	1.3
1907	5.6	4.6	1.0	2.9	2.6	0.3	2.3	2.6	—0.3	—	—	—	10.8	9.8	1.0
1908	5.7	6.0	—0.3	3.3	4.5	—1.2	2.4	2.3	0.1	—	—	—	11.4	12.8	—1.4
1909	6.9	7.2	—0.3	3.5	3.4	0.1	2.4	2.2	0.2	—	—	—	12.8	12.8	0.0
1910	6.2	7.7	—1.5	2.8	2.9	—0.1	2.2	2.2	0.0	—	—	—	11.2	12.8	—1.6
1911	7.4	7.5	—0.1	4.5	3.9	0.6	3.1	2.8	0.3	—	—	—	15.0	14.2	0.8
1912	8.6	8.0	0.6	4.5	4.8	—0.3	3.5	3.3	0.2	—	—	—	16.6	16.1	0.5
1913	9.5	10.6	—1.1	4.7	5.2	—0.5	3.9	3.5	0.4	—	—	—	18.1	19.3	—1.2
1914	11.2	11.3	—0.1	5.5	5.6	—0.1	5.3	4.0	1.3	—	—	—	22.0	20.9	1.1
1915	13.1	11.5	1.6	5.2	5.2	0.0	3.3	5.1	—1.8	—	—	—	21.6	21.8	—0.2
1916	13.8	13.4	0.4	5.7	5.3	0.4	4.5	4.2	0.3	—	—	—	24.0	22.9	1.1
1917	14.0	15.8	—1.8	5.9	5.6	0.3	4.1	4.0	0.1	—	—	—	24.0	25.4	—1.4
1918	13.5	13.3	0.2	6.2	6.1	0.1	4.3	3.6	0.7	—	—	—	24.0	23.0	1.0
1919	14.0	14.0	0.0	6.0	6.1	—0.1	4.4	3.9	0.5	—	—	—	24.4	24.0	0.4
1920	18.5	16.6	1.9	8.1	8.0	0.1	6.8	6.1	0.7	—	—	—	33.4	30.7	2.7
1921	22.5	23.2	—0.7	9.4	9.6	—0.2	7.2	7.0	0.2	—	—	—	39.1	39.8	—0.7
1922	24.1	22.7	1.4	9.6	9.4	0.2	6.5	6.5	0.0	—	—	—	40.2	38.6	1.6
1923	25.9	24.8	1.1	10.6	10.2	0.4	8.1	8.0	0.1	—	—	—	44.6	43.0	1.6
1924	25.7	26.4	—0.7	10.7	10.4	0.3	7.4	7.6	—0.2	—	—	—	43.8	44.4	—0.6
1925	30.9	29.7	1.2	10.6	11.1	—0.5	7.6	8.2	—0.6	—	—	—	49.1	49.0	0.1
1926	34.7	40.4	—5.7	12.3	12.2	0.1	8.1	7.8	0.3	46.3	44.8	1.5	101.4	105.2	—3.8
1927	41.6	38.1	3.5	14.2	14.4	—0.2	8.5	8.0	0.5	55.4	56.2	—0.8	119.7	116.7	3.0
1928	47.6	43.4	4.2	17.7	16.0	1.7	11.0	11.2	—0.2	64.9	63.1	1.8	141.2	133.7	7.5
1929	51.6	52.5	—0.9	17.1	17.0	0.1	10.7	9.3	1.4	55.9	65.9	—10.0	135.3	144.7	—9.4
1930	49.7	50.3	—0.6	16.9	16.1	0.8	10.3	9.4	0.9	57.1	49.1	8.0	134.0	124.9	9.1
1931	51.4	52.2	—0.8	20.0	16.4	3.6	12.8	9.0	3.8	53.7	51.0	2.7	137.9	128.6	9.3
1932	42.2	43.2	—1.0	18.2	15.5	2.7	12.6	10.2	2.4	52.1	59.0	—6.9	125.1	127.9	—2.8
1933	37.3	39.3	—2.0	16.7	13.6	3.1	10.3	9.5	0.8	54.7	52.3	2.4	119.0	114.7	4.3
[illegible]	[illegible]	38.8	2.4	17.8	14.0	3.8	10.4	9.3	1.1	58.0	55.4	2.6	127.4	117.5	9.9

[illegible]	[illegible]	[illegible]	[illegible]	[illegible]	[illegible]	4.3	11.3	10.8	0.5	64.7	63.1	1.6	137.5	127.3	10.2
1936	48.7	42.6	6.1	20.3	15.2	5.1	11.4	10.8	0.6	57.3	54.3	3.0	137.7	122.9	14.8
1937	48.3	42.9	5.4	16.9	17.4	—0.5	15.3	14.8	0.5	63.2	59.6	3.6	143.7	134.7	9.0
1938	54.3	55.5	—1.2	16.7	17.2	—0.5	15.2	14.1	1.1	55.1	64.3	—9.2	141.3	151.1	—9.8
1939	64.2	53.8	10.4	13.8	14.2	—0.4	12.2	12.8	—0.6	54.8	64.3	—9.5	145.0	145.1	—0.1
1940	68.6	78.1	—9.5	12.3	12.4	—0.1	11.6	10.6	1.0	55.7	50.0	5.7	148.2	151.1	—2.9
1941	79.7	78.5	1.2	12.9	12.7	0.2	11.6	10.7	0.9	58.5	54.2	4.3	162.7	156.1	6.6
1942	98.9	89.5	9.4	14.7	14.7	0.0	11.6	11.5	0.1	60.0	56.1	3.9	185.2	171.8	13.4
1943	103.9	105.9	—2.0	16.8	14.2	2.6	13.3	12.6	0.7	68.8	62.5	6.3	202.8	195.2	7.6
1944	127.8	122.8	5.0	13.6	14.8	—1.2	12.4	12.3	0.1	73.7	65.9	7.8	227.5	215.8	11.7
1945	159.2	144.5	14.7	27.3	31.3	—4.0	12.9	12.2	0.7	84.1	81.5	2.6	283.5	269.5	14.0
1946	166.1	164.3	1.8	32.6	34.3	—1.7	13.6	13.4	0.2	107.8	109.2	—1.4	320.1	321.2	—1.1
1947	230.9	218.2	12.7	64.7	58.0	6.7	22.3	23.7	—1.4	174.0	170.0	4.0	491.9	469.9	22.0
1948	244.5	245.4	—0.9	80.6	77.0	3.6	22.6	21.8	0.8	197.0	201.4	—4.4	544.7	545.6	—0.9
1949	277.1	270.4	6.7	88.2	87.5	0.7	27.6	27.3	0.3	254.6	244.2	10.4	647.5	629.4	18.1
1950	319.6	307.8	11.8	132.6	127.8	4.8	34.0	33.4	0.6	290.5	262.5	28.0	776.7	731.5	45.2
1951	382.9	369.2	13.7	166.5	165.8	0.7	38.6	39.1	—0.5	358.5	335.9	22.6	946.5	910.0	36.5
1952	483.9	428.1	55.8	261.0	192.9	68.1	82.2	57.8	24.4	543.9	439.9	104.0	1,371.0	1,118.7	252.3
1953	581.7	538.6	43.1	264.4	252.5	11.9	70.3	68.7	1.6	555.6	510.1	45.5	1,472.0	1,369.9	102.1
1954	715.5	657.7	57.8	350.3	333.4	16.9	86.6	82.7	3.9	603.9	590.6	13.3	1,756.3	1,664.4	91.9
1955	827.8	775.6	52.2	388.7	403.6	—14.9	82.5	88.9	—6.4	666.1	735.3	—69.2	1,965.1	2,003.4	—38.3
1956	1,025.2	966.4	58.8	435.4	513.4	—78.0	93.6	100.2	—6.6	692.9	990.0	—297.1	2,247.1	2,570.0	—322.9
1957	1,191.8	1,005.1	136.7	543.5	548.1	—4.6	130.9	122.8	8.1	900.0	861.6	38.4	2,766.2	2,587.6	178.6
1958	1,173.3	1,093.4	79.9	547.6	562.3	—14.7	125.5	135.8	—10.3	928.6	867.7	60.9	2,775.0	2,659.2	115.8
1959	974.6	990.5	—15.9	457.9	449.1	8.8	119.1	125.7	—6.6	942.9	802.8	140.1	2,494.5	2,368.1	126.4
1960	1,060.2	1,154.8	—94.6	604.3	544.7	59.6	135.4	127.8	7.6	1,192.1	1,177.1	15.0	2,992.0	3,004.4	—12.4

NOTES

The series include current revenue and expenditure of municipal motor bus services from their various years of establishment to 1958/9. In 1959 a National Omnibus Service was established to run all motor bus services in the municipalities. The figures from 1959/60 therefore exclude revenue and expenditure of the Omnibus Service, but are shown separately below.

	Revenue (£'000s)	Expenditure (£'000s)	
1959/60	1,166.8	1,228.4	(Covers April 1959 to June 1960)
1960/1	1,241.3	1,144.2	(Covers July 1960 to June 1961)

Sources: 1900–21, *Colonial Reports;* 1922/3 to 1930/1, *Annual Municipal Reports;* 1931/2 to 1939, *Blue Books;* 1939/40 to 1953/4, *Local Government Financial Statistics* (1954/5); 1954/5 to 1960/1, *Statistical Yearbooks 1961* and *1962*.

Table 31b. Municipal authorities: revenue by source and expenditure by function, 1950–60 (£000s)

Revenue

Year	Taxes and fees	Property income	Other sources	Transfers from govt.	Misc. transfers	Total revenue	Loans raised
1950	830.8	57.8	509.5	673.6	21.4	2,093.3	55.9
1951	982.5	76.2	615.0	821.5	19.4	2,514.6	45.8
1952	1,066.8	67.4	665.8	1,065.0	31.9	2,896.9	71.8
1953	1,485.1	70.3	495.9	1,617.4	34.7	3,703.4	147.0
1954	1,561.8	70.8	463.1	2,074.3	43.7	4,213.6	9.6
1955	1,854.7	615.3	537.9	2,226.3	327.5	5,561.7	129.5
1956	2,664.3	732.4	680.6	3,823.0	594.2	8,494.5	101.0
1957	2,318.2	804.6	644.5	3,243.5	387.9	7,398.7	59.5
1958	2,774.8	799.6	608.5	3,038.7	426.6	7,648.2	42.0
1959	2,939.5	511.5	665.7	2,835.4	468.0	7,420.1	30.0
1960	3,497.0	24.3	629.8	2,753.8	392.2	7,297.1	90.8

Expenditure

Year	Organs of State	Financial admin.	Police and justice	Other general services	Education and research	Health services	Construction
1950	254.6	92.1	165.8	24.6	215.7	302.1	268.8
1951	275.9	102.7	186.6	52.2	246.7	361.2	349.0
1952	305.4	120.7	216.0	94.2	320.6	431.8	789.7
1953	324.4	134.3	237.0	112.5	397.2	603.3	531.7
1954	335.6	169.5	307.6	18.1	546.2	791.2	597.0
1955	754.1	185.1	367.7	27.2	967.3	1,039.7	620.4
1956	1,168.0	211.6	507.2	29.9	1,630.7	1,449.8	815.7
1957	1,003.2	—	450.6	58.6	1,601.0	1,474.1	792.6
1958	830.9	—	413.8	65.8	1,709.8	1,513.0	781.0
1959	841.4	—	467.6	67.1	1,879.1	1,568.7	666.8
1960	771.2	—	398.5	120.9	1,960.6	1,461.7	794.9

Year	Agriculture	Transport	Other economic services	Miscellaneous	Current capital expenditure	Total expenditure
1950	23.6	—	—	170.0	496.0	1,517.3
1951	35.3	—	—	198.0	568.9	1,807.6
1952	39.6	11.6	—	337.2	720.1	2,666.8
1953	53.4	—	—	348.5	869.3	2,742.3
1954	47.5	19.4	—	268.2	907.6	3,100.3
1955	49.4	1,452.6	5.8	79.1	1,397.8	5,548.4
1956	56.0	2,318.2	13.5	55.3	2,194.9	8,255.9
1957	54.4	1,966.1	47.6	156.2	—	7,604.4
1958	42.1	2,060.5	62.1	93.4	—	7,572.4
1959	60.7	1,831.9	42.5	110.8	—	7,536.6
1960	43.0	1,449.1	76.3	96.7	—	7,172.9

Table 31b. Municipal authorities: revenue by source and expenditure by function, 1950–60 (£000s)—*continued*

NOTES

For all except Miscellaneous and Construction, the period 1955–6 relates to April 1955 to June 1956.

'Taxes and fees' relates to revenue from rates, licences, fees and duties and education fees.

'Property income' relates to revenue from interest and profits on business services.

'Other sources' relates to revenue from trading services, lorry revenue, justice and police, land and native rights, rent, ferries, precast cement and quarry works, municipal authorities.

'Transfers from govt.' relates to revenue from grants in aid, capital grants, education grants, reimbursement and other grants.

'Misc. transfers' relates to revenue from other works on repayment, transfer from loan accounts, transfer from reserves and miscellaneous.

'Other general services' relates to pensions and gratuities, temporary allowances and lands.

'Organs of State' relates to industry and commerce, and is available only from 1954–5 on.

'Financial administration' is available only until 1955–6. Source for the period 1954–5—1955–6 is the office of the Government Statistician.

'Construction' relates to Municipal Works Department, annually recurrent works, water supplies, engineers' branch, fire service, and housing and community facilities.

'Transport' relates to subsidy (contribution towards temporary additions to rates of pay of motor bus services) and loss on motor bus services, motor conservancy service and motor transport service. A Transport Authority designated Municipal Authority Service, which took over the Motor Transport Service from the Municipal and City Councils was set up in 1958–9. Figures for total receipts and payments for Municipal Transport Service are shown separately below. (The figures for 1959–60 relate to the period from 1 April 1959 to 30 June 1960.)

Receipts: 1958–9—295.5 1959–60—1,166.8 (£000s)
Payments: 1958–9—200.3 1959–60—1,228.4

Source: 1949–50—1953–4, Office of the Government Statistician; 1954–5—1959–60, Central Bureau of Statistics.

12. Transport and Communications

Table 32a. Railway financial returns, 1900–60 (£000s)

	Earnings				Working expenditure				Other expenditure*				
Year	Coaching	Goods	Misc.	Total	Ord. working expend.	Contr. to renewals s. fund	Total	Balance	Net revenue accounts	Interest	S. fund contr. & L. repaym.	Profit	Loss
1900	..	..	..	..	..	—	..	..	..	..	..	..	..
1901	..	..	..	..	..	—	..	..	..	..	..	..	..
1902	..	..	..	..	..	—	..	..	..	..	..	..	..
1903	12	53	1	66	47	—	47	19	..	..	..	..	..
1904	31	113	4	148	91	—	91	57	..	..	..	..	..
1905	29	101	3	133	82	—	82	50	..	..	..	..	..
1906	28	140	3	171	77	—	77	94	..	..	..	..	..
1907	32	128	6	166	77	—	77	89	..	..	..	..	..
1908	32	119	0	151	75	—	75	76	..	..	..	..	..
1909	36	147	2	185	74	—	74	111	..	..	..	..	..
1910	45	204	4	253	85	—	85	169	..	..	..	..	..
1911	62	220	4	286	102	—	102	184	..	..	..	..	..
1912	74	237	4	315	121	—	121	194	..	..	..	..	..
1913	90	264	7	361	150	—	150	211	..	..	..	..	..
1914	92	282	9	383	174	—	174	209	..	..	..	..	..
1915	109	330	8	447	184	—	184	263	..	..	..	..	..
1916	121	360	9	490	197	—	197	293	..	..	..	..	..
1917	116	366	12	494	195	—	195	299	..	..	..	..	..
1918	114	327	16	457	198	—	198	259	..	..	..	..	..
1919	166	489	17	672	234	—	234	438	..	..	..	..	..
1920	198	520	19	737	365	—	365	372	..	..	..	..	..
1921†	227	749	22	998	543	—	543	455	..	..	..	..	..
1922	188	655	35	878	398	—	398	480	..	309	49	115	
1923	203	772	37	1,012	431	98	529	484	10	293	47	133	
1924	202	826	39	1,067	454	98	552	515	12	293	47	162	
1925	215	850	37	1,102	470	98	568	534	70	271	52	141	
1926	224	894	38	1,156	472	101	573	584	14	374	77	118	
1927	268	905	43	1,216	507	96	603	613	15	386	80	131	
1928	282	918	43	1,243	527	71	598	645	17	408	85	134	
[illegible]	[illegible]	[illegible]	[illegible]	[illegible]	[illegible]	[illegible]	654	539	25	401	82	32	

[illegible]						[illegible]	[illegible]	[illegible]	2	403		67		121
1931	135	598	28	761	491	..	491	270	2	402		48		182
1932	130	529	24	683	..	..	421	262	..	404		62		203
1933	117	655	25	797	407	..	407	389	..	401		70		82
1934	151	634	26	811	408	80	488	323	2	399		70		148
1935	190	782	28	1,000	424	125	549	452	..	359		57	36	
1936	224	859	31	1,114	454	140	594	520	118‡	349		55		116
1937	220	668	36	924	498	22	520	404	..	349		54	1	
1938	213	945	34	1,192	502	262	764	428	2	347		54	24	
1939	202	768	35	1,005	578	94	672	333	..		393			60
1940	205	775	36	1,016	523	154	677	339	..		383			44
1941	230	829	45	1,104	554	158	712	392	1		384		7	
1942	340	940	30	1,311	673	147	820	491	3		377		111	
1943	402	1,148	40	1,590	786	149	935	655	3		377		275	
1944	413	1,212	52	1,677	864	148	1,012	665	1		376		288	
1945	..	..	..	..	..	..	..	..	..	..		..	..	..
1946	482	1,307	75	1,864	1,016	197	1,213	651	—119	180		..	590	
1947	456	1,167	67	1,691	1,231	200	1,430	261	11	179		..	72	
1948	528	1,668	54	2,250	1,434	280	1,714	536	—111	181		..	466	
1949	463	1,832	52	2,347	1,514	419	1,934	414	48	183		..	184	
1950	545	1,975	50	2,571	1,691	440	2,130	441	—94	186		39	310	
1951	632	2,094	57	2,783	2,067	465	2,532	250	117	199		49		113
1952	744	2,411	63	3,217	2,645	711	3,356	—139	—91	238		61		347
1953	683	2,476	61	3,220	2,758	628	3,386	—166	—182	335		128		447
1954	560	2,447	102	3,108	2,819	723	3,541	—433	—301	394		227		753
1955†	718	3,355	147	4,221	3,633	814	4,446	—226	—178	105		35		188
1956	595	3,053	133	3,781	3,039	745	3,784	—3	—168	89		30	47	
1957	635	2,746	146	3,528	3,354	765	4,119	—591	—201	254		30		508
1958	614	3,234	149	3,997	3,262	768	4,030	—33	—160	90		30	8	
1959	608	3,794	149	4,551	3,209	860	4,068	482	—64	92		31	424	
1960	671	4,371	166	5,208	3,390	860	4,250	958	—217	92		31	1,052	

NOTES
*Figures were not separately available until 1922. All loan charges and contributions to sinking funds before 1927 were borne by the central government.
†Fifteen months: data here are on the same basis as the fiscal year.
‡Includes £116,000 transferred to the renewals fund.
Source: *Railway Administration Reports.*

Table 32b. Railway freight traffic receipts, 1900–60 (£000s)

	Exported				Local goods			Imported goods		
Year	Cocoa	Manganese	Bauxite	Exported timber	Timber not exported	Firewood	Local produce	Coal oil petrol and kerosene	Other mainly imported	Total*
1900	..	—	—	..	..	—	..	..	..	..
1901	..	—	—	..	..	—	..	..	..	..
1902	..	—	—	..	..	—	..	..	..	..
1903	..	—	—	..	..	—	..	..	..	53.2
1904	0.1	—	—	0.8	0.4	—	0.5	..	..	113.4
1905	0.8	—	—	6.2	0.1	—	0.3	1.7	91.5	100.6
1906	0.7	—	—	4.8	—	—	1.0	2.0	131.4	139.9
1907	1.6	—	—	9.5	—	—	2.1	1.1	114.0	128.3
1908	3.3	—	—	6.2	—	—	2.2	2.6	104.4	118.7
1909	5.6	—	—	1.2	—	—	5.5	2.1	132.4	146.8
1910	5.9	—	—	1.8	—	—	5.4	2.4	188.8	204.3
1911	14.9	—	—	1.8	—	3.5	5.0	2.9	192.0	220.1
1912	35.0	—	—	2.5	—	3.6	7.5	2.6	186.0	237.2
1913	59.7	—	—	6.3	0.3	3.6	6.3	2.4	185.3	263.9
1914	69.8	—	—	5.0	0.3	5.6	7.6	2.5	191.0	281.8
1915	117.9	—	—	0.8	0.4	7.5	15.6	2.9	184.9	330.0
1916	122.8	1.4	—	1.0	0.2	10.1	8.7	5.7	210.1	360.0
1917	182.9	11.8	—	1.1	1.4	13.1	14.1	6.5	135.5	366.4
1918	163.4	11.9	—	0.8	3.8	14.9	25.3	5.7	101.4	327.2
1919	276.7	14.2	—	1.2	3.9	14.1	15.7	10.8	152.7	489.3
1920	262.7	17.9	—	5.8	2.5	15.3	12.3	13.2	190.8	520.5
1921†	293.6	3.0	—	6.6	1.7	16.1	12.2	14.0	164.8	512.0
1922	363.8	42.0	—	8.6	2.0	13.9	13.6	15.8	195.3	655.0
1923	425.1	67.1	—	10.4	2.5	11.3	13.0	18.8	223.7	771.0
1924	404.4	98.2	—	11.6	2.4	11.9	12.0	19.4	266.4	826.4
1925	387.0	133.4	—	10.1	1.8	10.9	10.1	21.2	275.7	850.2
1926	423.9	141.2	—	8.1	2.0	10.9	11.7	25.0	271.4	894.2
1927	355.7	121.0	—	9.0	2.0	12.6	10.7	41.1	352.7	904.8
1928	390.1	132.7	—	4.8	3.0	11.7	10.9	41.6	322.7	917.5
[illegible]	[illegible]	[illegible]	[illegible]	8.3	2.1	12.3	10.2	37.6	264.5	865.7

[illegible]	[illegible]	[illegible]	[illegible]	[illegible]	[illegible]	10.1	10.5	27.4	198.2	758.5
1931	330.0	78.3	—	3.0	2.2	10.2	7.0	28.0	139.7	598.4
1932	327.6	75.9	—	2.8	2.0	10.0	7.0	25.4	138.5	589.2
1933	373.0	92.4	—	3.9	2.1	12.3	7.4	24.1	139.1	654.3
1934	280.8	109.7	—	12.9	2.6	14.9	8.0	27.2	177.1	633.5
1935	312.5	151.3	—	12.9	3.3	15.7	11.0	24.6	251.7	782.1
1936	341.6	143.8	—	10.4	3.1	19.7	11.0	17.9	311.7	859.2
1937	82.4	184.0	—	11.5	4.5	13.0	14.7	69.9	285.7	665.7
1938	505.6	100.5	—	5.9	3.6	5.6	12.3	103.4	202.5	939.4
1939	..	..	—	..	..	..	..	..	..	767.9
1940	..	..	—	..	..	..	..	..	..	775.4
1941	..	..	—	..	..	..	..	..	..	820.5
1942	..	..	—	..	..	..	..	..	..	940.2
1943	..	..	—	..	..	..	..	..	..	1,147.5
1944	..	..	—	..	..	..	..	..	..	1,211.8
1945	..	..	—	..	..	..	..	..	..	..
1946	385.6	294.2	65.6	92.9	21.0	20.5	41.0	105.7	273.6	1,300.1
1947	290.3	234.9	55.2	96.8	34.5	20.0	31.7	102.9	295.2	1,161.5
1948	519.9	318.0	78.8	117.4	27.5	21.1	28.9	136.3	414.3	1,662.2
1949	641.2	309.1	104.8	128.9	58.6	19.5	24.3	174.2	367.4	1,828.0
1950	612.8	344.5	66.4	219.9	85.7	17.9	17.4	220.9	384.7	1,970.2
1951	619.6	403.2	51.5	177.1	81.4	14.3	20.8	241.6	476.8	2,086.5
1952	759.8	386.4	71.7	205.7	92.0	16.0	18.7	286.7	565.7	2,402.7
1953	721.8	363.7	61.8	363.8	138.9	18.4	15.1	296.3	488.2	2,468.0
1954	810.7	206.4	94.3	419.7	152.5	18.0	12.5	253.4	471.9	2,439.9
1955†	1,005.5	370.6	90.5	687.0	222.7	14.4	11.3	312.0	634.1	3,348.1
1956	1,000.8	372.7	120.9	717.7	158.5	11.6	8.7	228.4	427.1	3,046.8
1957	766.6	343.5	146.7	840.2	171.2	6.8	7.3	213.5	244.4	2,740.2
1958	981.3	270.7	116.7	1,210.1	223.0	6.4	8.2	231.9	178.9	3,227.2
1959	1,194.0	296.9	125.5	1,413.0	284.1	6.0	5.0	215.5	247.9	3,787.5
1960	1,335.2	273.9	173.9	1,850.6	286.7	4.9	5.0	159.7	274.2	4,364.1

NOTES

* From 1900 to 1947 relates to total receipts from goods traffic; from 1947 receipts from livestock were excluded.

† Fifteen months.

Source: *Railway Administration Reports.*

Table 32c. Railway freight traffic (excluding livestock), 1900–60 (000 tons)

	Exported				Local goods			Imported goods		
Year	Cocoa	Manganese	Bauxite	Exported timber	Timber not exported	Firewood	Local produce	Coal oil petrol and kerosene	Other mainly imported	Total
1900	..	—	—	..	..	..	..	..	..	..
1901	..	—	—	..	..	..	..	..	..	..
1902	..	—	—	..	..	..	..	..	..	..
1903	—	—	—	—	—	—	—	—	—	—
1904	0.1	—	—	1.2	0.5	—	0.4	0.0	—	—
1905	0.6	—	—	6.4	0.1	—	0.3	0.4	24.4	32.2
1906	0.1	—	—	5.6	0.0	—	0.6	0.6	40.5	47.4
1907	0.6	—	—	12.0	0.0	—	0.6	0.1	37.8	51.1
1908	0.8	—	—	8.2	0.0	—	4.8	0.7	31.7	46.2
1909	1.8	—	—	1.4	0.0	—	5.7	0.7	45.9	55.5
1910	1.9	—	—	2.1	0.0	—	6.3	0.8	71.3	82.4
1911	5.1	—	—	2.5	0.0	81.4	8.2	1.1	83.9	182.2
1912	20.8	—	—	4.1	0.0	72.0	11.2	1.3	88.0	197.4
1913	37.4	—	—	9.9	0.6	66.4	7.9	1.7	107.1	231.0
1914	41.1	—	—	7.8	0.6	80.3	10.6	1.9	116.3	258.6
1915	60.3	—	—	1.1	0.8	99.0	15.9	1.9	90.2	269.2
1916	57.4	4.3	—	1.4	0.6	122.6	11.6	2.6	97.3	297.8
1917	79.7	32.4	—	1.4	1.6	134.3	16.0	2.8	66.9	335.1
1918	73.8	25.9	—	1.1	3.3	139.7	26.7	1.9	44.0	316.4
1919	111.9	35.6	—	1.8	2.7	127.8	13.4	3.7	51.0	347.9
1920	95.5	43.1	—	6.6	2.3	132.0	10.7	3.8	77.4	371.4
1921†	109.1	7.1	—	7.6	1.3	141.9	12.7	3.9	74.0	357.6
1922	143.1	83.2	—	9.0	2.3	115.0	13.9	4.6	68.0	439.1
1923	164.3	189.6	—	10.8	2.1	97.3	11.4	6.1	114.1	595.7
1924	156.1	273.8	—	12.6	1.8	110.3	11.6	6.7	129.7	702.6
1925	150.3	372.5	—	11.7	1.3	103.7	13.1	7.2	137.1	796.9
1926	149.2	394.1	—	9.5	1.3	107.4	12.0	7.0	124.7	805.2
1927	131.2	377.5	—	11.6	1.6	116.4	10.6	10.2	130.8	789.9
1928	165.6	370.3	—	6.3	2.9	106.6	11.2	19.6	126.3	808.8
[illegible]	[illegible]	[illegible]	[illegible]	[illegible]	[illegible]	122.6	10.9	16.1	123.2	932.2

[illegible]	[illegible]	[illegible]	[illegible]	3.6	3.2	96.8	7.5	19.7	63.2	526.3
1932	122.0	73.1	—	5.6	—	99.6	—	—	—	391.1
1933	125.9	335.9	—	5.1	3.4	107.0	7.7	12.9	65.3	663.2
1934	122.4	357.6	—	16.3	4.3	113.5	11.2	12.9	91.7	729.9
1935	130.6	465.7	—	14.9	5.6	122.6	15.4	27.2	129.7	911.7
1936	140.1	442.4	—	15.2	6.7	143.4	14.8	35.2	157.5	955.3
1937	134.6	566.2	—	17.5	7.9	109.1	21.1	63.3	185.2	1,104.9
1938	207.8	268.1	—	8.1	8.7	84.5	19.8	79.1	154.6	830.7
1939	115.5	466.0	—	8.9	..	..	23.8	..	..	933.4
1940	141.7	427.2	—	21.7	..	..	22.4	..	..	883.4
1941	131.7	541.9	7.3	25.0	..	..	25.8	..	..	1,009.8
1942	103.6	563.9	67.8	40.3	..	..	47.9	..	..	1,167.5
1943	184.3	398.4	150.7	57.8	..	..	51.8	..	..	1,195.3
1944	..	..	..	..	..	..	..	..	..	1,466.8
1945	..	..	..	..	..	..	..	..	..	..
1946	182.3	784.5	117.5	109.3	28.0	124.7	50.3	81.3	158.4	1,636.3
1947	29.2	626.5	98.2	103.7	41.0	119.7	38.6	80.8	184.2	1,321.9
1948	77.4	748.3	141.2	113.5	27.7	118.9	33.7	102.6	209.4	1,572.7
1949	201.8	727.3	145.0	125.0	70.0	121.4	28.3	102.0	175.6	1,696.4
1950	193.0	810.6	126.5	190.7	122.8	120.0	22.6	90.1	288.2	1,964.5
1951	168.5	848.8	98.1	153.2	136.0	45.5	23.2	110.6	290.9	1,874.8
1952	164.1	813.4	136.5	151.3	124.8	37.5	21.2	109.4	299.9	1,858.1
1953	141.3	765.7	117.8	240.9	170.3	40.9	18.2	109.9	226.3	1,831.3
1954	159.9	434.1	179.6	272.9	175.3	42.7	16.1	100.3	230.0	1,610.9
1955†	186.6	741.5	141.7	426.2	233.7	32.5	14.9	119.6	274.9	2,171.6
1956	180.2	709.2	172.7	399.4	156.9	22.3	11.4	97.0	174.2	1,923.3
1957	155.9	654.2	209.8	427.5	167.1	10.8	9.3	96.1	114.0	1,844.7
1958	176.6	515.6	166.7	507.7	130.9	9.6	9.0	99.1	77.7	1,692.9
1959	225.5	565.5	178.7	587.6	148.2	9.2	8.1	85.9	121.8	1,930.5
1960	243.4	500.6	232.3	764.5	146.2	7.1	7.7	69.5	125.8	2,097.1

NOTES

† Fifteen months.
See also notes to Table 32b.

Table 33. Other railway statistics, 1900–60

Year	Value of capital (£000s)	Track miles open	No. of loco-motives	Passenger vehicles no.	Goods vehicles no.	No. of workers	Wage bill (£000s)	No. of passenger journeys (000s)
1900	..	..	..	..	..	..	..	..
1901	..	..	..	..	..	..	..	..
1902	..	39	..	..	..	..	..	..
1903	1,796	124	..	..	..	..	..	32
1904	1,756	168	..	..	..	..	..	94
1905	1,782	168	16	18	201	..	42	86
1906	1,818	168	16	18	226	..	37	89
1907	1,847	168	20	19	238	..	53	105
1908	1,837	168	20	19	232	..	53	110
1909	1,846	168	22	20	233	..	50	216
1910	1,857	168	22	26	245	..	54	362
1911	2,045	188	32	32	376	..	65	536
1912	2,415	222	34	33	424	..	77	638
1913	2,550	227	39	43	488	..	82	742
1914	2,851	227	43	49	501	..	92	775
1915	3,049	245	45	50	634	..	97	855
1916	3,171	248	47	63	617	2,765	109	888
1917	3,211	268	44	62	610	..	117	887
1918	3,255	269	46	62	610	2,522	112	845
1919	3,417	269	49	64	641	2,888	109	1,224
1920	4,198	269	49	64	685	3,520	159	1,334
1921*	6,081	276	64	93	809	3,797	196	1,228
1922	6,994	334	69	94	913	4,076	200	1,346
1923	6,720	379	79	94	954	4,186	226	1,335
1924	7,419	394	83	94	995	4,932	246	1,348
1925	8,049	394	88	107	1,060	4,921	258	1,487
1926	8,298	457	88	106	1,054	4,682	267	1,954
1927	8,433	480	86	107	1,033	5,341	269	2,303
1928	9,138	495	85	107	979	6,120	274	2,177
1929	9,180	500	83	105	986	3,576	279	1,874
1930	9,306	500	83	117	969	4,639	280	1,340
1931	9,308	500	79	119	979	4,017	256	1,005
1932	9,308	500	83	119	980	3,881	..	..
1933	9,242	500	83	118	972	3,808	211	1,061
1934	9,242	500	79	116	987	3,749	211	1,822
1935	9,247	500	77	123	989	4,091	215	3,101
1936	9,354	500	82	146	991	4,168	220	3,537
1937	9,375	500	81	144	938	4,278	228	3,436
1938	8,686	500	83	155	1,115	4,633	232	3,358
1939	..	..	88	164	1,112	4,781	..	3,216
1940	..	..	88	163	1,100	4,711	..	3,249
1941	..	..	84	151	1,034	4,722	..	3,682
1942	..	..	81	151	1,043	5,138	..	5,326
1943	..	..	98	151	1,354	5,279	..	6,575
1944	..	..	98	167	1,407	6,117	..	6,140
1945	..	..	..	..	..	..	..	..
1946	8,654	635	92	165	1,383	..	425	6,800
1947	8,868	636	92	164	1,508	5,439	599	6,338
1948	9,094	639	93	163	1,582	5,808	557	5,237
1949	10,039	641	108	189	1,791	5,534	578	4,678

Year	Value of capital (£000s)	Track miles open	No. of loco-motives	Passenger vehicles no.	Goods vehicles no.	No. of workers	Wage bill (£000s)	No. of passenger journeys (000s)
1950	10,616	642	110	177	1,882	5,791	643	5,451
1951	11,670	643	139	177	1,883	6,922	1,035	5,650
1952	12,563	646	138	186	1,869	7,152	995	6,402
1953	14,295	654	138	168	1,996	7,411	1,016	4,672
1954	17,148	675	148	192	2,436	6,591	996	4,803
1955*	18,871	749	152	220	2,425	8,213	1,275	6,300
1956	19,762	727	153	247	2,633	8,229	1,177	4,991
1957	20,326	750	160	251	2,634	7,280	1,451	5,189
1958	22,357	750	160	248	2,716	8,516	1,438	5,199
1959	24,778	750	194	246	2,826	9,212	1,532	5,340
1960	25,534	762	180	237	2,763	10,932	1,823	5,370

NOTES

* Fifteen months.

Source: *Railway Administration Reports.*

Table 34a. Tonnage of cargo unloaded at Ghana ports, 1920–60 *

Year	No. of vessels †	Total tonnage (000s)	Takoradi (000s)	Cape Coast (000s)	Winneba (000s)	Accra (000s)	Keta (000s)	Other (000s)
1920	450	222.7	..	..	..	..	..	..
1921	507	177.6	..	..	..	..	..	..
1922	557	184.7	..	..	..	..	..	..
1923	628	248.6	..	..	..	..	..	..
1924	700	253.8	..	..	..	..	..	..
1925	760	309.6	..	..	..	..	..	..
1926	867	336.3	..	..	..	..	..	..
1927	900	422.4	..	..	..	..	..	..
1928	985	422.5	..	..	..	..	..	..
1929	999	393.2	..	..	..	..	..	..
1930	940	365.3	..	..	..	..	..	..
1931	772	204.8	..	..	..	..	..	..
1932	636	213.6	..	..	..	..	..	..
1933	678	223.4	..	..	..	..	..	..
1934	768	232.7	..	..	..	..	..	..
1935	836	342.9	..	..	..	..	..	..
1936	842	419.5	..	..	..	..	..	..
1937	888	593.2	..	..	..	..	..	..
1938	846	430.6	298.6	16.4	11.4	92.4	5.4	—
1939	751	433.2	..	..	..	..	..	..
1940	570	340.2	..	..	..	..	..	..
1941	560	545.1	..	..	..	..	..	..
1942	612	713.6	..	..	..	..	..	..
1943	556	522.9	..	..	..	..	..	..
1944	476	364.8	..	..	..	..	..	..
1945	593	350.0	280.8	—	—	68.2	—	..
1946	705	414.1	319.9	—	—	93.4	—	..
1947	673	518.0	354.9	5.0	1.5	156.0	0.7	..
1948	898	645.1	443.8	9.4	4.9	183.5	3.5	..
1949	969	864.2	555.8	15.3	13.1	273.4	6.7	..
1950	985	880.7	584.6	22.3	20.9	244.8	8.1	..
1951	1,005	1,047.2	674.7	26.1	20.8	319.5	6.1	..
1952	1,373	1,055.2	711.0	17.1	11.8	311.6	3.7	..
1953	1,558	1,157.8	716.6	22.4	19.0	390.3	9.5	..
1954	1,552	1,159.3	719.1	22.9	20.6	386.6	10.1	..
1955	1,582	1,426.6	854.5	24.0	25.4	511.7	11.0	..
1956	1,581	1,374.5	789.7	24.0	22.9	528.5	9.4	..
1957	1,576	1,472.6	874.2	24.2	26.9	542.9	4.4	..
1958	2,079	1,616.9	1,524.7	4.4	22.9	64.9	..	..
1959	2,476	1,830.3	1,720.1	7.3	21.6	81.3	..	..
1960	2,437	2,035.7	1,895.4	12.4	38.9	89.0	..	..

NOTES

* Data other than total tonnage loaded and unloaded are not available for years 1920–37 and 1939–44.

† Figures given for number of vessels unloaded and loaded at Ghana ports for 1920–51 relate to number of vessels entered and cleared respectively.

Source: *Railway Administration Reports.*

Year	No. of vessels	Total tonnage (000s)	Takoradi (000s)	Cape Coast (000s)	Winneba (000s)	Accra (000s)	Keta (000s)	Other (000s)
1920	441	236.8	..	..	..	..	..	..
1921	506	200.0	..	..	..	..	..	..
1922	556	358.1	..	..	..	..	..	..
1923	613	356.9	..	..	..	..	..	..
1924	685	501.8	..	..	..	..	..	..
1925	757	616.7	..	..	..	..	..	..
1926	865	661.2	..	..	..	..	..	..
1927	891	648.9	..	..	..	..	..	..
1928	982	613.1	..	..	..	..	..	..
1929	1,010	734.4	..	..	..	..	..	..
1930	948	677.2	..	..	..	..	..	..
1931	770	534.9	..	..	..	..	..	..
1932	636	312.7	..	..	..	..	..	..
1933	680	533.3	..	..	..	..	..	..
1934	766	621.8	..	..	..	..	..	..
1935	831	725.8	..	..	..	..	..	..
1936	844	772.7	..	..	..	..	..	..
1937	891	852.3	..	..	..	..	..	..
1938	840	653.3	470.4	12.2	23.5	129.0	2.5	—
1939	742	662.3	..	..	..	..	..	..
1940	577	790.5	..	..	..	..	..	..
1941	548	738.5	..	..	..	..	..	..
1942	617	745.1	..	..	..	..	..	..
1943	560	866.0	..	..	..	..	..	..
1944	473	979.3	..	..	..	..	..	..
1945	601	1,234.8	1,135.3	—	..	99.4	..	..
1946	700	1,301.1	1,206.1	—	4.2	90.8	..	..
1947	674	1,064.7	986.1	6.8	13.7	58.0	..	..
1948	893	1,258.6	1,179.3	7.5	16.2	55.6	..	..
1949	974	1,409.8	1,318.6	6.2	19.7	65.2	..	..
1950	985	1,372.5	1,279.5	8.0	18.8	66.2	..	..
1951	1,015	1,463.4	1,377.7	7.6	17.2	60.9	..	..
1952	1,360	1,399.2	1,316.5	6.6	20.9	55.2	..	..
1953	1,563	1,502.9	1.402.7	5.3	25.9	69.0	..	..
1954	1,552	1,244.8	1,156.8	5.7	22.6	59.7	..	..
1955	1,582	1,371.2	1,272.3	4.3	23.8	68.8	2.0	..
1956	1,587	1,633.6	1,528.6	3.9	22.5	77.9	0.7	..
1957	1,568	1,794.9	1,679.0	5.0	30.4	80.5	—	..
1958	2,078	1,396.6	763.5	19.7	23.4	583.0	7.0	..
1959	2,484	1,544.8	815.1	18.6	22.2	674.5	14.4	..
1960	2,434	1,843.8	1,007.5	23.0	22.4	790.9	—	..

NOTES

See notes to Table 34a.

Table 35. Total number and tonnage of vessels entered at and cleared from Ghana ports, 1900–60

Year	Entered: No. of vessels	Entered: Tonnage (000s)	Cleared: No. of vessels	Cleared: Tonnage (000s)
1900	445	714	436	701
1901	456	711	449	706
1902	511	859	501	838
1903	587	1,011	579	1,002
1904	577	1,032	584	1,018
1905	605	1,088	593	1,072
1906	589	1,073	581	1,064
1907	636	1,173	630	1,160
1908	579	1,121	566	1,095
1909	650	1,262	640	1,236
1910	679	1,308	670	1,291
1911	666	1,349	652	1,327
1912	687	1,449	660	1,400
1913	693	1,516	678	1,471
1914	637	1,413	629	1,398
1915	362	826	347	803
1916	360	783	358	783
1917	336	722	331	725
1918	256	539	253	542
1919	367	849	353	822
1920	450	1,190	441	1,169
1921	507	1,255	506	1,254
1922	557	1,392	556	1,383
1923	628	1,664	613	1,634
1924	700	1,852	685	1,820
1925	760	2,091	757	2,090
1926	867	2,408	865	2,407
1927	900	2,459	891	2,438
1928	985	2,741	982	2,722
1929	999	2,758	1,010	2,782
1930	940	2,628	948	2,639
1931	772	2,241	770	2,235
1932	636	1,775	636	1,773
1933	678	1,920	680	1,927
1934	768	2,143	766	2,136
1935	836	2,364	831	2,347
1936	842	2,422	844	2,436
1937	888	2,610	891	2,614
1938	846	2,412	840	2,405
1939	751	2,181	742	2,154
1940	570	1,768	577	1,797
1941	560	1,596	548	1,549
1942	612	1,817	617	1,843
1943	556	1,865	560	1,886
1944	475	1,561	473	1,546

Table 35. Total number and tonnage of vessels entered at and cleared from Ghana ports, 1900–60—*continued*

Year	Entered		Cleared	
	No. of vessels	Tonnage (000s)	No. of vessels	Tonnage (000s)
1945	593	1,930	600	1,958
1946	705	2,573	700	2,554
1947	673	2,145	674	2,156
1948	898	2,785	893	2,777
1949	969	3,068	974	3,082
1950	985	3,234	985	3,223
1951	1,005	3,300	1,015	3,342
1952	1,031	3,276	1,012	3,226
1953	1,108	3,622	1,120	3,645
1954	1,129	3,666	1,128	3,661
1955	1,169	3,789	1,170	3,806
1956	1,187	3,725	1,193	3,741
1957	1,279	3,990	1,269	3,972
1958	1,572	4,727	1,574	4,731
1959	1,827	5,407	1,818	5,383
1960	1,738	5,513	1,741	5,527
1961	1,783	5,776	1,791	5,791
1962	1,836	5,904	1,830	5,898
1963	1,740	5,712	1,729	5,683

NOTES

Figures given relate to total number and tonnage of vessels entered at and cleared from Ghana ports. If a vessel calls at more than one port without an intervening call at a port abroad, the vessel is recorded as ' entered ' at one only of such ports on arrival and cleared at one only of such ports on departure.

Sources: *Blue Books, Trade Reports* and *Digest of Statistics.*

Table 36a. Roads maintained by the Public Works Department, 1900–60 (selected years) (miles)

	Eastern	Central	Western	Ashanti	Northern	Total
1903	99	88	9	..	..	196
1910	99	88	9	..	..	196
1915	137	131	42	..	..	310
1920	196	231	72	145	190	834
1925	377	375	269	275	231	1,527
1930	467	419	364	329	276	1,855
1935	470	410	371	408	273	1,932
1939	606	432	433	559	285	2,315
1945	661	430	438	577	282	2,388
1950	(788)	(825)	(414)	(787)	(438)	3,525*
1955	815	833	434	807	977	4,127†
1960	..	..	..	..	..	4,420

NOTES

* Includes 273 miles in the Volta Region.

† Includes 261 miles in the Volta Region.

Bracketed figures are interpolations.

Sources: 1903–55, *Public Works Department, Reports*; 1960, *Statistical Yearbook, 1962*.

Table 36b. Roads other than those maintained by the Public Works Department, 1921–35 (miles)

	Eastern	Central	Western	Ashanti	Northern	Total
1921	838	443	85	475	400	2,241
1922	1,015	..	97	532	1,200	..
1923	1,057	..	140	781	1,200	..
1924	1,266	477	156	836	1,242	3,977
1925	1,306	..	214	1,019	1,785	..
1926	1,319	521	259	1,080	1,931	5,110
1927	1,444	587	354	1,142	2,000	5,527
1928	1,506	..	390	1,158	2,300	..
1929	1,525	633	443	1,175	2,335	6,111
1930	1,525	713	500	1,228	2,772	6,738
1931	..	..	..	..	..	6,400
1932	..	..	..	..	..	6,168
1933	..	..	..	..	..	6,200
1934	..	..	..	..	..	6,200
1935	..	..	..	..	..	6,200

NOTES

Roads maintained by the Public Works Department were not the only roads in the colony. The tables above show what other roads existed for those periods for which estimates are available.

Sources: 1921–31; Cardinal, *The Gold Coast*; 1932–5, *Colonial Reports*.

Table 37. Motor licences by type of vehicle, 1909–60

	Valid Licences									New Registrations								
	Cars*	Motor cycles	Public† conveyances	Goods vehicles	Trailers and caravans	Special purpose vehicles	Public service vehicles	Tractors and mech. equip.	Total	Cars*	Motor cycles	Public† conveyances	Goods vehicles	Trailers and caravans	Special purpose vehicles	Public service vehicles	Tractors and mech. equip.	Total
1909	..	..	..	..	..	..	..	..	..	11	12	—	16	..	..	..	..	39
1910	..	..	..	..	..	..	..	..	..	16	22	—	32	..	..	..	..	70
1911	..	..	..	..	..	..	..	..	..	5	12	—	16	..	..	..	..	33
1912	..	..	..	..	..	..	..	..	..	5	22	—	17	..	..	..	..	44
1913	..	..	..	..	..	..	..	..	..	5	38	—	23	..	..	..	..	66
1914	..	..	..	..	..	..	..	..	..	20	71	—	29	26	..	..	..	146
1915	..	..	..	..	..	..	..	..	..	28	102	—	56	37	..	..	..	223
1916	..	..	..	..	..	..	..	..	..	81	162	—	125	102	..	..	..	470
1917	..	..	..	..	..	..	..	..	..	65	72	—	99	59	..	..	..	295
1918	..	..	..	..	..	..	..	..	..	29	42	—	57	58	..	..	..	186
1919	..	..	..	..	..	..	..	..	..	95	75	—	213	74	..	..	..	457
1920	..	..	..	..	..	..	..	..	..	214	101	—	586	183	..	..	..	1,084
1921	..	..	..	..	..	..	..	..	..	84	96	—	196	79	..	..	..	455
1922	..	..	..	..	..	..	..	..	..	109	58	—	150	108	..	..	..	425
1923	..	..	..	..	..	..	..	..	3,287	..	..	..	..	..	..	..	..	1,278
1924	..	..	..	..	..	..	..	..	3,828	..	..	..	..	..	..	..	..	1,909
1925	..	..	..	..	..	..	..	..	4,636	..	..	..	..	..	..	..	..	2,207
1926	..	..	..	..	..	..	..	..	5,601	..	..	..	..	..	..	..	..	2,471
1927	1,100	727	—	4,250	1,060	—	—	—	7,137	..	..	..	..	..	..	..	..	3,458
1928	1,591	697	—	3,889	787	—	—	—	6,964	..	..	..	..	..	..	..	..	2,820
[illegible]	[illegible]	[illegible]	[illegible]	3,893	571	—	—	—	6,960	..	..	..	..	..	..	..	..	2,956

[illegible]	[illegible]	[illegible]	—	[illegible]	[illegible]	—	—	—	8,921	..	..	..	..	..	..	..	..	2,058
1931	2,004	722	—	5,057	641	—	—	—	8,424	..	..	..	..	..	..	..	..	1,752
1932	2,036	464	—	5,022	595	—	—	—	8,117	..	..	..	..	..	..	..	..	1,431
1933	1,757	649	—	4,818	571	—	—	—	7,795	..	..	..	..	..	..	..	..	1,153
1934	1,772	557	—	4,513	787	—	—	—	7,629	..	..	..	..	..	..	..	..	1,470
1935	1,818	475	—	4,990	1,198	—	—	—	8,481	..	..	..	..	..	..	..	..	..
1936	1,862	380	—	5,481	1,691	—	—	—	9,414	..	..	..	..	..	..	..	..	..
1937	2,182	315	—	6,104	1,527	—	—	—	10,127	..	..	..	..	..	..	..	..	..
1938	2,094	284	—	5,618	2,106	—	—	—	10,103	..	..	..	..	..	..	..	..	..
(Data not available 1939–49)																		
1950	..	..	..	..	..	..	..	..	..	1,695	269	33	2,544	488	253	7	29	5,318
1951	6,880	840	99	8,528	1,536	315	315	122	18,635	2,121	310	15	2,259	451	317	7	50	5,530
1952	8,090	1,037	186	9,523	1,570	220	220	179	21,025	2,179	332	44	2,268	361	233	23	93	5,533
1953	7,475	924	208	9,314	1,251	1,375	1,375	127	22,049	2,490	316	70	3,020	310	404	34	126	6,770
1954	10,735	1,140	331	11,771	1,330	1,027	98	436	26,868	2,842	271	149	3,422	266	457	20	197	7,624
1955	11,886	1,371	398	12,583	1,218	1,266	101	500	29,323	3,107	519	106	3,379	339	595	29	184	8,258
1956	13,395	1,619	545	13,677	1,317	1,807	177	683	33,220	3,741	596	170	3,903	355	781	25	234	9,805
1957	14,518	1,756	784	14,026	1,301	2,063	170	750	35,368	4,062	584	349	3,410	314	748	29	240	9,736
1958	15,546	2,123	1,270	13,205	1,229	2,317	177	829	36,696	3,678	825	572	2,071	297	722	18	177	8,360
1959	17,590	2,449	1,952	13,471	1,344	2,757	181	964	40,708	4,719	925	899	2,448	309	922	12	257	10,491
1960	20,663	2,842	2,779	13,747	1,464	3,078	205	1,115	45,893	5,832	998	1,233	2,871	356	1,109	31	301	12,731

NOTES

*Includes taxis.

†Includes vehicles other than buses licensed to carry goods and passengers.

Sources: *Colonial Reports*, *Police Department Reports*, *Quarterly Digest of Statistics* and *Statistical Yearbook 1962*.

Table 38a. Number of Post Offices and amount of mail matter and parcels handled, 1900–60 *

Year	No.† of Post Offices	Letters and postages			Registered articles			Newspapers, book packets and samples			Total	Parcel post
		Posted	Delivered	Total	Posted	Delivered	Total	Posted	Delivered	Total		
1900	34	610	407	1,017	49	43	92	66	1,608	1,674	2,783	8
1901	41	1,294	2,922	4,216	83	58	141	45	3,203	3,248	7,605	13
1902	41	830	1,737	2,567	102	64	166	28	1,234	1,262	3,995	23
1903	45	1,069	2,126	3,195	126	91	217	70	585	655	4,067	31
1904	50	1,279	1,587	2,866	138	104	242	175	524	699	3,806	33
1905	51	1,229	1,241	2,470	239	115	354	142	481	623	3,446	43
1906	58	1,282	1,075	2,357	158	105	263	139	466	605	3,225	38
1907	61	1,296	1,177	2,473	163	107	270	142	479	621	3,364	44
1908	61	1,911	1,396	3,307	192	110	302	174	506	680	4,290	49
1909	61	2,140	1,783	3,923	190	159	349	212	575	787	5,060	62
1910	61	1,956	2,266	4,222	236	167	403	243	710	953	5,579	80
1911	73	1,865	2,177	4,042	229	185	414	253	713	966	5,424	83
1912	69	1,521	2,455	3,976	243	231	474	113	972	1,085	5,535	84
1913	71	1,697	2,339	4,036	244	209	453	168	877	1,045	5,533	104
1914	74	2,026	2,151	4,177	231	186	417	356	1,290	1,646	6,242	96
1915	83	1,989	2,304	4,293	315	261	576	196	908	1,104	5,974	98
1916	88	2,604	3,345	5,949	320	248	568	258	923	1,181	7,699	132
1917	103	2,289	2,829	5,118	255	273	528	240	559	799	6,446	81
1918	108	2,110	2,014	4,124	188	163	351	185	600	785	5,261	63
1919	110	2,330	2,147	4,477	289	212	501	118	622	740	5,718	90
1920	121	2,478	1,796	4,274	293	229	522	153	1,178	1,331	6,126	154
1921	135	1,846	2,252	4,098	224	185	409	94	573	667	5,175	93
1922–3	159	2,676	3,165	5,841	317	254	571	152	1,063	1,215	7,627	116
1923–4	164	3,001	3,430	6,431	321	343	664	242	1,239	1,481	8,575	123
1924–5	171	3,239	4,671	7,910	642	336	978	211	797	1,008	9,896	128

[illegible]	[illegible]	[illegible]	[illegible]	[illegible]	456	385	841	329	1,436	1,765	10,458	157
1926–7	198	3,951	4,324	8,275	475	432	907	327	1,385	1,712	10,894	152
1927–8	214	4,483	5,275	9,758	536	504	1,040	386	1,511	1,897	12,696	183
1928–9	231	5,465	1,267‡	6,732	499	64‡	563	302	952‡	1,254	8,549	163
1929–30	264	4,870	1,136‡	6,006	611	92‡	703	354	1,260‡	1,614	8,322	162
1930–1	274	4,617	4,775	9,393	518	484	1,002	375	1,374	1,749	12,144	126
1931–2	281	2,994	3,119	6,114	402	381	783	349	1,183	1,532	8,429	80
1932–3	287	2,890	3,059	5,949	356	322	679	379	1,058	1,437	8,064	69
1933–4	282	3,019	3,282	6,301	384	349	733	366	1,192	1,558	8,592	64
1934–5	288	4,104	3,734	7,838	405	396	801	501	1,320	1,822	10,461	75
1936	277	5,702	5,230	10,932	505	400	905	570	1,403	1,973	13,810	72
1937	286	5,900	5,897	11,796	452	426	878	475	2,074	2,500	15,174	92
1938	286	4,707	4,878	9,584	430	391	821	447	1,682	2,129	12,534	83
§												
1945	322	6,904	1,554‡	8,458	611	58‡	669	1,146	373‡	1,519	10,646	60
1946	331	10,716	2,562‡	13,278	781	64‡	845	1,151	1,128‡	2,279	16,404	97
1947	349	10,927	2,572‡	13,499	797	100‡	897	1,760	1,821‡	3,581	17,976	111
1948	366	12,307	3,376‡	15,683	1,099	100‡	1,199	1,603	1,720‡	3,323	20,205	164
1949	374	14,040	12,815	26,855	1,183	1,056	2,239	1,924	3,705	5,629	34,724	141
§												
1955	577	25,240	..	..	1,971	..	..	..	..	..	..	..
1956	623	26,771	..	..	2,153	..	..	..	..	..	..	..
1957	649	33,987	..	..	2,262	..	..	..	..	..	..	..
1958	662	37,260	..	..	2,680	..	..	..	..	..	..	..
1959	714	46,843	..	..	4,722	..	..	..	..	..	..	..
1960	743	60,215	..	..	3,219	..	..	..	..	..	..	..

NOTES
*Includes official mails.
†Includes postal agencies.
‡Figures exclude number of local letters, etc. delivered and are therefore not comparable with others.
§Figures during the war years and from 1950 to 1955 are not available.
Sources: *Post and Telecommunications Department Reports; Blue Books.*

Table 38b. Telegraph and telephone services of the Post and Telecommunications Department, 1900–60

	Telegraph		Telegrams*			Telephones		
Year	No. of offices	Miles of line	Inland messages (000s)	Foreign messages (000s)	Total	No. of sub-scribers	No. of points	Radiogram messages no.
1900	27	688	132	8	140	..	..	..
1901	31	716	184	15	199	..	..	..
1902	32	810	248	11	259	..	..	..
1903	36	916	264	13	277	..	..	..
1904	39	1,078	..	..	..	..	..	..
1905	40	1,108	194	11	205	..	..	..
1906	43	1,129	206	12	218	104	..	..
1907	46	1,280	231	14	245	111	..	..
1908	46	1,280	256	16	272	98	..	..
1909	50	1,363	248	13	261	139	..	..
1910	50	1,424	257	21	278	147	..	..
1911	48	1,492	259	14	273	153	..	..
1912	41	1,592	254	16	270	179	..	..
1913	41	1,492	269	15	284	155	..	171
1914	50	1,295	279	15	294	171	..	223
1915	51	1,331	290	22	312	166	..	225
1916	55	1,333	232	26	258	182	..	587
1917	59	1,905	259	26	285	224	..	127
1918	61	2,743	287	31	318	218	..	15
1919	60	2,762	385	33	418	255	..	640
1920	65	2,767	461	39	500	338	..	1,382
1921	70	2,782	431	36	467	259	..	1,434
1922	81	4,935	413	41	454	360	..	1,719
1923	90	5,616	376	37	413	464	..	1,702
1924	94	6,482	416	33	449	519	..	1,708
1925	96	6,972	393	31	424	578	..	1,725
1926	112	8,490	426	34	460	628	..	2,292
1927	120	4,329	476	35	511	730	1,283	1,926
1928	134	4,350	488	35	523	926	..	2,185
1929	148	4,298	513	34	547	1,051	..	3,054
1930	157	4,411	438	31	469	1,152	2,411	..
1931	159	4,713	304	21	325	..	2,046	..
1932	167	4,713	263	19	282	..	1,907	..
1933	169	4,657	256	21	277	..	1,886	..
1935	173	4,675	276	27	303	..	2,058	..
1936	173	4,517	382	29	411	..	2,072	3,235
1937	180	4,707	426	25	451	..	2,291	4,231
1938	193	5,082	542	28	570	..	2,661	3,153
1939	192	..	575	32	607	..	2,766	1,614
1940	201	..	615	56	671	..	3,027	86
1941	206	5,012	711	101	812	..	3,278	177
1942	210	5,054	741	112	853	..	3,511	1,094
1943	212	..	888	90	978	..	3,602	378
1944	..	..	844	60	904	..	3,848	..
1945	221	..	858	54	912	..	4,084	1,193
1946	222	..	986	53	1,039	..	4,479	2,119
1947	231	..	1,029	54	1,083	..	4,786	2,790
1948	240	..	1,191	62	1,253	..	5,657	3,591
1949	252	..	1,157	67	1,224	..	5,939	3,632
1955	..	..	977	36	1,013	8,330	13,419	..

Table 38b. Telegraph and telephone services of the Post and Telecommunications Department, 1900–60—*continued*

Year	Telegraph: No. of offices	Telegraph: Miles of line	Telegrams*: Inland messages (000s)	Telegrams*: Foreign messages (000s)	Telegrams*: Total	Telephones: No. of subscribers	Telephones: No. of points	Radiogram messages no.
1956	..	..	1,014	37	1,051	9,005	15,588	..
1957	..	..	993	49	1,042	9,826	16,100	..
1958	..	..	861	45	906	10,769	19,193	..
1959	..	..	752	46	798	11,824	21,498	..
1960	..	..	751	47	798	12,892	23,837	..

NOTES

* Includes official messages forwarded and received.

Sources: *Post and Telecommunications Department Reports*; *Statistical Yearbooks, 1961* and *1962*.

Table 38c. Post Office Savings Bank returns, 1900–60

Year	No. of live accounts at end of period (000s)	Balance at beginning (£000s)	Deposits (£000s)	Interest (£000s)	Withdrawals (£000s)	Balance at end of financial year (£000s)
1900	0.3	5.0	3.4	0.1	4.0	4.5
1901	0.3	4.5	3.5	0.1	3.6	4.5
1902	0.4	4.5	4.1	0.09	3.4	5.3
1903	0.3	5.3	6.2	0.1	5.9	5.8
1904	0.4	5.8	6.6	0.1	5.6	7.0
1905	0.6	7.0	5.6	0.2	3.8	9.0
1906	0.9	9.0	9.0	0.2	5.4	12.8
1907	1.3	12.8	12.8	0.3	10.6	15.3
1908	1.7	15.3	16.6	0.4	11.7	20.7
1909	2.2	20.7	17.1	0.02	13.6	24.7
1910	2.3	24.7	20.2	0.6	16.3	29.2
1911	3.1	29.2	24.0	0.7	19.1	34.8
1912	3.9	34.8	25.4	0.8	22.5	38.6
1913	4.3	38.6	30.1	0.9	24.3	45.3
1914	5.6	45.3	33.2	1.1	27.7	51.9
1915	5.1	51.9	37.3	1.2	34.8	55.6
1916	5.8	55.6	43.5	1.3	39.0	61.4
1917	5.9	61.4	39.9	1.4	45.0	57.8
1918	5.8	51.8	33.0	1.2	33.9	52.1
1919	5.8	52.1	42.0	1.2	40.9	54.4
1920	6.0	54.4	31.5	1.2	35.1	52.1
1921	6.3	52.1	28.1	1.4	30.3	51.2
1922	5.3	51.2	30.3	1.4	31.4	51.1
1923	5.8	51.1	34.1	1.4	35.7	51.0
1924	6.3	51.0	39.6	1.4	37.3	54.7

Table 38c. Post Office Savings Bank returns, 1900–60—*continued*

Year	No. of live accounts at end of period (000s)	Balance at beginning (£000s)	Deposits (£000s)	Interest (£000s)	Withdrawals (£000s)	Balance at end of financial year (£000s)
1925	7.3	54.7	45.5	1.5	40.9	60.9
1926	8.4	60.9	50.7	1.7	44.8	68.5
1927	10.0	68.5	72.6	2.0	59.2	84.0
1928	11.2	84.0	66.8	2.3	62.3	90.8
1929	12.4	90.8	81.3	2.5	76.1	98.4
1930	13.4	98.4	66.4	2.5	78.1	89.3
1931	..	89.1	66.3	2.4	63.6	94.2
1932	..	94.2	71.2	2.6	65.3	102.7
1933	..	102.7	79.9	2.9	70.5	115.0
1934	..	115.0	95.2	2.9	70.9	142.2
1935	..	142.2	120.1	3.5	94.3	171.6
1936	..	189.9	202.5	4.5	118.8	278.0
1937	..	278.0	147.5	5.9	184.6	246.8
1938	..	246.8	163.9	5.7	140.6	275.8
1939	..	275.8	161.3	6.1	148.7	294.6
1940	45.6	294.6	166.0	6.3	148.6	318.3
1941	61.0	318.3	299.7	8.3	170.9	455.4
1942	85.3	455.4	516.9	12.6	259.4	725.5
1943	125.0	725.5	804.0	20.8	419.2	1,131.2
1944	158.7	1,131.2	925.2	29.7	544.1	1,542.0
1945	195.9	1,542.0	1,473.8	40.1	868.1	2,187.8
1946	225.6	2,187.8	2,137.3	51.5	1,862.3	2,514.3
1947	256.5	2,514.3	1,684.6	62.6	1,204.0	3,057.5
1948	283.7	3,057.5	2,179.3	75.3	1,438.0	3,874.1
1949	308.8	3,874.1	1,807.1	90.2	1,726.2	4,045.3
1950	337.9	4,045.3	2,328.5	98.0	1,781.7	4,683.0
1951	365.7	4,683.0	2,124.3	113.1	1,804.3	5,116.0
1952	396.7	5,116.0	2,000.0	121.4	1,920.8	5,317.5
1953	426.2	5,317.5	1,846.3	123.7	1,983.8	5,303.6
1954	455.9	5,303.6	1,801.9	118.3	2,127.5	5,096.6
1955	488.4	5,096.6	1,851.7	120.9	1,774.6	5,294.5
1956	522.0	5,294.5	1,900.0	124.9	1,913.2	5,406.2
1957	547.3	5,406.2	1,574.2	122.3	1,983.7	5,119.0
1958	572.3	5,119.0	1,588.1	120.2	1,784.7	5,042.7
1959	592.2	5,042.7	1,454.8	114.7	1,719.6	4,892.6
1960	621.8	4,892.6	1,751.3	117.6	1,599.3	5,162.1

NOTES

1901–35, Years ending 31 December; 1936–7—1962–3, Years ending 31 March.
Source: *Post Office Savings Bank Annual Reports.*

Table 38d. Value of money orders and number and value of postal orders issued and paid, 1900–60

	Money orders				Postal orders			
	Issued		Cashed		Issued		Cashed	
Year	For payment in Ghana (£000s)	For payment abroad (£000s)	Issued in Ghana (£000s)	Advised from abroad (£000s)	No. (000s)	Value (£000s)	No. (000s)	Value (£000s)
1900	3.8	18.1	..	..	..	2.3	..	..
1901	5.2	28.1	..	..	..	2.5	..	..
1902	6.8	35.6	..	..	..	3.7	..	..
1903	9.7	39.3	..	4.6	..	5.0	..	..
1904	13.9	41.1	..	5.7	..	8.6	..	..
1905	10.7	25.6	..	8.8	..	31.4	..	..
1906	9.4	17.9	9.4	9.0	74.9	51.7	..	..
1907	25.4	21.9	25.2	8.9	95.7	63.8	..	..
1908	21.4	25.8	21.2	9.9	110.1	73.4	..	..
1909	26.2	22.9	26.2	6.0	123.3	82.6	..	..
1910	20.5	29.6	20.2	6.1	151.7	98.6	53.6	39.9
1911	22.0	27.5	22.3	7.8	157.7	105.8	57.3	42.6
1912	24.6	23.3	23.8	5.0	168.9	116.3	64.1	48.6
1913	26.8	23.9	26.9	15.3	197.3	138.7	67.4	51.8
1914	33.6	23.7	34.5	5.3	186.1	132.9	69.6	53.6
1915	46.5	27.7	45.6	2.7	182.5	131.8	76.1	59.1
1916	57.6	31.6	57.1	3.0	202.4	138.1	78.1	59.4
1917	63.6	24.8	63.5	1.9	137.7	101.2	84.5	65.9
1918	69.2	12.4	69.2	3.1	105.6	78.4	84.2	65.4
1919	64.2	41.6	67.7	5.2	188.2	132.7	68.0	53.7
1920	97.0	70.0	79.7	7.5	291.7	214.8	91.4	74.0
1921	66.0	50.0	84.6	5.5	183.0	135.7	82.3	66.1
1922	84.5	53.8	84.0	3.8	234.2	171.9	95.8	75.0
1923	94.2	44.3	94.2	2.4	250.0	181.8	104.3	80.6
1924	99.3	42.1	99.4	1.7	280.3	199.8	122.1	92.0
1925	114.1	41.5	113.4	2.0	295.7	208.8	131.0	98.7
1926	127.8	47.7	127.0	1.8	315.6	229.6	147.6	110.8
1927	168.7	57.0	168.3	2.7	370.5	285.1	171.0	129.6
1928	174.2	49.3	173.9	2.8	364.5	272.6	183.2	140.0
1929	177.8	42.7	178.4	3.5	372.2	275.1	193.9	146.5
1930	128.8	29.7	129.4	2.4	298.8	211.2	176.7	128.9
1931	115.9	24.2	116.4	2.3	237.3	167.7	146.6	103.5
1932	128.7	23.1	127.3	1.9	217.7	153.8	132.9	94.4
1933	128.0	19.6	129.0	1.5	208.5	141.7	128.3	88.0
1934	140.4	22.1	139.3	2.0	239.6	156.8	148.6	95.2
1935	158.4	26.3	159.1	2.4	261.3	173.8	163.6	106.8
1936	196.6	33.9	195.3	3.4	302.9	206.9	181.1	119.7
1937	209.2	37.2	209.4	3.5	311.9	213.3	179.2	125.9
1938	213.9	40.4	213.3	3.8	324.1	224.1	203.4	134.2
1939	235.7	27.8	234.3	2.6	303.2	205.3	212.1	137.1
1940	273.8	21.2	275.1	3.1	245.0	168.0	196.3	127.6
1941	317.6	29.1	314.0	5.3	248.4	179.0	197.6	130.1
1942	364.0	39.9	363.0	5.3	305.7	227.5	259.7	177.8
1943	423.8	44.9	422.7	9.0	350.5	271.3	299.6	215.4
1944	434.5	46.4	435.0	9.7	377.1	291.5	362.8	266.3

Table 38d. Value of money orders and number and value of postal orders issued and paid, 1900–60—*continued*

	Money orders				Postal orders			
	Issued		Cashed		Issued		Cashed	
Year	For payment in Ghana (£000s)	For payment abroad (£000s)	Issued in Ghana (£000s)	Advised from abroad (£000s)	No. (000s)	Value (£000s)	No. (000s)	(Value (£000s)
1945	441.0	54.8	440.4	11.8	446.0	342.1	461.0	347.3
1946	478.3	65.0	474.8	15.1	552.5	424.5	425.6	307.0
1947	555.0	65.2	552.9	18.3	643.0	506.8	458.0	338.0
1948	707.1	93.7	634.2	16.2	828.5	670.6	547.5	411.5
1949	673.8	93.5	600.3	18.0	869.6	726.0	548.6	429.1
1950	..	..	..	..	..	..	..	..
1951	..	..	..	..	..	..	..	..
1952	..	..	..	..	..	..	..	..
1953	..	..	..	..	..	..	..	..
1954	..	..	..	..	..	..	..	..
1955	..	..	..	..	..	..	..	..
1956	..	..	..	..	..	..	..	..
1957	..	..	..	..	..	..	..	..
1958	..	..	..	..	..	..	..	..
1959	735.0	39.0	712.0	16.6	369.2	657.8	322.7	554.7
1960	781.6	36.1	762.8	15.5	663.8	1,280.0	657.3	1,248.9

NOTES

Source: *Post and Telecommunications Department Reports.*

13. Education

Table 39. Enrolment in primary and middle schools, 1900–60

Year	Infants			Primary				Middle					Total primary and middle	Boys	Girls
	Class 1	Class 2	Class 3	Class 4 Std 1	Class 5 Std 2	Class 6 Std 3	Total	Form 1 Std 4	Form 2 Std 5	Form 3 Std 6	Form 4 Std 7	Total			
1900	..	6,293	..	1,012	831	731	8,867	584	426	308	144	1,462	11,996	9,919	2,077
1901	..	6,278	..	1,070	876	702	8,926	550	358	238	76	1,222	12,018	9,859	2,159
1902	..	6,809	..	1,121	888	729	9,547	552	397	239	87	1,275	14,862	12,190	2,672
1903	..	6,950	..	1,192	977	858	9,977	628	416	281	117	1,442	16,326	13,390	2,936
1904	..	7,836	..	1,312	1,096	874	11,118	725	494	722	143	1,634	16,520	13,587	2,933
1905	..	8,592	..	1,392	1,199	1,041	12,224	747	605	355	169	1,876	17,658	14,563	3,095
1906	..	8,852	..	1,404	1,290	1,073	12,619	806	617	442	228	2,093	17,878	14,836	3,042
1907	..	8,187	..	1,644	1,233	1,119	12,183	855	601	416	278	2,150	21,265	18,084	3,181
1908	..	8,475	..	1,692	1,269	1,130	12,566	914	748	433	288	2,383	19,011	15,758	3,253
1909	..	9,876	..	1,729	1,391	1,221	14,217	916	694	509	308	2,427	20,648	16,953	3,695
1910	..	10,306	..	1,795	1,537	1,295	14,933	998	721	549	369	2,637	22,377	18,456	3,921
1911*	..	10,874	..	2,057	1,592	1,307	15,830	1,040	821	558	387	2,806	21,695	17,772	3,923
1912	..	10,971	..	1,863	1,620	1,318	15,772	983	840	536	355	2,714	23,072	18,744	4,328
1913	..	10,806	..	2,042	1,607	1,392	15,847	1,059	791	516	345	2,711	24,841	20,679	4,162
1914	..	11,813	..	1,992	1,831	1,395	17,031	1,143	860	601	387	2,991	28,406	23,743	4,663
1915–9	..	..	..	..	..	..	..	..	..	..	..	..	24,090	20,010	4,080
1920–4	..	..	..	..	..	..	..	..	..	..	..	..	32,599	26,722	5,877
1925–9	..	..	..	..	..	..	..	..	..	..	..	..	36,780	29,243	7,537
1930–4	..	..	..	..	..	..	..	..	..	..	..	..	54,819	42,115	12,704
1935–9†	..	..	..	..	..	..	..	..	..	..	..	..	75,525	57,677	17,848
1940–4†	..	..	..	..	..	..	..	..	..	..	..	..	105,627	81,599	24,028
1945–7	..	..	..	..	..	..	..	..	..	..	..	..	105,891	72,287	33,604
1948	56,307	40,216	38,623	38,638	33,645	29,630	237,059	15,652	13,178	11,580	9,252	49,662	286,721	217,994	68,727
1949	29,751	22,569	22,230	25,014	23,420	22,374	145,358	17,128	13,480	11,172	9,841	51,621	291,519	220,411	71,108

Table 39. Enrolment in primary and middle schools, 1900–60—*continued*

Year	Infants			Primary				Middle							
	Class 1	Class 2	Class 3	Class 4 Std 1	Class 5 Std 2	Class 6 Std 3	Total	Form 1 Std 4	Form 2 Std 5	Form 3 Std 6	Form 4 Std 7	Total	Total primary and middle	Boys	Girls
1950‡	50,566	34,553	32,348	33,768	31,298	29,461	211,994	20,839	16,042	12,462	10,597	59,940	271,954	202,981	68,973
1951‡	59,739	38,043	34,793	35,775	33,511	32,631	234,492	21,525	18,634	14,260	11,794	66,213	300,705	223,136	77,569
1952	132,045	54,086	43,144	39,507	35,172	34,314	337,268	27,437	21,760	18,522	13,934	81,653	418,921	301,914	117,007
1953	117,475	86,508	52,825	44,758	38,661	35,455	375,682	28,452	26,237	20,463	17,284	92,436	468,118	330,334	137,784
1954	109,496	81,184	76,500	54,444	43,281	38,296	403,201	30,995	28,625	25,684	19,281	104,585	507,786	355,012	152,774
1955	114,579	77,302	72,933	71,592	50,933	42,179	429,518	34,174	29,581	27,104	23,030	113,889	543,407	375,524	167,883
1956	117,880	76,428	71,532	68,294	65,442	47,126	446,702	35,012	29,765	25,971	24,864	115,612	562,404	384,769	177,635
1957	122,699	81,919	72,006	67,237	63,064	61,096	468,021	40,487	33,401	28,311	25,318	127,517	595,538	406,610	188,928
1958	123,343	86,094	74,481	66,927	61,066	59,109	471,020	49,156	36,275	29,684	24,686	139,801	610,821	413,626	197,195
1959	128,937	88,599	77,048	69,617	61,245	57,979	483,425	49,679	44,273	33,856	26,918	154,726	638,151	429,637	208,514
1960	134,957	92,519	80,705	72,308	63,865	58,801	503,155	48,902	44,612	39,568	28,095	161,177	664,332	443,119	221,213

NOTES

Sources: *Education Department Reports*, *Education Statistics* and *Statistical Yearbooks 1961* and *1962*.

Figures other than those for 1915–28 and 1945–7 relate to enrolment in public and known private schools.

*Excludes enrolment in Wesleyan schools.

† Excludes enrolment in Achimota primary and middle schools for the years 1939–42.

‡ Figures for the middle forms of private schools are not available and therefore not included.

Table 40a. Standard VII examination results, 1900–60 (selected years)

	Entered	Passed
1900	114	..
1905	169	..
1910	369	..
1914	387	..
1921	878	581
1925	1,710	591
1930	2,543	732
1935	2,085	928
1938	2,340	1,382
1942	3,035	2,124
1946	6,361	4,532
1950	10,571	6,429
1955	22,180	13,243
1956	29,701	15,656
1957	24,398	14,567
1958	19,568	11,114
1959	25,915	17,068
1960	28,555	19,068

NOTES

The examination was abolished in 1951 but restored in 1955.

Source: *Education Department Reports.*

Table 40b. Secondary school enrolment and examination performance, 1905–60 (selected years)

	Enrolment	Cambridge School Certificate Examination*		Sixth form enrolment and Higher School Certificate Examination		
	Forms I–V	Entered	Passed	Enrolment	Entered	Passed
1905	65	..	..	..	..	..
1910	382	..	..	..	..	..
1915	465	..	..	..	..	..
1920	387	..	..	..	..	..
1925	242	..	..	..	..	..
1930	450	34	23	..	..	..
1935	629	113	65	..	..	..
1938	919	180	83	..	..	..
1942	2,138	358	205	..	..	..
1946	4,150	391	263	..	..	..
1950	6,162	920	572	..	..	..
1951	6,901	1,108	539	..	21	21
1952	7,742	1,292	588	80	34	32
1953	8,443	1,336	669	246	38	36
1954	8,310	1,357	806	400	202	149
1955	9,723	1,065	751	375	176	131
1956	10,625	1,166	760	440	187	145
1957	11,688	1,654	1,074	431	264	200
1958	12,709	1,794	1,060	487	251	181
1959	14,687	1,824	1,045	630	324	208
1960	15,411	1,668	1,078	701	378	219

NOTES

* Excludes private candidates.

Source: *Education Department Reports.*

14. Miscellaneous

Table 41. Production of cocoa by main cocoa producing countries, 1898–1963 (5 year averages) (000 tons)

Country	1898/9–1902/3	1903/4–1907/8	1908/9–1912/13	1913/14–1917/18	1918/19–1922/3	1923/4–1927/8	1928/9–1932/3	1933/4–1937/8	1938/9–1942/3	1943/4–1947/8	1948/9–1952/3	1953/4–1957/8	1958/9–1962/3
New World Total	91.2	119.9	151.3	180.5	192.7	187.4	193.9	237.3	228.6	210.0	252.1	302.9	300.4
Percentage	79.0	73.6	63.1	58.6	45.6	37.4	34.1	33.4	33.3	34.4	33.2	37.0	28.1
Brazil	18.5	25.3	31.8	45.3	56.3	68.9	82.8	124.5	130.5	109.4	129.8	160.0	144.6
Ecuador	23.4	24.8	37.3	42.8	37.7	23.9	14.4	17.9	13.8	15.7	23.6	30.7	36.8
Dominican Republic	6.5	13.9	18.3	20.9	22.2	22.5	21.0	24.3	24.2	27.6	30.0	33.7	35.8
British West Indies	17.5	28.1	32.3	12.3	17.3	32.3	31.7	21.8	12.6	9.4	13.2	13.1	12.7
Africa Total	19.6	37.3	81.2	120.4	223.1	304.9	364.7	463.6	448.9	393.5	499.9	502.6	747.1
Percentage	17.0	22.9	33.8	39.1	52.7	60.9	64.2	65.3	65.4	64.5	65.8	61.5	69.9
Ghana	1.3	8.4	34.4	73.6	155.8	216.1	236.7	266.8	250.9	210.1	253.3	234.7	366.7
Nigeria	0.2	0.8	3.4	9.9	25.7	42.0	59.0	91.0	108.5	90.0	105.4	100.0	68.2
Cameroons	0.5	1.6	4.1	3.5	3.1	5.9	12.5	24.9	24.0	35.1	52.3	62.8	71.9
Ivory Coast	..	..	..	0.2	1.9	8.8	24.1	47.2	37.4	27.2	53.8	61.8	78.0
Spanish Equatorial Region	1.1	2.0	3.6	4.3	5.0	7.1	10.7	11.7	14.1	15.4	15.7	20.5	25.9
Sao Thome and Principe	16.5	24.1	34.6	27.6	27.5	17.4	12.8	10.0	6.4	9.6	8.0	8.0	8.8
Other	4.6	5.5	7.3	7.0	7.3	8.6	9.3	9.0	8.5	6.6	7.9	12.0	20.7
Percentage	4.0	3.5	3.1	2.3	1.7	1.7	1.7	1.3	1.3	1.1	1.0	1.5	2.0
World Total	115.0	163.0	240.0	308.0	423.0	501.0	568.0	710.0	686.0	610.0	760.0	818.0	1,068.2

Table 42. Cocoa Marketing Board receipts and payments, 1947/8–1959/60 (£000s)

	1947/8	1948/9	1949/50	1950/1	1951/2	1952/3	1953/4	1954/5	1955/6	1956/7	1957/8	1958/9	1959/60
Receipts													
Proceeds of Cocoa Sales	41,520	37,545	45,102	70,300	51,612	57,120	74,703	77,487	52,333	50,686	62,875	70,946	69,896
Cocoa stocks held by C.M.B.	4	58	—	—	—	—	—	—	—	—	—	—	—
Interest on investments	251	601	797	1,087	1,542	1,741	1,851	2,089	2,345	1,942	2,016	1,765	1,874
Rents	4	6	6	6	6	6	9	10	13	20	26	36	59
Surplus on sale of bags	4	2	6	25	31	64	129	138	143	245	115	95	56
Other	—	—	—	—	—	—	—	—	—	2	1	262	—
Total:	41,783	38,212	45,912	71,419	53,191	58,931	76,693	79,724	54,834	52,895	65,033	73,104	71,885
Payments													
Cost of cocoa purchased	16,723	35,746	23,540	36,992	34,015	35,247	30,428	32,007	37,897	43,270	30,319	37,171	45,172
Export duty on cocoa	371	1,683	3,497	13,372	14,741	15,986	34,041	38,358	14,596	11,959	26,269	25,551	19,382
Shipping and Transport expenses:													
Railway freight	432	613	560	593	586	829	707	790	895	1,011	791	1,053	1,321
Lighterage and harbour dues	87	110	107	126	119	162	146	205	222	270	222	261	321
Other	53	101	110	113	118	131	102	93	191	284	265	276	425
Transfer and Bank charges	32	66	42	84	42	109	125	136	120	128	123	97	177
Administrative expenses	15	21	25	28	37	41	47	60	66	72	97	94	129
Other	1	5	9	2	4	6	21	17	14	1,094	408	60	703
Total	17,713	38,346	27,890	51,310	49,662	52,511	65,617	71,666	54,001	58,088	58,494	64,563	67,671
Operating surplus (+) deficit (—)	24,069	—134	180,22	20,109	3,530	6,420	11,075	8,058	833	—5,194	6,539	8,542	4,215
Payments from surplus and reserves*													
Premium paid on investments	392	152	21	129	—	—	—	—	—	—	—	—	—
Housing projects and equipment	—	10	35	11	1	1	3	20	34	63	33	235	132
Rehabilitation scheme	300	350	300	500	1,000	2,500	2,250	2,000	2,367	2,821	2,940	3,752	5,972
Local development grants	—	—	—	70	198	71	207	817	1,089	330	3,134	544	1,219
Grant to University			1,000	—	—	—	—	—	870	80	70	—	—
W.A. Cocoa Research Institute	690	—	—	—	—	—	—	1,347	—	—	—	—	—
Other	79	78	39	50	11	251	1,995	821	159	1,400	652	1,375	1,663
Total	1,461	590	1,395	760	1,210	2,823	4,455	5,005	4,519	4,694	6,829	5,906	8,986

NOTES

*Excludes loans granted to the central government and investments in government stocks.
Source: Cocoa Marketing Board Annual Reports.

Table 43. Public Works Department; pattern of expenditure (selected years), 1905–58 (£000s)

	1905	1912	1922	1928	1932	1937	1949	1958
Personal emoluments	14	32	118	145	112	97	180	1,071
Machinery, cars, office equipment, etc.	—	1	8	3	—	3	26	50
Living quarters (construction, maintenance, etc.)	10	36	25	153	4	70	146	259
Public buildings:								
Administration	16	16	19	64	2	41	122	1,463
Defence	—	—	—	9	—	—	—	—
Other	—	—	—	2	35	—	—	—
Community works:								
Sanitation and water works	1	44	43	62	16	81	134	1,215
Survey and research	—	—	—	9	12	—	1	—
Town improvements	5	7	82	45	21	38	62	81
Community buildings and markets	1	2	—	8	—	1	—	—
Plants and workshops	1	5	20	33	4	8	41	108
Schools and training centres	—	4	8	2	—	7	42	—
Hospitals	1	4	108	26	—	16	21	—
Post offices and telegraphs	—	2	1	26	1	1	1	5
Roads and bridges	7	53	149	289	142	292	573	2,469
Railways	—	1	31	2	1	—	—	—
Harbours	—	—	—	25	—	—	—	—
Electricity	—	—	—	—	—	—	—	2,138
Other	10	18	50	49	14	107	302	76
Total	66	223	663	950	365	765	1,652	8,936

NOTES

Figures refer to total expenditure, i.e. recurrent, extraordinary, special department and loan works expenditure.

Sources: *Public Works Department Reports* and *Treasury Department Reports.*

Year	No. of companies mining: Lode	No. of companies mining: Alluvial	No. of companies producing: Lode	No. of companies producing: Alluvial	Non-African employed	African employed
1900	..		..		..	..
1901	..		..		..	..
1902	..		..		..	..
1903	12		..		611	17,000
1904	..		..		611	..
1905	17		..		504	12,500
1906	17		..		..	..
1907	..		..		..	..
1908	11		..		589	15,200
1909	16		..		500	15,400
1910	12		..		672	18,500
1911	12		..		770	18,400
1912	15		..		..	16,900
1913	16		..		..	16,100
1914	14		..		..	17,400
1915	14		..		..	17,300
1916	17		15		447	14,500
1917	16		13		408	15,000
1918	16		15		330	10,800
1919	13		11		287	11,000
1920	13		11		205	9,800
1921	14		10		252	10,300
1922	16		10		273	12,100
1923	16		12		257	10,000
1924	15		9		229	10,300
1925	13		11		190	9,100
1926	11		9		195	8,200
1927	10		8		202	7,800
1928	9		8		209	7,800
1929	9		5		200	7,400
1930	..	..	..	..	..	..
1931	5	1	4	1	166	7,940
1932	6	2	4	2	199	8,882
1933	9	..	5	..	255	10,452
1934	23	2	8	..	389	15,163
1935	28	3	9	1	621	23,535
1936	27	4	10	1	755	27,091
1937	17	1	11	1	783	27,313
1938	17	2	13	2	872	30,534
1939	19	2	14	2	855	33,724
1940	19	2	14	2	767	33,837
1941	13	3	12	3	677	34,541
1942	12	2	12	2	586	30,335
1943	7	2	7	2	444	21,738
1944	7	1	7	1	370	22,733
1945	7	1	7	1	439	25,454
1946	12	1	9	1	622	30,101
1947	14	2	9	2	722	31,148
1948	13	2	10	2	749	30,180

Table 44a. Mines; general statistics, 1900–60 (Gold)—*continued*

Year	No. of companies mining: Lode	No. of companies mining: Alluvial	No. of companies producing: Lode	No. of companies producing: Alluvial	Non-African employed	African employed
1949	13	2	9	1	757	29,543
1950	11	1	10	1	784	31,072
1951	11	1	11	1	782	29,868
1952	11	1	11	1	776	28,050
1953	11	1	9	1	848	27,890
1954	10	1	9	1	823	25,295
1955	10	1	9	1	794	19,855
1956	8	1	6	1	722	21,210
1957	7	1	6	1	685	21,350
1958	6	1	6	1	670	21,991
1959	6	1	6	1	668	22,024
1960	6	1	6	1	628	20,589

NOTES

Source: Department of Mines.

Table 44b. Mines; general statistics, 1920–60 (Manganese, Diamonds and Bauxite)

Year	No. of companies mining	Non-African employed	African employed	No. of companies mining	Non-African employed	African employed	No. of companies mining	Non-African employed	African employed
1920	..	..	..	..	..	..	..	..	..
1921	..	..	..	..	..	..	..	..	..
1922	..	..	..	..	..	..	..	..	..
1923	..	..	..	..	..	..	..	..	..
1924	..	..	..	..	..	..	..	..	..
1925	..	..	..	..	..	..	..	..	..
1926	..	..	..	..	..	..	..	..	..
1927	..	..	..	..	..	..	..	..	..
1928	..	..	..	..	..	..	..	..	..
1929	..	..	..	..	..	..	..	..	..
1930	..	..	..	..	..	..	..	..	..
1931	1	23	758	4	36	2,960	..	..	..
1932	1	18	631	4	36	2,667	..	..	..
1933	1	18	705	4	46	3,638	..	..	..
1934	1	25	1,059	5	51	4,118	..	..	..
1935	1	35	1,319	6	53	4,376	..	..	..
1936	1	37	1,396	6	55	4,553	..	..	..
1937	1	46	1,203	5	49	5,164	..	..	..
1938	1	42	1,065	5	43	5,005	..	..	..
1939	1	40	1,748	5	37	4,149	..	..	..
1940	2	38	2,115	5	32	3,459	..	..	..
1941	2	41	2,757	5	31	3,138	1	5	1,011
1942	2	39	2,675	4	32	3,390	1	15	2,276
1943	2	42	2,752	4	32	3,141	2	26	3,312
1944	2	31	2,646	4	29	3,204	2	19	886
1945	2	38	2,998	4	29	2,926	1	15	608
1946	2	42	2,747	4	31	2,723	1	15	637
1947	1	42	2,693	4	36	3,239	1	15	674
1948	1	42	3,408	4	40	3,382	1	20	776
1949	2	45	4,266	4	43	3,175	1	19	843
1950	2	49	5,383	4	43	3,462	1	21	695
1951	2	56	6,251	4	50	3,807	1	27	763
1952	1	63	6,129	5	51	3,758	1	30	908
1953	1	57	5,822	5	51	3,774	1	27	634
1954	1	45	4,096	5	58	3,918	1	24	548
1955	1	43	4,204	5	76	4,320	1	22	487
1956	1	47	4,574	5	78	4,711	1	20	462
1957	1	40	4,593	5	109	5,101	1	20	465
1958	1	43	4,085	6	113	4,674	1	19	442
1959	1	36	3,070	4	115	4,230	1	17	432
1960	1	34	2,820	4	117	4,226	1	16	435

NOTES

Source: Department of Mines.

Table 44c. Mines; general statistics, 1900–60 (Total employment)

Year	Non-African employed: Surface	Non-African employed: Underground	African employed: Surface	African employed: Underground	Fatal accidents: Non-African	Fatal accidents: African
1900	..	..	..	..	..	..
1901	..	..	..	..	..	..
1902	..	..	..	..	..	..
1903	..	..	..	..	..	..
1904	..	..	..	..	..	..
1905	338	166	8,900	3,700	—	27
1906	355	160	8,200	4,800	5	68
1907	359	179	8,600	6,100	1	41
1908	325	171	8,800	5,600	4	55
1909	329	264	8,700	6,500	1	41
1910	434	238	11,600	6,800	—	36
1911	513	257	10,900	7,400	1	39
1912	..	..	8,900	8,000	5	48
1913	..	..	8,100	3,900	5	68
1914	..	..	7,600	9,700	—	..
1915	..	..	7,300	10,100	3	50
1916	270	180	7,900	7,000	1	32
1917	264	151	8,800	7,200	1	30
1918	222	114	7,200	6,400	—	41
1919	196	96	6,400	5,300	—	25
1920	197	76	6,500	4,000	—	25
1921	199	67	7,400	3,900	—	16
1922	201	78	7,400	5,200	—	7
1923	201	80	7,900	4,200	2	27
1924	211	75	8,800	4,300	1	28
1925	209	57	9,100	4,100	—	19
1926	200	69	6,700	4,100	—	15
1927	189	79	6,900	3,800	—	13
1928	207	77	7,800	3,600	—	21
1929	218	68	8,800	3,300	—	19
1930	..	..	..	..	—	..
1931	168	64	7,805	4,034	—	21
1932	182	79	8,224	4,095	—	24
1933	259	106	11,654	4,799	1	22
1934	430	193	18,537	7,998	4	77
1935	582	257	23,470	9,933	—	44
1936	614	294	24,332	11,018	1	57
1937	663	314	26,047	11,739	3	53
1938	700	323	26,690	12,432	1	70
1939	708	325	27,879	13,133	1	34
1940	611	233	25,765	14,118	5	50
1941	545	209	26,770	14,677	—	46
1942	514	158	25,867	12,810	1	32
1943	420	124	22,703	8,240	—	21
1944	343	106	20,470	8,999	—	20
1945	400	121	22,074	9,912	—	14
1946	542	180	25,082	11,655	—	33
1947	616	201	25,541	12,261	2	31
1948	649	205	24,481	13,527	1	38

Table 44c. Mines; general statistics, 1900–60 (Total employment)— *continued*

Year	Non-African employed: Surface	Non-African employed: Underground	African employed: Surface	African employed: Underground	Fatal accidents: Non-African	Fatal accidents: African
1949	631	234	24,894	13,009	2	47
1950	627	270	27,448	13,166	1	29
1951	661	264	27,971	12,897	—	44
1952	656	264	26,590	12,255	1	28
1953	708	275	24,646	12,626	1	30
1954	683	295	21,571	12,529	1	32
1955	635	318	19,031	9,981	—	27
1956	630	282	20,302	11,022	4	34
1957	606	282	19,927	11,837	1	32
1958	610	259	18,791	12,578	1	25
1959	597	264	17,118	12,827	—	27
1960	564	256	16,043	12,204	—	31

NOTES

Source: Department of Mines.

Table 45. Police and prisons, 1900–60

Year	No. of police*	No. of persons convicted†	Daily av. no. of prisoners‡	Av. daily cost per head‡ (shillings)
1900	534	..	402	..
1901	606 ‖	..	..	..
1902	678	4,169	..	..
1903	594	7,110	..	..
1904	611	9,528	653	..
1905	613	7,802	770	..
1906	621	7,904	763	..
1907	628	8,479	791	..
1908	699	8,422	884	3.0
1909	693	10,511	988	3.3
1910	742	12,339	931	3.33
1911	770	10,397	978	3.04
1912	838	11,478	1,046	3.42
1913	897	9,447	966	3.52
1914	1,041	12,334	1,033	3.19
1915	1,118	15,163	1,201	3.67
1916	1,104	11,148	1,320	3.81
1917	1,154	8,974	1,447	3.92
1918	1,086	8,683	1,502	3.0
1919	1,259	9,169	1,572	2.81
1920	1,449	10,797	1,592	5.77
1921	1,270	10,633	1,763	4.64
1922	1,327	10,549	1,655	3.54
1923	1,350	10,401	1,463	3.33
1924	1,522	12,248	1,390	3.05

Table 45. Police and prisons, 1900–60—*continued*

Year	No. of police*	No. of persons convicted†	Daily av. no. of prisoners‡	Av. daily cost per head‡ (shillings)
1925	1,546	15,329	1,433	2.9
1926	1,606	15,997	1,620	3.0
1927	1,667	17,669	1,701	3.03
1928	1,765	20,413	1,806	2.83
1929	2,065	23,490	1,754	2.85
1930	2,025	22,162	1,825	2.88
1931	1,981	20,743	1,715	2.91
1932	2,017 ‖	22,875	1,927	2.85
1933	2,053	22,399	1,984	3.01
1934	2,054	24,225	1,967	2.96
1935	2,037	25,267	1,904 ‖	2.87
1936	2,099	30,029	1,840	2.4
1937	..	28,360	1,978	2.56
1938	..	29,695	1,963	2.47
1939	..	27,923	1,959	2.31
1940	..	25,392	2,265	2.74
1941	..	25,315	2,346	3.12
1942	..	19,331	2,560	3.16
1943	..	28,491	2,818	..
1944	..	..	2,928	..
1945	..	..	2,941	7.55
1946	..	..	2,977	7.81
1947	..	..	3,266	8.11
1948	3,200	20,230	2,998	8.84
1949	3,501	24,424	3,054	8.93
1950	..	..	3,428	9.10
1951	..	..	3,341	10.01
1952	..	..	3,539	19.72
1953	..	26,905	3,523	22.47
1954	..	29,082	3,531	22.55
1955	5,381	35,609	4,004	23.98
1956	5,653	37,270	4,208 ‖	23.49 ‖
1957	5,920	35,075	4,412	23.0
1958	5,959	37,310	4,519	21.5
1959	6,271	26,185	5,026	21.0
1960	7,366	31,202	5,296	21.0
			5,567	21.0

NOTES

* Source: *Police Department Reports.*

† Sources: 1900 to 1923, *Blue Books.* 1924 to 1938, *Colonial Reports.* 1939 to 1943, *Blue Books.* 1948 to 1960, *Police Department Reports.*

‡ Source: *Prison Departmental Reports.*

‖ Estimated.

	Beds	Inpatients	Outpatients	Total no. treated
1900	..	1,157	..	..
1905	..	1,989	38,284	40,273
1910	..	..	..	43,932
1915	..	3,269	45,323	48,592
1920	..	..	..	58,585
1925	..	..	..	82,476
1930	952	15,963	233,163	249,126
1935	1,269	25,397	248,079	273,476
1940	1,390	28,076	315,117	343,193
1945	1,600	37,107	493,962	531,069
1950	1,866	60,766	747,231	807,997
1955	2,582	58,922	420,123	479,045

NOTES

Source: *Medical Department Reports*

Table 47. Number of banks and branches, 1906–60 (selected years)

	Bank of West Africa	Barclays Bank	Ghana Commercial Bank	Total
1906	9*	—	—	9
1910	10*	—	—	10
1915	10*	—	—	10
1920	12	6	—	18
1925	12	6	—	18
1930	16	9	—	25
1935	10	9	—	19
1940	11	9	—	20
1944	9	8	—	17
1951	12	7	—	19
1952	13	7	—	20
1953	16	11	1	28
1954	..	..	..	
1955	19	14	2	35
1956	..	..	..	
1957	26	33	2	61
1958	34	49	3	86
1959	..	..	..	..
1960	40	53	6	99

NOTES

* Includes agencies.

The Bank of West Africa was established in the colony in 1897 but data did not become available until 1906. Barclays was established in 1917 but figures did not become available until 1920.

Sources: 1900–44, *Blue Books*; 1951–60, *Handbooks of Trade and Commerce.*

Index